PUBLICATIONS OF THE NEWTON INSTITUTE

Semantics and Logics of Computation

Publications of the Newton Institute

Edited by H. P. F. Swinerton-Dyer
Executive Director, Isaac Newton Institute for Mathematical Sciences

The Isaac Newton Institute of Mathematical Sciences of the University of Cambridge exists to stimulate research in all branches of the mathematical sciences, including pure mathematics, statistics, applied mathematics, theoretical physics, theoretical computer science, mathematical biology and economics. The four six-month long research programmes it runs each year bring together leading mathematical scientists from all over the world to bring together leading mathematical scientists from all over the world to exchange ideas through seminars, teaching and informal interaction.

Associated with the programmes are two types of publication. The first contains lecture courses, aimed at making the latest developments accessible to a wider audience and providing an entry to the area. The second contains proceedings of workshops and conferences focusing on the most topical aspects of the subjects.

Semantics and Logics of Computation

Edited by

Andrew M. Pitts
Computer Laboratory, Cambridge University

Peter Dybjer
Institutionen för Datavetenskap, Chalmers Tekniska Högskola

CAMBRIDGE
UNIVERSITY PRESS

CAMBRIDGE UNIVERSITY PRESS
Cambridge, New York, Melbourne, Madrid, Cape Town, Singapore, São Paulo, Delhi

Cambridge University Press
The Edinburgh Building, Cambridge CB2 8RU, UK

Published in the United States of America by Cambridge University Press, New York

www.cambridge.org
Information on this title: www.cambridge.org/9780521118460

First published 1997
This digitally printed version 2009

A catalogue record for this publication is available from the British Library

ISBN 978-0-521-58057-1 hardback
ISBN 978-0-521-11846-0 paperback

Contents

Metalanguages and Applications
Eugenio Moggi

Operationally-Based Theories of Program Equivalence
Andrew Pitts

Categories in Concurrency
Glynn Winskel and Mogens Nielsen

Index   355

Contributors

Samson Abramsky Department of Computer Science, University of Edinburgh, The King's Buildings, Mayfield Road, Edinburgh EH9 3JZ, UK

Thierry Coquand Institutionen för Datavetenskap, Chalmers Tekniska Högskola, S-412 96 Göteborg, Sweden

Peter Dybjer Institutionen för Datavetenskap, Chalmers Tekniska Högskola, S-412 96 Göteborg, Sweden

Martin Hofmann Fachbereich Mathematik, Technische Hochschule Darmstadt, Schlossgartenstrasse 7, D-64289 Darmstadt, Germany

Martin Hyland Department of Pure Mathematics and Mathematical Statistics, Cambridge University, 16 Mill Lane, Cambridge CB2 1SB, UK

Eugenio Moggi Dipartimento di Informatica, Università di Genova, via Dodecaneso 35, 16146 Genova, Italy

Mogens Nielsen Department of Computer Science, Aarhus Universitet, Ny Munkegade, Bldg. 540, DK-8000 Aarhus C., Denmark

Andrew Pitts Computer Laboratory, Cambridge University, Pembroke Street, Cambridge CB2 3QG, UK

Glynn Winskel Department of Computer Science, Aarhus Universitet, Ny Munkegade, Bldg. 540, DK-8000 Aarhus C., Denmark

Preface

This book is based on material presented at a summer school on Semantics and Logics of Computation that took place at the Isaac Newton Institute for Mathematical Sciences, Cambridge UK, in September 1995. The school was sponsored by the EU ESPRIT Basic Research Action on *Categorical Logic in Computer Science* (CLiCS I & II) and aimed to present some modern developments in semantics and logics of computation in a series of graduate-level lectures. Most of the material presented here has not previously been accessible in such a coherent and digestible form. This Preface gives a thematic overview of the contents of the book. It also briefly sketches the history of the two CLiCS projects which came to an end with the summer school.

Games, proofs and programs One of the most exciting recent developments in programming semantics has been the use of games and strategies to provide a more fine grained semantics than that provided by domain-theoretic models. This 'intensional semantics' aims to combine the good mathematical and structural properties of traditional denotational semantics with the ability to capture dynamical and interactive aspects of computation, and to embody the computational intuitions of operational semantics. More pragmatically, game semantics have been used to solve long-standing 'full abstraction' problems for PCF (a simple language for Programming Computable arithmetic Functions of higher type) and Idealised Algol. In other words games have provided syntax-independent models of these languages which precisely capture the operationally defined notion of 'contextual equivalence' of program expressions.

Abramsky's chapter on *Semantics of Interaction: an Introduction to Game Semantics* and Hyland's chapter on *Game Semantics* together provide an excellent introduction to these developments. They both present basic notions of games and strategies, although from somewhat different perspectives. The connection between strategies and partial computation and between winning strategies and terminating computation is discussed. Games and strategies are organised into a category with sufficient structure to model Linear Logic. Abramsky describes the use of games for modelling relationally parametric polymorphism. Hyland describes an exponential comonad and the associated cartesian closed co-Kleisli category. He goes on to introduce the 'dialogue games' which he and Ong used for constructing a fully abstract model of PCF. (Another fully abstract game semantics of PCF due to Abramsky, Jagadeesan, and Malacaria instead uses games and history-free strategies.)

Games are also one of the themes in Coquand's chapter on the *Computational Content of Classical Logic*. This area of research has developed rapidly during the last few years partly because of its connection to classical Linear Logic and to theories of 'continuation-passing' semantics. Coquand discusses three ways of extracting computational content from proofs in classical logic: the negative translation of classical proofs into intuitionistic proofs; the interpretation of formulas and proofs in classical logic as games and strategies; and the use of formal topology. He makes a special point of connecting the old tradition of proof theory of classical logic with recent developments in computer science. He also follows Gentzen in analysing a number of actual mathematical examples.

Categories, types and computation Type theories of one kind or another form an integral part of many computer-oriented formalisations of mathematics. For example, several mechanised proof assistants for intuitionistic type theory have been developed (notably as part of CLiCS's sister project, the ESPRIT Basic Research Action on *Types for Proofs and Programs*). Within the context of semantics and logics of computation, dependent types have been incorporated into metalanguages for denotational semantics.

Hofmann's chapter on the *Syntax and Semantics of Dependent Types* describes the category-theoretic interpretation of intuitionistic type theory. He shows how categorical notions can be used to clarify what it means to be a model of a theory with dependent types and thus to facilitate metamathematical studies. He begins by giving an introduction to dependent types and to some of the most important type theories such as Martin-Löf's Type Theory and The Calculus of Constructions. He then discusses several kinds of models, both syntactic and semantic. The chapter ends by using the categorical machinery to prove conservativity of Martin-Löf's Logical Framework over ordinary type theory.

Moggi's chapter on *Metalanguages and Applications* develops an incremental approach to the denotational semantics of programming languages making use of the categorical notion of 'strong monad'. The basic idea is to use monads as a structuring device. Monads have been shown to capture in abstract form essential common properties of various types of computation (such as partial, imperative, non-deterministic, parallel, and exception-raising computation); and for this reason they have also recently become popular as a structuring device in functional programming. In his chapter, Moggi also makes essential use of a metalanguage of dependent types (of the kind discussed in Hofmann's chapter) when presenting denotational semantics. The chapter ends with a treatment of recursive definitions in the context of metalanguages, incorporating some ideas from recent axiomatic and synthetic treatments of domain theory.

Operationally-Based Theories of Program Equivalence Pitts' chapter describes techniques for proving properties of programs which are based directly on the syntax and operational semantics of programming languages. A central result is the co-inductive characterisation of contextual equivalence between programs in a lazy functional programming language. As a consequence contextual equivalences between programs can be proved by co-induction. This technique has already been exploited extensively in concurrency theory, where it is used for proving bisimulation equivalence between processes. Pitts gives a number of concrete example of how the technique is used for proving equivalences between lazy functional programs. Although this operationally-based approach bypasses some of the mathematical intricacies of denotational semantics, it also borrows denotational ideas. This is illustrated in the last part of the chapter where a syntactic analogue of Scott's induction principle for fixpoint recursion is developed.

Categories in Concurrency   The chapter by Winskel and Nielsen presents a range of models for parallel and concurrent computation. They consider both interleaving models such as transition system, synchronisation trees and languages, and models where concurrency is represented more explicitly ('true concurrency') by a form of causal independence, such as Petri Nets, event structures, pomsets and Mazurkiewicz traces. They show how these models can be unified by putting them in a category-theoretic framework. As a consequence they are able to give language independent characterisations of various constructs such as parallel composition. They also discuss bisimulation equivalence, the most important notion of equivalence for transition systems, and show how the categorical framework helps to find an appropriate corresponding notion for other models such as Petri nets.

The CLiCS projects   The summer school which gave rise to this book marked the end of six years of funding by the EU of ESPRIT Basic Research Actions on *Categorical Logic in Computer Science*. The first CLiCS project started in October 1989 and was succeeded by CLiCS-II which continued until December 1995. The following universities and research institutes participated: Aarhus in Denmark; Cambridge, Imperial College, Manchester, and Sussex in England; ENS, Paris and INRIA (Rocquencourt) in France; Darmstadt and GMD (Bonn) in Germany; Genova and Parma in Italy; and Chalmers in Sweden. One purpose of this book is to publish in accessible form some of the highlights of the research which evolved during these projects.

The initial aim of CLiCS was to bring together a group of mathematicians and theoretical computer scientists to work on foundational problems in computer science. This was motivated by the belief that significant advances in language design, programming methodology, and even language implementation and computer architecture, are based on the insights and analytical techniques made available by theoretical work. As the name of the project suggests a unifying theme was the application of concepts and techniques from Category Theory and Categorical Logic. The project encompassed four main areas: domain theory; semantics and logics of programming languages; concurrency theory and linear logic; and type theory and constructive mathematics. It was organised into nine research topics: sequentiality and stability; duality in domain theory; logic of inductive and recursive datatypes; subtypes and polymorphism in higher order languages; higher order modal program logics; monadic programming language semantics; applied linear logic; computational content of classical logic; and symbolic computation. Material on many, but by no means all, of these topics may be found in the chapters that follow.

Acknowledgements We wish to thank the European Union and the Isaac Newton Institute for Mathematical Sciences for the funding which made the summer school possible; to thank the lecturers and participants for making it such an enjoyable, if exhausting week; and to thank the staff of the Newton Institute for their quiet efficiency. Finally, we would like to thank David Tranah at CUP for his encouragement and assistance in turning the lectures into this book.

Andrew Pitts
Peter Dybjer   September 1996

Semantics of Interaction: an Introduction to Game Semantics

Samson Abramsky

Contents

1 Introduction

The "classical" paradigm for denotational semantics models data types as *domains*, i.e. structured sets of some kind, and programs as (suitable) *functions* between domains. The semantic universe in which the denotational modelling is carried out is thus a category with domains as objects, functions as morphisms, and composition of morphisms given by function composition. A sharp distinction is then drawn between denotational and operational semantics. Denotational semantics is often referred to as "mathematical semantics" because it exhibits a high degree of mathematical structure; this is in part achieved by the fact that denotational semantics abstracts away from the dynamics of computation—from time. By contrast, operational semantics is formulated in terms of the syntax of the language being modelled; it is highly intensional in character; and it is capable of expressing the dynamical aspects of computation.

The classical denotational paradigm has been very successful, but has some definite limitations. Firstly, fine-structural features of computation, such as sequentiality, computational complexity, and optimality of reduction strategies, have either not been captured at all denotationally, or not in a fully satisfactory fashion. Moreover, once languages with features beyond the purely functional are considered, the appropriateness of modelling programs by functions is increasingly open to question. Neither concurrency nor "advanced" imperative features such as local references have been captured denotationally in a fully convincing fashion.

1

This analysis suggests a desideratum of *Intensional Semantics*, interpolating between denotational and operational semantics as traditionally conceived. This should combine the good mathematical structural properties of denotational semantics with the ability to capture dynamical aspects and to embody computational intuitions of operational semantics. Thus we may think of Intensional semantics as "Denotational semantics + time (dynamics)", or as "Syntax-free operational semantics".

A number of recent developments (and, with hindsight, some older ones) can be seen as contributing to this goal of Intensional Semantics. We will focus on the recent work on Game semantics, which has led to some striking advances in the Full Abstraction problem for PCF and other programming languages (Abramsky *et al.* 1995) (Abramsky and McCusker 1995) (Hyland and Ong 1995) (McCusker 1996a) (Ong 1996). Our aim is to give a genuinely elementary first introduction; we therefore present a simplified version of game semantics, which nonetheless contains most of the essential concepts. The more complex game semantics in (Abramsky *et al.* 1995) (Hyland and Ong 1995) can be seen as refinements of what we present. Some background in category theory, type theory and linear logic would be helpful in reading these notes; suitable references are (Crole 1994), (Girard *et al.* 1989), (Girard 1995) (which contain much more than we will actually need).

Acknowledgements   I would like to thank the Edinburgh "interaction group" (Kohei Honda, Paul-André Melliès, Julo Chroboczek, Jim Laird and Nobuko Yoshida) for their help in preparing these notes for publication, Peter Dybjer for his comments on a draft version, and Peter Dybjer and Andy Pitts for their efforts in organizing the CLiCS summer school and editing the present volume.

Notation

If X is a set, X^* is the set of finite sequences (words, strings) over X. We use $s, t,$ u, v to denote sequences, and a, b, c, d, m, n to denote elements of these sequences. Concatenation of sequences is indicated by juxtaposition, and we won't distinguish notationally between an element and the corresponding unit sequence. Thus as denotes the sequence with first element a and tail s.

If $f : X \longrightarrow Y$ then $f^* : X^* \longrightarrow Y^*$ is the unique monoid homomorphism extending f. We write $|s|$ for the length of a finite sequence, and s_i for the ith element of s, $1 \leq i \leq |s|$.

Given a set S of sequences, we write S^{even}, S^{odd} for the subsets of even- and odd-length sequences respectively.

We write $X + Y$ for the disjoint union of sets X, Y.

If $Y \subseteq X$ and $s \in X^*$, we write $s \upharpoonright Y$ for the sequence obtained by deleting all elements not in Y from s. In practice, we use this notation in the context where

$X = Y + Z$, and by abuse of notation we take $s \restriction Y \in Y^*$, *i.e.* we elide the use of injection functions.

We write $s \sqsubseteq t$ if s is a prefix of t, *i.e.* $t = su$ for some u.

$\text{Pref}(S)$ is the set of prefixes of elements of $S \subseteq X^*$. S is *prefix-closed* if $S = \text{Pref}(S)$.

2 Game Semantics

We give a first introduction to game semantics. We will be concerned with two-person games. Why the magic number 2? The key feature of games, by comparison with the many extant models of computation (labelled transition systems, event structures, etc. etc.) is that they provide an *explicit representation of the environment*, and hence model interaction in an intrinsic fashion. By contrast, interaction is modelled in, say, labelled transition systems using some additional structure, typically a "synchronization algebra" on the labels. One-person games would degenerate to transition systems; it seems that multi-party interaction can be adequately modeled by two-person games, in much the same way that functions with multiple arguments can be reduced to one-place functions and tupling. We will use such games to model interactions between a System and its Environment. One of the players in the game is taken to represent the System, and is referred to as Player or Proponent; the other represents the Environment and is referred to as Opponent. Note that the distinction between System and Environment and the corresponding designation as Player or Opponent depend on *point of view*:

> If Tom, Tim and Trevor converse in a room, then from Tom's point of view, he is the System, and Tim and Trevor form the Environment; while from Tim's point of view, he is the System, and Tom and Trevor form the Environment.

A single 'computation' or 'run' involving interaction between Player and Opponent will be represented by a sequence of *moves*, made alternately by Player and Opponent. We shall adopt the convention that *Opponent always makes the first move*. This avoids a number of technical problems which would otherwise arise, but limits what we can successfully model with games to the *negative fragment* of Intuitionistic Linear Logic. (This is the $\otimes$, $\multimap$, $\&$, $!$, $\forall$ fragment).

A game specifies the set of possible runs (or 'plays'). It can be thought of as a
tree

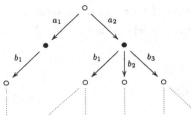

where hollow nodes ∘ represent positions where Opponent is to move; solid nodes •
positions where Player is to move; and the arcs issuing from a node are labelled with
the moves which can be made in the position represented by that node.

Formally, we define a game G to be a structure (M_G, λ_G, P_G), where

- M_G is the set of *moves* of the game;

- $\lambda_G : M_G \longrightarrow \{P, O\}$ is a labelling function designating each move as by
  Player or Opponent;

- $P_G \subseteq^{\mathrm{nepref}} M_G^{\mathrm{alt}}$, *i.e.* P_G is a non-empty, prefix-closed subset of M_G^{alt}, the set
  of alternating sequences of moves in M_G.

More formally, M_G^{alt} is the set of all $s \in M_G^*$ such that

$$\forall i : 1 \leq i \leq |s| \qquad \mathrm{even}(i) \implies \lambda_G(s_i) = P$$
$$\wedge \quad \mathrm{odd}(i) \implies \lambda_G(s_i) = O$$

i.e.

$$
\begin{array}{ccccccc}
s & = & a_1 & a_2 & \cdots & a_{2k+1} & a_{2k+2} & \cdots \\
\lambda_G & & \downarrow & \downarrow & & \downarrow & \downarrow \\
& & O & P & & O & P
\end{array}
$$

Thus P_G represents the game tree by the prefix-closed language of strings labelling
paths from the root. Note that the tree can have infinite branches, corresponding to
the fact that there can be infinite plays in the game. In terms of the representation
by strings, this would mean that all the finite prefixes of some infinite sequence of
moves would be valid plays.

For example, the game

$$
\begin{array}{ccccccc}
(\{a_1, a_2, b_1, b_2, b_3\}, \{ & a_1 & , & a_2 & , & b_1 & , & b_2 & , & b_3 & \}, \{\epsilon, a_1, a_1b_1, a_2, a_2b_2, a_2b_3\} \\
& \downarrow & & \downarrow & & \downarrow & & \downarrow & & \downarrow \\
& O & & O & & P & & P & & P
\end{array}
$$

represents the tree

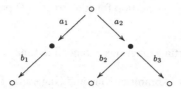

We are using games to represents *types* (objects in the semantic category). A game can be seen as specifying the possible interactions between a System and its Environment. In the traditional interpretation of types as structured sets of some kind, types are used to classify *values*. By contrast, games classify *behaviours*. *Programs* will be modelled by *strategies*, *i.e.* rules specifying how the System should actually play.

Formally, we define a (deterministic) strategy σ on a game G to be a subset $\sigma \subseteq P_G^{\text{even}}$ of the game tree, satisfying:

- $\epsilon \in \sigma$

- $sab \in \sigma \implies s \in \sigma$

- $sab, sac \in \sigma \implies b = c$

To understand this definition, think of

$$s = a_1 b_1 \cdots a_k b_k \in \sigma$$

as a record of repeated interactions with the Environment following σ. It can be read as follows:

> If the Environment initially does a_1,
>> then respond with b_1;
> If the Environment then does a_2,
>> then respond with b_2;
> $\vdots$
> If the Environment finally does a_k,
>> then respond with b_k.

The first two conditions on σ say that it is a sub-tree of P_G of even-length paths. The third is a determinacy condition.

This can be seen as generalizing the notion of graph of a relation, *i.e.* of a set of ordered pairs, which can be read as a set of stimulus-response instructions. The generalization is that ordinary relations describe a single stimulus-response event only (giving rules for what the response to any given stimulus may be), whereas strategies describe repeated interactions between the System and the Environment. We can regard $sab \in \sigma$ as saying: 'when given the stimulus a in the context s, respond with b'. Note that, with this reading, the determinacy condition generalizes the usual single-valuedness condition for (the graphs of) partial functions. Thus a useful slogan is:

"Strategies are (partial) functions extended in time."

(*cf.* interaction categories (Abramsky, Gay and Nagarajan 1996b)).

Notation 2.1 We write $\mathrm{dom}(\sigma) = \{sa \mid \exists b.sab \in \sigma\}$, and then by the determinacy condition we have a well-defined partial function, which we shall also write as σ ($M_G^P = \lambda_G^{-1}(P)$):

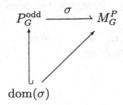

Example 2.1 Let $\mathbb{B}$ be the game

$$(\{*, tt, ff\}, \{* \mapsto O, tt \mapsto P, ff \mapsto P\}, \{\epsilon, *, *tt, *ff\})$$

This game can be seen as representing the data type of booleans. The opening move $*$ is a request by Opponent for the data, which can be answered by either tt or ff by Player. The strategies on $\mathbb{B}$ are as follows:

$$\{\epsilon\} \quad \mathrm{Pref}\{*tt\} \quad \mathrm{Pref}\{*ff\}$$

The first of these is the undefined strategy ('$\perp$'), the second and third correspond to the boolean values tt and ff. Taken with the inclusion ordering, this "space of strategies" corresponds to the usual flat domain of booleans:

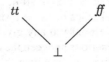

Constructions on games

We will now describe some fundamental constructions on games.

Tensor Product

Given games A, B, we describe the tensor product $A \otimes B$.

$$
\begin{aligned}
M_{A \otimes B} &= M_A + M_B \\
\lambda_{A \otimes B} &= [\lambda_A, \lambda_B] \\
P_{A \otimes B} &= \{ s \in M_{A \otimes B}^{\text{alt}} \mid s{\upharpoonright}M_A \in P_A \wedge s{\upharpoonright}M_B \in P_B \}
\end{aligned}
$$

We can think of $A \otimes B$ as allowing play to proceed in *both* the subgames A and B in an interleaved fashion. It is a form of 'disjoint (*i.e.* non-communicating or interacting) parallel composition'.

A first hint of the additional subtleties introduced by the explicit representation of both System and Environment is given by the following result.

Proposition 2.1 *(Switching condition)*
In any play $s \in P_{A \otimes B}$, if successive moves s_i, s_{i+1} are in different subgames (i.e. one is in A and the other in B), then $\lambda_{A \otimes B}(s_i) = P$, $\lambda_{A \otimes B}(s_{i+1}) = O$.

In other words, only Opponent can switch from one subgame to another; Player must always respond in the same subgame that Opponent just moved in.

To prove this, consider for each $s \in P_{A \otimes B}$ the 'state'

$$
\ulcorner s \urcorner = (\text{parity}(s \upharpoonright A), \text{parity}(s \upharpoonright B))
$$

We will write O for even parity, and P for odd parity, since *e.g.* after a play of even parity, it is Opponent's turn to move. Initially, the state is $\ulcorner \epsilon \urcorner = (O, O)$. Note that O can move in either sub-game in this state. If O moves in A, then the state changes to (P, O). P can now only move in the first component. After he does so, the state is back to (O, O). Thus we obtain the following 'state transition diagram':

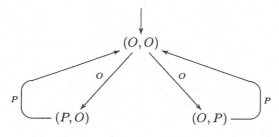

We see immediately from this that the switching condition holds; and also that the state (P, P) can never be reached (*i.e.* for no $s \in P_{A \otimes B}$ is $\ulcorner s \urcorner = (P, P)$).

Linear Implication

Given games A, B, we define the game $A \multimap B$ as follows:

$$M_{A \multimap B} = M_A + M_B$$
$$\lambda_{A \otimes B} = [\overline{\lambda_A}, \lambda_B] \qquad \text{where } \overline{\lambda}_A(m) = \begin{cases} P \text{ when } \lambda_A(m) = O \\ O \text{ when } \lambda_A(m) = P \end{cases}$$
$$P_{A \multimap B} = \{s \in M^{\text{alt}}_{A \multimap B} \mid s \upharpoonright M_A \in P_A \wedge s \upharpoonright M_B \in P_B\}$$

This definition is *almost* the same as that of $A \otimes B$. The crucial difference is the inversion of the labelling function on the moves of A, corresponding to the idea that on the left of the arrow the rôles of Player and Opponent are interchanged.

If we think of 'function boxes', this is clear enough:

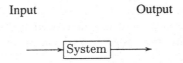

Input   Output

On the output side, the System is the producer and the Environment is the consumer; these rôles are reversed on the input side.

Note that $M^{\text{alt}}_{A \multimap B}$, and hence $P_{A \multimap B}$, are in general quite different to $M^{\text{alt}}_{A \otimes B}$, $P_{A \otimes B}$ respectively. In particular, the first move in $P_{A \multimap B}$ must always be in B, since the first move must be by Opponent, and all opening moves in A are labelled P by $\overline{\lambda_A}$.

We obtain the following switching condition for $A \multimap B$:

> If two consecutive moves are in different components, the first was by Opponent and the second by Player; so only Player can switch components.

This is supported by the following state-transition diagram:

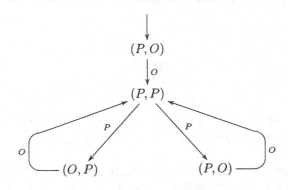

Example 2.2 The copy-cat strategy.

For any game A, we define a strategy on $A \multimap A$. This will provide the identity morphisms in our category, and the interpretation of logical axioms $A \vdash A$.

To illustrate this strategy, we undertake by the power of pure logic to beat either Kasparov or Short in chess. To do this, we play two games, one against, say, Kasparov, as White, and one against Short as Black. The situation is as follows:

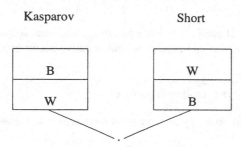

We begin with the game against Short. He plays his opening move, and we play his move in our game against Kasparov. After Kasparov responds, we play his move as our response to Short. In this way, we *play the same game twice*, but *once as White* and *once as Black*. Thus, whoever wins, we win one game. Otherwise put, we act as a buffer process, indirectly playing Kasparov off against Short.

This copy-cat process can be seen as a 'dynamic tautology', by contrast with classical propositional tautologies, which are vacuous static descriptions of states of affairs. The logical aspect of this process is a certain 'conservation of flow of information' (which ensures that we win one game).

In general, a copy-cat strategy on A proceeds as follows:

$$A \quad \multimap \quad A$$

Time		
1		a_1 O
2	a_1	P
3	a_2	O
4		a_2 P
$\vdots$	$\vdots$	$\vdots$

$$\mathrm{id}_A = \{ s \in P^{\mathrm{even}}_{A_1 \multimap A_2} \mid \forall t \text{ even-length prefix of } s : t{\upharpoonright}A_1 = t{\upharpoonright}A_2 \}$$

Here, we write A_1, A_2 to index the two occurrences of A in $A \multimap A$ for ease of reference. Note also that we write $s \upharpoonright A_1$ rather than $s{\upharpoonright}M_{A_1}$. We will continue with both these notational "abuses").

We indicate such a strategy briefly by $\overbrace{A \multimap A}$, alluding to axiom links in the proof nets of Linear Logic.

Example 2.3 Application (*Modus Ponens*).

$$\mathrm{Ap}_{A,B} : (A \multimap B) \otimes A \multimap B$$

This is the conjunction of two copy-cat strategies

$$(A \quad \multimap \quad B) \quad \otimes \quad A \quad \multimap \quad B$$

Note that A and B each occur once positively and once negatively in this formula; we simply connect up the positive and negative occurrences by 'copy-cats'.

$$\mathrm{Ap}_{A,B} = \{ s \in P^{\text{even}}_{(A_1 \multimap B_1) \otimes A_2 \multimap B_2} \mid$$
$$\forall t \text{ even-length prefix of } s : \ t{\upharpoonright}A_1 = t{\upharpoonright}A_2 \ \wedge \ t{\upharpoonright}B_1 = t{\upharpoonright}B_2 \}$$

To understand this strategy as a protocol for function application, consider the following play:

	(	A	$\multimap$	B	)	$\otimes$	A	$\multimap$	B	
O									ro	
P				ro						
O		ri								ro — request for output
P								ri		ri — request for input
O									id	id — input data
P		id								od — output data
O				od						
P									od	

The request for output to the application function is copied to the output side of the function argument; the function argument's request for input is copied to the other argument; the input data provided at the second argument is copied back to the function argument; the output from the function argument is copied back to answer the original request. It is a protocol for *linear* function application since the state of both the function and the argument will change as we interact with them; we have no way of returning to the original state. Thus we "consume" our "resources" as we produce the output. In this way there is a natural match between game semantics and linear logic.

The Category of Games $\mathcal{G}$

- Objects: Games

- Morphisms: $\sigma : A \longrightarrow B$ are strategies σ on $A \multimap B$.

- Composition: interaction between strategies.

This interaction can be described as "parallel composition plus hiding".

$$\frac{\sigma : A \to B \quad \tau : B \to C}{\sigma ; \tau : A \to C}$$

$$\sigma;\tau \;=\; (\sigma \,\|\, \tau)/B \;=\; \{s{\restriction}A,C \mid s \in \sigma \,\|\, \tau\}$$
$$\sigma \,\|\, \tau \;=\; \{s \in (M_A + M_B + M_C)^* \mid s{\restriction}A,B \in \sigma \,\wedge\, s{\restriction}B,C \in \tau\}.$$

(Note that we are extending our abuse of notation for restriction here; by $s{\restriction}A, B$ we mean the restriction of s to $M_A + M_B$ as a "subset" of $M_A + M_B + M_C$, and similarly for $s{\restriction}A, C$ and $s{\restriction}B, C$.) This definition looks very symmetric, but the actual possibilities are highly constrained by the switching condition.

$$A \xrightarrow{\;\sigma\;} B \qquad B \xrightarrow{\;\tau\;} C$$

$$
\begin{array}{ccc}
 & & c_1 \\
 & b_1 & \\
b_1 & & \\
b_2 & & \\
 & b_2 & \\
\vdots & \vdots & \\
 & b_k & \\
b_k & & \\
a_1 & &
\end{array}
$$

Initially, Opponent must move in C (say with c_1). We consider τ's response. If this is in C, then this is the response of $\sigma; \tau$ to c_1. If τ responds in B, say with b_1, then a move by Player in B in $B \multimap C$ is a move by Opponent in $A \multimap B$. So it makes sense to consider σ's response to b_1. If it is in A, this is the overall response of $\sigma; \tau$ to c_1. If σ responds with b_2 in B, then b_2 is a move by Opponent in $B \multimap C$, and we consider τ's response. Continuing in this way, we obtain a uniquely determined sequence.

$$c_1 b_1 b_2 \cdots b_k \cdots$$

If the sequence ends in a visible action in A or C, this is the response by the strategy $\sigma; \tau$ to the initial move c_1, with the internal dialogue between σ and τ in B being hidden from the Environment. Note that σ and τ may continue their internal dialogue in B forever. This is "infinite chattering" in CSP terminology, and "divergence by an infinite τ-computation" in CCS terminology.

As this discussion clearly shows, composition in $\mathcal{G}$ is interaction between strategies. The following fact is useful in the analysis of composition.

The map $s \mapsto s{\restriction}A, C$ induces a surjective map

$$\psi : \sigma \,\|\, \tau \longrightarrow \sigma;\tau.$$

Covering Lemma. ψ is injective (and hence bijective) so for each $t \in \sigma; \tau$ there is a unique $s \in \sigma \,\|\, \tau$ such that $s \restriction A, C = t$.

If $t = m_1 m_2 .... m_k$, then s has the form

$$m_1 u_1 m_2 u_2 .... u_{k-1} m_k$$

where $u_i \in M_B^*$, $1 \le i < k$.

Exercise 2.1 Prove the Covering lemma by formalizing the preceding discussion.

Proposition 2.2 $\mathcal{G}$ *is a category.*

In particular, $\mathrm{id}_A : A \longrightarrow A$ is the copy-cat strategy described previously.

Exercise 2.2 Verify this Proposition.

Exercise 2.3 Define a strategy not: $\mathbb{B} \longrightarrow \mathbb{B}$ on the boolean game defined previously to represent Boolean complement. Calculate explicitly the strategies

$$\bot; \mathtt{not} \qquad \mathit{tt}; \mathtt{not} \qquad \mathit{ff}; \mathtt{not}$$

and hence show that this strategy does indeed represent the intended function. (For this purpose, treat strategies σ on $\mathbb{B}$ as strategies $\sigma : I \longrightarrow \mathbb{B}$ where

$$I = (\emptyset, \ \emptyset, \ \{\varepsilon\})$$

is the empty game, so that the above compositions make sense).

Exercise 2.4 Embed the category of sets and partial functions faithfully into $\mathcal{G}$. Is your embedding full? What about the category of flat domains and monotone maps?

Tensor structure of $\mathcal{G}$

We will now see (in outline) that $\mathcal{G}$ is an "autonomous" = symmetric monoidal closed category, and hence a model for IMLL, Intuitionistic Multiplicative Linear Logic.

We have already defined the tensor product $A \otimes B$ on objects. Now we extend it to morphisms:

$$\frac{\sigma : A \to B \quad \tau : A' \to B'}{\sigma \otimes \tau : A \otimes A' \to B \otimes B'}$$

$$\sigma \otimes \tau = \{s \in P_{A \otimes A' \multimap B \otimes B'}^{\mathrm{even}} \mid s \restriction A, B \in \sigma \ \wedge \ s \restriction A', B' \in \tau\}.$$

This can be seen as disjoint (i.e. non-communicating) parallel composition of σ and τ.

Exercise 2.5 Check functoriality, i.e. the equations

- $(\sigma \otimes \tau); (\sigma' \otimes \tau') = (\sigma; \sigma') \otimes (\tau; \tau')$.
- $\mathrm{id}_A \otimes \mathrm{id}_B = \mathrm{id}_{A \otimes B}$.

The tensor unit is defined by:

$$I = (\emptyset, \emptyset, \{\varepsilon\})$$

The canonical isomorphisms are conjunctions of copy-cat strategies.

$\mathrm{assoc}_{A,B,C}:$
$$(A \otimes B) \otimes C \xrightarrow{\sim} A \otimes (B \otimes C)$$

$$(A \quad \otimes \quad B) \quad \otimes \quad C \quad \multimap \quad A \quad \otimes \quad (B \quad \otimes \quad C)$$

$\mathrm{symm}_{A,B}:$
$$A \otimes B \xrightarrow{\sim} B \otimes A$$

$$A \quad \otimes \quad B \quad \multimap \quad B \quad \otimes \quad A$$

$\mathrm{unitl}_A:$
$$(I \otimes A) \xrightarrow{\sim} A$$

$$(I \quad \otimes \quad A) \quad \multimap \quad A$$

$\mathrm{unitr}_A:$
$$(A \otimes I) \xrightarrow{\sim} A$$

$$(A \quad \otimes \quad I) \quad \multimap \quad A$$

The application (or evaluation) morphisms

$$\mathrm{Ap}_{A,B} : (A \multimap B) \otimes A \longrightarrow B$$

have already been defined. For currying, given

$$\sigma : A \otimes B \multimap C$$

define

$$\Lambda(\sigma) : A \longrightarrow (B \multimap C)$$

by

$$\Lambda(\sigma) = \{\alpha^*(s) \mid s \in \sigma\}$$

where $\alpha : (M_A + M_B) + M_C \xrightarrow{\sim} M_A + (M_B + M_C)$ is the canonical isomorphism in **Set**.

Exercise 2.6 Verify that the above definitions work! *E.g.* verify the equations $\text{Ap} \circ (\Lambda(\sigma) \otimes \text{id}_A) = \sigma$:

$$(A \multimap B) \otimes A \xrightarrow{\;\text{Ap}\;} B$$

with $\Lambda(\sigma) \otimes \text{id}_A$ pointing up from $C \otimes A$ and σ the diagonal from $C \otimes A$ to B.

and $\Lambda(\text{Ap} \circ (\tau \otimes \text{id}_A)) = \tau$ for $\tau : C \longrightarrow (A \multimap B)$.

Exercise 2.7 Prove that I is terminal in $\mathcal{G}$, i.e. for each A there is a unique morphism $t_A : A \longrightarrow I$.

This shows that $\mathcal{G}$ is really a model of Affine Logic, in which (unlike in Linear Logic proper) the Weakening rule is valid. Indeed, tensor has "projections":

$$A \otimes B \xrightarrow{\text{id}_A \otimes t_B} A \otimes I \xrightarrow{\text{unitr}} A.$$

Exercise 2.8 Given A, B define $A\&B$ by

$$
\begin{aligned}
M_{A\&B} &= M_A + M_B \\
\lambda_{A\&B} &= [\lambda_A, \lambda_B] \\
P_{A\&B} &= \{\text{inl}^*(\text{s}) \mid \text{s} \in P_A\} \cup \{\text{inr}^*(\text{t}) \mid \text{t} \in P_B\}.
\end{aligned}
$$

(Draw a picture of the game tree of $A\&B$; it is formed by gluing together the trees for A and B at the root. There is no overlap because we take the disjoint union of the alphabets.) Prove that $A\&B$ is the product of A and B in $\mathcal{G}$, i.e. define projections

$$A \xleftarrow{\;\text{fst}\;} A\&B \xrightarrow{\;\text{snd}\;} B$$

and pairing

$$\langle\, ,\, \rangle : \mathcal{G}(C, A) \times \mathcal{G}(C, B) \longrightarrow \mathcal{G}(C, A\&B)$$

and verify the equations

$$
\begin{aligned}
\langle \sigma, \tau \rangle; \text{fst} &= \sigma \\
\langle \sigma, \tau \rangle; \text{snd} &= \tau \\
\langle v; \text{fst}, v; \text{snd} \rangle &= v \quad \text{for } v : C \longrightarrow A\&B.
\end{aligned}
$$

Exercise 2.9 Try to define coproducts in $\mathcal{G}$. What is the problem?

Exercise 2.10 A strategy σ on A is *history-free* if it satisfies

- $sab, tac \in \sigma \;\Rightarrow\; b = c.$

- $sab, t \in \sigma, ta \in P_A \;\Rightarrow\; tab \in \sigma.$

Prove that id_A, $\text{assoc}_{A,B,C}$, $\text{sym}_{A,B}$, $\text{Ap}_{A,B}$, unitl_A, unitr_A, $\text{fst}_{A,B}$, $\text{snd}_{A,B}$ are all history-free; and that if σ and τ are history free so are $\sigma\,;\,\tau$, $\sigma \otimes \tau$, and $\Lambda(\sigma)$. Conclude that the sub-category $\mathcal{G}^{\text{hf}}$, of history-free strategies is also a model of IMLL. What about the pairing operation $\langle \sigma, \tau \rangle$? Does $\mathcal{G}^{\text{hf}}$ have binary products?

3   Winning Strategies

As we have seen, deterministic strategies can be viewed as partial functions extended in time. This partiality is appropriate when we aim to model programming languages with general recursion, in which the possibility of non termination arises. However we would also like to use game semantics to model logical systems satisfying Cut Elimination or Strong Normalization. We would therefore like to find a condition on strategies generalizing totality of functions. The obvious candidate is to require that at each stage of play, a strategy σ on A has some response to every possible move by opponent.

$$(\mathbf{tot}) \qquad s \in \sigma, sa \in P_A \Rightarrow \exists b : sab \in \sigma.$$

Call a strategy *total* if it satisfies this condition. However, totality as so defined does not suffice ; in particular, it is not closed under composition.

Exercise 3.1 Find games A, B, C and strategies $\sigma : A \to B$ and $\tau : B \to C$, such that

- σ and τ are total

- $\sigma ; \tau$ is not total.

(Hint: use infinite chattering in B.)

The best analogy for understanding this fact is with the untyped λ-calculus: the class of strongly normalizing terms is not closed under application. Thus in the Tait/Girard method for proving strong normalization in various systems of typed λ-calculus, one introduces a stronger property which does ensure closure under application. The approach we will pursue with strategies can be seen as a semantic analogue of this idea.

Before introducing this approach, we make a brief digression to allow the ideas to be presented at an appropriate level of generality. For further references on specification structures see (Abramsky *et al.* 1996a).

Specification Structures

Our aim is to "refine" a category $\mathcal{C}$ with a more subtle notion of type. A *specification structure* on $\mathcal{C}$ is given by:

- a set PA of "properties over A" for each object A of $\mathcal{C}$.

- a relation $\mathcal{R}_{A,B} \subseteq PA \times \mathcal{C}(A, B) \times PB$ for all $A, B \in Obj(\mathcal{C})$.

We write this as $\phi\{f\}\psi$, rather than $\mathcal{R}_{A,B}(\phi, f, \psi)$ - the "Hoare triple relation". This data is required to satisfy the following axioms:

(ss1) $\phi\{f\}\psi, \psi\{g\}\theta \Rightarrow \phi\{f;g\}\theta$

(ss2) $\phi\{\mathrm{id}_A\}\phi.$

We can then form a new category $\mathcal{C}_S$ as follows:

- objects are pairs (A, ϕ), $A \in Obj(\mathcal{C})$, $\phi \in PA$

- morphisms; $f : (A, \phi) \to (B, \psi)$ are $\mathcal{C}$-morphisms $f : A \to B$ such that $\phi\{f\}\psi$.

There is now an evident faithful functor

$$\mathcal{U}_S : \mathcal{C}_S \to \mathcal{C}, \qquad \mathcal{U}_S(A, \phi) = A, \qquad \mathcal{U}_S(f) = f$$

Exercise 3.2 For each of the following categories $\mathcal{C}$ and specification structures S, identify $\mathcal{C}_S$ as a known category.

(i) $\mathcal{C} = \mathbf{Set}$, $PX = X$, $x\{f\}y \stackrel{\mathrm{def}}{\equiv} f(x) = y$.

(ii) $\mathcal{C} = \mathbf{Set}, PX = \{R \subseteq X^2 \mid R \text{ is a partial order}\}$,
$R\{f\}S \stackrel{\mathrm{def}}{\equiv} R(x,y) \Rightarrow S(f(x), f(y))$.

(iii) $\mathcal{C} = \mathbf{Rel}, PX = \{R \subseteq X^2 \mid R \text{ is symmetric and irreflexive}\}$,
$R\{\rho\}S \stackrel{\mathrm{def}}{\equiv} R(x,y), \rho(x,u), \rho(y,v) \Rightarrow S(u,v)$.

(iv) $\mathcal{C} = \mathbf{Set}, PX = \{e : \omega \rightharpoonup X \mid e \text{ is surjective}\}$,
$e\{f\}e' \stackrel{\mathrm{def}}{\equiv} \exists n \in \omega, \forall m \in \omega : f \circ e(m) \simeq e' \circ \phi_n(m)$,
where $(\phi_n \mid n \in \omega)$ is an acceptable numbering of the partial recursive functions.

Exercise 3.3 Show that a specification structure on $\mathcal{C}$ is equivalently defined as a lax functor

$$R : \mathcal{C} \to \mathbf{Rel}$$

In particular, the axioms **(ss1)**, **(ss2)** correspond exactly to lax functoriality:

$$R(f); R(g) \subseteq R(f; g)$$

$$\mathrm{id}_{R(A)} \subseteq R(\mathrm{id}_A)$$

Exercise 3.4 (i) Show that every faithful functor

$$F : \mathcal{D} \to \mathcal{C}$$

gives rise to a specification structure on $\mathcal{C}$.

(ii) Show that there is a bijective correspondence between faithful functors into $\mathcal{C}$ and lax functors from $\mathcal{C}$ to $\mathbf{Rel}$.

(iii) (Pavlovic) Extend (ii) to a correspondence between arbitrary functors into $\mathcal{C}$ and lax functors from $\mathcal{C}$ into the bicategory **Span**.

If C already has some structure, e.g. is autonomous, we can lift this structure to C_S by endowing the structure on C with suitable "actions" on S. For example, to lift a tensor product we require actions

$$\otimes_{A,B} : PA \times PB \to P(A \otimes B)$$
$$* : \mathbf{1} \to PI$$

satisfying:

$$\phi\{f\}\phi' \wedge \psi\{g\}\psi' \Rightarrow \phi \otimes_{A,A'} \phi' \{f \otimes g\} \psi \otimes_{B,B'} \psi'$$

$$(\phi \otimes_{A,B} \psi) \otimes_{A\otimes B,C} \theta \{\mathtt{assoc}_{A,B,C}\} \phi \otimes_{A,B\otimes C} (\psi \otimes_{B,C} \theta)$$

$$\phi \otimes_{A,B} \psi \{\mathtt{symm}_{A,B}\} \psi \otimes_{B,A} \phi$$

$$\phi \otimes_{A,I} * \{\mathtt{unitr}_A\} \phi$$

$$* \otimes_{I,A} \phi \{\mathtt{unitl}_A\} \phi$$

For the closed structure, we must add:

$$\multimap_{A,B}: PA \times PB \to P(A \multimap B)$$

satisfying:

$$(\phi \multimap_{A,B} \psi) \otimes \phi \{\mathtt{Ap}_{A,B}\} \psi$$

$$\phi \otimes \psi \{f\} \theta \Rightarrow \phi \{\Lambda(f)\} \psi \multimap \theta.$$

Given a specification structure S with these actions on an autonomous category C, we can define an autonomous structure on C_S by:

$$(A, \phi) \otimes (B, \psi) = (A \otimes B, \phi \otimes_{A,B} \psi)$$
$$(A, \phi) \multimap (B, \psi) = (A \multimap B, \phi \multimap_{A,B} \psi)$$
$$(I, *)$$

The axioms guarantee that the morphisms used to witness the autonomous structure of C lift to C_S. Moreover, the faithful functor $\mathcal{U}_S : C_S \to C$ preserves the autonomous structure.

Exercise 3.5 What actions are needed to lift products from C to C_S? Cartesian closure?

Exercise 3.6 Define suitable actions for the examples of specification structures given in Exercise 3.2.

Winning Strategies

We now return to the problem of strengthening the properties to be required of total strategies to ensure closure under composition. The idea is to take *winning* strategies. We will formalize this via a suitable specification structure.

Given a game A, define P_A^∞, the infinite plays over A, by

$$P_A^\infty = \{s \in M_A^\omega \mid \mathrm{Pref}(s) \subseteq P_A\}$$

(By $\mathrm{Pref}(s)$ we mean the set of *finite* prefixes.)

Thus the infinite plays correspond exactly to the infinite branches of the game tree. Now define a specification structure $\mathcal{W}$ on $\mathcal{G}$ thus:

$$PA = \{W \mid W \subseteq P_A^\infty\}$$

So properties are sets of infinite plays over A: such a set can be interpreted as designating those infinite plays which are "wins" for Player. Now we say that σ is a winning strategy with respect to W (notation: $\sigma \models W$), if:

- σ is total

- $\{s \in P_A^\infty \mid \mathrm{Pref}(s) \subseteq \sigma\} \subseteq W$.

Thus σ is winning if at each finite stage when it is Player's turn to move it has a well defined response, and moreover every infinite play following σ is a win for Player. Now we define actions on the properties by:

$$\otimes_{A,B}(V, W) = \{s \in P_{A \otimes B}^\infty \mid s \restriction A \in P_A \cup V \wedge s \restriction B \in P_B \cup W\}$$

$$\multimap_{A,B}(V, W) = \{s \in P_{A \otimes B}^\infty \mid s \restriction A \in P_A \cup V \Rightarrow s \restriction B \in W\}$$

Finally we define, for $V \in P_A$, $\sigma : A \to B$, $W \in P_B$:

$$V\{\sigma\}W \equiv \sigma \models V \multimap_{A,B} W.$$

Proposition 3.1 *The above definitions satisfy the axioms for a specification structure on an autonomous category. Thus $\mathcal{G}_\mathcal{W}$ is an autonomous category.*

To spell things out, objects of $\mathcal{G}_\mathcal{W}$ are pairs (A, W_A) where A is a game as before, and $W_A \subseteq P_A^\infty$ is the designated set of winning infinite plays for Player. Morphisms $\sigma : (A, W_A) \to (B, W_B)$ are strategies $\sigma : A \to B$ such that σ is total, and for all $s \in P_{A \multimap B}^\infty$,

$$\mathrm{Pref}(s) \subseteq \sigma \wedge s \restriction A \in P_A \cup W_A \Rightarrow s \restriction B \in W_B.$$

We will verify the key point that axiom (**ss1**) is satisfied by $\mathcal{W}$, so that we indeed have a category of total strategies closed under composition, leaving the rest of the proof of the proposition as an **Exercise**.

Suppose then that $\sigma : (A, W_A) \to (B, W_B)$ and $\tau : (B, W_B) \to (C, W_C)$. We want to prove that $\sigma; \tau$ is total, i.e. that there can be no infinite chattering in B. Suppose for a contradiction that there is an infinite play

$$t = sb_0 b_1 \cdots \in \sigma \| \tau$$

with all moves after the finite prefix s in B. Then $t \upharpoonright A, B$ is an infinite play in $A \multimap B$ following σ, while $t \upharpoonright B, C$ is an infinite play in $B \multimap C$ following τ. Since σ is winning and $t \upharpoonright A$ is finite, we must have $t \upharpoonright B \in W_B$. But then since τ is winning we must have $t \upharpoonright C \in W_C$, which is impossible since $t \upharpoonright C$ is finite.

Exercise 3.7 *Give a direct proof (not using proof by contradiction) that winning stratregies compose.*

Exercise 3.8 (i) Verify that the total strategies

$$\sigma : \mathbb{B} \to \mathbb{B}$$

correspond exactly to the total functions on the booleans.
(ii) Embed the category of non-empty sets and functions faithfully into $\mathcal{G}_{\mathcal{W}}$. Is your embedding full? What about the empty set?

Exercise 3.9 Consider a game of binary streams Str

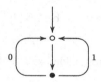

with plays $*b_1 * b_2 * b_3 \ldots$, alternating between requests for data by Opponent and bits supplied by Player. Let W_{Str} be all infinite plays of this game. Verify that the winning strategies on $(\mathsf{Str}, W_{\mathsf{Str}})$ correspond exactly to the infinite binary sequences. Verify that the winning strategies

$$\sigma : (\mathsf{Str}, W_{\mathsf{Str}}) \to (\mathsf{Str}, W_{\mathsf{Str}})$$

induce functions which map infinite streams to infinite streams. Can you characterize exactly which functions on the domain

$$\{0, 1\}^* \cup \{0, 1\}^\omega$$

with the prefix ordering are induced by winning strategies?

4 Polymorphism

Our aim now is to use game semantics to give a model for polymorphism. We extend our notation for types with type variables $X, Y, \ldots$ and with second order quantifiers

$$\forall X.A$$

As a test case, we want our model to have the property that the interpretation it yields of the polymorphic (affine) booleans

$$\forall X.X \multimap (X \multimap X)$$

has only two elements, corresponding to the denotations of the terms

$$tt \stackrel{\text{def}}{\equiv} \Lambda X.\lambda x, y : X.x$$

$$ff \stackrel{\text{def}}{\equiv} \Lambda X.\lambda x, y : X.y$$

Firstly, we need some control over the *size* of the universe of types. To achieve this, we assume a non empty set $\mathcal{V}$ satisfying

$$\mathcal{V} + \mathcal{V} \subseteq \mathcal{V}$$

(for example take $\mathcal{V} = \{0,1\}^*$).
Now we define a game $\mathcal{U}$ by:

$$\mathbf{M}_{\mathcal{U}} = \mathcal{V} + \mathcal{V}$$
$$\lambda_{\mathcal{U}} = [\mathbf{K}P, \mathbf{K}O]$$
$$\mathbf{P}_{\mathcal{U}} = \mathbf{M}_{\mathcal{U}}^{alt}.$$

(Here $\mathbf{K}P$ is the constant function valued at P.) We can define a partial order on games by:

$$A \trianglelefteq B \stackrel{\text{def}}{\equiv} \mathbf{M}_A \subseteq \mathbf{M}_B \wedge \lambda_A = \lambda_B \restriction \mathbf{M}_A \wedge \mathbf{P}_A \subseteq \mathbf{P}_B$$

Now define

$$\mathcal{G}_{\mathcal{U}} = \{A \in Obj(\mathcal{G}) \mid A \trianglelefteq \mathcal{U}\}$$

We define a *variable type* (in k variables) to be a function (monotone with respect to $\trianglelefteq$)

$$F : \mathcal{G}_{\mathcal{U}}^k \to \mathcal{G}_{\mathcal{U}}$$

Note that

$$A, B \in \mathcal{G}_{\mathcal{U}} \Rightarrow A \otimes B, A \multimap B \in \mathcal{G}_{\mathcal{U}}$$

(that was the point of having $\mathcal{V} + \mathcal{V} \subseteq \mathcal{V}$)

Exercise 4.1 (If you care about details) The above is not *quite* true. Amend the definition of $A \otimes B$, $A \multimap B$ slightly to make it true.

Thus variable types will be closed under $\otimes$ and $\multimap$. Given $F, G : \mathcal{G}_{\mathcal{U}}^k \to \mathcal{G}_{\mathcal{U}}$, we can define

$$F \otimes G(\vec{A}) = F(\vec{A}) \otimes G(\vec{A})$$
$$F \multimap G(\vec{A}) = F(\vec{A}) \multimap G(\vec{A})$$

A *uniform strategy* σ on a variable type F is defined to be a strategy on $F(\vec{\mathcal{U}})$ such that, for all $\vec{A} \in \mathcal{G}_{\mathcal{U}}^k$, $\sigma_{\vec{A}}$ is a well-defined strategy on $F(\vec{A})$, where $\sigma_{\vec{A}}$ is defined inductively by

$$\sigma_{\vec{A}} = \{\epsilon\} \ \cup \ \{sab \mid s \in \sigma_{\vec{A}}, sa \in P_{F(\vec{A})}, sab \in \sigma\}$$

(NB: in this notation, $\sigma = \sigma_{\vec{\mathcal{U}}}$).

Exercise 4.2 Show that the following properties hold for a uniform strategy σ on F:

   (i) $\vec{A} \trianglelefteq \vec{B}$ (component-wise) $\Rightarrow \sigma_{\vec{A}} = \sigma_{\vec{B}} \cap P_{F(\vec{A})} \subseteq \sigma_{\vec{B}}$

   (ii) if $(\vec{A}_i \mid i \in I)$ is a $\trianglelefteq$-directed family in $\mathcal{G}_{\mathcal{U}}^k$, then
$$\sigma_{\bigvee_{i \in I} \vec{A}_i} = \bigcup_{i \in I} \sigma_{\vec{A}_i} \qquad \text{where}$$
$\bigvee_{i \in I} \vec{A}_i$ is the directed join of the $\vec{A}_i$ (defined by component-wise union), and $\bigcup_{i \in I} \sigma_{\vec{A}_i}$ is the directed union of the strategies $\sigma_{\vec{A}_i}$.

Our aim now is to show that, for each $k \in \omega$, we obtain a category $\mathcal{G}(k)$ with:

    objects   :   variable types $F : \mathcal{G}_{\mathcal{U}}^k \to \mathcal{G}_{\mathcal{U}}$

    morphisms : $\sigma : F \to G$ are uniform strategies σ on $F \multimap G$

Moreover $\mathcal{G}(k)$ is an autonomous category.

The idea is that all the structure is transferred pointwise from $\mathcal{G}$ to $\mathcal{G}(k)$. E.g if $\sigma : F \multimap G$, $\tau : G \multimap H$, then $\sigma; \tau : F \to H$ is given by $\sigma; \tau = \sigma_{\vec{\mathcal{U}}}; \tau_{\vec{\mathcal{U}}}$.

Exercise 4.3 Check that $\sigma; \tau$ is a well-defined uniform strategy on $F \multimap H$.

Similarly, we define

$$\mathrm{id}_F = \mathrm{id}_{F(\vec{\mathcal{U}})}$$
$$\mathrm{Ap}_{F,G} = \mathrm{Ap}_{F(\vec{\mathcal{U}}), G(\vec{\mathcal{U}})}$$

etc.

Now we define a "base category" $\mathbb{B}$ with the objects $\mathcal{G}_{\mathcal{U}}^k$, $k \in \omega$, and $\trianglelefteq$-monotone functions as morphisms. For each object $\mathcal{G}_{\mathcal{U}}^k$ of $\mathbb{B}$, we have the autonomous category $\mathcal{G}(k)$. For each monotone

$$F = \langle F_1, \ldots, F_l \rangle : \mathcal{G}_{\mathcal{U}}^k \to \mathcal{G}_{\mathcal{U}}^l$$

we can define a functor

$$F^* : \mathcal{G}(l) \to \mathcal{G}(k)$$

by

$$F^*(G)(\vec{A}) = G(F(\vec{A}))$$
$$F^*(\sigma_{\vec{A}}) = \sigma_{F(\vec{A})}$$

Proposition 4.1 *The above defines a (strict) indexed autonomous category.*

At this point, we have enough structure to interpret types and terms with type variables. It remains to interpret the quantifiers. For notational simplicity, we shall focus on the case $\forall X.A(X)$ where X is the only type variable free in A. Semantically A will be interpreted by a function $F : \mathcal{G}_\mathcal{U} \to \mathcal{G}_\mathcal{U}$. We must define a game $\Pi(F) \in \mathcal{G}_\mathcal{U}$ as the interpretation of $\forall X.A$

Corresponding to the polymorphic type inference rule

$$(\forall - \text{elim}) \quad \frac{\Gamma \vdash t : \forall X.A}{\Gamma \vdash t\{B\} : A[B/X]}$$

we must define a uniform strategy

$$\pi : \mathbf{K}\Pi(F) \to F.$$

(Here $\mathbf{K}\Pi(F) : \mathcal{G}_\mathcal{U} \to \mathcal{G}_\mathcal{U}$ is the constant function valued at $\Pi(F)$. Note that $\mathbf{K} = t_\mathcal{U}^*$ where $t : \mathcal{U} \to \mathbf{1} = \mathcal{G}_\mathcal{U}^0$ is the map to the terminal object in $\mathbb{B}$.)

Corresponding to the type inference rule

$$(\forall - \text{intro}) \quad \frac{\Gamma \vdash t : A}{\Gamma \vdash \Lambda X.t : \forall X.A} \quad \text{if } X \notin FTV(\Gamma)$$

we must prove the following universal property:

for every $C \in \mathcal{G}_\mathcal{U}$ and uniform strategy $\sigma : \mathbf{K}C \to F$ there exists a unique strategy $\Lambda^2(\sigma) : C \to \Pi(F)$ such that

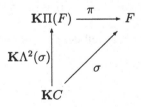

This says that there is an adjunction

$$\mathcal{G}_\mathcal{U} = \mathcal{G}_\mathcal{U}(0) \underset{\underset{\Pi(F)}{\longleftarrow}}{\overset{t_\mathcal{U}^*}{\longrightarrow}} \mathcal{G}_\mathcal{U}(1)$$

Furthermore, we must show that the Beck-Chevalley condition holds (see (Crole 1994)).

Remark 4.1 *More generally, we should show the existence of adjunctions*

$$\mathcal{G}_{\mathcal{U}} = \mathcal{G}_{\mathcal{U}}(k) \underset{\Pi_k(F)}{\overset{p^*}{\rightleftarrows}} \mathcal{G}_{\mathcal{U}}(k+1)$$

where $p : \mathcal{G}_{\mathcal{U}}^{k+1} \to \mathcal{G}_{\mathcal{U}}^k$ *is the projection function.*

Now, how are we to construct the game $\Pi(F)$? Logically, Π is a second-order quantifier. Player must undertake to defend F at any instance $F(A)$, where A is specified by Opponent. If Opponent were to specify the entire instance A at the start of the game, this would in general require an infinite amount of information to be specified in a finite time, violating a basic continuity principle of computation ("Scott's axiom"). Instead we propose the metaphor of the "veil of ignorance" (*cf.* John Rawls, *A Theory of Justice*). That is, initially nothing is known about which instance we are playing in. Opponent progressively reveals the "game board" ; at each stage, Player is constrained to play within the instance *thus far revealed* by Opponent.

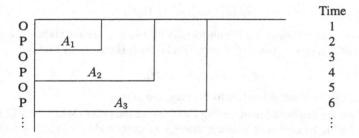

This intuition is captured by the following definition.

$$M_{\Pi(F)} = M_{F(\mathcal{U})}$$

$$\lambda_{\Pi(F)} = \lambda_{F(\mathcal{U})}$$

$P_{\Pi(F)}$ is defined inductively as follows:

$$P_{\Pi(F)} = \quad \{\epsilon\}$$
$$\cup \quad \{sa \mid s \in P_{\Pi(F)}^{\text{even}} \wedge \exists A.sa \in P_{F(A)}\}$$
$$\cup \quad \{sab \mid sa \in P_{\Pi(F)}^{\text{odd}} \wedge \forall A.sa \in P_{F(A)} \Rightarrow sab \in P_{F(A)}\}$$

The first clause in the definition of $P_{\Pi(F)}$ is the basis of the induction. The second clause refers to positions in which it is Opponent's turn to move. It says that Opponent may play in any way which is valid in *some* instance (extending the current one). The final clause refers to positions in which it is Player's turn to move. It says that Player can only move in a fashion which is valid in *every* possible instance.

For the polymorphic projection

$$\Pi(F) \overset{\pi_A}{\to} F(A)$$

π_A plays copy-cat between $\Pi(F)$ and $F(A)$. This is uniform, witnessed by the "global copy-cat" $\mathrm{id}_{F(\mathcal{U})}$.

Why does this definition work? Consider the situation

$$\Pi(F) \quad \to \quad \underset{a}{F(A)}$$
$$a$$

At this stage, it is Opponent's turn to move, and of course there are many moves in $\Pi(F)$ which would not be valid in $F(A)$. However, Opponent in $\Pi(F)$ in contravariant (i.e negative) position must play as Player in $\Pi(F)$, and hence is constrained to respond to a only in a fashion which is valid in *every* instance in which a can be played, and which in particular is valid in $F(A)$. Hence Opponent's response can safely be copied back into $F(A)$.

Now for the universal property. Given uniform $\sigma : KC \to F$, we define

$$\Lambda^2(\sigma) = \sigma : C \to \Pi(F)$$

That this is valid follows from the uniformity of σ so that at each stage its response must be valid in *any* instance that we might be in. It is then clear that

$$K\Lambda^2(\sigma); \pi = \sigma; \mathrm{id}_{F\mathcal{U}} = \sigma$$

and hence that this definition fulfills the required properties.

Since we are interested in modeling IMLL2 (second order IMLL) we will refine our model with the notion of winning strategy, as explained in the previous section.

Firstly, we briefly indicate the additional structure required of a specification structure in order to get a model for IMLL2 in the refined category.

We assume that variable types are modeled by monotone functions $F : \mathcal{G}_\mathcal{U} \to \mathcal{G}_\mathcal{U}$ equipped with actions

$$F_A : PA \to P(FA)$$

for each $A \in \mathcal{G}_\mathcal{U}$.

Also there is an action:

$$\Pi_F : \mathbf{1} \to P(\Pi(F))$$

satisfying:

($\forall$ − elim) $\Pi_F\{\pi_A\}\phi$ $(A \in \mathcal{G}_\mathcal{U}, \phi \in P(FA))$

($\forall$ − intro) $(\forall A \in \mathcal{G}_\mathcal{U}, \psi \in PA. \phi\{\sigma_A\}F_A(\psi)) \Rightarrow \phi\{\Lambda^2(\sigma)\}\Pi_F.$

Now in the case of the specification structure W for winning strategies, we define:

$$\Pi_F = \{s \in \mathrm{P}^\infty_{\Pi(F)} \mid \forall A \in \mathcal{G}_\mathcal{U}, W \subseteq \mathrm{P}^\infty_A . s \in \mathrm{P}^\infty_{F(A)} \Rightarrow s \in F_A(W)\}.$$

Exercise 4.4 Verify that this satisfies ($\forall$-intro) and ($\forall$-elim).

Thus we have a game semantics for IMLL2 in which terms denote winning strategies. How good is this semantics? As a basic test, let us look at the type

$$\forall X. X \multimap (X \multimap X)$$

which we write as

$$\forall X. X_1 \multimap (X_2 \multimap X_3)$$

using indices to refer to the occurrences of X. What are the winning strategies for this type? Note that the first move must be in X_3. Because of the definition of Π, Player can only respond by playing the same move in a negative occurrence of X, i.e X_1 or X_2. Suppose Player responds in X_2:

$$\forall X. X_1 \multimap (X_2 \quad \multimap \quad X_3) \atop a$$
$$a$$

At this point, by the switching condition Opponent must respond in X_2, say with a move b; what can Player do next? If he were playing as the term $\Lambda X.\lambda x, y : X.y$, then he should copy b back to X_3. However there is another possiblity (pointed out by Sebastian Hunt): namely, Player can *play a in X_1*, and continue thereafter by playing copy-cat between X_1 and X_3. This certainly yields a winning strategy, but does not correspond to the denotation of any term.

To eliminate such undesirable possibilities, we introduce a constraint on strategies. Recall from Exercise 1.10 that a strategy is *history-free* if its response at any point depends only on the last move by Opponent: that is, if it satisfies:

$$sab \in \sigma, t \in \sigma, ta \in P_A \;\Rightarrow\; tab \in \sigma.$$

The history-free strategies suffice to model the multiplicatives and polymorphism, so we get a model $\mathcal{G}_{\mathcal{W}}^{\text{hf}}$ of IMLL2.

Now consider again the situation

$$\forall X. X_1 \multimap (X_2 \quad \multimap \quad X_3)$$
$$a$$
$$a$$
$$b$$

Player can only respond to b by copying b into X_3 if he is following a history-free strategy: the option of playing a in X_1 is not open to him, because a is not "visible" to him. Thus he can only proceed by

$$\forall X. X_1 \multimap (X_2 \quad \multimap \quad X_3)$$
$$a$$
$$a$$
$$b$$
$$b$$

Moreover, Player must continue to play copy-cat between X_2 and X_3 ever thereafter, since the information available to him at each stage is only the move just played by Opponent.

Note also that Player must play in the same way, regardless of which move is initially made by Opponent. For example, suppose for a contradiction that Player responded to a_1, by copying it to X_1, and to a_2 by copying it to X_2. Now consider the situation:

$$\forall X. \quad X_1 \quad \multimap \quad (X_2 \quad \multimap \quad X_3)$$
$$a_1$$
$$a_1$$
$$b_1$$
$$b_1$$
$$a_2$$
$$a_2$$

Since Player is following a history-free strategy, he must *always* respond to a_2 by copying it to X_2; but the above position is clearly not valid, since there is an instance A with $P_A = \text{Pref}\{a_1 b_1 a_2\}$ in which a_2 cannot be played as an initial move.

Thus we conclude that for our test case the model $\mathcal{G}_{\mathcal{W}}^{\text{hf}}$ does indeed have the required property that the only strategies for the game

$$\forall X. X_1 \multimap (X_2 \multimap X_3)$$

are the denotations of the terms:

$$\Lambda X.\lambda x, y : X.x \qquad\qquad \Lambda X.\lambda x, y : X.y$$
copycat between X_1 and X_3 \qquad copycat between X_2 and X_3.

Exercise 4.5 *Show that the only two strategies in $\mathcal{G}_{\mathcal{W}}^{\text{hf}}$ for the game*

$$\forall X. (X \otimes X) \multimap (X \otimes X)$$

are those corresponding to the identity and the twist map.

Open problem For which class of (closed) types of IMLL2 do we get a "Full Completeness" result, i.e. that all strategies at that type in $\mathcal{G}_{\mathcal{W}}^{\text{hf}}$ are definable in IMLL2? See Abramsky and Jagadeesan (1994).

5 Relational Parametricity

In this section, we investigate how the notion of relational parametricity can be adapted to the setting of games.

Firstly, we go back to the general level of Specification Structures. We use some notions due to Andy Pitts (1996).

Given $\phi, \psi \in PA$, we define:

$$\phi \leq \psi \;\equiv\; \phi\{\mathrm{id}_A\}\psi.$$

This is always a preorder by (ss1) and (ss2). Say that the specification structure S is *posetal* if it is a partial order (i.e. antisymmetric). Now the notion of meet of properties $\bigwedge_{i \in I} \phi_i$ can be defined on PA. Say that S is *meet-closed* if it is posetal and each PA has all meets.

Now we define a notion of *relations* on games. We shall focus on binary relations. Say that R is a relation from A to B (notation: $R \subseteq A \times B$) if R is a non-empty subset $R \subseteq P_A \times P_B$ satisfying:

- $R(s, t) \;\Rightarrow\; |s| = |t|$.

- $R(sa, tb) \;\Rightarrow\; R(s, t)$.

So R is a length-preserving non-empty prefixed closed subset).

We shall define a specification structure R on the product category $\mathcal{G} \times \mathcal{G}$ by taking $P(A, B)$ to be the set of relations $R \subseteq A \times B$. Given a relation $R \subseteq A \times B$, we lift it to a relation $\widehat{R}$ between strategies on A and strategies on B, by the following definition:

$$
\begin{aligned}
\widehat{R}(\sigma, \tau) \iff \forall s \in \sigma, t \in \tau.\, & R(sa, ta') \\
\Rightarrow\; & [(sa \in dom(\sigma) \Leftrightarrow ta' \in dom(\tau)) \\
& \wedge\, sab \in \sigma, ta'b' \in \tau \;\Rightarrow\; R(sab, ta'b')]
\end{aligned}
$$

This definition is "logical relations extended in time"; it relativizes the usual clause:

$$R(x, y) \iff [(fx{\downarrow} \Leftrightarrow gy{\downarrow}) \wedge (fx{\downarrow}, gy{\downarrow} \Rightarrow R(fx, gy))]$$

to the context (previous history) s. It can also be seen as a form of bisimulation:

> "If σ and τ reach related states at P's turn to move, then one has a response iff the other does, and the states after the response are still related."

Also, if $R \subseteq A \times A'$ and $S \subseteq B \times B'$, then we define:

$$
\begin{aligned}
R \otimes_{(A, A'), (B, B')} S \;=\; \{\; (s,t) \in P_{A \otimes B} \times P_{A' \otimes B'} \mid\; & R(s{\restriction}A, t{\restriction}A') \wedge S(s{\restriction}B, t{\restriction}B') \\
& \wedge\, \mathrm{out}^*(s) = \mathrm{out}^*(t)) \;\}
\end{aligned}
$$

where $\mathrm{out} : M_A + M_B \to \{0, 1\}$ is given by:

$$\mathrm{out} = [\mathbf{K0}, \mathbf{K1}]$$

Similarly we define:

$$R \multimap_{(A,\,A'),\,(B,\,B')} S \;=\; \{\;(s,t) \in P_{A \to B} \times P_{A' \to B'} \;| $$
$$R(s{\restriction}A, t{\restriction}A') \,\wedge\, S(s{\restriction}B, t{\restriction}B')$$
$$\wedge\; out^*(s) = out^*(t))\;\}$$

Now we define:

$$R\{(\sigma, \tau)\}S \;\equiv\; \widehat{R \multimap S}(\sigma, \tau)$$

Proposition 5.1 *This is a specification structure in $\mathcal{G} \times \mathcal{G}$. In particular,*

$$R\{(\sigma, \tau)\}S, \; S\{(\sigma', \tau')\}T \;\Longrightarrow\; R\{(\sigma; \sigma', \tau; \tau')\}T$$

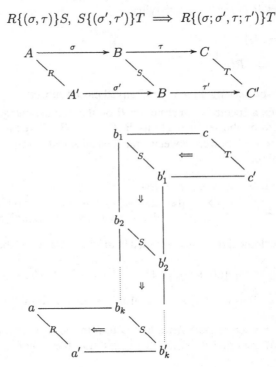

Exercise 5.1 Prove this! (The above "logical waterfall" diagram gives the idea of the proof.)

We shall in fact be more interested in "pulling back" this specification structure along the diagonal functor $\Delta : \mathcal{G} \to \mathcal{G} \times \mathcal{G}$. That is, we are interested in the category $\mathcal{G}_R$ with objects (A, R) where $R \subseteq A \times A$ and morphisms $\sigma : (A, R) \to (B, S)$ which are strategies $\sigma : A \to B$ such that $\widehat{R \multimap S}(\sigma, \sigma)$. We are also interested in the category $\mathcal{G}^{\mathrm{hf}}_{\mathcal{W}R}$ where we combine the winning strategy and relational structures so that objects are (A, W_A, R_A), where W_A is a set of designated winning plays, and $R_A \subseteq A \times A$ is a relation and $\sigma : (A, W_A, R_A)$ is a strategy $\sigma : A \to B$ such that $W_A\{\sigma\}W_B \wedge R_A\{\sigma\}R_B$.

Now we build a model of IMLL2 by refining our previous model with this specification structure R. A variable type will now be a monotone function

$$F : (\mathcal{G}_u, \trianglelefteq) \to (\mathcal{G}_u, \trianglelefteq)$$

with an action

$$F_A : PA \to P(FA).$$

We assume that the specification structure is monotone, in the sense that:

$$A \trianglelefteq B \implies PA \subseteq PB$$

(this is easily seen to hold for R and W), and that

$$
\begin{array}{ccc}
PA & \longrightarrow & PB \\
F_A \Big\downarrow & & \Big\downarrow F_B \\
P(FA) & \longrightarrow & P(FB)
\end{array}
$$

We also require that if $\phi \in PA, \psi \in PA, A \trianglelefteq A'$ and $B \trianglelefteq B'$, then

$$\phi\{F\}_{A,B}\psi \iff \phi\{F\}_{A',B'}\psi.$$

We further assume that the specification structure is meet-closed. Then we define:

$$\Pi_F \overset{df}{=} \bigwedge\{F_A(\phi) \mid A \in \mathcal{G}_u, \phi \in PA\} = \bigwedge\{F_A(\phi) \mid \phi \in P\mathcal{U}\} \quad (5.1)$$

(This latter equality holds because of the above monotonicity properties).

The fact that ($\forall$-intro) and ($\forall$-elim) are satisfied then holds automatically because of the definition of Π_F as a meet.

To apply this construction to R, we must show that it is meet-closed.

Firstly, we characterise the partial order on properties in R.

Proposition 5.2

$$
R \leq S \iff
\begin{array}{lll}
R^{\text{even}}(s, t) \wedge S(sa, tb) & \implies & R(sa, tb) \\
\wedge \quad S^{\text{odd}}(s, t) \wedge R(sa, tb) & \implies & S(sa, tb).
\end{array}
$$

We can read this as: at O-moves $S \subseteq R$ and at P-moves $R \subseteq S$.

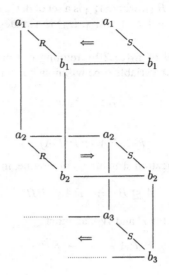

Proposition 5.3 $\bigwedge_{i \in I} R_i$ *is defined inductively by:*

$$\begin{aligned}
\bigwedge_{i \in I} R_i \;=\; & \{(\varepsilon, \varepsilon)\} \\
\cup\; & \{(sa, ta') \mid \quad (s, t) \in \bigwedge_{i \in I} R_i^{\text{even}} \land \\
& \qquad\qquad \exists i \in I.R_i(sa, ta')\} \\
\cup\; & \{(sab, ta'b') \mid \quad (sa, ta') \in \bigwedge_{i \in I} R_i^{\text{odd}} \land \\
& \qquad\qquad \forall i \in I.R_i(sa, ta') \;\Rightarrow\; R_i(sab, ta'b')\}.
\end{aligned}$$

Note the similarity between this definition and that of $P_{\Pi(F)}$, which is in fact the unary case of the above, indexed over all $P \subseteq^{\text{nepref}} P_{F(U)}$.

Exercise 5.2   1. Verify these propositions.

2. For the specification structure $\mathcal{W}$, show that:

- $V \leq W \;\Leftrightarrow\; V \subseteq W.$
- $\bigwedge_{i \in I} W_i = \bigcap_{i \in I} W_i.$

Thus we obtain a model $\mathcal{G}_{\mathcal{W}R}^{\text{hf}}$ of IMLL, incorporating both:

- the refinement to winning strategies
- a notion of "relational parametricity".

References

Abramsky, S., S. J. Gay and R. Nagarajan (1996a). Specification structures and propositions-as-types for concurrency. In G. Birtwhistle and F. Moller (Eds), *Logics for Concurrency: Structure vs. Automata. Proceedings of the VIIIth Banff Higher Order Workshop*, Volume 1043 of *Lecture Notes in Computer Science*, pp. 5–40. Springer-Verlag, Berlin.

Abramsky, S., S. J. Gay and R. Nagarajan (1996b). Interaction Categories and Foundations of Typed Concurrent Programming. In M. Broy (Ed.), *Deductive Program Design: Proceedings of the 1994 Marktoberdorf International Summer School, NATO ASI Series F: Computer and Systems Sciences*, pp. 35–113. Springer-Verlag, Berlin.

Abramsky, S. and R. Jagadeesan (1994). Games and full completeness for multiplicative linear logic, *Journal of Symbolic Logic, 59(2)*, 543–574.

Abramsky, S., R. Jagadeesan and P. Malacaria (1995). Full abstraction for PCF. Submitted for publication.

Abramsky, S. and G. McCusker (1995). Games for recursive types. In C. L. Hankin, I. C. Mackie and R. Nagarajan (Eds), *Theory and Formal Methods of Computing 1994: Proceedings of the Second Imperial College Department of Computing Workshop on Theory and Formal Methods*, Imperial College Press.

Abramsky, S., G. McCusker (1995). Games and full abstraction for the lazy λ-calculus. In *10th Annual Symposium on Logic in Computer Science*, pp. 234–243. IEEE Computer Society Press, Washington.

Crole, R. (1994). *Categories for Types*. Cambridge University Press.

Danos, V., H. Herbelin, and L. Regnier (1996). Games and abstract machines. In *11th Annual Symposium on Logic in Computer Science*, pp. 394–405. IEEE Computer Society Press, Washington.

Girard, J.-Y., Y. Lafont and P. Taylor (1989). *Proofs and types*. Cambridge University Press.

Girard, J.-Y. (1995). A survey of Linear Logic. In Y. Lafont (Ed.), *Advances in Linear Logic*. Cambridge University Press.

Hyland, J. M. E. and C.-H. L. Ong (1995). On full abstraction for PCF: I, II, and III. Submitted for publication.

McCusker, G. (1996a). Games and full abstraction for FPC In *11th Annual Symposium on Logic in Computer Science*, pp. 174–183. IEEE Computer Society Press, Washington.

McCusker, G. (1996b). Games and full abstraction for a functional metalanguage with recursive types. Phd thesis, University of London, to appear.

Nickau, H. (1994). Hereditarily sequential functionals. In A. Nerode and Yu. N. Matiyasevich (Eds.) *Logical Fondations of Computer Science, Proceedings 1994*, Volume 813 of *Lecture Notes in Computer Science*. Springer Verlag, Berlin.

Ong, C.-H. L. (1996). A semantic view of classical proofs. In *11th Annual Symposium on Logic in Computer Science*, pp. 230–241. IEEE Computer Society Press, Washington.

Pitts, A. M. (1996). Relational properties of domains. *Information and Computation 127*, 66–90.

Computational Content of
Classical Logic

Thierry Coquand

Contents

1 Introduction

This course is an *introduction* to the research trying to connect the proof theory of classical logic and computer science. We omit important and standard topics, among them the connection between the computational interpretation of classical logic and the programming operator callcc[1].

Instead, here we put the emphasis on actual mathematical examples. We analyse the following questions: what can be the meaning of a non-effective proof of an existential statement, a statement that claims the existence of a finite object that satisfies a decidable property? Is it clear that a non-effective proof has a meaning at all? Can we always say that this proof contains implicitly, if not explicitly, some effective witness? Is this witness unique? By putting the emphasis on actual mathematical examples, we follow Gentzen who founded natural deduction by analysing concrete mathematical examples, like Euclid's proof of the infinity of prime numbers.

We present general *methods* that can be used to compute effectively such witnesses. The three methods we shall analyse are[2]

1. The negative translation. This is a quite natural translation of classical logic in intuitionistic logic, which is both simple and powerful.

---

[1] See the references at the end of part I.

[2] A method that is not analysed here is the "no counter example" interpretation, due to Kreisel, and explained in detail in Girard's book "Proof Theory and Logical Complexity", Bibliopolis.

2. A game-theoretic interpretation of classical logic, which is a suggestive reformulation of Gentzen-Novikov's sequent calculus, and may be in some
   cases more convenient than negative translation.

3. Use of formal topology. It consists of realising some conditions in a topological model. In some cases, it is possible then to realise these conditions
   effectively, while the "absolute" realisation of these conditions is impossible. Though the extent of this method is not completely elucidated yet, it
   has given unexpected results in difficult cases where the negative translation
   cannot be used. (We present among applications a new proof of Herbrand's
   theorem, and an analysis of one proof of van der Waerden's theorem on arithmetical progressions.)

2 The Negative Translation

Two systems that we analyse are Peano Arithmetic, written PA, and Heyting Arithmetic, written HA.[3]

The system HA is a theory in first order intuitionistic logic. We add function
symbols for primitive recursive functions, and the axioms are the defining equations
of these equations, and the induction schema. See [TroeDal] and [Gentzen69] for
the complete presentation of this formal system.

The system PA can be defined as the system HA where we add the schema $\neg A \lor A$
or, equivalently, $\neg\neg A \Rightarrow A$. We recall that $\neg\phi$ can be seen as an abbreviation for
$\phi \Rightarrow \bot$.

2.1 Markov's rule

Markov's principle is the schema, for a quantifier-free formula ϕ

$$\neg\neg\exists x\ \phi \Rightarrow \exists x\ \phi \qquad (MP).$$

More generally, we can consider the schema

$$[\forall x\ [\phi \lor \psi]], [\neg\forall x\ \phi] \Rightarrow [\exists x\ \psi], \qquad (MP')$$

for arbitrary formulae ϕ and ψ. This schema implies (MP) for a decidable formula
ϕ.

This schema is *not* derivable.

We should make the meaning of this last sentence more precise, especially the
meaning of the word "schema". An example of a derivable schema is

$$\neg\exists x\phi \Rightarrow \forall x\neg\phi,$$

---

[3]These names are quite misleading because in the form they are now presented, both systems are
expressed in first order logic, while both Peano and Heyting formulated their systems using higher
order logic, i.e. with quantification over variables ranging over properties.

and by this, we mean that it is provable by the laws of intuitionistic logic if ϕ is $P\,x$, where P is a new predicate variable. Indeed, the formula

$$\neg \exists x P\,x \Rightarrow \forall x \neg P\,x,$$

is provable from the elimination rule for existential quantification, recalling that $\neg\,\phi$ is defined as $\phi \Rightarrow \bot$. The claim is that such a justification is not possible for the schema (MP').

There are at least two proofs of this fact, both interesting. The first one uses modified realizability (and was the motivation for the introduction of this notion Kreisel59]). The second one uses topological, or Beth, models. Both are in the exercises.

It can appear at first counter-intuitive that this principle does not hold intuitionistically, and this may seem a kind of incompleteness of the system HA. It seems that we do have an algorithm that will compute a witness: test successively $\phi\,0$ or $\psi\,0$, $\phi\,1$ or $\psi\,1 \ldots$ until one finds a value n_0 such that $\psi\,n_0$. Such an algorithm is not accepted intuitionistically, because we don't have any justification that this search will stop (only that it is impossible that it goes on forever).

However, if Markov's principle is not derivable, it is valid as a *rule*. By this we mean the following. Given a decidable formula ϕ, if $\neg\forall x.\neg\phi$ is provable in HA, then $\exists x.\phi$ is provable in HA.

We will prove this for an atomic formula ϕ. (The case of a quantifier-free formula is an exercise.) Notice however that if ϕ is decidable, we can always consider an extension of HA with a new predicate variable P such that $P\,x$ is equivalent to ϕ. (In exercise 5, it is shown how to reduce the case of a decidable formula to a quantifier free formula without extending HA.)

One can read this principle as: if $\exists x\phi$ is provable classically, then it is provable intuitionistically. In this form, this was shown by Novikov [Novikov43], and implicitly by Gentzen. An elegant proof is given by Friedman [Friedman78], and it is this proof that we present. The analogy with the monad of exceptions, used in functional programming, is striking, and we present a small example that illustrates this analogy.

2.2 Closure under Markov's rules

We present Friedman's proof that if $\neg\neg\exists x\ \phi$ is provable in HA, then so is $\exists x\ \phi$, where ϕ is quantifier free. This relies on the following translation:

- P^* is $P \vee A$, if P is atomic,
- $(B \vee C)^*$ is $B^* \vee C^*$,
- $(B \wedge C)^*$ is $B^* \wedge C^*$,
- $(B \Rightarrow C)^*$ is $B^* \Rightarrow C^*$,

- $(\forall x \ B)^*$ is $\forall x \ B^*$,

- $(\exists x \ B)^*$ is $\exists x \ B^*$,

- $\perp^*$ is A,

where A is the formula $\exists x \ \phi$.

Proposition: If B is provable in HA, then so is B^*.

This is direct.

Remark: If B is $\neg \forall x \ \neg \phi$, then B^* is equivalent to A.

Theorem: If $\neg \forall x \ \neg \phi$ is provable in HA (with ϕ quantifier free), then so is $\exists x \ \phi$.

Proof: Let B be $\neg \forall x \ \neg \phi$. If B is provable in HA, then so is B^* by the proposition. By the remark, B^* is equivalent to $\exists x \ \phi$, and hence $\exists x \ \phi$ is provable. $\square$

This translation is strongly reminiscent of the use of the exception monad [Moggi,SpiWad90] used in functional programming. The existential formula A corresponds to a fixed data type of error messages, and the operation on types is $T X = X + A$, which corresponds to the translation of atomic formulae.

Notice that we don't start from a classical proof of $\exists x.\phi$. Only an intuitionistic proof that it is impossible not to have an x such that ϕ holds. The next section will show how to transform a proof of $\exists x.\phi$ in PA into a proof of the same statement in HA.

2.3   Negative Translation

This translation can be traced back to Kolmogorov. A propositional form of this result was then stated by Glivenko, and it is not clear how much this has influenced the work of Gödel, Gentzen and Bernays. The references can be found in Gödel's collected work [God86]. The form stated in Kolmogorov is quite strong, since he claimed that, via the double negation translation, one can establish that a finitary result proved with the principle of excluded middle can be proved without using this principle. This strong form is still open however, and, as we shall see, the negative translation does not work in the presence of the Axiom of Choice.

The intuition behind this translation can be described as follows. There is a difference between the connective $\wedge$ and universal quantification on one side, and on the other side, disjunction and existential quantification. If a classical mathematician claims to have a proof of $A \wedge B$, he claims that he has a proof of A and a proof of B, like in intuitionistic logic. But if he claims to have a proof of $A \vee B$, he may claim only to have deduced a contradiction from the hypothesis that neither A not B hold. In the same way, if he claims to have a proof of $\exists x \ A$, he may mean only that he has arrived at a contradiction from the hypothesis that A never holds.

Notice that the connectives $\exists$ and $\vee$ have a special status. This point is discussed in Gentzen's collected works [Gentzen69].

Theorem: If $\exists x\ \phi$ is provable in PA (with ϕ decidable), then it is provable in HA.

This theorem does not hold if ϕ is not a decidable formula. It may even happen that $\exists x\ \phi$ is provable in PA, but that $\phi(n_0)$ is not provable in PA for any given numeral n_0 (see the exercises).

The proof of the theorem relies on the following translation:

- P^* is ∇P, if P is atomic,

- $(B \wedge C)^*$ is $B^* \wedge C^*$,

- $(B \Rightarrow C)^*$ is $B^* \Rightarrow C^*$,

- $(\forall x\ B)^*$ is $\forall x\ B^*$,

- $(B \vee C)^*$ is $\nabla\ (B^* \vee C^*)$,

- $(\exists x\ B)^*$ is $\nabla(\exists x\ B^*)$,

- $\perp^*$ is A,

where A is the formula $\exists x\ \phi$, and $\nabla\ B$ is $(B \Rightarrow A) \Rightarrow A$.

Proposition: If B is provable in PA, then B^* is provable in HA.

The proof is direct by induction on the proof of B. We comment rather on cases where this proposition *cannot* be applied. A good example is the fundamental theorem if algebra on the existence of roots. In this case, it happens to be possible to compute effectively the roots of a given polynomial, but this does not follow directly from a general meta-theorem. But the form of the statement "there exists a root x_0" of a given polynomial P is not, contrary to what it may seem, purely existential. Indeed, the statement $P(x_0) = 0$ is not decidable, but a universally quantified statement. To prove constructively this existence statement, one possibility is to prove first that there exists a rational x_1 such that $P(x_1)$ is "small", and then to use Newton's method to compute a zero of P from x_1.

The following proposition gives an example where a computational content is not possible. If f is a continuous function over $[0, 1]$ and $f(0) < 0$, $f(1) > 0$, then there exists x such that $f(x) = 0$. This holds classically, but it is not possible to extract an algorithm parametric in f that computes a root of f [TroeDal].

In functional programming, there is a monad closely connected to this translation. Given a data type A, one defines the "continuation monad" by $T\ X = (X \to A) \to A$. Notice that the operator ∇ on propositions can be seen as a modal operator and satisfies the law corresponding to the laws of a monad [SpiWad90].

- $B \Rightarrow \nabla B$,

- ∇B and $B \Rightarrow \nabla C$ entail ∇C.

Wadler [SpiWad90] has shown how to represent in an elegant way non functional operations in a purely functional programming language. This suggests that it should be possible to "simulate" classical reasoning by working in an intuitionistic framework with such a modality. The next section presents such a simulation on a simple example, due to U. Berger and H. Schwichtenberg.

2.4   Monads on Propositions

The goal of this section is to show that we can use monads as well on propositions. They can be used to simulate "impure features", here the use of excluded middle, in a pure Type Theory.

Here is the reasoning we want to simulate. Given a function f : N→N, with a proof h_1 : $\forall x \exists y\ x < f\ y$, and given x_0 : N with a proof h_2 : $f\ 0 \leq x_0$, we want to find n such that $f\ n \leq x_0$ and $x_0 < f\ (S\ n)$. That is we want to prove constructively $P = \exists\ n.f\ n \leq x_0 \wedge x_0 < f\ (S\ n)$. (This example is due to U. Berger and H. Schwichtenberg.)

Here is a classical proof (impure). Suppose $\neg P$, that is

$$h_3 : \forall n\ f\ n \leq x_0 \Rightarrow x_0 < f\ (S\ n) \Rightarrow \perp$$

we prove

$$\forall n\ f\ n \leq x_0 \qquad\qquad (*)$$

by induction on n.

For $n = 0$, it holds by h_2.

If $f\ n \leq x_0$, we cannot have $x_0 < f(Sn)$ by h_3, hence $f\ (S\ n) \leq x_0$.

But $(*)$ contradicts h_1, hence by excluded middle, we have P.

We simulate this impure reasoning by using the monad/modality ∇ : Set→Set defined by $\nabla X = X \vee P$.

Notice that we have unit : $X \Rightarrow \nabla X$ and bind : $\nabla X \Rightarrow [X \Rightarrow \nabla Y] \Rightarrow \nabla Y$. The following rule is derived from bind by induction

$$\frac{\nabla\ (A\ 0) \quad A\ n \Rightarrow \nabla\ (A\ (S\ n))}{\nabla\ (A\ n)} \qquad (**).$$

This holds for a general monad.

For this particular monad we have furthermore

$$lem_1 : \forall X \forall n\ f\ n \leq x_0 \Rightarrow x_0 < f\ (S\ n) \Rightarrow \nabla X$$

and
$$lem_2 : \forall X \; \neg X \Rightarrow \nabla \, X \Rightarrow P$$

Now, we prove
$$\forall n \; \nabla \, (f \, n \le x_0)$$

by using the rule $(**)$.

For $n = 0$, using h_2 and unit.

If $f \, n \le x_0$, then there are two cases. If $f \, (S \, n) > x_0$, we have $\nabla \, (f \, (S \, n) \le x_0)$
by lem_1 and if $f \, (S \, n) \le x_0$, we have $\nabla \, (f \, (S \, n) \le x_0)$ by unit.

This reasoning follows closely the classical reasoning.

We can now compute y_0 such that $x_0 < f \, y_0$ by h_1. Since we have

$$\nabla \, (f \, y_0 \le x_0)$$

we deduce P by lem_2.

What is the extracted program behind this reasoning?

In Gofer/Haskell [Augustsson], we would introduce

```
M a = Ok a | Exit Int
```

and program

```
exitM :: Int -> Ok a
exitM n = Exit n

g :: Int -> M ()

g 0 = unitM ()

g (n+1) =
g n 'bindM' \ _ ->
if x_0 < f (n+1)
    then exitM n
    else unitM ()
```

This program can be seen to be the Gofer version of our monadic proof.

The correctness of this program takes the form: if $x_0 < f \, n$, then $g \, n$ will be of
the form Exit p, with $p < n$ such that $f \, p \le x_0 < f \, (S \, p)$.

2.5 Exercises on Part I

1. Show that adding the schema $\neg A \lor A$ or the schema $\neg\neg A \Rightarrow A$ leads to the
   same theory.

2. We have $[\neg\neg A \wedge \neg\neg B] \Rightarrow \neg\neg[A \wedge B]$. Notice that there are two ways, not symmetric in A, B to prove this.

   Deduce from this that $\neg\neg A$ is provable intuitionistically iff A is provable classically for propositional logic.

   For infinite conjunction, we need Spector's "double negation shift" $\bigwedge \neg\neg A_i \Rightarrow \neg\neg \bigwedge A_i$. Show that the schema $\forall x \ \neg\neg A \Rightarrow \neg\neg\forall x \ A$ does not hold intuitionistically. (Hint: show otherwise that the negative translation of the Axiom of Choice would be provable and use the results of Part III.)

3. Using a Gödel sentence, give an example of a formula ϕ such that **PA** proves $\exists x \ \phi$, but $\phi(n_0)$ is not provable in **PA** for any given numeral n_0. (Hint: let ψ a decidable formula such that $G = \forall n \ \neg \ \psi$ is not provable in **PA** but $\psi[n_0]$ holds for no given numeral n_0. Consider the formula $\exists n \ [\psi \vee G]$.)

4. A *positive formula* is a formula built from atomic formula, existential quantification, finite conjunction and disjunction. A *geometric formula* is a formula of the form $\forall x_1, \ldots, x_n \ [\phi \Rightarrow \psi]$ where ϕ and ψ are positive formulae. Finally, a *geometric theory* is a set of geometric formulae. Prove that if a geometric formula is provable in **PA** $+ \ T$ where T is geometric, then it is provable in **HA** $+ \ T$.

5. Extend the proof of closure under Markov's rule to the case of quantifier-free formula. (G. Huet) Define a "semantical" negative translation such that ϕ^* is $\nabla\phi$ if ϕ is provably decidable in **HA**, that is **HA** $\vdash \phi \vee \neg\phi$. Use this to prove that if $\exists x \ \phi$ is provable in **PA** and ϕ is decidable in **HA**, then $\exists x \ \phi$ is provable in **HA**. For another proof, see Troelstra and van Dalen, Constructivism in Mathematics, volume I, exercise 4.4.8.

6. (U.Berger and H. Schwichtenberg) Let f be a function such that the formula

$$\forall x \ \exists y \ x < f \ y$$

   is provable in **HA**. Prove in **PA**

$$\forall x \ [f \ 0 \leq x \Rightarrow \exists y \ f \ y \leq x < f \ (y+1)].$$

   and notice that the natural non-constructive proof of this statement is actually a proof of

$$\forall x \ [f \ 0 \leq x \Rightarrow \neg\neg\exists y \ f \ y \leq x < f \ (y+1)].$$

   in **HA**. What is the algorithm implicit in this non-constructive argument? Given x_0, apply Friedman's translation by considering the modality $\nabla \ A = A \vee P$, where P is the proposition $\exists y \ f \ y \leq x_0 < f \ (y+1)]$.

7. (U.Berger and H. Schwichtenberg) Same exercise as the previous one, with the following problem: given a decidable property ϕ on binary tree, and a binary tree that satisfies ϕ, find a binary tree that satisfies ϕ such that no proper subtree satisfies ϕ.

8. Markov's principle is not derivable in HA (of course, it holds directly in PA, why?). One way to see this is by modified realizability [Kre59]: we interpret proofs of HA as programs defined by primitive recursion, and we see that, if Markov's principle was provable, we could solve the halting problem. This was actually Kreisel's motivation for introducing the notion of modified realizability. The other way is by building a boolean model of HA in which Markov's principle does not hold.

For this, consider the boolean algebra B freely built on countably many propositional letters A_0, A_1, ... Propositions of HA are interpreted as ideals of this boolean algebra. We have $\neg\neg \bigvee A_n$, because 0 is the only element of B less or equal than all $\neg A_n$, but $\bigvee A_n$, which is the ideal generated by all the A_i, is not the unit ideal.

9. Let f be a parameter, ranging over functions from integers to integers. We can prove classically

$$[\exists x \forall y \; f(y) \le x] \vee [\forall x \exists y \; x < f(y)]$$

and deduce from each case

$$\exists x_1, x_2, x_3 \; [x_1 < x_2 < x_3 \wedge f(x_1) \le f(x_2) \le f(x_3)].$$

For some concretely given f, compute witnesses for this statement using Friedman's method.

10. (G. Stolzenberg) Let f be a parameter, ranging over functions from integers to booleans. Give a proof in natural deduction of the "infinite box principle"

$$\forall x_0 \exists y_0 [x_0 \le y_0 \wedge f(y_0) = 0] \vee \forall x_1 \exists y_1 [x_1 \le y_1 \wedge f(y_1) = 1].$$

Use this to prove classically

$$\exists a \exists b \; [a < b \wedge f(a) = f(b)]$$

using as lemmas (that are valid intuitionistically)

$$\forall x_0 \exists y_0 [x_0 \le y_0 \wedge f(y_0) = 0] \Rightarrow \exists a \exists b \; [a < b \wedge f(a) = f(b)],$$

and

$$\forall x_1 \exists y_1 [x_1 \le y_1 \wedge f(y_1) = 1] \Rightarrow \exists a \exists b \; [a < b \wedge f(a) = f(b)].$$

Use Gödel-Gentzen-Friedman translation in order to transform these proofs into a functional $F(f) = (a, b)$ that, given f, computes a pair (a, b) such that $a < b$ and $f(a) = f(b)$. Is this functional the same as the one that computes $f(0)$ $f(1)$ and $f(2)$ and looks for two equal values among these three?

11. A "classical" example of a non-constructive proof is the following argument for the existence of two irrational numbers x and y such that x^y is rational. Consider a^a for $a^2 = 2$. Classically, either it is rational, and we can then take $x = y = a$, or it is irrational and we can take $x = a^a$, and $y = a$.

Since the statement proved is *not* a purely existential statement about "concrete" objects, but about real numbers, it is not possible a priori to give an effective meaning to this reasoning.

Compare this with the following argument: for each x in $[2, 3]$ there exists $y = g(x) > 0$ such that $x^y = 2$. Notice that g is one-to-one. Consider all pairs $(x, g(x))$ such that x is irrational. There are uncountably many such pairs. Hence, using the fact that g is one-to-one, there are uncountably many pairs such that both x and $g(x)$ are irrational (suggested by M. Hofmann). Give an effective version of this argument (Hint: the function g is continuous. Enumerate all rationals u_k and build a nested sequence of rational intervals I_k such that both I_k and $g(I_k)$ contains no u_j for $j < k$.)

2.6   References

[Augustsson] L. Augustsson. "Haskell B. user's manual." available over WWW from hhtp://www.cs.chalmers.se:80/pub/haskell/chalmers.

[God86] K. Gödel *Collected Works*. Oxford University Press. Volume I and II.

The formulation of PA and HA: can be traced back to Herbrand and Gödel, see the introduction of Gödel's article on negative translation by Troelstra in the volume I. Herbrand's system and Gentzen's system were *open* systems, very much like Martin-Löf's Intuitionistic Type Theory.

[Berg93] U. Berger and H. Schwichtenberg "Program Development by Proof Transformation." Proof and Computation, proceeding of the Marktoberdof Summer School 1993, NATO ASI Series.

Contains a description of analysis of classical proofs on a machine, and some examples of pruning.

[TroeDal] A.S. Troelstra and D. van Dalen *Constructivism in Mathematics*. Volume I, North-Holland.

Interesting historical introduction, and a lot of nice exercises. Highly recommended.

[Kreisel59] G. Kreisel "Interpretation of analysis by means of constructive functionals." In A. Heyting ed. *Constructivity in Mathematics*, North-Holland.

Among other things, contains the first mention of modified realisability, used to show that Markov's principle is not valid in HA.

[Friedman78] H. Friedman, "Classically and intuitionistically provably recursive functions," in Springer Lecture Notes in Computer Science, Volume 669.

Contains an incredibly easy and clear proof of closure under Markov's rule and a proof that if an existential statement is provable in PA, then it is provable in HA. As an application a function is provably recursive in PA iff it is so in HA. This can be extended to stronger ystems, but it is yet unknown for systems that combine Excluded Middle and the Axiom of Choice.

Novikov43] P.S. Novikoff "On the consistency of a certain logical calculus." Matematiceskij sbornik (Recueil Mathématique) T. 12 (54), pp. 230-260.

Contains an early proof of closure under Markov's rule.

Gentzen69] G. Gentzen *Collected Works*. M.E. Szabo ed., North-Holland.

Presents a version of the negative translation (discovered about the same time as Jödel's). The introduction of the first paper on consistency proofs for classical arithmetic contains a deep analysis of the difference between the "actualist" (non-effective) and the "intuitionistic" (effective) interpretation of logical connectives.

Moggi] E. Moggi "Notions of Computation and Monad", Information and Computation, vol. 93, p. 55-62, 1991.

Shows the relevance of the notion of monads in structuring the denotational description of programming languages.

SpiWad90] P. Wadler "The essence of functional programming", in POPL 92.

M. Spivey "A functional theory of exceptions", Science of Computer Programming 14, 990.

Presents an elegant way of simulating exceptions, and other "imperative features" in a pure functional programming language. This suggests that similar techniques could be applied to proof systems, and that we can simulate "non-effective features" in a pure intuitionistic system.

deGroot95] Ph. de Groote "A Simple Calculus of Exception Handling." In proceeding of TLCA 95, LNCS 902.

Presents a logical analysis of ML exceptions. Furthermore, it contains an extended bibliography of related works.

Here are some comments on this reference list.

One paper by Barbanera and Berardi contains another way to extract witnesses, presented in Prawitz's book on Natural Deduction.

The Ph. D. thesis of Ch. Murthy presents the connection between Friedman's translation and CPS transformation.

The paper of T. Griffin started the connections between analysis of classical proofs, and control operators.

The papers of M. Parigot contain an elegant generalisation of the λ-calculus, called $\lambda\mu$-calculus, that extends in some way the Curry-Howard correspondence between proofs and λ-terms to non-effective proofs. They have references to papers by J.L. Krivine that contain deep remarks about the connection between classical logics and imperative features.

The paper by J.Y. Girard contains, among other things, an optimised version of the translation of H. Friedman, that is analysed in the LICS 91 paper of Ch. Murthy.

Weyl] H. Weyl "Ueber die neue Grundlagenkrise der Mathematik", Mathematische Zeitschrift, 10, 1921.

3 Sequent Calculus

In this second part, we present another way of making constructive sense of classical reasoning: the sequent calculus. First, we analyse the formulation as it appears in Gentzen first proof of consistency for classical arithmetic. Next, we present a simplified version of Novikov's calculus, written with Hugo Herbelin, and a game-theoretic interpretation of this calculus.

3.1 Gentzen's calculus

3.1.1 Presentation of the system

The language is the same as in HA, PA, but Gentzen restricts it to the fragment defined by the connectives $\forall, \wedge, \neg$. The logic is represented by Natural Deduction with sequents of the form $\Gamma \vdash A$ where Γ is a set of formulae. We write Γ, A for $\Gamma \cup \{A\}$, and Γ, Δ for $\Gamma \cup \Delta$. The intuitionistic logical rules are

- if A is in Γ then $\Gamma \vdash A$,

- if $\Gamma \vdash A \wedge B$ then $\Gamma \vdash A$ and $\Gamma \vdash B$,

- if $\Gamma \vdash A$ and $\Gamma \vdash B$ then $\Gamma \vdash A \wedge B$,

- if $\Gamma \vdash A(x)$ and x is not free in Γ then $\Gamma \vdash \forall x\, A(x)$,

- if $\Gamma \vdash \forall x\, A(x)$ then $\Gamma \vdash A(t)$ for all terms t,

- if $\Gamma, A \vdash \perp$ then $\Gamma \vdash \neg A$,

- if $\neg A$ is in Γ, and $\Gamma \vdash A$ then $\Gamma \vdash \perp$.

There are two remaining rules. The induction rule is: from $\Gamma \vdash F(1)$ and $\Delta, F(a) \vdash F(a+1)$, follows $\Gamma, \Delta \vdash F(t)$, provided a fresh w.r.t. $\Gamma, \Delta, F(1), F(t)$. Finally, the double negation rule is that $\Gamma \vdash A$ follows from $\Gamma \vdash \neg\neg A$.

Notice that it is a finitary inductive definition of $\vdash$. (See [Aczel78] for an introduction to the notion of inductive definition.)

3.1.2 First Analysis

As analysed by Gentzen, the more problematic rule is the double negation rule that $\Gamma \vdash A$ follows from $\Gamma \vdash \neg\neg A$. Without this rule, we have a formalisation of the intuitionistic system HA, and this system has a direct intuitionistic meaning.

Gentzen has then an interesting discussion on "finitary" versus "infinitary", or non-effective interpretation of this system. He notices that the rules can be justified by a non-effective interpretation.

3.1.3 Non-standard interpretation

Gentzen then gives another, "non-standard" effective interpretation of the system. "The propositions of actualist mathematics seem to have a certain utility, but no *sense*. The major part of my consistency proof, however, consists precisely in *ascribing a finitary sense* to actualist propositions." This gives yet another computational content of classical proofs. This computational content is described by Gentzen as a *non-deterministic* algorithm. I will describe it as an *interactive* algorithm.

3.1.4 Reduction rule on sequents

This is an interactive algorithm between the "proof" and an opponent. All the formulae of the sequents are closed, and we can compute the truth value of any atomic statement. The opponent plays as long as the conclusion formula is not atomic, by "reducing" the sequent according to the following rules

- $\Gamma \vdash A \wedge B$ can be reduced to $\Gamma \vdash A$ or $\Gamma \vdash B$,

- $\Gamma \vdash \forall x\, A(x)$ can be reduced to any $\Gamma \vdash A(n_0)$,

- $\Gamma \vdash \neg A$ is reduced to $\Gamma, A \vdash \perp$.

The interaction stops if the conclusion is atomic and true. If the conclusion is atomic and false, it is the turn of the "proof" to play. The "proof" plays as long as the conclusion is atomic and false, and there is no atomic and false formulae among the antecedent formulae. It plays also by reducing the sequent, in the following way

- if $A \wedge B$ is in Γ then $\Gamma \vdash \perp$ can be reduced to $A, \Gamma \vdash \perp$, or to $B, \Gamma \vdash \perp$,

- if $\forall x\, A(x)$ is in Γ then $\Gamma \vdash \perp$ can be reduced to any $A(n_0), \Gamma \vdash \perp$,

- if $\neg A$ is in Γ then $\Gamma \vdash \perp$ can be reduced to $\Gamma \vdash A$ (and then it is the opponent turn to play, if the formula A is not atomic and false).

Thus during a play, the proof and its opponent try alternatively to reduce the sequent. The proof tries either to make the end formula atomic and true, or to make one antecedent formula atomic and false.

The finitary interpretation is a "reduction rule", i.e. a strategy for the proof. After finitely many interaction steps, the proof should reach a situation where either there is a true atomic conclusion formula, or there is a false atomic conclusion formula and a false atomic antecedent formula.

A strategy for the proof that achieves this, against any opponent (even if the opponent does not follow any fixed strategy), will be the "finitary meaning" of the sequent.

For instance, $\forall x\, P(x) \vdash \forall x\, P(x)$ has such a finitary meaning, if P is decidable. The strategy is as follows: the opponent has to give a value $x = x_0$ for x, and the sequent reduces then to $\forall x\, P(x) \vdash P(x_0)$. If $P(x_0)$ is true, then the game is finished. Otherwise, the proof can play by choosing also the same value $x = x_0$ reducing the sequent to $P(x_0), \forall x\, P(x) \vdash P(x_0)$ where $P(x_0)$ is a false atomic formula.

What is important here is that this strategy is an effective object, though we cannot decide of the truth value of the formula $\forall x\, P(x)$.

Finally, notice that it is the *sequent* itself that is "reduced" by the proof and its opponent; the "reduction" does not concern the proof, which is a strategy for doing this "reduction".

3.1.5 What Gentzen proves

Gentzen proves then that any provable sequent has a reduction rule. Since the sequent $\vdash 1 = 2$ has no reduction rule, it will follow that $\vdash 1 = 2$ is not provable.

Notice also that if $\forall x\, \neg P(x) \vdash \perp$ has a reduction rule, then this reduction rule gives us x_0 such that $P(x_0)$ holds. So we get that $\exists x\, P(x)$ holds intuitionistically if it is provable in **PA**. This result is mathematically weaker than Friedman/Dragalin's result, but it is enough for extracting computations from classical proofs.

The key step in the proof is the *cut lemma*: from a reduction rule for $\Gamma \vdash B$ and $\Delta, B \vdash A$, to give a reduction rule for $\Gamma, \Delta \vdash A$.

For instance, this gives an interpretation of the elimination of the double negation.

3.1.6 Cut lemma

The cut lemma that provides a reduction rule for $\Gamma, \Delta \vdash A$ given one for $\Gamma \vdash B$ and $\Delta, B \vdash A$ is proved by case analysis of the cut formula B.

If B is atomic, if it is true, we can simulate the reduction rule of $\Delta, B \vdash A$, and if it is false, we can simulate the reduction rule of $\Gamma \vdash B$.

The general case is more complicated and we refer the reader to Gentzen's original article or to Bernays' presentation of this proof.

3.1.7 Inductive definitions

Instead, we show next how to give an alternative presentation, using generalised inductive definitions instead of talking about interactions.

- If $\Gamma \Rightarrow A(n_0)$ for all n_0, then $\Gamma \Rightarrow \forall x\, A(x)$,

- if $\Gamma \Rightarrow A$ and $\Gamma \Rightarrow B$, then $\Gamma \Rightarrow A \wedge B$,

- if $A, \Gamma \Rightarrow \perp$, then $\Gamma \Rightarrow \neg A$,

- if A is atomic and true, then $\Gamma \Rightarrow A$,

- if $\forall x\ A(x)$ is in Γ, and $A(n_0), \Gamma \Rightarrow \perp$, then $\Gamma \Rightarrow \perp$,

- if $A \wedge B$ is in Γ, and $A, \Gamma \Rightarrow \perp$ or $B, \Gamma \Rightarrow \perp$, then $\Gamma \Rightarrow \perp$,

- if $\neg A$ is in Γ, and $\Gamma \Rightarrow A$, then $\Gamma \Rightarrow \perp$,

- if there is a false atomic formula in Γ, then $\Gamma \Rightarrow \perp$.

The idea is to embed our finitary system for HA in this infinitary system, that is to show that if $\Gamma \vdash A$, then $\Gamma \Rightarrow A$. This corresponds to the association of a reduction rule to any provable formula. The proof is direct. The cut lemma will be reformulated as the fact that the cut rule is admissible for this extended calculus. This means that $\Gamma \Rightarrow B$ and $\Delta, B \Rightarrow A$ imply $\Gamma, \Delta \Rightarrow A$. The proof is more involved and consists in a double induction, first in the cut formula B and then in the proofs. We will make this argument precise for a simpler sequent calculus in the next section. What should be emphasised is that the argument in this form is much easier to check than the original argument by Gentzen, or its presentation by Bernays [Bernays].

Notice the similarity between this infinitary system and the intuitionistic truth semantics of HA.

This notion of admissibility has indeed been introduced by Lorenzen, while thinking about Gentzen's consistency proof. See "Einfuehrung in die operative Logik und Mathematik", Springer, 1955, p. 5.

3.2 Tait/Novikov calculus

We present a simplification both of Tait's calculus, inspired by a game theoretical analogy between a proof and a winning strategy for a game, and of a calculus presented by Novikov 1943, which contains an elegant proof that if a purely existential statement is provable in classical arithmetic, then it holds intuitionistically.

3.2.1 Formulae and validity

The *positive* and *negative* formulae are defined inductively [Aczel78].

- if A_i is a family of negative formulae over a countable set, then $\bigvee A_i$ is a positive formula,

- if A_i is a family of positive formulae over a countable set, then $\bigwedge A_i$ is a negative formula,

We can define inductively the negation of a formula: $\overline{A}$ is $\bigwedge \overline{A_i}$ (resp. $\bigvee \overline{A_i}$) if A is $\bigvee A_i$ (resp. $\bigwedge A_i$). Notice that we can represent the false positive formula by taking $0 = \bigvee A_i$ where (A_i) is the empty family of negative formulae. The negative formula 1 is dually defined as $1 = \bigwedge A_i$ where (A_i) is the empty family of positive formulae. To each negative formula A corresponds a positive formula $[A]$ that we get by considering the family of negative formula with only one element A.

The notion of classical validity, as described by Novikoff [Novikoff43], defines inductively when a finite multiset of positive formulae is valid. We shall denote by $L, M, N, \ldots$ such multisets, and write L, A the addition of the positive formula A to the multiset L. Similarly we write the addition of the multisets L and M as L, M.

The multiset L, A, where $A = \bigvee A_i$, is valid if there exists i_0 such that A_{i_0} is a negative formula $\bigwedge A_{i_0 j}$ such that, for all j, the multiset $L, A, A_{i_0 j}$ is valid.

3.2.2 Main properties

In this section, we survey the basic properties of this notion of validity.

Proposition 1: If L is a multiset of positive formulae, and $A = \bigvee A_i$ a positive formula, then the multiset $L, A, \overline{A_i}$ is valid.

Proof: By induction on the formula A. We have $A_i = \bigwedge \overline{A_{ij}}$ and, by induction hypothesis, the multiset $L, A, \overline{A_i}, A_{ij}$ is valid for all j. Hence the multiset $L, A, \overline{A_i}$ is valid by definition. □

Proposition 2: If L is a valid multiset of positive formulae, and $A = \bigvee A_i$ a positive formula, then the multiset L, A is valid.

Proof: Direct by induction on the proof of validity of L. □

To simplify the presentation of the proofs, we will say that a multiset L, M is valid because of the L part, if it is valid because L can be written L', B where $B = \bigvee B_j$ is a positive formula such that $L', M, B_{j_0 l}$ is valid for one index j_0 and all index l.

Proposition 3: If L is a multiset of positive formulae, and $A = \bigvee A_i$ a positive formula, then the multiset L, A, A is valid iff L, A is valid.

Proof: One direction follows from proposition 2. Conversely, let us prove by induction on the proof of validity of L, A, A that L, A is valid.

This is direct if L, A, A is valid because of the L part.

Otherwise, it is because there exists an index i_0 such that $L, A, A, A_{i_0 k}$ is valid for all k. By induction hypothesis, $L, A, A_{i_0 k}$ is then valid for all k and hence L, A is valid. □

Notice that for propositions 2 and 3, we did not have to do an induction on formulae, but only on proofs of validity.

Proposition 4: If $A = \bigvee A_i$ is such that L, A is valid and $M, \overline{A_i}$ is valid for all , then L, M is valid.

Proof: By induction, first on the proposition A, then on the proof that L, A is valid. It is direct if L, A is valid because of the L part. If it is valid because there exists an index i_0 such that $L, A, A_{i_0 j}$ is valid for all j, then by induction hypothesis, we have that $L, M, A_{i_0 j}$ is valid for all j. By induction on the formula, we have that L, M, M is valid. By proposition 3, we deduce that L, M is valid. $\square$

This direct inductive proof of the admissibility of cut should be contrasted with the argument of [Tait68], that needs first an inversion lemma.

3.2.3 Example

In this section, we want to illustrate on one example that our formalism is well suited for representing proofs in classical arithmetics and for analysing their computational content. The mathematical content of the example may seem trivial, but it has revealed what seems to be a deep problem of symmetry in the operation of cut-elimination or negative interpretation.

Here is the non-constructive argument whose constructive content we shall analyse. Given a function f on integers that takes only the value 0 or 1, there exists $i < j$ such that $f(i) = f(j)$. Either there exists infinitely many 0's in the range of f, or infinitely many 1's. In the first case, choose i, j two distinct numbers on which f is 0. In the other case, choose i, j two distinct numbers on which f is 1.

This is a highly nonconstructive proof. It is composed of one main lemma: the function f takes infinitely many times the value 0, or infinitely many times the value , and two symmetric lemmas: if the function f takes infinitely many time the value , which can be 0 or 1, then there exists $i < j$ such that $f(i) = f(j)$.

For the translation of this proof in our formalism, we represent each decidable formula as the positive formula 0 if it is false, and the positive formula [1] if it is true.

We define

- $A_n = \bigvee_{m \geq n} . f(m) = 0$,

- $B_n = \bigvee_{m \geq n} . f(m) = 1$,

- $C = \bigvee_{i < j} f(i) = f(j)$.

The main lemma can be seen as stating the validity of A_{n_0}, B_{n_1} for all n_0, n_1 and the two other lemmas as stating the validity of $\bigvee \overline{A_n}, C$ and $\bigvee \overline{B_n}, C$.

The validity of A_{n_0}, B_{n_1} is clear by computing $f(\max(n_0, n_1))$.

The validity of $\bigvee \overline{A_n}, C$ can be seen as follows. We prove the validity of the sequent $\overline{A_{0m}}, \bigvee \overline{A_n}, C$ for all $m \geq 0$. This is direct if $f(m) \neq 0$. Otherwise, we show the validity of $\overline{A_{(m+1)m'}}, \overline{A_{0m}}, \bigvee \overline{A_n}, C$ for all $m' \geq m + 1$. This is direct if $f(m') \neq 0$. Otherwise, we have found $f(m) = f(m') = 0$ and $m < m'$, and so we have a witness for the formula C.

The validity of $\bigvee \overline{B_n}, C$ is established in the same way.

The following multisets

$$C, \bigvee \overline{A_n} \qquad C, \bigvee \overline{B_n} \qquad A_{n_0}, B_{n_1}$$

are valid.

It follows that C, C and hence C is valid. However, there are at least two ways of computing this proof of C.

We can first use proposition 4 on

$$C, \bigvee \overline{A_n} \qquad A_{n_0}, B_{n_1}$$

getting that C, B_{n_1} is valid for all n_1, and then again proposition 4 on

$$C, \bigvee \overline{B_n} \qquad C, B_{n_1}$$

getting that C, C is valid.

The other way is to use proposition 4 on

$$C, \bigvee \overline{B_n} \qquad A_{n_0}, B_{n_1}$$

getting that C, A_{n_0} is valid for all n_0, and then again proposition 4 on

$$C, \bigvee \overline{A_n} \qquad C, A_{n_0}$$

getting that C, C is valid.

As the reader can check, these two ways will give two different witnesses. Which one should be considered as "the" witness contained implicitly in this non-effective proof? Or should we consider that the non-effective proof contains in some mysterious ways both witnesses? This kind of question, while rather fundamental, is surprisingly unexplored.

3.3   Game-theoretic Interpretation of Sequent Calculus

The notion of intuitionistic validity

- 1 is valid,

- $\bigvee_i \phi_i$ is valid iff there exists i_0 such that ϕ_{i_0} is valid,

- $\bigwedge_i \phi_i$ is valid iff ϕ_i is valid for all i,

has a natural game theoretical interpretation. The game is played by two players, Vbelard and ∃loise, who quarrel about the truth of a given formula. The player ∃loise, who argues in favour, plays when the formula is existential, say $\bigvee_i \phi_i$, by choosing an index i_0 ("∃loise's Choice"), after which the game is continued with the formula ϕ_{i_0}. The player Vbelard, who argues against, plays when the formula is universal, say $\bigwedge_j \phi_j$, by choosing an index j_0, after which the game is continued with the formula ϕ_{j_0}. The game ends when either Vbelard or ∃loise chooses the formula 0 or 1. Evidently, the game always terminates. If either ∃loise or Vbelard chooses 1, then ∃loise wins the game and Vbelard looses. Dually, if either ∃loise or Vbelard chooses 0, then Vbelard wins the game and ∃loise looses.

We have the following completeness result: the player ∃loise has a winning strategy for the game associated to the existential formula ϕ if and only if this formula ϕ is intuitionistically valid. (Every formula is equivalent to an existential formula by prefixing it with a singleton disjunction.)

For instance, there is no winning strategy for the formula

$$\bigwedge_k \bigvee_{n \geq k} \bigwedge_{m \geq k} f(n) \leq f(m),$$

because it is not possible to compute effectively such a minimum value for a function f.

The notion of classical validity, as described by Novikoff [Novikoff43], is inductively defined by the clauses

- 1 is valid,

- $\bigvee_i \phi_i$ is valid iff there exists i_0 such that ϕ_{i_0} is 1, or is an universal formula $\bigwedge_j \phi_{i_0 j}$ such that, for all j, the formula $\phi_{i_0 j} \vee \bigvee_i \phi_i$ is valid,

- $\bigwedge_i \phi_i$ is valid iff ϕ_i is valid for all i.

This definition may seem not well-founded, but it correctly defines classical validity as the smallest set satisfying the above closure properties.

For instance, a formula of the form $\psi \vee \bigvee_i \phi_i \vee \overline{\phi_{i_0}}$ is always valid. This is shown by induction on the formula $\bigvee_i \phi_i$. Firstly, recall that $\overline{\phi}$ is the usual defined complement of ϕ, changing $\bigvee$'s into $\bigwedge$'s, 1's in 0's, and conversely. Second, ϕ_{i_0} is either 0 or 1, or a universal formula $\bigwedge_j \phi_{i_0 j}$ by the alternation of $\bigvee$'s and $\bigwedge$'s. In the first two cases, it is trivial to choose the index of a valid disjunct in the formula above. In the third case, choose the index such that we get the formula $\psi \vee \bigvee_i \phi_i \vee \overline{\phi_{i_0}} \vee \phi_{i_0 j}$, which is valid for all j by the induction hypothesis.

The game semantics has to be adapted to the classical notion of validity: in the case of a disjunction $\bigvee_i \phi_i$, the game proceeds with the formula $\bigwedge_j [\phi_{i_0 j} \vee \bigvee_i \phi_i]$.

The other cases do not change. A tentative interpretation of this definition is that it describes exactly a winning strategy for a game between ∀belard and ∃loise. This strategy is suggested by the inductive definition of classical validity: in the case of an existential formula, and after a choice j_0 of ∀belard, ∃loise should try again and choose a new i in

$$\phi_{i_0 j_0} \vee \bigvee_i \phi_i,$$

using information drawn from $\phi_{i_0 j_0}$ (if this latter formula is 1, then ∃loise should choose this formula, of course).

There is such a winning strategy for the formula

$$\bigwedge_k \bigvee_{n \geq k} \bigwedge_{m \geq k} \phi_{nm},$$

with $\phi_{nm} = f(n) \leq f(m)$, which can be described as follows. The game starts by ∀belard giving a value k. The player ∃loise answers choosing an arbitrary value $n \geq k$, say $n = k$ and ∀belard answers by playing $m = m_0 \geq k$. The formula becomes

$$\phi_{km_0} \vee \bigvee_{n \geq k} \bigwedge_{m \geq k} \phi_{nm}.$$

If ϕ_{km_0} is true, then ∃loise wins. If ϕ_{km_0} is false, the strategy for ∃loise is to choose the last value given by ∀belard. After ∀belard chooses a value $m = m_1 \geq k$, the formula becomes

$$\phi_{km_0} \vee \phi_{m_0 m_1} \vee \bigvee_{n \geq k} \bigwedge_{m \geq k} \phi_{nm}.$$

The player ∃loise wins if $f(m_0) \leq f(m_1)$. In this way, to each game corresponds a sequence $m_0, m_1, \ldots$ such that $\phi_{km_0}, \phi_{m_0 m_1}, \ldots$ are all false, i.e. such that $f(m_0) > f(m_1) > \ldots$ Since N is well-founded, ∃loise will win eventually by following this strategy.

3.4 Sequent Calculus versus Negative Translation

Both the negative translation and sequent calculus present a constructive explanation of some parts of mathematics that use the law of excluded middle.

It is instructive to compare both explanations in some concrete examples. On the 0/1 example, the sequent calculus seems much more suggestive than the negative translation, especially if we use the game-theoretic intuition.

3.5 Exercises on Part II

1. Do extraction of witnesses using sequent calculus, and compare with the Friedman's method. For instance, apply the sequent calculus to the exercises 9 and 10 of part I.

2. A concrete example of non-effective argument analysed by H. Schwitzenberg and U. Berger is the following proof for the existence of a greatest common divisor of two numbers a and b, with $b > 0$: the ideal (a, b) generated by a and b, contains an element $b > 0$, hence it contain a least element $c > 0$. Then c is the greatest common divisor of a and b. Apply the method of "trial and error" to guess what would be the computational content of this proof. (Hint: there are two parts in the proof, the first is the existence of a least element $c > 0$, the second that this least element c divides both a and b. The second part is effective. The first part is not: the interpretation is an algorithm that starts by claiming $c = b$, and whenever it is given an element $x \in (a, b)$ such that $0 < x < c$, "changes its mind" and take $c = x$ instead.)

3.6 References

[Aczel78] P. Aczel "An introduction to inductive definitions." In Handbook of mathematical logic, J. Barwise ed., North-Holland, p. 739-782.

Presents the notion of inductive definitions in a simple and clear way.

[Buchholz] W. Buchholz, S. Feferman, W. Pohlers and W. Sieg *Iterated Inductive Definitions and Subsystems of Analysis*. LNM 897.

One quite important point is that the negative translation does not work in presence of generalised inductive definitions. (In the next section, we will see that it does not work in presence of the Axiom of Choice.) If one thinks of generalised inductive definitions as least prefixed point of *strictly* positive operators (see [Aczel78]), one needs least prefixed point of positive operators, not necessarily strictly positive.

One main theme of this book is to present various methods that explain effectively the combination of generalised inductive definitions and classical logic. Three such methods are presented, and two of them are based on sequent calculus. Interestingly, cut-elimination is not proved in general, but only for sequents that have only positive occurrence of the inductively defined predicate.

[Bernays] "On the original Gentzen consistency proof for number theory" in Intuitionism and Proof Theory, Kino, Myhill, Vesley eds, pp. 409-417

[Gentzen69] G. Gentzen *Collected Works*. M.E. Szabo ed., North-Holland.

The reading of the original paper of Gentzen, especially the beginning of his first paper on consistency proof for classical arithmetic, and the presentation by Bernays are quite instructive. In particular, the paper of Gentzen contains a remarkable formal analysis of Euclid's proof of the infinity of prime numbers. In both papers there appears clearly the characteristic "multi-conclusion" feature of classical logic, which seems to indicate that a classical proof of an existential statement may contain potentially several witnesses, in opposition to a constructive proof.

[Tait68] W. W. Tait "Normal Derivability in Classical Logic." Springer Lecture Notes in Mathematics 72, J. Barwise ed, pp. 204-236.

The presentation is elegant and the goals and methods clearly stated. Let us cite a part of the introduction. "Also we will be dealing with infinitary propositions and infinite derivations of them, we will deal with these constructively—not, of course, in the narrow sense of Hilbert's finitism, but in the wider sense which admits (potential) infinities, in the form of rules of construction, as objects. As a consequence of this, we will obtain a constructive foundation for infinitary classical logic and for those parts of mathematics contained in it." It is to be noticed that Tait's paper had a deep influence on further proof-theoretic analysis of subsystems of second order arithmetic, as can be seen in the survey on inductive definitions [Buchholz].

[ML68] P. Martin-Löf *Notes on Constructive Mathematics*. Almqvist & Wiksell ed.

Another elegant presentation of sequent calculus is contained in the monograph of Martin-Löf. It presents a constructive explanation of the notion of Borel sets for Cantor space, using a sequent calculus where formulae are Borel sets. In this work there also appears clearly the fact that cut-elimination can be formulated as the *admissibility* of the cut rule in a system that presents inductively the cut-free provability of a sequent. This can be traced back to the first proof of Gentzen, and to Lorenzen, who introduced the notion of admissibility of a rule while analysing Gentzen's work.

[Novikov43] P.S. Novikoff "On the consistency of certain logical calculus." Matematiceskij sbornik (Recueil Mathématique) T. 12 (54), pp. 230-260.

[Coquand95] Th. Coquand "A Semantics of Evidence of Classical Arithmetic." Journal of Symbolic Logic 60 (1995), pp. 325–337.

Contains an analysis of cut-elimination based on a game-theoretic interpretation of proofs. Cut-elimination is seen as an interaction between two strategies, and the termination of cut-elimination is proved by an analysis of the structure of this interaction.

4   Axiom of Choice and Hilbert's Program

It is known that the Axiom of Choice is constructively valid, and this fact has been emphasised by Martin-Löf [Martin-Lof73]. As discussed in Bishop's book on constructive analysis, the well-known problems or "paradoxical consequences" of the Axiom of Choice in non-constructive mathematics, like the non-effective "existence" of a well-ordering of the reals or the Banach-Tarski paradox, use in an essential way a combination of this axiom with the law of excluded middle.

In the first part, we analyse in detail a logical problem that arises from this combination. We can thus formulate one of the open problems in proof-theory connected to this part: is it always possible to transform a proof of an existential statement that uses classical logic and the axiom of choice into a constructive proof of the same statement? This chapter is in part extracted from the paper [Berardi95].

We end with a short presentation of Hilbert's program.

4.1   Presentation of HA^ω

In order to formulate precisely what is the problem with the combination of the Axiom of Choice and the Law of Excluded Middle, we describe a formal system

HA^ω that allows quantification over functions (but in a quite "weak" way, since it is conservative over HA even extended with the Axiom of Choice, this is Goodman's result.)

4.1.1 Types

The types of HA^ω are N and with τ, τ' also $\tau \to \tau'$. Here and below types will be denoted by lower case Greek letters $\tau, \tau', \ldots$.

4.1.2 Terms

The terms of HA^ω are built from (typed) variables and constants using lambda abstraction and (well typed) application. There are countably many variables $x, y, z, \ldots$ for each type τ. The constants are: $0 : N$, $s : N \to N$ and finally $R_\tau : \tau \to (N \to \tau \to \tau) \to N \to \tau$ for every type τ. Terms are denoted by $M, M', N, \ldots$, and $M : \tau$ expresses that the term M has type τ.

4.1.3 Formulae

Prime formulae are equations of the form $M = M'$, with $M, M' : N$. Higher type equations, say $M = M'$ with $M, M' : N \to N$, are abbreviations of equations of lowest type, such as $Mx = M'x$ with x fresh. The set of formulae of HA^ω is generated in the usual way from the prime formulae by the boolean connectives $\wedge, \Rightarrow, \bot$ and the quantifiers $\forall, \exists$. We use $\phi, \phi', \ldots$ to denote formulae. We abbreviate $\phi \Rightarrow \bot$ by $\neg\phi$.

4.1.4 Theory

The theory HA^ω, intuitionistic higher order arithmetic, is built up from three parts: (i) axioms and rules for first order many-sorted intuitionistic predicate logic; (ii) equality axioms and the axiom schema of induction; (iii) lambda calculus axioms and rules and the defining equations of the constants R_τ, which are: $R_\tau xy0 = x$, $R_\tau xy(sz) = yz(R_\tau xyz)$. Thus our theory HA^ω essentially coincides with HA^ω from [Troelstra344], the only difference being that we consider $\vee$ as defined and use the lambda version instead of the combinator version. The theory HA_c^ω is HA^ω with classical logic; HA_-^ω, minimal higher order arithmetic, is HA^ω without the axiom schema $\bot \Rightarrow \phi$.

4.1.5 The Axiom of Choice

Theories of classical (intuitionistic) analysis can be obtained from HA_c^ω (HA^ω) by adding the axiom of choice. The axiom of choice of types τ, τ', denoted by $AC(\tau, \tau')$, is the axiom schema

$$[\forall x : \tau \; \exists y : \tau' \; \phi(x, y)] \Rightarrow \exists f : \tau \to \tau' \; \forall x : \tau \; \phi(x, fx)$$

(schematic in formula ϕ). Here we will mainly consider $\mathsf{AC}(\mathsf{N}, \tau)$ (schematic in τ), that we may abbreviate to AC. The axiom AC is sufficiently strong to formalise a large part of classical analysis. Intuitionistically, AC is not a strong axiom, as may be expected from the Brouwer–Heyting–Kolmogorov interpretation of a $\forall\exists$ prefix. More formally, it follows from results of Goodman [Goodman70] that adding $\mathsf{AC}(\mathsf{N}, \mathsf{N})$ and $\mathsf{AC}(\mathsf{N}, \mathsf{N}{\to}\mathsf{N})$ to HA^ω is conservative over Heyting Arithmetic.

4.1.6   A negative interpretation

We will use the notation $\nabla\,\phi$ for $\neg\neg\phi$. This notation is justified by the fact that $\neg\neg$ can be thought of as a modal operator on formulae; indeed we can prove that $\nabla\,\phi$ follows from ϕ, and $\nabla\,\psi$ from $\nabla\,\phi$ and $\phi \Rightarrow \nabla\,\psi$.

Since absurdity is not interpreted by the empty type, we cannot realise $\bot \Rightarrow \phi$ for all ϕ. We overcome this problem by exercising some care in the negative interpretation. The idea is due to Kolmogorov. We employ the fact that $\bot \Rightarrow \nabla\,\phi$ can be proved for all ϕ without using the axiom schema $\bot \Rightarrow \phi$. Although our prime formulae are decidable, the negative interpretation of a prime formula ϕ will be $\nabla\,\phi$.

As negative interpretation we use a standard version of the double negation translation, i.e. prefixing prime formulae and $\exists$ by ∇. The negative interpretation of a formula ϕ, denoted by $\mathsf{D}\phi$, is inductively defined by:

- $\mathsf{D}\bot \equiv \bot$

- $\mathsf{D}\phi \equiv \nabla\,\phi$ if ϕ is a prime formula

- $\mathsf{D}[\phi \Rightarrow \psi] \equiv [\mathsf{D}\phi] \Rightarrow \mathsf{D}\psi$

- $\mathsf{D}[\phi \wedge \psi] \equiv \mathsf{D}\phi \wedge \mathsf{D}\psi$

- $\mathsf{D}\forall x : \tau\ \phi \equiv \forall x : \tau\ \mathsf{D}\phi$

- $\mathsf{D}\exists x : \tau\ \phi \equiv \nabla\,\exists x : \tau\ \mathsf{D}\phi$

Here and below, $\equiv$ denotes syntactical identity.

The negative interpretation satisfies the following preservation property: if ϕ is provable in HA^ω_c, then $\mathsf{D}\phi$ is provable in HA^ω_-. In the presence of AC, one cannot expect such a simple preservation result since, as we shall see below, AC is much stronger classically than it is intuitionistically.

The theory $\mathsf{HA}^\omega_- + \mathsf{D}\,\mathsf{AC}$ will be called *negative analysis*. We need the following technical results.

Lemma 1 *The following schemata are provable in* HA^ω_-:

(i) $\bot \Rightarrow \nabla\,\phi$;

(ii) $\neg \nabla \phi \iff \neg \phi;$

(iii) $\phi \Rightarrow \nabla \phi;$

(iv) $\mathsf{D}\phi \iff \nabla \mathsf{D}\phi,$

(v) $\mathsf{D}\exists x : \tau \ \phi \iff \nabla \exists x : \tau \ \phi$, *if ϕ is a prime formula;*

(vi) $\phi \Rightarrow \mathsf{D}\phi$, *if ϕ is a prenex formula not containing $\Rightarrow$;*

(vii) $\mathsf{D}\neg\phi \iff \neg\mathsf{D}\phi.$

Proof: The clauses (i)-(iii) and (vi),(vii) are trivial. For (iv), observe that the standard proof of this fact by formula induction does not use the axiom schema $\bot \Rightarrow \phi$. For all ϕ we have $\nabla \exists x : \tau \ \nabla \phi \iff \nabla \exists x : \tau \ \phi$ via $\neg \exists x : \tau \ \phi \iff \forall x : \tau \ \neg \phi$ using (ii), so we have (v).

The negative interpretation of AC, DAC, reads:

$$[\forall x : \mathsf{N} \ \nabla \ \exists y : \tau \ \mathsf{D}\phi(x,y)] \Rightarrow \nabla \ \exists f : \mathsf{N}{\to}\tau \ \forall x : \mathsf{N} \ \mathsf{D}\phi(x,fx).$$

By the stability[4] of formulae after the negative interpretation, which follows from Lemma 1.1 (iv), DAC is subsumed by the following axiom schema:

$$[\forall x : \mathsf{N} \ \nabla \ \exists y : \tau \ \neg\phi(x,y)] \Rightarrow \nabla \ \exists f : \mathsf{N}{\to}\tau \ \forall x : \mathsf{N} \ \neg\phi(x,fx)$$

Par abus de langage we will from now on denote this schema by DAC.

We can now extend the preservation property above to: if ϕ is provable in classical analysis, then $\mathsf{D}\phi$ is provable in negative analysis. The proof goes by inspection of the standard preservation proof, taking care that $\bot \Rightarrow \phi$ is avoided using the lemma above.

4.2 Classical Logic and the Axiom of Choice

In this section, we enumerate some known difficulties in giving a constructive interpretation of the Axiom of Choice in the presence of classical logic. The main remark is that DAC fails to be an intuitionistic consequence of the Axiom of Choice[5]. We point out three independent reasons:

- DAC makes problematic the constructive interpretation of the notion of function; actually, it refutes Church's Thesis;

- DAC is proof theoretically very strong, we can actually interpret by DAC impredicative second order comprehension, so that one cannot give any predicative interpretation of DAC;

---

[4] A formula is stable iff it is equivalent to the negation of another formula.

[5] This is to be contrasted with the induction schema over integers, whose negative interpretation is an instance of the induction schema.

- a standard computational interpretation of classical arithmetic, the one using infinitary propositional calculus, that we presented in part II, when extended to quantification over functions, fails to interpret the Axiom of Choice.

4.2.1   DAC refutes Church's Thesis

In the classical system $HA_c^\omega + AC$, we may define the characteristic function of any predicate. Indeed, for any statement $\phi(x)$, we have

$$\exists f \, \forall x \, [\phi(x) \iff [f(x) = 0]]$$

since, by the Excluded Middle,

$$\forall x \, \exists y \, [\phi(x) \iff [y = 0]].$$

If we take for ϕ some non-decidable formula, then we may prove in this way the existence of non-recursive functions in $HA_c^\omega + AC$.

In other words, we refute in $HA_c^\omega + AC$ the formula

$$\mathsf{CT} \equiv \forall f : \mathsf{N}{\to}\mathsf{N} \, \exists e : \mathsf{N} \, \forall x : \mathsf{N} \, \exists y : \mathsf{N} \, [T(e, x, y) \wedge U(y) = f(x)]$$

where $T(e, x, y)$ is the standard Kleene predicate (which can be formulated as an equation) and $U(y) = z$ means that the output of the computation with code y is z. This formula CT expresses Church's Thesis in an intuitionistic way, stating that every function f has a recursive code e.

This simple remark has some deep consequences. Since CT is a prenex formula, it implies its negative translation DCT by lemma 1.1 (vi). We can thus prove $\bot$ in the system $HA_-^\omega + \mathsf{DAC} + \mathsf{CT}$. In other words, if we assume $\mathsf{D\,AC}$, we can prove in HA_-^ω that not all functions are recursive (even if we cannot exhibit a counterexample!).

A direct corollary is that there cannot be any recursive realisation of $\mathsf{D\,AC}$. For exactly this reason, and because the semantics of the system NuPrl is based on recursive realizability, the work [Mur90] restricts itself to a fragment of classical logic that does not include the Axiom of Choice. This often forces one to encode functions as relations, and this encoding may be unnatural (see the discussion of Higman's lemma in [Mur90]).

4.2.2   Proof Theoretic Strength of $\mathsf{D\,AC}$

A second difficulty in interpreting $\mathsf{D\,AC}$ comes from the fact that in intuitionistic logic, $\mathsf{D\,AC}$ is proof-theoretically much stronger than AC.

We have seen already that $HA^\omega + \mathsf{AC}$ is conservative over HA [Goodman]. In contrast, by using the fact that in $HA_c^\omega + \mathsf{AC}$ we may define the characteristic function of any predicate, it is not difficult to see that we can interpret the second order comprehension axiom in $HA_\sim^\omega + D\ AC$. This system is proof theoretically much stronger than HA (see, for instance, Shoenfield's book on Mathematical Logic, Section 8.5), which implies that there cannot be any predicative way of modelling $HA_\sim^\omega + D\ AC$.

These remarks may explain a comment of Gödel after presenting the negative interpretation (see his Collected Work): "Intuitionism appears to introduce genuine restrictions only for analysis and set theory; these restrictions, however, are due to the rejection, not of the principle of Excluded Middle, but of notions introduced by impredicative definitions."

An important aspect that is not covered in this comment however is a more "intensional" aspect of logical systems, independently of their proof-theoretic strength. From an intuitionistic viewpoint, the proof object, that counts as evidence for the truth of a proposition, is of primary importance.

4.2.3 Problem in sequent calculus

Let us analyse now another way to get a possible computational content from classical arguments by considering Gentzen's sequent calculus formulation of classical arithmetic. One elegant approach is to use derivations in infinitary propositional logic. There is a general cut-elimination result for this logic which gives a computational interpretation of proofs. If we introduce countable disjunction and conjunction, we can interpret in this way classical quantification over natural numbers and give a computational interpretation of proofs in classical arithmetic.

A natural attempt is then to introduce disjunction and conjunction over the set of all number theoretic functions, and hope that we can interpret in this way classical quantification over number theoretic functions. However, as noticed in Tait's paper (see the reference in part II), there is a natural formulation of the Axiom of Choice in infinitary propositional logic. We start from atoms $\phi_{mn}, \overline{\phi_{mn}}$, and axioms

$$\Gamma, \phi_{mn}, \overline{\phi_{mn}}$$

and we ask whether it is possible to build a cut-free proof of

$$\bigvee_m \bigwedge_n \overline{\phi_{mn}}, \bigvee_f \bigwedge_m \phi_{mf(m)}, \tag{4.1}$$

from these axioms. It is not difficult to see that there cannot be such a cut-free proof. We will explain this in some detail.[6] Assume by contradiction Δ is a cut-free proof of (4.1).

First, observe that all conjunctions in (4.1) are countable, so by the subformula property all conjunctions in Δ are countable, so that Δ is at most countably branching. Since Δ is also well-founded, it follows that Δ is countable and that at most countably many functions $f_0, f_1, \ldots$ appear in Δ.

---

[6]Cf. Tait's paper. Tait describes this result as known already, but does not give further references. We think he was thinking to a proof using boolean models, as presented in the appendix.

Second, replace every subformula of the form $\bigvee_f \phi(f)$ in Δ by $\bigvee_k \phi(f_k)$ and call the resulting tree Δ'. Observe that $\bigvee_f \phi(f)$ can only be introduced in Δ from some $\phi(f_k)$. It follows that Δ' is indeed a proof of

$$\bigvee_m \bigwedge_n \overline{\phi_{mn}}, \bigvee_k \bigwedge_m \phi_{mf_k(m)}.$$

Third, the above conclusion of Δ' is false. This can be seen by taking f to be a function diagonalising over $f_0, f_1, \ldots$, e.g. $f(n) = f_n(n) + 1$, and $\phi_{mn} \iff f(m) = n$. Indeed, $\bigvee_m \bigwedge_n \overline{\phi_{mn}}$ is false since f is total, and $\bigvee_k \bigwedge_m \phi_{mf_k(m)}$ is false since f is by construction different from all f_k's.

4.3 Hilbert's Program

At the core of Hilbert's program [Hilbert], was the problem of making constructive sense of classical reasoning that uses the axiom of choice.

We recall here the idea of Hilbert for attacking this problem, idea that we shall reformulate in the next chapter in a constructive framework. The idea is to look at the axiom of choice in the form of an operator ϵ that is like an oracle that "chooses" an element. Typically, we introduce a functional $\epsilon(f)$ on functions such that

$$f(x) = 0 \Rightarrow f(\epsilon(f)) = 0.$$

The immediate problem is that we cannot describe effectively such a functional. This is clear by a continuity argument: were ϵ computable, only a finite number of values of f would be used in the computation of $\epsilon(f)$. If f_0 is the constant function 1, and $n_0 = \epsilon(f_0)$, we get a contradiction by considering the function g which is 1 only on n_0 and the values of f needed in the computation of $\epsilon(f_0)$, and 0 otherwise. We should have indeed $\epsilon(g) = \epsilon(f_0) = n_0$, but $g(n_0) = 1$ and there exists n such that $g(n) = 0$.

In order to solve this difficulty, Hilbert suggested looking at the operator ϵ as an "ideal" object, not having a "real" existence. Its purpose is only to simplify the theory, like the introduction of complex numbers in the theory of equations, or the introduction of ideal points at infinity in projective geometry. A main difference however is that complex numbers can be given a meaning as a pair of reals. Here, if it is not possible to explain what is this "ideal" object ϵ in general, to give a constructive model of it, Hilbert thought it would be possible to explain its meaning *in any given proof* of a concrete statement. The reason is intuitive: in any given proof, we can only have used a finite amount of information about this "ideal", "infinitary" object, and hence we should be able to replace it by a finite approximation. Notice that we did already meet this restriction to proofs of "finitary result" in Friedman's method. This method transforms non-effective proofs of a statement into an effective proof of the same statement only if this statement is purely existential.

What is important to notice here is that this interpretation by a finite approximation is relative to a given proof of a concrete statement. This is to be contrasted with he usual semantics, where the interpretation does depend only of the statement, and not of its proof.

Hilbert introduced a stratification of different uses of the axiom of choice in classical mathematics:

1. at the first level, we have the axiom of choice over natural numbers $AC(o, o)$,

2. the next level is the axiom of choice over functions $AC(o{\to}o, o)$,

3. the third level, used for proving for instance the existence of a well-ordering of the reals, requires the extensional form of $AC(o{\to}o, o)$.

The first level contains the problem of explaining constructively second order arithmetic. This is still an open problem. However, it is remarkable that in some mathematically interesting examples, it is possible to explain constructively the use of the Axiom of Choice by the technique of formal or point-free, topology.

4.4   Exercises on Part III

1. Show that it is not possible to give a negative translation for Martin-Löf's Intuitionistic Type Theory. (Hint: with the use of Σ types, it is possible to interpret the Axiom of Choice in Type Theory with one universe, while in Beeson's book for instance, it is shown that Type Theory with one universe is proof theoretically weaker than second order arithmetic.)

4.5   References

[Troelstra344] A. Troelstra "Metamathematical investigation of intuitionistic arithmetic and analysis" LNM 344.

[Beeson85] M. Beeson *Foundations of Constructive Mathematics*. Berlin, Springer-Verlag.

Contains interesting historical discussions, and a proof of Goodman's result that $HA^\omega +$ AC is conservative over HA.

[Mur90] Ch. Murthy "Extracting Computational Content from Classical Proofs." Ph. D. Thesis, Cornell.

The analysis of the non-effective proof of Higman's lemma explains clearly on a concrete mathematical example the problem of combining Excluded Middle with the Axiom of Choice.

[Martin-Lof73] P. Martin-Löf "An Intuitionistic Theory of Types: predicative part." Logic Colloquium 73, North-Holland, 1975, p. 73-118.

Presents a derivation of the Axiom of Choice in Type Theory, and emphasises the intuitionistic validity of the Axiom of Choice.

[Goodman] N. Goodman. *Intuitionistic arithmetic as a theory of constructions*. PhD thesis, Stanford University, 1968. There are more accessible references in JSL 37, p. 225-246 and in LNM 337.

Contains a proof that the Axiom of Choice added to HA$^\omega$ still leads to a theory conservative over HA. This is to be contrasted with the situation in classical logic, where the addition of the Axiom of Choice is not well understood yet.

[Hilbert] D. Hilbert "Die logischen Grundlagen der Mathematik." Math. Annalen 88 p. 151-65, 1923

"Ueber das Unendliche." Math. Annalen 95, 1926.

"Probleme der Grundlagen der Mathematik." Math. Annalen 102, 1929.

[Tait68] W. W. Tait "Normal Derivability in Classical Logic." Springer Lecture Notes in Mathematics 72, J. Barwise ed, pp. 204-236.

[Berardi95] S. Berardi, M. Bezem, Th. Coquand "On the computational content of the Axiom of Choice." In proceeding of TLCA 95, LNCS 902.

Contains a rather direct computational interpretation of the negative translation of the axiom of choice. The normalisation property is proved using excluded middle and dependent choices. The algorithmic structure of the interpretation of some proofs (like Higman's lemma) seems however interesting.

There is a theorem in topos theory (Barr's theorem) that claims that if a geometric statement is proved from a geometric theory using classical logic and axiom of choice, then it can be proved intuitionistically. However, the proof of this statement uses the axiom of choice and classical logic.

5 Formal Topology

The Axiom of Choice is often used, combined with the Law of Excluded Middle, in the form of Zorn's lemma to prove the existence of objects such as prime ideals, maximal ideals, Henkin sets, ultrafilters ... We have seen in the previous section that both negative translation and sequent calculus fail to explain constructively such use of the Axiom of Choice.

While it is still an open problem to have a general explanation, we present in this chapter a method that explains effectively some uses of Zorn's lemma. This method is best seen as a combination of two notions: the notion of *topological models*, where truth-values become open of suitable topological spaces, and the notion of *formal spaces*, by which we can describe in an effective way these models.

5.1 Historical Roots

The idea of point-free topology seems to go back to Whitehead (around 1910), and it was first presented by Russell (see [Russell14]). The 1935 paper by Moore [Moore35] presents a point-free version of the plane and the sphere, while Menger [Menger] presents a survey of some notions of point-free topology in 1940. The main application for Russell was an analysis of the use of mathematical abstractions n representing the physical world. The idea was to define the objects of mathematical physics as functions of observable sense-data, thus explaining abstract mathematical objects in term of concrete things. This is a kind of converse of the usual view, that explains sense-data as functions of physical objects. The advantage of his change of point of view is to make the application of mathematics to physics somewhat less mysterious.

This is the core of the idea of point-free/formal topology: to explain an ideal, nfinitary object like a point in terms of concrete finitary objects.

For instance, in some papers by Wiener [Wiener14], the notion of instant of time s analysed in terms of event.

One major problem that Russell mentions is the need to use the Axiom of Choice, 'or building points. Russell formulated the problem as follows: "It is shown that he existence of instants require hypotheses which there is no reason to suppose true - a fact which may be not without importance in physics." One of the hypotheses here was that "the whole class of events can be well ordered" [Russell36].

5.2 Formal Topology

5.2.1 Locales

The idea of point-free topology has been revived recently in the framework of locales [Stone] and, in computer science, with the notion of information systems [ML83,Scott82,Vickers89]. The problem of using the Axiom of Choice in the construction of points gets in this framework a subtle partial solution, that is described by Johnstone [1981]. In term of the theory of locales, it is noticed that "the category of locales is actually more convenient in many ways than the category of spaces" and that we can develop a constructive theory of spaces by staying at the level of the presentation of the spaces, without ever mentioning the points. Johnstone credits to Isbell the idea that the category of locales may have even better properties than the usual category of topological spaces.

5.2.2 Relevance to the analysis of the Axiom of Choice

In what way is the problem raised by Russell of the use of constructing points solved partially by the theory of locales?

This is best understood by looking at some examples of Stone's duality between the algebraic structure of boolean algebra and topological structure of totally disconnected compact spaces [Stone]. Any element of a boolean algebra can be seen as defining a closed open subset of the associated space, which, as a set, is the set of all ultrafilters of the boolean algebra. This duality gives a kind of dictionary between topological notions (infinitary) and algebraic notions (finitary). For instance: the notion of space correspond to the notion of algebra, continuous maps corresponds to algebraic morphisms, open subsets correspond to ideals.

A typical example is Cantor space $C = \{0, 1\}^N$. As a formal space, this is nothing but the boolean algebra built freely on a countable number of atoms.

An open subset of the space corresponds to an ideal of this boolean algebra seen as a ring. Namely, if U is an open subset, the set of closed open subsets included in U forms an ideal, and conversely we can associate to an ideal the open union of its elements thought of as closed open subsets. If we have a family of ideals I_k, the union of these ideals seen as an open of the space corresponds to the ideal ΣI_k which is the ideal of elements that can be written $x_{k_1} + \ldots + x_{k_p}$ for a finite family $x_{k_j} \in I_{k_j}$.

The fact that we can extract a finite covering from any covering becomes in this way the fact that if 1 belongs to an ideal ΣI_k where (I_k) is a family of ideals, then we can find $k_1, \ldots, k_p$ such that 1 belongs to $I_{k_1} + \ldots + I_{k_p}$. This is direct because if $1 \in \Sigma I_k$ we can by definition write $1 = x_{k_1} + \ldots + x_{k_p}$ for some $x_{k_j} \in I_{k_j}$ and hence 1 is already in some finite sum $I_{k_1} + \ldots + I_{k_p}$.

We see that the compactness of Cantor space is direct and constructive if expressed in a point-free way. This can be contrasted with the usual form of compactness whose proof is some form of König's lemma[7].

It is sometimes surprising how usual topological notions correspond in this way to usual algebraic notions. As we have seen, an open U corresponds to an ideal I (the ideal of closed open subsets that are subset of U). To say that U is everywhere dense is equivalent to $I^{\perp} = 0$, that is $x = 0$ whenever $xy = 0$ for all $y \in I$.

Sometimes however, an (apparently!) simple topological notion corresponds to a more subtle algebraic construction. For instance, if X_1, X_2 are respectively the spaces corresponding to the algebras B_1 and B_2, the product $X_1 \times X_2$ corresponds to a kind of tensor product $B_1 \otimes B_2$ whose direct algebraic description is subtle (it is *not* the algebraic product of B_1 and B_2 which corresponds to the sum of X_1 and X_2). In the other direction, we can give as example the Baire theorem, which corresponds to a simple lemma known as Tarski's lemma [Feferman].

What is striking from a proof theoretic viewpoint is that infinitary notions on one side are replaced by finitary notions on the other side. Often not only the use of the Axiom of Choice, but also of the law of excluded middle disappear on the algebraic side [Stone].

Formal topology generalises this to more general kind of topological spaces.

5.2.3 Formal Spaces

We now present one possible definition of formal spaces in a predicative framework. The importance of this restriction is that we want to analyse some impredicative proofs using the theory of locales in a predicative way. The definition we present is due to Sambin [Sambin87].

---

[7]More generally, one can define the product of spaces in a point-free way, and prove Tychonoff's theorem directly [Stone]. The classical version of this theorem is equivalent to the Axiom of Choice.

A formal space is a commutative monoid S with unit, together with a covering relation $x \lhd U$ between elements of S and subsets of S satisfying the following conditions.

- if $x \in U$, then $x \lhd U$,

- if $x \lhd U$, and $U \lhd V$ then $x \lhd V$, where $U \lhd V$ means that $u \lhd V$ for all $u \in U$,

- if $x \lhd U$ and $x \lhd V$, then $x \lhd UV$, where UV is the set of all elements uv for $u \in U$, $v \in V$,

- if $x \lhd U$ then $xy \lhd U$.

Intuitively the elements of S represents basic opens, the monoid operation the intersection of basic opens, and $x \lhd U$ means that the basic open x, as a set of points, is contained in the union of all basic open in U. A formal open in general is a subset of S, thought of as the union of its elements.

A *formal point* of a space $(S, 1, ., \lhd)$ is a predicate α on the set S such that[8]

- $\alpha(1)$,

- if $\alpha(x.y)$ then $\alpha(x)$,

- if $x \lhd U$, and $\alpha(x)$ then there exists $y \in U$ such that $\alpha(y)$,

- if $\alpha(x)$ and $\alpha(y)$ then $\alpha(x.y)$.

For instance, any boolean algebra B defines in a canonical way a formal space. We define $x \lhd U$ as meaning that x belongs to the ideal generated by U. We can then check that all four properties above are satisfied.

5.2.4 Phase Semantics

We will use often the following construction of formal spaces. Let S be a commutative monoid, and $Z \subseteq S$ a subset of S. For $U \subseteq S$, we define $U^{\perp}$ as $\{x \in S \mid xU \subseteq Z\}$ where xU is the set $\{xu \mid u \in U\}$. If $x \in S$ we write $x^{\perp}$ for $\{x\}^{\perp}$.

Proposition: If $Z \subseteq S$ is such that

- if $x \in Z$, $y \in S$ then $xy \in Z$,

- if $x^2 \in Z$, then $x \in Z$,

---

[8] We can see in the examples below the importance of a distinction between the "kind" of objects considered here: basic open are to be thought of as "concrete objects" while open in general are predicates. The points of a space also are predicates. These fundamental distinctions may be lost in a presentation of formal topology which uses freely impredicativity.

then the relation $x \lhd U$ defined by $U^{\perp} \subseteq x^{\perp}$ defines a covering on S.

This proposition has a direct proof. Notice that $U \lhd V$ iff $V^{\perp} \subseteq U^{\perp}$. It can be noticed that the complete Heyting algebra of saturated subsets, such that $U = U^{\perp\perp}$ is actually a complete *boolean* algebra. We refer to [Sambin] for an analysis of the notion of complete Heyting algebra in a predicative metalanguage like Intuitionistic Type Theory[9].

This space is called the *space of phases* defined by S and Z.

5.3 Topological models

The idea of seeing an open of an ordinary topological space as a generalised truth value goes back at least to Stone and Tarski.[10]

This is possible in general only if the logic is intuitionistic. The negation of an open U is interpreted as the interior of its complement, while its double negation is the interior of its closure, which does not coincide with U in general. Excluded middle is thus not validated by topological models in general.

This interpretation generalises directly if we use formal spaces. The method we use can then be described as follows.

We start from a set of conditions[11]. Often these conditions cannot be satisfied in an effective way, and we need Zorn's lemma to realise them. What we do instead is to realise *effectively* these conditions in a "relativised sense", where the conditions are interpreted as opens of a suitable formal space Y[12].

Of course, we have realised these conditions only in a "weak" sense. However, the next sections show that, if the formal space Y is non trivial, this "weak" realisation may be enough for some applications.

5.4 Prime Filters

A simple example of this "elimination of the use of the Axiom of Choice" is the existence of prime ideals for a distributive lattice. Given such a lattice D, we consider the elements of D as basic opens, and we define a covering relation $x \lhd U$, for U subset of D, by "there exists $x_1, \ldots, x_k \in U$ such that $x \leq x_1 \vee \ldots \vee x_k$." In particular, if $1 \lhd \emptyset$ then $1 \leq 0$ and the lattice has only one point. Notice also that $x \lhd y$ holds iff $x \leq y$.

---

[9]The key point is a distinction between *sets* (small collections) and *types* (large collections). The support of a complete lattice will be in general a *type* and what is required is the existence of a least upper bound for any *set*-indexed family of elements.

[10]They consider only propositional logic; this was generalised later to first order logic by Mostowski [Mostowski]. It should be noted the early paper by Tsao-Chen [Tsao] pointing out very clearly the connection between topology and modal logic.

[11]This set of conditions has to be expressed as a so-called geometric theory.

[12]It is important to remark that we can present effectively these models, and indeed, following [Sambin], this presentation can be done in Intuitionistic Type Theory.

What would be a point of this space? We can see it as a predicate $\mu(x)$ on D such that

- $\mu(1)$,
- $\neg\mu(0)$,
- $\mu(x), \mu(y) \to \mu(x \wedge y)$,
- $\mu(x \vee y) \to [\mu(x) \vee \mu(y)]$.

Thus a point of this space is exactly a prime filter of the distributive lattice D.

If we don't have the last condition, we can find explicitly such a predicate μ by taking $\mu(x)$ to be $z \leq x$ where z is an element such that $\neg[z \leq 0]$ holds. But, in general, it is *not* possible to describe effectively a predicate μ satisfying these conditions together with $\mu(x \vee y) \to [\mu(x) \vee \mu(y)]$.

If we interpret $\mu(x)$ as the basic open x of the space defined by $\vartriangleleft^{13}$, we do realise *effectively* all these conditions. For instance, the condition

$$\mu(x) \to [\mu(y) \to \mu(x \wedge y)]$$

is satisfied, because if $z \vartriangleleft x$ and $z \vartriangleleft y$ then $z \leq x$, $z \leq y$ and hence $z \leq x \wedge y$ and $z \vartriangleleft x \wedge y$. The last condition holds because $x \vee y$ is covered by $\{x, y\}$.

5.5   Prime Ideals

Let A be a commutative ring with unit. We list conditions on a predicate ν, such that $\nu(x)$ would say classically that x is *not* in a fixed prime ideal.

1. $\nu(1)$,
2. $\neg\nu(0)$,
3. $\nu(x), \nu(y) \to \nu(xy)$,
4. $\nu(xy) \to \nu(x)$,
5. $\nu(x + y) \to [\nu(x) \vee \nu(y)]$.

In general, it is not possible to realise effectively these conditions, i.e. to build a predicate that satisfies these conditions. However, if we require only that $\nu(x)$ is an open of a topological space, rather than a truth value, then it is possible to realise these conditions effectively.

---

[13] An open set is a subset of the set of all basic open, which represents formally the union of all its elements. Here $\mu(x)$ is interpreted as the subset $\{z \in D \mid z \leq x\}$.

We will define a formal space X such that it is possible to realise the previous conditions by giving values for $\nu(x)$ as opens of X. The goal is in some sense to show the consistency of the conditions above seen as a propositional theory by building a particular topological model.

We define $Z(x)$ to mean $\exists n[x^n = 0]$, that is x is nilpotent. We may expect that $\neg\nu(x)$ is provable iff $Z(x)$ holds, since classically, x is nilpotent iff it belongs to all prime ideals. We define

$$x \lhd U = \forall z\,[[\forall y \in U\; Z(y\,z)] \Rightarrow Z(x\,z)].$$

This relation satisfies the following properties

- $x \lhd 1$,

- if $x \in U$ then $x \lhd U$,

- if $x \lhd U$, and $U \lhd V$, then $x \lhd V$,

- if $x \lhd U$, then $x\,y \lhd U$,

- if $x \lhd U$ and $x \lhd V$, then $x \lhd UV$,

- $x + y \lhd \{x, y\}$.

All these conditions are directly checked. Hence, we can consider a formal space whose basic neighbourhoods are the elements of A and the covering relation is $\lhd$. Let X be this formal space.

Proposition: If $1 \lhd \emptyset$ in X, then $1 = 0$ in A.

This is direct because $1 \lhd \emptyset$ means $Z(1)$, which is equivalent to $1 = 0$.

A possible reformulation of this construction is the following: if $U \subseteq A$, let $U^\perp$ be $\{x \in A \mid xU \subseteq Z\}$, where Z is the radical of A, i.e. the set of nilpotent elements of A. Then $U \lhd V$ is equivalent to $V^\perp \subseteq U^\perp$ and X is the locale of subsets U of A such that $U = U^{\perp\perp}$. That is, the formal space we consider is the space of phases defined by A and Z.

If we interpret the proposition $\nu(x)$ as the basic open x of the space X, all the conditions on ν are satisfied. Hence we have a model of the propositional theory describing ν.

The first formal description of this space of prime ideals is due to A. Joyal.

This proposition can be used to prove that a given ideal J of a ring B contains 1: it is enough to show that the space X of prime ideals of the quotient ring $A = B/J$ is not consistent. This corresponds closely to the non-effective argument: if 1 is not in J, then deduce a contradiction from the existence of a prime ideal that contains J. However, it becomes in this way an effective argument: the inconsistency of X can be transformed to an actual derivation that 1 belongs to J.

This is this method that we shall illustrate in van der Waerden's example. Notice that we reformulate the problem of showing $1 \in J$ as the problem of showing a contradiction in a suitable theory.

5.6   Henkin Sets

Another suggestive example is the notion of Henkin sets. Given a first order classical theory T, its Tarksi-Lindenbaum algebra is a boolean algebra. A *Henkin set*
is a predicate μ on this boolean algebra which defines an ultrafilter μ such that
$\mu(\exists x \, A) \to \bigvee_t \mu(A[t])$.

It is possible to show that the space defined by this theory, called the Henkin
topology associated to T, is consistent if the theory T is consistent. Indeed, it is
enough to consider the phase space defined by $Z = \{A \mid A \vdash \bot\}$. It can be checked
that this provides a model for the predicate μ above.

Proposition: If $1 \lhd \emptyset$ then the first order theory T is inconsistent.

Proof: Direct using the phase model, since $1 \lhd \emptyset$ implies $1 \in Z$, that is $1 \vdash \bot$.
☐

This example is interesting because Henkin sets can be used to give an elegant
proof of completeness [Feferman]. We have given a constructive meaning to this
proof. It would be quite difficult to analyse this proof by negative translation, or by
using sequent calculus.

5.7   Jacobson's Theorem

As a first concrete example of an elimination of the use of the Axiom of Choice,
we take a simplified proof of a simple case of Jacobson's theorem.

Theorem: If A is a ring such that $x^3 = x$ for all $x \in A$, then A is commutative.

The general form is that commutativity follows from the fact that, for all x in A,
there exists $n(x) > 1$ such that $x^{n(x)} = x$.

The idea is to reduce the problem to the case where A is a division algebra. In
this case, the theorem is clear since $x^3 = x$ can be written $x(x - 1)(x + 1) = 0$
and hence implies $x = 0$ or $x = 1$ or $x = -1$. To reduce the problem to this case,
we must ensure the existence of enough maximal ideals. For this, we can either
classically use the axiom of choice, or alternatively, use topological models.

First, we state some lemmas that have a direct proof.

Lemma 1: If $x^2 = 0$, then $x = 0$.

Proof: we have then $x = x^2 x = 0$. ☐

Lemma 2: If $e^2 = e$, then $ex = xe$ for all x.

Proof: If $y = ex(1 - e)$ we have $y^2 = 0$, and hence by lemma 1, $y = 0$, that is
$ex = exe$. Similarly, we prove $xe = exe$. Hence $ex = xe$. ☐

Let B be the boolean algebra of all idempotents of A, that is, all elements $e \in A$
such that $e^2 = e$. This is a boolean algebra where the addition is defined by

$e_1 +' e_2 = e_1 + e_2 - 2e_1e_2$ and the multiplication is the multiplication of A. Lemma 2 is needed to check that $e_1 +' e_2$ is an idempotent if e_1, e_2 are idempotent. Notice that $x^2 \in B$ for all $x \in A$, and hence, for all $x \in A$, there exists $e \in B$ such that $xe = ex = x$.

5.7.1 First proof (non effective)

What follows is a simplified version of Jacobson's proof, which uses the Axiom of Choice. If $x \neq 0$, there exists a maximal ideal J on B such that x^2 is not in J. This follows from the fact that $x^2 \neq 0$ by lemma 1.

Lemma 3: if J is a maximal ideal of B, then $\bar{J} = \{x \in A \mid x^2 \in J\}$ is a double sided ideal of A such that $A/\bar{J}$ is a division algebra.

Proof: The verification that $\bar{J}$ is an ideal involves only elementary algebraic manipulations. We give them here for sake of completeness. First, if $x^2 \in J$ we have $(xy)^2 = x^2(xy)^2$ and hence $(xy)^2 \in J$. Similarly, $(yx)^2 = (yx)^2 x^2$ and hence $(yx)^2 \in J$. Thus $xy \in \bar{J}$ and $yx \in \bar{J}$ if $x \in \bar{J}$. Next, we claim that $x \in \bar{J}$ iff there exists $e \in J$ such that $xe = x$. In one direction, this follows from $xx^2 = x$. Conversely, if $e \in J$ and $xe = x$, then $x^2 e = x^2$ and hence $x^2 \in J$. If $x^2 \in J$ and $y^2 \in J$, we have $x^2 \vee y^2 = x^2 + y^2 - x^2y^2 \in J$ and $(x+y)(x^2 \vee y^2) = x + y$, hence $x + y \in \bar{J}$.

Finally, we prove that the quotient $A/\bar{J}$ is a division algebra if J is a maximal ideal of B. If $x \in A$, we have $x^2 \in J$ or $1 - x^2 \in J$. If $x^2 \in J$, then $x \in \bar{J}$. If $1 - x^2 \in J$, then x is its own inverse modulo $\bar{J}$. □

The quotient $A/\bar{J}$ is then a division algebra and we deduce $x = 0, 1$ or -1 modulo $\bar{J}$, hence the commutativity of each $A/\bar{J}$. Hence, $xy - yx = 0$ modulo each $\bar{J}$ and, by the remark above, $xy = yx$.

5.7.2 Second Proof (effective)

It is possible to eliminate the use the Axiom of Choice in the first argument by interpreting the proof in the topological model defined by the boolean algebra B, where truth values are ideals of B. We define $J_x = \{e \in B \mid xe = 0\}$. This is an ideal of B. The value of $x = y$ for $x, y \in A$ is defined as

$$[\![x = y]\!] = \{e \in B \mid xe = ye\} = J_{x-y}.$$

The following observation is the key to eliminate the use of maximal ideals.

Transfer Principle: If $x = y$ holds in the topological model defined by B, it holds in A.

Proof: If we have $[\![x = y]\!] = B$, we have $1 \in J_{x-y}$ and hence $x - y = 1(x - y) = 0$. □

The following formula is true under this interpretation

$$(\forall x \in A)[x = 0 \vee (\exists y \in A)[xy = 1]]$$

ndeed, this means $B = J_x + \Sigma_y J_{xy-1}$, which holds because $B = J_x + J_{xx-1}$ since $1 - x^2 \in J_x$ and $x^2 \in J_{xx-1}$. It follows that the following formula holds

$$(\forall x \in A)[x = 0 \vee x = 1 \vee x = -1],$$

and hence

$$(\forall x, y \in A)[xy = yx].$$

This means $[\![xy = yx]\!] = B$, and so, by the transfer principle $xy = yx$ in A.

5.7.3 Third Proof (effective)

It is possible to analyse completely this proof and to get a purely equational proof.

We analyse $[\![x = 0 \vee x = 1 \vee x = -1]\!] = B$. This means that, for any $x \in A$, we can find $e_1, e_2, e_3 \in B$ such that $1 = e_1 + e_2 + e_3$ and $xe_1 = 0$, $xe_2 = e_2$, $xe_3 = -e_3$.

Indeed, the analysis gives us $e_1 = 1 - u$, $e_2 = u(1 - v)$ and $e_3 = uv$ where $u = x^2$ and $v = (1 - x)^2$.

Using the fact that idempotents commute with any elements (lemma 2), it follows that

$$xy = e_1xy + e_2xy + e_3xy = e_2y - e_3y = e_1yx + e_2yx + e_3yx = yx.$$

This is really in the spirit of Hilbert's program; the use of maximal ideals has disappeared, and at the end, we get even a purely equational proof.

5.8   Van der Waerden's Theorem

Girard, in his book "Proof Theory and Logical Complexity", analyses a proof of Van der Waerden's theorem on arithmetical progression that uses some general lemmas of topological dynamics. Van der Waerden's theorem states that if k is given, there exists N such that for any partition A, B of $[1, N]$, either A or B contains an arithmetical progression of length k. This is a Π_2^0 statement, and it is natural to ask what is the computational content of its non-combinatorial proof. One general lemma used in this proof is the following: if X is a compact space and $f : X \to X$ a continuous map, there exists K compact non-empty such that $f(K) \subseteq K$ and if L compact non-empty such that $L \subseteq K$ and $f(L) \subseteq L$, then $K = L$. That is there exists a *minimal* invariant closed subspace.

Girard does not directly analyse this statement, but instead gives an equivalent statement, which is possible to analyse using the method of no counterexample, yet another method of extracting computational content of non-effective proofs, which is described in detail in Girard's book. It is possible to use formal topology and to give a topological model in which such a minimal invariant subspace exists in a relative sense, at least in the case where X is a *boolean* space, that is the Stone space of a boolean algebra B. This method provides an alternative analysis of the computational content(s) of this proof. Moreover, it extracts a purely algebraic and elementary lemma that can be seen as the "formal" statement of the existence of minimal invariant subspace.

In term of the boolean algebra B, a minimal invariant subspace can be described as a predicate μ such that

1. $\mu(1)$,

2. $\neg\mu(0)$,

3. if $\mu(x)$ and $x \subseteq y$, then $\mu(y)$,

4. if $\mu(x)$ and $\mu(y)$, then $\mu(x.y)$,

5. if $\mu(x)$, then $\mu(g(x))$,

6. $\mu(1 - x)$ or $\mu(\vee_{i \leq n} g^i(x))$ for one n.

Here g is a morphism $B \to B$ of boolean algebras, which corresponds to a continuous map $f : X \to X$.

We can read $\mu(x)$ as "the closed open subspace x of X contains the closed invariant subspace K," where K is invariant iff $f(K) \subseteq K$. Conversely, K is the intersection of all elements of B satisfying μ. If we add the condition $\neg\mu(x)$ for $x \in I$, where I is an invariant ideal of B, we describe a closed invariant subspace included in a given closed subspace of X.

Given such an ideal, we introduce the predicate $Z_I(x)$ meaning that there exists n such that $\wedge_{i \leq n} g^i(x) \in I$. The next three lemmas have direct proofs.

Lemma 1: If there exists n such that $Z_I(\wedge_{i \leq n} g^i(x))$, then $Z_I(x)$.

Lemma 2: If $Z_I(x)$ and $y \subseteq x$, then $Z_I(y)$.

Lemma 3: If $Z_I(x)$ and $y \in I$, then $Z_I(x \vee y)$.

Proof: Because I is closed under the morphism g. $\square$

Notice that, a priori, we cannot conclude that $Z_I(x \vee y)$ if we know only $Z_I(x)$ and $Z_I(y)$.

The main combinatorial property is:

Proposition 1: If $Z_I(y.(1 - x))$ and $Z_I(y.\vee_{i \leq n} g^i(x))$ for all n, then $Z_I(y)$.

Proof: We have n such that $\wedge_{i \leq n} g^i(y.(1 - x)) \in I$. By lemma 1, it is enough to show that $Z_I(\wedge_{i \leq n} g^i(y))$. This follows from lemmas 2, 3 and the inequality

$$\wedge_{i \leq n} g^i(y) \subseteq \wedge_{i \leq n} g^i(y.(1 - x)) \vee y.\vee_{i \leq n} g^i(x).$$

This inequality is a special case of the following remark: if $w \leq u_i \vee v_i$ for all , then $w \leq \wedge u_i \vee \vee v_i$. We apply this remark to the case $w = \wedge_{i \leq n} g^i(y)$ and $u_i = g^i(y.(1-x))$, $v_i = y.g^i(x)$. $\square$

We introduce next a covering relation on the set B

$$x \triangleleft U = (\forall z)[[(\forall y \in U)Z_I(z.y)] \Rightarrow Z_I(z.x)].$$

This defines a formal space M, following Sambin's definition of a formal topology [Sambin].

Proposition 2: The relation $x \triangleleft U$ satisfies

- if $x \in U$, then $x \triangleleft U$,

- if $x \triangleleft U$, and $U \triangleleft V$, then $x \triangleleft V$,

- if $x \triangleleft U$ and $x \triangleleft V$, then $x \triangleleft UV$,

- if $x \triangleleft U$ then $x.y \triangleleft U$,

- $x \triangleleft g(x)$,

- $1 \triangleleft 1 - x, \vee_n \vee_{i \leq n} g^i(x)$.

Proof: The first three conditions do not use any special properties of the predicate Z_I.

The fourth condition follows from lemma 2.

It is clear that if $Z_I(z.g(x))$, then $Z_I(z.x)$ and hence $x \triangleleft g(x)$.

The last condition follows from proposition 1. $\square$

We can use the previous construction to give a topological model of the predicate μ described above. For this, we interpret each proposition $\mu(x)$, for $x \in B$, as an open of the formal space M, namely as the basic open x. It can then be checked that all six properties characterising the property μ get interpreted by the open 1. Furthermore the condition $\neg \mu(x)$ holds for $x \in I$. This is used in [Coquand] in the proof-theoretical analysis of the topological proof of van der Waerden's theorem on arithmetical progression. In this case, the boolean algebra B is the Tarski-Lindenbaum algebra on countably many atomic propositions A_n and g is defined as the shift morphism $g(A_i) = A_{i+1}$.

As for the example of the spectrum of a ring, a possible reformulation of this construction is the following: if $U \subseteq B$, let $U^\perp$ be $\{x \in B \mid xU \subseteq Z_I\}$, where Z_I is the set of elements x such that $\wedge_{i \leq n} g^i(x) \in I$ for some n. Then $U \triangleleft V$ is equivalent to $V^\perp \subseteq U^\perp$ and X is the locale of subsets U of B such that $U = U^{\perp\perp}$. That is, the space we consider is the space of phases defined by B and Z_I.

Conclusion

In conclusion, we have given four different instances of uses of spaces of phases: for the spectrum of a distributive lattice, for the spectrum of a ring, for the space of Henkin sets, and finally for the space of minimal invariant subspaces. The use of formal topology in the example of Jacobson's theorem was of a different nature: we were using the space defined by the boolean algebra of idempotents of a ring.

5.9 References

[ML68] P. Martin-Löf *Notes on Constructive Mathematics*. Almqvist & Wiksell ed. The theory of the continuum by Brouwer can be described as a non-atomistic theory of non-discrete space. For instance Cantor space is not defined as a *set* of points, but as a spread. This is clearly explained in this book.

[Stone] P.J. Johnstone, *Stone Spaces*, Cambridge Studies in Advanced Mathematics

The introduction to the theory of locales. Contains the basic results and interesting references. In particular, the paper "The point of pointless topology", BAMS, is quite suggestive.

[ML83] P. Martin-Löf "Domain Interpretation of Type Theory" Workshop on the semantics of Programming Languages, Chalmers 1983

A very clear proof of the adequacy theorem for denotational semantics that connects it with operational semantics.

[Scott82] D. Scott "Domains for denotational semantics." Proceeding of ICALP 82, LNCS 140.

Presents the notion of information systems, that can be seen as a point-free presentation of domains.

[Tsao] Tang Tsao-Chen "Algebraic Postulates and a Geometric Interpretation for the Lewis Calculus of Strict Implication." BAMS 44 (1938), p. 737-744.

A clear geometric view of modal operators.

[Vickers89] S. Vickers, *Topology via Logic*, Cambridge Tracts in Theoretical Computer Science 5

Contains some connections between the theory of locales and domain theory.

[Wiener14] N. Wiener, "A Contribution to the Theory of Relative Position." Proc. Camb. Phil. Soc., Vol. 17

[Russell14] B. Russell, *Our Knowledge of the External World*, Cambridge University Press.

[Whitehead19] A.N. Whitehead, *The Concept of Nature*, Cambridge University Press.

[Russell36] B. Russell, "On order in time." In Logic and Knowledges, essays 1901-1950, R.C. Marsh editor.

Early references to the work in "point-free topology". Suggests some intriguing connections with physics.

[Moore35] R.L. Moore, Fundamenta Mathematicae 25.

Contains a point-free presentation of the plane.

Menger40] K. Menger "Topology without Points." Rice Institute Pamphlet.

In this survey, a large part is concerned with the construction of points from what Menger calls "lumps", that can be thought as basic neighbourhoods (Moore uses the terminology "pieces"). Let us cite Menger: "Such a topology of lumps seems to me closer to the physicist's concept of space than is the point set theoretical concept. For naturally all the physicist can measure and observe are pieces of space, and the individual points are merely given as the result of approximations."

Weyl] H. Weyl "Ueber die neue Grundlagenkrise der Mathematik", Mathematische Zeitschrift, 10, 1921.

This text contains an early presentation of the basic notions of first order logic (H. Weyl's thesis was about trying to explain Zermelo's formalisation of set theory, and he introduces these notions for this purpose; this later inspired Skolem), and the idea that an existential statement can be seen as an incomplete statement (an idea that was taken up in Hilbert-Bernays, and later motivated Kleene in formulating his realizability interpretation). It contains also a point-free definition of reals, continuous functions, and a sketch of a point-free definition of the notion of manifolds.

Mostowski] A. Mostowski. "Proofs of non-deducibility in intuitionistic functional calculus." Journal of Symbolic Logic 13, p. 204-207, 1948

First presentation of topological models for first order logic. (Formulae are interpreted by closed subsets!) It is used to show the non derivability of some formulae (we present similar examples in the appendix). The completeness of this method is conjectured.

Mulvey] Ch. Mulvey, J.W. Pelletier. "A Globalization of the Hahn-Banach Theorem." Advances in Mathematics, Vol. 89, p. 1-59, September 1991

Ch. Mulvey, J.W. Pelletier. "A geometric characterization concerning compact, convex sets." Math. Proc. Camb. Phil. Soc. , 109, p. 351-361, 1991

Quite elegant presentation of some basic results of functional analysis in a localic framework.

Vermeulen] J. Vermeulen, Ph.D. Thesis.

Contains an elegant formal presentation of reals and an intuitionistic proof of a localic version of Hahn-Banach, to be contrasted with Mulvey's paper, which presents the localic version, but proves it using Barr's theorem.

Sambin87] G. Sambin. "Intuitionistic Formal Spaces - a first communication." In Mathematical Logic and its applications, D. Skordev ed., Plenum, 187-204.

Dragalin87] A. Dragalin, two papers presented in the same volume where Sambin's paper appeared: Mathematical Logic and its applications, D. Skordev ed.

A formal space is given here as a partial order with a covering relation. This is closer to the notion of coverage presented in [Vickers] and [Stone].

Sambin 93] G. Sambin "The semantics of pretopologies", in: "Substructural logics", ed. P. Schroeder-Heister - K. Dosen, Clarendon, Oxford 1993, p. 293-307

Sambin 95] G. Sambin "Pretopologies and completeness proofs", J. Symbolic Logic 60 (1995), p. 863-878

[Feferman] review of Rasiowa-Sikorski, JSL 17, p. 72.

A quite clear presentation of a topological proof of completeness for first order logic.

[Ceder] J. Cederquist "A machine assisted formalization of pointfree topology in type theory." Technical Report, Chalmers University.

A beginning of a complete formalisation of pointfree topology in type theory. Contains still another alternative to the presentation of formal spaces.

[Coquand] Th. Coquand and J. Smith "An application of Constructive Completeness," to appear in the proceeding of the meeting Proof and Types, Torino 1995.

This is an application of formal spaces to give a constructive proof of a conservativity result, inspired by Dragalin's use of topological models.

Th. Coquand "Minimal Invariant Spaces in Formal Topology."

To appear in the Journal of Symbolic Logic. Shows that the localic version of the existence of minimal invariant subspaces can be applied in the same way as the usual existence in the topological proof of van der Waerden's theorem on arithmetical progression.

A   Appendix: Boolean Models

We present the basic definitions and some applications of the notion of boolean models: non derivability of Markov's principle, of the axiom of choice in some systems, and a new proof of Herbrand's theorem. The general idea is to replace the truth-value 0,1 by ideals of a fixed boolean algebra B. This is a special case of topological models. As usual, we denote by $I + J$ the ideal generated by $I \cup J$, while ΣI_α denotes the ideal generated by the union of all ideals I_α.

The notion of boolean models in metamathematics goes back to Tsao-Chen, Stone and Tarski (for modal and propositional logic) and Mostowski (for first order logic). One important and new point is that we can define and use this notion in an effective way, without using indirect reasoning. All the proofs that follow are effective, and indeed, can be represented in Intuitionistic Type Theory.

A.1   Semantics of First Order Logic

A.1.1   Intuitionistic First Order Logic

We suppose given an interpretation $[P] : \mathsf{D}^k \to \mathsf{B}$, for each atomic k-ary predicate P, and an interpretation $[f] : \mathsf{D}^k \to \mathsf{D}$ of each k-ary function symbol f. We can then interpret $[t]_\rho \in \mathsf{D}$ and $[\phi]_\rho$ as an ideal of B. For $\phi = P\, t_1 \ldots t_k$ $[\phi]_\rho$ is the principal ideal generated by $[P]\, [t_1]_\rho \ldots [t_k]_\rho$. We define $[\exists x\, \phi]_\rho$ to be $\Sigma_{d \in \mathsf{D}}\, [\phi]_{(\rho, x = d)}$ and $[\forall x\, \phi]_\rho$ to be $\bigcap_{d \in \mathsf{D}}\, [\phi]_{(\rho, x = d)}$. Notice that with this definition, each atomic formula is intended to be decidable. It would be possible to give a more general definition of models without this hypothesis, by requiring only to assign an ideal of B to each atomic proposition.

A.1.2   Classical First Order Logic

In order to get an interpretation of classical logic, we define first a negation operator on ideals of B: if I is an ideal, then $I^\perp$ is the ideal of $x \in B$ such that $xy = 0$ for all $y \in I$. It is then clear that $I^{\perp\perp}$ is an ideal that contains I, for any ideal I of B. We call an ideal I *regular* iff it is such that $I = I^{\perp\perp}$.

Proposition 1: We have the following properties

1. an intersection of an arbitrary family of regular ideals is a regular ideal,

2. for any ideal I, the ideal $(I + I^\perp)^\perp$ is the zero ideal 0,

3. any principal ideal is regular.

These assertions have a direct proof. We define then

$$[\![\exists x \ \phi(x)]\!] = (\Sigma_{d \in D}[\![\phi(d)]\!])^{\perp\perp}$$

and

$$[\![\phi \vee \psi]\!] = ([\![\phi]\!] + [\![\psi]\!])^{\perp\perp},$$

By the first property above, we can define:

$$[\![\forall x \ \phi(x)]\!] = \bigcap_{d \in D} [\![\phi(d)]\!].$$

and by the second property, we see that the law of excluded middle $\phi \vee \neg\phi$ is valid.

We say that such a model is a model of a theory T iff $[\![\psi]\!]$ is the principal ideal 1 for all $\psi \in T$. The following soundness property is proved directly by induction.

Proposition 2: If ϕ is provable in a theory T, then for any model of T, we have $[\![\phi]\!] = 1$.

A.2   Applications

A.2.1   Markov's principle

We consider the boolean algebra B generated by a countable number of elements $A_0, A_1, \ldots$[14] Notice that any element $x \in B$ "depends only on" a finite number of elements A_i. In particular if x is not 0, there are only finitely many i such that $x \leq A_i$ or $x \leq \neg A_i$. Thus, if $x \leq A_i$ or $x \leq \neg A_i$ for all i, then $x = 0$.

Over this boolean model, we can find a decidable predicate α such that the value $[\![\neg\neg\exists n \ (\alpha \ n)]\!]$ is 1 and $[\![\exists n \ (\alpha \ n)]\!]$ is not 1. Indeed, we can take $\alpha \ n = A_n$. Then, $[\![\neg\neg\exists n \ (\alpha \ n)]\!]$ is $(\bigcap_n A_n^\perp)^\perp$. But we have just seen that $\bigcap_n A_n^\perp = 0$ and hence $[\![\neg\neg\exists n \ (\alpha \ n)]\!]$ is 1. Next, $[\![\exists n \ (\alpha \ n)]\!]$ is ΣA_n, which is not the ideal 1 since, for instance, $\neg A_{27}$ does not belong to the ideal ΣA_n.

Mostowski introduced topological models of first order intuitionistic logic in order to show the non derivability of some formulae. However, a crucial difference is that he was using a non effective metalanguage.

---

[14] The algebra B can also be described as the unique countable atomless boolean algebra.

A.2.2 Herbrand's Theorem

As another application of Boolean models, here is a constructive proof of Herbrand's theorem. Let $\exists x\, A$ be a provable formula, with A quantifier-free. We let C be the usual Tarski-Lindenbaum boolean algebra of formulae, and I the ideal of C generated by all instantiation $A(t)$, for t term. Let B be the quotient algebra C/I.

We define a boolean model whose domain is the set D of terms, and by interpreting an atomic formula $P(t_1, \ldots, t_n)$ by the formula $P(t_1, \ldots, t_n)$ itself modulo I. Then $[\![\exists x\, A]\!]$ is 0 because each $A(t)$ gets the value 0 and each $[\![A]\!]_{x=t}$ is equal to $A(t)$ since A is quantifier-free.

Hence $0 = 1$ in B, that is $1 \in I$ in C, and there exists a finite number of terms $t_1, \ldots, t_k$ such that $A(t_1) \vee \ldots \vee A(t_k)$ is provable.

A.3 Semantics of Analysis

A.3.1 The language of Analysis

We give a model of HA^ω. The interpretations of terms are defined as usual, while the interpretations of formulae will be ideals of a fixed-boolean algebra. We can interpret $\mathsf{HA}^\omega + \mathsf{EM}$ by interpreting formulae as regular ideals.

A.3.2 Application to the Axiom of Choice

We exhibit a boolean model in which the formula

$$\exists f\, \forall n\, [[f\, n = 0] \equiv \alpha\, n]$$

is interpreted by the ideal 0. The boolean algebra we use is the boolean algebra B generated by $A_0, A_1, \ldots$ We interpret $\alpha\, n$ as the principal (and hence regular) ideal generated by A_n. The ideal $\exists f\, \forall n\, [[f\, n = 0] \equiv \alpha\, n]$ is then

$$\Sigma_f \bigcap_n [[f\, n = 0] \equiv \alpha_n].$$

But I claim that, for each given $f : \mathsf{N} \to \mathsf{N}$, the interpretation of $\bigcap_n [[f\, n = 0] \equiv \alpha_n]$ is 0. Indeed, for a given n, the interpretation $[[f\, n = 0] \equiv \alpha_n]$ is A_n if $f\, n = 0$ and $\neg A_n$ if $f\, n \neq 0$. The assertion follows then from the fact that if $x \leq A_n$ or $x \leq \neg A_n$ for all n, then $x = 0$ in B.

Syntax and Semantics of Dependent Types

Martin Hofmann

Contents

1 Introduction

Dependent types are types which unlike simple types, such as products, function spaces, or natural numbers, depend on or vary with values. An example of a dependent type is a type of vectors or arrays $Vec_\sigma(M)$ of a given length $M : \mathbf{N}$ over some type σ. Its objects are $nil_\sigma : Vec_\sigma(0)$ and $Cons_\sigma(U, V) : Vec_\sigma(Suc(M))$ where $U : \sigma$ and $V : Vec_\sigma(M)$. We can now consider a function which given $x: \mathbf{N}$ returns a vector (over $\mathbf{N}$) of length x and all entries 0. This function then has the type $\Pi x: \mathbf{N}. Vec_\mathbf{N}(x)$ — a type of functions with the property that the type of the result depends on the argument. The same algorithm could also be typed as $\mathbf{N} \to List(\mathbf{N})$. The point of the dependent typing is that it reveals more information about the function. Another example of this kind is the exception-free head function for vectors

$$Hd : \Pi x: \mathbf{N}. Vec_\sigma(Suc(x)) \to \sigma$$

which yields the first entry of a vector. The typing prevents the unwanted case that Hd gets applied to the empty list. In this way the dependent typing circumvents the need for partial functions in certain cases.

Another source for type dependency comes from type variables and type universes. For instance, the type of monoids with carrier X

$$MON(X) \stackrel{\text{def}}{=} ((X \times X) \to X) \times X$$

is a type depending on X. Type variables such as X above can be treated as ordinary variables using universes, that is types containing (names for) other types

79

as members. The function constructing the free monoid on a type X would then be given the type

$$\Pi X\colon U.MON(List(X))$$

where U is such a universe.

The third important source for dependent types comes from the propositions-as-types analogy under which propositions (in constructive logic) are seen as types, namely the type of their proofs. For instance, a proof of $\phi \wedge \psi$ consists of a proof of ϕ and a proof of ψ; a proof of $\phi \supset \psi$ consists of a procedure which transforms a hypothetical proof of ϕ into a proof of ψ. Therefore, conjunction and implication can be identified with cartesian product and function space, respectively. Under this correspondence, predicates, i.e. propositional functions, become dependent types. We will describe how to view the atomic equality predicate and universal and existential quantification as types and type formers. In fact universal quantification corresponds to the Π-type introduced above.

If propositions are ordinary types they can be part of other types. For instance, we can enrich the above-defined type of monoids of monoids by a proposition stating associativity and neutrality:

$$MON'(X) \overset{\text{def}}{=}$$
$$\Sigma\circ\colon (X \times X) \to X.$$
$$\Sigma e\colon X.$$
$$(\forall x, y, z\colon X. \circ (\circ(x,y),z) = \circ(x,\circ(y,z))) \;\wedge\; (\forall x\colon X. \circ(e,x) = x \wedge \circ(x,e) = e)$$

The Σ-type former is a generalisation of the cartesian product $\times$ to dependent types and corresponds under the propositions-as-types analogy to existential quantification. An object of the above generalised signature thus consists of

- an object $\circ$ of type $(X \times X) \to X$

- an object e of type X

- a proof that $\circ$ is associative and e is neutral

The main aim of this article is not so much to explain how to use dependent types to formalise constructive mathematics or to do program development and specification, but rather to introduce the reader to a tool for the meta-theoretic study of dependent type theory: category-theoretic semantics.

By semantics we understand a compositional assignment of mathematical objects to syntactic objects, for instance sets or sets to types and set-theoretic functions to (open) terms of the types. Such interpretation is performed with the aim of establishing consistency or conservativity of certain type-theoretic constructs, or simply in order to explain, motivate, and justify them. Due to type dependency the verification that such an interpretation indeed validates all the rules of type theory can be quite involved which is why it has proven useful to define a general abstract notion: the category-theoretic semantics, which is proven sound and complete once and for all. Then in order to obtain an interpretation of type theory one "only" needs to check that one has an instance of the semantic notion.

The semantics is not surprising (like maybe the set-theoretic semantics for first-order logic) in that we have an almost trivial completeness property like in the case of Heyting algebra semantics for intuitionistic logic. The point is that the soundness theorem is non-trivial and therefore some work can be saved when presenting a translation of the syntax as a model construction.

1.1 Overview

In the next section we give the syntax for an extensible calculus of dependent types which encompasses various "named" type theories like Martin-Löf's type theory or the Calculus of Constructions. In Sections 2.4 and 2.3 we introduce pre-syntax and syntactic context morphisms. Both are auxiliary syntactic notions required later to define the interpretation function and to construct a term model. Section 3 contains the material on category-theoretic semantics. It introduces *categories with families* which provide a category-theoretic counterpart of type dependency and form the backbone of the semantics. We compare this notion to related concepts and identify the additional structure required to model the type and term formers. Section 3 ends with the interpretation of the syntax in the semantic structures. Finally, Section 4 is devoted to an extended application of the material: we give an interpretation of types as "variable sets" (presheaves) and use it to establish conservativity of Martin-Löf's Logical Framework over ordinary type theory.

Every section or larger subsection except the last one ends with several exercises which either contain definitions or proofs which are similar to previously given ones and are required later, or contain applications of the material. The last section contains instead an overview of the literature on applications of semantic methods to dependent type theory as a suggestion for further reading.

This article is self-contained except for the presupposition of some very basic category theory in Sections 3 and 4 which has not been included since very good introductions are readily available. The required notions are summarised in the beginning of Section 3.

2   Formal systems for dependent types

A theory of dependent types is a formal system which mainly allows one to derive judgements of the form $M : \sigma$ (the term M has type σ) and σ *type* (σ is a type). As types may contain terms, typing affects typehood and both kinds of judgements must be defined simultaneously. For instance, $Vec_\sigma(M)$ is a type if σ is a type and $M : N$. Furthermore, we usually want a notion of definitional equality to be built into the theory, for example we wish to consider $0 : N$ and $0 + 0 : N$ as (definitionally) equal terms and hence $Vec_\sigma(0)$ and $Vec_\sigma(0 + 0)$ as definitionally equal types: if $M : Vec_\sigma(0)$ then also $M : Vec_\sigma(0 + 0)$. This leads to two more forms of judgement: $M = N : \sigma$ (M and N are definitionally equal terms of type σ) and $\sigma = \tau$ *type* (σ and τ are definitionally equal types). Finally, we must keep track of the types of the free variables occurring in a judgement; we cannot assert $x + y :$ N unless we know that x: N and y: N. Since such declarations may depend on each other like in x: N, y: $Vec_N(x)$ it is convenient to make all judgements relative to a list of variable declarations including at least the free variables occurring inside the judgement. Such lists of declarations are called *contexts* and sometimes also *type assignments*. Intuitively, a context $x_1: \sigma_1, \ldots, x_n: \sigma_n$ is well-formed if each σ_i is a type in the context $x_1: \sigma_1, \ldots x_{i-1}: \sigma_{i-1}$ and the x_i are pair-wise distinct. So typehood (and thus typing) affects context validity and we finally arrive at six kinds of judgements:

$\vdash \Gamma \ ctxt$	Γ is a valid context
$\Gamma \vdash \sigma \ type$	σ is a type in context Γ
$\Gamma \vdash M : \sigma$	M is a term of type σ in context Γ
$\vdash \Gamma = \Delta \ ctxt$	Γ and Δ are definitionally equal contexts
$\Gamma \vdash \sigma = \tau \ type$	σ and τ are definitionally equal types in context Γ
$\Gamma \vdash M = N : \sigma$	M and N are def. equal terms of type σ in context Γ.

Well-formedness and equality of contexts can be defined in terms of the other judgements, but it is technically easier to include them as primary notions.

Regardless of which rules we later introduce to describe particular type and term formers such as the natural numbers or Π-types we always have the following structural rules.

- Rules for context formation:

$$\frac{}{\vdash \diamond \ ctxt} \ \text{C-EMP} \qquad \frac{\Gamma \vdash \sigma \ type}{\vdash \Gamma, x: \sigma \ ctxt} \ \text{C-EXT}$$

$$\frac{\vdash \Gamma = \Delta \ ctxt \qquad \Gamma \vdash \sigma = \tau \ type}{\vdash \Gamma, x: \sigma = \Delta, y: \tau \ ctxt} \ \text{C-EXT-EQ}$$

The variables x and y in rules C-EXT and C-EXT-EQ are assumed to be fresh.

- The variable rule

$$\frac{\vdash \Gamma, x: \sigma, \Delta \ ctxt}{\Gamma, x: \sigma, \Delta \vdash x : \sigma} \ \text{VAR}$$

- Rules expressing that definitional equality is an equivalence relation:

$$\frac{\vdash \Gamma \ ctxt}{\vdash \Gamma = \Gamma \ ctxt} \ \text{C-EQ-R}$$

$$\frac{\vdash \Gamma = \Delta \ ctxt}{\vdash \Delta = \Gamma \ ctxt} \quad \text{C-Eq-S}$$

$$\frac{\vdash \Gamma = \Delta \ ctxt \qquad \vdash \Delta = \Theta \ ctxt}{\vdash \Gamma = \Theta \ ctxt} \quad \text{C-Eq-T}$$

$$\frac{\Gamma \vdash \sigma \ type}{\Gamma \vdash \sigma = \sigma \ type} \quad \text{Ty-Eq-R}$$

$$\frac{\Gamma \vdash \sigma = \tau \ type}{\Gamma \vdash \tau = \sigma \ type} \quad \text{Ty-Eq-S}$$

$$\frac{\Gamma \vdash \sigma = \tau \ type \qquad \Gamma \vdash \tau = \rho \ type}{\Gamma \vdash \sigma = \rho \ type} \quad \text{Ty-Eq-T}$$

$$\frac{\Gamma \vdash M : \sigma}{\Gamma \vdash M = M : \sigma} \quad \text{Tm-Eq-R}$$

$$\frac{\Gamma \vdash M = N : \sigma}{\Gamma \vdash N = M : \sigma} \quad \text{Tm-Eq-S}$$

$$\frac{\Gamma \vdash M = N : \sigma \qquad \Gamma \vdash N = O : \sigma}{\Gamma \vdash M = O : \sigma} \quad \text{Tm-Eq-T}$$

- Rules relating typing and definitional equality:

$$\frac{\Gamma \vdash M : \sigma \qquad \vdash \Gamma = \Delta \ ctxt \qquad \Gamma \vdash \sigma = \tau \ type}{\Delta \vdash M : \tau} \quad \text{Tm-Conv}$$

$$\frac{\vdash \Gamma = \Delta \ ctxt \qquad \Gamma \vdash \sigma \ type}{\Delta \vdash \sigma \ type} \quad \text{Ty-Conv}$$

- For convenience (cf. E2.7 below) we also introduce the following weakening and substitution rules where $\mathcal{J}$ ranges over one of the judgements $M : \sigma$, $\sigma \ type$, $M = N : \sigma, \sigma = \tau \ type$.

$$\frac{\Gamma, \Delta \vdash \mathcal{J} \qquad \Gamma \vdash \rho \ type}{\Gamma, x{:}\rho, \Delta \vdash \mathcal{J}} \quad \text{Weak}$$

$$\frac{\Gamma, x{:}\rho, \Delta \vdash \mathcal{J} \qquad \Gamma \vdash U : \rho}{\Gamma, \Delta[U/x] \vdash \mathcal{J}[U/x]} \quad \text{Subst}$$

Here $\mathcal{J}[U/x]$ (and similarly $\Delta[U/x]$) denotes the capture-free substitution of U for x in $\mathcal{J}$. This means that bound variables in $\mathcal{J}$ are systematically renamed so as to prevent any free variables in U from becoming bound in $\mathcal{J}[U/x]$. We will henceforth consider all contexts, types, and terms as equal if they agree up to names of bound variables and assume the existence of a capture-free substitution function on these equivalence classes. One can use a de Bruijn style presentation of the syntax to avoid this identification. A good reference is (Huet 1990). The de Bruijn presentation gives rise to canonical representatives of the equivalence classes and yields an algorithm implementing capture-free substitution.

2.1   Type formers

Type and term formers are introduced by formation, introduction, elimination, and equality rules. There is no definitive set of type formers and new ones can be invented as needed. We present several of them to give an idea of the general pattern.

2.1.1   Dependent function space

The *dependent function space* also called *dependent product or* Π-*type* corresponds to the set-theoretic notion of cartesian product over a family of sets $\Pi_{i \in I} B_i$ which has as elements functions mapping an index i to an element of the corresponding set B_i. In type theory this is expressed as follows:

$$\frac{\Gamma \vdash \sigma \; type \quad \Gamma, x\!:\!\sigma \vdash \tau \; type}{\Gamma \vdash \Pi x\!:\!\sigma.\tau \; type} \; \Pi\text{-F}$$

$$\frac{\Gamma \vdash \sigma_1 = \sigma_2 \; type \quad \Gamma, x\!:\!\sigma \vdash \tau_1 = \tau_2 \; type}{\Gamma \vdash \Pi x\!:\!\sigma_1.\tau_1 = \Pi x\!:\!\sigma_2.\tau_2 \; type} \; \Pi\text{-EQ}$$

The first rule expresses that a dependent function space consists of a type σ (possibly depending on other types recorded in Γ) and a type depending on σ (and Γ), viz. τ. The rule Π-EQ expresses that definitional equality is respected by the Π-former. The variable x becomes bound in $\Pi x\!:\!\sigma.\tau$ and thus this type is subject to the convention on renaming of variables set out above. To form elements of the Π-type we have the introduction rule with associated congruence rule:

$$\frac{\Gamma, x\!:\!\sigma \vdash M : \tau}{\Gamma \vdash \lambda x\!:\!\sigma.M^\tau : \Pi x\!:\!\sigma.\tau} \; \Pi\text{-I}$$

$$\frac{\Gamma, x\!:\!\sigma \vdash M_1 = M_2 : \tau \quad \Gamma \vdash \sigma_1 = \sigma_2 \; type \quad \Gamma, x\!:\!\sigma \vdash \tau_1 = \tau_2 \; type}{\Gamma \vdash \lambda x\!:\!\sigma_1.M_1^{\tau_1} = \lambda x\!:\!\sigma_2.M_2^{\tau_2} : \Pi x\!:\!\sigma_1.\tau_1} \; \Pi\text{-I-EQ}$$

So to give an element of $\Pi x\!:\!\sigma.\tau$ one must give an element of $\tau[x]$ in the presence of a variable x of type σ. The congruence rule Π-I-EQ expresses that definitional equality preserves Π-introduction (λ). We will henceforth refrain from writing down congruence rules. Such rules are silently understood for every type and term former we will introduce.

Elements of a Π-type are consumed using application like in the set-theoretic situation where an element of $\Pi_{i\in I}B_i$ and a specific $i_0 \in I$ gives an element of B_{i_0}:

$$\frac{\Gamma \vdash M : \Pi x\!:\!\sigma.\tau \quad \Gamma \vdash N : \sigma}{\Gamma \vdash App_{[x:\sigma]\tau}(M, N) : \tau[N/x]} \quad \Pi\text{-E}$$

Notice that the square brackets in the typing annotation $[x\!:\!\sigma]\tau$ are an integral part of the term former for application and indicate the binding of x in τ. Now we encounter a source for definitional equality: applying a function $\lambda x\!:\!\sigma.M^\tau$ to a term $N : \sigma$ results in M with x replaced by N:

$$\frac{\Gamma \vdash \lambda x\!:\!\sigma.M^\tau : \Pi x\!:\!\sigma.\tau \quad \Gamma \vdash N : \sigma}{\Gamma \vdash App_{[x:\sigma]\tau}(\lambda x\!:\!\sigma.M^\tau, N) = M[N/x] : \tau[N/x]} \quad \Pi\text{-C}$$

Notice that substitution plays a more prominent role in dependently typed calculi as it is needed to formulate even the typing rules, not only the conversion rules (as in the case of simply-typed lambda calculus).

The attribute "definitional" for en equation like Π-C is certainly arguable. It is motivated by the understanding of $\lambda x\!:\!\sigma.M^\tau$ as a *canonical* element of $\Pi x\!:\!\sigma.\tau$ and application as a *derived* concept defined by equation Π-C. This view becomes important if one wants to see type theory as a *foundation* of constructive mathematics which accordingly is to be justified by a philosophical argument rather than via an interpretation in some other system, see (Martin-Löf 1975;(1984)). For us the distinction between canonical and non-canonical elements is not important. However, we will use it to motivate further definitional equalities.

A more pragmatic explanation for Π-C is that in applications one often uses abstraction as a means for making definitions and application to instantiate a definition. Thus when the Π-type is used in this way then both sides of Π-C are indeed definitionally equal in the proper sense of the word.

2.1.2 Dependent sum

The next type former we introduce is the Σ-*type* (or *dependent sum*) corresponding to disjoint union in set theory. If we are given a family of sets $(B_i)_{i\in I}$ we can form the set $\Sigma_{i\in I}B_i \stackrel{\text{def}}{=} \{(i, b) \mid i \in I \wedge b \in B_i\}$ whose elements consist of an index i and an element of the corresponding set B_i. In type theory the corresponding formation and introduction rules look as follows.

$$\frac{\Gamma \vdash \sigma\ type \quad \Gamma, x\!:\!\sigma \vdash \tau\ type}{\Gamma \vdash \Sigma x\!:\!\sigma.\tau\ type} \quad \Sigma\text{-F} \qquad \frac{\Gamma \vdash M : \sigma \quad \Gamma \vdash N : \tau[M/x]}{\Gamma \vdash Pair_{[x:\sigma]\tau}(M, N) : \Sigma x\!:\!\sigma.\tau} \quad \Sigma\text{-I}$$

The elimination rule looks a bit complicated at first sight:

$$\frac{\Gamma, z\!:\!\Sigma x\!:\!\sigma.\tau \vdash \rho\ type \quad \Gamma, x\!:\!\sigma, y\!:\!\tau \vdash H : \rho[Pair_{x:\sigma.\tau}(x, y)/z] \quad \Gamma \vdash M : \Sigma x\!:\!\sigma.\tau}{\Gamma \vdash R^\Sigma_{[z:\Sigma x:\sigma.\tau]\rho}([x\!:\!\sigma.y\!:\!\tau]H, M) : \rho[M/z]} \quad \Sigma\text{-E}$$

Here the variable z in ρ and the variables x, y in H become bound inside R^Σ as indicated by the square brackets. The idea behind R^Σ is that in order to give a (possibly dependent) function out of $\Sigma x \colon \sigma.\tau$, it is enough to specify it on canonical elements, viz. the pairs. This is expressed by the following definitional equality

$$\frac{\Gamma \vdash \mathsf{R}^\Sigma_{[z:\Sigma x:\sigma.\tau]\rho}([x\colon\sigma, y\colon\tau]H, Pair_{[x:\sigma]\tau}(M, N)) : \rho[Pair_{[x:\sigma]\tau}/z]}{\begin{array}{c}\Gamma \vdash \mathsf{R}^\Sigma_{[z:\Sigma x:\sigma.\tau]\rho}([x\colon\sigma, y\colon\tau]H, Pair_{[x:\sigma]\tau}(M, N)) = \\ H[M/x, N/y] : \rho[Pair_{[x:\sigma]\tau}/z]\end{array}} \quad \Sigma\text{-}\mathsf{C}$$

which says that a function on $\Sigma x \colon \sigma.\tau$ defined using the eliminator R^Σ behaves on canonical elements as specified by the argument H. As an example we show how to define projections for the Σ-type. Assume $\Gamma \vdash \sigma$ *type*, $\Gamma, x \colon \sigma \vdash \tau$ *type*, and $\Gamma \vdash M : \Sigma x \colon \sigma.\tau$. We define

$$M.1 \stackrel{\text{def}}{=} \mathsf{R}^\Sigma_{[z:\Sigma x:\sigma.\tau]\sigma}([x\colon\sigma, y\colon\tau]x, M) : \sigma$$

Now, in the particular case where M is canonical, i.e. $M \equiv Pair_{[x:\sigma]\tau}(U, V)$ the rule Σ-C gives $\Gamma \vdash M.1 = U : \sigma$ as expected. A second projection can be defined similarly:

$$M.2 \stackrel{\text{def}}{=} \mathsf{R}^\Sigma_{[z:\Sigma x:\sigma.\tau]\tau[z.1/x]}([x\colon\sigma, y\colon\tau]y, M) : \tau[M.1]$$

Notice that the definiens (the right-hand side) is well-typed by virtue of rules Σ-C and Ty-Conv which allow us to conclude

$$\Gamma, x \colon \sigma, y \colon \tau \vdash y : \tau[(Pair_{[x:\sigma]\tau}(x, y).1)/x]$$

One can restrict the elimination operator R^Σ to those cases where the type ρ does not depend on $\Sigma x \colon \sigma.\tau$. One can then still define the first projection, but no longer the second one. This is called *weak Σ-elimination*, see (Luo 1994).

Important special cases of $\Pi x \colon \sigma.\tau$ and $\Sigma x \colon \sigma.\tau$ arise when τ does not actually depend on σ. In this case, i.e. when $\Gamma \vdash \sigma$ *type* and $\Gamma \vdash \tau$ *type* we write

$$\sigma \to \tau \stackrel{\text{def}}{=} \Pi x \colon \sigma.\tau$$

and

$$\sigma \times \tau \stackrel{\text{def}}{=} \Sigma x \colon \sigma.\tau$$

indicating that in these cases the Π- and Σ-types correspond to ordinary non-dependent function space and cartesian product, respectively.

A (constructive) proof of an existential statement $\exists x \colon \sigma.P(x)$ consists of an element M of σ (the witness) together with a proof that $P(M)$, that is an element of $P(M)$. Thus under the propositions-as-types analogy the Σ-type is the counterpart to existential quantification.

2.1.3 Natural numbers

An example of a basic type is provided by the type of natural numbers given by the rules

$$\frac{\vdash \Gamma\ ctxt}{\Gamma \vdash \mathbf{N}\ type}\ \text{N-F} \qquad \frac{\vdash \Gamma\ ctxt}{\Gamma \vdash 0 : \mathbf{N}}\ \text{N-I-0} \qquad \frac{\Gamma \vdash M : \mathbf{N}}{\Gamma \vdash Suc(M) : \mathbf{N}}\ \text{N-I-S}$$

The elimination rule is similar to the one for Σ-types; in order to define a (possibly dependent) function on $\mathbf{N}$ it is enough to give it on the canonical elements 0 and $Suc(M)$. In the case of $Suc(M)$ the function may be called (primitive) recursively for M.

$$\frac{\begin{array}{c} \Gamma, n{:}\,\mathbf{N} \vdash \sigma\ type \\ \Gamma \vdash H_z : \sigma[0/n] \\ \Gamma, n{:}\,\mathbf{N}, x{:}\,\sigma \vdash H_s : \sigma[Suc(n)/n] \\ \Gamma \vdash M : \mathbf{N} \end{array}}{\Gamma \vdash \mathsf{R}^{\mathbf{N}}_{[n{:}\mathbf{N}]\sigma}(H_z, [n{:}\,\mathbf{N}, x{:}\,\sigma]H_s, M) : \sigma[M/n]}\ \text{N-E}$$

The primitive-recursive behaviour of $\mathsf{R}^{\mathbf{N}}$ is expressed by the following two rules for definitional equality:

$$\frac{\Gamma \vdash \mathsf{R}^{\mathbf{N}}_{[n{:}\mathbf{N}]\sigma}(H_z, [n{:}\,\mathbf{N}, x{:}\,\sigma]H_s, 0) : \sigma[0/n]}{\Gamma \vdash \mathsf{R}^{\mathbf{N}}_{[n{:}\mathbf{N}]\sigma}(H_z, [n{:}\,\mathbf{N}, x{:}\,\sigma]H_s, 0) = H_z : \sigma[0/n]}\ \text{N-C-0}$$

$$\frac{\Gamma \vdash \mathsf{R}^{\mathbf{N}}_{[n{:}\mathbf{N}]\sigma}(H_z, [n{:}\,\mathbf{N}, x{:}\,\sigma]H_s, Suc(M)) : \sigma[Suc(M)/n]}{\begin{array}{c}\Gamma \vdash \mathsf{R}^{\mathbf{N}}_{[n{:}\mathbf{N}]\sigma}(H_z, [n{:}\,\mathbf{N}, x{:}\,\sigma]H_s, Suc(M)) = \\ H_s[M/n, \mathsf{R}^{\mathbf{N}}_{[n{:}\mathbf{N}]\sigma}(H_z, [n{:}\,\mathbf{N}, x{:}\,\sigma]H_s, M)/x] : \sigma[Suc(M)/n]\end{array}}\ \text{N-C-S}$$

The elimination rule for natural numbers allows for both the definition of functions by primitive recursion and proof of properties of the natural numbers by mathematical induction. For instance, we can define addition as follows

$$M + N \stackrel{\text{def}}{=} \mathsf{R}^{\mathbf{N}}_{[n{:}\mathbf{N}]\mathbf{N}}(N, [n{:}\,\mathbf{N}, x{:}\,\mathbf{N}]Suc(x), M) : \mathbf{N}$$

and—writing $\bar{n}$ for the closed term $\underbrace{Suc(\dots Suc(0)\dots)}_{n\ \text{times}}$—we have

$$\diamond \vdash \bar{n} + \bar{m} = \overline{m+n} : \mathbf{N}$$

for all (set-theoretic) natural numbers m, n by m-fold application of rule N-C-S followed by N-C-Z. We will see an example of the use of mathematical induction below.

2.1.4 Notation

We will henceforth freely suppress type annotations if this increases readability. For instance, we may write $\lambda x{:}\,\sigma.M$ or even $\lambda x.M$ instead of $\lambda x{:}\,\sigma.M^\tau$. We sometimes omit a prevailing context Γ and thus write $\vdash \mathcal{J}$ instead of $\Gamma \vdash \mathcal{J}$. We write $\diamond \vdash J$ if we want to emphasise that a judgement holds in the empty context. If σ contains among others the free variable x then we can write $\sigma[x]$ to emphasise this and use the notation $\sigma[M]$ for $\sigma[M/x]$ in this case.

In implementations of type theory many more such conventions are being used and sometimes they are even made part of the official syntax. It is always an important question whether such shorthands should be treated formally or informally. Here we have decided to have a syntax as explicit as possible so as to facilitate its meta-theoretic study. For doing proofs within the theory obviously the syntactic sugar is unavoidable.

2.1.5 Identity types

As we have explained, definitional equality is the congruence generated by the computational equations like N-C-Z and Π-C. Its main purpose is to facilitate the construction of inhabitants of types; in some examples, like the definition of the second projection for Σ-types above, its use is unavoidable. However, definitional equality is merely a judgement, and not a type, that is, not a proposition, and therefore cannot be established by induction, i.e., using R^N or R^Σ. Also, we cannot have definitional equalities as assumptions in a context. In order to enable equality reasoning inside type theory one is therefore lead to introduce a type corresponding to equality—the *identity type*. For every two terms of the same type we have a (not necessarily inhabited) type of proofs of their equality

$$\frac{\Gamma \vdash M : \sigma \qquad \Gamma \vdash N : \sigma}{\Gamma \vdash Id_\sigma(M, N) \; type} \quad \text{ID-F}$$

and the identity types have canonical inhabitants corresponding to reflexivity

$$\frac{\Gamma \vdash M : \sigma}{\Gamma \vdash Refl_\sigma(M) : Id_\sigma(M, M)} \quad \text{ID-I}$$

We call two terms $\Gamma \vdash M, N : \sigma$ *propositionally equal* if the type $\Gamma \vdash Id_\sigma(M, N)$ is inhabited. By the (implicit) congruence rules and rule TY-CONV propositional equality extends definitional equality, that is, we have $\Gamma \vdash Refl_\sigma(M) : Id_\sigma(M, N)$ provided $\Gamma \vdash M = N : \sigma$.

So far we only know that propositional equality is a reflexive relation. The further properties like symmetry, transitivity, Leibniz' principle are all consequences of the following elimination rule for identity types

$$\frac{\begin{array}{l} \Gamma \vdash \sigma \; type \\ \Gamma , x{:}\sigma, y{:}\sigma , p{:}Id_\sigma(x,y) \vdash \tau \; type \\ \Gamma, z{:}\sigma \vdash H : \tau[z/x, z/y, Refl_\sigma(z)/p] \\ \Gamma \vdash M{:}\sigma \qquad \Gamma \vdash N{:}\sigma \\ \Gamma \vdash P : Id_\sigma(M, N) \end{array}}{\Gamma \vdash R^{Id}_{[x:\sigma,y:\sigma,p:Id_\sigma(x,y)]\tau}([z{:}\sigma]H , M, N, P) : \tau[M/x, N/y, P/p]} \quad \text{ID-E}$$

and the associated equality rule

$$\frac{\Gamma \vdash R^{Id}_{[x:\sigma, y:\sigma, p:Id_\sigma(x,y)]\tau}([z:\sigma]H, M, M, Refl_\sigma(M)) : \tau[M/x, M/y, Refl_\sigma(M)/p]}{\begin{array}{c} \Gamma \vdash R^{Id}_{[x:\sigma, y:\sigma, p:Id_\sigma(x,y)]\tau}([z:\sigma]H, M, M, Refl_\sigma(M)) \\ = H[M/z] : \tau[M/x, M/y, Refl_\sigma(M)/p] \end{array}} \quad \text{ID-C}$$

The eliminator R^{Id} is an induction principle like R^N and R^Σ which roughly states that every element of an identity type behaves as if it were a canonical one of the form $Refl_\sigma(M)$. We demonstrate how to derive Leibniz' principle from R^{Id}: Suppose that $x:\sigma \vdash \rho[x]$ *type*, and that we are given two propositionally equal terms of type σ, i.e., $\vdash M, N : \sigma$ and $\vdash P : Id_\sigma(M, N)$. If $\vdash H : \rho[M]$ then we can construct an element $Subst_{[x:\sigma]\rho}(P, H)$ of $\rho[N]$ as follows. We define

$$\tau[x:\sigma, y:\sigma, p:Id_\sigma(x,y)] \stackrel{\text{def}}{=} \rho[x] \Rightarrow \rho[y]$$

Recall that $\phi \Rightarrow \psi$ abbreviates $\Pi x:\phi.\psi$.) Now $\lambda h:\rho[x].h$ is an inhabitant of $c:\sigma \vdash \tau[x, x, Refl_\sigma(x)]$, so

$$Subst_{[x:\sigma]\rho}(P, H) \stackrel{\text{def}}{=} App(R^{Id}_{[x:\sigma, y:\sigma, p:Id(x,y)]}([x:\sigma]\lambda h:\rho[x].h, M, N, P), H) : \rho[N]$$

and from ID-C and Π-C we get the derived rule $Subst_{[x:\sigma]\rho}(Refl_\sigma(M), H) = H : \rho[M]$.

From *Subst* we can derive symmetry, transitivity, and congruence properties of propositional equality in the usual way. For example, if $x:\sigma \vdash U[x] : \tau$ and $\vdash P : Id_\sigma(M, N)$ then

$$Resp_{\sigma,\tau}([x:\sigma]U, P) \stackrel{\text{def}}{=} $$
$$Subst_{[x:\sigma]Id_\tau(U[M], U[x])}(P, Refl_\tau(U[M])) : Id_\tau(U[M], U[N])$$

We can derive a similar congruence property in the case that τ depends on x; for this and other derived properties and combinators for propositional equality we refer to Nordström, Petersson, and Smith 1990; Streicher 1993; Hofmann 1995a).

We have now collected enough material to carry out the promised example of a proof by induction. We wish to construct an element of the type

$$m: N \vdash Id_N(m + 0, m) \text{ } type$$

where $+$ is the addition operation defined above. Notice that we have $n: N \vdash Refl_N(n) : Id_N(0 + n, n)$ immediately by N-E-Z and the definition of $+$. Let us define $\sigma[m: N] \stackrel{\text{def}}{=} Id_N(m + 0, m)$. So σ is now a type with a distinguished free variable m. By N-C-Z we have

$$\vdash Refl_N(0) : \sigma[0]$$

Now by N-E-S we have

$$m: N \vdash \sigma[Suc(m)] = Id_N(Suc(m), Suc(m + 0)) \text{ } type$$

Therefore,

$$m: \mathbf{N}, h: \sigma[m] \vdash Resp_{\mathbf{N},\mathbf{N}}([x: \mathbf{N}]Suc(x), h) : \sigma[Suc(m)]$$

and we can finally conclude

$$m: \mathbf{N} \vdash R^{\mathbf{N}}_{[m:\mathbf{N}]\sigma}(\ [t]Refl_{\mathbf{N}}(0),$$
$$[m: \mathbf{N}, h: \sigma]Resp_{\mathbf{N},\mathbf{N}}([x: \mathbf{N}]Suc(x), h),$$
$$m) : \sigma[m]$$

Again, we refer to (Nordström, Petersson, and Smith 1990) for more examples of this kind. The metatheory and the strength of the present and other formulations of the identity type have been analysed in (Hofmann 1995a;(1996);Streicher 1993).

We remark that propositional equality does not affect the definitional one which even in the presence of identity types remains confined to intensional equality. Therefore, type theory together with identity types as defined here is called *intensional type theory*, see (Martin-Löf 1982). There exists another formulation of identity types in which one may conclude $\Gamma \vdash M = N : \sigma$ from $\Gamma \vdash P : Id_\sigma(M, N)$. This rule is called *equality reflection* and makes it possible to derive "definitional" equalities by induction and thus makes it extensional. Therefore, type theory with equality reflection is called *extensional type theory*. Since the proof P is discarded upon application of this rule, definitional equality (then rather called *judgemental equality*) and thus typing become undecidable. See also E3.30.

2.1.6 Universes

A universe is a type containing codes for types. This is expressed by the following two rules

$$\frac{\vdash \Gamma\ ctxt}{\Gamma \vdash U\ type}\ \text{U-F} \qquad \frac{\Gamma \vdash M : U}{\Gamma \vdash El(M)\ type}\ \text{EL-F}$$

So if $M : U$ is such a "code" then we can form the type associated to M, namely $El(M)$. So far the universe does not contain any closed codes. This may be achieved by stipulating that the universe be closed under certain type formers. For instance, closure under Π-types is expressed by

$$\frac{\Gamma \vdash S : U \qquad \Gamma, s: El(S) \vdash T : U}{\Gamma \vdash \hat{\Pi}(S, [s: El(S)]T) : U}\ \text{U-}\Pi$$

$$\frac{\Gamma, s: El(S) \vdash M : El(T)}{\Gamma \vdash \hat{\lambda}s: El(S).M^{El(T)} : El(\hat{\Pi}(S, [s: El(S)]T))}\ \text{U-}\Pi\text{-I}$$

$$\frac{\Gamma \vdash M : El(\hat{\Pi}(S, [s: El(S)]T)) \qquad \Gamma \vdash N : El(S)}{\Gamma \vdash \hat{App}_{[s:El(S)]El(T)}(M, N) : El(T[N/s])}\ \text{U-}\Pi\text{-E}$$

$$\frac{\Gamma \vdash \hat{App}_{[s:El(S)]El(T)}(\hat{\lambda}s\colon El(S).M^{El(T)}, N) : El(T[N/s])}{\Gamma \vdash \hat{App}_{[s:El(S)]El(T)}(\hat{\lambda}s\colon El(S).M^{El(T)}, N) = M[N/s] : El(T[N/s])} \quad \text{U-}\Pi\text{-C}$$

A more economic syntax for universes closed under Π-types is obtained if we replace the last three above rules by a single new type equality

$$\frac{\Gamma \vdash \hat{\Pi}(S, [s\colon El(S)]T) : U}{\Gamma \vdash El(\hat{\Pi}(S, [s\colon El(S)]T)) = \Pi s\colon El(S).El(T) \; type} \quad \text{U-}\Pi\text{-TY}$$

which states that $El(\hat{\Pi}(S, [s\colon El(S)]T))$ *is* the product of the $El(T)$ rather than behaving like it. One does not need the new application and abstraction operators $\hat{\lambda}$ and $\hat{App}$ then. This syntax, which in fact is often used in the literature, has the disadvantage that it is no longer the case that equal types share the same outermost type former. This makes it more difficult to show that the type formers are injective; an auxiliary property required to establish the subject reduction property for an untyped rewrite system derived from definitional equality. Also, in many models rule U-Π-TY is not valid under the canonical interpretation of Π, see (Streicher 1991) and the example following Def. 3.20.

Closure under natural numbers is described by

$$\frac{\vdash \Gamma \; ctxt}{\Gamma \vdash \hat{N} : U} \quad \text{U-N}$$

and further rules introducing term formers $\hat{0}$, $\hat{Suc}$, and $\hat{R}^N$ witnessing that $El(\hat{N})$ behaves like N. Again we could instead impose the equality $\Gamma \vdash El(\hat{N}) = N \; type$ if the type theory already contains natural numbers.

In a similar way closure under other type formers including another universe can be stipulated. A final important closure property for universes is *impredicative quantification*:

$$\frac{\Gamma \vdash \sigma \; type \qquad \Gamma, x\colon \sigma \vdash T : U}{\Gamma \vdash \forall x\colon \sigma.T : U} \quad \text{U-}\forall$$

$$\frac{\Gamma, x\colon \sigma \vdash M : El(T)}{\Gamma \vdash \hat{\lambda}x\colon \sigma.M^{El(T)} : El(\forall x\colon \sigma.T)} \quad \text{U-}\forall\text{-I}$$

$$\frac{\Gamma \vdash M : El(\forall x\colon \sigma.T) \qquad \Gamma \vdash N : \sigma}{\Gamma \vdash \hat{App}_{[x:\sigma]El(T)}(M, N) : El(T[N/x])} \quad \text{U-}\forall\text{-E}$$

$$\frac{\Gamma \vdash \hat{App}_{[x:\sigma]El(T)}\hat{\lambda}x\colon \sigma.M^{El(T)}, N) : El(T[N/x])}{\Gamma \vdash \hat{App}_{[x:\sigma]El(T)}(\hat{\lambda}x\colon \sigma.M^{El(T)}, N) = M[N/x] : El(T[N/x])} \quad \text{U-}\forall\text{-C}$$

The difference to closure under Π-types is that the "domain-type" σ is arbitrary and not confined to a "small type" of the form $El(S)$. In particular σ can be U itself and we can form terms like

$$polyone = \forall c\colon U.\forall s\colon El(c).c$$

where $El(polyone)$ has the closed inhabitant

$$\diamond \vdash \hat{\lambda} C \colon U. \hat{\lambda} x \colon El(C).x \; : \; El(polyone)$$

—the polymorphic identity function known from polymorphic lambda calculus.

Universes are employed for modularisation and abstraction. For instance, they permit the definition of a type of a certain algebraic structure. In this way the type of semigroups with carrier $X : U$ can be defined as

$$SEM(X) \stackrel{\text{def}}{=} \Sigma \circ \colon El(X) \times El(X) \to El(X).$$
$$\Pi x \colon El(X).\Pi y \colon El(X).\Pi z \colon El(X).Id_{El(X)}(\circ(\circ(x,y),z)\; , \circ(x,\circ(y,z)))$$

An element of type $SEM(X)$ consists of a binary function on $El(X)$, and a proof that this function is associative. We can now write a function $F : \Pi X \colon U.MON(X) \to SEM(X)$ which "forgets" the neutral element. We can also form $\Sigma X \colon U.SEM(X)$; the type of semigroups. More complex examples of this kind may be found in (Luo 1991). An application of this pattern to semantics of modules in functional languages is (Harper and Mitchell 1993).

Under the propositions-as-types analogy we can view a universe also as a type of propositions. For instance, the type $\sigma \to U$ can be viewed as an analogue to the power-set of σ.

2.1.7 Miscellaneous types

A counterpart to absurdity in logic is the following empty type:

$$\frac{\vdash \Gamma \; ctxt}{\Gamma \vdash \mathbf{0} \; type} \; \text{0-F} \qquad \frac{\Gamma \vdash \sigma \; type \qquad \Gamma \vdash M : \mathbf{0}}{\Gamma \vdash \mathsf{R}^0_\sigma(M) : \sigma} \; \text{0-E}$$

There are no canonical elements in $\mathbf{0}$ so there is no "computation rule" like N-C-Z. It is sometimes useful to have a type with a single canonical element corresponding to the true proposition:

$$\frac{\vdash \Gamma \; ctxt}{\Gamma \vdash \mathbf{1} \; type} \; \text{1-F} \qquad \frac{\vdash \Gamma \; ctxt}{\Gamma \vdash \star : \mathbf{1}} \; \text{1-I}$$

$$\frac{\Gamma, x \colon \mathbf{1} \vdash \sigma \; type \qquad \Gamma \vdash H : \sigma[\star/x] \qquad \Gamma \vdash M : \mathbf{1}}{\Gamma \vdash \mathsf{R}^1_{[x\colon 1]\sigma}(H,M) : \sigma[M/x]} \; \text{1-E}$$

$$\frac{\Gamma \vdash \mathsf{R}^1_{[x\colon 1]\sigma}(H,\star) : \sigma[\star/x]}{\Gamma \vdash \mathsf{R}^1_{[x\colon 1]\sigma}(H,M) = H : \sigma[M/x]} \; \text{1-C}$$

There are a number of other types considered in the literature like co-product types corresponding to binary disjoint union, finite types with n elements for each natural number n, types of well-founded trees, subset types, and quotient types to name the most important ones. In implementations like LEGO and COQ new type formers can be defined "on the fly" by giving the rules for their canonical elements (like *Suc* and 0 in the case of N). The elimination rules are then generated automatically. In ALF this is also possible, but elimination rules are replaced by the more general device of *pattern-matching* on the form of the constructors.

Finally, we can consider arbitrary theories of dependent types defined by type symbols, constants, and equations. This is described in (Pitts 1997).

2.2 Examples of type theories

In this section we briefly describe some "named" type theories and how they fit into the formal framework described here.

2.2.1 Martin-Löf's type theory

This is a collective name for type theories containing several of the above-described type formers, but not a universe closed under impredicative quantification. A characteristic feature of Martin-Löf's type theory is the presence of identity types either with or without equality reflection. Martin-Löf invented his type theories with the aim of extending the propositions as types correspondence to predicate logic and to provide a universal language for constructive mathematics (Martin-Löf 1984; Martin-Löf 1975). A standard reference on Martin-Löf's type theories is (Nordström, Petersson, and Smith 1990). An implementation of extensional Martin-Löf type theory is the Nuprl system (Constable et al. 1986).

2.2.2 The Logical Framework

Martin-Löf's *Logical Framework* (LF), see Part IV of (Nordström, Petersson, and Smith 1990), is a type theory with Π-types and a universe. Its intended use is to define theories, in particular Martin-Löf type theory, as extensions of the LF by constants and equations.

The idea is that types and type formers are declared as constants in the universe and that term-formers are declared as constants of the appropriate *El*-types. To distinguish from object level type formers some different notation is used: the Π-type of the framework is written $(x{:}\,\sigma)\tau$ instead of $\Pi x{:}\,\sigma.\tau$ and $(\sigma)\tau$ instead of $\sigma \to \tau$. Iterated Π-types are written $(x_1{:}\,\sigma_1,\ldots,x_n{:}\,\sigma_n)\tau$ instead of $\Pi x_1{:}\,\sigma_1.\ldots.\Pi x_n{:}\,\sigma_n.\tau$. Abstraction is written as $[x{:}\,\sigma]M$ instead of $\lambda x{:}\,\sigma.M^\tau$ and application is written $M(N)$ instead of $App_{[x{:}\,\sigma]\tau}(M,N)$.[1] Iterated abstractions and applications are written $[x_1{:}\,\sigma_1,\ldots,x_n{:}\,\sigma_n]M$ and $M(N_1,\ldots,N_n)$, respectively. The lacking type information can be inferred. The universe is written *Set* instead of U. The *El*-operator is omitted.

---

[1] In loc. cit. and in the ALF system the type annotations in functional abstractions are omitted. We include them for the sake of consistency.

For example the Π-type is described by the following constant and equality declarations (understood in every valid context):

$$\vdash \Pi : (\sigma\colon Set, \tau\colon (\sigma)Set)Set$$
$$\vdash App : (\sigma\colon Set, \tau\colon (\sigma)Set, m\colon \Pi(\sigma,\tau), n\colon \sigma)\tau(m)$$
$$\vdash \lambda : (\sigma\colon Set, \tau\colon (\sigma)Set, m\colon (x\colon \sigma)\tau(x))\Pi(\sigma,\tau)$$
$$\sigma\colon Set, \tau\colon (\sigma)Set, m\colon (x\colon \sigma)\tau(x), n\colon \sigma \vdash$$
$$App(\sigma,\tau,\lambda(\sigma,\tau,m),n) = m(n)$$

Notice, how terms with free variables are represented as framework abstractions (in the type of λ) and how substitution is represented as framework application (in the type of *App* and in the equation).

In this way the burden of dealing correctly with variables, substitution, and binding is shifted from the object language to the Logical Framework and so can be handled once and for all.

Of course, the LF can also cope with type formers other than the dependent function space. Since we refer to it later in Section 4, we consider here an ad hoc type former (creating a copy of its argument) defined by the two rules

$$\frac{\Gamma \vdash \sigma \; type}{\Gamma \vdash \mathbf{L}(\sigma) \; type} \qquad \frac{\Gamma \vdash M : \sigma}{\Gamma \vdash \mathbf{l}(M) : \mathbf{L}(\sigma)}$$

In LF it would have to be rendered by two constants $\mathbf{L}$: $(Set)Set$ and $\mathbf{l} : (\sigma\colon Set, \sigma)\mathbf{L}(\sigma)$.

The ALF system (Magnusson and Nordström 1994) is based on the Logical Framework. It allows for the definition of types in *Set* simply by giving their constructors. Functions on the types are then defined by pattern-matching over the constructors as needed.

The Logical Framework can also be used to encode the syntax of other logical systems such as predicate logic and modal logic. The interested reader is referred to (Harper, Honsell, and Plotkin 1993).

2.2.3 The Calculus of Constructions

The *Calculus of Constructions* (CC) (Coquand and Huet 1988) is a type theory with Π-types and a universe closed under impredicative quantification (U-IMPR). The universe is traditionally denoted by *Prop* and the corresponding *El*-operator is either written $Prf(-)$ or omitted. The idea is that the universe *Prop* corresponds to a type of propositions and that $Prf(-)$ associates the type of proofs to a proposition. Originally, it was intended that *Prop* not only contains propositions, but also datatypes like the natural numbers which are definable by their "impredicative encodings", for instance one has

$$Nat \stackrel{\text{def}}{=} Prf(\forall c\colon Prop.\forall z\colon Prf(c).\forall s\colon Prf(c) \to Prf(c).c)$$

and for this type constants 0 and $Suc(-)$ can be defined as well as an operator permitting definition of functions by primitive recursion. The point is that Nat itself is of the form $Prf(-)$ and so can serve as the argument c to an element of Nat. Also other inductive datatypes like lists or trees can be defined in this way. Similarly, logical connectives can be defined on the type $Prop$ by their usual higher-order encodings (Coquand and Huet 1988).

The encoding of datatypes inside $Prop$ proved insufficient as no internal induction principles (like R^N) are available for these. This gave rise to two extensions of the pure Calculus of Constructions: Luo's *Extended Calculus of Constructions* (ECC) implemented in the LEGO system (Luo 1994; Luo and Pollack 1992) and the *Calculus of Inductive Definitions* (CID) implemented in the COQ system (Coquand and Paulin-Mohring 1989; Dowek et al. 1991). ECC extends the Calculus of Constructions by a sequence of universes $U_0, U_1, \ldots$ where each U_{i+1} contains a code for U_i and $Prop$ is contained in U_0. Datatypes reside in U_0 and are given by inductive rules like the ones for $\mathbf{N}$. The higher universes are used for modularisation as hinted at in the example above. $Prop$ is used for propositions only.

In the CID we have two universes both closed under impredicative quantification, Set and $Prop$. The datatypes reside in Set and are given by inductive rules as in ECC. The implementation of the CID, COQ, comes with a program extraction facility which extracts executable ML programs from derivations in CID essentially by removing all terms and types coming from the universe $Prop$, see also (Paulin-Mohring 1989).

2.3 Pre-syntax

The syntax of types, terms, and contexts has been given together with the typing and equality rules. For certain purposes it is convenient to have a simpler inductive definition of possibly non well-typed terms, out of which the actual ones are singled out by the rules. For instance, we might want to consider $App_{[x:\mathbf{N}]\mathbf{N}}(0,0)$ as a term albeit not a well-typed one. These pre-terms, -types, and -contexts have been used to give semantics to type theory in terms of untyped computation (Allen 1987; Martin-Löf 1984); we will use them as an auxiliary device in the definition of the interpretation of type theory in semantic structures and also in the definition of context morphisms below.

The pre-contexts (Γ), pre-types (σ, τ), and pre-terms (M, N) for a type theory with $\Pi-$, $\Sigma-$, identity types, and natural numbers are given by the following grammar.

$$\Gamma \quad ::= \quad \diamond$$
$$\qquad \qquad \mid \Gamma, x\!:\!\sigma \qquad \text{provided } x \text{ is not declared in } \Gamma$$

$$\sigma, \tau \quad ::= \quad \Pi x\!:\!\sigma.\tau \mid \Sigma x\!:\!\sigma.\tau \mid Id_\sigma(M, N) \mid \mathbf{N}$$

$$M, N, H, P \quad ::= \quad x \mid \lambda x\!:\!\sigma.M^\tau \mid App_{[x:\sigma]\tau}(M, N) \mid$$
$$Pair_{[x:\sigma]\tau}(M, N) \mid \mathsf{R}^\Sigma_{[z:(\Sigma x:\sigma.\tau)]\rho}([x\!:\!\sigma, y\!:\!\tau]H, M) \mid$$
$$Refl_\sigma(M) \mid \mathsf{R}^{Id}_{[x:\sigma,y:\sigma,p:Id_\sigma(x,y)]\tau}([z\!:\!\sigma]H , M, N, P) \mid$$
$$0 \mid Suc(M) \mid \mathsf{R}^{\mathbf{N}}_{[n:\mathbf{N}]\sigma}(H_z, [n\!:\!\mathbf{N}, x\!:\!\sigma]H_s, M)$$

Capture-free substitution and identification of terms with different bound variables can then be dealt with on the level of the pre-syntax. We will use the predicates well-formed or valid for those pre-terms/-types/-contexts which actually occur in derivable judgements. Note that the variables declared in a pre-context are pairwise distinct.

Exercises

E2.1 Construct an inhabitant of the type

$$m\!:\!\mathbf{N}, n\!:\!\mathbf{N} \vdash Id_{\mathbf{N}}(m + n, n + m) \; type$$

E2.2 Show that for arbitrary types $\Gamma \vdash \sigma \; type$, $\Gamma \vdash \tau \; type$, and $\Gamma, x\!:\!\sigma, y\!:\!\tau \vdash \rho \; type$ the following type corresponding to the *axiom of choice* is inhabited:

$$\Gamma \vdash (\Pi x\!:\!\sigma.\Sigma y\!:\!\tau.\rho) \Rightarrow (\Sigma f\!:\!\sigma \Rightarrow \tau.\Pi x\!:\!\sigma.\rho[(f\,x)/y]) \; type$$

E2.3 By analogy to the type of natural numbers define the rules for a list type former which to any type σ associates a type $List(\sigma)$ consisting of finite sequences of elements of σ. Hint: think of lists as inductively generated from the empty list by successive additions of elements of σ ("cons"). Define a length function of type $List(\sigma) \to \mathbf{N}$ and define a type $Vec_\sigma(M)$ of lists of length M for each $M : \mathbf{N}$ using lists, the identity type, and the Σ-type.

E2.4 Define a type of binary natural numbers with three constructors: $Zero$, Suc_0, and Suc_1 and define a conversion function from these binary representations to $\mathbf{N}$.

E2.5 Give the rules for a universe U containing a code $\hat{0}$ for the empty type 0 and a code $\hat{1}$ for the unit type 1. Show that in a type theory which supports natural numbers, this universe, and the empty type itself the following type in the empty context is inhabited

$$\diamond \vdash Id_{\mathbf{N}}(0, Suc(0)) \to 0 \; type$$

corresponding to Peano's fourth axiom $0 \neq 1$. Hint: define using R^N a function $f \colon N \to U$ such that $\diamond \vdash f0 = \hat{1} \colon U$ and $\diamond \vdash f(Suc(0)) = \hat{0} \colon U$. Later on we will show by a semantic argument that the above type is not inhabited in the absence of a universe (Smith 1988).

2.6* (Troelstra and van Dalen 1988) Show that in type theory without the empty type **0** such an empty type can be *defined* as $Id_N(0, Suc(0))$. The elimination operator R^0_σ must then be defined by induction on the structure of σ. Notice that in view of the semantic result anticipated in the previous exercise this definition hinges on the fact that there is no empty type in the first place.

2.7* Show that for any type theory containing some or all of the type formers described above the rules WEAK and SUBST are admissible.

2.8* (Weak Σ-types in the Calculus of Constructions) For $\vdash \sigma$ *type* and $x \colon \sigma \vdash P \colon Prop$ define

$$\exists x \colon \sigma.P \stackrel{\text{def}}{=} \forall c \colon Prop.(\forall x \colon \sigma.P \Rightarrow c) \Rightarrow c$$

where $X \Rightarrow Y$ abbreviates $\forall p \colon Prf(X).Y$. Define a pairing operation which to $M \colon \sigma$ and $N \colon Prf(P[M])$ associates an element $\exists\text{-I}(M, N) \colon Prf(\exists x \colon \sigma.P)$ and define in the case that $\sigma = Prf(S)$ for some $S \colon Prop$ a first projection $witness_S \colon Prf(\exists x \colon Prf(S).T) \to Prf(S)$. Show that for M and N as above one has $\vdash witness_S \exists\text{-I}(M, N) = M$.

2.9 Give the rules for a universe closed under impredicative quantification using the "economic syntax" exemplified in rule U-Π-TY

2.10* Prove that whenever $\Gamma \vdash M \colon \sigma$ and $\Gamma \vdash M \colon \tau$ then $\Gamma \vdash \sigma = \tau$ *type* by induction on derivations. Find some type annotations in term formers which can safely be omitted without violating this property. Discuss the properties a type theory must have so that the type annotation in application can be omitted. In other words when can we replace $App_{[x \colon \sigma]\tau}(M, N)$ by $App(M, N)$ in the official syntax without violating uniqueness of types. See (Streicher 1991) for a thorough discussion of this point.

2.4 Context morphisms

Definition 2.11 *Let* Γ *and* $\Delta \stackrel{\text{def}}{=} x_1 \colon \sigma_1, \ldots, x_n \colon \sigma_n$ *be valid contexts. If* $f \stackrel{\text{def}}{=} (M_1, \ldots, M_n)$ *is a sequence of* n *pre-terms we write*

$$\Gamma \vdash f \Rightarrow \Delta$$

and say that f is a context morphism *from Γ to Δ if the following n judgements hold:*

$$\Gamma \vdash M_1 : \sigma_1$$
$$\Gamma \vdash M_2 : \sigma_2[M_1/x_1]$$
$$\ldots$$
$$\Gamma \vdash M_n : \sigma_n[M_1/x_1][M_2/x_2]\ldots[M_{n-1}/x_{n-1}]$$

Examples. For any context Γ we have the empty context morphism () from Γ to $\diamond$ and this is the only context morphism from Γ to $\diamond$. If $\Gamma \equiv x_1: \sigma_1, \ldots, x_n: \sigma_n$ is a context and $\Gamma \vdash \sigma$ *type* and x is a fresh variable, then $(x_1, \ldots x_n)$ forms a context morphism from $\Gamma, x: \sigma$ to Γ which we denote by $\mathsf{p}(\Gamma, \sigma)$. A more concrete example is $(0, \mathit{Refl}_\mathbf{N}(0))$ which forms a context morphism from $\diamond$ to $n: \mathbf{N}, p: \mathit{Id}_\mathbf{N}(0, n)$ as $\diamond 0: \mathbf{N}$ and $\diamond \mathit{Refl}_\mathbf{N}(0) : (\mathit{Id}_\mathbf{N}(0, n))[0/n]$. The same sequence of terms also forms a context morphism from $\diamond$ to $n: \mathbf{N}, p: \mathit{Id}_\mathbf{N}(0, 0)$ which shows that the "target context" Δ is not uniquely determined by f. For any term $\Gamma \vdash M : \sigma$ we can form a context morphism $\Gamma \vdash \overline{M} \Rightarrow \Gamma, x: \sigma$ where $\overline{M} \equiv (x_1, \ldots, x_n, M)$ if $\Gamma \equiv x_1: \sigma_1, \ldots, x_n: \sigma_n$. Finally, we have the identity context morphism $\Gamma \vdash \mathit{id}_\Gamma \Rightarrow \Gamma$ given by $\mathit{id}_\Gamma \equiv (x_1, \ldots, x_n)$.

2.4.1 Generalised substitution

We denote syntactic identity up to renaming of variables by $\equiv$. If $\Gamma \vdash f \Rightarrow \Delta$ and τ is a pre-type we write $\tau[f/\Delta]$ for the simultaneous replacement of the Δ-variables in τ by the corresponding terms in f, more precisely, if $\Delta \equiv x_1: \sigma_1, \ldots, x_n: \sigma_n$ and $f \equiv (M_1, \ldots, M_n)$ then

$$\tau[f/\Delta] \equiv \tau[M_1/x_1][M_2/x_2]\ldots[M_n/x_n]$$

The attribute "simultaneous" means that the variables in Δ should be made disjoint from those in Γ before performing the substitution. We define $-[f/\Delta]$ analogously for pre-terms, pre-contexts, and judgements $\mathcal{J}$ of the form $M : \sigma, \sigma$ *type*, $M = N : \sigma, \sigma = \tau$ *type*.

By induction on the length of Δ and using rules WEAK and SUBST we can then establish the following property:

Proposition 2.12 *If $\Gamma \vdash f \Rightarrow \Delta$ and $\Delta, \Theta \vdash \mathcal{J}$ then $\Gamma, \Theta[f/\Delta] \vdash \mathcal{J}[f/\Delta]$.*

One is only interested in the case where $\Theta \equiv \diamond$ as this subsumes the general case with f replaced by the context morphism $\mathsf{q}(f, \Theta)$ from $\Gamma, \Theta[f/\Delta]$ to Δ, Θ given by $\mathsf{q}(f, \Theta) \equiv (f, z_1, \ldots, z_k)$ for $\Theta \equiv z_1: \theta_1, \ldots, z_k: \theta_k$. However, in order to get the inductive argument through one needs the case of non-empty Θ. When $\Theta \equiv \diamond$ and when no confusion can arise we write $\tau[f]$ for $\tau[f/\Delta]$ and similarly for terms, contexts, and judgements.

Notice the special case of the context morphism $\mathsf{p}(\Gamma, \sigma)$ defined above. If $\Gamma \vdash \mathcal{J}$ then $\Gamma, x: \sigma \vdash \mathcal{J}[\mathsf{p}(\Gamma, \sigma)]$, but $\mathcal{J} \equiv \mathcal{J}[\mathsf{p}(\Gamma, \sigma)]$ so the generalised substitution subsumes weakening. Similarly, for $\Gamma, x{:}\sigma \vdash \mathcal{J}$ and $\Gamma \vdash M : \sigma$ we have $\mathcal{J}[\overline{M}] \equiv \mathcal{J}[M/x]$ so ordinary substitution is subsumed, too.

The defined substitution operation allows us to establish the following derived typing rule for non-empty context morphisms:

$$\frac{\Gamma \vdash f \Rightarrow \Delta \qquad \vdash \Delta, x{:}\sigma \; ctxt \qquad \Gamma \vdash M : \sigma[f]}{\Gamma \vdash (f, M) \Rightarrow \Delta, x{:}\sigma} \quad \text{Mor-Cons}$$

This rule together with

$$\frac{\vdash \Gamma \; ctxt}{\Gamma \vdash () \Rightarrow \diamond} \quad \text{Mor-Empty}$$

generates all valid judgements of the form $\Gamma \vdash f \Rightarrow \Delta$.

If $\Gamma \vdash f \Rightarrow \Delta$ and $\Delta \vdash g \Rightarrow \Theta$ where $g \equiv (N_1, \ldots, N_k)$ we can form the list of terms $g \circ f \equiv (N_1[f], \ldots, N_k[f])$. In other words $g \circ f$ is obtained by simultaneously replacing the Δ-variables in g by the corresponding terms in f. This list $g \circ f$ forms a context morphism from Γ to Θ and $\circ$ as indicated is an associative operation. Although this can be seen directly with some intuition about substitutions we prefer to state it as a proposition together with some other properties which the reader is invited to prove by *simultaneous induction* on the length of g.

Proposition 2.13 *Assume* $B \vdash e \Rightarrow \Gamma$, $\Gamma \vdash f \Rightarrow \Delta$, *and* $\Delta \vdash g \Rightarrow \Theta$. *Furthermore let* $\Theta \vdash \sigma$ *type and* $\Theta \vdash M : \sigma$. *Then the following equations hold up to syntactic identity.*

$$\Gamma \vdash g \circ f \Rightarrow \Theta$$
$$\sigma[g \circ f] \equiv \sigma[g][f]$$
$$M[g \circ f] \equiv M[g][f]$$
$$(g \circ f) \circ e \equiv g \circ (f \circ e)$$

Hint for the proof: define $g \circ f$ inductively by $() \circ f \stackrel{\text{def}}{=} ()$ and $(g, M) \circ f \stackrel{\text{def}}{=} (g \circ f, M[f])$ where (g, M) denotes the list g extended by M. Use the fact that $\tau[f] \equiv \tau$ if none of the Δ-variables occurs in τ and that $\tau[N/x][f] \equiv \tau[f/\Delta][N[f]/x]$. $\qquad\square$

2.4.2 Context morphisms and definitional equality

Let $f \equiv (M_1, \ldots, M_n)$ and $g \equiv (N_1, \ldots, N_n)$. If $\Gamma \vdash f \Rightarrow \Delta$ and $\Gamma \vdash g \Rightarrow \Delta$ then we write $\Gamma \vdash f = g \Rightarrow \Delta$ as an abbreviation for the n judgements $\Gamma \vdash M_1 = N_1 : \sigma_1$, $\Gamma \vdash M_2 = N_2 : \sigma_2[M_1/x_1], \ldots, \Gamma \vdash M_n = N_n : \sigma_n[M_1/x_1] \ldots [M_{n-1}/x_{n-1}]$ if $\Delta \equiv x_1{:}\sigma_1, \ldots, x_n{:}\sigma_n$. Notice that we could equivalently replace the second judgement by $\Gamma \vdash M_2 = N_2 : \sigma_2[N_1/x_1]$ in view of the first one and the congruence rules for definitional equality. If $\Gamma \vdash f = g \Rightarrow \Delta$ we say that f and g are definitionally equal context morphisms from Γ to Δ. By straightforward induction it is now possible to derive congruence rules for the defined operators on context morphisms, w.r.t. this definitional equality and we also have that if $\vdash \Gamma = \Gamma'$ $ctxt$, $\vdash \Delta = \Delta'$ $ctxt$, and $\Gamma \vdash f = g \Rightarrow \Delta$ then $\Gamma' \vdash f = g \Rightarrow \Delta'$.

Exercises

E2.14   Show that the above-defined context morphisms $\mathsf{p}(\Gamma, \sigma)$, $\overline{M}$, and $\mathsf{q}(f, \Theta)$ have the following properties:

- If $\Gamma \vdash f \Rightarrow \Delta$ then $id_\Delta \circ f \equiv f \equiv f \circ id_\Gamma$.

- If $\Gamma \vdash M : \sigma$ then $\mathsf{p}(\Gamma, \sigma) \circ \overline{M} \equiv id_\Gamma$.

- If $\Gamma \vdash (f, M) \Rightarrow \Delta, x{:}\,\sigma$ then $\mathsf{p}(\Gamma, \sigma) \circ (f, M) \equiv f$ and $x[(f, M)] \equiv M$.

- If $\Gamma \vdash f \Rightarrow \Delta$ and $\vdash \Delta, x{:}\,\sigma\ ctxt$ then $\mathsf{p}(\Delta, \sigma) \circ \mathsf{q}(f, x{:}\,\sigma) \equiv f \circ \mathsf{p}(\Gamma, \sigma[f])$.

- If $\Gamma \vdash f \Rightarrow \Delta$ and $\Delta \vdash M : \sigma$ then $\overline{M} \circ f \equiv \mathsf{q}(f, x{:}\,\sigma) \circ \overline{M[f]}$.

- If $\Gamma \vdash \sigma\ type$ and x fresh then $id_{\Gamma, x{:}\,\sigma} \equiv (\mathsf{p}(\Gamma, \sigma), x)$.

E2.15   Show that if $\Delta \vdash \Pi x{:}\,\sigma.\tau\ type$ and $\Gamma \vdash f \Rightarrow \Delta$ then $(\Pi x{:}\,\sigma.\tau)[f] \equiv \Pi x{:}\,\sigma[f].\tau[\mathsf{q}(f, x{:}\,\sigma)]$. Hint: you may assume that x does not occur in Δ as types are identified up to renaming of bound variables.

3   Category-theoretic semantics of type theory

Now we develop an abstract notion of semantics for theories of dependent types of which most known interpretations of type theory form an instance. The main purpose in defining such an abstract semantics is that it is easier to show that a mathematical structure forms an instance of the abstract framework rather than defining an interpretation function for it directly. This is achieved by essentially three properties of the abstract semantics:

- Substitution is a primitive operation rather than inductively defined.

- Variables are replaced by combinators for substitutions.

- Definitional equality is modelled by true (set-theoretic) equality.

Category-theoretic semantics is based on an abstraction from the combinators (like $\circ$, p, $(-, -)$, $\mathsf{q}(-, -)$) and equations for context morphisms identified in the previous section. The key concept is the one of a category: a collection of objects (the contexts), and for any two objects a collection of morphisms (the context morphisms) together with an associative composition and identities. For lack of space we cannot give an introduction to categories here and need to presuppose some very basic notions, in particular categories, functors, natural transformations, isomorphisms, terminal objects, and the category of sets and functions. Reading the relevant parts of the first chapter of (Lambek and Scott 1985), for instance, should suffice to attain the required state of knowledge. If $\mathcal{C}$ is a category we write $|\mathcal{C}|$ or

C for its collection of objects and $C(A, B)$ for the collection of morphisms from A to B. We also write $f : A \to B$ instead of $f \in C(A, B)$. A final prerequisite: if ϕ is an informal proposition then we define the set $[\phi]$ by $[\phi] \equiv \{\star\}$ if ϕ is true and $[\phi] \equiv \emptyset$ if ϕ is false.

3.1 Categories with families

We choose the semantic framework of *categories with families* (CwFs) (Dybjer 1996) a variant of Cartmell's *categories with attributes* which have the advantage of being equationally defined, rather than using conditional equations. Furthermore, CwFs are closer to the syntax than categories with attributes and therefore—this is the hope of the author—should be easier to understand.

The definition of a CwF follows the structure of the judgements in type theory except that context morphisms and substitution are part of the structure rather than defined afterwards. Along with the explanation of CwFs we define two important instances: the term model $\mathcal{T}$ of the calculus of dependent types described in Section 2. and the set-theoretic model $\mathcal{S}et$ as running examples.

If we include context morphisms the syntax contains four kinds of objects: contexts, context morphisms, types, and terms. Accordingly, for each of these we have a domain of interpretation in the model. More precisely, a CwF C contains

- a category C of semantic contexts and context morphisms
- for $\Gamma \in C$ a collection $Ty_C(\Gamma)$ of semantic types
- for $\Gamma \in C$ and $\sigma \in Ty_C(\Gamma)$ a collection $Tm_C(\Gamma, \sigma)$ of semantic terms

Where appropriate we leave out the attribute "semantic" and write $Tm_C(\sigma)$ instead of $Tm_C(\Gamma, \sigma)$. We also omit the subscripts if they are clear from the context.

In the term model $\mathcal{T}$ the collection of contexts is the quotient by definitional equality of well-formed contexts, that is pre-contexts Γ such that $\vdash \Gamma\ ctxt$. Two such contexts Γ and Δ are identified if $\vdash \Gamma = \Delta\ ctxt$. We tend to denote equivalence classes by their representatives. A morphism from Γ to Δ is an equivalence class with respect to definitional equality of syntactic context morphisms $\Gamma \vdash f \Rightarrow \Delta$. This is well-defined in view of the observations in Section 2.4.2. Composition and identities are given by the corresponding operations on syntactic context morphisms. $Ty_{\mathcal{T}}(\Gamma)$ is the set of pre-types σ such that $\Gamma \vdash \sigma\ type$ again factored by definitional equality, that is σ and τ are identified if $\Gamma \vdash \sigma = \tau\ type$. Finally, $Tm(\Gamma, \sigma)$ is the set of pre-terms M with $\Gamma \vdash M : \sigma$ factored by definitional equality.

The set-theoretic model $\mathcal{S}et$ has as category of contexts the category of sets and functions. An element of $Ty_{\mathcal{S}et}(\Gamma)$ is a family of sets $(\sigma_\gamma)_{\gamma \in \Gamma}$ indexed over Γ. An element of $Tm_{\mathcal{S}et}(\Gamma, \sigma)$ is an assignment of an element $M(\gamma)$ of σ_γ for each $\gamma \in \Gamma$.

Next, we need constants and operations on these domains in order to interpret the rules of type theory. Moreover, substitution must be axiomatised in such a way that it corresponds to the defined syntactic substitution. The definition of CwFs only accounts for the structural rules common to all systems of dependent types as set out in Section 2. The interpretation of the various type and term formers will be given afterwards as additional structure.

Semantic substitution is described by two operations for each context morphism, one for types and one for terms: if $f : \Gamma \to \Delta$ then there is a function $-\{f\} : Ty(\Delta) \to Ty(\Gamma)$ and for $\sigma \in Ty(\Delta)$ a function $-\{f\} : Tm(\Delta, \sigma) \to Tm(\Gamma, \sigma\{f\})$. These operations must be compatible with composition and identities in the following sense. If $\Gamma, \Delta, \Theta \in \mathcal{C}, f : \Gamma \to \Delta$, $g : \Delta \to \Theta, \sigma \in Ty(\Theta)$, and $M \in Tm(\Theta, \sigma)$ then the following equations are required to hold:

$$
\begin{array}{rcccl}
\sigma\{id_\Theta\} & = & \sigma & \in & Ty(\Theta) & \quad\text{(Ty-Id)}\\
\sigma\{g \circ f\} & = & \sigma\{g\}\{f\} & \in & Ty(\Gamma) & \quad\text{(Ty-Comp)}\\
M\{id_\Theta\} & = & M & \in & Tm(\Theta, \sigma) & \quad\text{(Tm-Id)}\\
M\{g \circ f\} & = & M\{g\}\{f\} & \in & Tm(\Gamma, \sigma\{g \circ f\}) & \quad\text{(Tm-Comp)}
\end{array}
$$

Notice that the former two equations are required for the two latter to "typecheck". Notice also, that substitution together with equations *(Ty-Id)* and *(Ty-Comp)* makes Ty a contravariant functor from $\mathcal{C}$ to *Set*. The sets Tm can also be organised into a functor, see Section 3.1.1 below.

In the term model substitution is the "generalised substitution" defined in Section 2.4.1. This means that we have $\sigma\{f\} \stackrel{\text{def}}{=} \sigma[f]$ and $M\{f\} \stackrel{\text{def}}{=} M[f]$. In the set-theoretic model substitution is given by pre-composition. If $f : \Delta \to \Gamma$ is a function and $(\sigma_\gamma)_{\gamma \in \Gamma}$ is a family of sets then $\sigma\{f\}$ is the family of sets given by $\sigma\{f\}_\delta \stackrel{\text{def}}{=} \sigma_{f(\delta)}$. Similarly, if $M \in Tm(\Gamma, \sigma)$ then $M\{f\}(\delta) \stackrel{\text{def}}{=} M(f(\delta))$. It is easy to see that the required equations hold.

Next we want to interpret the context formation rules. To model the empty context we require a terminal object $\top$ in the category $\mathcal{C}$. We usually write $\langle\rangle_\Gamma$ for the unique morphism from Γ to $\top$. In the term model and in the set-theoretic model these terminal objects are the empty context and an arbitrary singleton set, respectively.

To interpret context extension we require for each $\Gamma \in \mathcal{C}$ and $\sigma \in Ty(\Gamma)$ a context $\Gamma.\sigma \in \mathcal{C}$ and a morphism $\mathsf{p}(\sigma) : \Gamma.\sigma \to \Gamma$. The context $\Gamma.\sigma$ is called the *comprehension* of σ and $\mathsf{p}(\sigma)$ is called the *projection associated to* σ. In the term model $\Gamma.\sigma$ is the extended context $\Gamma, x : \sigma$ and $\mathsf{p}(\sigma)$ is the context morphism given by $\Gamma, x : \sigma \vdash \mathsf{p}(\Gamma, \sigma) \Rightarrow \Gamma$ as defined in Section 2.4. In the set-theoretic model $\Gamma.\sigma$ is the disjoint union of the σ_γ, i.e. the set $\{ (\gamma, x) \mid \gamma \in \Gamma \wedge x \in \sigma_\gamma \}$. The function $\mathsf{p}(\sigma)$ then sends (γ, x) to γ.

The morphism $\mathsf{p}(\sigma)$ can be seen as the first projection out of the generalised product $\Gamma.\sigma$. The second projection takes the form of an element $\mathsf{v}_\sigma \in Tm(\Gamma.\sigma, \sigma\{\mathsf{p}(\sigma)\})$ corresponding to the judgement $\Gamma, x : \sigma \vdash x : \sigma$.

In the term model this is the term x in $\Gamma, x : \sigma \vdash x : \sigma$, whereas in the set-theoretic model we define it by the assignment $(\gamma, x) \mapsto x$. Note that, in this model,

$\sigma\{\mathsf{p}(\sigma)\}_{(\gamma, x)} = \sigma_\gamma.$

According to the definition of syntactic context morphisms we need an operation which extends a semantic context morphism by a terms. If $f : \Gamma \to \Delta, \sigma \in Ty(\Delta)$, and $M \in Tm(\Gamma, \sigma\{f\})$ then there is a context morphism $\langle f, M \rangle_\sigma : \Gamma \to \Delta.\sigma$—the extension of f by M—satisfying the following equations for $f : \Gamma \to \Delta$, $g : \mathrm{B} \to \Gamma, \sigma \in Ty(\Delta), M \in Tm(\Gamma, \sigma\{f\})$.

$\mathsf{p}(\sigma) \circ \langle f, M \rangle_\sigma$	$=$	f	$: \Gamma \to \Delta$	*(Cons-L)*
$\mathsf{v}_\sigma\{\langle f, M \rangle_\sigma\}$	$=$	M	$\in Tm(\Gamma, \sigma\{f\})$	*(Cons-R)*
$\langle f, M \rangle_\sigma \circ g$	$=$	$\langle f \circ g, M\{g\}\rangle_\sigma$	$: \mathrm{B} \to \Delta.\sigma$	*(Cons-Nat)*
$\langle \mathsf{p}(\sigma), \mathsf{v}_\sigma \rangle_\sigma$	$=$	$id_{\Delta.\sigma}$	$: \Delta.\sigma \to \Delta.\sigma$	*(Cons-Id)*

In the term model the extension of f by M is $\Gamma \vdash (f, M) \Rightarrow \Delta, x{:}\sigma$, whereas in the set-theoretic model we have $\langle f, M \rangle_\sigma(\gamma \in \Gamma) \overset{\text{def}}{=} (f(\gamma), M(\gamma))$. We include the "type" information σ in $\langle f, M \rangle_\sigma$ as it cannot be inferred from the "types" of f and M.

This completes the definition of categories with families. Let us summarise that a CwF is a structure $(\mathcal{C}, Ty, Tm, -\{-\}, \top, \langle\rangle_-, -.-, \mathsf{p}, \mathsf{v}_-, \langle -, - \rangle_-)$ of sorts and operations subject to the requirements set out above. (The substitution $-\{-\}$ is understood to work for both types and terms.)

3.1.1 A more abstract definition

We give in this section an equivalent, but more abstract and more compact definition of CwF based on family-valued functors and a universal property. The idea of using family-valued functors is due to Peter Dybjer.

Definition 3.1 *The category $\mathcal{F}am$ of* families of sets *has as objects pairs $B = (B^0, B^1)$ where B^0 is a set and $(B_b^1)_{b \in B^0}$ is a family of sets indexed over B^0. A morphism from B to $C = (C^0, C^1)$ is a pair (f^0, f^1) where $f^0 : B^0 \to C^0$ is a function and $f^1 = (f_b^1)_{b \in B^0}$ is a family of functions $f_b^1 : B^1(b) \to C^1(f^0(b))$.*

The carrier sets Ty and Tm of a CwF over category $\mathcal{C}$ can now be given more compactly as a single functor $\mathcal{F} : \mathcal{C}^{op} \to \mathcal{F}am$. Indeed, given Ty and Tm we obtain a functor functor $\mathcal{F}$ with object part

$$\mathcal{F}(\Gamma) = (Ty(\Gamma), (Tm(\Gamma, \sigma))_{\sigma \in Ty(\Gamma)})$$

The morphism part of $\mathcal{F}$ is induced by semantic substitution. Conversely, given a functor $\mathcal{F} : \mathcal{C}^{op} \to \mathcal{F}am$ we define $Ty(\Gamma) := F^0$ and $Tm(\Gamma, \sigma) = F^1(\sigma)$ where $\mathcal{F}(\Gamma) = (F^0, F^1)$. If $f : \Delta \to \Gamma$ then writing $\mathcal{F}(f) = (f^0, f^1)$ we have $f^0 : Ty(\Gamma) \to Ty(\Delta)$ and $f_\sigma^1 : Tm(\Gamma, \sigma) \to Tm(\Delta, f^0(\sigma))$ giving us semantic substitution. The required equations follow from functoriality of $\mathcal{F}$.

Definition 3.2 *Let C be a category and $\mathcal{F} = (Ty, Tm) : C^{op} \to \mathcal{F}am$ be a functor. Furthermore, let Γ be an object of C and $\sigma \in Ty(\Gamma)$. A comprehension of σ is given by an object $\Gamma.\sigma$ of C together with two projections $\mathsf{p}(\sigma) : \Gamma.\sigma \to \Gamma$ and $\mathsf{v}_\sigma \in Tm(\Gamma.\sigma, \sigma\{\mathsf{p}(\sigma)\})$ such that for each $f : \Delta \to \Gamma$ and $M \in Tm(\sigma\{f\})$ there exists a unique morphism $\langle f, M \rangle_\sigma : \Delta \to \Gamma.\sigma$ satisfying $\mathsf{p}(\sigma) \circ \langle f, M \rangle_\sigma = f$ and $\mathsf{v}_\sigma\{\langle f, M \rangle_\sigma\} = M$.*

Definition 3.3 (Dybjer) *A category with families is given by the following data.*

- *a category C with terminal object,*

- *a functor $\mathcal{F} = (Ty, Tm) : C^{op} \to \mathcal{F}am$,*

- *a comprehension for each $\Gamma \in C$ and $\sigma \in Ty(\Gamma)$.*

This definition is equivalent to the one in Section 3.1. The proof is left to the reader.

The fact that comprehensions enjoy a universal property and thus are unique up to isomorphism (see E3.12) means that up to a choice of representatives a CwF is fully determined by its underlying family-valued functor.

3.1.2   Terms and sections

Assume a CwF. If $M \in Tm(\Gamma, \sigma)$ then also $M \in Tm(\Gamma, \sigma\{id_\Gamma\})$ and thus

$$\overline{M} \stackrel{\text{def}}{=} \langle id_\Gamma, M \rangle_\sigma : \Gamma \to \Gamma.\sigma$$

By *(Cons-L)* we have $\mathsf{p}(\sigma) \circ \overline{M} = id_\Gamma$ thus $\overline{M}$ is a right inverse or a so-called *section* of $\mathsf{p}(\sigma)$. Conversely, if $f : \Gamma \to \Gamma.\sigma$ is a *section* of $\mathsf{p}(\sigma)$, that is, $\mathsf{p}(\sigma) \circ f = id_\Gamma$ then

$$\mathsf{v}_\sigma\{f\} \in Tm(\Gamma, \sigma\{\mathsf{p}(\sigma)\}\{f\}) = Tm(\Gamma, \sigma\{\mathsf{p}(\sigma) \circ f\}) = Tm(\Gamma, \sigma)$$

by *(Ty-Comp)*, *(Ty-Id)*, and assumption. These two operations establish a bijective correspondence between the collection $Sect(\mathsf{p}(\sigma))$ of sections of $\mathsf{p}(\sigma)$ and $Tm(\Gamma, \sigma)$, as $\mathsf{v}_\sigma\{\overline{M}\} = M$ by *(Cons-L)* and $\overline{\mathsf{v}_\sigma\{f\}} = \langle id_\Gamma, \mathsf{v}_\sigma\{f\} \rangle_\sigma = \langle \mathsf{p}(\sigma) \circ f, \mathsf{v}_\sigma\{f\} \rangle_\sigma = \langle \mathsf{p}(\sigma), \mathsf{v}_\sigma \rangle_\sigma \circ f = f$ by *(Cons-Nat)* and *(Cons-Id)*.

3.1.3   Weakening

Suppose that $f : B \to \Gamma$ and $\sigma \in Ty(\Gamma)$. A context morphism $\mathsf{q}(f, \sigma) : B.\sigma\{f\} \to \Gamma.\sigma$ called the *weakening of f by σ* is defined by

$$\mathsf{q}(f, \sigma) = \langle f \circ \mathsf{p}(\sigma\{f\}), \mathsf{v}_{\sigma\{f\}} \rangle_\sigma$$

In the term model $\mathsf{q}(f, \sigma)$ is the eponymous syntactic context morphism defined in Section 2.4; in the set-theoretic model we have $\mathsf{q}(f, \sigma)(\beta \in B, x \in \sigma_{f(\beta)}) = (f(\beta), x)$.

A *weakening map* is a morphism of the form $\mathsf{p}(\sigma) : \Gamma.\sigma \to \Gamma$ or (inductively) a morphism of the form $\mathsf{q}(w, \tau)$ where w is a weakening map. In the term model a weakening map takes the form of a projection from $\Gamma, x : \sigma, \Delta$ to Γ, Δ.

We introduce the abbreviations σ^+ and M^+ for $\sigma\{w\}$ and $M\{w\}$ if w is a weakening map which is clear from the context. Furthermore, if $f : \Gamma \to \Delta$ is any context morphism we may write f^+ for $\mathsf{q}(f, \sigma)$. For example, as demonstrated in E2.15 we have in the term model $\Pi x : \sigma.\tau\{f\} = \Pi x : \sigma\{f\}.\tau\{f^+\}$.

Exercises

E3.4 Show that in a CwF the defined morphisms $\mathsf{q}(f, \sigma)$ from Section 3.1.3 do satisfy the coherence requirements $\mathsf{q}(id_\Gamma, \sigma) = id_{\Gamma.\sigma}$ and $\mathsf{q}(f \circ g, \sigma) = \mathsf{q}(f, \sigma) \circ \mathsf{q}(g, \sigma\{f\})$.

E3.5 Transform the following equations into the explicit notation; prove them, and explain their intuitive meaning. (1) $\mathsf{p}(\sigma)^+ \circ \overline{\mathsf{v}_\sigma} = \mathsf{p}(\sigma^+) \circ \overline{\mathsf{v}_\sigma} = id_{\Gamma.\sigma}$; (2) $f^+ \circ \overline{M\{f\}} = \overline{M} \circ f$; (3) $f = \langle \mathsf{p}(\sigma) \circ f, \mathsf{v}_\sigma\{f\} \rangle_\sigma$. Also expand the expression $\Gamma.\sigma.\tau$ when $\sigma, \tau \in Ty\Gamma$.

E3.6 Check that equations *(Cons-L)* ... *(Cons-Id)* hold in the set-theoretic model.

E3.7 This exercise will be taken up in later sections and will lead us up to Jan Smith's proof of the independence of Peano's fourth axiom from Martin-Löf's type theory without universes (Smith 1988). Let $\mathcal{P}$ be the poset of truth values $\{\text{ff}, \mathbf{t}\}$ where $\text{ff} \le \mathbf{t}$ viewed as a category. Show that $\mathcal{P}$ has a terminal object, viz. $\mathbf{t}$. Extend $\mathcal{P}$ to a CwF by putting $Ty_{\mathcal{P}}(\mathbf{t}) = Ty_{\mathcal{P}}(\text{ff}) = \{\text{ff}, \mathbf{t}\}$ and $Tm_{\mathcal{P}}(\Gamma, \sigma) = [\Gamma \le \sigma]$. Hint: define comprehension by $\Gamma.\sigma \overset{\text{def}}{=} \Gamma \wedge \sigma$. An intuition for this model (or rather for the interpretation of the syntax in it) is to view $\mathbf{t}$ as "potentially inhabited" and ff as "always empty".

3.2 Other notions of semantics

In the literature other notions of model have been offered which mostly are equivalent to CwFs. A key property of these models is that substitution on terms is a defined concept rather than a primitive. To understand how this works we need the notion of pullback in a category.

Definition 3.8 *Let $\mathcal{C}$ be a category, $f : X \to Y$ and $g : Z \to Y$ morphisms with common codomain. A pullback of g along f is a pair of morphisms $p : P \to Y$ and $q : P \to Z$ such that $f \circ p = g \circ q$ and whenever $p' : P' \to X$ and $q' : P' \to Z$ are two morphisms with $f \circ p' = g \circ q'$ then there exists a unique morphism $h : P' \to P$*

such that $p \circ h = p'$ *and* $q \circ h = q'.$ [2]

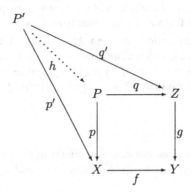

A quadruple (p, q, f, g) of morphisms with $f \circ p = g \circ q$ (a *commuting square*) is called *a* pullback if p and q form a pullback of g along f.

In the category *Set* the pullback of $g : Z \to Y$ along $g : X \to Y$ always exists and is (e.g.) given by $P \stackrel{\text{def}}{=} \{(x, z) \mid x \in X \land z \in Z \land f(x) = g(z)\}$. The two projections p, q send a pair $(x, z) \in P$ to x and z, respectively.

In *Set* we can view a morphism $g : Z \to Y$ as a family of sets indexed over Y, namely the family of sets $(g^{-1}(y))_{y \in Y}$ where $g^{-1}(y) \stackrel{\text{def}}{=} \{z \in Z \mid g(z) = y\}$. Conversely, if we are given a family of sets $(G_y)_{y \in Y}$ we can construct a function g into Y as the projection from the disjoint union

$$Z \stackrel{\text{def}}{=} \{(y, \gamma) \mid y \in Y \land \gamma \in G_y\}$$

to Y which sends (y, γ) to y. (This is precisely $\mathsf{p}((G_y)_{y \in Y})$ in the notation of Section 3.1.) Now a pullback of the thus defined $g : Z \to Y$ along $f : X \to Y$ is given by applying this construction to the composite family $(G_{f(x)})_{x \in X}$, more precisely, we can put

$$P \stackrel{\text{def}}{=} \{(x, \gamma) \mid x \in X \land \gamma \in G_{f(x)}\}$$

with projections $p(x, \gamma) = x$ and $q(x, \gamma) = (f(x), \gamma)$. Note that this is not equal to the canonical pullback of g along f which is $\{(x, (x', \gamma)) \mid x = x' \text{ and } \gamma \in G_{f(x')}\}$.

A more general correspondence between pullbacks and substitution arises in the framework of CwFs:

---

[2]This and the following diagrams were typeset using Paul Taylor's Latex diagram package the use of which is herewith gratefully acknowledged.

Proposition 3.9 *Let C be a CwF, $f : B \to \Gamma$, and $\sigma \in Ty(\Gamma)$. The following square is a pullback*

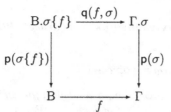

Proof. The diagram commutes by equation *(Cons-L)*. To see that it is indeed a pullback assume $p' : \Theta \to B$ and $q' : \Theta \to \Gamma.\sigma$ such that $f \circ p' = p(\sigma) \circ q'$. We can decompose q' as $q' = \langle p(\sigma), v_\sigma \rangle_\sigma \circ q' = \langle p(\sigma) \circ q', v_\sigma\{q'\} \rangle_\sigma = \langle f \circ p', N \rangle_\sigma$, where $N \stackrel{\text{def}}{=} v_\sigma\{q'\}$. We have $N \in Tm(\sigma\{p(\sigma)\}\{q'\}) = \sigma\{p(\sigma) \circ q'\} = \sigma\{f \circ p'\} = \sigma\{f\}\{p'\}$. Therefore,

$$h \stackrel{\text{def}}{=} \langle p', N \rangle_{\sigma\{f\}} : \Theta \to B.\sigma\{f\}$$

We have $p(\sigma\{f\}) \circ h = q'$ by *(Cons-L)* and

$$
\begin{aligned}
& q(f, \sigma) \circ h \\
= \ & \langle f \circ p(\sigma\{f\}), v_{\sigma\{f\}} \rangle_\sigma \circ h && \text{by definition} \\
= \ & \langle f \circ p(\sigma\{f\}) \circ h, v_{\sigma\{f\}}\{h\} \rangle_\sigma && \text{by \textit{(Cons-Nat)}} \\
= \ & \langle f \circ p', v_{\sigma\{f\}}\{h\} \rangle_\sigma && \text{by \textit{(Cons-L)}} \\
= \ & \langle f \circ p', v_\sigma\{q'\} \rangle_\sigma && \text{by \textit{(Cons-R)}} \\
= \ & \langle p(\sigma) \circ q', v_\sigma\{q'\} \rangle_\sigma && \text{by assumption} \\
= \ & q' && \text{by \textit{(Cons-Nat)} and \textit{(Cons-Id)}}
\end{aligned}
$$

For uniqueness assume a morphism $h' : \Theta \to B.\sigma\{f\}$ such that $p(\sigma\{f\}) \circ h' = p'$ and $q(f, \sigma) \circ h' = q'$. We must show $h' = h$. To see this, we expand h' as $\langle p(\sigma\{f\}) \circ h', v_{\sigma\{f\}}\{h'\} \rangle_{\sigma\{f\}}$ using *(Cons-Id)*, *(Id-L)*, *(Cons-Nat)*. By assumption we can rewrite this to $\langle p', M \rangle_{\sigma\{f\}}$ where

$$M \stackrel{\text{def}}{=} v_{\sigma\{f\}}\{h'\} \in Tm(\sigma\{f \circ p(\sigma\{f\}) \circ h'\}) = Tm(\sigma\{f \circ p'\}) = Tm(\sigma\{p(\sigma) \circ q'\})$$

Now we have

$$
\begin{aligned}
& v_\sigma\{q'\} \\
= \ & v_\sigma\{q(f, \sigma) \circ h'\} && \text{by assumption} \\
= \ & v_{\sigma\{f\}}\{h'\} && \text{by definition of q and \textit{(Cons-R)}} \\
= \ & M
\end{aligned}
$$

so we are done. $\square$

The pullback property of substitution may be taken as primitive thereby making substitution on terms superfluous.

Definition 3.10 *A* category with attributes *(Cartmell 1978; Moggi 1991; Pitts 1997) consists of*

- *A category* $\mathcal{C}$ *with terminal object* $\top$.

- *A functor* $Ty : \mathcal{C}^{op} \to Set$, *i.e., a set* $Ty(\Gamma)$ *for each* $\Gamma \in \mathcal{C}$ *and a function* $-\{f\} : Ty(\Gamma) \to Ty(B)$ *for each* $f : B \to \Gamma$ *such that (Ty-Id) and (Ty-Comp) from Section 3.1 hold.*

- *For each* $\sigma \in Ty(\Gamma)$ *an object* $\Gamma.\sigma$ *and a morphism* $\mathsf{p}(\sigma) : \Gamma.\sigma \to \Gamma$.

- *For each* $f : B \to \Gamma$ *and* $\sigma \in Ty(\Gamma)$ *a pullback diagram*

$$
\begin{array}{ccc}
B.\sigma\{f\} & \xrightarrow{\;\mathsf{q}(f,\sigma)\;} & \Gamma.\sigma \\
{\scriptstyle \mathsf{p}(\sigma\{f\})}\Big\downarrow & & \Big\downarrow{\scriptstyle \mathsf{p}(\sigma)} \\
B & \xrightarrow[\;f\;]{} & \Gamma
\end{array}
$$

such that $\mathsf{q}(id_\Gamma, \sigma) = id_{\Gamma.\sigma}$ *and* $\mathsf{q}(f \circ g, \sigma) = \mathsf{q}(f,\sigma) \circ \mathsf{q}(g, \sigma\{f\})$.

It follows from Prop. 3.9 and **E3.4** that every CwF is a category with attributes if we forget about the terms.

Conversely, given a category with attributes we can construct a CwF by putting $Tm(\Gamma, \sigma) \stackrel{\text{def}}{=} Sect(\mathsf{p}(\sigma))$ and for $M \in Tm(\Gamma, \sigma)$ defining $M\{f\}$ as the unique morphism with $\mathsf{p}(\sigma\{f\}) \circ M\{f\} = id_B$ and $\mathsf{q}(f, \sigma) \circ M\{f\} = M \circ f$.

For $f : B \to \Gamma, M \in Tm(B, \sigma\{f\})$ we put $\langle f, M \rangle_\sigma \stackrel{\text{def}}{=} \mathsf{q}(f, \sigma) \circ M$ and finally define v_σ as the unique morphism $\mathsf{v}_\sigma : \Gamma.\sigma \to \Gamma.\sigma.\sigma^+$ with $\mathsf{p}(\sigma^+) \circ \mathsf{v}_\sigma = \mathsf{p}(\sigma)^+ \circ \mathsf{v}_\sigma = id_{\Gamma.\sigma}$. We leave it as an exercise to verify that this defines indeed a CwF.

If one starts out with a category with attributes, constructs a CwF, and from this CwF again a category with attributes one ends up with the one to start off with. The other way round one gets back the original CwF with the set of terms $Tm(\Gamma, \sigma)$ replaced by the set of right inverses to $\mathsf{p}(\sigma)$ (cf. Section 3.1.2).

Notice that context extensions in categories with attributes are not unique up to isomorphism. For instance, if $\sigma \in Ty(\Gamma)$ nothing prevents us from defining $\Gamma.\sigma$ simply as Γ and the corresponding morphisms p and q as identities.

There are various other notions of model all of which are essentially equivalent as far as interpretation of type theory in them is concerned. Locally-cartesian closed categories (Seely 1984) and categories with display maps (Taylor 1986; Lamarche 1987; Hyland and Pitts 1989) are less general than CwFs because semantic types are identified with their associated projections. Usually, in these models the conditions corresponding to *(Ty-Comp)* and *(Ty-Id)* only hold up to isomorphism, which makes the definition of the interpretation function more complicated. See (Hofmann 1995b; Curien 1993). Models based on fibrations (Jacobs 1991; Jacobs 1993; Ehrhard 1988) and indexed categories (Curien 1989; Obtułowicz 1989) are more general since they allow for morphisms between semantic types. These morphisms make it possible to describe certain type formers more elegantly, but do not have a direct counterpart in the syntax. Mention must also be made of contextual categories where semantic contexts carry an explicit tree structure corresponding to context extensions (see (Streicher 1991; Cartmell 1978) and E3.13).

For a good taxonomy of the different notions and various back-and-forth constructions see (Jacobs 1993).

Exercises

E3.11 (Agnes Diller) Show that the requirement $q(id_\Gamma, \sigma) = id_{\Gamma.\sigma}$ in Def. 3.10 is actually redundant.

E3.12* Prove that comprehensions are indeed unique up to isomorphism in the following sense: If $\sigma \in Ty(\Gamma)$ and $p : \Sigma \to \Gamma$ and $v \in Tm(\sigma\{f\})$ is a comprehension of σ then there exists an isomorphism $f : \Gamma.\sigma \to \Sigma$ satisfying $p \circ f = p(\sigma)$ and $v\{\sigma\} = v_\sigma$.

Now give another proof of Prop. 3.9 by showing that $(\Theta, p', v_\sigma\{q'\})$ is a comprehension of $\sigma\{f\}$.

E3.13* A *contextual category* (Cartmell 1978; Streicher 1991) is a category C with terminal object $\top$ and a tree structure on the objects given by a function f on the objects of C such that $f(\top) = \top$ and f ("father") is injective on $C \setminus \{\top\}$ and for each $\Gamma \in C$ there is a minimal n—the level of Γ—such that $f^n(\Gamma) = \top$. Moreover, the assignment $Ty(\Gamma) = \{\Delta \mid f(\Delta) = \Gamma\}$ extends to a category with attributes over C. Spell this out without using the notion of a category with attributes and define a canonical construction of a contextual category out of a CwF. The objects of the contextual category are lists $(\sigma_1, \cdots, \sigma_k)$ where $\sigma_1 \in Ty(\top)$ and $\sigma_{i+1} \in Ty(\top.\sigma_1.\cdots.\sigma_i)$.

The advantage of contextual categories is that they rule out semantic contexts which do not arise from the empty context by successive applications of comprehension. This can be used to establish properties of semantic contexts by induction on the level. Examples of this can be found in (Streicher 1991).

E3.14* Assume a CwF C. For each $\Gamma \in C$ we define a category $\mathcal{D}(\Gamma)$ with objects the types over Γ and in which a morphism from σ to τ is a C-morphism $f : \Gamma.\sigma \to \Gamma.\tau$ such that $p(\tau) \circ f = p(\sigma)$. Equivalently a morphism from σ to τ can be defined as an element of $Tm(\Gamma.\sigma, \tau^+)$ (Why?). Explain why this defines indeed a category and find an extension of the assignment $\mathcal{D}$ to a contravariant functor from $\mathcal{C}$ to the category of categories.

Such a functor is called an *indexed category* and forms the heart of Curien and Ehrhard's notion of D-categories (Curien 1989; Ritter 1992).

3.3   Semantic type formers

In order to interpret a type theory in a CwF we must specify how the various type and term formers are to be interpreted. This results in certain requirements on a CwF which follow very closely the syntactic rules. We give a precise definition for closure under $\Pi, \Sigma, Id, \forall$ to convey the general pattern. The reader may then by herself define the conditions for the other type formers. Some are treated in the exercises.

Definition 3.15 *A CwF supports Π-types if for any two types $\sigma \in Ty(\Gamma)$ and $\tau \in Ty(\Gamma.\sigma)$ there is a type $\Pi(\sigma, \tau) \in Ty(\Gamma)$ and for each $M \in Tm(\Gamma.\sigma, \tau)$ there is a term $\lambda_{\sigma,\tau}(M) \in Tm(\Gamma, \Pi(\sigma, \tau))$ and for each $M \in Tm(\Gamma, \Pi(\sigma, \tau))$ and $N \in Tm(\Gamma, \sigma)$ there is a term $App_{\sigma,\tau}(M, N) \in Tm(\Gamma, \tau\{\overline{M}\})$ such that (the appropriately typed universal closures of) the following equations hold:*

$$
\begin{array}{rcll}
App_{\sigma,\tau}(\lambda_{\sigma,\tau}(M), N) & = & M\{\overline{N}\} & \Pi\text{-}C \\
\Pi(\sigma, \tau)\{f\} & = & \Pi(\sigma\{f\}, \tau\{q(f, \sigma)\}) \in Ty(B) & \Pi\text{-}S \\
\lambda_{\sigma,\tau}(M)\{f\} & = & \lambda_{\sigma\{f\},\tau\{q(f,\sigma)\}}(M\{q(f, \sigma)\}) & \lambda\text{-}S \\
App_{\sigma,\tau}(M, N)\{f\} & = & App_{\sigma\{f\},\tau\{q(f,\sigma)\}}(M\{f\}, N\{f\}) & App\text{-}S
\end{array}
$$

The third equation typechecks by virtue of the second. The last equation makes implicit use of *(Ty-Comp)* and the fact that

$$
q(f, \sigma) \circ \overline{M\{f\}} = \overline{M} \circ f
$$

which follows by rewriting both sides to $\langle f, M\{f\} \rangle_\sigma$.

We see that we stipulate exactly the same type and term formers as in the syntax together with an equation corresponding to Π-C. Congruence rules are not needed on the semantic level as everything preserves equality, but we need extra equations to specify that substitution commutes with the semantic type and term formers.

Since substitution is a primitive notion in the semantics we can obtain a more economic definition of dependent function spaces by restricting the *App*-combinator to variables and replacing it by an appropriate morphism.

Proposition 3.16 *A CwF supports dependent function spaces iff there are operations Π and λ as in Def. 3.15 and for any two types $\sigma \in Ty(\Gamma)$ and $\tau \in Ty(\Gamma.\sigma)$ a morphism*

$$
App_{\sigma,\tau} : \Gamma.\sigma.\Pi(\sigma, \tau)^+ \to \Gamma.\sigma.\tau
$$

such that

$$p(\tau) \circ App_{\sigma,\tau} = p(\Pi(\sigma,\tau)^+) \qquad\qquad App\text{-}T$$

and for every term $M \in Tm(\tau)$

$$App_{\sigma,\tau} \circ \overline{M\{p(\sigma)\}} = \overline{M} \qquad\qquad \Pi\text{-}C'$$

and, finally, for every morphism $f : B \to \Gamma$

$$App_{\sigma,\tau} \circ q(q(f,\sigma), \Pi(\sigma,\tau)\{q(f,\sigma)\}) = q(q(f,\sigma),\tau) \circ App_{\sigma\{f\},\tau\{q(f,\sigma)\}}$$

Proof. The first equation states that $App_{\sigma,\tau}$ leaves its first two arguments unchanged, and thus corresponds to a term of τ^+. The second equation corresponds to $\Pi\text{-}C$, and the third one to $App\text{-}S$; stability under substitution. From the App-morphism we can define an application combinator as follows. Given $M \in Tm(\Pi(\sigma,\tau))$ and $N \in Tm(\sigma)$ then $v_\tau\{App_{\sigma,\tau} \circ \langle N, M^+\rangle_{\Pi(\sigma,\tau)+}\} \in Tm(\tau\{p(\tau) \circ App_{\sigma,\tau} \circ \langle N, M^+\rangle_{\Pi(\sigma,\tau)+}\} = Tm(\tau\{\overline{N}\})$ by Eqn. $App\text{-}T$ and it follows from the other two equations that this term has the required properties. Conversely, suppose that a model supports dependent function spaces in the sense of Def. 3.15. Let Δ be $\Gamma.\sigma.\Pi(\sigma,\tau)^+$. We have $N \stackrel{\text{def}}{=} v_\sigma^+ \in Tm(\Delta, \sigma^{++})$ and $M \stackrel{\text{def}}{=} v_{\Pi(\sigma,\tau)+} \in Tm(\Delta, \Pi(\sigma,\tau)^{++}) = Tm(\Delta, \Pi(\sigma^{++}, \tau^{++}))$. Accordingly, we have

$$App_{\sigma,\tau}(M,N) \in Tm(\Delta, \tau^{++}\{N\}) = Tm(\Delta, \tau^+)$$

We define the application morphism as

$$\langle p(\Pi(\sigma,\tau)^+, App_{\sigma,\tau}(M,N)\rangle_\tau$$

The verifications are left to the reader. $\qquad\qquad\qquad\qquad\qquad\qquad\qquad\square$

This second definition of dependent function spaces allows for the following restriction by which $\lambda_{\sigma,\tau}(M)$ is required to be the unique element of $Tm(\Pi(\sigma,\tau))$ for which $\Pi\text{-}C'$ holds.

Definition 3.17 *A CwF supports Π-types in the strict sense if it supports them and whenever $M \in Tm(\Gamma.\sigma, \tau)$ and $U \in Tm(\Pi(\sigma,\tau))$ and $App_{\sigma,\tau} \circ \overline{U^+} = \overline{M}$ then $U = \lambda_{\sigma,\tau}(M)$.*

The syntactic counterpart to these strict Π-types is an η-rule which allows one to conclude $\Gamma \vdash \lambda x{:}\,\sigma.(M\,x)^\tau = M : \Pi x{:}\,\sigma.\tau$ from $\Gamma \vdash M : \Pi x{:}\,\sigma.\tau$.

If Π-types are supported in the strict sense then Eqn. $\lambda\text{-}S$ can be derived. Moreover, the operation $\Pi(\sigma, -)$ then becomes part of an adjunction, see, e.g. (Pitts 1997).

The term model of a type theory with Π-types supports Π-types with the obvious settings:

$$\Pi(\sigma,\tau) \stackrel{\text{def}}{=} \Pi x{:}\,\sigma.\tau$$

$$\lambda_{\sigma,\tau}(M) \stackrel{\text{def}}{=} \lambda x \colon \sigma.M^{\tau}$$

$$App_{\sigma,\tau}(M, N) \stackrel{\text{def}}{=} App_{[x:\sigma]\tau}(M, N)$$

The corresponding application morphism is the context morphism defined by $\Gamma, y \colon \sigma, z \colon \Pi x \colon \sigma.\tau \vdash (\vec{x}, App_{[x:\sigma]\tau}(z, y)) \Rightarrow \Gamma, x \colon \sigma, w \colon \tau$ where $\vec{x}$ are the variables in Γ. Notice that these Π-types are not strict unless we enrich our type theory with the abovementioned η-equation.

The set-theoretic model supports Π-types in the strict sense. If $(\sigma_\gamma)_{\gamma\in\Gamma} \in Ty(\Gamma)$ and $(\tau_{(\gamma,x)})_{(\gamma,x)} \in \Gamma.\sigma$ then we define $\Pi(\sigma,\tau)_\gamma \stackrel{\text{def}}{=} \Pi_{x\in\sigma_\gamma}\tau_{(\gamma,x)}$ and abstraction and application as their set-theoretic companions.

Definition 3.18 *A CwF supports Σ-types if the following data are given:*

- *for any two types $\sigma \in Ty(\Gamma)$ and $\tau \in Ty(\Gamma.\sigma)$ there is a type $\Sigma(\sigma,\tau) \in Ty(\Gamma)$ such that*

$$\Sigma(\sigma,\tau)\{f\} = \Sigma(\sigma\{f\}, \tau\{f^+\}) \qquad\qquad \Sigma\text{-S}$$

  whenever $f : B \to \Gamma$.

- *A morphism $Pair_{\sigma,\tau} : \Gamma.\sigma.\tau \to \Gamma.\Sigma(\sigma,\tau)$ such that $\mathsf{p}(\Sigma(\sigma,\tau)) \circ Pair_{\sigma,\tau} = \mathsf{p}(\sigma) \circ \mathsf{p}(\tau)$ and such that*

$$f^+ \circ Pair_{\sigma,\tau} = Pair_{\sigma\{f\},\tau\{f^+\}} \circ f^{++} \qquad\qquad Pair\text{-S}$$

  whenever $f : B \to \Gamma$.

- *For every type $\rho \in Ty(\Gamma.\Sigma(\sigma,\tau))$ and term $H \in Tm(\rho\{Pair_{\sigma,\tau}\})$ a term $\mathsf{R}^\Sigma_{\sigma,\tau,\rho}(H) \in Tm(\rho)$ such that*

$$\mathsf{R}^\Sigma_{\sigma,\tau,\rho}(H)\{Pair_{\sigma,\tau}\} = H \qquad\qquad \Sigma\text{-C}$$

  and

$$\mathsf{R}^\Sigma_{\sigma,\tau,\rho}(H)\{f^+\} = \\ \mathsf{R}^\Sigma_{\sigma\{f\},\tau\{f^+\},\rho\{f^+\}}(H\{f^{++}\}) \qquad\qquad \mathsf{R}^\Sigma\text{-S}$$

The term model supports Σ-types as follows: if $\Gamma, x \colon \sigma \vdash \tau$ *type* then $\Sigma(\sigma,\tau) \stackrel{\text{def}}{=} \Sigma x \colon \sigma.\tau$ and $Pair_{\sigma,\tau}$ is the context morphism

$$\Gamma, x \colon \sigma, y \colon \tau \vdash (\gamma, Pair_{[x:\sigma]\tau}(M, N)) \Rightarrow \Gamma, z \colon \Sigma x \colon \sigma.\tau$$

Finally, if $\Gamma, x \colon \sigma, y \colon \tau \vdash H : \rho[Pair_{[x:\sigma]\tau}(x, y)]$ then $\Gamma, z \colon \Sigma x \colon \sigma.\tau \vdash \mathsf{R}^\Sigma(H, z) : \rho$.

Also the set-theoretic model supports Σ-types as follows.

$$\Sigma(\sigma,\tau)_{\gamma\in\Gamma} \stackrel{\text{def}}{=} \{(x, y) \mid x \in \sigma_\gamma \wedge y \in \tau_{(\gamma,x)}\}$$

and
$$Pair_{\sigma,\tau}(\gamma, x, y) \overset{\text{def}}{=} (\gamma, (x, y))$$

This morphism $Pair$ is surjective and thus we can take Σ-C as the defining equation for $R^\Sigma_{\sigma,\tau,\rho}$ which also ensures that $R^\Sigma_{\sigma,\tau,\rho}(H)$ is the unique term with property Σ-C. Again, we say that Σ-types are supported in the strict sense if this is the case.

Definition 3.19 *A CwF supports (intensional) identity types if for each type $\sigma \in Ty(\Gamma)$ the following data are given:*

- *a type $Id_\sigma \in Ty(\Gamma.\sigma.\sigma^+)$,*

- *a morphism $Refl_\sigma : \Gamma.\sigma \to I(\sigma)$ where $I(\sigma) = \Gamma.\sigma.\sigma^+.Id_\sigma$ such that $p(Id_\sigma) \circ Refl_\sigma$ equals $\overline{v_\sigma} : \Gamma.\sigma \to \Gamma.\sigma.\sigma^+$; the diagonal morphism,*

- *for each $\tau \in Ty(I(\sigma))$ a function $R^{Id}_{\sigma,\tau} \in Tm(\tau\{Refl_\sigma\}) \to Tm(\tau)$*

in such a way that these data are stable under substitution w.r.t. morphisms $f : B \to \Gamma$ and such that whenever $\tau \in Ty(I(\sigma))$ and $H \in Tm(\tau\{Refl_\sigma\})$ then $R^{Id}_{\sigma,\tau}(H)\{Refl_\sigma\} = H$.

The term model of intensional type theory supports identity types with the following settings: if $\Gamma \vdash \sigma$ type then Id_σ is the type $\Gamma, x: \sigma, y: \sigma \vdash Id_\sigma(x, y)$ type and $Refl_\sigma$ is the context morphism

$$\Gamma, x: \sigma \vdash (\gamma, x, x, Refl_\sigma(x)) \Rightarrow \Gamma, x: \sigma, y: \sigma, p: Id_\sigma(x, y)$$

If $\Gamma, x: \sigma, y: \sigma, p: Id_\sigma(x, y) \vdash \tau[x, y, p]$ type and $\Gamma, x: \sigma \vdash H : \tau[x, x, Refl_\sigma(x)]$ then

$$\Gamma, x: \sigma, y: \sigma, p: Id_\sigma(x, y) \vdash R^{Id}([x: \sigma]H, x, y, p) : \tau[x, y, p]$$

which defines the required function.

The set-theoretic model supports identity types with $(Id_\sigma)_{(\gamma, x, y)} \overset{\text{def}}{=} [x = y]$ and $Refl_\sigma(\gamma, x) \overset{\text{def}}{=} (\gamma, x, x, \star)$. For $H \in Tm_{\mathcal{S}et}(\tau\{Refl_\sigma\})$ we put

$$R^{Id}_{\sigma,\tau}(H)(\gamma, x, y, p) \overset{\text{def}}{=} H(x)$$

which is type correct because in the presence of $p \in Id_\sigma(x, y)$ we have $x = y$ and furthermore p itself equals $\star$.

The semantic interpretation of natural numbers, unit types, empty types follows the pattern of the Σ-types and is left to the reader. We conclude the definition of semantic analogues to type formers by specifying the interpretation of a universe closed under impredicative quantification.

Definition 3.20 *A CwF supports the Calculus of Constructions if it supports Π-types and the following data are given:*

- *a type Prop $\in$ Ty($\top$). We write Prop also for $\top$.Prop,*

- *A type Prf $\in$ Ty(Prop),*

- *for $\sigma \in$ Ty(Γ) and $p : \Gamma.\sigma \to$ Prop a morphism $\forall_\sigma(p) : \Gamma \to$ Prop,*

- *a term former $\lambda_{\sigma,p}(-)$ and a morphism $App_{\sigma,p}$ like in Prop 3.16 establishing that Prf$\{\forall_\sigma(p)\}$ is a dependent function space of Prf$\{p\}$ over σ*

such that all these data are stable under substitution.

The term model is a model for the Calculus of Constructions with *Prop* equal to the type of propositions *Prop* in $\diamond \vdash$ *Prop type* and the type of proofs equal to *Prf*(x) in x: *Prop* $\vdash$ *Prf*(x) *type*. A morphism from $\Gamma.\sigma$ to *Prop* takes the form of a term Γ, x: $\sigma \vdash P$: *Prop*. Then $\Gamma \vdash \forall x$: $\sigma.P$: *Prop* is a morphism from Γ to *Prop* with the required properties.

The set-theoretic model is a model for the Calculus of Constructions with the settings *Prop* $\overset{\text{def}}{=} \{\text{ff}, \text{t}\}$ and *Prf*$_x \overset{\text{def}}{=} [x = \text{t}]$. If $p : \Gamma.\sigma \to$ *Prop* then we define $\forall_\sigma(p)(\gamma) \overset{\text{def}}{=} ["p(\gamma, x) = \text{t}$ for all $x \in \sigma_\gamma"]$.

Notice that in this model all elements of a type *Prf*(A) are equal. By "Reynolds' paradox" (Reynolds and Plotkin 1988) this has to be so in any set-theoretic interpretation of the Calculus of Constructions. In Section 3.4 below we describe a model where this is not the case.

Notice that *Prf*$\{\forall_\sigma(p)\}$ is not equal to $\Pi(\sigma, $ *Prf*$\{p\})$ but in bijective correspondence because if $p(\gamma, x) = \text{t}$ for each $x \in \sigma_\gamma$ then *Prf*$\{\forall_\sigma(p)\} = \{\star\}$, whereas $\Pi(\sigma, $ *Prf*$\{p\})_\gamma$ is the set of functions from σ_γ to $\{\star\}$ which is a singleton set, but not $\{\star\}$. However, this bijective correspondence enables us to define the required operations $\lambda_{\sigma,p}$ and $App_{\sigma,p}$.

Exercises

E3.21   Show that the truth value model from E3.7 supports Π and Σ-types each in the strict sense, as well as identity types with the settings $\Pi(\sigma, \tau) \overset{\text{def}}{=} \sigma \supset \tau$ and $\Sigma(\sigma, \tau) \overset{\text{def}}{=} \sigma \wedge \tau$ and $Id_\sigma \overset{\text{def}}{=} \text{t}$, where $\supset$ and $\wedge$ denote implication and conjunction of truth values.

E3.22*   Show that a CwF supports Σ-types in the strict sense iff it supports them and each morphism $Pair_{\sigma,\tau}$ is an isomorphism.

E3.23   Spell out what it means that *Id* and *Refl* are stable under substitution.

E3.24   Explain how a CwF $\mathcal{C}$ supports unit types if (but not only if) there exists $1 \in Ty(\top)$ such that $\top.1$ is a terminal object in $\mathcal{C}$ or equivalently $\top.1$ is isomorphic to $\top$.

E3.25 Define what it means for a model to support natural numbers. Show that the set-theoretic model supports natural numbers by $N \stackrel{\text{def}}{=} \omega$ and that the truth value model supports natural numbers by $N \stackrel{\text{def}}{=} t$.

E3.26* Define what it means to support an empty type in the sense of Section 2.1.7 and show that the set-theoretic model supports it by $0 \stackrel{\text{def}}{=} \emptyset$ and that the truth value model supports it by $0 \stackrel{\text{def}}{=} ff$ and that this interpretation is the only possibility. Conclude that if $M, N \in Tm(\Gamma, \sigma)$ in this model then the set $Tm(\Gamma.Id_\sigma\{\langle \overline{M}, N^+ \rangle_{\sigma^+}\}, 0)$ is empty.

E3.27 Show that the truth value model forms a model of the Calculus of Constructions with $Prop \stackrel{\text{def}}{=} t$, $Prf(\star) \stackrel{\text{def}}{=} t$, $\forall_\sigma(\star) \stackrel{\text{def}}{=} \star$.

E3.28* Define the semantics of a universe containing a code for the empty type and a code for the unit type. Show that the set-theoretic model supports such a universe, but that the truth value model does not.

E3.29* Let $\mathcal{Poset}$ be the category of posets and monotone functions. Extend $\mathcal{Poset}$ to a CwF by defining $Ty(\Gamma)$ for poset Γ as the set of down-closed subsets (ideals) of Γ. If $\sigma \in Ty(\Gamma)$ then define $\Gamma.\sigma$ as σ considered as a poset and let $p(\sigma)$ be the inclusion from σ to Γ. Finally, define $Tm(\Gamma, \sigma)$ as $[\Gamma = \sigma]$. For $\tau \in Ty(\Gamma.\sigma)$ let $\Pi'(\sigma, \tau) \in Ty(\Gamma)$ be $\{\gamma \in \Gamma \mid \forall x \in \sigma.x \leq \gamma \Rightarrow x \in \tau\}$. Show that $Tm(\Gamma, \Pi'(\sigma, \tau)) = Tm(\Gamma.\sigma, \tau)$, but that nevertheless Π' does not determine dependent function spaces on $\mathcal{Poset}$ because it is not stable under substitution. In fact, the CwF $\mathcal{Poset}$ does *not* support dependent function spaces.

E3.30* (Extensional type theory) Say that a CwF with identity types supports them in the strict sense if whenever $\sigma \in Ty(\Gamma)$ and $\tau \in Ty(I(\sigma))$ (recall that $I(\sigma) \stackrel{\text{def}}{=} \Gamma.\sigma.\sigma^+.Id_\sigma$) and $H \in Tm(\tau)$ then $H = R_{\sigma,\tau}^{Id}(H\{Refl_\sigma\})$. Note that this is the case for the CwFs *Set* and $\mathcal{P}$ (Why?). (1) Show that a CwF with identity types supports them in the strict sense iff the morphism $Refl_\sigma : \Gamma.\sigma \to I(\sigma)$ is an isomorphism (with inverse $Refl_\sigma^{-1} \stackrel{\text{def}}{=} (p(\sigma^+))^+$). (2) *Extensional type theory* is usually formulated as a type theory with identity types where rules ID-E and ID-C are replaced by the rules

$$\frac{\Gamma \vdash P : Id_\sigma(M, N)}{\Gamma \vdash M = N : \sigma} \ \text{REFLECTION} \qquad \frac{\Gamma \vdash P : Id_\sigma(M, N)}{\Gamma \vdash P = Refl_\sigma(M)} \ \text{ID-CAN}$$

Show that the term model of extensional type theory supports identity types in the strict sense. (3) Show that rule ID-CAN is independent of REFLECTION by considering the set-theoretic model with the setting $(Id_\sigma)_{(\gamma, x, y)} = \{\star, \star'\}$ if $x = y$

and $\emptyset$ otherwise. "Independence" is understood informally here; to establish that ID-CAN cannot be derived from REFLECTION one needs the soundness theorem 3.35 below. (4) Show that if a model supports identity types in the strict sense then it supports Σ-types iff it supports them in the strict sense.

3.4   The ω-set model

In this section we present another important CwF which provides a non-trivial interpretation of the Calculus of Constructions in which there is a proposition $\hat{N} \in Tm(Prop_\top)$ such that $Tm(Prf(\hat{N}))$ has more than one element.

An ω-set X consists of a set (denoted $|X|$ or X) and a relation $\Vdash_X \subseteq \omega \times |X|$ between natural numbers and elements of X with the property that for each $x \in |X|$ there is an $n \in \omega$ such that $n \Vdash_X x$. If $n \Vdash_X x$ one says that n realises x or codes x or is a code/realiser for x so the condition on $\Vdash_X$ means that every $x \in X$ has a realiser.

A morphism from ω-set X to Y is a function f from X to Y with the property that there exists a partial recursive function e (thought of as a natural number) such that whenever $n \Vdash_X x$ then $\{e\}(n)$—the application of e to n—is defined and realises $f(x)$. The ω-sets together with their morphisms form a category.

An example of an ω-set is N where $|N| = \omega$ and $n \Vdash_N m$ iff $n = m$. The morphisms in the category of ω-sets from N to N are exactly the total recursive functions. Another example is $\top$ with $|\top| = \{\star\}$ and $n \Vdash_\top \star$ for all $n \in \omega$. This ω-set is readily seen to be a terminal object. If X is a set then we form an ω-set $\triangle X$ by $|\triangle X| = X$ and $n \Vdash_{\triangle X} x$ for all $n \in \omega$ and $x \in X$.

The category of ω-sets can be extended to a CwF as follows. For ω-set Γ the set $Ty(\Gamma)$ consists of families of ω-sets indexed over Γ. Thus, $\sigma \in Ty(\Gamma)$ means that $\sigma = (\sigma_\gamma)_{\gamma \in \Gamma}$ and each σ_γ is an ω-set. A term $M \in Tm(\Gamma, \sigma)$ is a function assigning to each $\gamma \in \Gamma$ an element $M(\gamma) \in \sigma_\gamma$ such that there exists a partial recursive function e with the property that for each $\gamma \in \Gamma$ and $n \Vdash_\Gamma \gamma$ the computation $\{e\}(n)$ is defined and $\{e\}(n) \Vdash_{\sigma_\gamma} M(\gamma)$.

The ω-set $\Gamma.\sigma$ has as underlying set the disjoint union $\Sigma_{\gamma \in \Gamma} \sigma(\gamma)$ and $n \Vdash_{\Gamma.\sigma} (\gamma, x)$ if $L(n) \Vdash_\Gamma \gamma$ and $R(n) \Vdash_{\sigma(\gamma)} x$ where L and R are the inverses to a bijection like $P(m, n) \stackrel{def}{=} 2^m(2n + 1)$ from $\omega \times \omega$ to ω. The remaining components are left to the reader as an exercise.

The ω-set model supports Π-types with the setting $\Pi(\sigma, \tau)_\gamma = \{M \in \Pi x \in \sigma_\gamma.\tau_{(\gamma,x)} \mid \exists e$ such that $T(e, M)\}$ where $T(e, M)$ means that $n \Vdash_{\sigma_\gamma} x$ implies $\{e\}(n) \Vdash M(x)$ for all $x \in \sigma_\gamma$ and $n \in \omega$. If $M \in \Pi(\sigma, \tau)_\gamma$ and $e \in \Gamma$ then $e \Vdash_{\Pi(\sigma,\tau)_\gamma} M$ if $T(e, M)$. Application and abstraction are defined as in the set-theoretic model. The required realisers are obtained from untyped application and abstraction ("smn-theorem").

All the other type formers we have considered and many more are also supported by the ω-set model.

3.4.1 Modest sets

In an ω-set X two different elements can have the same realiser. An ω-set where this is not so is called a *modest set*. In other words a *modest set* consists of a set X and a partial surjective function $\Vdash_X$ from ω to X. More generally, $\sigma \in Ty(\Gamma)$ is modest if each σ_γ is a modest set. It is easy to see that if $\tau \in Ty(\Gamma.\sigma)$ is modest then so is $\Pi(\sigma, \tau)$ for arbitrary σ. A modest set X induces a symmetric, transitive relation $\sim_X$ (a *partial equivalence relation*, per) on the set ω of natural numbers by putting $m \sim_X n$ if there exists a (necessarily unique) $x \in X$ such that $m \Vdash_X x$ and $n \Vdash_X x$. Conversely, if $R \subseteq \omega \times \omega$ is any per we can define a modest set $Prf(R)$ having as underlying set the quotient of $\{n \mid nRn\}$ by R (which restricted to this set is an equivalence relation). We have $m \Vdash_{Prf(R)} [n]_R$ if mRn. If X is modest then X is isomorphic to $Prf(\sim_X)$ in the category of ω-sets and a per R is equal to $\sim_{Prf(R)}$. This suggests to interpret the Calculus of Constructions by putting $Prop = \triangle(PER)$ where PER is the set of symmetric and transitive relations on ω. Notice that $Prop$ is not modest. The above-defined operation Prf then yields a type $Prf \in Ty(Prop)$. If $p : \Gamma \to Prop$ then $p(\gamma)$ is a per for each $\gamma \in \Gamma$ and we have $Prf\{p\}_\gamma = Prf(p(\gamma))$.

If $p : \Gamma.\sigma \to Prop$ then we define $\forall_\sigma(p) : \Gamma \to Prop$ by $(\forall_\sigma(p))(\gamma) \stackrel{\text{def}}{=} \sim_{\Pi(\sigma, Prf\{p\})_\gamma}$. The verifications are tedious but essentially straightforward.

For mRn iff $m = n$ we have that $Prf(R)$ is isomorphic to the ω-set $\mathbf{N}$ which means that we can interpret a type theory in which the impredicative universe $Prop$ contains a code for the natural numbers. $Prop$ also contains codes for other reasonable data types and indeed the ω-sets furnish a model for the CID mentioned in Section 2.2.3. Beeson (1985) and Allen (1987) show how to model type theory with non-impredicative universes (no $\forall$) entirely within the pers.

Exercises

E3.31 Let X be any set. Show that every morphism in ω-set from $\triangle X$ to $\mathbf{N}$ is constant and that for arbitrary ω-set Y every set-theoretic function from Y to X is a morphism in ω-set from Y to $\triangle X$.

E3.32 Explain how the set-theoretic model supports lists, cf. E2.3.

E3.33 Explain how the ω-set model supports identity types in the strict sense.

E3.34* For any ω-set X a per $\mathcal{I}(X)$ is defined as the transitive closure of the relation which relates two numbers if they realise a common element of X. Define a morphism $\eta_X : X \to Prf(\mathcal{I}(X))$ which sends $x \in X$ to the equivalence class of a realiser of x. Show that if Y is a modest set and $f : X \to Y$ then there exists a unique morphism $\hat{f} : Prf(\mathcal{I}(X)) \to Y$ such that $f = \hat{f} \circ \eta_X$. This means that the modest sets form a *reflective sub-category* of the ω-sets. One can define impredicative quantification in the ω-set model by $\forall_\sigma (M)_{\gamma \in \Gamma} \stackrel{\text{def}}{=} \mathcal{I}(\Pi x \colon \sigma.Prf(M)_\gamma)$. In (Ehrhard 1989) such a reflection is made part of the definition of a model for the Calculus of Constructions.

3.5 Interpretation of the syntax

We have already implicitly spoken about interpretation of type theory in CwFs by appealing to the informal analogy between components of CwFs and type-theoretic entities. In this section we make this precise by defining an interpretation function and establishing a soundness property.

Assume for the rest of this section a fixed type theory and a CwF $\mathcal{C}$ supporting the type and term formers present in this theory. For simplicity we restrict our attention to Π-types.

We define a *partial* interpretation function $[\![-]\!]$ which maps:

- pre-contexts to objects of $\mathcal{C}$

- pairs $\Gamma \, ; \sigma$, where Γ is a pre-context and σ is a pre-type, to families in $Ty([\![\Gamma]\!])$

- pairs $\Gamma \, ; M$, where Γ is a pre-context and M is a pre-term to elements of $Tm(\sigma)$ for some $\sigma \in Ty([\![\Gamma]\!])$.

The definition is by induction on the lengths of the involved pre-terms, -types, and -contexts. We show below in Thm. 3.35 that the semantic function is defined on all contexts, types, and terms.

The semantic clauses are the following, where we adopt the convention that an expression containing an undefined subexpression is itself undefined. We also adopt the convention that expressions which do not "typecheck", like $\Gamma.\sigma$ if $\sigma \notin Ty(\Gamma)$, are undefined.

- $[\![\diamond]\!] = \top$

- $[\![\Gamma, x \colon \sigma]\!] = [\![\Gamma]\!].[\![\Gamma \, ; \sigma]\!]$ if x not in Γ, undefined otherwise.

- $[\![\Gamma \, ; \Pi x \colon \sigma.\tau]\!] = \Pi([\![\Gamma \, ; \sigma]\!], [\![\Gamma, x \colon \sigma \, ; \tau]\!])$

- $[\![\Gamma, x \colon \sigma \, ; x]\!] = \mathsf{v}_{[\![\Gamma \, ; \sigma]\!]}$

- $[\![\Gamma, x \colon \sigma, \Delta, y \colon \tau \, ; x]\!] = [\![\Gamma, x \colon \sigma, \Delta \, ; x]\!]\{\mathsf{p}([\![\Gamma, x \colon \sigma, \Delta \, ; \tau]\!])\}$

- $[\![\Gamma \, ; App_{[x \colon \sigma]\tau}(M, N)]\!] = App_{[\![\Gamma \, ; \sigma]\!],[\![\Gamma,x \colon \sigma \, ; \tau]\!]} \circ \langle \overline{[\![\Gamma \, ; M]\!]}, [\![\Gamma \, ; N]\!]^+\rangle_{[\![\Gamma \, ; \Pi x \colon \sigma.\tau]\!]^+}$

- $[\![\Gamma \, ; \lambda x \colon \sigma.M^\tau]\!] = \lambda_{[\![\Gamma \, ; \sigma]\!],[\![\Gamma,x \colon \sigma \, ; \tau]\!]}([\![\Gamma, x \colon \sigma \, ; M]\!])$

Notice that the semantics of variables is defined by induction on the depth of their declaration as an appropriate weakening of a v_--expression.

Theorem 3.35 *The interpretation function enjoys the following soundness properties*

- *If* $\Gamma \vdash$ *then* $[\![\Gamma]\!]$ *is an object of* $\mathcal{C}$.
- *If* $\Gamma \vdash \sigma$ *then* $[\![\Gamma\,;\sigma]\!]$ *is an element of* $Ty([\![\Gamma]\!])$.
- *If* $\Gamma \vdash M : \sigma$ *then* $[\![\Gamma\,;M]\!]$ *is an element of* $Tm([\![\Gamma\,;\sigma]\!])$.
- *If* $\vdash \Gamma = \Delta$ *ctxt then* $[\![\Gamma]\!] = [\![\Delta]\!]$.
- *If* $\Gamma \vdash \sigma = \tau$ *type then* $[\![\Gamma\,;\sigma]\!] = [\![\Gamma\,;\tau]\!]$.
- *If* $\Gamma \vdash M = N : \sigma$ *then* $[\![\Gamma\,;M]\!] = [\![\Gamma\,;N]\!]$.

The proof of this theorem, although essentially straightforward, presents surprising technical difficulties. The idea is to first establish a substitution lemma which relates syntactic substitution (and weakening) and semantic substitution $(-\{-\})$. This is necessary because the equations governing semantic type formers such as Π-C are formulated w.r.t. $-\{-\}$, whereas their syntactic counterparts (here Π-C) refer to syntactic substitution which is defined by structural induction. Due to type dependency one needs to account for substitution and weakening in the middle and not merely at the end of a context.

We need some notation first. For pre-contexts Γ, Δ and pre-type ρ we define the expression $\mathbf{P}(\Gamma; \rho; \Delta)$ inductively by

$$\mathbf{P}(\Gamma; \rho; \diamond) = \mathsf{p}([\![\Gamma\,;\rho]\!])$$
$$\mathbf{P}(\Gamma; \rho; \Delta, x{:}\,\sigma) = \mathsf{q}(\mathbf{P}(\Gamma; \rho; \Delta), [\![\Gamma, \Delta\,;\sigma]\!])$$

Now let Γ, Δ, ρ be as before and M be a pre-term. We define the expression inductively by the following clauses.

$$\mathbf{T}(\Gamma; \rho; \diamond; M) = \overline{[\![\Gamma\,;M]\!]}$$
$$\mathbf{T}(\Gamma; \rho; \Delta, x{:}\,\sigma; M) = \mathsf{q}(\mathbf{T}(\Gamma; \rho; \Delta), [\![\Gamma, z{:}\,\rho, \Delta\,;\sigma]\!]) \qquad z \text{ fresh}$$

The idea is that $\mathbf{P}(\Gamma; \rho; \Delta)$ is a morphism from $[\![\Gamma, z{:}\,\rho, \Delta]\!]$ to $[\![\Gamma, \Delta]\!]$ projecting out the ρ-part. Similarly, $\mathbf{T}(\Gamma; \rho; \Delta; M)$ is intended to go from $[\![\Gamma, \Delta[M/z]]\!]$ to $[\![\Gamma, z{:}\,\rho, \Delta]\!]$ yielding $[\![\Gamma\,;M]\!]$ at the $z{:}\,\rho$ position and variables otherwise. But that this is really the case has to be proved simultaneously with the weakening and substitution lemmas.

For possibly undefined expressions s, t we write $s \simeq t$ to mean that if either side is defined then so is the other and both agree (Kleene equality).

Lemma 3.36 (Weakening) *Let* Γ, Δ *be pre-contexts,* ρ, σ *be pre-types,* N *be a pre-term and* z *be a fresh variable. Let* $X \in \{\sigma, N\}$. *The expression* $\mathbf{P}(\Gamma; \rho; \Delta)$ *is defined iff* $[\![\Gamma, z{:}\,\rho, \Delta]\!]$ *and* $[\![\Gamma, \Delta]\!]$ *are defined and in this case is a morphism from the former to the latter. If* $[\![\Gamma, \Delta\,;X]\!]$ *is defined then*

$$[\![\Gamma, z{:}\,\rho, \Delta\,;X]\!] \simeq [\![\Gamma, \Delta\,;X]\!]\{\mathbf{P}(\Gamma; \rho; \Delta)\}$$

Lemma 3.37 (Substitution) *Let* Γ, Δ *be pre-contexts,* ρ, σ *be pre-types,* M, N *be pre-terms, and* z *a fresh variable. Let* $X \in \{\sigma, N\}$ *and suppose that* $[\![\Gamma\,;M]\!]$ *is defined.*

The expression $\mathbf{T}(\Gamma; \rho; \Delta; M)$ *is defined iff* $[\![\Gamma, \Delta[M/z]]\!]$ *and* $[\![\Gamma, z: \rho, \Delta]\!]$ *are both defined and in this case is a morphism from the former to the latter. If* $[\![\Gamma, z: \rho, \Delta\,;X]\!]$ *is defined then*

$$[\![\Gamma, \Delta[M/z]\,;X]\!] \simeq [\![\Gamma, z: \rho, \Delta]\!]\{\mathbf{T}(\Gamma; \rho; \Delta; M)\}$$

The proofs of both lemmas proceed by induction on the lengths of the involved pre-terms,-types, and -contexts. The most difficult case arises when the term N is a variable. One must then make a case distinction on whether it is declared in Γ or in Δ and perform some equational reasoning. The other cases follow by applying stability under substitution of the participating semantic type and term formers such as Π-S. If the type σ or the term N is a binder like $\Pi x\colon \phi.\psi$ the inductive hypothesis must be used with Δ extended by $z\colon \phi$. In order to prove the correct typing of the $\mathbf{P}$ and $\mathbf{T}$ morphisms one uses the second part of each lemma with shortened Δ.

After this introduction we leave the proofs themselves to the reader as following the calculations seems to require as much effort as doing them by oneself.

Given the above two lemmas the proof of the soundness theorem becomes a straightforward induction on derivations. For the same reason as before this proof will not be reproduced here; the reader is instead encouraged to carry out at least a few cases of the inductive argument by himself and in case of serious difficulty consult Streicher's monograph (1991) where the verification of the corresponding interpretation in contextual categories is spelt out in a very detailed fashion.

The method of partially interpreting pre-syntax first and proving definedness by induction on derivations was invented by Streicher (1991) and is used in order to ensure that the interpretation does not depend on the particular derivation chosen. Notice that derivations of a given judgement are not unique as instances of the conversion rules Ty-CONV and TM-CONV are not recorded in judgements. Alternatively, one could define the interpretation by induction on derivations and then use the device of pre-syntax to establish *coherence* of the semantics with respect to the conversion rules, but this would result in a more complicated proof. For a particular model this has been carried out in (Palmgren and Stoltenberg-Hansen 1990).

Exercises

E3.38 Extend the interpretation function to Σ-types

E3.39* Formulate a completeness theorem for the semantics and use the term model to prove it. Deduce from the term model that if $\Gamma \vdash M : \sigma$ and $\Gamma \vdash M : \tau$ then $\Gamma \vdash \sigma = \tau$ *type*.

E3.40   Explain why the interpretation function cannot be defined in the same way as we did in case application is not typed, i.e., with $App_{[x:\sigma]\tau}(M, N)$ replaced by $(M\ N)$. Also explain why it would not matter to leave out the type annotation τ in $\lambda x\!:\!\sigma.M^\tau$ and similar situations.

E3.41   Try to define the interpretation function on triples $\Gamma\ ;\ M\ ;\ \sigma$ of typed terms in context rather than on the pairs $\Gamma\ ;\ M$. What goes wrong?

E3.42*   Extend the interpretation function to syntactic context morphisms and state a general substitution lemma for context morphisms (Pitts 1997). It seems difficult to prove this general substitution lemma directly without using Lemmas 3.36 and 3.37.

E3.43   Deduce from E3.26 and the soundness theorem that the following type is not inhabited in a type theory without universes.

$$\diamond \vdash Id_{\mathbf{N}}(0, Suc(0)) \to \mathbf{0}\ type$$

E3.44   Use the ω-set model to derive that in the Calculus of Constructions with natural numbers there does not exist a term $\diamond \vdash M : Prop \to \mathbf{N}$ and propositions $\diamond \vdash P : Prop$ and $\diamond \vdash Q : Prop$ such that $\diamond \vdash App(M, P) = 0 : \mathbf{N}$ and $\diamond \vdash App(M, Q) = Suc(0) : \mathbf{N}$

E3.45*   Show that the interpretation of existential quantification $\exists x\!:\!\sigma.P$ as defined in E2.8 in the set-theoretic model is **t** if $P(x)$ is **t** for some $x \in [\![\sigma]\!]$ and **ff** otherwise. Conclude that the following extension of the Calculus of Constructions by a choice function is consistent in the sense that neither the empty type (if it exists) nor the type $Prf(\forall c\!:\!Prop.c)$ is inhabited in the empty context:

$$\frac{\Gamma \vdash H : Prf(\exists x\!:\!\sigma.P)}{\Gamma \vdash Choice(H) : \sigma}$$

It is known that such choice function becomes inconsistent if in addition one imposes the equation

$$\vdash Choice(\exists\text{-I}(M, N)) = M : \sigma$$

for all $M\!:\!\sigma$ and $N\!:\!Prf(P[M])$, see (Coquand 1990).

4   Extended example: presheaf models

In this section we encounter a family of interpretations of type theory which generalises the set-theoretic model in that types are interpreted as variable sets (presheaves) or families of such. There are various applications of such interpretations, see for example (Asperti and Martini 1992) and (Altenkirch, Hofmann, and Streicher 1996) where they are used to define models of the polymorphic lambda calculus in which type quantification is interpreted as cartesian product. We use a presheaf interpretation here to show that the Logical Framework in the sense of Section 2.2.2 forms a *conservative extension* of ordinary type theory. This result appears here for the first time; a more detailed version will be published elsewhere.

Preliminaries. Let $\mathcal{K}$ be a (small) category. A *presheaf* over $\mathcal{K}$ is a contravariant functor from $\mathcal{K}$ to the category *Set* of sets and functions. We denote by $\hat{\mathcal{K}}$ the functor category *Set*$^{\mathcal{K}^{op}}$ of presheaves over $\mathcal{K}$. We denote presheaf application by subscripting. That is, if $F \in \hat{\mathcal{K}}$ and $u \in \mathcal{K}(I, J)$ then $F_u : F_J \to F_I$. If $\mu \in \hat{\mathcal{K}}(F, G)$ then $\mu_I : F_I \to G_I$. We may think of $\mathcal{K}$ as a category of *stages* or *worlds* and of a presheaf as a set varying with these stages. The *Yoneda embedding* $y : \mathcal{K} \to \hat{\mathcal{K}}$ sending I to $\mathcal{K}(-, I)$ is a full and faithful embedding of the stages into $\hat{\mathcal{K}}$. See (Barr and Wells 1990) for more information on presheaves.

4.1   Presheaves as a CwF

Our aim is to construct a CwF which has $\hat{\mathcal{K}}$ as the category of contexts. This category has a terminal object given by $\top_I = \{\star\}$. We define types, substitution, terms, and comprehension in order. From now on we will use the generic letters $\Gamma, f, \sigma, \ldots$ to range over presheaves, natural transformations, families of presheaves, etc. if these arise in the context of a CwF.

If Γ is a presheaf then we form its *category of elements* $\int(\Gamma)$ with objects (I, γ) where $I \in \mathcal{K}$ and $\gamma \in \Gamma_I$. A morphism from (J, γ') to (I, γ) is a $\mathcal{K}$-morphism $u \in \mathcal{K}(J, I)$ such that $\Gamma_u(\gamma) = \gamma'$. In other words, if $u \in \mathcal{K}(J, I)$ and $\gamma \in \Gamma_I$ then u is an $\int(\Gamma)$-morphism from $(J, \Gamma_u(\gamma))$ to (I, γ). If appropriate we may also write (u, γ) for this morphism. Composition is inherited from $\mathcal{K}$.

For presheaf $\Gamma \in \hat{\mathcal{K}}$ we define the set $Ty(\Gamma)$ to consist of the presheaves over $\int(\Gamma)$. If $\sigma \in Ty(\Gamma)$ and $(I, \gamma) \in \int(\Gamma)$ then we write $\sigma_I(\gamma)$ rather than $\sigma_{(I,\gamma)}$ for σ at argument (I, γ) and similarly for morphisms. That σ is a presheaf means that if $u \in \mathcal{K}(J, I)$ and $\gamma \in \Gamma_I$ and $x \in \sigma_I(\gamma)$ then $\sigma_u(\gamma)(x) \in \sigma_J(\Gamma_u(\gamma))$ and this action is compatible with composition and identities in $\mathcal{K}$.

Now suppose that $f : \Delta \to \Gamma$ is a natural transformation. We define a functor $\int(f) : \int(\Delta) \to \int(\Gamma)$ by $\int(f)(I, \delta) = (I, f_I(\delta))$ and for $u \in \mathcal{K}(J, I)$, $\delta \in \Delta_I$ we define $\int(f)(u, \delta) = (u, f_I(\delta))$. Now if $\sigma \in Ty(\Gamma)$ is a family of presheaves then we define $\sigma\{f\} \in Ty(\Delta)$ as the composition $\sigma \circ \int(f)$. So, we have $\sigma\{f\}_I(\delta) = \sigma_I(f_I(\delta))$. It is clear that this has the required functoriality properties.

Next we define terms. If $\sigma \in Ty(\Gamma)$ then an element M of $Tm(\sigma)$ assigns to each stage I and element $\gamma \in \Gamma_I$ an element $M_I(\gamma) \in \sigma_I(\gamma)$ in such a way that if $u \in \mathcal{K}(J, I)$ then $\sigma_u(\gamma)(M_I(\gamma)) = M_J(\Gamma_u(\gamma))$. If $M \in Tm(\sigma)$ and $f : \Delta \to \Gamma$ then $M\{f\} \in Tm(\sigma\{f\})$ is given by composition as $M\{f\}_I(\delta) = M_I(f_I(\delta))$.

If $\sigma \in Ty(\Gamma)$ then the presheaf $\Gamma.\sigma$ is defined by $(\Gamma.\sigma)_I = \{(\gamma, x) \mid \gamma \in \Gamma_I, x \in \sigma_I(\gamma)\}$. If $u \in \mathcal{K}(J, I)$ and $(\gamma, x) \in (\Gamma.\sigma)_I$ then $(\Gamma.\sigma)_u(\gamma, x) = (\Gamma_u(\gamma), \sigma_u(\gamma)(x))$. The projection $\mathsf{p}(\sigma)$ is defined by $\mathsf{p}(\sigma)_I(\gamma, x) = \gamma$; the variable $\mathsf{v}_\sigma \in Tm(\sigma\{\mathsf{p}(\sigma)\})$ is defined by $(\mathsf{v}_\sigma)_I(\gamma, x) = x$. Finally, if $f : \Delta \to \Gamma$ and $M \in Tm(\sigma\{f\})$ then $(\langle f, M \rangle_\sigma)_I(\delta) = (f_I(\delta), M_I(\delta))$. The verifications are straightforward expansions of the definitions. We have thus established that presheaves over $\mathcal{K}$ furnish a CwF.

4.2 Type formers in $\hat{\mathcal{K}}$

The presheaf model supports most of the type formers the set-theoretic model supports, often by the very same constructions. The major difference is the interpretation of Π-types which is carried out in a way similar to the treatment of implication in Kripke models, and of course similar to the definition of exponentiation in functor categories.. Suppose that $\sigma \in Ty(\Gamma)$ and $\tau \in Ty(\Gamma.\sigma)$. Following the convention from Section 2.2.2 we will write $(\sigma)\tau$ rather than $\Pi(\sigma, \tau)$ for the dependent function space of σ and τ. It is defined as follows. If $I \in \mathcal{K}$ and $\gamma \in \Gamma_I$ then an element f of $(\sigma)\tau_I(\gamma)$ associates to $J \in \mathcal{K}$ and $w : J \to I$ and $x \in \sigma_J(\Gamma_w(\gamma))$ an element $f(w, x) \in \tau_J(\Gamma_w(\gamma), \sigma_w(\gamma)(x))$. Notice that $w \in \int(\Gamma)((J, \Gamma_w(\gamma)), (I, \gamma))$ and thus $\sigma_w(\gamma)(x) \in \sigma_I(\Gamma_w(\gamma))$. Moreover the assignment f must be natural in the sense that if in addition $w' : J' \to J$ then

$$f(w \circ w', \sigma_{w'}(\Gamma_w(\gamma))(x)) = \tau_{w'}(\Gamma_w(\gamma), \sigma_w(\gamma)(x))(f(w, x))$$

The generalisation to "later stages" J is necessary to make $(\sigma)\tau$ a presheaf and not merely an assignment of sets to stages. Indeed, if $v : I' \to I$ and $f \in (\sigma)\tau_I(\gamma)$ then we can define $(\sigma)\tau_v(\Gamma_v(\gamma))(f) \in (\sigma)\tau_{I'}(\Gamma_v(\gamma))$ by

$$(\sigma)\tau_v(\Gamma_v(\gamma))(f)(w : J \to I', x \in \sigma_J(\Gamma_w(\Gamma_v(\gamma)))) \stackrel{\text{def}}{=} f(v \circ w, x)$$

which is valid because $\Gamma_w(\Gamma_v(\gamma)) = \Gamma_{v \circ w}(\gamma)$.

If $M \in Tm(\Gamma.\sigma, \tau)$ then $\lambda_{\sigma, \tau}(M) \in Tm((\sigma)\tau)$ is given by

$$\lambda(M)_I(\gamma \in \Gamma_I, J \in \mathcal{K}, w : J \to I, x \in \sigma_J(\Gamma_w(\gamma))) \stackrel{\text{def}}{=} M_J(\Gamma_w(\gamma), x)$$

The application morphism $App_{\sigma, \tau} : \Gamma.\sigma.(\sigma)\tau^+ \to \Gamma.\sigma.\tau$ maps at stage I elements $\gamma \in \Gamma_I$ and $x \in \sigma_I(\gamma)$ and $f \in (\sigma)\tau_I(\gamma)$ to $f(id_I, x) \in \tau_I(\gamma, x)$. It is routine to check that this defines dependent function spaces in the strict sense.

The dependent sum $\Sigma(\sigma, \tau)$ of the presheaves above is given by stage-wise set-theoretic dependent sum. This means that

$$\Sigma(\sigma, \tau)_I(\gamma) = \{(x, y) \mid x \in \sigma_I(\gamma) \wedge y \in \tau_I(\gamma, x)\}$$

We omit the associated term formers. We remark without proof that $\hat{\mathcal{K}}$ supports natural numbers and other inductive types; it also supports universes if the ambient set theory w.r.t. which the presheaves are formed supports them.

4.3   Conservativity of the logical framework

Let $\mathcal{T}$ be a theory of dependent types like one of those set out in Section 2. The precise nature of $\mathcal{T}$ is unimportant.

Furthermore, we let $\mathcal{T}_{LF}$ denote the Logical Framework presentation of $\mathcal{T}$, i.e., a dependent type theory with Π-types and one universe Set together with constants and equations corresponding to the type and term formers in $\mathcal{T}$. We have a conversion map i translating terms, types, and judgements in $\mathcal{T}$ into ones in $\mathcal{T}_{LF}$ in such a way that judgements are preserved. More precisely, if $\Gamma \vdash \mathcal{J}$ in $\mathcal{T}$ then $\mathrm{i}(\Gamma) \vdash \mathrm{i}(\mathcal{J})$ in $\mathcal{T}_{LF}$. For distinction, we write $\vdash_{\mathcal{T}}$ and $\vdash_{\mathcal{T}_{LF}}$ for the judgement relations in the two type theories. For example, in $\mathcal{T}$ we might have

$$x\colon \mathrm{N} \vdash_{\mathcal{T}} \Pi y\colon \mathrm{N}.Id(x,y) \to Id(y,x) \ \textit{type}$$

Applying the translation yields the following judgement in $\mathcal{T}_{LF}$:

$$x\colon El(\hat{\mathrm{N}}) \vdash_{\mathcal{T}_{LF}} El(\hat{\Pi} y\colon El(\hat{\mathrm{N}}).\hat{Id}(x,y) \hat{\to} \hat{Id}(y,x)) \ \textit{type}$$

In other words, $\mathrm{i}(\mathrm{N}) = El(\hat{\mathrm{N}})$, etc. If we omit the El-operator and the $\hat{-}$-decorations then the translated judgement looks exactly like the one to start with. We will do so in the sequel and omit the coercion i.

Due to the presence of type variables $\mathcal{T}_{LF}$ is a proper extension of $\mathcal{T}$. Judgements like $\vdash$ Set $type$ or $F\colon \mathrm{N} \to Set \vdash F(0)$ are not in the image of i. A natural question to ask is whether $\mathcal{T}_{LF}$ is $conservative$ over $\mathcal{T}$. There is more than one way to extend the notion of conservativity from logic to theories of dependent types. We will here use the simplest one and prove the following theorem:

Theorem 4.1 *If* $\Gamma \vdash_{\mathcal{T}} \sigma$ *type and* $\Gamma \vdash_{\mathcal{T}_{LF}} M : \sigma$ *for some term* M *then there exists a term* M' *such that* $\Gamma \vdash_{\mathcal{T}} M' : \sigma$.

Notice that M itself need not be a legal $\mathcal{T}$-term, it could for instance contain a subterm like $([X\colon Set]Suc(0))(\mathrm{N})$ which is equal, but not identical to $Suc(0)$.

Our strategy for proving this theorem consists of exhibiting a model of $\mathcal{T}_{LF}$ with the property that the interpretation of $\mathcal{T}$ in it (notice that such a model also models $\mathcal{T}$) is full. That is to say, if $Tm([\![\Gamma\, ; \sigma]\!]) \neq \emptyset$ for some $\Gamma \vdash_{\mathcal{T}} \sigma$ $type$ then there exists M with $\Gamma \vdash_{\mathcal{T}} M : \sigma$. Such a model is furnished by the presheaf model $\hat{\mathcal{T}}$ where $\mathcal{T}$ is the (category of contexts of the) term model of $\mathcal{T}$. The fullness of the interpretation of $\mathcal{T}$ in $\hat{\mathcal{T}}$ is essentially a consequence of the Yoneda lemma and will be proved at the end of this section.

Let us first show how $\hat{\mathcal{T}}$ models the Logical Framework. We have already demonstrated that $\hat{\mathcal{T}}$ (like every presheaf model) supports dependent function spaces. We interpret $Set \in Ty_{\hat{\mathcal{T}}}(\top) \cong \hat{\mathcal{T}}$ as the presheaf $Ty_{\mathcal{T}}$ which to a context $\Gamma \in \mathcal{T}$ associates the $\mathcal{T}$-types in context Γ quotiented by definitional equality. The interpretation of $El \in Ty_{\hat{\mathcal{T}}}(\top.Set) \equiv \widehat{\int(Set)}$ is defined as the presheaf $Tm_{\mathcal{T}}$ which to $\Gamma \in |\mathcal{T}|$ and $\sigma \in Ty_{\mathcal{T}}(\Gamma) = Set_{\Gamma}$ associates the set $Tm_{\mathcal{T}}(\Gamma, \sigma)$ of terms of type σ in context Γ factored by definitional equality. This extends to a presheaf by term substitution.

For the demonstration that $\hat{\mathcal{T}}$ models $\mathcal{T}_{LF}$ it remains to show that Set contains codes for all the type and term formers present in $\mathcal{T}$. We will deal with this task by way of example and assume that $\mathcal{T}$ contains Π-types and the (ad hoc) operator $\mathbf{L}$ from Section 2.2.2.

We deal with the $\mathbf{L}$-operator first. In order to simplify the notation and in view of the soundness and completeness of the semantics we will use the syntax of type theory with named variables to denote entities in $\hat{\mathcal{T}}$. Thus we require an element $\hat{\mathbf{L}} \in Tm(\top, (Set)Set)$ and an element $\hat{\mathbf{l}} \in Tm(\top, (\sigma: Set, m: El(\sigma))El(\mathbf{L}(\sigma)))$. Since the dependent function spaces in $\hat{\mathcal{T}}$ are strict the first task is equivalent to exhibiting an element, for simplicity also denoted $\hat{\mathbf{L}}$, of $Tm_{\hat{\mathcal{T}}}(\sigma: Set, Set)$ which we describe explicitly by

$$\hat{\mathbf{L}}_\Gamma(\sigma \in Ty_{\mathcal{T}}(\Gamma)) \stackrel{\text{def}}{=} \mathbf{L}(\sigma)$$

Recall that $Set_\Gamma = Ty_{\mathcal{T}}(\Gamma)$. The naturality of this assignment amounts to checking that for $f : B \to \Gamma$ and $\sigma \in Ty_{\mathcal{T}}(\Gamma)$ we have $\mathbf{L}(\sigma)[f] = \mathbf{L}(\sigma[f])$ which is immediate from the properties of syntactic substitution.

Similarly, the second task is equivalent to finding a term

$$\hat{\mathbf{l}} \in Tm_{\hat{\mathcal{T}}}(\sigma: Set, M: El(\sigma), El(\hat{\mathbf{L}}(\sigma)))$$

Again, we define it explicitly by

$$\hat{\mathbf{l}}_\Gamma(\sigma \in Ty_{\mathcal{T}}(\Gamma), M \in Tm_{\mathcal{T}}(\Gamma, \sigma)) = \mathbf{l}(M) \in Tm_{\mathcal{T}}(\Gamma, \sigma)$$

Recall here that $El_\Gamma(\sigma) = Tm_{\mathcal{T}}(\Gamma, \sigma)$. Naturality is again a consequence of stability under substitution. Notice that up to the necessary abstraction e.g. from $Tm(\sigma: Set, Set)$ to $Tm((Set)Set)$ the required constants in $\hat{\mathcal{K}}$ are given exactly by their counterparts in $\mathcal{T}$.

In essence, this is also the case for the Π-type, but due to the binding behaviour we encounter a slight complication. We wish to construct an element of

$$Tm_{\hat{\mathcal{T}}}(\top, (\sigma: Set, \tau: (El(\sigma))Set)Set)$$

By "uncurrying" this amounts to constructing a term $\hat{\Pi}$ of

$$Tm_{\hat{\mathcal{T}}}(\sigma: Set, \tau: (El(\sigma))Set, Set)$$

At stage Γ the arguments to $\hat{\Pi}$ are a type $\sigma \in Ty_{\mathcal{T}}(\Gamma)$ and an element of $(El(\sigma))Set_\Gamma$. Call the latter set X temporarily. An element τ of X associates by definition of dependent function spaces in $\hat{\mathcal{K}}$ to $f : B \to \Gamma$ and $M \in Tm_{\mathcal{T}}(B, \sigma\{f\})$ a type $\tau(B, f, M) \in Ty(B)$. This assignment is natural in the sense that for $f' : B' \to B$ we have $\tau(B', f \circ f', M\{f'\}) = \tau(B, f, M)\{f'\} \in Ty(B')$.

But this means that the whole of τ can be reconstructed from its particular instance $\tau_0 \overset{\text{def}}{=} \tau(\Gamma.\sigma, \mathsf{p}(\sigma), \mathsf{v}_\sigma) \in Ty(\Gamma.\sigma)$. Indeed, for arbitrary $f : B \to \Gamma$ and $M \in Ty(\sigma\{f\})$ we have that $\tau(B, f, M) = \tau_0\{\langle f, M \rangle_\sigma\}$ by naturality and equations *(Cons-L)* and *(Cons-R)*. By *(Cons-Id)* we also get the converse and have thus established a bijective correspondence between the sets $(El(\sigma))Set_\Gamma$ and $Ty_\mathcal{T}(\Gamma.\sigma = Set_{\Gamma.\sigma}$. Therefore, the arguments at stage Γ to the term $\hat{\Pi}$ which we aim to construct amount to a type $\sigma \in Ty(\Gamma)$ and a type $\tau_0 \in Ty(\Gamma.\sigma)$. We define the result as the syntactic dependent function space $\Pi(\sigma, \tau_0)$ in $\mathcal{T}$. Summing up, we have defined

$$\Pi_\Gamma(\sigma \in Set_\Gamma, \tau \in (El(\sigma))Set) = \Pi_\mathcal{T}(\sigma, \tau(\Gamma.\sigma, \mathsf{p}(\sigma), \mathsf{v}_\sigma))$$

So up to the bijection between the function space $(El(\sigma))Set_\Gamma$ and the set of types in $\Gamma.\sigma$ the Π-constant in $\mathcal{T}_{LF}$ has again been obtained directly from its syntactic companion. The same goes for the other constants $\hat{\lambda}$ and $\hat{App}$ whose definition we omit. In the case of $\hat{\lambda}$ we face again an argument of the dependent function space type $(x{:}\,El(\sigma))El(\tau)$ which at stage Γ is isomorphic to $Tm_\mathcal{T}(\Gamma.\sigma, \tau)$ by an analysis similar to the one which led to the characterisation of $(El(\sigma))Set$ before.

One can more generally characterise the dependent function spaces of the form $(El(-))F$ for arbitrary presheaf F as certain "shifts" of F. This allows for a systematic translation of arbitrary type and term formers possibly binding variables from $\mathcal{T}$ to $\mathcal{T}_{LF}$. The general strategy should have become clear from the example of Π. The important point is that in $\hat{\mathcal{K}}$ the function space $(El(\sigma))Set$ is so strongly confined by the naturality condition that it only contains functions induced by a syntactic type with free variable of type σ.

Proof of Thm. 4.1 Suppose that $\Gamma \vdash_\mathcal{T} \sigma$ *type* and that $\Gamma \vdash_{\mathcal{T}_{LF}} M : \sigma$. By induction on derivations we find that the interpretations of Γ and σ in $\hat{\mathcal{T}}$ have the following properties:

$$[\![\Gamma]\!]_\Delta \cong \mathcal{T}(\Delta, \Gamma)$$

and

$$[\![\Gamma ; \sigma]\!]_\Delta (f \in \mathcal{T}(\Delta, \Gamma)) = \sigma[f] \in Set_\Delta$$

Thus, in particular, we have $[\![\Gamma ; \sigma]\!]_\Gamma (id_\Gamma) = \sigma$. Therefore, the interpretation of M in $\hat{\mathcal{T}}$ yields $[\![\Gamma ; M]\!]_\Gamma (id_\Gamma) \in Tm_\mathcal{T}(\Gamma, \sigma)$; thus $\Gamma \vdash_\mathcal{T} M' : \sigma$ for any representative M' in the class $[\![\Gamma ; M]\!]$. The theorem is proved. $\qquad\square$

One may consider a Logical Framework which does not only support Π-types, but several other type formers like Σ-types, e.g. for modularisation and natural numbers, e.g. to define syntax. As long as these type formers are supported by $\hat{\mathcal{T}}$ (Σ and $\mathbf{N}$ are) the conservativity theorem continues to hold by the same proof. Using a dependent version of the *gluing construction* (Crole 1993) it is possible to obtain the stronger property that the term M' in Thm. 4.1 is $\mathcal{T}_{LF}$-equal to M.

We also remark that we have not used any particular properties of the term model in the construction of the presheaf model so that it can be formed out of any CwF and thus gives a canonical way to lift a model of some type theory to a model for the presentation of this type theory in the Logical Framework.

5 Other applications of semantic methods

We give some directions for further reading on the subject of semantical methods in the study of theories of dependent types. Independence results are the subject of (Streicher 1992) and (Hofmann and Streicher 1994). Semantical methods in order to derive syntactic properties of type theories like strong normalisation and thus decidability of type checking have been used in (Hyland and Ong 1993; Altenkirch 1994; Goguen 1995). In (Moggi 1991) and (Harper, Mitchell, and Moggi 1990) categories with attributes are used to give an account of higher-order modules in functional programming. There is an intriguing connection with Paulin's work on program extraction in type theory (Paulin-Mohring 1989) and the "deliverables" approach to program development (Burstall and McKinna 1993). In each of these works a type is modelled as a type or a set together with a predicate or a dependent type and terms are modelled as terms which preserve these predicates. A similar interpretation has been used in (Hofmann 1995a) where a translation of a type theory with a quotient type former into ordinary type theory and other applications of syntactic models are described.

Connections between category-theoretic semantics and abstract machines have been noticed in (Curien 1986) and (Ehrhard 1988) and were subsequently exploited and applied in (Ritter 1992) where an evaluator for the Calculus of Constructions is derived from its category-theoretic semantics.

Last, but not least we mention the use of domain-theoretic interpretations of type theory in order to establish the consistency of general recursion and fixpoint combinators with dependent types (Palmgren and Stoltenberg-Hansen 1990). In a similar direction goes (Reus 1995) where an interpretation of type theory using *synthetic domain theory* has been employed to establish the consistency of a very powerful dependent type theory incorporating higher-order logic, general recursion, and impredicativity.

References

Allen, S. (1987). A non-type-theoretic account of Martin-Löf's types. In *Symposium on Logic in Computer Science*.

Altenkirch, T. (1994). Proving strong normalization of CC by modifying realizability semantics. In H. Barendregt and T. Nipkow (Eds.), *Types for Proofs and Programs, Springer LNCS Vol. 806*, pp. 3–18.

Altenkirch, T., M. Hofmann, and T. Streicher (1996). Reduction-free normalisation for a polymorphic system. In *Proc. of the 11th IEEE Symp. on Logic in Comp. Sci. (LICS), New Brunswick, New Jersey*.

Asperti, A. and S. Martini (1992). Categorical models of polymorphism. *Information and Computation 99*, 1–79.

Barr, M. and C. Wells (1990). *Category Theory for Computing Science*. International Series in Computer Science. Prentice Hall.

Beeson, M. (1985). *Foundations of Constructive Mathematics*. Springer.

Burstall, R. and J. McKinna (1993). Deliverables: An approach to program semantics in constructions. In *Proc. MFCS '93, Springer LNCS, Vol. 711*. Also as LFCS technical report ECS-LFCS-91-133.

Cartmell, J. (1978). *Generalized Algebraic Theories and Contextual Categories*. Ph. D. thesis, Univ. Oxford.

Constable, R. et al. (1986). *Implementing Mathematics with the Nuprl Development System*. Prentice-Hall.

Coquand, T. (1990). Metamathematical investigations of a calculus of constructions. In P. Odifreddi (Ed.), *Logic and Computer Science*, pp. 91–118. Academic Press Ltd.

Coquand, T. and G. Huet (1988). The Calculus of Constructions. *Information and Computation 76*, 95–120.

Coquand, T. and C. Paulin-Mohring (1989). Inductively defined types. In *LNCS 389*. Springer.

Crole, R. (1993). *Categories for Types*. Cambridge University Press.

Curien, P.-L. (1986). *Categorical Combinators, Sequential Algorithms and Functional Programming*. Pitman.

Curien, P.-L. (1989). Alpha-conversion, conditions on variables and categorical logic. *Studia Logica 3*, 318–360.

Curien, P.-L. (1993). Substitution up to isomorphism. *Fundamenta Informaticae 19*, 51–86.

Dowek, G. et al. (1991, Dec.). The COQ proof assistant user's guide, V5.6. Rapport technique 134, INRIA Rocquencourt.

Dybjer, P. (1996). Internal type theory. In *Proc. BRA TYPES workshop, Torino, June 1995, Springer LNCS*. To appear.

Ehrhard, T. (1988). *Une sémantique catégorique des types dépendants. Application au Calcul des Constructions*. Ph. D. thesis, Univ. Paris VII.

Ehrhard, T. (1989). Dictoses. In *Proc. Conf. Category Theory and Computer Science, Manchester, UK*, pp. 213–223. Springer LNCS Vol. 389.

Goguen, H. (1995). Typed operational semantics. In *Proc. TLCA '95, Edinburgh, Springer LNCS Vol. 902*.

Harper, R., F. Honsell, and G. Plotkin (1993, January). A framework for defining logics. *Journal of the ACM 40*(1), 143–184.

Harper, R. and J. C. Mitchell (1993). On the type structure of Standard ML. *ACM Trans. Programming Lang. and Systems 15*(2), 211–252.

Harper, R., J. C. Mitchell, and E. Moggi (1990). Higher-order modules and the phase distinction. In *Conference record of the 17th ACM Symposium on Principles of Programming Languages (POPL)*, San Francisco, CA USA, pp. 341–354.

Hofmann, M. (1995a). *Extensional Concepts in Intensional Type Theory*. PhD thesis, Univ. of Edinburgh.

Hofmann, M. (1995b). On the interpretation of type theory in locally cartesian closed categories. In J. Tiuryn and L. Pacholski (Eds.), *Proc. CSL '94, Kazimierz, Poland, Springer LNCS, Vol. 933*, pp. 427–442.

Hofmann, M. (1996). Conservativity of equality reflection over intensional type theory. In *Proc. BRA TYPES workshop, Torino, June 1995, Springer LNCS*. To appear.

Hofmann, M. and T. Streicher (1994). A groupoid model refutes uniqueness of identity proofs. In *Proceedings of the 9th Symposium on Logic in Computer Science (LICS), Paris*.

Huet, G. (1990). A uniform approach to type theory. In *Logical Foundations of Functional Programming*. Addison-Wesley.

Hyland, J. M. E. and C.-H. L. Ong (1993). Modified realisability toposes and strong normalisation proofs. In J. F. Groote and M. Bezem (Eds.), *Typed Lambda Calculi and Applications, Springer LNCS, Vol. 664*.

Hyland, M. and A. Pitts (1989). The Theory of Constructions: Categorical Semantics and Topos-Theoretic Models. In *Categories in Computer Science and Logic*. AMS.

Jacobs, B. (1991). *Categorical Type Theory*. Ph. D. thesis, University of Nijmegen.

Jacobs, B. (1993). Comprehension categories and the semantics of type theory. *Theoretical Computer Science 107*, 169–207.

Lamarche, F. (1987). A simple model for the theory of constructions. In J. W. Gray and A. Scedrov (Eds.), *Proc. of AMS Research Conf., Boulder, Colorado*, pp. 137–199. AMS.

Lambek, J. and P. Scott (1985). *Introduction to Higher-Order Categorical Logic*. Cambridge University Press.

Luo, Z. (1991). Program specification and data refinement in type theory. In S. Abramsky and T. S. E. Maibaum (Eds.), *Proc. TAPSOFT '91, Springer LNCS, Vol. 493*, pp. 142–168.

Luo, Z. (1994). *Computation and Reasoning*. Oxford University Press.

Luo, Z. and R. Pollack (1992). LEGO Proof Development System: User's Manual. Technical Report ECS-LFCS-92-211, University of Edinburgh.

Magnusson, L. and B. Nordström (1994). The ALF proof editor and its proof engine. In H. Barendregt and T. Nipkow (Eds.), *Types for Proofs and Programs, Springer LNCS Vol. 806*, pp. 213–237. Springer-Verlag.

Martin-Löf, P. (1975). An intuitionistic theory of types: Predicative part. In H. E. Rose and J. C. Sheperdson (Eds.), *Logic Colloquium 1973*, pp. 73–118. North-Holland.

Martin-Löf, P. (1982). Constructive mathematics and computer programming. In *Proceedings of the Sixth International Congress for Logic, Methodology and Philosophy of Science*, pp. 153–175.

Martin-Löf, P. (1984). *Intuitionistic Type Theory*. Bibliopolis·Napoli.

Moggi, E. (1991). A category-theoretic account of program modules. *Math. Struct. in Comp. Sci. 1*(1), 103–139.

Nordström, B., K. Petersson, and J. M. Smith (1990). *Programming in Martin-Löf's Type Theory, An Introduction*. Clarendon Press, Oxford.

Obtułowicz, A. (1989). Categorical and algebraic aspects of Martin-Löf type theory. *Studia Logica 3*, 299–317.

Palmgren, E. and V. Stoltenberg-Hansen (1990). Domain interpretation of Martin-Löf's partial type theory. *Ann. of Pure and Appl. Logic 48*, 135–196.

Paulin-Mohring, C. (1989). Extracting F_ω's programs from proofs in the calculus of constructions. In *Principles of Programming Languages (POPL)*, pp. 1–17. ACM.

Pitts, A. (1997). Categorical logic. In *Handbook of Logic in Computer Science (Vol. VI)*. Oxford University Press. To appear.

Reus, B. (1995). *Program verification in Synthetic Domain Theory*. Ph. D. thesis, LMU, München.

Reynolds, J. C. and G. D. Plotkin (1988, May). On functors expressible in the polymorphic typed lambda calculus. Technical Report ECS-LFCS-88-53, University of Edinburgh.

Ritter, E. (1992). *Categorical Abstract Machines for Higher-Order Typed Lambda Calculi*. Ph. D. thesis, University of Cambridge.

Seely, R. A. G. (1984). Locally cartesian closed categories and type theory. *Mathematical Proceedings of the Cambridge Philosophical Society 95*, 33–48.

Smith, J. (1988). The independence of Peano's fourth axiom from Martin-Löf's type theory without universes. *Journal of Symbolic Logic 53*(3).

Streicher, T. (1991). *Semantics of Type Theory*. Birkhäuser.

Streicher, T. (1992). Dependence and independence results for (impredicative) calculi of dependent types. *Math. Struct. Comp. Sci. 2*, 29–54.

Streicher, T. (1993). *Semantical Investigations into Intensional Type Theory*. Habilitationsschrift, LMU München.

Taylor, P. (1986). *Recursive Domains, Indexed Category Theory, and Polymorphism*. Ph. D. thesis, University of Cambridge.

Troelstra, A. and D. van Dalen (1988). *Constructivism in Mathematics, An Introduction*, Volume I. North-Holland.

Game Semantics

Martin Hyland

Contents

1 Introduction

The aim of these notes is to explain how games can provide an intensional semantics for functional programming languages, and for a theory of proofs. From the point of view of program semantics, the rough idea is that we can move from modelling computable functions (which give the 'extensional' behaviour of programs) to modelling 'intensional' aspects of the algorithms themselves. In proof theory, the tradition has been to consider syntactic representations of (what are presumably intended to be 'intensional') proofs; so the idea is to give a more intrinsic account of a notion of proof.

Three main sections follow this Introduction. Section 2 deals with games and partial strategies; it includes a discussion of the application of these ideas to the modelling of algorithms. Section 3 is about games and total strategies; it runs parallel to the treatment in Section 2, and is quite compressed. Section 4 gives no more than an outline of more sophisticated notions of game, and discusses them as models for proofs. Exercises are scattered through the text.

I very much hope that the broad outline of these notes will be comprehensible on the basis of little beyond an understanding of sequences (lists) and trees. However the statements of some results and some of the exercises presuppose a little knowledge of category theory, of domain theory and of linear logic. The main categorical ideas used in the notes are explained in Appendix A. I have tried to give references for other background information. I ask those unfamiliar with category theory not to be put off by the fact that occasionally category theoretic language is used to give succinct expression to a collection of (hopefully plausible) phenomena.

The ideas of games and strategies are very intuitive, indeed that is a strong point in favour of their use as a basis for semantics. The disadvantage of course is that compelling intuitions can be misleading. There may well be mistakes in this account, and a critical attitude is recommended.

1.1 Precursors

The well-established denotational semantics for (functional) programming languages, which makes use of domain theory, is a theory of functions in extension: the interpretation of programs is via certain 'extensional' functions which they may be regarded as computing. This point of view is already apparent in classical recursion theory: the notion of partial recursive functions is independent of any specific machine, but the notion of effective algorithm is apparently machine-dependent. It would be reasonable to conclude that the notion of algorithm is inevitably machine-dependent (or language-dependent or syntax-dependent). Hence the very idea of modelling algorithms naturally in some sufficiently abstract way is a brave one. The pioneers in this endeavour were Kahn and Plotkin (1978) (in English, Kahn and Plotkin (1993)) and Berry and Curien (1982). A succinct account of the main ideas[1] in the tradition of concrete data structures is given in Curien (1993).

A game theoretic approach to proof (or at least to provability) was suggested by Lorenzen (Lorenzen and Lorenz 1978). His ideas have been developed and made precise by a number of people, and form the basis for a distinctive tradition in philosophical logic. For a good survey of work in this area, see Felscher (1986).

Structured (or compositional) approaches to games and strategies trace their origins back to work of Blass (1972) and Conway (1976), though neither were motivated by semantical questions. Joyal gave a compositional account of Conway's work, defining a compact closed category of games. (For an introduction to compact closed categories see Kelly and Laplaza (1980).) Joyal's observation inspired me to think of games in connection with program semantics; but we still have no good understanding of (or applications of) the category of Conway games, and it will not play a role in these notes. Blass himself drew attention to the semantic possibilities of his ideas (Blass 1992). For a compositional approach see Abramsky and Jagadeesan (1994).

1.2 Categories of Games: Ideas

1.2.1 The protagonists

The games we consider involve two players, P (Player, $\exists$loise, Left, Us) and O (Opponent, $\forall$belard, Right, Them) who play moves alternately. I adopt the uncontentious nomenclature: Player vs Opponent. As the contrast between the

---

[1] Similar ideas were developed by Kleene in a series of papers; Gandy modified Kleene's ideas to the continuous case, and he together with his student Pani have recently obtained a number of interesting partial results which have yet to be published.

respective pairs of names suggests, it is a crucial feature of (the use of) our intuition about games that our attitude to the two participants should be quite different: we favour Player (Us, Left) over Opponent (Them, Right). Some aspects of this preference may be indicated by the following series of dichotomies[2].

Player	Opponent
Strategy	Counterstrategy
Actor	Environment
Programmer	Computer
Operating system	Users
Program	Data
Proof	Refutation
Event	Cell
Output	Input

It is worth stressing that the conceptual tools described here are not intended to deal with interaction between many agents, as considered for example in concurrency theory. There is no obvious generalisation of the theory of two-person games considered here to many-person games.

1.2.2 Perspective of categorical logic

From the point of view of categorical logic, the important aspect is compositionality. Hence our preference for Player and for things on the left. We wish to compose programs and proofs; or in alternative jargon we desire modular tools of program or proof construction. It will turn out that it is Player's strategies for games which we shall be able to compose in an appropriate way, and hence we focus on Player's role. What we shall do is in the mainstream tradition of the categorical interpretation of types theories and of proof systems, and I indicate the connections in the following table:

Object	Map	Categorical Composition
Type	Term	Application in context
Proposition	Proof	Composition via Cut rule
Type	Algorithm	Composition plus hiding
Game	Strategy	Scratchpad Composition

This table incorporates within it both the Curry-Howard isomorphism and basic ideas of categorical logic (here proof theory). Good general background in categorical logic can be found in Lambek and Scott (1986). For a view of categorical type theory see Crole (1993).

---

[2]Do not get carried away by duality! There are similar seeming dichotomies which it is as well not to put in this list, as they can be used to refer to aspects of games which are independent of the dichotomy Player vs Opponent. Examples are: Question vs Answer, Active vs Passive, Positive vs Negative. Questions and Answers play a substantial role in Section 4.

1.3 Fundamental structures

1.3.1 Simple games

In this introductory survey, we write G, H for the kinds of two-person games in which we are interested. It is a consequence of our interest in composition that in standard play, O starts the play. In the simplest form, the game will be completely determined by the succession of moves with O playing first. I call such games *simple*; they are called *negative* in Abramsky and Jagadeesan (1994).

There is something like a natural duality for games: one interchanges the roles of the two players. Of course the dual of a simple game is not a simple game since P has to start: indeed it is best not to regard it as a game, but rather as a 'co-game'. We write $G^{\perp}$ for the dual of the game G.[3]

1.3.2 Playing games in parallel

In the cases we are interested in, there are the following two operations on games, each involving interleaved plays from the two component games:

Tensor product $G \otimes H$: in this game, G and H are played in parallel. For simple G and H, it will automatically happen that P can only move in the game in which O has just played; however O is allowed to switch games. There is usually a unit I for the tensor product, namely the 'empty game' in which no player can move.

Linear maps $G \multimap H$: in this game the dual $G^{\perp}$ of G is played in parallel with H. For simple games G and H, it will automatically happen that O must start in H; P can play in either $G^{\perp}$ or H, and thereafter P is allowed to switch games; on the other hand O can only now move in the game in which P has just moved.

Note that the switching behaviour in $G \multimap H$ is dual to that in $G \otimes H$. This reflects the duality between *tensor* and *par* in linear logic (Girard 1987).[4]

1.3.3 Strategies

The crucial notion is that of strategy; it will be interpreted computationally as an algorithm, and logically as an argument. Intuitively a strategy is some means for

---

[3] There are more complex possibilities. In the games which concern Abramsky and Jagadeesan (1994), the possibility that P could start a game G plays a role: while it cannot be realised in the standard play of G, it may be realised in the standard play of games constructed from G. The same phenomenon arises in the context of Conway games. Such situations which will not be treated in these notes; but with them one has a genuine duality.

[4] In the case of more complex games, O may switch in $G \otimes H$, and P may switch in $G \multimap H$. The 'Blass Convention', in the spirit of linear logic, is that the other player cannot switch. The 'Conway Convention' allows the other player to switch as well.

determining the next move in a game, but a natural question arises.

What is the next move determined by?

Here are some possible answers.

- The easy answer is 'everything': this gives rise to what are called history-sensitive strategies.

- A surprising answer is 'the last move'; then one has what might best be described as a game of stimulus and response (a rally in tennis perhaps). This has been studied by Abramsky and his coworkers (Abramsky and Jagadeesan 1994; Abramsky, Jagadeesan, and Malacaria 1994).

- A natural answer is 'the current position', perhaps identified with the succeeding game. This is the basis for much work in traditional logic, but presents problems with regard to compositionality.

- A further (not quite obvious) answer couched in terms of 'views' will be discussed in Section 4.

Note again that the thrust of these notes is that we want a good notion of composition. We want to be able to compose strategies in a disciplined way, so as to be able to argue effectively about the behaviour of composed strategies in a structured fashion. (We are rather far from this ideal!) We give mathematical expression to the idea of a good composition by forming categories of games; then we can exploit their rich structure.

1.3.4 Categorical structure

Let us review the structure which we extract from consideration of the notion of a simple game. (The relevant categorical definitions are given in Appendix A.) We can identify the following significant ideas.

A notion of game Two-person games A, B, C, ... played between Opponent O (who plays first) and Player P. The games will be the objects of a category $\mathcal{G}$ of games.

A notion of strategy in a game A P-strategy $\sigma : A$ for the game A (for O going first) will become a map $\sigma : I \longrightarrow A$ (or element of A) in the category $\mathcal{G}$.

Tensor products of games The tensor product $A \otimes B$ of two games A and B is obtained by playing them in parallel. It gives rise to a symmetric monoidal structure on the category of games. The unit I for the tensor product is the empty game.

Linear function spaces of games The linear function space $A \multimap B$ of 'maps' from A to B is obtained by playing B in parallel with the dual $A^{\perp}$ of A. It gives rise to the closed structure on the category of games.

136   *Hyland*

Copy-cat strategy For each game A, there is a P-strategy in $A \multimap A$ which simply copies moves by Opponent in A (respectively $A^\perp$) as the corresponding moves for Player in $A^\perp$ (respectively A). This acts as the identity in the category.

Composition of strategies [5] We can compose P-strategies $\sigma : (A \multimap B)$ and $\tau : (B \multimap C)$ to obtain a strategy $\sigma;\tau : (A \multimap C)$. This gives the composition in the category.

From the above we derive the following general result.

Theorem *There is a symmetric monoidal closed category $\mathcal{G}$ of games and strategies.*

The import of this is that the category $\mathcal{G}$ is a model for the multiplicative fragment of intuitionistic linear logic. The models which we shall consider all have the property that the unit I for the tensor product is the terminal object of the category: $I \cong 1$. In the language of linear logic, the multiplicative and additive units coincide, so in fact we have models of affine linear logic.

We have further structure in the cases we shall consider.

Products on the category The terminal game 1 is the empty game. (We already noted the problem $I = 1$.) In the product $A \times B$ of games A and B, Opponent gets a choice as to which game to play. (In fact we shall have arbitrary products in $\mathcal{G}$.)

Monoidal comonad A symmetric monoidal functor $! : \mathcal{G} \longrightarrow \mathcal{G}$, and monoidal natural transformations $\varepsilon : ! \longrightarrow 1_{\mathcal{G}}$, $\delta : ! \longrightarrow !!$, forming a comonad.

Comonoid structure Monoidal natural transformations $e : ! \longrightarrow I$ and $d : ! \longrightarrow !\otimes!$ giving (free) $!$-coalgebras the structure of a symmetric comonoid. This comonoid structure is compatible with the comonad in the sense that it is preserved by coalgebra maps: thus, whenever $f : (!A, \delta_A) \rightarrow (!B, \delta_B)$ is a coalgebra map, then f is also a comonoid map.

We make some remarks about this additional structure. First, it is a quite general phenomenon that a symmetric monoidal closed category (SMCC) together with the structure of a monoidal comonad equipped with discard and duplication as above gives rise to a cartesian closed category (CCC) of coalgebras with objects the products of free coalgebras.

Theorem *Suppose that a SMCC $\mathcal{C}$ is equipped with a monoidal comonad, itself equipped with a commutative comonoid structure as above. Then the category of Eilenberg-Moore coalgebras has products; and the full subcategory on objects isomorphic to finite products of free coalgebras is cartesian closed.*

---
[5] As stressed by Abramsky, composition of strategies has a natural reading in process terms as 'parallel composition plus hiding'.

For a fuller discussion of these points see Benton, Bierman, de Paiva, and Hyland (1992), Bierman (1993) and Bierman (1995). The general result does have applications, but the categories of games which we consider have products. It follows that they satisfy Seely's axioms for a model of linear logic extended as in Bierman (1995), that is, they are new-Seely categories. This means that the Kleisli category of the comonad is equivalent to the one introduced in the last theorem. Thus we can give very concrete descriptions of the CCCs derived from our SMCCs of games.

Theorem *The Kleisli category $\mathcal{G}_!$ for the comonad* ! *on $\mathcal{G}$ forms a cartesian closed category of games and strategies.*

The simply typed λ-calculus lies at the heart of (typed) functional programming, and is more or less the static proof theory (in the sense of Girard) of the ($\Rightarrow$)-fragment of intuitionistic logic (minimal logic). The two interpretations of the λ-calculus give the Curry-Howard correspondence. It is natural and changes little to include products in a typed language, to include conjunction in the logic giving the $(\wedge, \Rightarrow)$-fragment, and so to add pairing to the λ-calculus. (See for example Girard (1989b).) The simply typed λ-calculus under $\beta\eta$-equality corresponds exactly to CCCs. (See Lambek and Scott (1986).) It follows that any CCC models proof theory. The primary aim in these notes is to consider the CCCs arising from games either as models for a functional programming language or as models for a theory of proofs.

1.3.5 Intensionality

We may contrast the notion of an algorithm which has a definite *intensional* component with that of the function which it computes regarded as determined by its *extensional* behaviour (its graph). It seems that this distinction can be reflected to some extent in a standard categorical notion.

Definition *A category C with terminal object 1, is* extensional *if and only if C has enough points, that is, if and only if whenever $f, g : A \rightarrow B$ in C,*

$$a; f = a; g \text{ for all } a : 1 \longrightarrow A, \text{ implies } f = g.$$

(One also says that 1 is a generator in C.)

Suppose that a category C, typically a cartesian closed category (CCC), is being used to model computations or proofs. We shall take the fact that C is not extensional in this technical sense, as indicating that it has intensional aspects.[6] Caution is indicated here. The converse looks worse than suspect as one can always add points, as in the Capitalisation Lemma of Freyd and Scedrov (1990). (This reference contains an interesting discussion of points in categories; and a forceful treatment of many other aspects of category theory.)

---

[6] This question of extensionality of models has nothing to do with the question of the η-rule in the λ-calculus. This automatically holds in CCCs.

1.4   Notation and prerequisites

In our formulation, a game A is determined by a tree of moves, so we start with some notation for finite sequences (lists) infinite sequences (streams) and trees.

Sequences   For finite (and occasionally for infinite) sequences p and q we write $q \preceq p$ for the *prefix* relation (equivalently p *extends* q or q *is an initial subsequence of* p); $q \prec p$ is the corresponding strict order relation (q is a *proper prefix of* p). We let juxtaposition or an infix dot denote *concatenation* of sequences or elements (moves): pa or $p.a$ (respectively pq or $p.q$) is the sequence p followed by element a (respectively sequence q).

Trees   A *tree* T on a set X is a prefix closed collection of finite sequences of elements of X; a *subtree* S of T is a subcollection of finite sequences of T which itself forms a tree. A tree on X is a subtree of the full tree X^* of all finite sequences on X.[7]

Projections   Suppose first that $X = Y + Z$ is given as a coproduct (or disjoint union). If $p \in X^*$, then we let *the projection of p on Y*, $p_Y \in Y^*$ be the sequence whose elements in order are those elements in order of the sequence p which lie in (the image of) Y. We extend projections to trees in the obvious way. If T is a tree, then *the projection of T on Y* is

$$T_Y = \{p_Y \mid p \in T\} \, ;$$

clearly T_Y is a tree on Y.
Secondly suppose that $X = Y \times \mathbb{N}$ is given as an N-indexed copower (sum) of Y. If $p \in X^*$, then we let *the kth projection of p*, $p_k \in Y^*$ be the sequence whose elements in order are those elements in order of the sequence p which lie in the kth copy of Y. We extend projections to trees in the obvious way. If T is a tree, then *the kth projection of T* is

$$T_k = \{p_k \mid p \in T\} \, ;$$

clearly T_k is a tree on Y.

Infinite sequences   For a set X, write $X^{\leq \omega} = X^* \cup X^\omega$ for the set of finite and infinite sequences of elements of X.
Suppose that T is a tree on a set X. Write

$$T^\infty = \{p \in X^\omega \mid q \in T \text{ for all } q \prec p \}$$

for the collection of infinite sequences generated by T, and

$$\overline{T} = \{p \in X^{\leq \omega} \mid q \in X^* \text{ implies } q \in T \text{ for all } q \preceq p \}$$

---

[7]Some readers will be acquainted with concurrency theory, and the use made in that subject of various notions of labelled tree; it may help to stress that our trees correspond to deterministic labelled trees.

for the complete set of all finite and infinite sequences determined by T. (IN game-theoretic terms, this will be the set of all *plays* in T.) Finally define the set of *maximal finite or infinite* sequences from T as follows

$$\widehat{T} = \{p \in \overline{T} \mid \text{ whenever } q \in \overline{T} \text{ then } p \preceq q \text{ implies } p = q\}\,.$$

(This will be the set of all *completed plays*.)

1.5 Acknowledgements

Much of the material in these notes was discussed in a series of lectures in Cambridge in Lent Term 1994. I owe a lot to my eclectic audience of computer scientists, logicians, mathematicians and philosophers. I owe a particular debt to Gavin Bierman and Luke Ong, with whom I have discussed models for linear logic in general and games in particular on numerous occasions. (They also allowed me to steal some of their TEXto help create these notes!) Finally I acknowledge use of Paul Taylor's diagram macros.

2 Games and computation

2.1 A monoidal closed category of games

2.1.1 Games and strategies

This section gives simple notions of game and of strategy from which to construct a category. The games are determined by trees of moves.

Definition 2.1 *A game for fun or* fun-game *A is given by a set $M = M_A$ of moves together with a non-empty tree T_A on M called the* game tree.
The elements p, q, .. of T_A are called positions *or* plays.
In a play $a_0.a_1.....a_n$, the moves a_0, a_2, ... , of even parity are moves played by the Opponent O; and the moves a_1, a_3, ... , of odd parity are moves played by the Player P.
If a play $a_0.a_1.....a_n$ is of odd length then O has just moved and it is P to move; we let O_A be the set of such odd positions in T_A. On the other hand if a play is of even length then P has just moved and it is O to move; we write P_A for the set of such even positions in T_A. (Note that in an odd position, an even move has just been played, and vice-versa.)
T_A is the disjoint union of the odd positions O_A and even positions P_A.

Throughout Section 2 we shall use *games* to refer to fun-games; but later we shall need to distinguish them from other kinds of games.

Player moves second and hence we can compose Player's strategies (P-strategies) to give a category structure on games. We give first a technically smooth definition.

Definition 2.2 *A P-strategy in a game A is given by a non-empty subtree S of T_A satisfying the following.*

If $p \in S \cap O_A$ then there is a unique move a with $p.a \in S$.

Remark It is probably more intuitive to present a strategy by means of a partial map[8] $\phi : O_A \longrightarrow M_A$, giving moves when Player is to move. We then stipulate that the domain dom$(\phi) \subseteq O_A$ is a prefix closed collection of odd positions, and that ϕ satisfies

(i) if $p \in \text{dom}(\phi)$, then $p.\phi(p) \in P_A$, and
(ii) if $p, q \in \text{dom}(\phi)$ and $q \prec p$, then $q.\phi(q) \prec p$.

The two notions of strategy determine one another via bijections $\phi \rightarrow S_\phi$ and $S \rightarrow \phi_S$ given as follows.

$$S_\phi = \{<>\} \cup \{q \mid q \preceq p.\phi(p) \text{ for some } p \in \text{dom}(\phi) \};$$

$$\phi_S(p) = a \text{ if and only if } p.a \in S.$$

We refer to the equivalent notions of strategy[9] as being either *in subtree mode* or *in function mode*. Greek letters $\sigma, \tau, ...$ will denote strategies without regard to mode of representation.

Exercises 1

1. Show that a strategy S given in subtree mode is determined by $S \cap P_A$.

2. Show that for any partial map $\psi : O_A \longrightarrow M_A$ there is a maximal partial map $\phi : O_A \longrightarrow M_A$ contained in ψ which is a strategy in function mode.

3. Show that a strategy is also determined by a subtree S of T_A such that (i) for $p \in S \cap O_A$, $p.a \in S$ and $p.b \in S$ imply $a = b$, and (ii) for any $p \in S \cap P_A$, $p.a \in O_A$ implies $p.a \in S$.

4. Formulate notions of non-deterministic partial strategy, and of deterministic and non-deterministic total strategy as functions and as subtrees along the lines of Definition 2.2.

2.1.2   Tensor product and linear function space

The idea behind the tensor product and linear function space of games was explained in Section 1.2, so we just give the formal definitions.

---

[8]Note that since strategies are given by partial functions, we are here dealing with partial but deterministic strategies. Other choices are clearly possible.

[9]Glynn Winskel drew to my attention that one can also think about strategies in terms of Petri nets. Regard the positions in O_A as conditions (or places), and those in P_A as events, where the initial position is a unique starting event. Then a strategy corresponds exactly to a possible state of the net.

Definition 2.3

The unit game I is defined by setting $M_I = \varnothing$. This determines the game tree which consists only of the empty sequence. (Thus I is a game in which no moves can be made.)

Given games A and B, the games $A \otimes B$ and $A \multimap B$ are defined as follows.
Moves *The moves are $M_{A \otimes B} = M_{A \multimap B} = M_A + M_B$, the coproduct (disjoint sum) of M_A and M_B.*
Game tree *The game tree $T_{A \otimes B}$ is the subtree of $(M_{A \otimes B})^*$ consisting of those sequences p whose projections $p_A = p_{M_A}$, and $p_B = p_{M_B}$ preserve parity of moves and are in T_A, T_B, respectively.*
The game tree $T_{A \multimap B}$ is the subtree of $(M_{A \multimap B})^*$ consisting of those sequences p such that the projection $p_A = p_{M_A}$ reverses, while $p_B = p_{M_B}$ preserves parity of moves and the projections are in T_A, T_B, respectively.

It is helpful to think of $A \multimap B$ as the result of playing the cogame $A^\perp$, which is A with the parity of moves reversed, in parallel with B. Suppose that we write $p_{A^\perp}$ for the sequence p_A with the parities of moves notionally reversed. Then in the definition of $A \multimap B$, we would say that $p_{A^\perp}$ and p_B preserve parity of moves and are in $T_{A^\perp}$, T_B respectively. This reformulation is helpful conceptually and technically (particularly in the case that $A = B$).

Exercises 2

1. *Show that it is indeed a design feature of these definitions that*

   - *in $A \otimes B$, O may switch between the games A and B, but P may not;*
   - *in $A \multimap B$, P may switch between the cogame $A^\perp$ and the game B, but O may not.*

2. *In a game of the form $(A \multimap B) \multimap C$, which of O and P can switch between which of the (co-)games (and when)? Do the same for a game of the form $A \multimap (B \otimes C)$. Explore a few more complicated examples!*

3. *Using the obvious intuitive notion of isomorphism of games, establish the following isomorphisms.[10]*

   - *$A \otimes (B \otimes C) \cong (A \otimes B) \otimes C$.*
   - *$I \otimes A \cong A \cong A \otimes I$.*
   - *$A \otimes B \cong B \otimes A$.*
   - *$A \multimap (B \multimap C) \cong (A \otimes B) \multimap C$.*

4. *Write S for the game which ends after a unique initial move.*
   (i) Give concrete descriptions of the games $S \otimes S$ and $S \multimap S$.

---

[10]Why do we not get identities in place of isomorphisms? In what sense is the coproduct $+$ of sets associative and commutative?

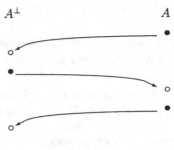

$$A^\perp \qquad\qquad\qquad A$$

Figure 1: Identity strategy.

(ii) Suppose that a game has just one initial move. Show that it is isomorphic to a game of the form $B \multimap S$ for some game B.

5. (i) For which games A do we have $A \cong A \otimes A$?
(ii) For which games A do we have $A \cong A \multimap A$?

2.1.3 The category $\mathcal{LFG}$ of linear games of fun

As explained earlier, the form of compositionality which we expect will give rise to the structure of a category with games as objects and strategies as maps. We now describe the relevant structure on the strategies.

Definition 2.4 *For any game A we define a strategy ι_A in $A \multimap A$ in subtree mode as follows.*

$$p \in \iota_A \cap P_A \text{ if and only if for all even } q \preceq p, \quad q_{A^\perp} = q_A.$$

Suppose that we have strategies $\sigma : A \multimap B$ and $\tau : B \multimap C$, in subtree mode. Their composite $\sigma; \tau$ is defined as follows.

$$p \in \sigma; \tau \cap P_{A \multimap B} \text{ if and only if}$$

$$\exists q \in \sigma \cap P_{A \multimap B}.\exists r \in \tau \cap P_{B \multimap C}. \, q_{A^\perp} = p_{A^\perp} \text{ and } q_B = r_{B^\perp} \text{ and } r_C = p_C.$$

The definitions of the identity maps and of composition are based on very simple ideas. The identity strategy simply copies moves from the copy of A to that of $A^\perp$ and vice-versa as in Figure 1. Composition can be understood by imagining that when playing $\sigma; \tau$ in $A \multimap C$, P keeps a scratchpad on which to record (corresponding pairs of) moves in B and $B^\perp$. A representative play is shown in Figure 2. The opponent starts the game $A \multimap C$ in C, and P plays in $B \multimap C$ a move according to τ which happens to be in $B^\perp$. (The situation where the move is in C is clearly straightforward.) P copies this over to B and regards that move as the start of a play in $A \multimap B$. Playing according to σ gives a move in B, which is copied over to $B^\perp$, where it is regarded as a move of O. P responds to that according to

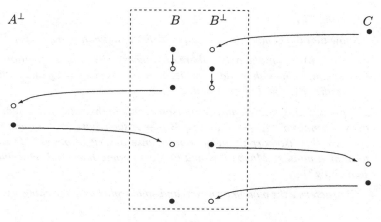

$$A^\perp \qquad\qquad B \qquad B^\perp \qquad\qquad\qquad C$$

Figure 2: Composition of strategies.

τ getting in the case illustrated a move in $B^\perp$. This in its turn is copied over to B where it is regarded as a response of O. P responds to that according to σ, getting a move in $A^\perp$. At last P is able to play a move 'for real' in the game $A \multimap C$. In the illustration O responds (necessarily) in $A^\perp$, and the game continues. (Further 'real moves' in C are shown.)

Let us now record the properties which say that we have a category.

Proposition 2.1 *Suppose that A and B are games with $\sigma : A \multimap B$; then $\iota_A; \sigma = \sigma = \sigma; \iota_B$.*
Suppose that A, B, C and D are games with $\rho : A \multimap B$, $\sigma : B \multimap C$ and $\tau : C \multimap D$; then $\rho; (\sigma; \tau) = (\rho; \sigma); \tau$. $\square$

In view of this proposition, we can define a category of games.

Definition 2.5 *The category $\mathcal{LFG}$ of* linear fun-games *has as objects, games as defined in definition 2.1; as maps from A to B, strategies in $A \multimap B$ as defined in definition 2.2; and identities and composition as in definition 2.4.*

We let $\mathcal{LFG}(A)$ denote the set of strategies in the game A and $\mathcal{LFG}(A, B)$ the set of maps from A to B in $\mathcal{LFG}$. So $\mathcal{LFG}(A, B) = \mathcal{LFG}(A \multimap B)$.

Exercises 3

1. *Show that the strategy ι_A can be defined in function mode by stipulating that $\iota_A(p.a) = c(a)$ for all $p.a \in O_{A \multimap A}$. ($c : M_{A \multimap A} \longrightarrow M_{A \multimap A}$ is the twist isomorphism on $M_{A \multimap A} = M_{A^\perp} + M_A = M_A + M_A$ which interchanges*

$M_{A^\perp}$ and M_A.) [11]

2. Show that the composite $\sigma; \tau$ can be defined in function mode as follows.

$\sigma; \tau(p) = d$ if and only if there are (necessarily unique) positions q consistent with σ and r consistent with τ with $q_B = r_B$ and with either $\sigma(q) = d$ or $\tau(r) = d$.

3. Suppose that games A and B are isomorphic in the categorical sense that there are maps $\sigma : A \longrightarrow B$ and $\tau : B \longrightarrow A$ such that $\sigma; \tau = \iota_A$ and $\tau; \sigma = \iota_B$. Are they isomorphic in the naive sense described above? (Just stop to think a minute. Maybe it would be worth going back and reformulating something?)

4. Characterise the monomorphisms and epimorphisms in the category $\mathcal{LFG}$.

2.1.4   Elementary structure on $\mathcal{LFG}$

This section contains a brief sketch of some elementary categorical structure on $\mathcal{LFG}$.

Symmetric monoidal closed structure on $\mathcal{G}$ Here is a brief indication of why $\mathcal{LFG}$ supports the structure of a symmetric monoidal closed category (SMCC).[12] First we have a choice of 'unit' I; and we have the construction $A \otimes B$ which is functorial in A and B. Secondly the isomorphisms from Exercises 2 give natural isomorphisms: associativity, $a_{ABC} : (A \otimes B) \otimes C \longrightarrow A \otimes (B \otimes C)$; identities $l_A : I \otimes A \longrightarrow A$ and $r_A : A \otimes I \longrightarrow A$; and symmetry $c_{AB} : A \otimes B \longrightarrow B \otimes A$. These satisfy the coherence conditions detailed in Appendix A, so that $\mathcal{G}$ has the structure of a symmetric monoidal category. Finally we have a natural isomorphism $\mathcal{LFG}(A \otimes B, C) \cong \mathcal{LFG}(A, B \multimap C)$ derived from the isomorphism $(A \otimes B) \multimap C \cong A \multimap (B \multimap C)$ and hence a closed structure on $\mathcal{LFG}$.

Categorical products The definition for finite products in $\mathcal{LFG}$ is given below; the extension to infinite products is obvious.

Definition 2.6

First define the terminal game 1 by stipulating that $M_1 = \varnothing$. Thus the terminal game 1 is just the unit game I. (The game tree consists only of the empty sequence, and no moves can be made in 1.)

Now suppose that A and B are games; the product game $A \times B$ is defined as

---

[11] In matrix notation one can write the map c in the definition of ι_A as

$$\begin{pmatrix} 0 & 1 \\ 1 & 0 \end{pmatrix}$$

Those who know the Geometry of Interaction (Girard 1989a) will recognise this matrix.

[12] This notion is explained in Appendix A, but if the reader just has in mind that the various isomorphisms given in Exercises 2 are intuitively natural, that will probably be enough.

follows:

Moves *The moves are* $M_{A \times B} = M_A + M_B$, *the coproduct or disjoint union of* M_A *and* M_B.

Game tree *The game tree* $T_{A \times B}$ *is the subtree of* $(M_{A \times B})^*$ *consisting of those sequences p with either* $p = p_{M_A} \in T_A$ *or* $p = p_{M_B} \in T_B$.

Proposition 2.2 *The object* 1 *is a terminal object in* $\mathcal{LFG}$.
For games A and B, there are maps **fst** $: A \times B \longrightarrow A$, **snd** $: A \times B \longrightarrow B$ *exhibiting* $A \times B$ *as a product in* $\mathcal{LFG}$.

Enrichment in domains We can regard $\mathcal{LFG}$ as a category enriched in some category of domains. We make do with an intuitive account of enrichment, but for more on this important topic see Kelly (1982). Here we presuppose some knowledge of domain theory. It is clear that the collection of all P-strategies $\mathcal{LFG}(A)$ in a game A forms a poset under inclusion (in either mode). We expect it to be some kind of domain or complete partial order (CPO).

Given an even position $p \in P_A$ of a game A, we define the least strategy $\sigma[p]$ giving rise to the play p by $\sigma[p] = \{q | q \preceq p\}$. (In function mode $\sigma[p](q) = a$ if and only if $q.a \preceq p$.)

Lemma 2.3 *(i) For any subset X of* $\mathcal{LFG}(A)$, *the supremum* $\bigsqcup X$ *exists if and only if* $\bigcup X$ *is a (partial) function, (in which case* $\bigsqcup X = \bigcup X$). *Hence each* $\mathcal{LFG}(A)$ *is a consistently complete* CPO.
(ii) A strategy $\sigma \in \mathcal{LFG}(A)$ *is compact if and only if σ is a finite partial function if and only if σ is a finite subtree. Hence each* $\mathcal{LFG}(A)$ *is algebraic and satisfies the finiteness axiom (I).*
(iii) A strategy $\sigma \in \mathcal{LFG}(A)$ *is prime if and only if it is* $\sigma[p]$ *for some position* $p \in P_A$ *(that is, if and only if as a subtree, it consists of a single path). Hence each* $\mathcal{LFG}(A)$ *is prime algebraic.*
It follows at once that the collection $\mathcal{LFG}(A)$ *of P-strategies in A ordered by inclusion is a dI-domain.*

Now we know that each $\mathcal{LFG}(B, C) = \mathcal{LFG}(B \multimap C)$ carries the structure of a dI-domain. To show that $\mathcal{LFG}$ is enriched in some category of domains, we should consider how the operations of $\mathcal{LFG}$ as a structured category are reflected in maps of dI-domains. Examples of such operations are the composition $\mathcal{LFG}(A, B) \times \mathcal{LFG}(B, C) \to \mathcal{LFG}(A, C)$ and tensor product $\mathcal{LFG}(A, B) \times \mathcal{LFG}(C, D) \to \mathcal{LFG}(A \otimes C, B \otimes D)$. Since strategies are determined by the prime strategies which they contain, it follows that all the relevant maps are affine (that is, preserve all nonempty sups) or biaffine as in the examples above. Hence we have the main result of this section.

Theorem 2.4 *The category* $\mathcal{LFG}$ *of games and strategies is a* SMCC *with products, enriched over the* SMCC *of dI-domains and affine maps.*

146   *Hyland*

This result on enrichment suggests that we think of the category of games as a kind of generalised (linear) domain theory. This perspective is useful in a number of ways. For example, one can present $\mathcal{LFG}$ as a category indexed over itself in such a way as to obtain a model for polymorphism (along the lines of Girard (1986), Coquand, Gunter, and Winskel (1989), Taylor (1986), and others). For another approach to polymorphism see Abramsky (1997).

Exercises 4

1. *Recall the game S with just one initial move after which the game is over.*
   (i) Show that any game is isomorphic to a (possibly infinite) product of games with just one initial move.
   (ii) Establish the following decomposition.[13] For any game A we can find games B_i for $i \in I$ with $A \cong \prod\{B_i \multimap S | i \in I\}$.
   (iii) Identify the least collection $\mathcal{W}$ of games containing S, closed under isomorphism and under finite products, and such that if $W \in \mathcal{W}$ then $W \multimap S \in \mathcal{W}$. Show that the full subcategory on such objects is a SMCC.

2. *Establish the following facts.*
   (i) The contravariant functor $(-) \multimap S$ is self dual on $\mathcal{LFG}$: we have

$$\mathcal{LFG}(A, B \multimap S) \cong \mathcal{LFG}(B, A \multimap S)$$

   naturally in A and B.
   (ii) The game $A \multimap S$ can be identified with $S(A)$, the game which is obtained from A by adding a fresh initial move, $\bullet$ say, for Opponent, and then letting play continue as in $A^\perp$.
   (iii) The self duality is enriched in the closed structure:

$$A \multimap S(B) \cong S(A \otimes B) \cong B \multimap S(A)$$

3. *A map $\rho : A \longrightarrow B$ in $\mathcal{LFG}$ is strict if and only if $\perp; \rho = \perp : I \longrightarrow B$. Write $\mathcal{LFG}_s(A, B)$ for the set of strict maps from A to B. On the basis of this definition establish the following facts.*
   (i) A map $\rho : A \longrightarrow B$ is strict just when ρ's response to an initial move (necessarily) in B is always a move in $A^\perp$.
   (ii) Let $L = S^2$ be the square of the functor S above. Show that L is the lift for our notion of strict map: that is, there is a natural isomorphism $\mathcal{LFG}(A, B) \cong \mathcal{LFG}_s(LA, B)$.
   (iii) Let $\eta_A : LA \to A$ be the strict map corresponding to the identity ι_A in the natural isomorphism. Show that $\rho : A \longrightarrow B$ is strict if and only if $L\rho; \eta_B = \eta_A; \rho$.

4. *Show that $\mathcal{LFG}$ does not have a coproduct, but that it does have a weak coproduct.*

---

[13]One can read this decomposition as follows. A game can do an O-move and become a cogame. Similarly a cogame can do a P-move and become a game. You may detect echoes of The Expansion Theorem for CCS in this question.

5. *Consider the category of games with history-free strategies in the sense of Abramsky and Jagadeesan (1994). Does this category have finite products?*

2.2 A cartesian closed category of games

2.2.1 The exponential comonad

The simple intuition behind the so-called exponential $!A$ of a game A is that it is an infinite ordered tensor product of (versions of) A.[14] We imagine that we are given instances $A_0, A_1, A_2, \cdots$ of the game A, and we play their infinite tensor product subject to the stipulation that O may not open (that is make the first move in) an instance A_{k+1} until all the A_i for $i \leq k$ have been opened. The formal definition is as follows.

Definition 2.7 *Suppose that A is a game for fun. Then the game $!A$ is defined as follows:*
Moves *The moves are $M_{!A} = M_A \times \mathbb{N}$, the countable copower of M_A.*
Game tree $T_{!A}$ *is the subtree of $(M_{!A})^*$ consisting of those sequences p such that (i) all the projections p_k are in T_A, and (ii) the first move in the $k+1$st copy is made after the first move in the kth.*

We devote this section to an explanation of that structure associated with the exponential which gives rise to a cartesian closed category of games.

! as a monoidal comonad It is routine to check that $!A$ is functorial in A; so that we have a functor $! : \mathcal{LFG} \longrightarrow \mathcal{LFG}$. In addition we can define mediating natural transformations $m_I : I \longrightarrow !I$ and $m_{AB} : !A \otimes !B \longrightarrow !(A \otimes B)$ making $!$ a *monoidal (endo)functor* on $\mathcal{LFG}$. The axioms for monoidal functors are explained in Appendix A; here we just describe the maps involved.

The map m_I This is uniquely determined since $!I \cong I \cong 1$.

The map m_{AB} This is more interesting; we have $(!A)^\perp$ and $(!B)^\perp$ in parallel with $!(A \otimes B)$. Player does the natural thing; moves in the successive versions of $A \otimes B$ are copied to moves in the successive versions of $A^\perp$ or $B^\perp$ as appropriate, and then also vice-versa. (This requires careful bookkeeping as which version corresponds to which is not determined in advance of a play. Figure 3 illustrates the case where O starts by playing in A in the first version of $A \otimes B$, then plays in B in the second version and then continues in A in the second version.)

We can further define the counit $\varepsilon_A : !A \longrightarrow A$ and the comultiplication $\delta_A : !A \longrightarrow !!A$ for a comonad as follows.

---

[14] Curien has considered in detail a more sophisticated exponential, which is already implicit in his early work on sequentiality, and which gives rise to the category of sequential algorithms. This underlies the recent treatment of full abstraction for extensions of PCF given in Cartwright, Curien, and Felleisen (1994). Curien's exponential is a retract of our crude exponential.

148   *Hyland*

$$A_0^\perp \ A_1^\perp \cdots \qquad B_0^\perp \ B_1^\perp \cdots \qquad (A \otimes B)_0 \ (A \otimes B)_1$$

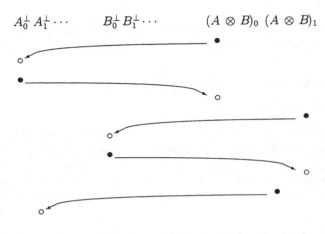

Figure 3: Mediating strategy.

Counit ε_A In the game $!A \multimap A$ we play $(!A)^\perp$ in parallel with A. In the strategy ε_A Player only makes use of the first copy of $A^\perp$ in $(!A)^\perp$, and simply copies moves across as in the identity (copy-cat) strategy. (The picture is like Figure 1, but with further unused copies of $A^\perp$ on the left.)

Comultiplication δ_A In the game $!A \multimap !!A$, we have $(!A)^\perp$ in parallel with $!!A$. In $!!A$, Opponent has in effect an $\mathbb{N} \times \mathbb{N}$-indexed collection of copies of A in which he may choose to play (of course with restriction on the legitimate order). In the strategy δ_A, Player makes use of his $\mathbb{N}$-indexed copies of $A^\perp$ in $(!A)^\perp$, to imitate the behaviour of Opponent; whenever O opens a new copy of A, P opens a corresponding new copy of $A^\perp$, thereby instituting a link between the respective copies; and thereafter whenever O plays in the one, P copies in the other. The idea is indicated in Figure 4. Moves from the first two versions of A in the first version of $!A$ and moves from the first version of A in the second version of $!A$ are shown copied.

It is routine to check that that ε_A and δ_A are the components of natural transformations $\varepsilon : ! \longrightarrow 1_{\mathcal{LFG}}$ and $\delta : ! \longrightarrow !!$; and that they are monoidal natural transformations in the sense explained in Appendix A. We can sum up this discussion in the following proposition.

Proposition 2.5 *The data* $(!, \varepsilon, \delta)$ *together with the ancillary structure* m_I *and* m_{AB} *form a monoidal comonad on* $\mathcal{LFG}$.

Comonoid structure on $!$ Now let us see how $!$ supports the operations of weakening and contraction associated with the 'exponential' of linear logic. The discard maps $e_A : !A \longrightarrow I$ and duplication maps $d_A : !A \longrightarrow !A \otimes !A$ are as follows.

Discard e_A The game $!A \multimap I$ is rather disappointing; it has no starting moves for O and so is isomorphic to I. Thus we have to let e_A be the unique 'empty

$$A_0^\perp \quad A_1^\perp \quad A_2^\perp \quad \cdots \qquad (A_{00} \ (A_{01} \ \cdots) \quad (A_{10} \ (A_{11} \cdots) \quad \cdots$$

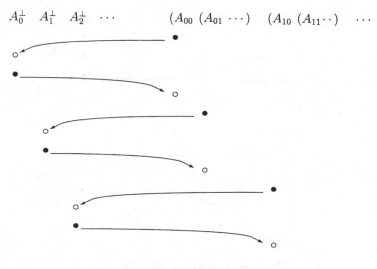

Figure 4: Comultplication strategy.

strategy' in $!A \multimap I$.

Duplication d_A The game $(!A \multimap !A \otimes !A)$ is more interesting. It amounts to playing $(!A)^\perp$ in parallel with two copies of $!A$. Opponent can switch between the copies of $!A$, while Player can switch between $(!A)^\perp$ and whichever copy of $!A$ is current. In the strategy d_A, Player systematically sets up a correspondence between fresh versions of A started by O in either of the two copies of $!A$, and fresh versions of $A^\perp$ in the copy of $(!A)^\perp$; he simply copies O's moves from any version to the corresponding one. So the picture is as in Figure 4 save that there are just the two (rather than countably many) copies of A on the right.

It is straightforward to check the desirable properties of discard and duplication.

Proposition 2.6 *The components of the natural transformations* $e_A \ : !A \ \rightarrow \ I$ *and* $d_A \ : !A \rightarrow !A \otimes !A$ *give each free coalgebra* $\delta_A \ : !A \rightarrow !!A$ *the structure of a commutative comonoid. This structure is compatible with the comonad in that it is preserved by coalgebra maps: whenever* $f : (!A, \delta_A) \rightarrow (!B, \delta_B)$ *is a coalgebra, then* f *is also a comonoid morphism.*

We could deduce at once that the category of Eilenberg-Moore coalgebras has products; and that the full subcategory on objects isomorphic to finite products of free coalgebras is cartesian closed. Fortunately, the category $\mathcal{LFG}$ has products. It follows that it satisfies Seely's axioms for a model of linear logic extended as in Bierman (1995), that is, it is a new-Seely category. Hence the Kleisli category of the comonad is the CCC in which we are interested.

150   *Hyland*

$$A_0^\perp \qquad A_1^\perp \qquad A_2^\perp \qquad\qquad\qquad B$$

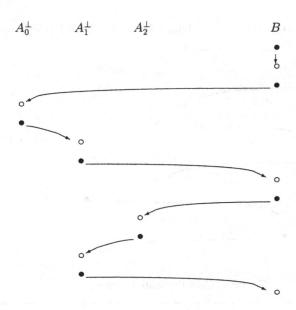

Figure 5: Play in the function space $A \Rightarrow B$.

___

Exercises 5

1. Is the counit $\varepsilon_A : !A \to A$ ever an isomorphism? Is the comultiplication $\delta_A : !A \to !!A$ ever an isomorphism?

2. For which games A do we have an isomorphism $A \cong !A$? For which games A do we have an isomorphism $!A \cong !!A$?

3. Give an example to show that $!A \otimes !B$ and $!(A \otimes B)$ need not be isomorphic.[15]

2.2.2 Description of the CCC $\mathcal{FG}$

Definition 2.8 *The category $\mathcal{FG}$ of fun-games (without qualification) is the Kleisli category for the comonad* ! *on* $\mathcal{LFG}$

The comonoid structure on the comonad $(!, \varepsilon, \delta)$ together with the existence of products in our category $\mathcal{LFG}$ ensures that the Kleisli category for ! is cartesian closed.

___

[15]The question why these objects are not isomorphic arose at the summer school. Nick Benton immediately gave a computational intuition. In $!(A \otimes B)$ there are always the same number of versions of A and B in which Opponent could be playing without having to 'call up' a fresh copy. But that is not true of $!A \otimes !B$.

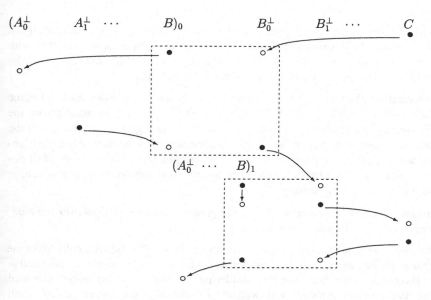

$(A_0^\perp \qquad A_1^\perp \quad \cdots \qquad B)_0 \qquad\qquad B_0^\perp \qquad B_1^\perp \quad \cdots \qquad C$

$(A_0^\perp \quad \cdots \quad B)_1$

Figure 6: Composition of $\sigma : A \Rightarrow B$ and $\tau : B \Rightarrow C$.

Proposition 2.7 *The category $\mathcal{FG}$ is cartesian closed. The categorical product is the product $A \times B$ and the function space $B \Rightarrow C$ is defined by*

$$B \Rightarrow C = !B \multimap C.$$

The standard adjunction induced by the comonad ! is a monoidal adjunction.

We write $\mathcal{FG}(A) = \mathcal{LFG}(A)$ for the elements (points) of A in $\mathcal{FG}$; then $\mathcal{FG}(A, B) = \mathcal{FG}(A \Rightarrow B) = \mathcal{LFG}(!A \multimap B)$.

Explicit description of $\mathcal{FG}$ The category $\mathcal{FG}$ of fun-games and (non-linear) strategies has the following description. The objects of the category are games as in Definition 2.1. The maps from A to B are strategies in the game $!A \multimap B = A \Rightarrow B$ obtained by playing a countable sequence of versions of $A^\perp$ in parallel with B. A typical play is illustrated in Figure 5, with a strategy for Player indicated by the arrows. The identity on a game A is given by the map $\varepsilon_A : !A \to A$. Finally we describe how to compose two maps $\sigma : A \Rightarrow B$ and $\tau : B \Rightarrow C$ in $\mathcal{FG}$. The strategies $\sigma : !A \multimap B$ and $\tau : !B \multimap C$ in $\mathcal{LFG}$ compose to give the composite

$$!A \xrightarrow{\;\delta\;} !!A \xrightarrow{\;!\sigma\;} !B \xrightarrow{\;\tau\;} C.$$

A play according to a composite strategy is indicated in Figure 6. Opponent opens in C and τ gives Player a move in the first copy $B_0^\perp$. This opens a scratchpad, and a few of Player's moves are shown given by σ. Eventually Player copies over a move as an O-move in $B_0^\perp$, and τ gives a response in $B_1^\perp$. This opens a fresh scratchpad, and calls up a fresh version of σ, and P-moves are made in accord with σ then with τ and then with σ again. In Figure 6 two scratchpads are shown, but more could be opened, and Player may well return to earlier scratchpads.

Enrichment The category $\mathcal{LFG}$ is enriched in the SMCC of dI-domains and affine maps. What about $\mathcal{FG}$? As $\mathcal{FG}(A, B) \cong \mathcal{LFG}(!A, B)$, we can again regard the hom-sets as dI domains. So we need to look at the maps giving the structure of the cartesian closed category. It is easy to see (for example in the case of composition) that we lose affineness; but the maps remain continuous. (The category of dI domains and continuous maps has products, and thus a symmetric monoidal structure; but it is not cartesian closed.)

Proposition 2.8 *The category $\mathcal{FG}$ of fun-games is a CCC enriched over the category of dI-domains and continuous maps.*

One can regard the CCC $\mathcal{FG}$ as as an intensional model of the typed λ-calculus in the sense explained in the Introduction: it does not have enough points. As indicated in the Exercises, one can see this by considering the object Σ whose unique maximal play consists of an O-move $\bullet$ followed by a P-move $\circ$. In the next sections we shall consider $\mathcal{FG}$ as a model PCF, and on the basis of that try to tease out the intuition that the category models intensional behaviour.

Exercises 6

> *1. Recall the game S with just an initial O-move. Show that the linear and general function spaces coincide: $S \Rightarrow S \cong S \multimap S$.*

> *2. (i) Show that $(S \Rightarrow S) \cong \Sigma$, the game with a unique maximal play consisting of an O-move $\bullet$ followed by a P-move $\circ$.*
> *(ii) Show that Σ has just two points.*
> *(iii) Show that there are infinitely many strategies in $\mathcal{FG}(\Sigma, \Sigma)$, and deduce that such strategies are not distinguished by the points of Σ.*

> *3. Can you construct games A with*
> *(i) $A \cong A \times A$;*
> *(ii) $A \cong A \Rightarrow A$;*
> *(iii) $A \cong A \times A \cong A \Rightarrow A$?*

> *4. If games A and B are isomorphic in $\mathcal{FG}$, are they isomorphic in $\mathcal{LFG}$?*

> *5. Recall the lift functor $L = S^2$ on $\mathcal{LFG}$. Does L act as a lift in the category $\mathcal{FG}$?*

2.3   Games as a model for intensional computation

We show how strategies for games provide a notion of algorithm[16] by explaining how our category provides a model for PCF. (A brief overview of PCF is given

---

[16] A better case is made by recent work of Abramsky modelling idealised ALGOL.

in Appendix B.) What is commonly called a denotational semantics for PCF is essentially an interpretation of (or model for) the type theory presented in Appendix B. The usual form of a model for PCF is that the types are interpreted as domains and the terms as continuous (or stable continuous) maps between domains. Here we describe a model in which the types are interpreted as games and the terms as strategies.

2.3.1 Interpretation of PCF types

First we define games $\mathbb{B}$ and N to model the ground types. These games are of a simple kind. In each game there is a unique opening move for O; in $\mathbb{B}$, P has two possible responses t and f, and then the game is over; in N, P has a countable number of possible responses n for each natural number n, and again then the game is over. The following is a formal definition.

Definition 2.9 *The* boolean game $\mathbb{B}$ *has moves* $M_{\mathbb{B}} = \{\bullet, t, f\}$, *and game tree* $T_{\mathbb{B}} = \{p \mid p \preceq \bullet.t \text{ or } p \preceq \bullet.f\}$.
The natural number *game* N *has moves* $M_N = \{\bullet, 0, 1, 2, 3, \cdots\}$, *and game tree* $T_N = \{p \mid p \preceq \bullet.n \text{ for some natural number } n\}$.

Now for any PCF-type A we define the interpretation $[\![A]\!]$ as a game recursively as follows:

$$[\![o]\!] \stackrel{\text{def}}{=} \mathbb{B},$$
$$[\![\iota]\!] \stackrel{\text{def}}{=} N,$$
$$[\![A_1 \Rightarrow A_2]\!] \stackrel{\text{def}}{=} [\![A_1]\!] \Rightarrow [\![A_2]\!];$$

where $\mathbb{B}$ and N are the boolean and natural number games just defined.

Exercises 7

1. *Show that the domains of strategies $\mathcal{FG}(\mathbb{B})$ and $\mathcal{FG}(N)$ are the traditional flat domains of booleans and natural numbers respectively. (Thus, our interpretation of PCF is standard in the sense of Plotkin (1977).)*

2. *Show that the function space domain $\mathcal{FG}(\mathbb{B} \Rightarrow \mathbb{B})$ is infinite.*

3. *What possibilities are there for the first four moves in a strategy in the domain $\mathcal{FG}(\mathbb{B} \times \mathbb{B} \Rightarrow \mathbb{B})$?*

4. *Construct a game whose domain of strategies is the traditional domain of lazy natural numbers.*

2.3.2 Interpretation of PCF: arithmetic and conditionals

Arithmetic The basic arithmetic constants are straightforwardly interpreted as strategies. The interpretations of $n : \iota$ and $t, f : o$ are the corresponding total strategies in the games $\mathbb{B}$ and N. We consider the interpretation of the successor function succ for illustration. The game in question $[\![\,(\iota,\iota)\,]\!] = (\mathbb{N} \Rightarrow \mathbb{N})$ has as set of moves

$$M_{\mathbb{N}} + M_{\mathbb{N}} = \{(0,\bullet),(0,n) \mid n \in \mathbb{N}\} \cup \{(1,\bullet),(1,n) \mid n \in \mathbb{N}\}$$

and an infinite game tree which we need not describe in detail. The strategy $[\![\,\text{succ} : (\iota,\iota)\,]\!]$ is best defined by giving the maximal plays in the subtree; these are

$$\{(1,\bullet).(0,\bullet).(0,n).(1,n+1) \mid n \in \mathbb{N}\}\,.$$

Conditionals We deal with the conditional at ι. The game in question $[\![\,(o,\iota,\iota,\iota)\,]\!] = (\mathbb{B} \Rightarrow \mathbb{N} \Rightarrow \mathbb{N} \Rightarrow \mathbb{N})$ has as set of moves

$$M_{\mathbb{B}} + M_{\mathbb{N}} + M_{\mathbb{N}} + M_{\mathbb{N}} = \{(0,\bullet),(0,t),(0,f)\}\cup$$

$$\{(1,\bullet),(1,n) \mid n \in \mathbb{N}\} \cup \{(2,\bullet),(2,n) \mid n \in \mathbb{N}\} \cup \{(3,\bullet),(3,n) \mid n \in \mathbb{N}\}$$

and an infinite game tree which we need not describe in detail. Again the strategy $[\![\,\text{cond}^{\iota} : (o,\iota,\iota,\iota)\,]\!]$ is defined by giving the maximal plays in the subtree; these are

$$\{(3,\bullet).(0,\bullet).(0,\text{t}).(1,\bullet).(1,n).(3,n) \mid n \in \mathbb{N}\}\cup$$

$$\{(3,\bullet).(0,\bullet).(0,\text{f}).(2,\bullet).(2,n).(3,n) \mid n \in \mathbb{N}\}\,.$$

Exercises 8

1. *Define strategies for predecessor,* pred, *and test for zero,* zero?, *by giving the maximal plays in the subtree as above.*

2. *(A misleading question!) What is wrong with the strategy whose maximal moves are*

$$\{(1,\bullet).(0,\bullet).(0,n).(0,\bullet).(0,n).(1,n+1) \mid n \in \mathbb{N}\}\,?$$

3. *Show inductively that the conditionals* cond^{ι} *and* cond^{o} *enable one to define conditionals at all types. The resulting conditional* $\text{cond}^{(\iota,\iota)}$ *is (probably) given by*

$$\text{cond}^{(\iota,\iota)} = \lambda x : o.\lambda f,g : (\iota,\iota).\lambda w : \iota.\text{cond}^{\iota}(x, f(w), g(w))\,.$$

Describe the strategy which is defined by this.

4. *(i) Define a strategy for a non-standard function test for one,* one?, *and compare what you give with the interpretation of*

$$\lambda x : \iota.\text{cond}^{\iota}(\text{zero?}(\text{pred}(x)), \text{cond}^{\iota}(\text{zero?}(x), \text{f}, \text{t}), \text{f})\,.$$

(ii) Describe the strategy which interprets the term

$$\lambda x : \iota.\text{cond}^{\iota}(\text{zero?}(x), \text{cond}^{\iota}(\text{one?}(x), 0, \Omega^{\iota}), \text{cond}^{\iota}(\text{zero?}(x), 0, \Omega^{\iota}))\,.$$

2.3.3 Fixed points

For any game (not just those which interpret PCF-types) A we shall describe a strategy in $(A \Rightarrow A) \Rightarrow A$ to interpret $\mathbf{Y}$. First we need to understand the structure of the game $(A \Rightarrow A) \Rightarrow A$. The game amounts to a sequence of cogames $(A \Rightarrow A)_i^{\perp}$ played in parallel with A, in such a way that P can switch games, but O cannot. We call the indicated version of A (in which O starts the game) the *main O-component*. Each $(A \Rightarrow A)_i^{\perp}$ amounts to playing a sequence A_{ij} in parallel with $A_i^{\perp}$, in such a way that O can switch games, but P cannot. We call the $A_i^{\perp}$, in which P starts, the *P-components*, and the games A_{ij} the *subsidiary O-components*. We list the components which we use to structure a discussion of play in $(A \Rightarrow A) \Rightarrow A$.

- *The main O-component.*

- *The P-components.*

- *Subsidiary O-components.*

We now proceed to describe a strategy $\mathbf{Y}$ in $(A \Rightarrow A) \Rightarrow A$. In a play according to the strategy we describe there will be a correspondence between O- and P-components. The first P-component to occur $A_0^{\perp}$ is the dual of the main O-component. The others in order they are started are the duals of the subsidiary O-components in order they are started. At any even position the duals will be copies of each other. The strategy can be succinctly described as follows: suppose O has just moved:

- *Case 1*. Opening move: P copies this to start the first P-component.

- *Case 2*. O starts a new subsidiary component: P copies this to start a new P-component.

- *Case 3*. O moves in some existing O-component (P-component): P copies the move in the dual P-component (O-component).

Arguing inductively it is easy to see this makes sense as a strategy.

Now we aim to show that $\mathbf{Y}$ is a fixed point operator. (In what follows, we shall not bother to distinguish between the strategy $\mathbf{Y} \in \mathcal{FG}((A \Rightarrow A) \Rightarrow A)$, the map $\mathbf{Y} : 1 \longrightarrow ((A \Rightarrow A) \Rightarrow A)$ in $\mathcal{FG}$, and its exponential transpose $\mathbf{Y} : (A \Rightarrow A) \longrightarrow A$.) Externally (or pointwise), that Y is a fixed point means just that the equation

$$\sigma(\mathbf{Y}(\sigma)) = \mathbf{Y}(\sigma)$$

holds for all $\sigma : A \Rightarrow A$. But as $\mathcal{FG}$ does not have enough points, this is not sufficient to provide a good model for PCF. Rather we need to show that

$$f : (A \Rightarrow A) \vDash f(\mathbf{Y}(f)) = \mathbf{Y}$$

holds in $\mathcal{FG}$. The expression $f(\mathbf{Y}(f))$ is interpreted as the composition

$$(A \Rightarrow A) \xrightarrow{\Delta} (A \Rightarrow A) \times (A \Rightarrow A) \xrightarrow{1 \times \mathbf{Y}} (A \Rightarrow A) \times A \xrightarrow{\text{ev}} A ,$$

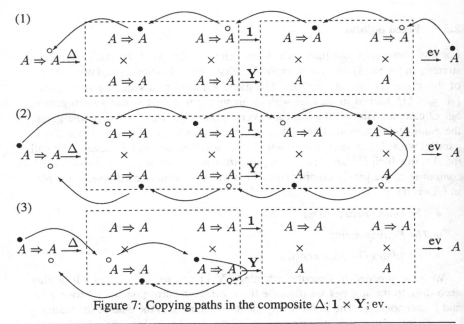

Figure 7: Copying paths in the composite Δ; $\mathbf{1} \times \mathbf{Y}$; ev.

where $\mathbf{1}$ is $\iota_{A \Rightarrow A}$. This composite is pictured (three times) in Figure 7 where "copying paths" are drawn to help explain the behaviour of the composite.[17]

In our discussion of the composite Δ; $\mathbf{1} \times \mathbf{Y}$; ev we use the terminology (main O-component, P-components, subsidiary components, the dual of a component) already introduced. We can tie down the behaviour of the composed strategy by making the following observations.

1. After the opening O-move in the main O-component, P copies along path (1) in Figure 7 to give a reply in the first P-component $A_0^\perp$ (the dual of the main O-component). Thereafter any O-move in either of the two components is answered by copying along path (1) (in either direction) to give a P-reply (which is just a "copy") in the dual component.

2. After the first O-move (if any) in the first subsidiary O-component A_{00}, P copies along path (2) to give a reply in the second P-component $A_1^\perp$ (its dual). Thereafter any O-move in either of these two components is answered by copying along path (2) (in either direction) to give a P-reply (just a "copy") in the dual component. Furthermore exactly the same applies *mutatis mutandis* in the case of any subsidiary O-component A_{0j}; after an opening move in A_{0j}, P opens the next available $A_k^\perp$, say, (its dual). [Perhaps it is worth noting that each of these further O-components involves P opening a fresh version of $\mathbf{Y}$ on the hidden scratch pad *i.e.* the "returning" portion of path (2) involves a fresh version of $\mathbf{Y}$ in each new case.]

---

[17]It does not seem accidental that the three paths in Figure 7 "cover" the whole picture.

3. After the first O-move (if any) in a subsidiary O-component $A_{(i+1)j}$, P copies along path (3) to give a reply in the next available P-component $A_l^\perp$, say,(its dual). Thereafter any O-move in either of these two components is answered by copying along path (3) (in either direction) to give P-reply (just a "copy") in the dual component.

It follows from the three observations above that the composed strategy behaves exactly like **Y**: that is

$$(A \Rightarrow A) \times (A \Rightarrow A) \xrightarrow{\mathbf{1} \times \mathbf{Y}} (A \Rightarrow A) \times A$$

$$
\begin{array}{ccc}
& \Delta \uparrow & \qquad\qquad & \downarrow \mathrm{ev} \\
A \Rightarrow A & \xrightarrow{\quad\mathbf{Y}\quad} & A
\end{array}
$$

commutes.

Exercises 9

1. Show that

$$f : A \Rightarrow B, g : B \Rightarrow A \vDash f(\mathbf{Y}(\lambda a.g(f(a)))) = \mathbf{Y}(\lambda b.f(g(b))) \,.$$

2. Show that

$$f : A \times A \Rightarrow A \vDash \mathbf{Y}(\lambda a.f(a, a)) = \mathbf{Y}(\lambda a.\mathbf{Y}(\lambda a'.f(a, a'))) \,.$$

3. Show that

$$f : A \Rightarrow A \vDash \mathbf{Y}(f) = \mathbf{Y}(\lambda a.f(f(a))) \,.$$

4. Recall that $\mathcal{FG}$ is enriched in a category of CPOs. *For a game A consider the map $\mathcal{FG}((A \Rightarrow A) \Rightarrow A) \to \mathcal{FG}((A \Rightarrow A) \Rightarrow A)$ taking a strategy ρ to the interpretation of $\lambda f : A \Rightarrow A.f(\rho(f))$. Let $\tilde{\mathbf{Y}} : (A \Rightarrow A) \Rightarrow A$ be the least fixed point of this map.*
(i) Show that $\tilde{\mathbf{Y}}$ is a fixed point operator.
(ii) (For the more experienced.) Show that $\tilde{\mathbf{Y}} = \mathbf{Y}$.

2.3.4 Catch

We wish to consider a revealing strategy in the game $(\mathbb{N} \times \mathbb{N} \Rightarrow \mathbb{N}) \Rightarrow \mathbb{N}$. In the spirit of Cartwright, Curien, and Felleisen (1994) we extend PCF by a constant catch : $((\iota \times \iota, \iota), \iota)$, whose interpretation will be this strategy. The game in question has as set of moves

$$M_\mathbb{N} + M_\mathbb{N} + M_\mathbb{N} + M_\mathbb{N} = \{(0, \bullet), (0, n) \mid n \in \mathbb{N}\} \cup$$

$$\{(1, \bullet), (1, n) \mid n \in \mathbb{N}\} \cup \{(2, \bullet), (2, n) \mid n \in \mathbb{N}\} \cup \{(3, \bullet), (3, n) \mid n \in \mathbb{N}\}$$

and an infinite game tree which we need not describe in detail. The strategy $[\![\text{catch} : ((\iota \times \iota, \iota), \iota)]\!]$ is again defined by giving the maximal plays in the subtree; these are

$$\{(3, \bullet).(2, \bullet).(2, k).(3, k + 2) \mid k \in \mathbb{N}\} \cup$$
$$\{(3, \bullet).(2, \bullet).(0, \bullet), (3, 0)\} \cup \{(3, \bullet).(2, \bullet).(1, \bullet).(3, 1)\}\,.$$

This algorithm inspects its argument, the algorithm $\sigma : \mathbb{N} \times \mathbb{N} \Rightarrow \mathbb{N}$ say, in a non-extensional way. If σ outputs a value k at once, then the algorithm returns $k + 2$. Otherwise if σ starts by 'looking at its first argument' it returns 0, and if it starts by 'looking at its second argument' it returns 1. If σ does nothing, then the algorithm returns nothing.

Let us explain the sense in which $[\![\text{catch}]\!]$ is a non-extensional strategy. Consider the following two algorithms $+_l : \mathbb{N} \times \mathbb{N} \Rightarrow \mathbb{N}$ and $+_r : \mathbb{N} \times \mathbb{N} \Rightarrow \mathbb{N}$ for addition. The game in question has moves $M_\mathbb{N} + M_\mathbb{N} + M_\mathbb{N}$, and the maximal plays are for $+_l$,

$$\{(2, \bullet).(0, \bullet).(0, n).(1, \bullet).(1, m).2, n + m) \mid n, m \in \mathbb{N}\},$$

and for $+_r$,

$$\{(2, \bullet).(1, \bullet).(1, m).(0, \bullet).(0, n).2, n + m) \mid n, m \in \mathbb{N}\}.$$

The two algorithms $+_l$ and $+_r$ are extensionally equivalent: the composites with any algorithms $n : \mathbb{N}$ and $m : \mathbb{N}$ are the same. On the other hand, $[\![\text{catch}]\!](+_l) = 0 : \mathbb{N}$ while $[\![\text{catch}]\!](+_r) = 1 : \mathbb{N}$, so catch is sensitive to the intensional difference.

One of the central results of Cartwright, Curien, and Felleisen (1994) is that the category of sequential algorithms (Curien 1993) is fully abstract for an extension of PCF by catch. One can obtain the category of sequential algorithms as a kind of retract of $\mathcal{FG}$, but the details are not simple. In any case the algorithms which are the strategies of $\mathcal{FG}$ are of much wider scope; in functional terms, they allow notice to be taken of arguments which vary according to the circumstances under which they are called.

Exercises 10

1. *Define an extended form of* catch, catch$_r$: $((\iota^r, \iota).\iota)$ *so that* catch $=$ catch$_2$.
   (i) What are catch$_0$ *and* catch$_1$? *Are they extensional?*
   (ii) Show that catch$_1$ *can not be modelled in the standard Scott domain model for* PCF, *and hence is not* PCF-*definable. Is* catch$_1$ *stable?*
   (iii) Is catch$_r$ PCF-*definable from* catch?

2. *Consider the following strategy* $[\![\text{lin0?}]\!]$ *in* $(\mathbb{N} \Rightarrow \mathbb{N}) \Rightarrow \mathbb{B}$. $[\![\text{lin0?}]\!]$ *inspects the algorithm* $\sigma : \mathbb{N} \Rightarrow \mathbb{N}$ *which is its argument. If* σ *outputs a value at once, then* $[\![\text{lin0?}]\!]$ *returns* f. *Otherwise if* σ *starts by 'looking at its argument',* $[\![\text{lin0?}]\!]$ *asks for the value of* σ *at* 0; *then if* σ *at once gives a value* $[\![\text{lin0?}]\!]$

returns t; *on the other hand if σ continues by again 'asking about its argument',* ⟦ lin0? ⟧ *returns* f. *If at any point σ does nothing, then the algorithm returns nothing.*

(i) Write down the maximal plays for ⟦ lin0? ⟧.
(ii) Describe what ⟦ lin0? ⟧ *does? In what sense is it intensional?*
(iii) Is lin0? *PCF-definable from* catch?

3. *Consider the strategy in the game* $(\mathbb{N} \Rightarrow \mathbb{N}) \Rightarrow \mathbb{N}$ *whose maximal plays are of the form*

$$(2, \bullet).(1, \bullet).(0, \bullet).(0, 0).(0, \bullet).(0, 1) \cdots (0, \bullet).(0, n).(1, m).(2, n + m).$$

What does this strategy do?

3   Games and logic

In the previous section we presented a category of games as an intensional model for computation. Now we want to present a corresponding model for constructive proof theory.

It is worth reflecting briefly on the contrast between traditional models of computable (programmable) functions and models for proofs. The point is that the Curry-Howard isomorphism between types and propositions (programs and proofs) has its limitations. A CCC which models the most general forms of computation will in some way involve partial functions. Thus in a category of domains, all the domains are inhabited (by the bottom element ⊥). So under the Curry-Howard isomorphism, all propositions are provable. To avoid this, we think of CCCs which model proof theory as involving total functions, and accept that the Curry-Howard isomorphism is most convincing in the context of programming in a language (such as Martin-Löf Type Theory) in which all functions are total.

This suggests at once that in order to model constructive proof theory we should consider total strategies. But care is needed to get a composition. In terms of the discussion of Section 2, the problem is that one may stay in the scratchpad of Figure 2 for ever, and so the next move may be undefined. Somehow one has to force a conclusion to the computation of the next move. This is fine if all games are 'well-founded'; but such a restriction presents problems for any simple-minded form of the exponential.[18] The good general way round the problem is to have a notion of winning, and only to compose winning strategies. In the simplest formulation we incorporate into the structure of a game a decision, for each infinite play of the game, as to whether that play is winning for Player or for Opponent. (Our presentation is definitely non-constructive. A constructive version of the material is possible, but its formulation requires care.)

---

[18]For finite games, an exponential in the style of Curien can overcome this problem.

3.1 A monoidal category of games and total strategies

In this section we define a specific category of games and total strategies.

3.1.1 Games and total strategies

We need to consider infinite plays, and shall use the notation for infinite sequences given in the Introduction.

Definition 3.1 *A game to win or win-game A is given by a set $M = M_A$ of moves, a non-empty tree T_A on M called the* game tree, *and a function $| - |_A = | - | :$ $T_A^\infty \longrightarrow \{W, L\}$ giving for all infinite plays in T_A the result which is either W, a win for Player, or L, a loss for Player, in the game A.*
Extend the function $| - |$ at once from T_A^∞ to $\overline{T_A}$ by setting

$$|p| = \begin{cases} W & \text{if } p \in O_A; \\ L & \text{if } p \in P_A. \end{cases}$$

The elements p, q, .. of T_A are again called positions *or* plays, *and we adopt from Definition 2.1 the notions of moves of even and odd parity and of the sets O_A of odd positions and P_A of even positions in T_A.*

The definition of the function $| - |$ for all finite plays is the *normal play* convention in Conway (1976). Variations lead to interesting pathologies.

As before, we aim to compose strategies for Player, the P-strategies, but now we want total winning strategies. In this section we refer to these simply as P strategies. As before, we give the definition in subtree mode, just adding clauses to ensure that the strategy is total and wins.

Definition 3.2 *A P-strategy in a game A is a non-empty subtree S of T_A satisfying the following three conditions.*

(1) If $p \in S \cap O_A$ then there is a unique move a with $p.a \in S$.
(2) If $p \in S \cap P_A$ then for any a, $p.a \in O_A$ implies $p.a \in S$.
(3) If $p \in \widehat{S}$, then $|p| = W$.

Remark Again we can present a strategy as a partial map $\phi : O_A \longrightarrow M_A$, with domain $\text{dom}(\phi) \subseteq O_A$ a prefix closed collection of odd positions, that is, $\text{dom}(\phi) = \{q \in O_A | \exists p \in \text{dom}(\phi). q \preceq p\}$. We require that

    (i) if $p \in \text{dom}(\phi)$, then $p.\phi(p) \in P_A$,
    (ii) if $p, q \in \text{dom}(\phi)$ and $q \prec p$, then $q.\phi(q) \prec p$,
    (iii) if $\phi(p) = a$ and $p.a.b \in O_A$ then $p.a.b \in \text{dom}(\phi)$, and
    (iv) if $p \in \widehat{T}$ and if $q \prec p$ odd implies $q.\phi(q) \preceq p$, then $|p| = W$.

The two notions of strategy[19] determine one another as in 2.1.1.

---

[19] Our strategies are now total and deterministic.

Exercises 11

1. Show that one can replace the total condition in the tree definition of strategy by the condition $\widehat{S} \subseteq \widehat{T}$.

2. Suppose that S is a set of positive integers and t a positive integer. Consider the following game.

Opponent starts by choosing a number $n_0 \in \mathbb{N}$ with $n_0 \geq t$; Player chooses $n_1 \in \mathbb{N}$ with $s_1 = (n_0 - n_1) \in S$; Opponent then chooses $n_2 \in \mathbb{N}$ with $s_2 = (n_1 - n_2) \in S$; and so on.

(i) Show that while the game is infinite, there are no infinite plays.

(ii) Who wins the game?

(iii) Vary the game by allowing $0 \in S$ but insisting that we never have $s_{k-1} = s_k$ (where conventionally $s_1 = 0$). What happens now?

3. Consider the strategy for the fixed point operation $\mathbf{Y}$ from Section 2. This is a total strategy as is the identity strategy $\mathbf{1} : A \Rightarrow A$.[20] Now consider the interpretation of $\mathbf{Y}(\mathbf{1})$ which is the composite

$$1 \xrightarrow{\;(\mathbf{1}, \mathbf{Y})\;} (A \Rightarrow A) \times ((A \Rightarrow A) \Rightarrow A) \xrightarrow{\;\text{ev}\;} A$$

(where ev *is the evaluation map). What is this strategy?*

3.1.2 Tensor product and linear function space

Inevitably conditions on wins must come into the definition of operations on games. We first give full definitions of the tensor product and linear function space of games.

Definition 3.3

The unit game I is defined by setting $M_I = \varnothing$; this determines the game tree which consists only of the empty sequence. (Thus I is a game in which no moves can be made.) There is a unique maximal position in I, which is automatically a win for Player.

Given games A and B, the games $A \otimes B$ and $A \multimap B$ are defined as follows.

Moves *The moves are $M_{A \otimes B} = M_{A \multimap B} = M_A + M_B$, the coproduct of M_A and M_B.*

Game tree *The game tree $T_{A \otimes B}$ is the subtree of $(M_{A \otimes B})^*$ consisting of those sequences p whose projections $p_A = p_{M_A}$ and $p_B = p_{M_B}$ preserve parity of moves and are in T_A, T_B, respectively.*

The game tree $T_{A \multimap B}$ is the subtree of $(M_{A \multimap B})^*$ consisting of those sequences p such that the projection $p_A = p_{M_A}$ reverses, while $p_B = p_{M_B}$ preserves parity of moves and the projections are in T_A, T_B, respectively.

---

[20] However $(A \Rightarrow A) \Rightarrow A$ is not a logical truth, though $A \Rightarrow A$ is one!

Winning positions *The (maximal) winning positions*[21] *in* $T_{A \otimes B}$ *are determined by*

$$|p| = W \text{ if and only if } |p_A| = W \text{ and } |p_B| = W.$$

The (maximal) winning positions in $T_{A \multimap B}$ *are determined by*

$$|p| = W \text{ if and only if } |p_A| = W \text{ implies } |p_B| = W.$$

Again it may be helpful to think of $A \multimap B$ as the result of playing a cogame $A^{\perp}$ in parallel with B. The cogame $A^{\perp}$ is A with the parity of moves reversed, and with outcomes W and L interchanged. So we write $p_{A^{\perp}}$ for the sequence p_A with the polarities of moves notionally reversed, and with $|p_{A^{\perp}}| = W$ if and only if $|p_A| = L$. Then in the definition of $A \multimap B$ we could say that $p_{A^{\perp}}$ and p_B preserve parity of moves and are in $T_{A^{\perp}}$, T_B respectively; and that $|p| = W$ if and only if $|p_{A^{\perp}}| = W$ or $|p_B| = W$.

Exercises 12

1. *Establish the following isomorphisms.*

   - $A \otimes (B \otimes C) \cong (A \otimes B) \otimes C.$
   - $I \otimes A \cong A \cong A \otimes I.$
   - $A \otimes B \cong B \otimes A.$
   - $A \multimap (B \multimap C) \cong (A \otimes B) \multimap C.$

   (The fresh point is that the winning positions correspond.)

2. *(i) Show that a maximal play p in $A \otimes B$ need not have both its projections p_A and p_B maximal. Do the same for $A \multimap B$.*
   (ii) Suppose that p is a maximal position in $T_{A \otimes B}$, but that p_A is not maximal in T_A. Show that p_B is maximal in T_B, and that p_A is even (so that necessarily $|p_A| = W$). If p_B is a finite play is it odd or even?
   (iii) Suppose that p is a maximal position in $T_{A \multimap B}$, but that $p_{A^{\perp}}$ is not maximal in $T_{A^{\perp}}$. Show that p_B is maximal in T_B, and that $p_{A^{\perp}}$ is odd (so that necessarily $|p_{A^{\perp}}| = L$). If p_B is a finite play is it odd or even? Repeat the other way round.
   (iv) Deduce that the definition of winning conditions given above accords with the normal play convention.

3. *Show that one can reformulate the condition for P winning in $A \otimes B$ purely in terms of the notion of winning on maximal plays in A and B as follows: P wins a maximal play p in $A \otimes B$ if and only if P wins each p_A, p_B which is maximal.*

---

[21] It is worth noting that in a maximal position p in $T_{A \otimes B}$ (respectively in $T_{A \multimap B}$), at least one of p_A and p_B is maximal.

4. *Let S be the game with just one initial move, after which the game ends as a loss for Player. Give concrete descriptions of the games $S \otimes S$ and $S \multimap S$. Set $\Sigma = (S \multimap S)$. Give concrete descriptions of the games $\Sigma \otimes \Sigma$ and $\Sigma \multimap \Sigma$.*

5. *Let R be the game in which there is just one infinite maximal play which (regrettably) is a loss for P. Describe the maximal plays in $R \otimes R$ and $R \multimap R$.*

3.1.3 The category $\mathcal{LWG}$ of games: elementary structure

We adopt the definition of identity strategy and composition of strategies from 2.4; but since we now require winning strategies, there is something to prove.

Proposition 3.1 *For any game A, the strategy ι_A is a winning strategy. And if $\sigma : A \multimap B$ and $\tau : B \multimap C$ are winning strategies, then so is their composite $\sigma; \tau$.*

We indicate briefly how insisting on winning strategies ensures that composed strategies stay total.[22] The problem when composing $\sigma : A \multimap B$ and $\tau : B \multimap C$ is the possibility of making an infinite play on the scratchpad B with $B^{\perp}$, out of which we do not emerge to play a further move in the game $A \multimap C$. Let us see roughly why this cannot occur. Suppose for simplicity that neither of the resulting plays in $A^{\perp}$ or C is maximal. Then we know that the values of the positions in $A^{\perp}$ and in C are both L. But the value on the scratchpad will be

either L for $B^{\perp}$ and W for B, so the value of the play in $B \multimap C$ is L,

or W for $B^{\perp}$ and L for B, so the value of the play in $A \multimap B$ is L.

In the first case we have a play according to τ which is not winning, and in the second case we have a play according to σ which is not winning.

It is now straightforward to check that we do as before have the structure of a category; winning works out well.

Proposition 3.2 *Suppose that A and B are games with $\sigma : A \multimap B$; then $\iota_A; \sigma = \sigma = \sigma; \iota_B$.*
Suppose that A, B, C, and D are games with $\rho : A \multimap B$, $\sigma : B \multimap C$ and $\tau : C \multimap D$; then $\rho; (\sigma; \tau) = (\rho; \sigma); \tau$.

Hence we can define a category.

Definition 3.4 *The category $\mathcal{LWG}$ of* linear win-games *has as objects, win-games as defined in Definition 3.1; as maps from A to B, winning strategies in $A \multimap B$ as defined in Definition 3.2; and identities and composition as in Definition 2.4.*

---

[22]This is a bit misleading, as in a suitable formulation Proposition 3.1 is constructive.

We let $\mathcal{LWG}(A)$ denote the set of (total winning) strategies in the game A and $\mathcal{LWG}(A,B)$ the set of maps from A to B in $\mathcal{LWG}$. Then we have $\mathcal{LWG}(A,B) = \mathcal{LWG}(A \multimap B)$.

Now consider the elementary structure on $\mathcal{LWG}$. Naturally this parallels the corresponding structure for $\mathcal{LFG}$ in Section 2 closely.

Symmetric monoidal closed structure on $\mathcal{LWG}$ This is exactly as in the case of $\mathcal{LFG}$ from Section 2, and presents no difficulties.

Categorical products in $\mathcal{LWG}$ We now have to deal with winning and losing, but otherwise the definition is as in Section 2. So we just display the clauses concerned with winning.

Winning positions *The terminal game 1 is again the unit game I, with no moves and with the empty position winning for Player.*

For $p \in \widehat{T_{A \times B}}$, $|p|_{A \times B} = W$ if and only if $|p|_A = W$ or $|p|_B = W$.

It is easy to see that all this works just as before.

Proposition 3.3 *The object 1 is a terminal object in $\mathcal{LWG}$.*
For games A and B, there are maps **fst** $: A \times B \longrightarrow A$, **snd** $: A \times B \longrightarrow B$ *exhibiting $A \times B$ as a product in $\mathcal{LFG}$.*

We sum up what we have so far.

Theorem 3.4 *The category $\mathcal{LWG}$ of games and strategies is a* SMCC *with products.*

Enrichment in spaces Recall that the collection of all P-strategies $\mathcal{LFG}(A)$ of a fun game A forms a dI-domain. For a game to win A, there is a corresponding fun game $F(A)$ in which we forget about winning. Each $\mathcal{LWG}(A)$ is a subset of (the maximal elements in) $\mathcal{LFG}(F(A))$ and so inherits the structure of a topological space. The spaces which arise are rather special, but it is clear that all the hom-sets $\mathcal{LWG}(B,C)$ are naturally spaces of some kind. So we should consider how the operations of $\mathcal{LWG}$ as a structured category are reflected in maps of spaces. This has been set as an exercise.

Exercises 13

1. *Any win-game A can be thought of as a fun-game, $F(A)$ say, simply by forgetting about winning.*
   (i) Show that F gives rise to a functor $F : \mathcal{LWG} \longrightarrow \mathcal{LFG}$.
   (ii) Is the forgetful functor F a monoidal functor?
   (iii) Does the forgetful functor $F : \mathcal{LWG} \longrightarrow \mathcal{LFG}$ preserve products?

2. *Establish the following facts.*
   (i) The contravariant functor $(-) \multimap S$ is self dual on $\mathcal{G}$.

(ii) The game $A \multimap S$ can be identified with $S(A)$, say, the game which is obtained from A by adding a fresh initial move $\bullet$ say for O, and then letting play continue as in $A^\perp$.

(iii) The self duality is enriched in the closed structure:

$$A \multimap S(B) \cong S(A \otimes B) \cong B \multimap S(A)$$

3. *Does $\mathcal{LWG}$ have coproducts? Does it have weak coproducts?*

4. *Find an appealing monoidal closed category of spaces in which to enrich $\mathcal{LWG}$.*

3.2 A cartesian closed category of games

3.2.1 The exponential comonad and the CCC

Again we take the exponential $!A$ of a game A to be in effect an infinite ordered tensor product of (versions of) A. We now have to deal with winning, and for completeness give the full definition.

Definition 3.5 *Suppose that A is a game to win as above. Then the game $!A$ is defined as follows:*
Moves *The moves are $M_{!A} = M_A \times \mathbb{N}$ the countable copower of M_A.*
Game tree *$T_{!A}$ is the subtree of $(M_{!A})^*$ consisting of those sequences p such that (i) all the projections p_k are in T_A, and (ii) the first move in the $k + 1$st copy is made after the first move in the kth.*
Winning plays *For a maximal play $p \in \widehat{T_{!A}}$, we set $|p| = W$ if and only if $p_k = W$ for all k.*

The monoidal structure $m_I : I \longrightarrow !I$ and $m_{AB} : !A \otimes !B \longrightarrow !(A \otimes B)$, the comonad structure $\varepsilon_A : !A \longrightarrow A$ and $\delta_A : !A \longrightarrow !!A$, and the operations $e_A : !A \longrightarrow I$ and $d_A : !A \longrightarrow !A \otimes !A$ of discard and duplication, can all be defined as in Section 2. One can check that all the strategies given there are in fact total winning ones. Thus the structure satisfies the same crucial properties as the corresponding structure on $\mathcal{LFG}$.

Proposition 3.5 *The components of the natural transformations $e_A : !A \to I$ and $d_A : !A \to !A \otimes !A$ give each free coalgebra $\delta_A : !A \to !!A$ the structure of a commutative comonoid. And this structure is preserved by coalgebra maps: whenever $f : (!A, \delta_A) \to (!B, \delta_B)$ is a coalgebra, then f is also a comonoid morphism.*

As before this means that there must be a cartesian closed category of games, and (as before) the existence of products means that we can concentrate on the Kleisli category.

Definition 3.6 *The category* $\mathcal{WG}$ *of* win-games *(without qualification) is the Kleisli category for the comonad* $!$ *on* $\mathcal{LWG}$

Again general considerations show what we want.

Proposition 3.6 *The category* $\mathcal{WG}$ *is cartesian closed. The categorical product is the product* $A \times B$ *and the function space* $B \Rightarrow C$ *is defined by*

$$B \Rightarrow C = !B \multimap C.$$

The standard adjunction induced by the comonad $!$ *is a monoidal adjunction.*

A concrete description of the CCC is as in the case of partial strategies, and now the hom-sets in $\mathcal{WG}$ are naturally spaces. We do not go into details.

Exercises 14

1. (i) Show that a maximal play in $!A$ *can involve starting only the first version* A_0 *of* A *and then playing a maximal play.*
(ii) Show that a maximal play in $!A$ *can involve starting all of the ordered sequence of versions of* A *in term, but completing none of them.*
(iii) Suppose that there is an infinite play in A. *Show that there are infinite plays in* $!A$ *which involve finishing all the versions* A_k *with the chosen infinite play. (How many of them are there?)*

2. (i) Suppose that we have a play in $A \Rightarrow B$ *where* P *infinitely often starts a new version of* A, *none of which are finished. Who wins?*
(ii) Suppose that we have a play in a game of the form

$$((A \Rightarrow B) \Rightarrow C) \Rightarrow D$$

in which (i) O *opens in* D, *(ii)* P *replies by starting* $C^{\perp}$, *(iii)* O *responds by starting* B, *(iv)* P *responds by starting* A *and (v) thereafter* P *responds to every move of* O *by starting a fresh version of* A. *Who wins?*

3. Recall the game S *with just an initial O-move. Show that the general and linear function spaces coincide:* $S \Rightarrow S \cong S \multimap S$.

4. Show that the category $\mathcal{WG}$ *is not extensional.*

3.2.2 $\mathcal{WG}$ as a model for constructive proofs

The category $\mathcal{WG}$ is a CCC in which not all objects have points, so prima facie it is a reasonable model of proof theory, and we ask how good it is.

Write $\Phi(\vec{p})$ and $\Psi(\vec{p})$ for propositional formulae in the $(\wedge, \Rightarrow)$-fragment of propositional logic with free propositional variables among the list $\vec{p} = p_1, \ldots p_n$. Every interpretation in $\mathcal{WG}$ of $\vec{p} = p_1, \ldots p_n$ as games $\vec{A} = A_1, \ldots A_n$ gives rise to interpretations written $\Phi(\vec{A})$ and $\Psi(\vec{A})$ of Φ and Ψ as games. It is this interpretation which we wish to assess.

Ideally we would look for a 'full completeness' theorem in the sense of Abramsky and Jagadeesan (1994). This would take something like the following form.

Strong completeness for C Every sequence $\Phi(\vec{A}) \longrightarrow \Psi(\vec{A})$ of maps uniform in $\vec{A}$, is the interpretation of a unique (up to $\beta\eta$-equality) proof of $\Phi \vdash \Psi$. (Equivalently, it is the interpretation of a unique (up to $\beta\eta$-equality) λ-term.)

To make this precise in the case of $\mathcal{WG}$ would require us to elucidate a suitable sense of 'uniform' in terms of some form of polymorphism. Let us concern ourselves only with a weaker question.

Weak completeness for C If there is a map $\Phi(\vec{A}) \longrightarrow \Psi(\vec{A})$ in C for every $\vec{A}$, then $\Phi \vdash \Psi$ is provable in intuitionistic logic. (Equivalently, there is a λ-term of type $\Phi(\vec{p}) \longrightarrow \Psi(\vec{p})$.)

Let us consider the question of whether $\mathcal{WG}$ is weakly complete for the $(\wedge, \Rightarrow)$-fragment of intuitionistic logic. The answer seems a little delicate. We start by considering determined games, that is games in which one or other of the players has a winning strategy. Suppose that A and B are determined games. Then so is $A \Rightarrow B$, indeed the conditions are obvious.

P wins $A \Rightarrow B$ if and only if P wins B or P wins $A^\perp$.
O wins $A \Rightarrow B$ if and only if O wins B and O wins $A^\perp$.

It follows that if $\Phi \vdash \Psi$ in classical logic, then for all determined games $\vec{A}$ there is a map $\Phi(\vec{A}) \longrightarrow \Psi(\vec{A})$ in $\mathcal{WG}$. But the converse is equally trivial. Suppose that $\Phi \nvdash \Psi$ in classical logic. Take an interpretation of $\vec{p}$ making Φ true and Ψ false; set

$$A_i = \begin{cases} I & \text{if } p_i \text{ is set true;} \\ S & \text{if } p_i \text{ is set false.} \end{cases}$$

I and S are determined and are wins for P and O respectively. Arguing inductively, we see that $\Phi(\vec{A})$ is a win for P, and $\Psi(\vec{A})$ is a win for O. Hence the game $\Phi(\vec{A}) \Rightarrow \Psi(\vec{A})$ is a win for O, and there is no map $\Phi(\vec{A}) \longrightarrow \Psi(\vec{A})$ in $\mathcal{WG}$.

If we restricted to games which are determined, then $\mathcal{WG}$ would be an excessively complicated model, weakly complete for classical logic. (The two-valued semantics seems a bit simpler.) But there are non-determined games (Mycielski 1964), and the general situation is not clear. Under the assumption of the Axiom of Choice, I believe that one can adapt and extend arguments from Blass (1972) to show the following conjecture.

Plausible Conjecture Assuming the Axiom of Choice, the category $\mathcal{WG}$ is weakly complete for intuitionistic conjunctive-implicational logic.

The dependence on set-theoretic combinatorics here is quite unsatisfactory, and it seems better to take uniformity seriously. That is not a topic for these notes, but see Abramsky (1997).

Exercises 15

1. Check explicitly that some propositional formulae of your choice are not validated in the model $W\mathcal{G}$.

2. Show directly that the strategy $\mathbf{Y}_A$ is not winning for some specific game A. Is there a game A for which $\mathbf{Y}_A$ is a winning strategy?

3. Check the claim made in the discussion about winning $A \Rightarrow B$ when A and B are deterministic. (There are a couple of trivial points to make.)

4. Take the games $((A \Rightarrow B) \Rightarrow A) \Rightarrow A$ corresponding to the Pierce formula. Find winning strategies in the case of some specific games A and B. Can you detect a sense in which your strategies are not produced by a uniform algorithm?

5. (Blass 1972) Fix $\mathcal{U}$ a non-principal ultrafilter on $\mathbb{N}$. Consider the game A with $M_A = \mathbb{N}$ and $T_A = \{p \in \mathbb{N}^* | p_0 < p_1 < p_2 < \cdots\}$. For $p \in \ldots$ set $E(p) = \{n | p_{2k} \le n, p_{2k+1}$ for some $k\}$.
(i) Show that Opponent has a winning strategy for the game $A \otimes A$.
(ii) Recall $S(A) \cong (A \multimap S)$ from Exercises 13. Show that Opponent has a winning strategy for the game $S(A) \otimes S(A)$.
(iii) Deduce that the game A is not determined.

4 Dialogue Games

A feature of the main strategies considered in Section 2 is that a discipline of questions and answers ran through the resulting plays. This is obvious in the case of the games $\mathbb{N}$ and $\mathbb{B}$ in which an initial question $\bullet$ is answered by an appropriate value; but that is a trivial instance of a more general feature of all strategies denoting PCF-terms. In this part we explain in rough outline how making this intuition precise leads to a richer notion of game (a dialogue game) and to a restricted notion of strategy (an innocent strategy); and we indicate applications both to computation and to logic.

4.1 Categories of Dialogue Games

4.1.1 Moves in dialogue games

Questions and answers In a dialogue game, the moves are of four distinct kinds: Player's question which we represent generically as "(", Opponent's answer ")", Opponent's question "[" and Player's answer "]". The representation of questions and answers as left and right matching parentheses respectively reflects the following convention: Player's question can only be answered by Opponent, and *vice versa*. In addition every answer will be associated with a unique question. Questions need not be immediately answered; the immediate response to a question may either be an answer, or some further question.

A play in a dialogue game is required to satisfy the following basic condition.[23]

> **Principle of Pertinence** Whenever an answer occurs in a play, it answers the latest unanswered question.

Another way of putting this discipline of questions and answers is that questions pending in a dialogue are answered on a "last-asked-first-answered" basis. This has the following global consequence. If one looks at the pattern of brackets in any play of a game, it will be *potentially well-bracketed*, that is, the sequence can be extended to one in which the brackets match up in the standard way. Indeed, we may as well restrict ourselves to games in which the finite total plays are well bracketed, and in which any finite play extends to a finite total one.

Justification Some discipline is also maintained on the subsidiary questions which may be asked in response to a question (and answered before that question is answered). This is done by the use of a notion of explicit justification which can be thought of as providing a pointer from the given move (or the resulting position) to an earlier position. Restrictions on these pointers are given by the following convention.

> **Justification Convention** The justification for a P-question (must be an instance of some earlier O-question [which is not yet answered. The justification for an O-question [must be either the initial position of the game (so the question does not require justification), or else an instance of some earlier P-question (which is not yet answered. Answers are taken to be justified by the unique instance of the question which they answer.

Let us call pointers in accord with this convention *Justification Pointers*. It is natural for what follows to think of them as pointing from instances of moves to instances of moves. (When the pointer is to the initial position, think of it as pointing to the First Cause.)

Moves In the earlier parts of these notes it made sense to regard moves as tokens carrying no specific information. Where there is a structure of justification this is less satisfactory, and it is better to think of moves as carrying with them their justification history and possible futures[24]. However this effects nothing that we need worry about here and we omit the details.

---

[23] The Principle of Pertinence can be found in the established tradition in game semantics of intuitionistic logic, see *e.g.* Felscher's survey paper (Felscher 1986). I learnt of its importance for the theory of algorithms from Robin Gandy who invented it independently and called it the 'no-dangling-question-mark condition'.

[24] This is in line with a reading of dialogue games as involving 'menu-driven' computation.

4.1.2 Dialogue games and innocent strategies

Views Suppose now that we are given a play in some game which is a sequence of (explicitly justified) questions and answers satisfying the Principle of Pertinence and the Justification Convention. Call such a sequence well-formed. Suppose that P is to reply. We are going to require that P's strategy makes use only of some relevant part of this history: this is the *P-view* of the play.

Definition 4.1 *The* Player's view, *or* P-view, $\ulcorner p \urcorner$ *of a well-formed sequence p of moves is defined recursively. Let q range over well-formed sequences of moves, and r over segments of well-formed sequences.*

$$
\begin{aligned}
\ulcorner [\urcorner &\stackrel{\text{def}}{=} [& &\text{if "[" is initial,}\\
\ulcorner q \cdot (\cdot r \cdot [\urcorner &\stackrel{\text{def}}{=} \ulcorner q \urcorner \cdot (\cdot [& &\text{if "(" explicitly justifies "[",}\\
\ulcorner q \cdot) \urcorner &\stackrel{\text{def}}{=} \ulcorner q \urcorner \cdot) & &\\
\ulcorner q \cdot [\cdot r \cdot] \urcorner &\stackrel{\text{def}}{=} \ulcorner q \urcorner & &\text{if "]" explicitly answers "[",}\\
\ulcorner q \cdot (\urcorner &\stackrel{\text{def}}{=} \ulcorner q \urcorner \cdot (&
\end{aligned}
$$

The P-view of a well-formed sequence of moves has the typical shape

$$[\cdot(\cdot)\cdot(\cdot)\cdot(\cdot[\cdot(\cdot)\cdot(\cdot)\cdot(\cdot[\cdot(\cdot)\cdots$$

By construction, whenever there is a pattern "$(\cdot[$" in a P-view, the O-question "[" is explicitly justified by the P-question "(". Also there can be no segments of the form "$[\cdots]$" in a P-view. This may be read in the following two ways:

(i) Player simply ignores answers to questions posed by Opponent;

(ii) Player imagines that Opponent always answers questions directly.

There is a dual definition of *Opponent's view, or O-view,* $\llcorner p \lrcorner$ of a well-formed sequence p of moves:

$$
\begin{aligned}
\llcorner q \cdot [\cdot r \cdot (\lrcorner &\stackrel{\text{def}}{=} \llcorner q \lrcorner \cdot [\cdot(& &\text{if "[" explicitly justifies "(",}\\
\llcorner q \cdot] \lrcorner &\stackrel{\text{def}}{=} \llcorner q \lrcorner \cdot] & &\\
\llcorner q \cdot (\cdot r \cdot) \lrcorner &\stackrel{\text{def}}{=} \llcorner q \lrcorner & &\text{if ")" explicitly answers "(",}\\
\llcorner q \cdot [\lrcorner &\stackrel{\text{def}}{=} \llcorner q \lrcorner \cdot [&
\end{aligned}
$$

The O-view of an empty sequence is the empty sequence. Since a well-formed sequence never begins with a P-question, we omit the case of $\llcorner (\lrcorner$. An O-view can never have a segment of the form $(\cdots)$: Opponent ignores answers to questions posed by Player. An O-view may, for example, have the shape

$$[\cdot(\cdot[\cdot]\cdot[\cdot]\cdot[\cdot(\cdot[\cdot]\cdot[\cdot(\cdots$$

The following properties of P-view and O-view are easy to verify:

- If $q \cdot (\cdot r \cdot)$ is a well-formed sequence and if "(" explicitly justifies ")", then

$$\ulcorner q \cdot (\cdot r \cdot) \urcorner \;\; = \;\; \ulcorner q \urcorner \cdot (\cdot).$$

Dually if $q \cdot [\cdot r \cdot]$ is a well-formed sequence and if "[" explicitly justifies "]", then

$$\llcorner q \cdot [\cdot r \cdot] \lrcorner \;\; = \;\; \llcorner q \lrcorner \cdot [\cdot].$$

- If p is a well-formed sequence ending with an O-move (respectively P-move), then the last move of p is preserved by P-view (respectively O-view); that is to say, the last move of $\ulcorner p \urcorner$ (respectively $\llcorner p \lrcorner$) comes from the same last move of p.

Legal positions The idea is that moves in a P-strategy should be determined, not by the position itself, but by the P-view of the position. However there is a problem. In the above definitions we tacitly assume that the justification pointers take care of themselves. In fact they need not do so; the justifying move may disappear in the P-view. So we need a further condition on justification pointers.

> **Visibility Condition** The visibility condition for a sequence q is as follows. For any initial subsequence $p \cdot ($ of the sequence q, the O-question "[" explicitly justifying the P-question "(" occurs in the P-view of p. Similarly for any initial subsequence $p \cdot [$ of the sequence q, the P-question explicitly justifying "[" occurs in the O-view of p.

Definition 4.2 *A play in a game of questions and answers is a* legal position *if it satisfies the Principle of Pertinence, the Justification Convention and the Visibility Condition.*

Clearly the set of legal positions is prefix closed. Furthermore for legal positions, the justification pointers do take care of themselves.

Proposition 4.1 *If p is a legal position, then both the O-view and the P-view of p are legal positions.*

Definition 4.3 *A* dialogue game for fun *or* dialogue fun game *consists of a nonempty tree (that is, prefix closed collection) of legal positions.*

Innocent strategies We are now in a position to describe a restricted notion of strategy. It is simplest to give this in function mode.

Definition 4.4 *Suppose that A is a simple dialogue game.*
A P-strategy (as in Section 2 but presented in function mode) $\sigma : O_A \longrightarrow M_A$ is an innocent strategy *if and only if whenever p and q are odd and $\ulcorner p \urcorner = \ulcorner q \urcorner$ then $\sigma(p) = \sigma(q)$ (in the usual sense that if one is defined then so is the other).*
The force of the definition is that an innocent strategy only makes use of the P-view. Hence it makes sense to regard the innocent strategy as being given by its restriction to P-views. Then a finite innocent strategy *is one whose restriction to P-views is a finite function.*

4.1.3 Categories of dialogue games

We now describe some categories of dialogue games. These come in two flavours: games for fun (with partial strategies) and games to win (with total strategies). We can follow the pattern already established in Sections 2 and 3. So first, there is a tensor product and linear function space for dialogue fun-games and for dialogue win-games. We can adopt the definition of identity strategy and composition of strategies from Definition 2.4; but, since we are now dealing with innocent strategies, there is something to prove. The basic (non-trivial) combinatorial fact is that innocent strategies compose.

Proposition 4.2 *For any dialogue game A, the strategy ι_A is innocent. And if $\sigma : A \multimap B$ and $\tau : B \multimap C$ are innocent, then so is their composite $\sigma; \tau$.*

As an immediate consequence, we have SMCCs of games.

Theorem 4.3 *There is a SMCC $\mathcal{LDFG}$ of linear dialogue fun-games, and a SMCC $\mathcal{LDWG}$ of linear dialogue win-games.*

In each case, there is a comonad $(!, \varepsilon, \delta)$ carrying a comonoid structure. Hence we get CCCs of games, and since we have products in the linear categories, these may be taken to be the Kleisli categories.

Theorem 4.4 *The Kleisli category of the comonad $(!, \varepsilon, \delta)$ on the SMCC $\mathcal{LDFG}$ of linear dialogue fun-games is a CCC $\mathcal{DFG}$ of dialogue fun-games. The Kleisli category of the comonad $(!, \varepsilon, \delta)$ on the SMCC $\mathcal{LDWG}$ of linear dialogue fun-games is a CCC $\mathcal{DWG}$ of dialogue win-games.*

A subcategory of $\mathcal{DFG}$ is described in detail in Hyland and Ong (1995) where it is used as the basis for the construction of an intensionally fully abstract model for PCF.[25]

Exercises 16

 1. *Show that in any play satisfying the Principle of Pertinence the number of questions is always greater than or equal to the number of answers. (Recall that this is the simple algorithm for checking correct bracketing of expressions.)*

 2. *Show that the operation of taking the P-view is idempotent. Similarly for taking the O-view.*

 3. *Describe the sequences of the form $\ulcorner \llcorner p \lrcorner \urcorner$, and of the form $\llcorner \ulcorner p \urcorner \lrcorner$. What do you notice?*

 4. *Show that what goes for questions goes for answers, that is, that the explicitly justifying question of every P-answer (respectively O-answer) in a legal position appears in the P-view (respectively O-view) of the legal position up to that point.*

[25] A model is intensionally fully abstract just when its observational or contextual quotient is fully abstract.

4.2 Dialogue Games and Logic

4.2.1 A Compactness Theorem for Strategies

In this section we identify a subcategory of the category $\mathcal{DWG}$ of dialogue win-games which is suited to modelling the proof theory of finitary logic.

Let us say that a game is *acyclic* just when there are no justification cycles, and *finitary* just when in addition, the number of questions and answers is finite. These are simple and plausible requirements on a game for finitary logic. We need an additional more subtle property.

Justice Suppose that p is an infinite play in a (finitary) game. We wish to catch the intuition that it is either P's fault or O's fault that the play has gone on so long; and that it is the one at fault who should lose. We do not go into the formal details, but give the basic idea.

> **Principle of Justice** Suppose that p is an infinite play in a game A, that Player asks questions justified by a specific instance of [infinitely often in such a way Player can see (from his view) that he asks infinitely often; then we may say that Player is *time-wasting*. Similarly Opponent may be time-wasting. However in a given play only one can be time wasting. We say that A *satisfies the principle of justice* if and only if for every infinite play p, if Player is time-wasting then Player loses, and similarly for Opponent.

Definition 4.5 *A dialogue win game is just if and only if it is finitary and satisfies the principle of justice.*

Proposition 4.5 *The collection of just games forms a full subCCC $\mathcal{JG}$ of the CCC $\mathcal{DWG}$.*

For just games there is a finiteness or compactness theorem, which seems fundamental for a good theory of proofs.

Theorem 4.6 *(Compactness Theorem) All winning strategies in a just game are finite.*[26]

4.2.2 Categories of Games of Argument

Our intention now is to obtain an appealing model for proofs, while avoiding questions of polymorphism or uniformity.[27] The approach is quite intuitive in as much as it relies on an idea which is fundamental to the Lorenzen tradition.

---

[26] Recall that an innocent strategy is finite just when the partial function (on views) giving the strategy is finite.

[27] We focus here on games with total strategies, though a version involving partial strategies is possible.

Start by fixing a set C of claims or confessions. All definitions and results are parameterised over this fixed set (which is to be regarded as a set of propositional constants).

Definition 4.6 *A* game of argument *is a dialogue win-game whose questions are indexed by elements of C; and where every question has as unique answer its index from C.*
In a play in a game of argument, both players may answer or admit $c \in C$ (possibly many times). A play *is* good *if and only if Player never admits $c \in C$ before Opponent does.*

The notions of tensor product and of linear function space carry over to this variation on the notion of a dialogue game. While the general notion of strategy (see Definitions 2.2 and 3.2) should by now be sufficiently clear, we are interested in rather special total strategies.

Definition 4.7 *A total P-strategy in an argument is*

- innocent *so long as it only makes use of the P-view of a position;*
- good *so long as all plays in accord with it are good;*
- winning *so long as all plays in accord with it are wins for Player.*

We again adopt the definition of identity strategy and composition of strategies from Definition 2.4; but now we need to show that good winning innocent strategies compose. We have commented on innocence in Section 4.1.2, dealt with winning in Section 3.1.1 and fortunately goodness takes care of itself.

Proposition 4.7 *For any argument A, the strategy $\iota_A : A \multimap B$ is a good, winning, innocent strategy. And if $\sigma : A \multimap B$ and $\tau : B \multimap C$ are good, winning innocent strategies, then so is their composite $\sigma; \tau : A \multimap C$.*

As an immediate consequence, we have SMCCs of games.

Theorem 4.8 *There is a* SMCC $\mathcal{LAG}$ *of linear games of argument.*

Again there is a comonad $(!, \varepsilon, \delta)$ carrying a comonoid structure. Hence we get a CCC of games, and since we have products in the linear categories, this may be taken to be the Kleisli categories.

Theorem 4.9 *The Kleisli category of the comonad $(!, \varepsilon, \delta)$ on the* SMCC $\mathcal{LAG}$ *of linear linear games of argument is a* CCC $\mathcal{AG}$ *of games of argument.*

4.2.3 $\mathcal{AG}$ as a model for constructive proofs

Regard the collection C of answers in the arguments as a set of propositional constants (or type constants). An interpretation of the proof theory of the $(\wedge, \Rightarrow)$-fragment of intuitionistic logic (or equivalently of the corresponding typed λ-calculus) is given by an interpretation of the elements of C as arguments.

Definition 4.8 *The* canonical interpretation *is given by interpreting each $c \in C$ as the argument in which O has just one opening question which can (only) be immediately answered by c.*

Inspection of this interpretation motivates the definition of 'good play'. In such a complex play, P acts in a cautious fashion and maintains no proposition which O has not already conceded.

The canonical interpretation is weakly complete for intuitionistic logic.

Theorem 4.10 *Let Φ and Ψ be propositional formulae in $(\wedge, \Rightarrow)$-logic with constants from C. Suppose that in the canonical interpretation there is a map $\Phi \longrightarrow \Psi$. Then $\Phi \vdash \Psi$ is provable in intuitionistic logic, and (equivalently) there is a λ-term of type $\Phi \Rightarrow \Psi$.*

The canonical interpretation in $\mathcal{AG}$ is far from being strongly complete; but this could reasonably be regarded as a positive feature. We get a new CCC and with it a more generous notion of proof. Let us close by considering briefly how the category $\mathcal{AG}$ (based on C) is related to the free CCC (on objects from C), or equivalently to the simply typed lambda calculus under $\beta\eta$-equality (with base types from C). Suppose we vary the notion of a game of argument so that once an answer has been given, all the outstanding questions must be answered in order. Then as the answers are determined by the questions, they are effectively redundant, and there is simply an option to call a halt. This gives us yet another CCC $\mathcal{RAG}$ of restricted games of argument: the objects are those of $\mathcal{AG}$, but the strategies are restricted. A restricted strategy can be read straightforwardly as a strategy, and so the CCC $\mathcal{RAG}$ embeds in the CCC $\mathcal{AG}$. This is hardly surprising in view of the following result.

Theorem 4.11 *The CCC $\mathcal{RAG}$ based on C is a free CCC generated by the set of objects C.*

This is a form of strong completeness: the proof is a simplified version of the definability result in Hyland and Ong (1995). Closely related ideas are in Felscher (1986), and Herbelin has independently made essentially the same observation from a somewhat different point of view.

Exercises 17

1. *Show that a play p in $A \otimes B$ can be good without its projection p_A being good.*

2. *Any argument A can be thought of as a win-game* $W(A)$. *Show that* W
   extends to a functor $\mathcal{LA} \longrightarrow \mathcal{LWG}$. *Is* W *a monoidal functor?*

3. *Test Theorem 4.10, by checking that, in the canonical interpretation, the
   Pierce formula does not hold.*

4. *How many maps* $A \times A \longrightarrow A$ *can you find in* $\mathcal{AG}$?

5. *Investigate further the relation between* $\mathcal{AG}$ *and* $\mathcal{RAG}$.

A Appendix: Monoidal Categories

The standard definitions of symmetric monoidal closed category, of monoidal functor and of monoidal natural transformation are as follows.

A *monoidal category* is a category $\mathcal{V}$ equipped with a functor $\otimes : \mathcal{V} \times \mathcal{V} \longrightarrow \mathcal{V}$, an object I of $\mathcal{V}$, and natural isomorphisms

$$a_{UVW} : (U \otimes V) \otimes W \longrightarrow U \otimes (V \otimes W),$$

$$l_U : I \otimes U \longrightarrow U \text{ and } r_U : U \otimes I \longrightarrow U,$$

such that the *coherence diagrams*

$$((U \otimes V) \otimes W) \otimes X \xrightarrow{a} (U \otimes V) \otimes (W \otimes X) \xrightarrow{a} U \otimes (V \otimes (W \otimes X))$$

$$\begin{array}{ccc}
a \otimes 1 \downarrow & & \uparrow 1 \otimes a \\
(U \otimes (V \otimes W)) \otimes X & \xrightarrow{\quad a \quad} & U \otimes ((V \otimes W) \otimes X)
\end{array}$$

$$(U \otimes I) \otimes V \xrightarrow{\quad a \quad} U \otimes (I \otimes V)$$

$$r \otimes 1 \searrow \quad \swarrow 1 \otimes l$$

$$U \otimes V$$

commute.
A *symmetry* for a monoidal category is a natural isomorphism

$$c_{UV} : U \otimes V \longrightarrow V \otimes U$$

with $c^2 = 1$, and such that the *coherence diagrams*

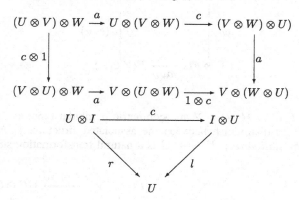

$$U \otimes I \xrightarrow{\quad c \quad} I \otimes U$$

$$r \searrow \qquad \swarrow l$$

$$U$$

commute.

A *closed structure* on a (symmetric) monoidal category is given by a bifunctor
$[-,-] : \mathcal{V}^{\mathrm{op}} \times \mathcal{V} \to \mathcal{V}$ together with an isomorphism

$$\mathcal{V}(U \otimes V, W) \cong \mathcal{V}(U, [V, W])$$

natural in U, V and W.

A *symmetric monoidal closed category* (SMCC) is a monoidal category equipped
with a symmetry and a closed structure.

Suppose that $\mathcal{U}$ and $\mathcal{V}$ are SMCCs. (We shall not trouble to distinguish between the
respective structures on the categories.) A *symmetric monoidal functor* is a functor
$F : \mathcal{U} \longrightarrow \mathcal{V}$ equipped with *mediating natural transformations*

$$m_I : I \longrightarrow F(I)$$

$$m_{UV} : F(U) \otimes F(V) \longrightarrow F(U \otimes V)$$

such that the diagrams

$$
\begin{array}{ccc}
FI \otimes FU & \xrightarrow{m_{IU}} & F(I \otimes U) \\
{\scriptstyle m_I \otimes 1_{FU}} \downarrow & & \downarrow {\scriptstyle F(l_U)} \\
I \otimes FU & \xrightarrow{\quad l_{FU} \quad} & FU
\end{array}
\qquad
\begin{array}{ccc}
FU \otimes FI & \xrightarrow{m_{UI}} & F(U \otimes I) \\
{\scriptstyle 1_{FU} \otimes m_I} \downarrow & & \downarrow {\scriptstyle F(\rho_A)} \\
FU \otimes I & \xrightarrow{\quad \rho_{FU} \quad} & FU
\end{array}
$$

$$
\begin{array}{ccccc}
(FU \otimes FV) \otimes FW & \xrightarrow{m_{UV} \otimes 1_{FW}} & F(U \otimes V) \otimes FW & \xrightarrow{m_{(U \otimes V)W}} & F((U \otimes V) \otimes W) \\
{\scriptstyle a} \downarrow & & & & \downarrow {\scriptstyle Fa} \\
FU \otimes (FV \otimes FW) & \xrightarrow{\quad 1_{FU} \otimes m_{VW} \quad} & FU \otimes F(V \otimes W) & \xrightarrow{\quad m_{U(V \otimes W)} \quad} & F(U \otimes (V \otimes W))
\end{array}
$$

$$FU \otimes FV \xrightarrow{m_{UV}} F(U \otimes V)$$

$$c_{UV} \downarrow \qquad\qquad \downarrow F(c_{UV})$$

$$FV \otimes FU \xrightarrow[m_{VU}]{} F(V \otimes U)$$

commute.

Suppose that $F, G : \mathcal{U} \longrightarrow \mathcal{V}$ are symmetric monoidal functors. (Again we do not trouble to distinguish between the associated structures.) A *monoidal natural transformation* $\alpha : F \longrightarrow G$ is a natural transformation such that the diagrams

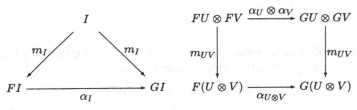

commute.

It is straightforward to compose symmetric monoidal functors and monoidal natural transformations.

Proposition SMCCs, *symmetric monoidal functors and monoidal natural transformations form a 2-category.*

A *monoidal comonad* on a SMCC $\mathcal{G}$ consists of a symmetric monoidal functor $! : \mathcal{G} \to \mathcal{G}$ (equipped with mediating natural transformations) together with monoidal natural transformations $\varepsilon : ! \longrightarrow 1_{\mathcal{G}}$ and $\delta : ! \longrightarrow !!$ which give a comonad on $\mathcal{G}$. (Thus a monoidal comonad is just a comonad in the 2-category of SMCCs.)

Definition A.1 *A Linear category is a SMCC $\mathcal{C}$, together with a monoidal comonad $(!, \varepsilon, \delta, m_{AB}, m_I)$ on $\mathcal{C}$, which is equipped with monoidal natural transformations with components $e_A : !A \to I$ and $d_A : !A \to !A \otimes !A$ which give each free coalgebra $\delta_A : !A \to !!A$ the structure of a commutative comonoid, this structure being preserved by coalgebra morphisms between free coalgebras.*

The condition that $(!A, d_A, e_A)$ forms a commutative comonoid means that the following three diagrams commute.

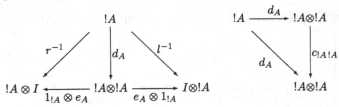

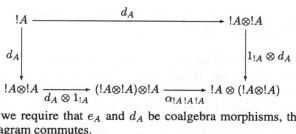

In addition we require that e_A and d_A be coalgebra morphisms, that is, that the following diagram commutes.

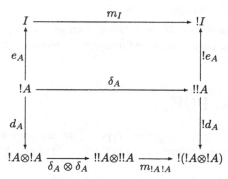

Finally all coalgebra morphisms between (free) coalgebras are also comonoid morphisms: if $f : !A \longrightarrow !B$ is a coalgebra morphism, then it is also a comonoid morphism between the comonoids $(!A, e_A, d_A)$ and $(!B, e_B, d_B)$, i.e. it makes the following diagram commute.

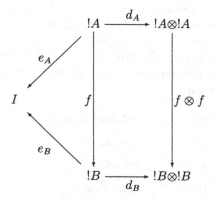

These conditions were introduced in Benton, Bierman, de Paiva, and Hyland (1992), and their consequences were closely studied in Bierman (1993). The crucial point is the following.

Theorem *A Linear category, C, is a categorical model for (intuitionistic) multiplicative exponential linear logic.*

Things simplify markedly in the presence of product, as first noticed by Seely, and further analysed by Bierman (1995).

Definition A.2 *A* new-Seely category *is a* SMCC *with finite products, C, together with a comonad, $(!,\varepsilon,\delta)$ and natural isomorphisms, $n_I : I \longrightarrow !1$ and n_{AB} : $!A \otimes !B \longrightarrow !(A \times B)$, such that the adjunction, $\langle F, G, \eta, \varepsilon \rangle$, between C and the (co-)Kleisli category $C_!$ is a* monoidal *adjunction.*

In the presence of products, a Linear Category will be a new-Seely category, and we shall have the following basic result.

Theorem (Seely, Bierman) *Given a Linear Category with products, C, the co-Kleisli category $C_!$ is cartesian closed and the adjunction between C and $C_!$ is a* monoidal *adjunction.*

B Appendix: PCF

PCF is a typed programming language. Types of the language are Church's simple types (Church 1940) also referred to as PCF-types. They are defined as follows:

$$A \ ::= \ \iota \qquad \text{natural numbers}$$
$$| \quad o \qquad \text{booleans}$$
$$| \quad A \Rightarrow A \quad \text{arrow or function type.}$$

Let the meta-variable β range over ground types ι and o. As usual $\Rightarrow$ associates to the right: $A_1 \Rightarrow A_2 \Rightarrow A_3$ is read as $A_1 \Rightarrow (A_2 \Rightarrow A_3)$. Each simple type can be uniquely expressed as $A_1 \Rightarrow A_2 \cdots \Rightarrow A_n \Rightarrow \beta$ $(n \geq 0)$; in the traditional notation of type theory this is abbreviated as $(A_1, \cdots, A_n, \beta)$. For example the type $((\iota \Rightarrow \iota) \Rightarrow \iota \Rightarrow \iota) \Rightarrow \iota \Rightarrow \iota$ is abbreviated as $(((\iota, \iota), \iota, \iota), \iota, \iota)$.

For each type A, fix a denumerable set of variables. Raw PCF-terms are defined by the following grammar:

$$s \ ::= \ \Omega^A \qquad \text{undefined term}$$
$$| \quad c^A \qquad \text{constant}$$
$$| \quad x \qquad \text{variable}$$
$$| \quad (s \cdot s) \qquad \text{application}$$
$$| \quad (\lambda x : A.s) \quad \text{abstraction}$$
$$| \quad \mathbf{Y}^A(s) \qquad \text{general recursive term, or Y-term;}$$

where c^A ranges over the basic arithmetic constants. Type information is omitted where irrelevant. The application $(s \cdot t)$ is written st, and application associates to the left: $st_1 \cdots t_n$ abbreviates $(\cdots((st_1)t_2)\cdots t_n)$. The phrase $s : A$ means that the type of the term s is A, derived according to the following rules:

$$\Omega^A : A \qquad\qquad c^A : A$$

$$\frac{s : A \Rightarrow A}{\mathbf{Y}^A(s) : A} \qquad \frac{s : A_1 \Rightarrow A_2 \quad t : A_1}{(s \cdot t) : A_2} \qquad \frac{s : A_2}{(\lambda x : A_1.s) : A_1 \Rightarrow A_2}$$

The basic arithmetic constants are as follows:

$$
\begin{array}{lll}
n & : \quad \iota & \text{numerals, for each natural number } n \geqslant 0 \\
\mathsf{t}, \mathsf{f} & : \quad o & \text{booleans: truth and falsity} \\
\mathsf{succ} & : \quad \iota \Rightarrow \iota & \text{successor} \\
\mathsf{pred} & : \quad \iota \Rightarrow \iota & \text{predecessor} \\
\mathsf{zero?} & : \quad \iota \Rightarrow o & \text{test for zero} \\
\mathsf{cond}^\iota & : \quad o \Rightarrow \iota \Rightarrow \iota \Rightarrow \iota & \text{natural number conditional} \\
\mathsf{cond}^o & : \quad o \Rightarrow o \Rightarrow o \Rightarrow o & \text{boolean conditional.}
\end{array}
$$

The notion of free and bound variables is completely standard; a closed term is a term without any free variables. Term substitution is written $s[t/x]$.

Operational Semantics *Programs* of PCF are closed terms of ground type. Values are λ-abstractions and constants of ground type; the meta-variable v ranges over values. Following the function paradigm, to compute a program in PCF is to evaluate it. The operational semantics of PCF is given in terms of a Martin-Löf style evaluation relation: $s \Downarrow v$ meaning "the closed term s evaluates to the value v".

$$v \Downarrow v \qquad \frac{u[t/x] \Downarrow v}{(\lambda x.u)t \Downarrow v} \qquad \frac{s \Downarrow v \quad vt \Downarrow v'}{st \Downarrow v'}$$

$$\frac{s \Downarrow \mathsf{t} \quad u \Downarrow v}{\mathsf{cond}^\beta suu' \Downarrow v} \qquad \frac{s \Downarrow \mathsf{f} \quad u' \Downarrow v}{\mathsf{cond}^\beta suu' \Downarrow v}$$

$$\frac{s\mathbf{Y}^A(s) \Downarrow v}{\mathbf{Y}^A(s) \Downarrow v}$$

$$\frac{s \Downarrow n}{\mathsf{succ} s \Downarrow n+1} \qquad \frac{s \Downarrow n+1}{\mathsf{pred} s \Downarrow n} \qquad \frac{s \Downarrow 0}{\mathsf{pred} s \Downarrow 0}$$

$$\frac{s \Downarrow 0}{\mathsf{zero?} s \Downarrow \mathsf{t}} \qquad \frac{s \Downarrow n+1}{\mathsf{zero?} s \Downarrow \mathsf{f}}$$

The type theory PCF The operational semantics for PCF reflects an intuitive understanding of the meaning of the terms. In this view the reductions are justified as the replacement of a term by an equal term. Thus the intuitive semantics can be given expression in an equational theory. In the case of PCF this amounts to a type theory related to Scott's original formulation. A (core) type theory for PCF $\mathbb{T}$ is given as follows. Take the typing rules already given, and define a relation $s = t$ on typed terms (in context) by taking, in addition to the usual rules for equality, the following:

$$(\lambda x : A.s)t = s[t/x] \qquad \lambda x : A.sx = s \quad \text{(if x not free in s)}$$
$$\text{cond}^\beta tst = s \qquad \text{cond}^\beta fst = t$$
$$s(\mathbf{Y}^A(s)) = \mathbf{Y}^A(s)$$
$$\text{succ } n = n+1 \qquad \text{pred } n+1 = n \qquad \text{pred } 0 = 0$$
$$\text{zero?}0 = t \qquad \text{zero?}n+1 = f$$

It is important that there be a good relation between the reduction relation $\Downarrow$ of the operational semantics and the equality of the type theory. This is given by the following result.

Proposition *For any programs s and t, if s and t are equal in the type theory* $\mathbb{T}$ *then for any ground value v $s \Downarrow v \iff t \Downarrow v$.*

What is commonly called a denotational semantics for PCF is essentially some kind of interpretation of (model for) the type theory which we have just introduced. The usual form of a model for PCF is that the types are interpreted as domains and the terms as continuous (or stable continuous) maps between domains. The major concern in modelling programming languages is with issues of 'adequacy' and 'full abstraction'. For a survey of the famous full abstraction problem for PCF see Ong (1986). Game theoretic solutions to the problem are offered in Abramsky, Jagadeesan, and Malacaria (1994) Abramsky, Jagadeesan, and Malacaria (1995) and in Hyland and Ong (1995). For other recent approaches to sequentiality see Brookes and Geva (1992), Bucciarelli and Ehrhard (1994), Plotkin and Winskel (1994) and Winskel (1994).

References

Abramsky, S. (1997). Semantics of interaction. In this volume, pp 1–32.

Abramsky, S. and R. Jagadeesan (1994). Games and full completeness for multiplicative linear logic. *Journal of Symbolic Logic 59*, 543–574.

Abramsky, S., R. Jagadeesan, and P. Malacaria (1994). Full abstraction for PCF (extended abstract). In *Theoretical Aspects of Computer Software: TACS'94*, Volume 789 of *Lecture Notes in Computer Science*, pp. 1–15. Springer-Verlag.

Abramsky, S., R. Jagadeesan, and P. Malacaria (1995). Games and full abstraction of PCF. Submitted to Information and Computation.

Benton, P. N., G. M. Bierman, V. C. V. de Paiva, and J. M. E. Hyland (1992). Term assignment for intuitionistic linear logic. Technical Report 262, Computer Laboratory, University of Cambridge.

Berry, G. and P.-L. Curien (1982). Sequential algorithms on concrete data structures. *Theoretical Computer Science 20*, 265–321.

Bierman, G. M. (1993). *On Intuitionistic Linear Logic.* Ph. D. thesis, Computer Laboratory, Cambridge University.

Bierman, G. M. (1995). What is a categorical model of linear logic? In *Proceedings of Second International Conference on Typed Lambda Calculi and Applications*, Volume 902 of *Lecture Notes in Computer Science*, pp. 78–93. North-Holland.

Blass, A. (1972). Degrees of indeterminacy of games. *Fundamenta Mathematica 77*, 1972.

Blass, A. (1992). A game semantics for linear logic. *Annals of Pure and Applied Logic 56*, 183–220.

Brookes, S. and S. Geva (1992). Stable and sequential functions on scott domains. Technical Report CMU-CS-92-121, School of Computer Science, Carnegie-Mellon Univeristy.

Bucciarelli, A. and T. Ehrhard (1994). Sequentiality in an extensional framework. *Information and Computation 110*, 265–296.

Cartwright, R., P.-L. Curien, and M. Felleisen (1994). Fully abstract semantics for observably sequential languages. *Information and Computation 111*, 297–401.

Church, A. (1940). A formulation of a simple theory of types. *Journal of Symbolic Logic 5*, 56–68.

Conway, J. H. (1976). *On Numbers and Games.* Academic Press.

Coquand, T., C. A. Gunter, and G. Winskel (1989). Domain theoretic models of polymorphism. *Information and Computation 81*, 123–167.

Crole, R. L. (1993). *Categories for Types.* Cambridge University Press.

Curien, P.-L. (1993). *Categorical Combinators, Sequential Algorithms and Sequential Functions.* Birkhauser.

Felscher, W. (1986). Dialogues as a foundation for intuitionist logic. In D. Gabbay and F. Guenther (Eds.), *Handbook of Philosophical Logic*, Volume III, pp. 341–372. D. Reidel.

Freyd, P. J. and A. Scedrov (1990). *Categories and Allegories.* North-Holland.

Girard, J.-Y. (1986). The system f of variable types, fifteen years later. *Theoretical Computer Science 45*, 159–192.

Girard, J.-Y. (1987). Linear logic. *Theoretical Computer Science 50*, 1–102.

Girard, J.-Y. (1989a). Geometry of interaction i: interpretation of system f. In Ferro, Bonotto, Valantini, and Zanardo (Eds.), *Proceedings of Logic Colloquium '88*, pp. 221–260. North-Holland.

184

Girard, J.-Y. (1989b). *Proofs and Types.* Cambridge University Press.

Hyland, J. M. E. and C.-H. L. Ong (1995). On full abstraction for PCF: I, II and III. Submitted to Information and Computation.

Kahn, G. and G. D. Plotkin (1978). Domaines concrets. Technical Report 336, INRIA-LABORIA.

Kahn, G. and G. D. Plotkin (1993). Concrete domains. *Theoretical Computer Science 121*, 187–277.

Kelly, G. M. (1982). *Basic Concepts of Enriched Category Theory.* LMS Lecture Notes. Cambridge University Press.

Kelly, G. M. and M. L. Laplaza (1980). Coherence for compact closed categories. *Journal of Pure and Applied Algebra 19*, 193–213.

Lambek, J. and P. J. Scott (1986). *Introduction to Higher Order Categorical Logic.* Cambridge University Press.

Lorenzen, P. and K. Lorenz (1978). *Dialogische Logik.* Wissenschaft Buchgesellschaft.

Mycielski, J. (1964). On the axiom of determinateness. *Fundamenta Mathematica 53*, 205–224.

Ong, C.-H. L. (1986). Correspondence between operational and denotational semntics. In S. Abramsky, D. Gabbay, and T. S. E. Maibaum (Eds.), *Handbook of Logic in Computer Science*, Volume 4, pp. 341–372. Oxford University Press.

Plotkin, G. D. (1977). LCF as a programming language. *Theoretical Computer Science 5*, 223–255.

Plotkin, G. D. and G. Winskel (1994). Bistructures, bidomains and linear logic. Technical Report RS-94-9, BRICS.

Taylor, P. (1986). *Recursive Domains, Indexed Category Theory and Polymorphism.* Ph. D. thesis, DPMMS, Cambridge University.

Winskel, G. (1994). Stable bistructure models of PCF. Technical Report RS-94-13, BRICS.

Metalanguages and Applications

Eugenio Moggi

Contents

1 Introduction

The aim of these notes is to describe the monadic and incremental approaches to the denotational semantics of programming languages. This is done via the use of suitable typed metalanguages, which capture the relevant structure of semantic categories. The monadic and incremental approaches are formulated in the setting of a type-theoretic framework for the following reasons:

- a type theory with **dependent types** allows a precise, concise and general description of the two approaches, based on *signatures* as abstract representations for languages;

- there are various implementations (e.g. LEGO and CoQ) which provide computer assistance for several type-theories, and without computer assistance it seems unlikely that either of the two approaches can go beyond toy languages.

On the other hand, the monadic and incremental approaches can be described already with a naive set-theoretic semantics. Therefore, knowledge of Domain Theory and Category Theory becomes essential only in Section 6.

The presentation adopted differs from advanced textbooks on denotational semantics in the following aspects:

- it makes significant use of type theory as a tool for describing languages and calculi, while this is usually done via a set of formation or inference rules;

185

- it incorporates ideas from Axiomatic and Synthetic Domain Theory into metalanguages, while most metalanguages for denotational semantics are variants of LCF;

- it stresses the use of metalanguages to give semantics via translation (using the monadic and incremental approaches), but avoids a detailed analysis of the categories used in denotational semantics.

The remaining sections are organised as follows:

- Section 2 introduces some toy languages used in examples.

- Section 3 gives a brief overview of different approaches to programming language semantics, in order to place the use of metalanguages into context.

- Section 4 introduces a logical framework suitable for our applications, and explains how it may be used.

- Section 5 explains possible uses of typed metalanguages for giving semantics to programming languages. Then, it introduces computational types and describes the monadic and incremental approaches.

- Section 6 addresses the issue of recursive definitions in the context of metalanguages. This is done by incorporating ideas from axiomatic and synthetic domain theory. Finally, it revises the notion of computational types (and its applications) in this richer setting.

Acknowledgements. These notes are partly based on joint work with P. Cenciarelli, some unpublished work by A. Simpson, and the MSc thesis of N. Signa. I would like to thank several people for discussions on Axiomatic and Synthetic Domain Theory: B. Reus, M. Fiore, P. Freyd, M. Hyland, A. Pitts, P. Rosolini, A. Simpson and T. Streicher. This notes were completed during my stay at the Newton Institute, and I would like to thank the Institute and the organisers of the program on "Semantics of Computation" for inviting me and providing such a pleasant working environment. I have used Paul Taylor's package for diagrams.

2   Toy programming languages

In this section we introduce some toy programming languages. They will be used as running examples to illustrate the use of metalanguages in describing the denotational semantics of programming languages.

These toy languages include a simple functional language and simple extensions of it obtained by adding the following features: divergence, mutable store, exception handling, non-determinism, parallelism.

We present the functional language first, by giving its syntax, its typing rules, and two operational semantics (one call-by-value and one call-by-name). Then we introduce its extensions, by saying how their presentations differ from that of the simple functional language.

Here programming languages are given via an operational semantics, since this requires very little mathematical sophistication and it is enough to give meaning to *observations*. However, in Section 3 we will describe alternative approaches, the trade-offs involved, and criteria to compare different semantics for the same language.

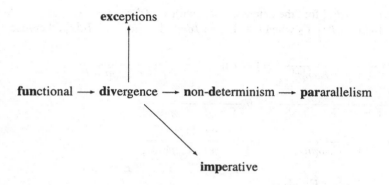

2.1 A simple functional language

A simple way of describing the syntax of a programming language is first to define *pseudo-expressions* by a BNF, and then define *well-formed expressions* by a set of typing rules. Often, the operational semantics can be defined for pseudo-expressions, while the denotational semantics is given by induction on the derivation that an expression is well-formed.

2.1.1 Syntax

The syntax for types and expressions of the language is given by the following BNF:

types $\tau \in T ::= unit \mid bool \mid nat \mid \tau_1 {\Rightarrow} \tau_2$

identifiers $x \in Id ::=$ an infinite set

expressions $e \in Exp ::= x \mid$
$\qquad * \mid$
$\qquad tt \mid ff \mid if(e, e_1, e_2) \mid$
$\qquad 0 \mid s(e) \mid It(e_0, (\lambda x : \tau.e_s), e) \mid$
$\qquad (\lambda x : \tau_1.e_2) \mid ap(e, e_1)$

188 *Moggi*

2.1.2 Typing rules

We give a set of rules to derive judgements of the form $\Gamma \vdash e : Exp[\tau]$, i.e. "expression e has type τ in typing context Γ". A **typing context** Γ is a sequence $x_1 : Id[\tau_1], \ldots, x_n : Id[\tau_n]$ s.t. the x_i are distinct.

Notation 2.1 We write:

- $DV(\Gamma)$ for the set of the x_i, i.e. "the set of declared variables in Γ";

- $\Gamma(x_i)$ for $Id[\tau_i]$, i.e. "the type of x_i in Γ";

- $\Gamma; x : Id[\tau]$ for "the extension of Γ with $x : Id[\tau]$", i.e.
  $\Gamma_1, x : Id[\tau], \Gamma_2$ when $\Gamma \equiv \Gamma_1, x : Id[\tau'], \Gamma_2$ and $\Gamma, x : Id[\tau]$ otherwise.

$$var \frac{}{\Gamma \vdash x : Exp[\tau]} \ \Gamma(x) = Id[\tau] \qquad * \frac{}{\Gamma \vdash * : Exp[unit]}$$

$$tt \frac{}{\Gamma \vdash tt : Exp[bool]} \qquad ff \frac{}{\Gamma \vdash ff : Exp[bool]}$$

$$0 \frac{}{\Gamma \vdash 0 : Exp[nat]} \qquad s \frac{\Gamma \vdash e : Exp[nat]}{\Gamma \vdash s(e) : Exp[nat]}$$

$$if \frac{\Gamma \vdash e : Exp[bool] \quad \Gamma \vdash e_1, e_2 : Exp[\tau]}{\Gamma \vdash if(e, e_1, e_2) : Exp[\tau]} \qquad It \frac{\Gamma \vdash e : Exp[nat] \quad \Gamma \vdash e_0 : Exp[\tau] \quad \Gamma; x : Id[\tau] \vdash e_s : Exp[\tau]}{\Gamma \vdash It(e_0, (\lambda x : \tau.e_s), e) : Exp[\tau]}$$

$$ap \frac{\Gamma \vdash e : Exp[\tau_1 \Rightarrow \tau_2] \quad \Gamma \vdash e_1 : Exp[\tau_1]}{\Gamma \vdash ap(e, e_1) : Exp[\tau_2]} \qquad ab \frac{\Gamma; x : Id[\tau_1] \vdash e_2 : Exp[\tau_2]}{\Gamma \vdash \lambda x : \tau_1.e_2 : Exp[\tau_1 \Rightarrow \tau_2]}$$

Remark 2.2 There are some basic properties of the typing rules one would like: it should be decidable whether a judgement $\Gamma \vdash e : Exp[\tau]$ is derivable, and its derivation should be unique, so that the interpretation of a judgement can be given unambiguously by induction on its derivation.

2.1.3 CBV operational semantics

The call-by-value (CBV) operational semantics is given by an evaluation relation $\Downarrow \subset Exp \times Val$, where $Val \subset Exp$ is the set of values:
$$v \in Val ::= \quad x \mid * \mid tt \mid ff \mid 0 \mid s(v) \mid (\lambda x : \tau_1.e_2)$$
The evaluation relation is defined by giving a set of rules for deriving judgements of the form $e \Downarrow v$, i.e. "expression e evaluates to value v".

$$val \frac{}{v \Downarrow v}$$

$$s\frac{e \Downarrow v}{s(e) \Downarrow s(v)}$$

$$if\frac{\begin{array}{c}e \Downarrow tt\\ e_1 \Downarrow v\end{array}}{if(e, e_1, e_2) \Downarrow v} \qquad if\frac{\begin{array}{c}e \Downarrow ff\\ e_2 \Downarrow v\end{array}}{if(e, e_1, e_2) \Downarrow v}$$

$$It\frac{\begin{array}{c}e \Downarrow 0\\ e_0 \Downarrow v\end{array}}{It(e_0, (\lambda x : \tau.e_s), e) \Downarrow v} \qquad It\frac{\begin{array}{c}e \Downarrow s(v_n)\\ It(e_0, (\lambda x : \tau.e_s), v_n) \Downarrow v_s\\ e_s[x := v_s] \Downarrow v\end{array}}{It(e_0, (\lambda x : \tau.e_s), e) \Downarrow v}$$

$$ap\frac{\begin{array}{c}e \Downarrow (\lambda x : \tau_1.e_2)\\ e_1 \Downarrow v_1\\ e_2[x := v_1] \Downarrow v\end{array}}{ap(e, e_1) \Downarrow v}$$

where $e'[x := v]$ is the substitution of identifier x with value v in expression e' (with a suitable renaming of the bound variables in e' to avoid clashes with the free variables in v).

Remark 2.3 Although the operational semantics is given independently from the typing rules, one expects some properties relating the two, e.g. **subject reduction**: $\emptyset \vdash e : Exp[\tau]$ and $e \Downarrow v$ implies $\emptyset \vdash v : Exp[\tau]$. This operational semantics is deterministic, i.e. there is at most one v s.t. $e \Downarrow v$, but this is not a property one may expect in general.

2.1.4 CBN operational semantics

The call-by-name (CBN) operational semantics is similar to CBV. The only differences are the definition of value (identifiers range over expressions) and the rule for evaluating $ap(e, e_1)$ (e_1 is not evaluated before substitution).

$$v \in Val ::= \quad * \mid tt \mid ff \mid 0 \mid s(v) \mid (\lambda x : \tau_1.e_2)$$

The Set of rules defining the CBN evaluation relation are those for CBV except

$$ap\frac{\begin{array}{c}e \Downarrow (\lambda x : \tau_1.e_2)\\ e_2[x := e_1] \Downarrow v\end{array}}{ap(e, e_1) \Downarrow v}$$

where $e'[x := e]$ is the substitution of identifier x with expression e in e'.

2.2 Extensions to the functional language

For each extension we give the corresponding additions to the syntax and typing rules of the functional language, and the modifications to the CBV operational semantics (the modifications to CBN operational semantics are left as an exercise).

2.2.1 Extension with divergence

- Syntax

types	$\tau \in T ::= \ldots$
identifiers	$x \in Id ::= \ldots$
expressions	$e \in Exp ::= \ldots \mid \bot$

- Typing rules

$$\bot \, \frac{}{\Gamma \vdash \bot : Exp[\tau]}$$

- CBV operational semantics

  $\Downarrow \subset Exp \times Val$, there are no changes to Val and the evaluation rules.

2.2.2 Extension with mutable store

- Syntax

types	$\tau \in T ::= \ldots$
identifiers	$x \in Id ::= \ldots$
locations	$l \in Loc ::= $ a set
expressions	$e \in Exp ::= \ldots \mid l \mid l := e$

- Typing rules

$$get \, \frac{}{\Gamma \vdash l : Exp[nat]} \; l \in Loc \qquad set \, \frac{\Gamma \vdash e : Exp[nat]}{\Gamma \vdash (l := e) : Exp[unit]} \; l \in Loc$$

- CBV operational semantics

  $\Downarrow \subset (Exp \times St) \times (Val \times St)$, there are no changes to Val, and St is the set of stores $s \in St \triangleq Loc \Rightarrow Val$

  the evaluation rules for the functional language are changed, e.g.

$$val \, \frac{}{v, s \Downarrow v, s} \qquad ap \, \frac{\begin{array}{c} e, s_0 \Downarrow (\lambda x.e_2), s_1 \\ e_1, s_1 \Downarrow v_1, s_2 \\ e_2[x := v_1], s_2 \Downarrow v, s_3 \end{array}}{ap(e, e_1), s_0 \Downarrow v, s_3}$$

  the following evaluation rules are added

$$get \, \frac{}{l, s \Downarrow v, s} \; v = s(l) \qquad set \, \frac{e, s_0 \Downarrow v, s_1}{l := e, s_0 \Downarrow *, s_1[l \mapsto v]}$$

  where $s[l \mapsto v]$ is the function which maps l to v and is like s elsewhere.

2.2.3 Extension with exception handling

- Syntax

types	$\tau \in T ::= \ldots$
identifiers	$x \in Id ::= \ldots$
exception names	$n \in Exn ::=$ a set
expressions	$e \in Exp ::= \ldots \mid raise(n) \mid handle(n, e_1, e_2)$

- Typing rules

$$raise\frac{}{\Gamma \vdash raise(n) : Exp[\tau]} \; n \in Exn$$

$$handle\frac{\Gamma \vdash e_1, e_2 : Exp[\tau]}{\Gamma \vdash handle(n, e_1, e_2) : Exp[\tau]} \; n \in Exn$$

- CBV operational semantics

$\Downarrow \subset Exp \times (Val + Exn)$ there are no changes to Val

the evaluation rules for the functional language are changed, e.g.

$$val\frac{}{v \Downarrow v}$$

$$ap\frac{e \Downarrow (\lambda x.e_2) \\ e_1 \Downarrow v_1 \\ e_2[x := v_1] \Downarrow r}{ap(e, e_1) \Downarrow r} \quad ap\frac{e \Downarrow (\lambda x.e_2) \\ e_1 \Downarrow n}{ap(e, e_1) \Downarrow n} \quad ap\frac{e \Downarrow n}{ap(e, e_1) \Downarrow n}$$

the following evaluation rules are added

$$raise\frac{}{raise(n) \Downarrow n}$$

$$handle\frac{e_2 \Downarrow n \\ e_1 \Downarrow r}{handle(n, e_1, e_2) \Downarrow r} \quad handle\frac{e_2 \Downarrow r}{handle(n, e_1, e_2) \Downarrow r} \; r \not\equiv n$$

2.2.4 Extension with non-deterministic choice

- Syntax

types	$\tau \in T ::= \ldots$
identifiers	$x \in Id ::= \ldots$
expressions	$e \in Exp ::= \ldots \mid or(e_1, e_2)$

- Typing rules

$$or\frac{\Gamma \vdash e_1, e_2 : Exp[\tau]}{\Gamma \vdash or(e_1, e_2) : Exp[\tau]}$$

- CBV operational semantics

  $\Downarrow \subset Exp \times Val$, there are no changes to Val and the evaluation rules the following evaluation rule is added

  $$or \frac{e_i \Downarrow v}{or(e_1, e_2) \Downarrow v}$$

2.2.5 Extension with parallelism

- Syntax

types	$\tau \in T ::= \ldots$
identifiers	$x \in Id ::= \ldots$
expressions	$e \in Exp ::= \ldots \mid por(e_1, e_2) \mid pap(e_1, e_2)$

- Typing rules

  $$por \frac{\Gamma \vdash e_1, e_2 : Exp[\tau]}{\Gamma \vdash por(e_1, e_2) : Exp[\tau]} \qquad pap \frac{\begin{array}{c} \Gamma \vdash e : Exp[\tau_1 \Rightarrow \tau_2] \\ \Gamma \vdash e_1 : Exp[\tau_1] \end{array}}{\Gamma \vdash pap(e, e_1) : Exp[\tau_2]}$$

- small step CBV operational semantics

  $\Rightarrow \subset Exp \times Exp$, there are no changes to Val

  the evaluation rules for the functional language are changed, e.g.

  $$if \frac{e \Rightarrow e'}{if(e, e_1, e_2) \Rightarrow if(e', e_1, e_2)}$$

  $$if \frac{}{if(tt, e_1, e_2) \Rightarrow e_1} \qquad if \frac{}{if(ff, e_1, e_2) \Rightarrow e_2}$$

  $$s \frac{e \Rightarrow e'}{s(e) \Rightarrow s(e')} \qquad \ldots$$

  $$ap \frac{e \Rightarrow e'}{ap(e, e_1) \Rightarrow ap(e', e_1)} \qquad ap \frac{e_1 \Rightarrow e_1'}{ap(v, e_1) \Rightarrow ap(v, e_1')}$$

  $$ap \frac{}{ap((\lambda x.e_2), v_1) \Rightarrow e_2[x := v_1]}$$

  the following evaluation rules are added

  $$pap \frac{e \Rightarrow e'}{pap(e, e_1) \Rightarrow pap(e', e_1)} \qquad pap \frac{e_1 \Rightarrow e_1'}{pap(e, e_1) \Rightarrow pap(e, e_1')}$$

  $$pap \frac{}{pap((\lambda x.e_2), v_1) \Rightarrow e_2[x := v_1]}$$

  $$por \frac{e_1 \Rightarrow e_1'}{por(e_1, e_2) \Rightarrow por(e_1', e_2)} \qquad por \frac{e_2 \Rightarrow e_2'}{por(e_1, e_2) \Rightarrow por(e_1, e_2')}$$

$$por\,\frac{}{por(v, e_2) \Rightarrow v} \qquad por\,\frac{}{por(e_1, v) \Rightarrow v}$$

3 Equivalence of programs

So far we have considered only operational semantics. In this section we review the denotational and algebraic (axiomatic) approaches, and explain how one can compare different semantics. The denotational approach assigns meaning to well-formed expressions (by induction on the derivation that they are well-formed), while the algebraic approach gives a set of rules for deriving when two well-formed expressions are equivalent. The denotational approach is particularly useful to validate reasoning principles, including equational rules, which can be used to prove properties of programs formally (without direct reference to the denotational model).

3.1 Observational equivalence

Operational semantics (even for the same programming language) can be substantially different. However one can compared the induced *observational equivalences*, which are equivalence relations (indeed congruences) on well-formed expressions. In fact, to associate an observational equivalence/preorder to an operational semantics one has to fix a notion of observation on *programs*, e.g. "program p has value tt", a notion of program context $C[\_]$, and an (operational) interpretation of observations. We exemplify these notions for some of the operational semantics introduced so far:

- p is a program ($p \in Prg$ for short) $\overset{\Delta}{\Longleftrightarrow}$ p is a well-formed expression of type *bool* without free variables, i.e. $\vdash p : Exp[bool]$ is derivable.

- $C[\_]$ is a program context for expressions of type τ in typing context Γ $\overset{\Delta}{\Longleftrightarrow}$ $C[\_]$ is an *expression with one hole* s.t. $C[e] \in Prg$, whenever $\Gamma \vdash e : Exp[\tau]$ is derivable.

- given an operational semantics of the form $\Downarrow \subseteq Exp \times Val$ we say that "p has value tt" $\overset{\Delta}{\Longleftrightarrow}$ ($p \in Prg$ and) $p \Downarrow tt$

- given two well-formed expressions $\Gamma \vdash e_i : Exp[\tau]$ we say that

  $\Gamma \vdash e_1 \leq^{op} e_2 : Exp[\tau]$ (observational preorder) $\overset{\Delta}{\Longleftrightarrow}$
  $C[e_1] \Downarrow tt$ implies $C[e_2] \Downarrow tt$, whenever $C[\_]$ is a program context for expressions of type τ in typing context Γ

  $\Gamma \vdash e_1 =^{op} e_2 : Exp[\tau]$ (observational equivalence) $\overset{\Delta}{\Longleftrightarrow}$
  $\Gamma \vdash e_1 \leq^{op} e_2 : Exp[\tau]$ and $\Gamma \vdash e_2 \leq^{op} e_1 : Exp[\tau]$.

Definition 3.1 *Given two programming languages* PL_i *and corresponding (operational) semantics* $\Downarrow_i$ *s.t. the well-formed expressions of* PL_1 *are included in those of* PL_2 *(i.e.* $\Gamma \vdash_1 e : Exp[\tau]$ *implies* $\Gamma \vdash_2 e : Exp[\tau]$*), we say that*

- $\Downarrow_2$ *is* **computationally adequate** *w.r.t.* $\Downarrow_1 \stackrel{\Delta}{\Longleftrightarrow}$ *the meaning of observations agrees, i.e.* $p \Downarrow_1 tt$ *iff* $p \Downarrow_2 tt$ *for any program* p *of* PL_1.

- $\Downarrow_2$ *is* **equationally sound** *w.r.t.* $\Downarrow_1 \stackrel{\Delta}{\Longleftrightarrow} \Gamma \vdash_2 e_1 =^{op} e_2 : Exp[\tau]$ *implies* $\Gamma \vdash_1 e_1 =^{op} e_2 : Exp[\tau]$*, whenever* e_i *are well-formed expressions of* PL_1 *(i.e.* $\Gamma \vdash_1 e_i : Exp[\tau]$*)*

- $\Downarrow_2$ *is* **abstraction preserving** *w.r.t.* $\Downarrow_1 \stackrel{\Delta}{\Longleftrightarrow}$ *(it is equationally sound and)* $\Gamma \vdash_1 e_1 =^{op} e_2 : Exp[\tau]$ *implies* $\Gamma \vdash_2 e_1 =^{op} e_2 : Exp[\tau]$.

Under reasonable assumptions about programs and program contexts (which we do not spell out), the following result hold.

Proposition 3.2 *If* $\Downarrow_2$ *is computationally adequate (w.r.t.* $\Downarrow_1$*), then it is also sound.*

Let us consider the following operational semantics: $\Downarrow_{f\_v}$ (CBV for the functional language), $\Downarrow_{f\_n}$ (CBN for the functional language), $\Downarrow_v$ (CBV for the functional language with divergence), $\Downarrow_n$ (CBN for the functional language with divergence).

Proposition 3.3 *The following relations holds:*

- $p \Downarrow_{f\_v} tt$ *iff* $p \Downarrow_{f\_n} tt$, *so the two semantics induce the same observational equivalence* $=^{op}$;

- $\Downarrow_v$ *and* $\Downarrow_n$ *are computationally adequate w.r.t.* $\Downarrow_{f\_v}$;

- $\Downarrow_v$ *and* $\Downarrow_n$ *are not computationally adequate w.r.t. each other, e.g.* $p \Downarrow_n tt$ *but* $p \not\Downarrow_v tt$ *when* $p = (\lambda x : \tau.tt)\bot$.

If one compares the observational equivalences $=^{op}$, $=^{op}_v$ and $=^{op}_n$ on the well-formed expressions of the functional language, then $=^{op}_v$ and $=^{op}_n$ are incomparable, and both are properly included in $=^{op}$. In fact:

- $x, y : Id[unit] \vdash x = y : Exp[unit]$ holds for $=^{op}$ and $=^{op}_v$, but not for $=^{op}_n$

- $y : Id[unit], f : Id[unit \Rightarrow unit] \vdash ap(\lambda x : unit.y, ap(f, *)) = y : Exp[unit]$ holds for $=^{op}$ and $=^{op}_n$, but not for $=^{op}_v$,

Remark 3.4 Instead of observing "p has value tt" (where $\vdash p : Exp[bool]$), we could have observed "p has a value" (where $\vdash p : Exp[\tau]$ for some type τ). The observational equivalences considered above are affected by this change as follows:

- $=^{op}$ collapses to the equivalence which identifies well-formed expressions of the same type;

- $=_v^{op}$ is unchanged;

- $=_n^{op}$ discriminates more, e.g. $f : Id[\tau_1 \Rightarrow \tau_2] \vdash \lambda x : \tau_1.ap(f, x) = f : Exp[\tau_1 \Rightarrow \tau_2]$ is no longer true.

3.2 Denotational semantics

The general pattern of a set-theoretic semantics for the functional language (and its extensions) is:

- types, like τ, syntactic categories, like $Exp[\tau]$, and typing contexts, like Γ, are interpreted as sets

- well-formed expressions, like $\Gamma \vdash e : Exp[\tau]$, are interpreted as functions from the interpretation of Γ to that of $Exp[\tau]$.

The same pattern applies, mutatis mutandis, to the interpretation in any category (e.g. the category of cpos), just replace sets with objects and functions with morphisms.

In fact, we will view the interpretation of $\Gamma \vdash e : Exp[\tau]$ as a family $\langle a_\rho | \rho \in [\![\Gamma]\!]\rangle$ assigning to each *environment* ρ the interpretation of e in it. This is closer to the usual Tarski's semantics for predicate calculus, but it does not generalise as easily to other categories. The interpretation is defined by induction on the syntax, in the case of a well-formed expression this means by induction on the derivation of $\Gamma \vdash e : Exp[\tau]$.

As a sample we give the *standard* set-theoretic interpretation of the functional language and two interpretations of the extension with divergence, which *correspond* to CBV and CBN (in a sense to be made precise later).

3.2.1 Standard semantics of the functional language

- The interpretation of types, syntactic categories and typing contexts is:

$$
\begin{aligned}
[\![unit]\!] &= \{*\} \\
[\![bool]\!] &= \{tt, f\!f\} \\
[\![nat]\!] &= \mathbb{N}, \text{ the set of natural numbers} \\
[\![\tau_1 \Rightarrow \tau_2]\!] &= [\![\tau_1]\!] \to [\![\tau_2]\!], \text{ the set of total functions} \\
[\![Id[\tau]]\!] &= [\![\tau]\!] \\
[\![Exp[\tau]]\!] &= [\![\tau]\!] \\
[\![\Gamma]\!] &= [\![Id[\tau_1]]\!] \times \ldots \times [\![Id[\tau_n]]\!]
\end{aligned}
$$

where Γ is $x_1 : Id[\tau_1], \ldots, x_n : Id[\tau_n]$.

- The interpretation of well-formed expressions (of functional type) is:

$$
\begin{array}{rl}
[\![\Gamma \vdash x_i : Exp[\tau_i]]\!]_\rho = & \pi_i^n(\rho) : A_i \\[6pt]
\dfrac{[\![\Gamma, x : Id[\tau_1] \vdash e_2 : Exp[\tau_2]]\!]_{\rho,a} =}{[\![\Gamma \vdash \lambda x : \tau_1.e_2 : Exp[\tau_1 \Rightarrow \tau_2]]\!]_\rho =} & \begin{array}{l} b_a : A_2 \\ \lambda a \in A_1.b_a \end{array} \\[12pt]
\dfrac{\begin{array}{l}[\![\Gamma \vdash e : Exp[\tau_1 \Rightarrow \tau_2]]\!]_\rho = \\ [\![\Gamma \vdash e_1 : Exp[\tau_1]]\!]_\rho = \end{array}}{[\![\Gamma \vdash ap(e, e_1) : Exp[\tau_2]]\!]_\rho =} & \begin{array}{l} f : A_1 \to A_2 \\ a : A_1 \\ f(a) \end{array}
\end{array}
$$

where $A = [\![\tau]\!]$ and $A_i = [\![\tau_i]\!]$.

3.2.2 CBV semantics of the functional language with divergence

- CBV semantics differs from standard semantics in the interpretation of $\tau_1 \Rightarrow \tau_2$ and $Exp[\tau]$:

$$
\begin{aligned}
[\![\tau_1 \Rightarrow \tau_2]\!] &= [\![\tau_1]\!] \to [\![Exp[\tau_2]]\!] \\
[\![Exp[\tau]]\!] &= [\![\tau]\!] + \{\bot\}
\end{aligned}
$$

- while the interpretation of well-formed expressions has to be changed consistently (and extended in the obvious way):

$$
\begin{array}{rl}
[\![\Gamma \vdash x_i : Exp[\tau_i]]\!]_\rho = & in_1(\pi_i^n(\rho)) : A_i + \{\bot\} \\[8pt]
[\![\Gamma \vdash \bot : Exp[\tau]]\!]_\rho = & in_2(\bot) : A + \{\bot\} \\[8pt]
\dfrac{[\![\Gamma, x : Id[\tau_1] \vdash e_2 : Exp[\tau_2]]\!]_{\rho,a} =}{[\![\Gamma \vdash \lambda x : \tau_1.e_2 : Exp[\tau_1 \Rightarrow \tau_2]]\!]_\rho =} & \begin{array}{l} b_a : A_2 + \{\bot\} \\ in_1(\lambda a \in A_1.b_a) \end{array} \\[12pt]
\dfrac{\begin{array}{l}[\![\Gamma \vdash e : Exp[\tau_1 \Rightarrow \tau_2]]\!]_\rho = \\ [\![\Gamma \vdash e_1 : Exp[\tau_1]]\!]_\rho = \end{array}}{[\![\Gamma \vdash ap(e, e_1) : Exp[\tau_2]]\!]_\rho =} & \begin{array}{l} f : (A_1 \to (A_2 + \{\bot\})) + \{\bot\} \\ a : A_1 + \{\bot\} \\ \begin{cases} ga_1 & \text{if } f = in_1(g), a = in_1(a_1) \\ in_2(\bot) & \text{otherwise} \end{cases} \end{array}
\end{array}
$$

where $A = [\![\tau]\!]$ and $A_i = [\![\tau_i]\!]$.

3.2.3 CBN semantics of the functional language with divergence

- The CBN semantics differs from CBV semantics in the interpretation of $\tau_1 \Rightarrow \tau_2$ and $Id[\tau]$:

$$
\begin{aligned}
[\![\tau_1 \Rightarrow \tau_2]\!] &= [\![Exp[\tau_1]]\!] \to [\![Exp[\tau_2]]\!] \\
[\![Id[\tau]]\!] &= [\![\tau]\!] + \{\bot\}
\end{aligned}
$$

- while the interpretation of well-formed expressions has to be changed consistently:

$$
\begin{array}{rl}
[\![\Gamma \vdash x_i : Exp[\tau_i]]\!]_\rho = & \pi_i^n(\rho) : A_i + \{\bot\} \\[2mm]
[\![\Gamma \vdash \bot : Exp[\tau]]\!]_\rho = & in_2(\bot) : A + \{\bot\} \\[2mm]
\hline
[\![\Gamma, x : Id[\tau_1] \vdash e_2 : Exp[\tau_2]]\!]_{\rho,a} = & b_a : A_2 + \{\bot\} \\
[\![\Gamma \vdash \lambda x : \tau_1.e_2 : Exp[\tau_1 \Rightarrow \tau_2]]\!]_\rho = & in_1(\lambda a \in A_1.b_a) \\[2mm]
\hline
[\![\Gamma \vdash e : Exp[\tau_1 \Rightarrow \tau_2]]\!]_\rho = & f : ((A_1 + \{\bot\}) \to (A_2 + \{\bot\})) + \{\bot\} \\
[\![\Gamma \vdash e_1 : Exp[\tau_1]]\!]_\rho = & a : A_1 + \{\bot\} \\
\hline
[\![\Gamma \vdash ap(e,e_1) : Exp[\tau_2]]\!]_\rho = & \begin{cases} g(a) & \text{if } f = in_1(g) \\ in_2(\bot) & \text{otherwise} \end{cases}
\end{array}
$$

where $A = [\![\tau]\!]$ and $A_i = [\![\tau_i]\!]$.

3.2.4 Denotational versus observational equivalence

An interpretation $[\![\_]\!]$ of well-formed expressions induces an equivalence relation indeed a congruence (under reasonable assumptions about $[\![\_]\!]$):

- $[\![\Gamma \vdash e_1 = e_2 : Exp[\tau]]\!]$ (denotational equivalence) $\overset{\Delta}{\Longleftrightarrow}$ the interpretations $[\![\Gamma \vdash e_i : Exp[\tau]]\!]$ are equal.

However, one can also associate an observational equivalence/preorder to a denotational semantics. What is needed is to fix the interpretation of observations (and proceed like in Section 3.1), e.g.:

- "p has value tt" $\overset{\Delta}{\Longleftrightarrow}$ $[\![\vdash p = tt : Exp[bool]]\!]$.

Remark 3.5 At this point we can relate the three denotational semantics considered in this section with the operational semantics considered in Section 3.1:

- $[\![\vdash p = tt : Exp[bool]]\!]_{fun}$ iff $p \Downarrow_{fun} tt$
- $[\![\vdash p = tt : Exp[bool]]\!]_v$ iff $p \Downarrow_v tt$
- $[\![\vdash p = tt : Exp[bool]]\!]_n$ iff $p \Downarrow_n tt$

i.e. corresponding semantics agree on the interpretation of observations.

In general, denotational and observational equivalence for a given denotational semantics do not coincide, but under reasonable assumptions about $[\![\_]\!]$, the following result hold.

Proposition 3.6 *Denotational equivalence implies observational equivalence.*

It is usually easier to establish denotational equivalence than observational equivalence, since the latter involves a universal quantification over program contexts. Therefore, the result above gives a simpler way to prove observational equivalence (on the other hand, it is easy to prove that two expressions are not observationally equivalent, just find a discriminating program context!).

Definition 3.7 *Given a denotational semantics $[\![\_]\!]$ for a programming language PL (and an interpretation of observations), we say that*

- $[\![\_]\!]$ *is* **fully abstract** $\stackrel{\Delta}{\Longleftrightarrow}$ *denotational and observational equivalence coincide.*

Remark 3.8 A broader and deeper discussion on "good fit criteria" between operational and denotational semantics can be found in (Meyer and Cosmodakis 1988).

3.3 Equational calculi

A simple way to prove observational equivalence is to identify inference rules which are *admissible* w.r.t. denotational equivalence, and use them to derive formally $\Gamma \vdash e_1 = e_2 : Exp[\tau]$. It is usually easy to check that an inference rule is admissible w.r.t. denotational equivalence (just check that the conclusion of the rule is true in the model, whenever the premises are!). When one cannot rely on a denotational model, one can establish that provable equivalence implies observational equivalence, by analogy with Section 3.2.4:

- first express observations in the equational calculus, e.g.

  "p has value tt" $\stackrel{\Delta}{\Longleftrightarrow}$ "$\vdash p = tt : Exp[bool]$" is derivable

- then prove that: $\vdash p = tt : Exp[bool]$ is derivable iff $p \Downarrow tt$.

Under reasonable assumptions about program contexts this entails that provable equivalence implies observational equivalence. Note that this is weaker than "the inference rules are admissible w.r.t. observational equivalence".

For each of the denotational semantics considered in Section 3.2 we give a set of admissible rules for deriving denotational equivalence (we skip the congruence rules, which are always admissible):

- standard equational calculus

$$\beta' \frac{}{\Gamma \vdash ap(\lambda x : \tau_1.e_2, x) = e_2 : Exp[\tau_2]}$$

$$\eta' \frac{}{\Gamma \vdash \lambda x : \tau_1.ap(f, x) = f : Exp[\tau_1 \Rightarrow \tau_2]}$$

$$sub \frac{\Gamma \vdash e_i : Exp[\tau_i] \quad (i = 1, \ldots, n)}{\Gamma \vdash e[\overline{x} := \overline{e}] = e'[\overline{x} := \overline{e}] : Exp[\tau]}$$

- CBV equational calculus, like the standard calculus but (*sub*) is replaced by

$$sub_v \frac{\Gamma \vdash e_i : Exp[\tau_i] \quad (i = 1, \ldots, n) \qquad x_1 : Id[\tau_1], \ldots, x_n : Id[\tau_n] \vdash e = e' : Exp[\tau]}{\Gamma \vdash e[\overline{x} := \overline{e}] = e'[\overline{x} := \overline{e}] : Exp[\tau]} \quad e_i \text{ values}$$

where values are either variables or lambda-abstractions

- CBN equational calculus, like the standard calculus but without (η').

4 Abstract syntax and encoding in LF

In this section we introduce a *logical framework* with a cumulative hierarchy of predicative universes (in this way we don't need to distinguish between contexts Γ and signatures Σ). Our main motivation for introducing a logical framework is to have precise and concise descriptions of (the well-formed expressions of) languages and translations: languages are described by signatures and translations by signature realisations.

4.1 The logical framework LF

The logical framework is given by a set of inference rules for deriving judgements of the following forms:

- $\Gamma \vdash$, i.e. Γ is a context

- $\Gamma \vdash A : Type_i$, i.e. A is a type (in the i-th universe) in context Γ

- $\Gamma \vdash M : A$, i.e. M is a term of type A in context Γ

where M and A range over pseudo-terms described by the following BNF:

identifiers $\quad x \in Id ::=$ an infinite set
pseudo-terms $\quad A, M \in Exp ::= x \mid Type_i \mid \Pi x : A_1.A_2 \mid \lambda x : A.M \mid M_1 M_2$

$$\text{empty} \frac{}{\emptyset \vdash}$$

$$\text{ext} \frac{\Gamma \vdash A : Type_i}{\Gamma, x : A \vdash} \quad x \notin DV(\Gamma)$$

$$\text{type-} \in \frac{\Gamma \vdash}{\Gamma \vdash Type_i : Type_{i+1}} \quad i \geq 0$$

$$\text{type-} \subset \frac{\Gamma \vdash A : Type_i}{\Gamma \vdash A : Type_j} \quad i < j$$

$$\text{var} \frac{\Gamma \vdash}{\Gamma \vdash x : A} \quad A = \Gamma(x)$$

$$\Pi\frac{\Gamma \vdash A_1 : Type_i \qquad \Gamma, x : A_1 \vdash A_2 : Type_i}{\Gamma \vdash (\Pi x : A_1.A_2) : Type_i}$$

$$\lambda\frac{\Gamma \vdash A_1 : Type_i \qquad \Gamma, x : A_1 \vdash M_2 : A_2}{\Gamma \vdash (\lambda x : A_1.M_2) : (\Pi x : A_1.A_2)}$$

$$\text{app}\frac{\Gamma \vdash M : (\Pi x : A_1.A_2) \qquad \Gamma \vdash M_1 : A_1}{\Gamma \vdash MM_1 : A_2[x := M_1]}$$

$$\text{conv}\frac{\Gamma \vdash M : A_1 \qquad \Gamma \vdash A_2 : Type_i}{\Gamma \vdash M : A_2} \; A_1 =_{\beta\eta} A_2$$

where $=_{\beta\eta}$ is $\beta\eta$-conversion on pseudo-terms, i.e. the congruence induced by α-conversion, $(\lambda x : A.M_2)M_1 = M_2[x := M_1]$ and $(\lambda x : A.Mx) = M$ provided $x \notin \text{FV}(M)$.

Remark 4.1 The meta-theory of LF is rather delicate because of the (conv) rule and the failure of the Church-Rosser property for $\beta\eta$-reduction on pseudo-terms. Anyway one can prove the following properties (see (Harper, Honsell, and Plotkin 1987; Geuvers 1992; Luo 1994)):

- it is decidable whether $\Gamma \vdash M : A$ is derivable

- if $\Gamma \vdash M_i : A$ (for $i = 1, 2$) is derivable, then $M_1 =_{\beta\eta} M_2$ is decidable.

It is convenient to separate the initial part of a context, which is intended to consist of constants, from the remaining part, consisting of variables. Therefore, we introduce the following derived notation:

- a LF-signature Σ is a well-formed context $\Sigma \vdash$

- a relativised judgement $\Gamma \vdash_\Sigma J$ stands for $\Sigma, \Gamma \vdash J$.

4.2 Set-theoretic semantics

The set-theoretic interpretation of LF has the following pattern (to model the cumulative hierarchy of universes we need a sequence of inaccessible cardinals α_i, so that $Type_i$ is interpreted by the set V_{α_i} of the von Neumann's hierarchy):

- the interpretation $[\![\Gamma \vdash]\!]$ of a context is a set I

- the interpretation $[\![\Gamma \vdash A : Type_j]\!]$ of a type is a family of sets $\langle X_i | i \in I \rangle$ s.t. $X_i \in V_{\alpha_j}$

- the interpretation $[\![\Gamma \vdash M : A]\!]$ of a term is a family of elements $\langle x_i | i \in I \rangle$ s.t. $x_i \in X_i$.

Remark 4.2 Because of the (conv) rule one may have different derivations of the same judgement, therefore the interpretation of a judgement cannot be defined by induction on the derivation. In any case, for defining the interpretation it is better to work with an equivalent semantic system (see (Geuvers and Werner 1994)), in which one has also judgements of the form $\Gamma \vdash M_1 = M_2 : A$. One can proceed in two ways: either define the interpretation of a derivation and prove that derivations of the same judgement are interpreted in the same way (this is called a coherence result), or give a partially defined interpretation of pseudo-judgements (by induction on their *size*) and prove that whenever a pseudo-judgement is derivable its interpretation is defined (and satisfies certain properties).

We follow the second approach and define a partial function $[\![\Gamma \vdash M : A]\!]$ by induction on $s(\Gamma) + s(M)$, where $s(\_)$ gives the number of *symbols* in $\_$.

Notation 4.3 Given a set X and a family of sets $\langle Y_x | x \in X \rangle$ we write $\Sigma x \in X.Y_x$ for the set $\{(x, y) | x \in X, y \in Y_x\}$ and $\Pi x \in X.Y_x$ for the set of all functions with domain X s.t. $\forall x \in X.f(x) \in Y_x$. Moreover, we identify a function $\lambda x \in X.y_x$ with its graph, i.e. the set $\{(x, y_x) | x \in X\}$, and write $X \times Y$ and $X \to Y$ instead of $\Sigma x \in X.Y_x$ and $\Pi x \in X.Y_x$, when Y_x is constantly Y.

empty	$[\![\emptyset \vdash]\!] = 1 = \{*\}$
ext	$[\![\Gamma \vdash A]\!] = \langle X_i | i \in I \rangle$
	$[\![\Gamma, x : A \vdash]\!] = \Sigma i \in I.X_i$
type-$\in$	$[\![\Gamma \vdash]\!] = I$
	$[\![\Gamma \vdash Type_j]\!] = \langle V_{\alpha_j} | i \in I \rangle$
var	$[\![\Gamma \vdash]\!] = I$
	$[\![\Gamma \vdash x]\!] = \langle \pi_x^\Gamma(i) | i \in I \rangle$
Π	$[\![\Gamma \vdash A_1]\!] = \langle X_i | i \in I \rangle$
	$[\![\Gamma, x : A_1 \vdash A_2]\!] = \langle Y_{(i,x)} | i \in I, x \in X_i \rangle$
	$[\![\Gamma \vdash (\Pi x : A_1.A_2)]\!] = \langle \Pi x \in X_i.Y_{(i,x)} | i \in I \rangle$
λ	$[\![\Gamma \vdash A_1]\!] = \langle X_i | i \in I \rangle$
	$[\![\Gamma, x : A_1 \vdash M_2]\!] = \langle y_{(i,x)} | i \in I, x \in X_i \rangle$
	$[\![\Gamma \vdash (\lambda x : A_1.M_2)]\!] = \langle \lambda x \in X_i.y_{(i,x)} | i \in I \rangle$
app	$[\![\Gamma \vdash M]\!] = \langle f_i | i \in I \rangle$
	$[\![\Gamma \vdash M_1]\!] = \langle x_i | i \in I \rangle$
	$[\![\Gamma \vdash MM_1]\!] \simeq \langle f_i(x_i) | i \in I \rangle$

Note that it is only in the last case that the interpretation can be undefined even when the premisses are satisfied. At this point one can prove (by induction on the derivation of a judgement in the semantic system), that:

- if $\Gamma \vdash$ is derivable, then $[\![\Gamma \vdash]\!] = I$ for some set I

- if $\Gamma \vdash M : A$ is derivable, then
  $[\![\Gamma \vdash M]\!] = \langle x_i | i \in I \rangle$, $[\![\Gamma \vdash A]\!] = \langle X_i | i \in I \rangle$ and $\forall i \in I.x_i \in X_i$
  for some set I and I-indexed families x and X

  therefore we can define $[\![\Gamma \vdash M : A]\!]$ as $[\![\Gamma \vdash M]\!]$

- if $\Gamma \vdash M = N : A$ is derivable, then
  $[\![\Gamma \vdash M]\!] = \langle x_i | i \in I \rangle = [\![\Gamma \vdash N]\!]$, $[\![\Gamma \vdash A]\!] = \langle X_i | i \in I \rangle$ and
  $\forall i \in I.x_i \in X_i$
  for some set I and I-indexed families x and X.

Given a model for a LF-signature, i.e. $M \in [\![\Sigma]\!]$, one can define the interpretation $[\![\Gamma \vdash_\Sigma J]\!]^M$ of relativised judgements in M in the obvious way, e.g. $[\![\Gamma \vdash_\Sigma]\!]^M \triangleq \{i | M * i \in I\}$, where $I = [\![\Sigma, \Gamma \vdash]\!]$ and $*$ is concatenation.

4.3   Encodings

One can give a compact and uniform description of the typing rules for the functional language (and the other languages introduced in Section 2) in terms of a LF-signature.

Notation 4.4 We use the convention of writing: $Type$ for some unspecified $Type_i$ with i big enough, $A_1 \to A_2$ for $\Pi x : A_1.A_2$ with $x \notin FV(A_2)$, $A_1, \ldots, A_n \to A$ for $A_1 \to \ldots A_n \to A$.

- LF-signature Σ_{fun} for the functional language:

types	$T : Type$
	$unit, bool, nat : T$
	$\Rightarrow : T, T \to T$
ident	$Id : T \to Type$
expr	$Exp : T \to Type$
	$var : \Pi X : T.Id(X) \to Exp(X)$
unit	$* : Exp(unit)$
bool	$tt, f\!\!f : Exp(bool)$
	$if : \Pi X : T.Exp(bool), Exp(X), Exp(X) \to Exp(X)$
nat	$0 : Exp(nat)$
	$s : Exp(nat) \to Exp(nat)$
	$It : \Pi X : T.Exp(X), (Id(X) \to Exp(X)), Exp(nat) \to Exp(X)$
$\Rightarrow$	$ab : \Pi X_1, X_2 : T.(Id(X_1) \to Exp(X_2)) \to Exp(X_1 \Rightarrow X_2)$
	$ap : \Pi X_1, X_2 : T.Exp(X_1 \Rightarrow X_2), Exp(X_1) \to Exp(X_2)$

The correspondence between the syntax of the functional language and the LF-signature Σ_{fun} is expressed by the following adequacy result (more examples of encodings and similar adequacy results can be found in (Harper, Honsell, and Plotkin 1987)).

Proposition 4.5 (Syntactic adequacy) *There is a translation $\_^*$ of types $\tau \in T$ and expressions $e \in Exp$ of the functional language into pseudo-terms of LF s.t.:*

- $\vdash_{\Sigma_{fun}} \tau^* : T$, *whenever* $\tau \in T$

- $\Gamma^* \vdash_{\Sigma_{fun}} e^* : Exp(\tau^*)$, *whenever* $\Gamma \vdash_{fun} e : Exp[\tau]$.

Moreover, the translation induces the following bijections

- *types $\tau \in T \Longleftrightarrow$ pseudo-terms M (up to $\beta\eta$-conversion) s.t. $\vdash_{\Sigma_{fun}} M : T$*

- *expression $e \in Exp$ (up to α-conversion) s.t. $\Gamma \vdash_{fun} e : Exp[\tau] \Longleftrightarrow$ pseudo-terms M (up to $\beta\eta$-conversion) s.t. $\Gamma^* \vdash_{\Sigma_{fun}} M : Exp(\tau^*)$.*

LF-signatures for the other languages of Section 2 can be obtain by a simple extension of Σ_{fun} (and similar syntactic adequacy results can be proved):

- LF-signature extension Σ_{div}

  $\perp : \Pi X : T.Exp(X)$

- LF-signature extension Σ_{imp}

  locations $Loc : Type$
  $get : Loc \to Exp(nat)$
  $set : Loc, Exp(nat) \to Exp(unit)$

- LF-signature extension Σ_{exc}

  exception
  names $Exn : Type$
  $raise : \Pi X : T.Exn \to Exp(X)$
  $handle : \Pi X : T.Exn, Exp(X), Exp(X) \to Exp(X)$

- LF-signature extension Σ_{nd}

  $or : \Pi X : T.Exp(X), Exp(X) \to Exp(X)$

- LF-signature extension Σ_{par}

  $por : \Pi X : T.Exp(X), Exp(X) \to Exp(X)$
  $pap : \Pi X_1, X_2 : T.Exp(X_1 {\Rightarrow} X_2), Exp(X_1) \to Exp(X_2)$

4.4   Semantics via translation

A model M for the LF-signature Σ_{fun} induces an interpretation of the functional language via the **encoding** $\_^*$ as follows:

- the interpretation $[\![\tau]\!]^{\mathrm{M}}$ of a type τ is (the only element in the family) $[\![\vdash_{\Sigma_{fun}} \tau^* : T]\!]^{\mathrm{M}}$

- the interpretation $[\![\Gamma \vdash e : Exp[\tau]]\!]_{\rho}^{M}$ of a well-formed expression e in an environment ρ is $[\![\Gamma^{*} \vdash_{\Sigma_{fun}} e^{*} : Exp[\tau^{*}]]\!]_{\rho}^{M}$.

Moreover, the standard semantics for the functional language can be recovered by a suitable choice of M.

In general, given a translation $\_^{*} : L' \to L$ from the language/formalism L' to L, we can turn an interpretation $[\![\_]\!]$ of L into an interpretation $[\![\_]\!]'$ of L' by defining $[\![\_]\!]'$ to be the interpretation of the translation of $\_$, i.e. $[\![\_^{*}]\!]$. We call this way of defining an interpretation **semantics via translation**.

When one considers only languages induced by a LF-signature (this is not a strong restriction because of syntactic adequacy results), translations can be described in a compact way as signature *realisations*:

- given a LF-signature Σ, let $L(\Sigma)$ be the set of all derivable judgements of the form $\Gamma \vdash_{\Sigma} J$

- given two LF-signatures Σ and Σ', a **realisation** $I : \Sigma' \to \Sigma$ of Σ' in Σ is a sequence of substitutions, one for each constant declared in Σ'. The precise definition is given by induction on the length of Σ':

  - $\emptyset : \emptyset \to \Sigma$
  - $(I, x := M) : (\Sigma', x : A) \to \Sigma$ iff $I : \Sigma' \to \Sigma$ and $\vdash_{\Sigma} M : A[I]$ is derivable, where $A[I]$ is the substitution instance of A obtained by applying in parallel all substitutions in I

- given a realisation $I : \Sigma' \to \Sigma$ between LF-signatures, the induced translation (also denoted by I) from $L(\Sigma')$ to $L(\Sigma)$ maps $\Gamma \vdash_{\Sigma'} J$ to $\Gamma[I] \vdash_{\Sigma} J[I]$.

In the sequel, we will describe languages by LF-signatures and translations by realisations. However, for readability we will often use some derived notation or suppress some type information, which can be recovered from the context.

5 Metalanguages for denotational semantics

In this section we specialise the technique of giving semantics via translation to the case of programming languages. The general idea is to define the denotational semantics of a programming language PL by translating it into a typed metalanguage ML. The idea is as old as denotational semantics (see Scott 1993), so the main issue is whether it can be made into a viable technique capable of dealing with complex programming languages.

Before being more specific about metalanguages, let us discuss what are the main advantages in using them to give semantics via translation:

- to reuse the same ML for translating several programming languages.

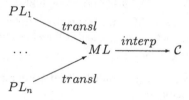

Here we are implicitly assuming that defining a translation from PL to ML is simpler than directly defining an interpretation of PL.

In this case it is worth putting some effort into the study of ML. In fact, once certain properties of ML have been established (e.g. reasoning principles or computational adequacy), it is usually *easy* to transfer them to PL via the translation.

- to choose ML according to certain criteria, which are usually not met by programming languages, for instance:

    – a metalanguage which is built around few *orthogonal* concepts will be simpler to study, on the contrary programming languages often introduce *syntactic sugar* for the benefit of programmers;

    – ML may be equipped with a logic so that it can be used for formalising reasoning principles or for translating specification languages;

    – ML may be chosen as the *internal language* for a class of categories (e.g. cartesian closed or order-enriched categories) or for a specific semantic category (e.g. the category of sets or cpos).

- to use ML for hiding details of semantic categories (see Gordon 1979).

    For instance, when ML is the internal language for a class of categories, it has one intended interpretation in each of them, therefore a translation into ML will induce a variety of interpretations

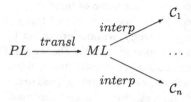

Even when ML has only one intended interpretation, it may be difficult to work with the semantic category directly.

A good starting point for a metalanguage is to build it on top of a fairly standard typed λ-calculus. More controversial issues are:

- whether the metalanguage should be equipped with some logic (ranging from equational logic to higher order predicate logic).

  We believe that it should, since this is the simplest way to abstract from the semantics of the metalanguage, and still have something usable to establish properties of programs.

- whether the metalanguage should be itself a programming language (i.e. have an operational semantics).

  In fact, this may force one to choose among a variety of operational semantics (CBV or CBN), to place restrictions on the types (dependent types would be problematic), and to use *non-standard* equational axiomatisations (see Section 3.3).

- whether one gains something by giving semantics to a (complex) programming language PL via translation into a metalanguage ML instead of giving the semantics of PL directly. In particular, it would be unsatisfactory if giving either the translation of PL into ML, or the semantics of ML are as difficult as giving the semantics of PL directly.

  We will discuss how the monadic approach can help in structuring the translation from PL to ML by the introduction of **auxiliary notation** (see Mosses 1990a; Moggi 1991)

$$PL \xrightarrow{\ transl\ } ML(\Sigma) \xrightarrow{\ transl\ } ML$$

and in incrementally defining the semantics of auxiliary notation (see Cenciarelli and Moggi 1993)

$$PL \xrightarrow{\ transl\ } ML(\Sigma_n) \xrightarrow{\ transl\ } \ldots \xrightarrow{\ transl\ } ML(\Sigma_0) \xrightarrow{\ transl\ } ML$$

Remark 5.1 The metalanguages we consider can be described in terms of LF-signatures. This may cause problems in defining their interpretation in semantic categories other than sets, since some of them (e.g. the category of cpos) are not suitable for interpreting LF. One way around this is to define the interpretation of these metalanguages directly, without going via LF. An alternative way, is to follow the approach of *Synthetic Domain Theory* (SDT) and view these semantic categories as fully embedded in a constructive set-theoretic universe, like a *topos* or *quasitopos*, in which one can interpret LF (and much more). The latter approach has considerable advantages, provided one can *avoid* (e.g. by axiomatising the relation between the semantics category and the constructive set-theoretic universe) the extra mathematical sophistication involved in SDT models.

5.1 Typed lambda-calculi

The metalanguages we consider are extensions of the simply typed $\lambda\beta\eta$-calculus (with type variables). Formally they will be described by LF-signatures, but we will introduce and use more standard syntax and notational conventions as shorthand for the formal (and almost unreadable) notation.

5.1.1 Equational logic and extensionality

An integral part of any typed lambda-calculi is the set of equational rules, which often give a complete characterisation of types (like the universal properties used in Category Theory). Therefore, we consider LF-signatures which incorporate equational logic.

- LF-signature Σ_{eq} for equational logic:

propositions	$Prop : Type$
proofs	$pr : Prop \rightarrow Type$

we write ϕ for $pr(\phi)$, identifying a prop with the type of its proofs

logical constants

equality $\quad eq : \Pi X : Type.X, X \rightarrow Prop$

we write $M_1 =_\tau M_2$ or $M_1 = M_2$ for $eq(\tau, M_1, M_2)$

axioms

reflexivity $\quad \Pi X : Type.\Pi x : X.x = x$

substitutivity $\quad \Pi X : Type, P : X \rightarrow Prop, x, y : X.x = y, P(x) \rightarrow P(y)$

We have not introduced explicit constants for reflexivity of equality and substitutivity of equals (in propositions), since they are never needed for defining signature extensions.

One can show that the following rules are derivable (in equational logic), where A is derivable (in equational logic) formally means that there exists a term M such that $\vdash_{\Sigma_{eq}} M : A$.

- symmetry, i.e. $x = y \rightarrow y = x$

- transitivity, i.e. $x = y, y = z \rightarrow x = x$

- congruence for application, i.e. $x =_{\tau_1} y, f =_{(\tau_1 \rightarrow \tau_2)} g \rightarrow fx =_{\tau_2} gy$

  this cannot be extended to arbitrary Π-types, because fx and gy may have different types, nevertheless the following rule is derivable

  $$f =_{(\Pi x:\tau.Xx)} g \rightarrow fx =_{Xx} gx$$

Remark 5.2 Instead of equational logic one can start with the more powerful Higher Order Logic, taking as sole logical constant universal quantification $\forall : \Pi X : Type.(X \rightarrow Prop) \rightarrow Prop$. Then one defines implication $\phi_1 \supset \phi_2$ as $\forall p : \phi_1.\phi_2$ and equality $x =_\tau y$ as Leibniz' equality $\forall P : \tau \rightarrow Prop.P(x) \supset P(y)$.

Although in LF one can identify functional types with Π-types, extensionality for functions is not derivable (from Σ_{eq}). Therefore, it has to be included explicitly as additional rule.

- LF-signature extension Σ_{ext} for extensionality rules:

Π-ext $\quad \Pi X : Type, F : X \to Type, f, g : (\Pi x : X.Fx).$
$$(\Pi x : X.fx = gx) \to f = g$$
$Prop$-ext $\quad \Pi \phi_1, \phi_2 : Prop.(\phi_1 \to \phi_2) \to (\phi_2 \to \phi_1) \to \phi_1 = \phi_2$
pr-irrel $\quad \Pi \phi : Prop, x, y : \phi.x = y$

Π-extensionality generalises extensionality for functions, $Prop$-extensionality says that logical equivalence implies equality, and proof-irrelevance says that all proofs of a given proposition are equal.

In this extension one can easily derive (using only Π-ext) extensionality for functions, i.e. $(\Pi x : \tau_1.fx =_{\tau_2} gx) \to f =_{(\tau_1 \to \tau_2)} g$.

The standard set-theoretic interpretation of Σ_{eq} (and Σ_{ext}) is as follows:

$$
\begin{aligned}
[\![Prop]\!] &= \quad 2 \triangleq \{\emptyset, \{\emptyset\}\} \text{ the set of truth values} \\
[\![pr]\!](\phi) &= \quad \phi \\
[\![eq]\!](\tau, x, y) &= \quad \begin{cases} 1 & \text{if } x = y \\ 0 & \text{otherwise} \end{cases}
\end{aligned}
$$

Remark 5.3 Other interesting models of Σ_{eq}, including intensional ones (which fail to satisfy Σ_{ext}), can be obtained by interpreting LF in realizability toposes.

5.1.2 Products, sums and natural numbers

We describe products, sums and the type of natural numbers as extensions of the LF-signature Σ_{eq} for equational logic.

- LF-signature extension $\Sigma_\times$ for product types

types
unit $\quad 1 : Type$
product $\quad \times : Type, Type \to Type$
we write $\tau_1 \times \tau_2$ for $\times (\tau_1, \tau_2)$

operations
$\quad * : 1$
pairing $\quad pair : \Pi X_1, X_2 : Type.X_1, X_2 \to X_1 \times X_2$
we write $\langle M_1, M_2 \rangle$ for $pair(\tau_1, \tau_2, M_1, M_2)$
projections $\quad \pi_i : \Pi X_1, X_2 : Type.(X_1 \times X_2) \to X_i$
we write $\pi_i(M)$ for $\pi_i(\tau_1, \tau_2, M)$

axioms
$\quad \Pi x : 1.x = *$
$\quad \Pi X_1, X_2 : Type, x_1 : X_1, x_2 : X_2.\pi_i(\langle x_1, x_2 \rangle) = x_i$
$\quad \Pi X_1, X_2 : Type, x : X_1 \times X_2.\langle \pi_1(x), \pi_2(x) \rangle = x$

- LF-signature extension Σ_+ for sum types

  types

empty	$0 : Type$
sum	$+ : Type, Type \to Type$

  we write $\tau_1 + \tau_2$ for $+(\tau_1, \tau_2)$

  operations

  $$0 : \Pi X : Type.0 \to X$$

  inclusions $\quad in_i : \Pi X_1, X_2 : Type.X_i \to (X_1 + X_2)$

  we write $in_i(M)$ for $in_i(\tau_1, \tau_2, M)$

  case $\quad case : \Pi X_1, X_2, X : Type.$
  $$(X_1 \to X), (X_2 \to X) \to (X_1 + X_2) \to X$$

  we write $case(M_1, M_2, M)$ for $case(\tau_1, \tau_2, \tau, M_1, M_2, M)$

  axioms

  $$\Pi X : Type, x : 0, y : X.0(X, x) = y$$
  $$\Pi X_1, X_2 : Type, f_1 : (X_1 \to X), f_2 : (X_2 \to X), x : X_i.$$
  $$case(f_1, f_2, in_i(x)) = f_i(x)$$
  $$\Pi X_1, X_2, X : Type, f : (X_1 \times X_2) \to X.$$
  $$case(f \circ in_1, f \circ in_2) = f$$

  we may write (case M of $x_1.M_1 | x_2.M_2$) for $case(\lambda x_1 \; : \; \tau_1.M_1, \lambda x_2 \; : \; \tau_2.M_2, M)$

- LF-signature extension Σ_N for natural numbers

  types

NNO	$N : Type$

  operations

zero	$0 : N$
successor	$s : N \to N$
iteration	$I : \Pi X : Type.X, (X \to X) \to N \to X$

  we write $M^n(N)$ for $I(\tau, N, M, n)$

  axioms

  $$\Pi X : Type, x : X, f : (X \to X).f^0(x) = x$$
  $$\Pi X : Type, x : X, f : (X \to X), n : N.f^{s(n)}(x) = f(f^n(x))$$
  $$\Pi X : Type, x : X, f : (X \to X), h : (N \to X), n : N.$$
  $$h(0) = x, (\Pi m : N.h(sm) = f(hm)) \to h(n) = f^n(x)$$

Remark 5.4 there are stronger axiomatisations of natural numbers (and other types) as *inductive types* (see Coquand and Paulin 1988), which introduce also additional conversion rules on pseudo-terms:

types	
NNO	$N : Type$

operations	
zero	$0 : N$
successor	$s : N \to N$
induction	$R : \Pi P : N \to Type.P(0) \to$
	$(\Pi n : N.P(n) \to P(sn)) \to \Pi n : N.P(n)$

axioms

$$\Pi P : N \to Type, x : P(0), f : (\Pi n : N.P(n) \to P(sn)).$$
$$R(P, x, f, 0) = x$$
$$\Pi P : N \to Type, x : P(0), f : (\Pi n : N.P(n) \to P(sn)), n : N.$$
$$R(P, x, f, s(n)) = f(n, R(P, x, f, n))$$

Iteration $I(\tau, a, f)$ can be defined by induction as $R(\lambda n : N.\tau, a, \lambda n : N.f)$. The first two axioms for I follow easily from the two axioms for R, while the third axiom for I is proved by induction. Namely, given proofs $b : (h(0) = a)$ and $c : (\Pi n : N.h(sn) = f(hn))$, one can construct a proof $g : (\Pi n : N.P(n) \to P(sn))$, where $P(n)$ stands for $h(n) = f^n(a)$. Therefore, $R(P, b, g, n) : P(n)$ proves the conclusion of the third axiom for I.

The stronger axiomatisation of natural numbers becomes equivalent to the weaker one only in an *extensional* version of LF, where convertibility and equality coincide. However, in this extensional version of LF it is no longer decidable whether a judgement is derivable.

5.2 Computational types and structuring

A typical problem of denotational and operational semantics is the following: when a programming language is extended, its semantics may need to be extensively redefined. For instance, in Section 2 we kept redefining the operational semantics of the functional part, every time we considered a different extension. The problem remains even when the semantics is given via translation in a typed lambda-calculus (like the one introduce so far): one would keep redefining the translation of the functional part. In (Mosses 1990b) this problem is identified very clearly, and it is stressed how the use of **auxiliary notation** may help in making semantic definitions more reusable.

(Moggi 1991) identifies *monads* as an important structuring device for denotational semantics (but not for operational semantics!). The basic idea is that there is a unary type constructor T, called a **notion of computation**, and terms of type $T\tau$, called a **computational type**, should be thought as programs which computes values of type τ. The interpretation of T is not fixed, it varies according to the *computational features* of the programming language under consideration. Nevertheless, one can identifies some operations (for specifying the order of evaluation) and basic properties of them, which should be common to all notions of computation. This suggests translating a programming language PL into a metalanguage

$ML_T(\Sigma)$ with computational types, where the signature Σ gives additional operations (and their basic properties). In summary, given a programming language PL, the **monadic approach** to denotational semantics consists of three steps:

- identify a suitable metalanguage $ML_T(\Sigma)$, this hides the interpretation of T and Σ like an interface hides the implementation of an abstract datatype,

- define a translation of PL into $ML_T(\Sigma)$,

- construct a model of $ML_T(\Sigma)$, e.g. via translation into a metalanguage ML without computational types.

By a suitable choice of Σ, one can find a simple translation from PL to $ML_T(\Sigma)$ (in comparison to a direct translation into ML), which usually does not have to be redefined when PL is extended, and at the same time one can keep the translation of $ML_T(\Sigma)$ into ML fairly manageable.

- LF-signature extension Σ_T for computational types

types

T $T : Type \to Type$

operations

val $val^T : \Pi X : Type.X \to TX$

let $let^T : \Pi X_1, X_2 : Type.(X_1 \to TX_2), TX_1 \to TX_2$

we write $val^T(M)$ for $val^T(\tau, M)$ and similarly for let^T

we drop the superscript T, when it is clear from the context

axioms

$\Pi X_1, X_2 : Type, x : X_1, f : (X_1 \to TX_2).let(f, val(x)) = f(x)$

$\Pi X : Type, c : TX.let(val, c) = c$

$\Pi X_1, X_2, X_3 : Type, c : TX_1, f : (X_1 \to TX_2), g : (X_2 \to TX_3).$
$let(g, let(f, c)) = let(let(g) \circ f, c)$

Notation 5.5 We introduce some derived notation for computational type:

- $[e]_T$ stands for $val^T(e)$

- $let_T\ x \Leftarrow e_1\ in\ e_2$ stands for $let^T(\lambda x : \tau_1.e_2, e_1)$

- $Tf : T\tau_1 \to T\tau_2$, where $f : \tau_1 \to \tau_2$, stands for $\lambda c : T\tau_1.let\ x \Leftarrow c\ in\ [f(x)]$

- $\mu : T^2\tau \to T\tau$ stands for $\lambda c : T^2\tau.let\ x \Leftarrow c\ in\ x$

- $let\ \overline{x} \Leftarrow \overline{e}\ in\ e$ stands for $let\ x_1 \Leftarrow e_1\ in\ (\ldots(let\ x_n \Leftarrow e_n\ in\ e)\ldots)$

- $\langle \overline{x} \Leftarrow \overline{e}, e \rangle$ stands for $let\ \overline{x}, x \Leftarrow \overline{e}, e\ in\ [\langle \overline{x}, x \rangle]$

- $let\ \langle \overline{x} \rangle \Leftarrow c\ in\ e(x_1, \ldots, x_n)$ stands for $let\ x \Leftarrow c\ in\ e(\pi_1(x), \ldots, \pi_n(x))$.

Intuitively, the program $[e]$ simply returns the value e, while (let $x \Leftarrow e_1$ in e_2) first evaluates e_1 and binds the result to x, then evaluates e_2. With the above notation the third axiom becomes

$$\text{let } x_2 \Leftarrow (\text{let } x_1 \Leftarrow e_1 \text{ in } e_2) \text{ in } e_3 = \text{let } x_1 \Leftarrow e_1 \text{ in } (\text{let } x_2 \Leftarrow e_2 \text{ in } e_3)$$

which says that only the order of evaluation matters.

Unlike the previous types, computational types are not uniquely determined (up to isomorphism) by their equational axioms.

Example 5.6 We give a list of possible interpretations of computational types in Set, and indicate which *computational feature* they try to capture. It is left as an exercise to find a suitable interpretation of *val* and *let* and verify the equational axioms.

- Given a single sorted algebraic theory Th (i.e. a signature and a set of equational axioms), let $TX = |T_{Th}(X)|$, i.e. the carrier of the free Th-algebra $T_{Th}(X)$ over X. By a suitable choice of Th one can obtain interesting notions of computation, e.g.:

  - $TX = X$, which captures terminating functional programs
  - $TX = X + \{\bot\}$, which captures functional programs which may diverge, where $\bot$ represents programs which diverge
  - $TX = \mathcal{P}_{fin}(X)$ the set of finite subsets of X, which captures non-deterministic programs
  - $TX = (X + E)$, which captures programs with exceptions, where E is the set of exceptions
  - $TX = \mu X'.\mathcal{P}_{fin}(X + X')$ the set of finite trees with leaves labelled in X, which captures parallel programs

- $TX = (X \times S)^S$, which captures imperative programs, where S is the set of states, while $TX = X^S$ captures programs that can only look at the state

- $TX = R^{(R^X)}$, which captures programs with a continuation, where R is the set of final results

- $TX = X \times N$, which captures programs with timers, where N is the set of natural numbers

One could consider variations and combinations of the examples above, e.g.

- variations for non-deterministic programs are: $TX = \mathcal{P}(X)$ the set of subsets of X, and $TX = \mathcal{P}_\omega(X)$ the set of countable subsets of X

- two possible combinations for imperative programs with exceptions are: $TX = ((X + E) \times S)^S$ and $TX = ((X \times S) + E)^S$

- $TX = \mu X'.\mathcal{P}_{fin}(X + (A \times X'))$, which captures parallel programs which interact, where A is the set of actions (in fact TX is the set of finite synchronisation trees up to strong bisimulation)

- $TX = \mu X'.\mathcal{P}_{fin}((X + X') \times S)^S$, which captures parallel imperative programs (in fact TX is closely related to resumptions).

One could give further examples (in the category of cpos) based on the denotational semantics for various programming languages (see Schmidt 1986; Gunter and Scott 1990; Mosses 1989).

To exemplify the use of computational types, for each of the programming languages introduced in Section 2 we define a translation into a metalanguage $ML_T(\Sigma)$ with computational types, for a suitable choice of Σ, and indicate a possible interpretation for computational types and Σ. More formally, we give a realisation of the LF-signature Σ_{PL} for a programming language PL (as given in Section 4.3) in the LF-signature $\Sigma_{ML} + \Sigma_T + \Sigma$ for the metalanguage, where Σ_{ML} can be taken as $\Sigma_{eq} + \Sigma_\times + \Sigma_+ + \Sigma_N$. Incidentally, the axioms for the metalanguage could be safely ignored when defining the realisation.

5.2.1 CBV translation of the functional language with divergence

We define a translation of $\Sigma_{fun} + \Sigma_{div}$ into $ML_T(\Sigma)$. For this translation the LF-signature extension Σ is

operations
divergence $\quad \perp : \Pi X : Type.T(X)$

$$T^* := Type$$

types
$$unit^* := 1$$
$$bool^* := 1 + 1$$
$$nat^* := N$$
$$\Rightarrow^*(X_1, X_2) := X_1 \rightarrow T(X_2)$$
$$Id^*(X) := X$$
$$Exp^*(X) := T(X)$$

expressions

$$var^*(X, x) := [x]$$
$$*^* := [*]$$
$$tt^* := [in_1(*)]$$
$$ff^* := [in_2(*)]$$
$$if^*(X, c, c_1, c_2) := \text{let } x \Leftarrow c \text{ in (case } x \text{ of } \_ : 1.c_1|\_ : 1.c_2)$$
$$0^* := [0]$$
$$s^*(c) := \text{let } n \Leftarrow c \text{ in } [s(n)]$$
$$It^*(X, c_0, f, c) := \text{let } n \Leftarrow c \text{ in } g^n(c_0) \text{ , where}$$
$$g \triangleq \lambda c : TX.\text{let } c \Leftarrow x \text{ in } f(x)$$
$$ab^*(X_1, X_2, f) := [f]$$
$$ap^*(X_1, X_2, c, c_1) := \text{let } f \Leftarrow c \text{ in (let } x \Leftarrow c_1 \text{ in } f(x))$$
$$\bot^* := \bot$$

One gets the CBV denotational semantics by taking $TX = X + \{\bot\}$, and the standard semantics (for the fragment Σ_{fun} without divergence) by taking $TX = X$.

5.2.2 CBN translation of the functional language with divergence

We define a translation of $\Sigma_{fun} + \Sigma_{div}$ into $ML_T(\Sigma)$. Also for this translation the LF-signature extension Σ is

operations
divergence $\bot : \Pi X : Type.T(X)$

We give only those clauses where the CBN translation differs from the CBV translation

types
$$\Rightarrow^*(X_1, X_2) := T(X_1) \rightarrow T(X_2)$$
$$Id^*(X) := T(X)$$
$$Exp^*(X) := T(X) \text{ , this is like CBV}$$

expressions
$$var^*(X, c) := c$$
$$ap^*(X_1, X_2, c, c_1) := \text{let } f \Leftarrow c \text{ in } f(c_1)$$

One gets the CBN denotational semantics by taking $TX = X + \{\bot\}$, and again the standard semantics (for the fragment without divergence) by taking $TX = X$.

5.2.3 CBV translation of $\Sigma_{fun} + \Sigma_{imp}$

For this translation the LF-signature extension Σ is

types
locations $L : Type$

operations
lookup $lkp : L \rightarrow TN$
update $upd : L, N \rightarrow T1$

We give only those clauses which extend the CBV translation

types
$$Loc^* := \quad L$$
expressions
$$get^*(l) := \quad lkp(l)$$
$$set^*(l, c) := \quad \text{let } x \Leftarrow c \text{ in } upd(l, x)$$

One gets a CBV denotational semantics for the imperative language by taking $L = Loc$, $TX = (X \times \mathsf{S})^{\mathsf{S}}$ with $\mathsf{S} = Loc \to N$, $lkp(l) = \lambda s : \mathsf{S}.\langle s(l), s \rangle$, and $upd(l, n) = \lambda s : \mathsf{S}.\langle *, s[l \mapsto n] \rangle$. More precisely, one could prove this semantics to be computationally adequate with respect to the CBV operational semantics, when observing "p has value tt".

5.2.4 CBV translation of $\Sigma_{fun} + \Sigma_{exc}$

For this translation the LF-signature extension Σ is

types

exceptions	$E : Type$

operations

test	$eq : E, E \to 1 + 1$
raise	$raise : \Pi X : Type.E \to TX$
handle	$handle : \Pi X : Type.(E \to TX), TX \to TX$

We give only those clauses which extend the CBV translation

types
$$Exn^* := \quad E$$
expressions
$$raise^* := \quad raise$$
$$handle^*(X, n, c_1, c_2) := \quad handle(X, (\lambda x : E.\text{case } eq(x, n) \text{ of}$$
$$c_1 \mid raise(x)), c_2)$$

One gets a CBV denotational semantics for the language with exceptions by taking $E = Exn$, $TX = (X + E)$, $eq(n_1, n_2)$ is the equality on E, $raise(n) = in_2(n)$, $handle(f, in_1(x)) = x$ and $handle(f, in_2(n)) = f(n)$.

5.2.5 CBV translation of $\Sigma_{fun} + \Sigma_{nd}$

For this translation the LF-signature extension Σ is

operations

choice $\quad or : \Pi X : Type.TX, TX \to TX$

We give only those clauses which extend the CBV translation

expressions

$or^* := \quad or$

One gets a CBV denotational semantics for the non-deterministic language by taking $TX = \mathcal{P}_{fin}(X)$ and $or(x_1, x_2) = x_1 \cup x_2$. More precisely, one could prove this semantics to be computationally adequate with respect to the CBV operational semantics, when observing "p **may** have value tt".

5.2.6   CBV translation of $\Sigma_{fun} + \Sigma_{par}$

For this translation the LF-signature extension Σ is

operations

one-step $\delta : \Pi X : Type.TX \to TX$

or-parallelism $por : \Pi X : Type.TX, TX \to TX$

and-parallelism $pand : \Pi X_1, X_2 : Type.TX_1, TX_2 \to T(X_1 \times X_2)$

we write $\delta(M)$ for $\delta(\tau, M)$ and similarly for the others

Unlike the previous examples of CBV translations, here we need both to extend and redefine the CBV translation of expressions. For brevity we consider only the redefinition of constructors associated to boolean and functional types

expressions

$$var^*(X, x) := [x]$$
$$tt^* := [in_1(*)]$$
$$ff^* := [in_2(*)]$$
$$if^*(X, c, c_1, c_2) := \text{let } x \Leftarrow c \text{ in } \delta(\text{case } x \text{ of } \_ : 1.c_1|\_ : 1.c_2)$$
$$ab^*(X_1, X_2, f) := [f]$$
$$ap^*(X_1, X_2, c, c_1) := \text{let } f \Leftarrow c \text{ in } (\text{let } x \Leftarrow c_1 \text{ in } \delta(fx))$$
$$pap^*(X_1, X_2, c, c_1) := \text{let } \langle f, x \rangle \Leftarrow pand(c, c_1) \text{ in } \delta(fx)$$
$$por^* := por$$

One gets a *trace semantics* of the parallel language by taking $TX = \mathcal{P}_{fne}(N \times X)$ the set of finite nonempty subsets of $N \times X$, where $\langle n, x \rangle$ represents a sequence of n steps with final result x. The operations $pand$ and por can be defined as the additive functions such that

$$pand(\langle n_1, x_1 \rangle, \langle n_2, x_2 \rangle) = \{\langle n_1 + n_2, \langle x_1, x_2 \rangle\rangle\}$$

$$por(\langle n_1, x_1 \rangle, \langle n_2, x_2 \rangle) = \{\langle n_1 + m, x_1 \rangle | 0 \leq m \leq n_2\}$$
$$\cup \{\langle n_2 + m, x_2 \rangle | 0 \leq m \leq n_1\}$$

these correspond to an interleaved implementation of $pand$ and por, a concurrent (lock-step) implementation would be better represented as follows

$$pand(\langle n_1, x_1 \rangle, \langle n_2, x_2 \rangle) = \{\langle max(n_1, n_2), \langle x_1, x_2 \rangle\rangle\}$$

$$por(\langle n_1, x_1 \rangle, \langle n_2, x_2 \rangle) = \{\langle n_1, x_1 \rangle | n_1 \leq n_2\} \cup \{\langle n_2, x_2 \rangle | n_2 \leq n_1\}$$

Remark 5.7 The translation for the parallel language could be considered a refinement of that for the functional language, obtained by inserting δ in few places. One can consider many variations of the above translation, which differ only in the use of δ, each of them corresponds to a different choice of *granularity* for the steps of the operational semantics.

5.3   Translations and incremental approach

The monadic approach to denotational semantics outlined in Section 5.2 has a caveat. When the programming language PL is complex, the signature Σ identified by the monadic approach can to get fairly large, and the translation of $ML_T(\Sigma)$ into ML may become quite complicated. There is no magic, but one can alleviate the problem by adopting an **incremental approach** in defining the translation of $ML_T(\Sigma)$ into ML.

The basic idea is to adapt to this setting the techniques and modularisation facilities advocated for formal software development, in particular the desired translation of $ML_T(\Sigma)$ into ML corresponds to the implementation of an abstract datatype (in some given language). In an incremental approach, the desired implementation is obtained by a sequence of steps, where each step constructs an implementation for a more complex datatype from an implementation for a simpler datatype. To make the approach viable, we need a collection of self-contained parameterized modules with the following features:

- they should be *polymorphic*, i.e. for any signature Σ (or at least for a wide range of signatures) the module should take an implementation of Σ and construct an implementation of $\Sigma + \Sigma_{new}$, where Σ_{new} is fixed

- they could be *parametric*, i.e. the construction and the signature Σ_{new} may depend on parameters of some fixed signature Σ_{par}.

The polymorphic requirement can be easily satisfied, when one can implement Σ_{new} without changing the implementation of Σ (this is often the case in software development). However, the constructions we are interested in are not *persistent*, since they involve a re-implementation of computational types, and consequently of Σ. The translations we need to consider are of the form

$$I : ML_T(\Sigma_{par} + \Sigma + \Sigma_{new}) \to ML_T(\Sigma_{par} + \Sigma)$$

where Σ_{new} are the new symbols defined by I, Σ are the old symbols *redefined* by I and Σ_{par} are the parameters of the construction (which are unaffected by I). In general I can be decomposed in

- a translation $I_{new} : ML_T(\Sigma_{par} + \Sigma_{new}) \to ML_T(\Sigma_{par})$ defining the new symbols (in Σ_{new}) and redefining computational types,

- translations $I_{op} : ML_T(\Sigma_{op}) \to ML_T(\Sigma_{par} + \Sigma_{op})$ redefining an old symbol op in *isolation* (consistently with the redefinition of computational types), for each possible type of symbol one may have in Σ.

Remark 5.8 An obvious question is: why do we not apply the incremental approach directly to programming languages? One reason is that we take programming languages as given, so we have no scope to make them suitable to an incremental approach. A deeper reason is that programming languages cannot separate computational types from other type constructors, so one could not delimit the part of the language which needs to be redefined as sharply as in metalanguages.

We exemplify the ideas above with a variety of translations for adding one computational feature at a time and do the necessary redefinitions. For each translation we give

- LF-signature extensions Σ_{par} and Σ_{new}

- an LF-signature realisation

$$\Sigma_{ML} + \Sigma_{par} + \Sigma_T + \Sigma_{op} + \Sigma_{new} \to \Sigma_{ML} + \Sigma_{par} + \Sigma_T + \Sigma_{op}$$

where Σ_{op} is the following LF-signature extension

$A, B : Type$
old $op : \Pi X : Type.A, (B \to TX) \to TX$
we write $op(a, f)$ for $op(\tau, a, f)$

The realisation leaves unchanged the symbols in $\Sigma_{ML} + \Sigma_{par}$ and the types A and B in Σ_{op}, so they are not explicitly redefined. For simplicity the axiom part of signatures is ignored.

5.3.1 Translation I_{se} for adding side-effects

- LF-signature Σ_{par} for parameter symbols

  states $S : Type$

- LF-signature Σ_{new} for new symbols

  lookup $lkp : TS$
  update $upd : S \to T1$

- LF-signature realisation

  redefinition of computational types
  $$T^*X := S \to T(X \times S)$$
  $$val^*(X, x) := \lambda s : S.[\langle x, s \rangle]$$
  $$let^*(X, Y, f, c) := \lambda s : S.\text{let } \langle x, s' \rangle \Leftarrow c(s) \text{ in } f(x, s')$$
  definition of new symbols
  $$lkp^* := \lambda s : S.[\langle s, s \rangle]$$
  $$upd^*(s) := \lambda s' : S.[\langle *, s \rangle]$$
  redefinition of old operation
  $$op^*(X, a, f) := \lambda s : S.op(X \times S, a, \lambda b : B.f(b, s))$$

Remark 5.9 The operations lkd and upd do not fit (by a suitable instantiation of A and B) the format for a redefinable operation, as specified in Σ_{op}. However, they can be massaged to fit into the required format. In fact, given an operation of the form $op' : A \rightarrow TB$ (like lkd and upd) one can define an operation $op : \Pi X : Type.A, (B \rightarrow TX) \rightarrow TX$ of the right format by taking $op(X, a, f) =$ let $b \Leftarrow op'(a)$ in $f(b)$. Moreover, op' can be recovered from op as follows $op'(a) = op(B, a, val(B))$.

5.3.2 Translation I_{ex} for adding exceptions

- LF-signature Σ_{par} for parameter symbols

  exceptions $E : Type$

- LF-signature Σ_{new} for new symbols

  raise $raise : \Pi X : Type.E \rightarrow TX$
  handle $handle : \Pi X : Type.(E \rightarrow TX), TX \rightarrow TX$

- LF-signature realisation

  redefinition of computational types
  $$T^*X := T(X + E)$$
  $$val^*(X, x) := [in_1(x)]$$
  $$let^*(X, Y, f, c) := \text{let } u \Leftarrow c \text{ in (case } u \text{ of } x : X.f(x) \mid$$
  $$n : E.raise^*(Y, n))$$
  definition of new symbols
  $$raise^*(X, n) := [in_2(n)]$$
  $$handle^*(X, f, c) := \text{let } u \Leftarrow c \text{ in (case } u \text{ of } x : X.val^*(X, x) \mid$$
  $$n : E.f(n))$$
  redefinition of old operation
  $$op^*(X) := op(X + E)$$

Remark 5.10 In this translation we have improperly used the symbols to be realised on the right-hand side of the realisation. This could always be replaced with a proper realisation, since we have been careful enough to avoid circular definitions.

In this translation the redefinition of op is particularly simple, and one can show that the same redefinition works for a more general type of operations, given by the following LF-signature extension

  $F : Type \rightarrow Type$
old $op : \Pi X : Type.F(TX)$

5.3.3 Translation I_{co} for adding complexity

- LF-signature Σ_{par} for parameter symbols

  monoid $M : Type$
  $\quad\quad\quad 1 : M$
  $\quad\quad\quad * : M, M \rightarrow M$
  we write $m * n$ for $*(m, n)$

- LF-signature Σ_{new} for new symbols

  cost $\delta : M \to T1$

- LF-signature realisation

  redefinition of computational types
  $$T^*X := T(X \times M)$$
  $$val^*(X, x) := [\langle x, 1 \rangle]$$
  $$let^*(X, Y, f, c) := \text{let } \langle x, m \rangle \Leftarrow c \text{ in } (\text{let } \langle y, n \rangle \Leftarrow f(x) \text{ in } [\langle y, m * n \rangle])$$
  definition of new symbols
  $$\delta^*(m) := [\langle *, m \rangle]$$
  redefinition of old operation
  $$op^*(X) := op(X \times M)$$

Remark 5.11 We should have added to Σ_{par} axioms saying that $(M, 1, *)$ is a monoid. In fact, without them one cannot prove that the redefinition of computational types satisfies the axioms in Σ_T.

5.3.4   Translation I_{con} for adding continuations

- LF-signature Σ_{par} for parameter symbols

  results $R : Type$

- LF-signature Σ_{new} for new symbols

  abort $abort : \Pi X : Type.R \to TX$
  call-cc $call_{cc} : \Pi X, Y : Type.((X \to TY) \to TX) \to TX$

- LF-signature realisation

  redefinition of computational types
  $$T^*X := (X \to TR) \to TR$$
  $$val^*(X, x) := \lambda k.k(x)$$
  $$let^*(X, Y, f, c) := \lambda k.c(\lambda x : X.f(x)k)$$
  definition of new symbols
  $$abort^*(X, r) := \lambda k.[r]$$
  $$call_{cc}^*(X, Y, f) := \lambda k.f(\lambda x : X.\lambda k'.abort^*(X, kx))k$$
  redefinition of old operation
  $$op^*(X, a, f) := \lambda k.op(R, a, \lambda b : B.f(b)k)$$

Remark 5.12 The operation $call_{cc}$ does not fit the format for a redefinable operation, as specified in Σ_{op} (nor the more general one). This translation is quite different from the others, since computational types are used very little on the left-hand side of the realisation.

5.3.5 Other Translations

One can consider also a translation I_{res} for adding resumptions, i.e. $T^*X :=$ $\mu X'.T(X + X')$. However, in the category of sets the type expression on the right-hand side does not have a semantics, unless one makes strong restrictions on T. A proper treatment of resumptions can be done only after extending the metalanguages $ML_T(\Sigma)$ with suitable machinery for dealing with recursive definitions. We have not provided any translation for adding non-determinism. In fact, it seems that this (and some other notions of computation) should be used as starting point for the incremental approach.

5.3.6 Incremental approach at work

Now that we have introduced several translations for adding one computational feature at a time, one can compose them to obtain more complex translations and richer metalanguages $ML_T(\Sigma)$, as advocated by the incremental approach. We consider the realisation of computational types given by some of the composite translations, and indicate the kind of programming languages for which they could be used:

- $I_{ex}(I_{se}T)X = S \to T((X + E) \times S)$

  this is suitable for imperative language with exceptions, like Standard ML

- $I_{se}(I_{ex}T)X = S \to T((X \times S) + E)$

  this is suitable for languages with recovery blocks, where an error is handled by executing some alternative piece of code starting from a checkpoint state

- $I_{se}(I_{con}T)X = (X \to S \to TR) \to S \to TR$

  this is suitable for imperative languages with goto

- $I_{con}(I_{se}T)X = (X \to S \to T(R \times S)) \to S \to T(R \times S)$

  as above but with R replaced by $R \times S$

- $I_{res}(I_{se}T)X = \mu X'.S \to T((X + X') \times S)$

  this is suitable for parallel imperative languages, when T is suitable for non-deterministic languages (e.g when T is the finite powerset)

- $I_{se}(I_{res}T)X = S \to \mu X'.T((X \times S) + X')$

  this is suitable for transaction based languages, where a change of state can happen only after the interaction with other processes has been successfully completed.

One can pursue further the analogies with formal software development. For instance, an important issue that we have ignored so far is: what properties of the symbols defined by a realisation can be proved, knowing that the symbols used on the right-hand side of the realisation have certain properties? Of course, one wants to know that the redefinition of computational types preserves at least the axioms given in Σ_T. More interesting properties of translations one can investigate are:

- Which equations for the new operations are validated by the translation?

  For instance, I_{se} validates the following equations

  $upd(s); lkp = upd(s); [s]$
  $upd(s); upd(s') = upd(s')$
  let $s \Leftarrow lkp$ in $upd(s) = [*]$
  $lkp; c = c$

  while I_{ex} validates

  let $x \Leftarrow raise(n)$ in $f(x) = raise(n)$
  $handle(f, [x]) = [x]$
  $handle(f, raise(n)) = f(n)$
  $handle(raise, c) = c$
  $handle(f_2, handle(f_1, c)) = handle(\lambda n : E.handle(f_2, f_1(n)), c)$

- Which equations for the old operation are preserved by the translation?

  For instance, one can show that all translations preserve algebraic equations such as commutativity, associativity and idempotency for a binary polymorphic operation $op : \Pi X : Type.TX, TX \to TX$.

6 Metalanguages and recursive definitions

The typed metalanguages considered so far do not allow for recursive definitions of programs or types. The extensions we consider are inspired by Synthetic Domain Theory (SDT) and Axiomatic Domain Theory (ADT). From SDT we take the idea that predomains should be part of a set-theoretic universe with an expressive logic. From ADT we take equational reasoning principles, which are valid in many categories used in Denotational Semantics, such as the category of cpos. We have not taken the more traditional approach of LCF (see Scott 1993), in which predomains come equipped with a partial order, because in some semantic categories (e.g. complete extensional PERs and effective morphisms) the order structure is not the most important one, while in others (e.g. in dI-domains and stable functions) some of the LCF axioms fail. The axiomatisation is structured as follows:

- axioms clarifying the relation between predomains and the predicative universes $Type_i$;

- axioms for *lifting* as the classifier of partial *computable* functions, at this point we introduce the derived notion of partial map, domain and strict map;

- axioms asserting that the category of predomains and partial maps is algebraically compact (see Freyd 1992), from which one derives the existence of a fix-type and a unique uniform fix-point combinator. At this point, we mention an equivalent axiomatisation, based on the fix-type and existence of special invariant objects.

- revised axioms for computational types, which take into account recursive definitions.

6.1 The category of cpos

The category $\mathbf{Cpo}$ of cpos is the *intended* model of ADT, and we use it to exemplify the ADT part of the axiomatisation. In this section we recall the basic definitions, and the key properties of $\mathbf{Cpo}$ and related categories.

- A **cpo** (also called **predomain**) is a poset $\underline{X} = (X, \leq_X)$ (the subscript on $\leq$ is omitted when clear from the context) s.t. every ω-chain $\langle x_i | i \in \omega \rangle$ has least upper bound (lub) $\sqcup_i x_i$, where

  an ω-chain is a sequence $\langle x_i \in X | i \in \omega \rangle$ s.t. $\forall i. x_i \leq x_{i+1}$, and

  the lub of a sequence/set $\langle x_i \in X | i \in I \rangle$ is the unique $x \in X$ s.t. $\forall y \in X.(\forall i \in I. x_i \leq y) \leftrightarrow x \leq y$.

- A **cppo** (also called **domain**) is a cpo $\underline{X}$ with least element $\bot_X$, where

  the least element of a cpo/poset $\underline{X}$ is the unique $x \in X$ s.t. $\forall y \in X. x \leq y$.

- A **continuous** function $f : \underline{X} \to \underline{Y}$ between cpos is a function $f : X \to Y$ which is monotonic, i.e. $x_1 \leq x_2 \supset f(x_1) \leq f(x_2)$, and preserves lubs of ω-chains, i.e. $f(\sqcup_i x_i) = \sqcup_i f(x_i)$.

- An **open** subset X' of a cpo $\underline{X}$ is an upward closed subset of X, i.e. $x_1 \in X'$ and $x_1 \leq_X x_2$ imply $x_2 \in X'$, s.t. $(\sqcup_i x_i) \in X'$ implies $\exists i. x_i \in X'$ for any ω-chain $\langle x_i | i \in \omega \rangle$. We write $\underline{X}'$ for the cpo $(X', \leq_X \cap (X' \times X'))$, i.e. X' with the induced order.

- A **partial** continuous function $f : \underline{X} \rightharpoonup \underline{Y}$ between cpos is a partial function $f : X \rightharpoonup Y$ s.t. its domain X' is an open subset of $\underline{X}$ and f is continuous on $\underline{X}'$, i.e. $f : \underline{X}' \to \underline{Y}$.

- A **strict** function $f : \underline{X} \circ\!\!\longrightarrow \underline{Y}$ between cppos is a continuous function $f : \underline{X} \to \underline{Y}$ which preserves the least element, i.e. $f(\bot) = \bot$.

There are four categories of domains and predomains one could consider:

- $\mathbf{Cpo}$ is the category of predomains and continuous functions,

- $\mathbf{Cpo}_\bot$ is the category of predomains and partial continuous functions,

- **Cppo** is the category of domains and continuous functions,

- **Cpo**$^\perp$ is the category of domains and strict functions.

Remark 6.1 Cpo is a biCCC (i.e. a cartesian closed category with finite coproducts) with NNO and the category **Set** of sets is a full sub-biCCC of **Cpo** with the same NNO, therefore it is the appropriate replacement for **Set**. **Cppo** is a full sub-CCC of **Cpo** and every endomorphism has a fix point, therefore it is the right setting for a fix-point combinator. **Cpo**$_\perp$ is algebraically compact, therefore it is the right setting for solving domain equations. Moreover, the inclusion of **Cpo** in **Cpo**$_\perp$ is bijective on objects and reflects isomorphisms, therefore a solution in **Cpo**$_\perp$ to a domain equation is also a solution in **Cpo**. In fact, **Cpo**$^\perp$ is isomorphic to **Cpo**$_\perp$, but in other models of ADT the situation can be different.

6.2   The category of predomains

The main slogan of SDT is "predomains are sets". In LF this can be formalised by adding a new universe $Pdom$ included in $Type_0$ and closed under Π-types over $Type_0$, i.e.

$$\Pi \frac{\Gamma \vdash A_1 : Type_0 \qquad \Gamma, x : A_1 \vdash A_2 : Pdom}{\Gamma \vdash (\Pi x : A_1.A_2) : Pdom}$$

One could impose additional properties on $Pdom$:

- $Pdom$ is a full reflective subcategory of $Type_0$, this ensures that many universal constructions in $Pdom$ are as in $Type_0$, and so "predomain constructions are set constructions";

- $Pdom$ is an impredicative universe, i.e.

$$\Pi \frac{\Gamma \vdash A_1 : Type_i \qquad \Gamma, x : A_1 \vdash A_2 : Pdom}{\Gamma \vdash (\Pi x : A_1.A_2) : Pdom}$$

  this is satisfiable in realizability models, and it is particularly useful when modelling programming languages with polymorphic types.

It is consistent to assume that $Prop \subset Pdom$, while $Prop \in Pdom$ is inconsistent with $Pdom$ being an impredicative universe (and with other axioms for predomains introduced in the sequel). The rest of the axiomatisation of predomains is rather independent from the above assumptions. This reflects the ADT approach, which tries to identify only the essential structure and properties to give meaning to recursive definitions.

6.3   The classifier for partial computable functions

The axiomatisation of predomains has sole additional structure a monad (L, η, let^L) on the category of predomains. Other structure introduced by the axiomatisation consists of universal constructions, and therefore is unique up to isomorphism. Intuitively, $L\tau$ is the type of partial (deterministic) computations, which may either diverge or produce a value in τ. The intended interpretation in **Cpo** is as follows:

- $L\underline{X}$ is the lifting $\underline{X}_\perp$ of $\underline{X}$, i.e. the domain $(\{\perp\} + X, \leq)$ s.t. $\perp < in(x)$ and $in(x) \leq in(x') \leftrightarrow x \leq x'$, i.e. L adds an element $\perp$ below $\underline{X}$;

- $\eta : \underline{X} \to L\underline{X}$ is given by $\eta(x) = in(x)$;

- $let^L : (L\underline{Y})^{\underline{X}} \times L\underline{X} \to L\underline{Y}$ is given by $let^L(f, \perp) = \perp$ and $let^L(f, in(x)) = f(x)$.

Moreover, (L, η) **classifies** partial continuous maps, i.e. there is a one-one correspondence between partial continuous maps $f : \underline{X} \rightharpoonup \underline{Y}$ and continuous maps $g : \underline{X} \to L\underline{Y}$ given by

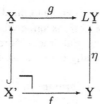

- LF-signature extension Σ_L for lifting

types

lifting	$L : Pdom \to Pdom$

operations

val	$\eta : \Pi X : Pdom.X \to LX$
diverge	$\perp : \Pi X : Pdom.LX$
let	$let^L : \Pi X_1, X_2 : Pdom.(X_1 \to LX_2), LX_1 \to LX_2$

same conventions as for computational types in Section 5.2

axioms

$L.0$	$\Pi X_1, X_2 : Pdom, x : X_1, f : (X_1 \to LX_2).$
	$\qquad\qquad\qquad\qquad\qquad let(f, \eta(x)) = f(x)$
$L.1$	$\Pi X_1, X_2 : Pdom, f : (X_1 \to LX_2).let(f, \perp) = \perp$
$L.2$	$\Pi X_1, X_2 : Pdom, f, g : (LX_1 \to X_2).$
	$\qquad f(\perp) = g(\perp), (\Pi x : X_1.f(\eta(x)) = g(\eta(x))) \to f = g$
$L.3$	$\Pi X : Pdom, x, y : X.\eta(x) = \eta(y) \to x = y$
$L.4$	$\Pi X : Pdom, f, g : (LX \to X).$
	$\qquad (\Pi x : X_1.f(\eta(x)) = x), (\Pi x : X_1.g(\eta(x)) = x) \to f = g$

derived properties

$\Pi X : Pdom, c : LX.let(\eta, c) = c$

$\Pi X_1, X_2, X_3 : Pdom, c : LX_1, f : (X_1 \to LX_2),$
$\qquad g : (X_2 \to LX_3).let(g, let(f, c)) = let(let(g) \circ f, c)$

Remark 6.2 We have not axiomatised that (L, η) is a partial map classifier, because it is too clumsy to do so. We will indicate explicitly, when this extra axiom would have been useful.

Some comments about the axioms. $(L.0)$ is the only axiom for computational types we need to assume, since the others are derivable. $(L.1)$ says that $\bot$ represents the diverging program. $(L.2)$ says that $[\eta, \bot] : X + 1 \to LX$ is epic in $Pdom$, but not in $Type$. $(L.3)$ says that $\eta : X \to LX$ is monic in $Pdom$ as well as $Type$, this is true for any partial map classifier. $(L.4)$ says that there is at most one left inverse to $\eta : X \to LX$, this axiom is convenient but not essential.

In **Cpo** there are only three partial map classifiers: lifting $\underline{X}_\bot$, topping $\underline{X}^\top$ and $\underline{X} + 1$. Only the first two satisfy $(L.4)$. In a preorder (viewed as a category) the only monad, which satisfies (trivially) all the axioms, is the one mapping every object to the terminal one.

Various domain-theoretic notions can be defined solely in terms of L. When L is the lifting monad in **Cpo** these notions agree with those introduced already for cpos, and defined in terms of the partial order. Moreover, most of their properties, valid in **Cpo**, can be derived formally from the axioms for L.

- $(X, \alpha_X : LX \to X)$ (i.e. is a **domain**) iff

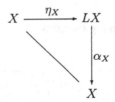

We often say that X is a domain, since by $(L.4)$ the left inverse is unique, and write Dom for the collection of domains.

- $f : X \rightharpoonup Y$ (i.e. is **partial**) iff $f : X \to LY$, therefore predomains and partial maps are the Kleisli category for the monad L.

- Given X and Y domains, $f : X \circ\!\!\longrightarrow Y$ (i.e. is **strict**) iff $f(\alpha_X(\bot)) = \alpha_Y(\bot)$.

The following assertions are derivable:

- $\bot$ is the unique element satisfying $(L.1)$, i.e.
  $$\Pi X : Pdom, c : LX.(\Pi f : X \to LX.let(f, c) = c) \to c = \bot$$

- If X and Y are domains and $f : X \multimap Y$, then

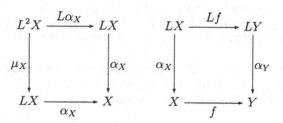

therefore domains and strict maps are the category of Eilenberg-Moore algebras for the monad L.

- If $X \lhd Y$ via (m, e), i.e. $m; e = \mathrm{id}_X$, and Y is a domain, then X is a domain and e is strict.

- 1, $Y_1 \times Y_2$ and $X_1 \to Y_2$ are domains, provided Y_1 and Y_2 are domains.

6.4 Algebraic compactness

The main contribution of Domain Theory to Denotational Semantics consists of general techniques (applicable to a variety of categories) for giving semantics to recursive definitions. Recursive definitions come in two forms: $x = f(x)$ where f is a function on a domain, or $X \cong FX$ where F is a type constructor. The more traditional approach to recursive definitions works in the context of **Cpo**-categories (see Smyth and Plotkin 1982; Tennent 1991). More recently Freyd has identified *algebraic compactness* as the general abstract property to give semantics to recursive definitions (see Freyd 1990; Freyd 1992).

Definition 6.3 (Freyd) *Given a category* C *we say that:*

- $\sigma_F : F(\mu F) \to \mu F$ *is a* **free** *algebra for the functor* $F : C \to C$, *when* σ_F *is an initial F-algebra (and hence in particular is an isomorphism with inverse* σ_F^{-1}*) and* σ_F^{-1} *is a final F-coalgebra;*

- C *is* **algebraically complete** *iff every* $F : C \to C$ *has an initial algebra*

- C *is* **algebraically cocomplete** *iff every* $F : C \to C$ *has a final coalgebra*

- C *is* **algebraically compact** *iff every* $F : C \to C$ *has a free algebra.*

Remark 6.4 The quantification over *every* endofunctor should be understood 2-categorically. Algebraic compactness implies that $0 \cong 1$, therefore it is equationally inconsistent with C being cartesian closed. We will consider only covariant domain equations. However, one can solve also domain equations of mixed variance, since $C^{op} \times C$ is algebraically compact when C is.

Neither **Set** nor **Cpo** are algebraically complete (or cocomplete), even with respect to *strong* functors, e.g. take $FX = (X \rightarrow 2) \rightarrow 2$. The category PER (Partial Equivalence Relations over Kleene's partial applicative structure) is algebraically complete and cocomplete with respect to *realisable* functors.

Theorem 6.5 *The category* $C_\perp$ *of predomains and partial maps is algebraically compact with respect to* **Cpo***-functors, where* $F : C_\perp \rightarrow C_\perp$ *is a* **Cpo***-functor iff its action on morphisms is given by continuous maps* $F : (LY)^X \rightarrow L(FY)^{FX}$.

Proof This follows from a general result on **Cpo**-categories (see Smyth and Plotkin 1982). More explicitly, the free F-algebra μF is given by the set (with the point-wise order)

$$\{x \in \Pi_n L(F^n 0) | \forall n : N.x_n = let(F^n!.x_{n+1}) \wedge \exists n : N, x' : F^n 0.x_n = \eta(x')\}$$

where ! is the unique map in $F0 \rightarrow L0$, i.e. $!(x') = \perp$. ∎

The following axioms say that for each endofunctor $F : C_L \rightarrow C_L$, F-algebra $\alpha : F\tau \rightharpoonup \tau$ and F-coalgebra $\beta : \tau \rightharpoonup F\tau$ there exist unique $\alpha^\dagger$ and $\beta_\dagger$ such that

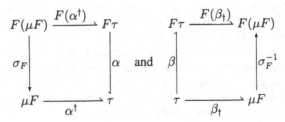

The precise axiomatisation is quite complicated in comparison to the above description. First, one has to represent by a suitable type $Endo_L$ the collection of endofunctors on the Kleisli category C_L, to do this one uses the cumulative hierarchy of universes. Then, one has to introduce some common conventions for functors. Finally, one can introduce the following LF-signature.

- LF-signature extension $\Sigma_{\mu\nu}$ for free algebras

  types
  free $\mu : Endo_L \rightarrow Pdom$

  _____

  operations
  $\sigma : \Pi F : Endo_L.F(\mu F) \rightarrow \mu F$
  $\sigma^{-1} : \Pi F : Endo_L.\mu F \rightarrow F(\mu F)$
  $I : \Pi F : Endo_L, X : Pdom.(FX \rightarrow LX), (\mu F) \rightarrow LX$
  $J : \Pi F : Endo_L, X : Pdom.(X \rightarrow L(FX)), X \rightarrow L(\mu F)$
  we write $\alpha^\dagger$ for $I(F, \tau, \alpha)$ and $\alpha_\dagger$ for $J(F, \tau, \alpha)$

  _____

axioms

iso $\Pi F : Endo_L, x : F(\mu F).\sigma_F^{-1}(\sigma_F x) = x$

         $\Pi F : Endo_L, x : \mu F.\sigma_F(\sigma_F^{-1}x) = x$

initial $\Pi F : Endo_L, X : Pdom, \alpha : (FX \to LX), x : F(\mu F).$

$$\alpha^\dagger(\sigma_F x) = let^L(\alpha, F(\alpha^\dagger)x)$$

         $\Pi F : Endo_L, X : Pdom, \alpha : (FX \to LX), f : (\mu F \to LX).$

$$(\Pi x : F(\mu F).let^L(\alpha, F(f)x)) \to f = \alpha^\dagger$$

final $\Pi F : Endo_L, X : Pdom, \beta : (X \to L(FX)), x : F(X).$

$$let^L(L\sigma_F^{-1}, \beta_\dagger x) = let^L(F(\beta_\dagger), \beta x)$$

         $\Pi F : Endo_L, X : Pdom, \beta : (X \to L(FX)), f : (X \to L(\mu F)).$

$$(\Pi x : X.let^L(F\sigma_F^{-1}, fx) = let^L(Ff, \beta x)) \to f = \beta_\dagger$$

Remark 6.6 To be faithful to the definition of algebraic compactness, we should have required σ_F to be an isomorphism in $\mathcal{C}_L$ instead of $\mathcal{C}$. In fact, when L is a partial map classifier (we have not axiomatised this) one can show that: the inclusion of $\mathcal{C}$ in $\mathcal{C}_L$ reflects isomorphisms, and that an initial F-algebra in $\mathcal{C}_L$ is initial also in $\mathcal{C}$, when F cuts down to $\mathcal{C}$.

There are several functors on $\mathcal{C}$, which can be extended to $\mathcal{C}_L$

- binary products, although $\tau_1 \times \tau_2$ is not the product of τ_1 and τ_2 in $\mathcal{C}_L$

- binary sums, and $\tau_1 + \tau_2$ is also the coproduct of τ_1 and τ_2 in $\mathcal{C}_L$

a restricted form of exponentiation, which suffices for most applications to Denotational Semantics, is also available

Proposition 6.7 *If $T : \mathcal{C}_L \to \mathcal{C}_L$ factors through $\mathcal{C}^L$, i.e. FX is a domain and Ff is (the image of) a strict map, then T cuts down to $\mathcal{C}$ and*

- *the functor $\_ \to T\_ : \mathcal{C}^{op} \times \mathcal{C} \to \mathcal{C}$ extends to a functor from $\mathcal{C}_L^{op} \times \mathcal{C}_L$ to $\mathcal{C}_L$ which factors through $\mathcal{C}^L$;*

- *the free T-algebra $T(\mu T) \to \mu T$ in $\mathcal{C}_L$ is also a free T-algebra in $\mathcal{C}$.*

Remark 6.8 One could have assumed algebraic compactness for $\mathcal{C}^L$, i.e. the category of domains and strict maps, rather than for $\mathcal{C}_L$. In our opinion, it is preferable to use $\mathcal{C}_L$. In fact, in $\mathcal{C}^L$ one can define by recursion only domains (not predomains), and some additional type constructors, i.e. $\otimes$ (smash product) and $\multimap$ (strict function spaces), for dealing with CBV programming languages.

It is very cumbersome to work directly with functors. However, one can define once for all functors *corresponding* to (some) type constructors, and then *canonically* associate functors to type expressions, by exploiting the usual closure properties for functors. In fact, most metalanguages for denotational semantics avoid the problem by working with restricted forms of type expressions, which are guaranteed to have a *corresponding* functor.

At this point we can introduce some constructions with universal properties, whose existence follows from algebraic compactness: the fix-type (introduce by Crole and Pitts 1992) and a uniform fix-point combinator (see Simpson 1992).

6.4.1 The fix-type

The monad L extends to an endofunctor L' on the category $\mathcal{C}_L$ of predomains and partial maps, namely $L'f = Lf; \mu_Y; \eta_Y$ whenever $f : X \to LY$. Let $\sigma_L : L(\Omega) \to \Omega$ be the free L'-algebra in $\mathcal{C}_L$, then one can prove that it is also the free L-algebra in $\mathcal{C}$. In fact, (Crole and Pitts 1992) introduces the equivalent (but apparently weaker) notion of fix-type, which is enough for defining a uniform fix-point combinator and proving the *consistent algebraic compactness* of $\mathcal{C}_L$ and $\mathcal{C}^L$ (see Simpson 1992).

- LF-signature extension Σ_Ω for the fix-type

  types

fix-type	$\Omega : Pdom$

  operations

  $\sigma : L\Omega \to \Omega$

  $I_L : \Pi X : Pdom.(LX \to X), \Omega \to X$

  $\omega : \Omega$

  we write $\alpha^\dagger$ for $I_L(X, \alpha)$, $\underline{0}$ for $\sigma_L(\bot)$ and $\underline{s}$ for $\eta; \sigma_L$

  axioms

$\Omega.1$	$\Pi X : Pdom, \alpha : (LX \to X), c : L\Omega.\alpha^\dagger(\sigma c) = \alpha(L(\alpha^\dagger)c)$
	$\Pi X : Pdom, \alpha : (LX \to X), f : (\Omega \to X).$
	$\qquad\qquad (\Pi c : L\Omega.f(\sigma c) = \alpha(L(f)c)) \to f = \alpha^\dagger$
$\Omega.2$	$\underline{s}(\omega) = \omega$
	$\Pi x : L\Omega.\underline{s}(x) = x \to x = \omega$

  additional axioms

$\Omega.3$	$\Pi X : Pdom, f, g : (\Omega \to X).$
	$\qquad (\Pi n : N.f(\underline{s}^n(\underline{0})) = g(\underline{s}^n(\underline{0}))) \to f = g$

Remark 6.9 ($\Omega.1$) says that σ_L is the initial L-algebra. ($\Omega.2$) that there exists a unique fix-point for $\underline{s}$, or equivalently a unique L-coalgebra morphism from $\eta : 1 \to L1$ to σ_L^{-1}. These axioms are enough to derive **consistent algebraic compactness** of $\mathcal{C}_L$, i.e. any initial algebra (when it exists) is also a free algebra. Therefore, in the presence of a fix-type algebraic completeness of $\mathcal{C}_L$ implies algebraic compactness.

The axiom ($\Omega.3$) involves a NNO N in *Type*, and it is not derivable from algebraic compactness. It amounts to computational induction for the fix-point combinator (defined in terms of the fix-type), which is a useful proof principle.

In **Cpo** (when L is lifting) the fix-type can be described as follows:

- Ω is the domain $\{0 < 1 < \ldots < n < n + 1 < \ldots \omega\}$, i.e. the set of ordinals $\leq \omega$ with the natural order.

  There is a one-one correspondence between continuous maps $f : \Omega \to \underline{X}$ and ω-chains $\langle x_i | i \in \omega \rangle$ given by $f(n) = x_n$ for $n \in N$ and $f(\omega) = \sqcup_i x_i$.

- $\sigma : L\Omega \to \Omega$ is the map such that $\sigma(\bot) = 0$, $\sigma(in(n)) = n + 1$ and $\sigma(in(\omega)) = \omega$.

  Moreover one has that $\underline{0} = 0$, $\underline{s}(n) = n + 1$ and $\underline{s}(\omega) = \omega$. Therefore, ω is the unique fix-point of $\underline{s}$, and the unique $e : N \to \Omega$ such that $e(n) = \underline{s}^n(\underline{0})$ is $e(n) = n$.

- Given $\alpha : L\underline{X} \to \underline{X}$, the unique $\alpha^\dagger : \Omega \to \underline{X}$ such that

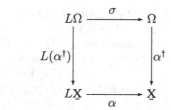

  is $\alpha^\dagger n = \underline{s}_\alpha^n(\alpha(\bot))$ and $\alpha^\dagger \omega = \sqcup_n \alpha^\dagger n$, where $\underline{s}_\alpha(x) = \alpha(\eta x)$.

- It is easy to see (because of continuity) that $e : N \to \Omega$ is an epic in **Cpo**, so the additional axiom $(\Omega.3)$ is valid.

When $L\underline{X}$ is $\underline{X}^\top$ or $\underline{X} + 1$ the initial L-algebra exists, but $\underline{s}$ has no fix-points.

6.4.2 The fix-point combinator

Following (Crole and Pitts 1992), we use the fix-type to define a *canonical* fix-point for a map $f : X \to X$ over a domain X, namely $\mathrm{fix}(f) = f^*(\omega)$, where $f^* : \Omega \to X$ is the unique map such that

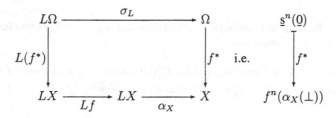

- LF-signature extension Σ_{fix} for the fix-point combinator

operations	
	$\text{fix} : \Pi X : Dom.(X \to X) \to X$
	we write $\text{fix} f$ for $\text{fix}(\tau, f)$

axioms	
fix-point	$\Pi X : Dom, f : (X \to X).\text{fix} f = f(\text{fix} f)$
uniform	$\Pi X_1, X_2 : Dom, f_1 : (X_1 \to X_1), f_2 : (X_2 \to X_2),$
	$\quad h : (X_1 \circ\!\!\longrightarrow X_2).f_2 \circ h = h \circ f_1 \to \text{fix} f_2 = h(\text{fix} f_1)$

additional axioms	
comp-ind	$\Pi X_1 : Dom, X_2 : Pdom, f : (X_1 \to X_1),$
	$\quad g_1, g_2 : (X_1 \to X_2).(\Pi n : N.\phi(f^n(\bot))) \to \phi(\text{fix} f)$
	where $\phi(M)$ stands for $g_1(M) = g_2(M)$ and $\bot$ for $\alpha_\tau(\bot)$.
Bekic	$\Pi X_1, X_2 : Dom, f : (X_1 \times X_2 \to X_1 \times X_2).$
	$\quad\quad (\text{fix} f) = \langle \text{fix}(F_1), F_2(\text{fix}(F_1)) \rangle$
	where $F_2(x_1) = \text{fix}(\lambda x_2.\pi_2(f(\langle x_1, x_2 \rangle)))$
	and $F_1(x_1) = \lambda x_1.\pi_1(f(\langle x_1, F_2(x_1) \rangle))$

Remark 6.10 From the axioms for the fix-type one can prove that there exists a unique fix satisfying (fix-point) and (uniform).

(Bekic) involves products in $Pdom$ and follows from algebraic compactness. Basically, it says that to solve a (finite) system of recursive equations, it does not matter in which order one constructs a solution, the result is anyway the same.

(comp-ind) follows from $(\Omega.3)$ and closure of $Pdom$ under equalisers computed in $Type$ (which is true when $Pdom$ is a full reflective sub-category of $Type$). However a weaker form of induction, called Scott's induction

$$\phi(\bot), (\Pi x : \phi(x) \to \phi(fx)) \to \phi(\text{fix} f)$$

follows from the axioms for the fix-type (and the assumption about equalisers).

In **Cpo** the fix-point combinator obtained from the fix-type Ω coincides with the least prefix-point combinator.

Definition 6.11 (Least prefixed point) *Given a domain $\underline{X}$ and a map $f : \underline{X} \to \underline{X}$, the least x such that $f(x) \le x$ exists, and it is given by* $\text{fix}(f) \stackrel{\Delta}{=} \sqcup_i f^i(\bot)$.

6.4.3 Special invariant objects

Instead of assuming algebraic compactness (of $\mathcal{C}_L$) and then deriving a fix-type and fix-point combinator, we can proceed in another way. More precisely, first assume a fix-type, which is enough to prove that there exists a unique uniform fix-point combinator, then assume the existence of *special invariant objects*.

- LF-signature extension Σ_{inv} for special invariant objects

types

invariant $\quad \mu : Endo_L \to Pdom$

---

operations

$$\sigma : \Pi F : Endo_L.F(\mu F) \to \mu F$$
$$\sigma^{-1} : \Pi F : Endo_L.\mu F \to F(\mu F)$$

---

axioms

iso $\quad \Pi F : Endo_L, x : \mu F.\sigma(\sigma^{-1}x) = x$

$\qquad \Pi F : Endo_L, x : F(\mu F).\sigma^{-1}(\sigma x) = x$

special $\quad \Pi F : Endo_L.\mathrm{fix}(\lambda f : \mu F \to L(\mu F).(L\sigma) \circ (Ff) \circ \sigma^{-1}) = \eta$

Remark 6.12 The definition of special invariant object is taken from (Simpson 1992) (which differs from Freyd's definition). In the presence of a fix-type, one can prove that for any endofunctor F over $\mathcal{C}_L$ an isomorphism $\sigma : FX \to X$ is a free F-algebra (a global property) iff it is a special invariant object (a local property). This correspondence generalises the equivalence, established in (Smyth and Plotkin 1982), between O-limits and ω-colimits for an ω-chain of embeddings.

6.5 Computational types revised

Once the monad L has been introduced, it is natural to revise the axioms for computational types given in Section 5.2. More specifically, T should act on predomains rather then arbitrary types, moreover one wants the possibility of defining programs by recursion and using T in recursive domain equations.

- LF-signature extension Σ_T for revised computational types

  types

  T $\qquad T : Pdom \to Pdom$

  ---

  operations

  val $\quad val^T : \Pi X : Pdom.X \to TX$

  let $\quad let^T : \Pi X_1, X_2 : Pdom.(X_1 \to TX_2), TX_1 \to TX_2$

  dom $\quad \alpha^T : \Pi X : Pdom.L(TX) \to TX$

  same conventions as in Section 5.2

  ---

  axioms

  $\qquad \Pi X_1, X_2 : Pdom, x : X_1, f : (X_1 \to TX_2).$
  $$let(f, val(x)) = f(x)$$
  $\qquad \Pi X : Pdom, c : TX.let(val, c) = c$

  $\qquad \Pi X_1, X_2, X_3 : Pdom, c : TX_1, f : (X_1 \to TX_2),$
  $\qquad\qquad g : (X_2 \to TX_3).let(g, let(f, c)) = let(let(g) \circ f, c)$

  $T.1 \quad \Pi X : Pdom, c : TX.\alpha(\eta(c)) = c$

  $T.2 \quad \Pi X_1, X_2 : Pdom, f : (X_1 \to TX_2).let(f, \bot) = \bot$

  $\qquad$ where $\bot$ stands for $\alpha_\tau(\bot)$

The first three axioms are the ones already introduced in Section 5.2. $(T.1)$ says that TX is a domain, therefore it has a fix-point combinator (because of the fix-type), which we can be use to define programs by recursion. $(T.2)$ says that $let(f) : TX \to TY$ is strict; this has two important consequences.

Proposition 6.13 *Let* in_X *be* $LX \circ\!\!\xrightarrow{\;L(val)\;} L(TX) \circ\!\!\xrightarrow{\;\alpha\;} TX$, *then*

- $in : LX \circ\!\!\longrightarrow TX$ *is the unique strict monad morphism from* L *to* T, *i.e.*
  $in([x]_L) = [x]_T$ *and* $in(\text{let}_L\ x\!\Leftarrow\!c\ \text{in}\ f(x)) = \text{let}_T\ x\!\Leftarrow\!in(c)\ \text{in}\ in(fx)$

- *the functor* $T : \mathcal{C} \to \mathcal{C}$ *extends to an endofunctor* T' *on* $\mathcal{C}_L$ *which factors through* $\mathcal{C}^L$, *namely* $T'f$ *is (the image of)*

$$TX \circ\!\!\xrightarrow{\;Tf\;} T(LY) \circ\!\!\xrightarrow{\;T(in)\;} T^2Y \circ\!\!\xrightarrow{\;\mu\;} TY$$

The second consequence of $(T.2)$ says not only that we can use T in recursive domain equations, but we can also exponentiate it (see Proposition 6.7).

6.6   Structuring and incremental approach revised

At this point we can replace the metalanguages $ML_T(\Sigma)$ introduced in Section 5.2 with more expressive ones, which distinguish between predomains $Pdom$ and type $Type$, and moreover incorporate the monad L, algebraic compactness of $\mathcal{C}_L$, the fix-type and fix-point combinator, and the revised LF-signature for computational types. Therefore, one can give semantics to more realistic programming languages via translation into these metalanguages. On the other hand, the more complex LF-signature for computational types requires only a minor overhead to the incremental approach, since we have to check two additional axioms (the structure α^T is unique). One can easily check that all translations given in Section 5.3 preserve these two axioms.

As a sample application, we define a translation I_{res} for adding resumptions, which uses recursive types, and show a better way to give semantics to the parallel language by translating it into a metalanguage with a fix-point combinator.

6.6.1   Translation for adding resumptions

In this section we define a translation parameterized with respect to an endofunctor H on $\mathcal{C}$ (not necessarily on $\mathcal{C}_L$). To deal with the simple parallel language introduced in Section 2 the parameter H should be instantiated to the identity functor. However, different instances of H may be needed for more complex parallel languages. We proceed as in Section 5.3, by given LF-signature extensions Σ_{par} and Σ_{new}, and an LF-signature realisation

$$\Sigma_{ML} + \Sigma_{par} + \Sigma_T + \Sigma_{op} + \Sigma_{new} \to \Sigma_{ML} + \Sigma_{par} + \Sigma_T + \Sigma_{op}$$

but now we should use the variant of LF incorporating predomains, Σ_{ML} should be $\Sigma_{eq} + \Sigma_\times + \Sigma_+ + \Sigma_N + \Sigma_L + \Sigma_{\mu\nu}$ and Σ_T is the LF-signature of Section 6.5.

- LF-signature Σ_{par} for parameter symbols

  resumptions $\quad H : Endo$
  $\qquad$ where $Endo$ is the type of endofunctors on $\mathcal{C}$

- LF-signature Σ_{new} for new symbols

  step $\quad S : \Pi X : Pdom.H(TX) \to TX$
  case $\quad C : \Pi X, Y : Pdom.(X \to TY), (H(TX) \to TY), TX \to TY$

- LF-signature realisation

  redefinition of computational types
  $$T^*X := T(\mu(G_X))$$
  $$\text{where } G_X : Endo_L \text{ is } G_X(X') = X + H(TX')$$
  $$val^*(X, x) := [in_1(x)]$$
  $$let^*(X, Y, f) := \text{fix}(\lambda f' : T^*X \to T^*Y.$$
  $$C^*(X, Y, f, \lambda x' : H(T^*X).S^*(Y, H(f')x')))$$
  definition of new symbols
  $$S^*(X, x') := [in_2(x')]$$
  $$C^*(X, Y, f, g, c) := \text{let } u \Leftarrow c \text{ in } (\text{case } u \text{ of } x : X.val^*(x) \mid$$
  $$x' : H(TX).g(x'))$$
  redefinition of old operation
  $$op^*(X) := op(X + H(T^*X))$$

In the definition above we have been somewhat imprecise, in order to keep the translation concise and readable:

- the exact definition of the endofunctor G_τ, where $\tau : Pdom$, is

$$G_\tau = \mathcal{C}_L \xrightarrow{\quad T' \quad} \mathcal{C} \xrightarrow{\quad \tau + H \quad} \mathcal{C} \hookleftarrow \mathcal{C}_L$$

  where T' was defined in Proposition 6.13

- we have not explicitly written the isomorphisms $\sigma_{G_\tau} : G_\tau(\mu G_\tau) \to \mu G_\tau$ nor their inverses.

Remark 6.14 The translation I_{ex} for adding exceptions can be viewed as an instance of I_{res} obtained by instantiating H to a constant functor.

$C(f, g, c)$ performs a case analysis on the *first step* of c: when the result is in X it applies f, when the result is in $H(T^*X)$ it applies g. When $H(X') = E$ the operation $handle(X, f, c)$ defined by I_{ex} can be expressed in terms of C as $C(X, X, val^*, f, c)$.

The definition of $let^*(f)$ uses the fact that $T^*X \to T^*Y$ is a domain (as T^*Y is), and so it has a fix-point combinator.

As for the other translations, one can investigate the equations for the new operations validated by the translation. For convenience, we divide the equations in two groups.

- Rewriting rules for C

$$C(f, g, [x]) = f(x)$$
$$C(f, g, S(c)) = g(c)$$
$$C(f_2, g_2, C(f_1, g_1, c)) = C(C(f_2, g_2) \circ f_1, C(f_2, g_2) \circ g_1, c)$$

these follow from the equational axioms for computational types

- special invariant property of T

$$\Pi X : Pdom.\text{fix}(\lambda h : TX \to TX.C(val, S \circ (Hh))) = (\lambda c : TX.c)$$

This follows from the special invariant property for $\mu(G_\tau)$. Using this property in combination with computational induction, one can prove that an equation $\phi(c) \equiv (g_1(c) = g_2(c))$ is true for any $c : TX$ by proving (e.g. by induction on N) that $\Pi n : N.\phi(c^n)$, where $c^n \overset{\Delta}{=} \Phi^n(\lambda c : TX.\bot)$ and $\Phi(h) \overset{\Delta}{=} C(val, S \circ (Hh))$.

A consequence of this property (and the rewriting rules for C) is existence and uniqueness of $h : TX \to TY$ such that $h = C(f, g \circ (Hh))$, where $f : X \to TY$ and $g : H(TY) \to TY$ are fixed.

In particular, $let(f)$ is the unique h such that $h = C(f, S \circ (Hh))$, and $\lambda c : TX.c$ is the unique h such that $h = C(val, S \circ (Hh))$.

Besides studying which equations for the old operation are preserved by the translation, one can also study whether equations for the old operation imply new equations involving the old operation and the new operations. For instance one can easily prove that:

- If before translation op **distributes** over let, i.e.

$$\Pi X, Y : Pdom, a : A, h : (B \to TX), f : (X \to TY).$$
$$let(f, op(a, h)) = op(a, \lambda b : B.let(f, hb))$$

then after the I_{res} translation op distributes over C, i.e.

$$\Pi X, Y : Pdom, a : A, h : (B \to TX), f : (X \to TY),$$
$$g : (H(TX) \to TY).C(f, g, op(a, h)) = op(a, \lambda b : B.C(f, g, hb))$$

6.6.2   Revised CBV translation of $\Sigma_{fun} + \Sigma_{par}$

In Section 5.2 we gave a translation of the parallel language into a fairly ad hoc metalanguage $ML_T(\Sigma)$, where Σ was the LF-signature:

one-step $\delta : \Pi X : Pdom.TX \to TX$
or-parallelism $por : \Pi X : Pdom.TX, TX \to TX$
and-parallelism $pand : \Pi X_1, X_2 : Pdom.TX_1, TX_2 \to T(X_1 \times X_2)$

This was not very satisfactory, because most of the operations in Σ are not obtained via the incremental approach. We now show that such operations are definable (by making an essential use of the fix-point combinator) from non-deterministic choice and the operations introduced by the translation I_{res} for adding resumptions when $HX' = X'$:

choice $or : \Pi X : Pdom.TX, TX \rightarrow TX$

step $S : \Pi X : Pdom.TX \rightarrow TX$

case $C : \Pi X, Y : Pdom.(X \rightarrow TY), (TX \rightarrow TY), TX \rightarrow TY$

The translation makes essential use of the fix-point combinator:

$$\delta(X) \triangleq S(X)$$
$$por(X) \triangleq \text{fix}(\ \lambda h : TX, TX \rightarrow TX.\lambda c_1, c_2 : TX.$$
$$or(C(val, \lambda c_1'.S(h(c_1', c_2))), c_1),$$
$$C(val, \lambda c_2'.S(h(c_1, c_2'))), c_2)))$$
$$pand(X_1, X_2) \triangleq \text{fix}(\ \lambda h : TX_1, TX_2 \rightarrow T(X_1 \times X_2).\lambda c_1 : TX_1, c_2 : TX_2.$$
$$or(C(\lambda x_1.S(\text{let } x_2 \Leftarrow c_2 \text{ in } [\langle x_1, x_2 \rangle]), \lambda c_1'.S(h(c_1', c_2))), c_1),$$
$$C(\lambda x_2.S(\text{let } x_1 \Leftarrow c_1 \text{ in } [\langle x_1, x_2 \rangle]), \lambda c_2'.S(h(c_1, c_2'))), c_2)))$$

Remark 6.15 The computations $por(c_1, c_2)$ and $pand(c_1, c_2)$ are quite similar. In both cases the computations c_1 and c_2 are interleaved. However, $por(c_1, c_2)$ may terminate as soon as one of the c_i has terminated, while $pand(c_1, c_2)$ terminates only when both c_i have terminated.

One can derive various *expected* properties of por and $pand$ from the properties of S and C validated by the translation for adding resumptions and the following properties of or:

- algebraic properties

$$or(c_1, or(c_2, c_3)) = or(or(c_1, c_2), c_3)$$
$$or(c_1, c_2) = or(c_2, c_1)$$
$$or(c, c) = c$$

- distributivity

$$C(f, g, or(c_1, c_2)) = or(C(f, g, c_1), C(f, g, c_2))$$

We exemplify a fairly general technique for proving algebraic properties of these and other derived operations, by proving associativity of por:

- first prove, by induction on $m + n + p$, that

$$\Pi X : Pdom.c_1, c_2, c_3 : TX.por(c_1^m, por(c_2^n, c_3^p)) = por(por(c_1^m, c_2^n), c_3^p)$$

- then, by repeatedly applying computational induction, conclude that

$$\Pi X : Pdom.c_1, c_2, c_3 : TX.por(c_1, por(c_2, c_3)) = por(por(c_1, c_2), c_3)$$

Remark 6.16 The operations S and C, in combination with the fix-point operator, can be used to define many other forms of parallel composition or other kinds of combinators. Moreover, by instantiating H with different functors one can deal with other (parallel) languages, e.g.:

- $HX' = L \times X'$ is suitable for processes which can only synchronise with signals in L (like pure CCS);

- $HX' = X' + L \times (V \to X') + L \times V \times X'$ is suitable for processes which can communicate values in V using channels in L;

- $HX' = I \to (O \times X')$ is suitable for I/O-automata, with input alphabet I and output alphabet O.

References

Cenciarelli, P. and E. Moggi (1993). A syntactic approach to modularity in denotational semantics. In *Proceedings of the Conference on Category Theory and Computer Science, Amsterdam, Sept. 1993*. CWI Tech. Report.

Coquand, T. and C. Paulin (1988). Inductively defined types. In *Conference on Computer Logic*, Volume 417 of *LNCS*. Springer Verlag.

Crole, R. and A. Pitts (1992). New foundations for fixpoint computations: Fix hyperdoctrines and the fix logic. *Information and Computation 98*.

Freyd, P. (1990). Recursive types reduced to inductive types. In J. Mitchell (Ed.), *Proc. 5th Symposium in Logic in Computer Science*, Philadelphia. I.E.E.E. Computer Society.

Freyd, P. (1992). Algebraically complete categories. In A. Carboni, M. Pedicchio, and G. Rosolini (Eds.), *Category Theory '90*, Volume 1144 of *Lecture Notes in Mathematics*, Como. Springer-Verlag.

Geuvers, H. (1992). The Church-Rosser property for $\beta\eta$-reduction in typed lambda calculi. In A. Scedrov (Ed.), *Proc. 7th Symposium in Logic in Computer Science*, Santa Cruz. I.E.E.E. Computer Society.

Geuvers, H. and B. Werner (1994). On the Church-Rosser property for expressive type systems and its consequences for their metatheory. In S. Abramsky (Ed.), *Proc. 9th Symposium in Logic in Computer Science*, Paris. I.E.E.E. Computer Society.

Gordon, M. (1979). *The Denotational Description of Programming Languages*. Springer-Verlag.

Gunter, C. and D. Scott (1990). Semantic domains. Technical report.

Harper, R., F. Honsell, and G. Plotkin (1987). A framework for defining logics. In R. Constable (Ed.), *Proc. 2th Symposium in Logic in Computer Science*, Ithaca, NY. I.E.E.E. Computer Society.

Luo, Z. (1994). *Computation and Reasoning: A Type Theory for Computer Science*. International Series of Monographs on Computer Science. Oxford University Press.

239

Meyer, A. and S. Cosmodakis (1988). Semantic paradigms: Notes for an invited lecture. In *3rd LICS Conf.* IEEE.

Moggi, E. (1991). Notions of computation and monads. *Information and Computation 93*(1).

Mosses, P. (1989). Denotational semantics. Technical Report DAIMI-PB-276, CS Dept., Aarhus University. to appear in North Holland Handbook of Theoretical Computer Science.

Mosses, P. (1990a). *Action Semantics*. Cambridge Tracts in Theoretical Computer Science. Cambridge University Press.

Mosses, P. (1990b). Denotational semantics. In J. van Leeuwen (Ed.), *Handbook of Theoretical Computer Science*. North Holland.

Schmidt, D. (1986). *Denotational Semantics: a Methodology for Language Development*. Allyn & Bacon.

Scott, D. (1993). A type-theoretic alternative to CUCH, ISWIM, OWHY. *Theoretical Computer Science 121*.

Simpson, A. (1992). Recursive types in Kleisli categories. Available via FTP from theory.doc.ic.ac.uk.

Smyth, M. and G. Plotkin (1982). The category-theoretic solution of recursive domain equations. *SIAM Journal of Computing 11*.

Tennent, R. (1991). *Semantics of Programming Languages*. Prentice Hall.

Operationally-Based Theories of Program Equivalence

Andrew Pitts

Contents

1 Introduction

This article describes some mathematical methods for verifying properties of programs in higher-order, functional languages. We focus on methods for reasoning about equivalence of expressions. Such methods are often based upon a denotational semantics of the programming language in question, using the mathematical theory of domains (Scott 1982; Plotkin 1981a). Here I will describe some methods which are based upon *operational semantics* (Plotkin 1981b). These operationally-based techniques have several attractive features. For example, there is relatively little mathematical overhead involved in developing the basic theory—in contrast with that needed to develop the existence and properties of recursively defined domains, the *sine qua non* of denotational semantics. On the other hand, domain theory provides an extremely powerful tool for analysing recursive program constructs. I believe that any serious attempt to develop a useful theory for verification of program properties has to involve *both* operational and denotational techniques.

Highlights The main purpose of this article is to advertise the usefulness, for proving equivalences between functional programs, of co-inductive techniques more familiar in the context of concurrency theory (de Roever 1978; Park 1981; Milner 1989). They were imported into the world of lambda calculus and functional programming by several people: see Dybjer and Sander (1989); Abramsky (1990); Howe (1989, Howe (1996); Egidi, Honsell, and della Rocca (1992); and Gordon 1994. I will also present proofs of some 'domain-theoretic' properties of the operational semantics. To keep things simple, but non-trivial, the example programming language used throughout is an extension of PCF (Plotkin 1977) with products and lazy lists. The technical highlights are:

- An 'operational extensionality' theorem (Theorem 3.8) for the example programming language. This is a generalisation of the context lemma of Milner (1977) and characterises ground contextual equivalence as a certain co-inductively defined notion of bisimilarity. This result yields a co-induction principle for proving instances of contextual equivalence, whose utility we illustrate with several examples (section 3). The use of *ground* contextual equivalence introduces some differences between the appropriate notion of bisimilarity and the 'applicative bisimulation' studied by Abramsky (and Howe) for 'lazy' lambda calculi. As far as I know Gordon (1995a) was the first person to give an operational extensionality theorem for ground contextual equivalence in non-strict, recursively typed languages. His notion of bisimilarity is based upon a labelled transition system for the language. Here we use a notion of bisimilarity based simply upon the evaluation (or 'big-step') semantics. Each approach has its uses. The proof of operational extensionality we give uses an adaptation of a method due to Howe (1989, Howe (1996); we postpone it to an Appendix in order not to interrupt the paper's flow. However, it is the technique rather than the result for the particular example language which is important, and so we urge readers not to neglect this Appendix.

- A proof of some order-theoretic properties of fixpoint recursion with respect to the contextual preorder (section 4). They are syntactic analogues of the ω-chain completeness and continuity properties used in domain-theoretic denotational semantics. Although these properties of the contextual preorder can be derived from a computationally adequate denotational semantics of the language, in keeping with the spirit of this article I give a proof directly from the operational semantics. Mason, Smith, and Talcott (1996) carry out a similar program based on a transition (or 'small-step') semantics, whereas here I use the evaluation semantics.

Prerequisites We assume the reader is familiar with some flavour of functional programming. The textbooks by Abelson and Susman (1985), Paulson (1991), and Bird and Wadler (1988) all provide good introductions. I will also assume familiarity with the use of inductive definitions to specify the syntax and operational semantics of programming languages (especially ones based upon typed lambda calculus). The recent text books by Gunter (1992) and Winskel (1993) both provide good introductions to this topic (and much else besides).

Acknowledgements I have had many stimulating discussions with Andrew Gordon on the topic of operationally-based notions of bisimilarity and co-induction.

His lecture notes (1995b) provide a somewhat different perspective on many of the topics covered here, and are recommended. Much of the material which follows is a reworking of other people's work: sources are given in the text as appropriate. Any errors are, of course, all my own work.

2 Contextual Equivalence

Loosely speaking, two expressions M and M' of a programming language are contextually equivalent if any occurrences of M and M' in complete programs can be interchanged without affecting the results of executing the programs. To formalise this for a particular language (as will be done in Definition 2.9 below), one has to specify precisely how programs are executed, i.e. specify an operational semantics, and one has to specify what the observable results of execution should be. These two key ingredients of contextual equivalence account for the fact that it is often referred to in the literature as *observational*, or *operational*, *equivalence*. As we shall see later (section 5), changing either of the parameters may or may not affect the properties of the resulting notion of contextual equivalence.

For most of this article we study properties of contextual equivalence with respect to a simple functional programming language for recursively defined, higher order functions and lazy lists. We coin the acronym PCFL for this language— standing for 'Programming Computable Functions on pairs and lazy Lists'. As the name suggests, PCFL is obtained from PCF (Plotkin 1977), the mother of all toy programming languages, by adding type constructors for pairs and lazy lists. It has the property of being extremely simple (so that the theory to be developed is not obscured by too many syntactical and semantical complications) whilst containing some potentially infinite data structures, for which co-inductive techniques seem particularly effective.

PCFL syntax

PCFL is a language of terms of various types (integers, booleans, function, product, and list types). Function definitions and recursive definitions in PCFL are handled anonymously, rather than through some explicit mechanism of environments binding identifiers to their definitions. This simplifies the theoretical development at the expense of making PCFL terms somewhat unwieldy.

The terms are built up from constants (for boolean and integer values and for the empty list) and variables, using the constructs which are given in Figure 1 and whose intended meaning is as follows. if B then M else N is a term which evaluates like M or N, according to whether the boolean term B evaluates to true or false. M op N is a binary operation or relation applied to two integer expressions. $\lambda x \, . \, F(x)$ is a name for the function mapping x to $F(x)$. $F \, A$ is the function F applied to the argument A. fix $x \, . \, F(x)$ is a recursively defined term, solving the

$$
\begin{array}{lll}
M ::= & x & \text{variables} \\
& |\ \underline{b} & \text{booleans} \\
& |\ \text{if } M \text{ then } M \text{ else } M & \text{boolean conditional} \\
& |\ \underline{n} & \text{numerals} \\
& |\ M \text{ op } M & \text{arithmetic operation} \\
& |\ \lambda x \,.\, M & \text{function abstraction} \\
& |\ M\,M & \text{function application} \\
& |\ \text{fix}\,x \,.\, M & \text{fixpoint recursion} \\
& |\ \langle M, M \rangle & \text{pairing} \\
& |\ \text{fst}(M) & \text{first projection} \\
& |\ \text{snd}(M) & \text{second projection} \\
& |\ \text{nil} & \text{empty list} \\
& |\ M :: M & \text{cons list} \\
& |\ \text{case } M \text{ of } \{\text{nil} \to M \mid x :: x \to M\} & \text{list conditional}
\end{array}
$$

where

$$
\begin{array}{ll}
x \in \textit{Var} & \text{a fixed, infinite set of variables,} \\[4pt]
b \in \mathbb{B} \stackrel{\text{def}}{=} \{\text{true}, \text{false}\} & \text{the set of booleans,} \\[4pt]
n \in \mathbb{Z} \stackrel{\text{def}}{=} \{\ldots, -2, 1, 0, 1, 2, \ldots\} & \text{the set of integers,} \\[4pt]
\text{op} \in \{=, -, =, \leq, \ldots\} & \text{a fixed, finite set of arithmetic} \\
& \text{operation and relation symbols.}
\end{array}
$$

Figure 1: PCFL syntax

fixpoint equation $x = F(x)$. $\langle M, N \rangle$ is the ordered pair with first and second components M and N. $\text{fst}(P)$ is the first component of the pair P. $\text{snd}(P)$ is the second component of the pair P. $H :: T$ is the list with head H and tail T. Finally, $\text{case } L \text{ of } \{\text{nil} \to M \mid h :: t \to N(h, t)\}$ is a term which evaluates like M or $N(H, T)$, according to whether the term L of list type evaluates to the empty list nil, or to a non-empty list $H :: T$.

More precisely, the **PCFL terms** are given by the syntax trees generated by the grammar in Figure 1, modulo α-equivalence. Recall that two expressions in a calculus with variable binding constructs are called α-**equivalent** if they are syntactically identical up to renaming of bound variables. In PCFL, function abstraction, fixpoint recursion and list destructors are variable binding constructs: occurrences of x in M are bound in $\lambda x \,.\, M$ and $\text{fix}\,x \,.\, M$, whilst occurrences of h and t in N are bound in case L of $\{\text{nil} \to M \mid h :: t \to N\}$. Any other occurrences of variables are free.

Warning Any reasonable semantics of a programming language with binding constructs will identify α-equivalent expressions. So since we are here concerned with semantic rather than implementation issues, we take the terms of the language PCFL to be α-equivalence classes of syntax trees. It would probably be better, both from an implementation as well as a semantic point of view, to use a more abstract form of representation without explicit bound variables—such as de Bruijn's notation (see Barendregt 1984, Appendix C). However such a representation tends to be hard to read, so we will stick with the more familiar form of syntax given in Figure 1. But be warned that *we will not make a notational distinction between a PCFL syntax tree and the term (α-equivalence class) it determines.*

Notation 2.1. We will use the following notation for the finite set of free variables of a PCFL term:

$$fvar(M) \stackrel{\text{def}}{=} \text{the set of free variables of } M.$$

If M and N are PCFL terms and x is a variable, then $N[M/x]$ will denote the PCFL term resulting from substituting M for all free occurrences of x in N. As usual with calculi with variable binding constructs, this operation of substitution is induced by textual substitution at the level of syntax trees, taking care to avoid capture of free variables (i.e. one must pick a representative tree for N whose bound variables are not in $fvar(M)$). More generally, given a list $M_1, \ldots, M_n$ of terms and a list $x_1, \ldots, x_n$ of distinct variables

$$N[M_1/x_1, \ldots, M_n/x_n], \quad \text{or just} \quad N[\vec{M}/\vec{x}]$$

will denote the result of simultaneously substituting each term M_i in the list for all free occurrences in N of the corresponding variable x_i.

PCFL type assignment

The terms of Plotkin's PCF (1977) contain explicit type information. For PCFL we have chosen to leave out type information from the terms. Nevertheless, PCFL is a typed language, in the sense that we will only consider a term to be well formed if it can be assigned a type, given an assignment of types to the free variables occurring in the term. **PCFL-types** are given by the following grammar:

$\sigma ::=$	γ	ground type
$\mid$	$\sigma \to \sigma'$	function type
$\mid$	$\sigma \times \sigma'$	product type
$\mid$	$[\sigma]$	list type

where

$$\gamma ::= \quad bool \qquad \text{type of booleans}$$
$$| \quad int \qquad \text{type of integers.}$$

A PCFL **typing assertion** takes the form

$$\Gamma \vdash M : \sigma \qquad\qquad (2.1)$$

where Γ is a finite partial function from variables to types, M is a PCFL term, and σ is a type. The **type assignment relation** for PCFL consists of all typing assertions that can be derived from the axioms and rules in Figure 2. If (2.1) is derivable, we simply say that it is **valid**. The notation $\Gamma, x : \sigma$ used in the rule ($\vdash$ abs) denotes the partial function which *properly* extends Γ by mapping x to σ. Implicit in its use is the assumption that x is not in $dom(\Gamma)$, the domain of definition of Γ. With this notational convention, strictly speaking the side condition on the rule is unnecessary, but has been included for people who only look at Figure 2 without reading the preceding sentence. Similar remarks apply to the rules ($\vdash$ fix) and ($\vdash$ case). If $dom(\Gamma)$ consists of the distinct variables $x_1, \ldots, x_n$ and $\Gamma(x_i) = \sigma_i$ say, then we will sometimes write (2.1) as $x_1 : \sigma_1, \ldots, x_n : \sigma_n \vdash M : \sigma$.

Lemma 2.2. *(i) If $\Gamma \vdash M : \sigma$ is a valid typing assertion, then $fvar(M) \subseteq dom(\Gamma)$.*

(ii) If $\Gamma \vdash M : \sigma$ and $x \notin dom(\Gamma)$, then $\Gamma, x : \sigma' \vdash M : \sigma$ (for any σ').

(iii) If $\Gamma, \Gamma' \vdash M : \sigma$ and $fvar(M) \subseteq dom(\Gamma)$, then $\Gamma \vdash M : \sigma$. Here (and elsewhere), Γ, Γ' indicates the union of the partial functions Γ and Γ', under the assumption that their domains of definition are disjoint.

(iv) If $\Gamma \vdash M_i : \sigma_i$ for $i = 1, \ldots, n$ and $\Gamma, x_1 : \sigma_1, \ldots, x_n : \sigma_n \vdash N : \sigma$, then $\Gamma \vdash N[M_1/x_1, \ldots, M_n/x_n] : \sigma$.

Proof. Parts (i), (ii) and (iii) are proved by induction on the derivation of $\Gamma \vdash M : \sigma$. Part (iv) is proved by induction on the derivation of $\Gamma, x_1 : \sigma_1, \ldots, x_n : \sigma_n \vdash N : \sigma$, using part (ii). $\square$

Definition 2.3. Let $Exp_\sigma(\Gamma)$ denote the set of PCFL terms that can be assigned type σ, given Γ:

$$Exp_\sigma(\Gamma) \overset{\text{def}}{=} \{M \mid \Gamma \vdash M : \sigma\}.$$

By part (i) of the above lemma, any $M \in Exp_\sigma(\Gamma)$ has its free variables contained in $dom(\Gamma)$. In particular, in the case Γ is the empty partial function, M is a **closed term**, that is, one with no free variables. (A term which does have free variables is called **open**.) We will write Exp_σ for $Exp_\sigma(\Gamma)$ in this case. The elements of Exp_σ are called the closed PCFL terms of type σ. A closed term is **typeable** if it belongs to Exp_σ for some type σ.

$$\Gamma \vdash x : \sigma \quad \text{(if } \Gamma \text{ is defined at } x \text{ with value } \sigma) \qquad (\vdash \text{var})$$

$$\Gamma \vdash \underline{b} : bool \quad \text{(if } b \in \mathbb{B}) \qquad (\vdash \text{bool})$$

$$\frac{\Gamma \vdash B : bool \qquad \Gamma \vdash M_1 : \sigma \qquad \Gamma \vdash M_2 : \sigma}{\Gamma \vdash \text{if } B \text{ then } M_1 \text{ else } M_2 : \sigma} \qquad (\vdash \text{cond})$$

$$\Gamma \vdash \underline{n} : int \quad \text{(if } n \in \mathbb{Z}) \qquad (\vdash \text{int})$$

$$\frac{\Gamma \vdash M_1 : int \qquad \Gamma \vdash M_2 : int}{\Gamma \vdash M_1 \text{ op } M_2 : \gamma} \text{ (if } \gamma \text{ is the result type of op)} \qquad (\vdash \text{op})$$

$$\frac{\Gamma, x : \sigma \vdash M : \sigma'}{\Gamma \vdash \lambda x . M : \sigma \to \sigma'} \, (x \notin dom(\Gamma)) \qquad (\vdash \text{abs})$$

$$\frac{\Gamma \vdash F : \sigma \to \sigma' \qquad \Gamma \vdash A : \sigma}{\Gamma \vdash F A : \sigma'} \qquad (\vdash \text{app})$$

$$\frac{\Gamma, x : \sigma \vdash F : \sigma}{\Gamma \vdash \text{fix} \, x . F : \sigma} \, (x \notin dom(\Gamma)) \qquad (\vdash \text{fix})$$

$$\frac{\Gamma \vdash M_1 : \sigma \qquad \Gamma \vdash M_2 : \sigma'}{\Gamma \vdash \langle M_1, M_2 \rangle : \sigma \times \sigma'} \qquad (\vdash \text{pair})$$

$$\frac{\Gamma \vdash P : \sigma \times \sigma'}{\Gamma \vdash \text{fst}(P) : \sigma} \qquad (\vdash \text{fst})$$

$$\frac{\Gamma \vdash P : \sigma \times \sigma'}{\Gamma \vdash \text{snd}(P) : \sigma'} \qquad (\vdash \text{snd})$$

$$\Gamma \vdash \text{nil} : [\sigma] \qquad (\vdash \text{nil})$$

$$\frac{\Gamma \vdash H : \sigma \qquad \Gamma \vdash T : [\sigma]}{\Gamma \vdash H :: T : [\sigma]} \qquad (\vdash \text{cons})$$

$$\frac{\Gamma \vdash L : [\sigma] \quad \Gamma \vdash M_1 : \sigma' \quad \Gamma, h : \sigma, t : [\sigma] \vdash M_2 : \sigma'}{\Gamma \vdash \text{case } L \text{ of } \{\text{nil} \to M_1 \mid h :: t \to M_2\} : \sigma'} \, (h, t \notin dom(\Gamma)) \quad (\vdash \text{case})$$

Figure 2: Rules for type assignment in PCFL

Evaluation of PCFL terms

Typically, a program in a typed functional language consists of some definitions (usually, recursive definitions) of data of various types, together with a term of a type whose values are printable (integers, booleans, character strings, etc) to

$$C \Downarrow C \qquad (\Downarrow \text{can})$$

$$\frac{B \Downarrow \text{true} \qquad M_1 \Downarrow C}{\text{if } B \text{ then } M_1 \text{ else } M_2 \Downarrow C} \qquad (\Downarrow \text{cond1})$$

$$\frac{B \Downarrow \text{false} \qquad M_2 \Downarrow C}{\text{if } B \text{ then } M_1 \text{ else } M_2 \Downarrow C} \qquad (\Downarrow \text{cond2})$$

$$\frac{M_1 \Downarrow \underline{n_1} \qquad M_2 \Downarrow \underline{n_2}}{M_1 \text{ op } M_2 \Downarrow \underline{c}} \ (\text{if } c = n_1 \text{ op } n_2) \qquad (\Downarrow \text{op})$$

$$\frac{F \Downarrow \lambda x \,.\, M \qquad M[A/x] \Downarrow C}{F A \Downarrow C} \qquad (\Downarrow \text{app})$$

$$\frac{F[\text{fix } x \,.\, F/x] \Downarrow C}{\text{fix } x \,.\, F \Downarrow C} \qquad (\Downarrow \text{fix})$$

$$\frac{P \Downarrow \langle M_1, M_2 \rangle \qquad M_1 \Downarrow C}{\text{fst}(P) \Downarrow C} \qquad (\Downarrow \text{fst})$$

$$\frac{P \Downarrow \langle M_1, M_2 \rangle \qquad M_2 \Downarrow C}{\text{snd}(P) \Downarrow C} \qquad (\Downarrow \text{snd})$$

$$\frac{L \Downarrow \text{nil} \qquad M_1 \Downarrow C}{\text{case } L \text{ of } \{\text{nil} \to M_1 \mid h :: t \to M_2\} \Downarrow C} \qquad (\Downarrow \text{case1})$$

$$\frac{L \Downarrow H :: T \qquad M_2[H/h, T/t] \Downarrow C}{\text{case } L \text{ of } \{\text{nil} \to M_1 \mid h :: t \to M_2\} \Downarrow C} \qquad (\Downarrow \text{case2})$$

Figure 3: Rules for evaluating PCFL terms

be evaluated modulo the given definitions. In PCFL definitions are given anonymously within a term, and we take the types with printable values to be just the ground types, *bool* and *int*. Therefore, a PCFL **program** is defined to be a closed term of ground type.

Executing such a program consists of evaluating the term to see which integer or boolean it denotes, if any. The process of evaluation will usually involve evaluation of subexpressions of non-ground type. There are at least two standard ways to specify this process of evaluation: by means of a transition relation between terms and by means of an evaluation relation between terms and terms in canonical form. Both are examples of the structural operational semantics of Plotkin (1981b), in as much as the inductive definition of the relation follows the structure of the term being evaluated. Here we will use the second (and more abstract) approach, and give an inductively defined **evaluation relation**.The relation takes the form

$$M \Downarrow C$$

where M and C are closed, typeable PCFL terms and C is in **canonical form**:

$$C ::= \underline{b} \mid \underline{n} \mid \lambda x . M \mid \langle M, M \rangle \mid \text{nil} \mid M :: M.$$

The evaluation relation is inductively defined by the axioms and rules in Figure 3.

The canonical forms and evaluation rules embody certain choices which have been made about how PCFL programs behave: evaluation does not continue under a lambda abstraction, or within the components of a pair or list-cons; and an argument is passed unevaluated to the body of a lambda abstraction in function application. Of course, these choices affect the properties of contextual equivalence for PCFL. Other choices and their effect on theories of program equivalence will be discussed in section 5.

Proposition 2.4. *Evaluation is deterministic and preserves typing, that is*

(i) (Determinacy) If $M \Downarrow C$ and $M \Downarrow C'$, then $C = C'$.

(ii) (Subject reduction) If $M \Downarrow C$ and $M \in Exp_\sigma$, then $C \in Exp_\sigma$.

Proof. Both properties can easily be proved by induction on the derivation of $M \Downarrow C$ (using Lemma 2.2(iv)). □

Exercise 2.5. Terms of type $[\sigma]$ in PCFL are notations for potentially infinite lists of the data described by terms of type σ. Here is how the standard example of the infinite list of natural numbers, $[0, 1, 2, \dots]$ can be coded in PCFL. Consider the terms

$$nats \overset{\text{def}}{=} \text{fix}\, \ell . \underline{0} :: map(\lambda x . x + \underline{1})\ell$$

$$map \overset{\text{def}}{=} \text{fix}\, m . \lambda f . \lambda \ell .$$
$$\text{case}\, \ell\, \text{of}\, \{\text{nil} \to \text{nil} \mid h :: t \to fh :: mft\}$$

$$head \overset{\text{def}}{=} \lambda \ell . \text{case}\, \ell\, \text{of}\, \{\text{nil} \to \bot \mid h :: t \to h\}$$

$$tail \overset{\text{def}}{=} \lambda \ell . \text{case}\, \ell\, \text{of}\, \{\text{nil} \to \text{nil} \mid h :: t \to t\}$$

$$\bot \overset{\text{def}}{=} \text{fix}\, x . x$$

Show that for any types σ and σ'

$$\emptyset \vdash \bot : \sigma$$
$$\emptyset \vdash head : [\sigma] \to \sigma$$
$$\emptyset \vdash tail : [\sigma] \to [\sigma]$$
$$\emptyset \vdash map : (\sigma \to \sigma') \to ([\sigma] \to [\sigma'])$$

and hence that $\emptyset \vdash nats : [int]$. Prove that $nats$ is a notation for the infinite list $[0, 1, 2, \ldots]$ in the sense that for all $n \in \mathbb{N}$, $head(tail^n\ nats) \Downarrow \underline{n}$, where

$$tail^0 \stackrel{\text{def}}{=} \lambda x . x$$

$$tail^{n+1} \stackrel{\text{def}}{=} \lambda x . tail(tail^n\ x).$$

PCFL contexts

Recall the informal definition of contextual equivalence with which we began this section. For our example language PCFL, so far we have decided upon what constitutes a program (namely, a closed term of ground type) and what the observable results of execution should be (namely, the integer or boolean constant to which the program evaluates, if any). It remains to formalise the notion of interchanging occurrences of terms in programs. To do so, we use 'contexts'—syntax trees containing parameters (or place-holders, or 'holes') which yield a term when the parameters are replaced by terms. Thus the **PCFL contexts**, $\mathcal{C}$, are the syntax trees generated by the grammar in Figure 1 augmented by the clause

$$\mathcal{C} ::= \cdots \mid \mathsf{p}$$

where p ranges over some fixed set of parameters. Note that the syntax trees of PCFL terms are particular contexts, namely the ones with no occurrences of parameters.

Context substitution $\mathcal{C}'[\mathcal{C}/\mathsf{p}]$ will denote the PCFL context obtained from a context $\mathcal{C}'$ by replacing all occurrences of p with the context $\mathcal{C}$. It should be emphasised that this form of substitution may well involve capture of free variables in $\mathcal{C}$ by binding variables in $\mathcal{C}'$. For example, if $\mathcal{C} = x$ and $\mathcal{C}' = \lambda x . \mathsf{p}$, then $\mathcal{C}'[\mathcal{C}/\mathsf{p}] = \lambda x . x$. For this reason, the operation of substituting $\mathcal{C}$ for p does not preserve the relation $\equiv^\alpha$ of α-equivalence. For example if x and y are distinct variables, then $\lambda x . \mathsf{p} \equiv^\alpha \lambda y . \mathsf{p}$, but $(\lambda x . \mathsf{p})[x/\mathsf{p}] = \lambda x . x \not\equiv^\alpha \lambda y . x = (\lambda y . \mathsf{p})[x/\mathsf{p}]$. However, one can easily prove by induction on the structure of $\mathcal{C}'$ that

$$\mathcal{C}_1 \equiv^\alpha \mathcal{C}_2 \Rightarrow \mathcal{C}'[\mathcal{C}_1/\mathsf{p}] \equiv^\alpha \mathcal{C}'[\mathcal{C}_1/\mathsf{p}].$$

In other words, substituting α-equivalent contexts results in α-equivalent contexts. It follows that the operation of substituting for a parameter in a context induces a well-defined operation on α-equivalence classes of PCFL syntax trees, that is, on PCFL terms.

It is possible to give a treatment of contexts and contextual equivalence which does not descend below the level of abstraction of α-equivalence classes of expressions (or equivalently, a treatment which applies to expressions using de Bruijn indices rather than explicit bound variables), at the expense of introducing 'function variables'. The interested reader is referred to (Pitts 1994, Section 4).

Notation 2.6. Most of the time we will use contexts only involving a single parameter, which we write as $-$. We write $C[-]$ to indicate that C is a context containing no parameters other than $-$. If M is a PCFL term, then $C[M]$ will denote the term resulting from choosing a representative syntax tree for M, substituting it for the parameter in C, and forming the α-equivalence class of the resulting PCFL syntax tree (which from the remarks above, is independent of the choice of representative for M).

Typed contexts We will assume given a function that assigns types to parameters. We write $-_\sigma$ to indicate that a parameter $-$ has type σ. Just as we only consider a PCFL term to be well-formed if it can be assigned a type, we will restrict attention to contexts that can be typed. The relation

$$\Gamma \vdash C : \sigma$$

assigning a type σ to a context C given a finite partial function Γ assigning types to variables, is inductively generated by axioms and rules just like those in Figure 2 together with the following axiom for parameters:

$$\Gamma \vdash -_\sigma : \sigma. \tag{2.2}$$

Warning: when the axioms and rules of Figure 2 are applied to syntax trees rather than α-equivalence classes of syntax trees (as is the case when typing contexts), it should be borne in mind that they enforce a separation between free and bound variables and hence are not closed under α-equivalence. For example, if $x \neq y$, then $x : int \vdash \lambda y . -_{int} : int \to int$ is a valid typing assertion, whereas $x : int \vdash \lambda x . -_{int} : int \to int$ is not.

Definition 2.7. Let $Ctx_\sigma(\Gamma)$ denote the set of PCFL contexts that can be assigned type σ, given Γ:

$$Ctx_\sigma(\Gamma) \overset{\text{def}}{=} \{C \mid \Gamma \vdash C : \sigma\}.$$

We write Ctx_σ for $Ctx_\sigma(\emptyset)$. Given $C[-_\sigma] \in Ctx_{\sigma'}(\Gamma)$, we write $traps(C[-_\sigma])$ for the set of variables that occur in $C[-_\sigma]$ associated to binders containing the hole $-_\sigma$ within their scope. Thus any free variables of M in $traps(C[-_\sigma])$ become bound in $C[M]$.

The operation $M \mapsto C[M]$ of substituting a PCFL term for a parameter in a context to obtain a new PCFL term respects typing in the following sense.

Lemma 2.8. *Suppose* $M \in Exp_\sigma(\Gamma, \Gamma')$, $C[-_\sigma] \in Ctx_{\sigma'}(\Gamma)$, *and that* $dom(\Gamma') \subseteq traps(C[-_\sigma])$. *Then* $C[M] \in Exp_{\sigma'}(\Gamma)$.

Proof. By induction on the derivation of $\Gamma \vdash C[-_\sigma] : \sigma'$. $\qquad\qquad\square$

Definition 2.9 (Ground contextual equivalence). As usual, let Γ be a finite partial function from variables to PCFL types. Given $M, M' \in Exp_\sigma(\Gamma)$, we write

$$\Gamma \vdash M \leq_\sigma^{\mathrm{gnd}} M'$$

to mean that for all $C[-_\sigma] \in Ctx_{bool}$ with $dom(\Gamma) \subseteq traps(C[-_\sigma])$

$$\forall b \in \mathbb{B}\,(C[M] \Downarrow \underline{b} \Rightarrow C[M'] \Downarrow \underline{b})$$

and for all $C[-_\sigma] \in Ctx_{int}$ with $dom(\Gamma) \subseteq traps(C[-_\sigma])$

$$\forall n \in \mathbb{Z}\,(C[M] \Downarrow \underline{n} \Rightarrow C[M'] \Downarrow \underline{n}).$$

(Note that by virtue of Lemma 2.8, $C[M]$ and $C[M']$ are indeed closed terms of type γ when $C[-_\sigma] \in Ctx_\gamma$ satisfies $dom(\Gamma) \subseteq traps(C[-_\sigma])$.)

The relation $\leq^{\mathrm{gnd}}$ will be called the **ground contextual preorder** between PCFL terms (of the same type, given a typing of their free variables). **Ground contextual equivalence** is the symmetrization of this relation:

$$\Gamma \vdash M \cong_\sigma^{\mathrm{gnd}} M' \stackrel{\mathrm{def}}{\Leftrightarrow} (\Gamma \vdash M \leq_\sigma^{\mathrm{gnd}} M' \ \& \ \Gamma \vdash M' \leq_\sigma^{\mathrm{gnd}} M).$$

In section 5 we will consider some variations on the notion of contextual equivalence, in which contexts of non-ground type are used. Until then we will drop the adjective 'ground' and just refer to $\leq^{\mathrm{gnd}}$ and $\cong^{\mathrm{gnd}}$ as the **contextual preorder** and **contextual equivalence**. For closed terms $M, M' \in Exp_\sigma$, we will just write

$$M \leq_\sigma^{\mathrm{gnd}} M' \quad \text{and} \quad M \cong_\sigma^{\mathrm{gnd}} M'$$

for $\emptyset \vdash M \leq_\sigma^{\mathrm{gnd}} M'$ and $\emptyset \vdash M \cong_\sigma^{\mathrm{gnd}} M'$ respectively.

Remark 2.10. The relations of contextual preorder and contextual equivalence remain the same if in Definition 2.9 we restrict to contexts yielding terms of type *bool* only, or of type *int* only, or restrict attention to evaluation to a fixed integer or boolean constant, or just to convergence to something. For example

$$\Gamma \vdash M \leq_\sigma^{\mathrm{gnd}} M' \Leftrightarrow \forall C[-]\,(C[M] \Downarrow \underline{42} \Rightarrow C[M'] \Downarrow \underline{42}). \tag{2.3}$$

To see this, given any context $C[-]$, for each $n \in \mathbb{Z}$ note that the context

$$C_n[-] \stackrel{\mathrm{def}}{=} \text{if } C[-] = \underline{n} \text{ then } \underline{42} \text{ else } \underline{0}$$

has the property that for all M

$$C_n[M] \Downarrow \underline{42} \Leftrightarrow C[M] \Downarrow \underline{n}.$$

Similarly, the contexts

$$C_{\mathsf{true}}[-] \stackrel{\mathrm{def}}{=} \text{if } C[-] \text{ then } \underline{42} \text{ else } \underline{0}$$

$$C_{\mathsf{false}}[-] \stackrel{\mathrm{def}}{=} \text{if } C[-] \text{ then } \underline{0} \text{ else } \underline{42}$$

satisfy

$$C_{\text{true}}[M] \Downarrow \underline{42} \Leftrightarrow C[M] \Downarrow \text{true}$$
$$C_{\text{false}}[M] \Downarrow \underline{42} \Leftrightarrow C[M] \Downarrow \text{false}.$$

Property (2.3) follows immediately.

Exercise 2.11. Writing $M\Downarrow_{int}$ to mean $\exists n \in \mathbb{Z} \, (M \Downarrow \underline{n})$, show that

$$\Gamma \vdash M \leq_\sigma^{\text{gnd}} M' \Leftrightarrow \forall C[-] \, (C[M]\Downarrow_{int} \Rightarrow C[M']\Downarrow_{int}).$$

[Hint: note that $\perp \overset{\text{def}}{=} \text{fix} \, x . \, x$ is a closed term (typeable to any type) which does not evaluate to anything. (Why?) Given any $C[-]$, use $\perp$ to define a new context $C'[-]$ satisfying for any M that $C'[M]\Downarrow_{int}$ if and only if $C[M] \Downarrow \underline{42}$. Now use Remark 2.10.]

Properties of PCFL contextual equivalence

Having given the precise definition of contextual equivalence for our example language PCFL we must now develop its theory—its general properties which one can use to establish that particular PCFL terms are, or are not, contextually equivalent. To show that two terms are *not* contextually equivalent is usually quite easy: one just has to find a suitable context of ground type for which the terms yield different results when the rules for evaluation in Figure 3 are applied. For example, the fact that $\underline{0} :: (\underline{1} :: \text{nil})$ and $\underline{0} :: \text{nil}$ are contextually inequivalent terms of type $[int]$, is witnessed by the context $C[-] \overset{\text{def}}{=} head(tail-)$, where $head$ and $tail$ are the terms defined in Exercise 2.5. For $C[\underline{0} :: (\underline{1} :: \text{nil})] \Downarrow \underline{1}$, whereas $C[\underline{0} :: \text{nil}]$ does not evaluate to anything.

The job of establishing that a contextual equivalence *does* hold can be much harder. For example, $\cong^{\text{gnd}}$ satisfies β-conversion:

$$\Gamma \vdash (\lambda x . \, M) \, A \cong_{\sigma'}^{\text{gnd}} M[A/x]$$

where $\Gamma, x : \sigma \vdash M : \sigma'$ and $\Gamma \vdash A : \sigma$. However, it is not immediately obvious from Definition 2.9 why this is so. The problem lies mainly in the quantification over all contexts that occurs in the definition of $\leq^{\text{gnd}}$ and $\cong^{\text{gnd}}$. One might try to construct a proof which proceeds by induction on the structure of contexts, but it is not so easy to find a sufficiently strong inductive hypothesis to make all the steps (involving evaluation of subexpressions at non-ground types) go through. We will take up the challenge of such problems seriously in the next section when we introduce PCFL bisimilarity—another, and more tractable, notion of equivalence which turns out to coincide with PCFL contextual equivalence. We conclude this section by stating some of the properties of $\leq^{\text{gnd}}$ and $\cong^{\text{gnd}}$ that will be proved in these notes.

(In)equational logic

$$\Gamma \vdash M : \sigma \Rightarrow \Gamma \vdash M \leq_\sigma^{\text{gnd}} M \tag{2.4}$$

$$(\Gamma \vdash M \leq_\sigma^{\text{gnd}} M' \ \& \ \Gamma \vdash M' \leq_\sigma^{\text{gnd}} M'') \Rightarrow \Gamma \vdash M' \leq_\sigma^{\text{gnd}} M'' \tag{2.5}$$

$$(\Gamma \vdash M \leq_\sigma^{\text{gnd}} M' \ \& \ \Gamma \vdash M' \leq_\sigma^{\text{gnd}} M) \Leftrightarrow \Gamma \vdash M \cong_\sigma^{\text{gnd}} M' \tag{2.6}$$

$$\Gamma, x : \sigma \vdash M \leq_{\sigma'}^{\text{gnd}} M' \Rightarrow \Gamma \vdash \lambda x \,.\, M \leq_{\sigma \to \sigma'}^{\text{gnd}} \lambda x \,.\, M' \tag{2.7}$$

$$\Gamma, x : \sigma \vdash M \leq_\sigma^{\text{gnd}} M' \Rightarrow \Gamma \vdash \text{fix}\, x \,.\, M \leq_\sigma^{\text{gnd}} \text{fix}\, x \,.\, M' \tag{2.8}$$

$$(\Gamma \vdash L \leq_{[\sigma]}^{\text{gnd}} L' \ \& \ \Gamma \vdash M \leq_{\sigma'}^{\text{gnd}} M' \tag{2.9}$$

$$\& \ \Gamma, h : \sigma, t : [\sigma] \vdash N \leq_{\sigma'}^{\text{gnd}} N')$$

$$\Rightarrow \Gamma \vdash \ (\text{case}\, L \,\text{of}\, \{\text{nil} \to M \mid h :: t \to N\}) \leq_{\sigma'}^{\text{gnd}}$$

$$(\text{case}\, L' \,\text{of}\, \{\text{nil} \to M' \mid h :: t \to N'\})$$

$$(\Gamma \vdash M \leq_\sigma^{\text{gnd}} M' \ \& \ \Gamma \subseteq \Gamma') \Rightarrow \Gamma' \vdash M \leq_\sigma^{\text{gnd}} M' \tag{2.10}$$

$$\Gamma \vdash M \leq_\sigma^{\text{gnd}} M' \ \& \ \Gamma, x : \sigma \vdash N : \sigma' \tag{2.11}$$

$$\Rightarrow \Gamma \vdash N[M/x] \leq_{\sigma'}^{\text{gnd}} N[M'/x]$$

$$\Gamma \vdash M : \sigma \ \& \ \Gamma, x : \sigma \vdash N \leq_{\sigma'}^{\text{gnd}} N' \tag{2.12}$$

$$\Rightarrow \Gamma \vdash N[M/x] \leq_{\sigma'}^{\text{gnd}} N'[M/x]$$

Properties (2.4)–(2.9) are all straightforward consequences of the definition of $\leq^{\text{gnd}}$ and $\cong^{\text{gnd}}$. By contrast, (2.12) is not so straightforward to establish, because the operation $N \mapsto N[M/x]$ is not necessarily of the form $N \mapsto \mathcal{C}[N]$ for some context $\mathcal{C}[-]$. The fact that (2.12) holds is intimately tied up with the fact that PCFL contextual equivalence satisfies the β-rule (2.13) given below: see Lemma A.10.

β-rules

$$(\Gamma, x : \sigma \vdash M : \sigma' \ \& \ \Gamma \vdash A : \sigma) \Rightarrow \Gamma \vdash (\lambda x \,.\, M)\, A \cong_{\sigma'}^{\text{gnd}} M[A/x] \tag{2.13}$$

$$(\Gamma \vdash M : \sigma \ \& \ \Gamma \vdash M' : \sigma') \Rightarrow \tag{2.14}$$

$$(\Gamma \vdash \text{fst}(\langle M, M' \rangle) \cong_\sigma^{\text{gnd}} M \ \& \ \Gamma \vdash \text{snd}(\langle M, M' \rangle) \cong_{\sigma'}^{\text{gnd}} M')$$

$$(\Gamma \vdash M : \sigma' \ \& \ \Gamma, h : \sigma, t : [\sigma] \vdash N : \sigma') \Rightarrow \tag{2.15}$$

$$\Gamma \vdash \text{case nil of}\, \{\text{nil} \to M \mid h :: t \to N\} \cong_{\sigma'}^{\text{gnd}} M$$

$$(\Gamma \vdash H : \sigma \ \& \ \Gamma \vdash T : [\sigma] \ \& \ \Gamma \vdash M : \sigma' \ \& \ \Gamma, h : \sigma, t : [\sigma] \vdash N : \sigma') \Rightarrow \tag{2.16}$$

$$\Gamma \vdash \text{case } H :: T \text{ of } \{\text{nil} \to M \mid h :: t \to N\} \cong_\sigma^{\text{gnd}} N[H/h, T/t]$$
$$(\Gamma \vdash M : \sigma \,\&\, \Gamma \vdash M' : \sigma) \Rightarrow \qquad\qquad\qquad (2.17)$$
$$(\Gamma \vdash \text{if true then } M \text{ else } M' \cong_\sigma^{\text{gnd}} M \,\&\,$$
$$\Gamma \vdash \text{if false then } M \text{ else } M' \cong_\sigma^{\text{gnd}} M')$$
$$(n \text{ op } n' = c) \Rightarrow \emptyset \vdash \underline{n} \text{ op } \underline{n'} \cong_\gamma^{\text{gnd}} \underline{c} \qquad\qquad\qquad (2.18)$$

The fact that these β-rules are valid follows from the characterisation of $\cong^{\text{gnd}}$ in terms of PCFL bisimilarity to be given in the next section (Theorem 3.8). For in each case, (closed instantiations of) the term on the left hand side of $\cong^{\text{gnd}}$ evaluates to a canonical C if and only if (closed instantiations of) the right hand term evaluates to the *same* canonical form. Thus each of (2.13)–(2.18) follows from the fact, shown in Proposition 3.9, that 'Kleene equivalence' is contained in the relation of contextual equivalence, together with the first of the following extensionality properties.

Extensionality properties

For all $N, N' \in Exp_\sigma(x_1 : \sigma_1, \ldots, x_n : \sigma_n)$:

$$x_1 : \sigma_1, \ldots, x_n : \sigma_n \vdash N \leq_\sigma^{\text{gnd}} N' \Leftrightarrow$$
$$\forall M_1 \in Exp_{\sigma_1}, \ldots, M_n \in Exp_{\sigma_n} \, (N[\vec{M}/\vec{x}] \leq_\sigma^{\text{gnd}} N'[\vec{M}/\vec{x}]) \quad (2.19)$$

For all $M, M' \in Exp_\gamma$ (γ a ground type):

$$M \leq_\gamma^{\text{gnd}} M' \Leftrightarrow \forall c \, (M \Downarrow \underline{c} \Rightarrow M' \Downarrow \underline{c}) \qquad\qquad (2.20)$$

For all $F, F' \in Exp_{\sigma \to \sigma'}$:

$$F \leq_{\sigma \to \sigma'}^{\text{gnd}} F' \Leftrightarrow \forall A \in Exp_\sigma \, (F A \leq_{\sigma'}^{\text{gnd}} F' A) \qquad\qquad (2.21)$$

For all $P, P' \in Exp_{\sigma \times \sigma'}$:

$$P \leq_{\sigma \times \sigma'}^{\text{gnd}} P' \Leftrightarrow$$
$$\text{fst}(P) \leq_\sigma^{\text{gnd}} \text{fst}(P') \,\&\, \text{snd}(P) \leq_{\sigma'}^{\text{gnd}} \text{snd}(P') \quad (2.22)$$

For all $L, L' \in Exp_{[\sigma]}$:

$$L \leq_{[\sigma]}^{\text{gnd}} L' \Leftrightarrow (L \Downarrow \text{nil} \Rightarrow L' \Downarrow \text{nil}) \,\&\,$$
$$\forall H, T \, (L \Downarrow H :: T \Rightarrow \exists H', T' \, (L' \Downarrow H' :: T' \,\&\,$$
$$H \leq_\sigma^{\text{gnd}} H' \,\&\, T \leq_{[\sigma]}^{\text{gnd}} T')) \quad (2.23)$$

Analogous extensionality properties hold by construction for the notion of PCFL similarity introduced in the next section. Thus (2.19)–(2.23) will follow once we have proved that this coincides with $\leq^{\text{gnd}}$ (Theorem 3.8).

The η-rule for functions and the surjective pairing rule for products follow by combining these extensionality properties with the corresponding β-rules:

$$(\Gamma \vdash F : \sigma \to \sigma' \;\&\; x \notin dom(\Gamma)) \Rightarrow \Gamma \vdash F \cong^{\mathrm{gnd}}_{\sigma \to \sigma'} (\lambda x . F) x \qquad (2.24)$$

$$\Gamma \vdash P : \sigma \times \sigma' \Rightarrow \Gamma \vdash P \cong^{\mathrm{gnd}}_{\sigma \times \sigma'} \langle \mathsf{fst}(P), \mathsf{snd}(P) \rangle \qquad (2.25)$$

Unfolding recursive terms

$$\Gamma, x : \sigma \vdash M : \sigma \Rightarrow \Gamma \vdash \mathsf{fix}\, x . M \cong^{\mathrm{gnd}}_{\sigma} M[\mathsf{fix}\, x . M/x] \qquad (2.26)$$

This holds for the same reason as the β-rules given above—it is an instance of 'Kleene equivalence', and so will follow from Proposition 3.9 below.

Syntactic bottom

The term $\bot \stackrel{\mathrm{def}}{=} \mathsf{fix}\, x . x$ acts as a least element with respect to $\leq^{\mathrm{gnd}}$:

$$\Gamma \vdash M : \sigma \Rightarrow \Gamma \vdash \bot \leq^{\mathrm{gnd}}_{\sigma} M \qquad (2.27)$$

As for the previous property, this will be deduced from Proposition 3.9.

Rational completeness and syntactic continuity

In addition to the unfolding property (2.26), terms of the form $\mathsf{fix}\, x . F$ enjoy a least prefixed point property: if $F \in Exp_{\sigma}(x : \sigma)$ and $M \in Exp_{\sigma}$, then

$$F[M/x] \leq^{\mathrm{gnd}}_{\sigma} M \Rightarrow \mathsf{fix}\, x . F \leq^{\mathrm{gnd}}_{\sigma} M. \qquad (2.28)$$

Sands (1995, Appendix) gives a direct, operationally-based proof of the analogous property of recursive functions definitions, making use of a transition relation rather than just an evaluation relation. We will deduce this least prefixed point property from a stronger property which we now explain.

For each natural number n, let $\mathsf{fix}^{(n)} x . F$ be the term given as follows:

$$\mathsf{fix}^{(0)} x . F \stackrel{\mathrm{def}}{=} \bot,$$

$$\mathsf{fix}^{(n+1)} x . F \stackrel{\mathrm{def}}{=} F[\mathsf{fix}^{(n)} x . F/x].$$

It follows from (2.11) and (2.27) that these terms form an ascending chain

$$\bot = \mathsf{fix}^{(0)} x . F \leq^{\mathrm{gnd}}_{\sigma} \mathsf{fix}^{(1)} x . F \leq^{\mathrm{gnd}}_{\sigma} \cdots.$$

We claim that $\mathsf{fix}\, x . F$ is a least upper bound with respect to $\leq^{\mathrm{gnd}}$ for this chain. In other words, for each $M \in Exp_{\sigma}$

$$\mathsf{fix}\, x . F \leq^{\mathrm{gnd}}_{\sigma} M \Leftrightarrow \forall n \, (\mathsf{fix}^{(n)} x . F \leq^{\mathrm{gnd}}_{\sigma} M). \qquad (2.29)$$

Thus the collection of PCFL terms preordered by $\leq^{\text{gnd}}$ enjoys a restricted amount of chain-completeness. Moreover, the operations of PCFL preserve these least upper bounds: for each context $\mathcal{C}[-]$ it is the case that

$$\mathcal{C}[\text{fix } x \, . \, F] \leq_\sigma^{\text{gnd}} M \Leftrightarrow \forall n \, (\mathcal{C}[\text{fix}^{(n)} x \, . \, F] \leq_\sigma^{\text{gnd}} M). \tag{2.30}$$

Properties (2.29) and (2.30) will be proved in Section 4, using operationally-based methods (which seem different from those used for the same purpose in (Smith 1992; Mason, Smith, and Talcott 1996)). Such properties can also be established via an adequate denotational semantics of PCFL—see (Pitts 1994) for example.

Note that (2.28) can be deduced from (2.29), since if $F[M/x] \leq^{\text{gnd}} M$, then one can show by induction on n that $\text{fix}^{(n)} x \, . \, F \leq_\sigma^{\text{gnd}} M$. The base case $n = 0$ is just (2.27); and the induction step follows from the hypothesis using (2.11) and (2.5).

3 Similarity and Bisimilarity

Look again at the extensionality properties (2.19)–(2.23) which we claim hold of the contextual preorder, $\leq^{\text{gnd}}$. Property (2.21) expresses the preordered version of a familiar extensionality property for functions—namely that two functions are equal if (and only if) they yield equal results when applied to any argument. In particular, (2.21) serves to express $\leq^{\text{gnd}}$ at a function type $(\sigma \to \sigma')$ in terms of $\leq^{\text{gnd}}$ at a simpler type (σ'). For the simply typed language PCF, $\to$ is the only type constructor and a typical PCF type takes the form $\sigma_1 \to (\sigma_2 \to \ldots (\sigma_n \to \gamma) \ldots)$ with γ a ground type and $n \geq 0$. Consequently, for this simpler language one can express the contextual preorder at any type in terms of application and evaluation of terms of ground type:

Milner's Context Lemma for PCF. *For any closed PCF terms M and M'*

$$M \leq_{\sigma_1 \to (\sigma_2 \to \ldots (\sigma_n \to \gamma) \ldots)}^{\text{gnd}} M' \Leftrightarrow$$
$$\forall A_1, \ldots, A_n, c \, (M A_1 \ldots A_n \Downarrow \underline{c} \Rightarrow M' A_1 \ldots A_n \Downarrow \underline{c}).$$

Proof. See Milner (1977). □

For PCFL with its types of (potentially infinite) lists, $[\sigma]$, the situation is not so straightforward. Property (2.23) does not serve to define $\leq^{\text{gnd}}$ at a list type $[\sigma]$ in terms of $\leq^{\text{gnd}}$ at type σ, since the occurrence $T \leq_{[\sigma]}^{\text{gnd}} T'$ on the right hand side of the bi-implication is not necessarily 'simpler' (for any measure of simplicity) than the occurrence $L \leq_{[\sigma]}^{\text{gnd}} L'$ on the left hand side. (For example, when $L = \text{fix} \, \ell \, . \, \underline{0} :: \ell \in Exp_{[int]}$, then $L \Downarrow \underline{0} :: L$, so T in this case is syntactically identical to L.) In other words, there may be many binary relations between closed PCFL terms which satisfy (2.23). The crucial observation is not just that $\leq^{\text{gnd}}$ is such a relation, but that it is the *greatest* such—indeed, is the greatest relation satisfying just the left-to-right implication in (2.23).

Greatest post-fixed points of monotone operators

Recall that a **complete lattice** is a partially ordered set $(X, \leq)$ for which every subset $S \subseteq X$ has a least upper bound, $\bigvee S$, with respect to $\leq$:

$$\forall x \in X \, (\bigvee S \leq x \Leftrightarrow \forall s \in S \, (s \leq x)).$$

(As is well known, this is equivalent to requiring that every subset has a greatest lower bound.)

A **monotone operator** on $(X, \leq)$ is a function $\Phi : X \longrightarrow X$ satisfying

$$\forall x, x' \in X \, (x \leq x' \Rightarrow \Phi(x) \leq \Phi(x')).$$

The **greatest post-fixed point** of Φ is the (necessarily unique) element $\nu(\Phi)$ of X satisfying

$$\nu(\Phi) \leq \Phi(\nu(\Phi)) \tag{3.1}$$

$$\forall x \in X \, (x \leq \Phi(x) \Rightarrow x \leq \nu(\Phi)). \tag{3.2}$$

Theorem 3.1 (Tarski-Knaster Fixed Point Theorem). *Every monotone operator Φ on a complete lattice $(X, \leq)$ possesses a greatest post-fixed point, $\nu(\Phi)$. This element is in fact the greatest element of the set $\{x \in X \mid x = \Phi(x)\}$ of fixed points of Φ.*

Proof. The proof is probably familiar to you, but in case not, here it is.

The monotonicity of Φ ensures that the least upper bound of any set of post-fixed points for Φ is again a post-fixed point. It follows that

$$\nu(\Phi) \overset{\text{def}}{=} \bigvee \{x \in X \mid x \leq \Phi(x)\}$$

is the greatest post-fixed point of Φ. Since

$$x = \Phi(x) \Rightarrow x \leq \Phi(x) \Rightarrow x \leq \nu(\Phi)$$

to prove the second sentence of the theorem, it suffices to see that $\nu(\Phi)$ *is* a fixed point of Φ. Since it is a post-fixed point, it suffices to show that $\Phi(\nu(\Phi)) \leq \nu(\Phi)$. But since $\nu(\Phi) \leq \Phi(\nu(\Phi))$ and Φ is monotone, one has that $\Phi(\nu(\Phi)) \leq \Phi(\Phi(\nu(\Phi)))$, that is, $\Phi(\nu(\Phi))$ is a post-fixed point of Φ. Since $\nu(\Phi)$ is the greatest such we have $\Phi(\nu(\Phi)) \leq \nu(\Phi)$, as required. $\qquad\qquad \square$

Definition 3.2. Throughout this section we will be concerned with one particular complete lattice, $(Rel, \leq)$. The elements of Rel are type-indexed families $\mathcal{R} = (\mathcal{R}_\sigma \mid \sigma)$ of binary relations $\mathcal{R}_\sigma$ between the closed PCFL terms of type σ. Thus each component of $\mathcal{R}$ is a subset $\mathcal{R}_\sigma \subseteq Exp_\sigma \times Exp_\sigma$. The partial ordering on Rel is defined to be set-theoretic inclusion in each component:

$$\mathcal{R} \leq \mathcal{R}' \overset{\text{def}}{\Leftrightarrow} \forall \sigma \, (\mathcal{R}_\sigma \subseteq \mathcal{R}'_\sigma).$$

Clearly, the least upper bound of a subset of Rel is given by set-theoretic union in each component.

PCFL simulations and bisimulations

Given $\mathcal{R} \in Rel$, the elements $\langle \mathcal{R} \rangle$ and $[\mathcal{R}]$ of Rel are defined as follows.

$$B \langle \mathcal{R} \rangle_{bool} B' \stackrel{\text{def}}{\Leftrightarrow} \forall b \in \mathbb{B} \, (B \Downarrow \underline{b} \Rightarrow B' \Downarrow \underline{b}) \tag{3.3a}$$

$$N \langle \mathcal{R} \rangle_{int} N' \stackrel{\text{def}}{\Leftrightarrow} \forall n \in \mathbb{Z} \, (N \Downarrow \underline{n} \Rightarrow N' \Downarrow \underline{n}) \tag{3.3b}$$

$$F \langle \mathcal{R} \rangle_{\sigma \to \sigma'} F' \stackrel{\text{def}}{\Leftrightarrow} \forall A \in Exp_\sigma \, (F \, A \, \mathcal{R}_{\sigma'} \, F' \, A) \tag{3.3c}$$

$$P \langle \mathcal{R} \rangle_{\sigma \times \sigma'} P' \stackrel{\text{def}}{\Leftrightarrow} \mathsf{fst}(P) \, \mathcal{R}_\sigma \, \mathsf{fst}(P') \, \& \, \mathsf{snd}(P) \, \mathcal{R}_{\sigma'} \, \mathsf{snd}(P') \tag{3.3d}$$

$$\begin{aligned} L \langle \mathcal{R} \rangle_{[\sigma]} L' \stackrel{\text{def}}{\Leftrightarrow} \; & (L \Downarrow \mathsf{nil} \Rightarrow L' \Downarrow \mathsf{nil}) \\ & \& \, \forall H, T \, (L \Downarrow H :: T \Rightarrow \\ & \qquad \exists H', T' \, (L' \Downarrow H' :: T' \, \& \, H \, \mathcal{R}_\sigma \, H' \, \& \, T \, \mathcal{R}_{[\sigma]} \, T')) \end{aligned} \tag{3.3e}$$

$$B [\mathcal{R}]_{bool} B' \stackrel{\text{def}}{\Leftrightarrow} \forall b \in \mathbb{B} \, (B \Downarrow \underline{b} \Leftrightarrow B' \Downarrow \underline{b}) \tag{3.4a}$$

$$N [\mathcal{R}]_{int} N' \stackrel{\text{def}}{\Leftrightarrow} \forall n \in \mathbb{Z} \, (N \Downarrow \underline{n} \Leftrightarrow N' \Downarrow \underline{n}) \tag{3.4b}$$

$$F [\mathcal{R}]_{\sigma \to \sigma'} F' \stackrel{\text{def}}{\Leftrightarrow} \forall A \in Exp_\sigma \, (F \, A \, \mathcal{R}_{\sigma'} \, F' \, A) \tag{3.4c}$$

$$P [\mathcal{R}]_{\sigma \times \sigma'} P' \stackrel{\text{def}}{\Leftrightarrow} \mathsf{fst}(P) \, \mathcal{R}_\sigma \, \mathsf{fst}(P') \, \& \, \mathsf{snd}(P) \, \mathcal{R}_{\sigma'} \, \mathsf{snd}(P') \tag{3.4d}$$

$$\begin{aligned} L [\mathcal{R}]_{[\sigma]} L' \stackrel{\text{def}}{\Leftrightarrow} \; & (L \Downarrow \mathsf{nil} \Leftrightarrow L' \Downarrow \mathsf{nil}) \\ & \& \, \forall H, T \, (L \Downarrow H :: T \Rightarrow \\ & \qquad \exists H', T' \, (L' \Downarrow H' :: T' \, \& \, H \, \mathcal{R}_\sigma \, H' \, \& \, T \, \mathcal{R}_{[\sigma]} \, T')) \\ & \& \, \forall H', T' \, (L' \Downarrow H' :: T' \Rightarrow \\ & \qquad \exists H, T \, (L \Downarrow H :: T \, \& \, H \, \mathcal{R}_\sigma \, H' \, \& \, T \, \mathcal{R}_{[\sigma]} \, T')). \end{aligned} \tag{3.4e}$$

Clearly, $\mathcal{R} \mapsto \langle \mathcal{R} \rangle$ and $\mathcal{R} \mapsto [\mathcal{R}]$ are both monotone operators on Rel. So we can apply Theorem 3.1 and form their greatest (post-)fixed points.

Definition 3.3. A family of relations $\mathcal{S} \in Rel$ satisfying $\mathcal{S} \leq \langle \mathcal{S} \rangle$ will be called a **PCFL simulation**; the greatest such will be called **PCFL similarity** and written $\preceq$. A family of relations $\mathcal{B} \in Rel$ satisfying $\mathcal{B} \leq [\mathcal{B}]$ will be called a **PCFL bisimulation**; the greatest such will be called **PCFL bisimilarity** and written $\simeq$.

Let us spell out what the conditions $\mathcal{S} \leq \langle \mathcal{S} \rangle$ and $\mathcal{B} \leq [\mathcal{B}]$ mean. A PCFL simulation $\mathcal{S}$ is specified by a type-indexed family of binary relations, $\mathcal{S}_\sigma \subseteq Exp_\sigma \times Exp_\sigma$, satisfying the conditions in Figure 4. A PCFL bisimulation is specified by a type-indexed family of binary relations, $\mathcal{B}_\sigma \subseteq Exp_\sigma \times Exp_\sigma$, satisfying the conditions in Figure 5.

Note in particular that the notion of (bi)simulation requires one to consider evaluation at ground and list types, but not at product and function types. The reason for this is that we wish to obtain a notion of bisimilarity which coincides with PCFL contextual equivalence as defined in the previous section. Some variations on the definition of $\cong^{\text{gnd}}$ and the corresponding changes in a coextensive notion of bisimilarity will be considered in 5.

$$(B\ \mathcal{S}_{bool}\ B'\ \&\ B \Downarrow \underline{b}) \Rightarrow B' \Downarrow \underline{b} \qquad\qquad\text{(sim 1)}$$

$$(N\ \mathcal{S}_{int}\ N'\ \&\ N \Downarrow \underline{n}) \Rightarrow N' \Downarrow \underline{n} \qquad\qquad\text{(sim 2)}$$

$$F\ \mathcal{S}_{\sigma\to\sigma'}\ F' \Rightarrow \forall A \in Exp_\sigma\ (F\ A\ \mathcal{S}_{\sigma'}\ F'\ A) \qquad\qquad\text{(sim 3)}$$

$$P\ \mathcal{S}_{\sigma\times\sigma'}\ P' \Rightarrow (\mathsf{fst}(P)\ \mathcal{S}_\sigma\ \mathsf{fst}(P')\ \&\ \mathsf{snd}(P)\ \mathcal{S}_{\sigma'}\ \mathsf{snd}(P')) \qquad\text{(sim 4)}$$

$$(L\ \mathcal{S}_{[\sigma]}\ L'\ \&\ L \Downarrow \mathsf{nil}) \Rightarrow L' \Downarrow \mathsf{nil} \qquad\qquad\text{(sim 5)}$$

$$(L\ \mathcal{B}_{[\sigma]}\ L'\ \&\ L \Downarrow H :: T) \Rightarrow \qquad\qquad\text{(sim 6)}$$
$$\exists H', T'\ (L' \Downarrow H' :: T'\ \&\ H\ \mathcal{B}_\sigma\ H'\ \&\ T\ \mathcal{B}_{[\sigma]}\ T')$$

Figure 4: Simulation conditions

$$(B\ \mathcal{B}_{bool}\ B'\ \&\ B \Downarrow \underline{b}) \Rightarrow B' \Downarrow \underline{b} \qquad\qquad\text{(bis 1a)}$$

$$(B\ \mathcal{B}_{bool}\ B'\ \&\ B' \Downarrow \underline{b'}) \Rightarrow B \Downarrow \underline{b'} \qquad\qquad\text{(bis 1b)}$$

$$(N\ \mathcal{B}_{int}\ N'\ \&\ N \Downarrow \underline{n}) \Rightarrow N' \Downarrow \underline{n} \qquad\qquad\text{(bis 2a)}$$

$$(N\ \mathcal{B}_{int}\ N'\ \&\ N' \Downarrow \underline{n'}) \Rightarrow N \Downarrow \underline{n'} \qquad\qquad\text{(bis 2b)}$$

$$F\ \mathcal{B}_{\sigma\to\sigma'}\ F' \Rightarrow \forall A \in Exp_\sigma\ (F\ A\ \mathcal{B}_{\sigma'}\ F'\ A) \qquad\qquad\text{(bis 3)}$$

$$P\ \mathcal{B}_{\sigma\times\sigma'}\ P' \Rightarrow (\mathsf{fst}(P)\ \mathcal{B}_\sigma\ \mathsf{fst}(P')\ \&\ \mathsf{snd}(P)\ \mathcal{B}_{\sigma'}\ \mathsf{snd}(P')) \qquad\text{(bis 4)}$$

$$(L\ \mathcal{B}_{[\sigma]}\ L'\ \&\ L \Downarrow \mathsf{nil}) \Rightarrow L' \Downarrow \mathsf{nil} \qquad\qquad\text{(bis 5a)}$$

$$(L\ \mathcal{B}_{[\sigma]}\ L'\ \&\ L' \Downarrow \mathsf{nil}) \Rightarrow L \Downarrow \mathsf{nil} \qquad\qquad\text{(bis 5b)}$$

$$(L\ \mathcal{B}_{[\sigma]}\ L'\ \&\ L \Downarrow H :: T) \Rightarrow \qquad\qquad\text{(bis 6a)}$$
$$\exists H', T'\ (L' \Downarrow H' :: T'\ \&\ H\ \mathcal{B}_\sigma\ H'\ \&\ T\ \mathcal{B}_{[\sigma]}\ T')$$

$$(L\ \mathcal{B}_{[\sigma]}\ L'\ \&\ L' \Downarrow H' :: T') \Rightarrow \qquad\qquad\text{(bis 6b)}$$
$$\exists H, T\ (L \Downarrow H :: T\ \&\ H\ \mathcal{B}_\sigma\ H'\ \&\ T\ \mathcal{B}_{[\sigma]}\ T').$$

Figure 5: Bisimulation conditions

Remark 3.4. Note that by Theorem 3.1, PCFL similarity and bisimilarity are fixed points (rather than just post-fixed points) of their associated monotone operators, that is, $\preceq = \langle\preceq\rangle$ and $\simeq = [\simeq]$.

Proposition 3.5 (Co-induction principle for $\simeq$ and $\preceq$). *Given* $M, M' \in Exp_\sigma$, *to prove that* $M \simeq_\sigma M'$ *holds, it suffices to find a PCFL bisimulation* $\mathcal{B}$ *such that* $M\ \mathcal{B}_\sigma\ M'$. *Similarly, to prove* $M \preceq_\sigma M'$, *it suffices to find a PCFL simulation* $\mathcal{S}$ *with* $M\ \mathcal{S}_\sigma\ M'$.

Proof. If $\mathcal{B} \leq [\mathcal{B}]$, then $\mathcal{B} \leq \simeq$ (since $\simeq$ is the greatest post-fixed point of $[-]$), so that $\mathcal{B}_\sigma \subseteq \simeq_\sigma$. Thus if $M \, \mathcal{B}_\sigma \, M'$, then $M \simeq_\sigma M'$. $\qquad\square$

Once we have proved that bisimilarity and contextual equivalence coincide for PCFL this proposition will provide a powerful tool for proving contextual equivalences. For the moment, we use it to establish some basic facts about (bi)similarity, the last of which depends very much upon the deterministic nature of evaluation in PCFL.

Proposition 3.6. *PCFL similarity is a preorder and PCFL bisimilarity is the equivalence relation induced by it. In other words, for all types σ and all closed terms $M, M', M'' \in Exp_\sigma$, one has:*

(i) $M \preceq_\sigma M$

(ii) $(M \preceq_\sigma M' \ \& \ M' \preceq_\sigma M'') \Rightarrow M \preceq_\sigma M''$

(iii) $M \simeq_\sigma M' \Leftrightarrow (M \preceq_\sigma M' \ \& \ M' \preceq_\sigma M)$.

Proof. Note that the element of *Rel* whose component at type σ is $\{(M, M) \mid M \in Exp_\sigma\}$ is trivially a PCFL simulation. So (i) holds by Proposition 3.5. Similarly, to prove (ii), it suffices to check that

$$\{(M, M'') \in Exp_\sigma \times Exp_\sigma \mid \exists M' \in Exp_\sigma \, (M \preceq_\sigma M' \ \& \ M' \preceq_\sigma M'')\}$$

determines a PCFL simulation. But this follows immediately from the fact that $\preceq$ is itself a PCFL simulation.

For (iii), note that since $\simeq$ satisfies the bisimulation conditions in Figure 5, both $\{(M, M') \mid M \simeq_\sigma M'\}$ and $\{(M, M') \mid M' \simeq_\sigma M\}$ determine PCFL simulations. Hence both are contained in $\preceq$, and thus we have the left-to-right implication in (iii). Conversely, the fact that $\preceq$ is a PCFL simulation and the fact that evaluation in PCFL is deterministic (Proposition 2.4(i)) together imply that $\{(M, M') \mid M \preceq_\sigma M' \ \& \ M' \preceq_\sigma M\}$ satisfies the conditions in Figure 5, and hence is contained in $\simeq_\sigma$. $\qquad\square$

We extend $\preceq$ and $\simeq$ from closed terms to all typeable PCFL terms by considering closed instantiations of open terms. (Cf. the property (2.19), which we are claiming the contextual preorder satisfies.) It is convenient to introduce a notation for this process.

Definition 3.7. Suppose $\mathcal{R} \in Rel$. For any finite partial function Γ assigning types to variables

$$\Gamma : x_1 \mapsto \sigma_1, x_2 \mapsto \sigma_2, \ldots, x_n \mapsto \sigma_n$$

for any type σ, and for any terms $N, N' \in Exp_\sigma(\Gamma)$, define

$$\Gamma \vdash N \, \mathcal{R}_\sigma^\circ \, N' \overset{\text{def}}{\Leftrightarrow}$$
$$\forall M_1 \in Exp_{\sigma_1}, \ldots, M_n \in Exp_{\sigma_n} \, (N[\vec{M}/\vec{x}] \, \mathcal{R}_\sigma \, N'[\vec{M}/\vec{x}]) \quad (3.5)$$

We will call $\mathcal{R}^\circ$ the **open extension** of $\mathcal{R}$. Applying this construction to $\preceq$ and $\simeq$, we get relations $\preceq^\circ$ and $\simeq^\circ$ on open terms, which we will still call similarity and bisimilarity respectively.

Armed with these definitions, we can state the co-inductive characterisation of contextual equivalence for PCFL.

Theorem 3.8 (Operational Extensionality for PCFL). *Contextual preorder (respectively, equivalence) coincides with similarity (respectively, bisimilarity):*

$$\Gamma \vdash M \leq^{gnd}_\sigma M' \Leftrightarrow \Gamma \vdash M \preceq^\circ_\sigma M'$$

$$\Gamma \vdash M \cong^{gnd}_\sigma M' \Leftrightarrow \Gamma \vdash M \simeq^\circ_\sigma M'.$$

In particular, the following **co-induction principle** *for $\cong^{gnd}$ holds:*

> *To prove that two closed PCFL terms are contextually equivalent, it suffices to find a PCFL bisimulation which relates them.*

The proof of this theorem will be given in the next section. In the rest of this section we explore some of its consequences and then give some examples of the use of co-induction to prove contextual equivalences.

First note that in view of the definition of $\preceq^\circ$ from $\preceq$, the extensionality property (2.19) of $\leq^{gnd}$ is an immediate consequence of Theorem 3.8. The other extensionality properties (2.20)–(2.23) also follow from the theorem, using the fact that $\preceq = \langle \preceq \rangle$.

Proposition 3.9 (Kleene equivalence). *For each type σ consider the following binary relations on Exp_σ:*

$$M \leq^{kl}_\sigma M' \stackrel{\text{def}}{\Leftrightarrow} \forall C\, (M \Downarrow C \Rightarrow M' \Downarrow C)$$

$$M \cong^{kl}_\sigma M' \stackrel{\text{def}}{\Leftrightarrow} M \leq^{kl}_\sigma M' \,\&\, M' \leq^{kl}_\sigma M.$$

If $M \cong^{kl}_\sigma M'$ holds we will say that M and M' are **Kleene equivalent.**[1] *Then*

$$M \leq^{kl}_\sigma M' \Rightarrow M \preceq_\sigma M' \tag{3.6}$$

$$M \cong^{kl}_\sigma M' \Rightarrow M \simeq_\sigma M'. \tag{3.7}$$

Hence in view of Theorem 3.8, Kleene equivalent closed PCFL terms are contextually equivalent.

Proof. Property (3.7) follows from property (3.6) by Proposition 3.6(iii). For (3.6), it suffices to check that the relations $\{(M, M') \mid M \leq^{kl}_\sigma M'\}$ (for each type σ) satisfy the conditions in Figure 4.

---

[1] Following Harper (1995), this terminology is adopted from the logic of partially defined expressions, where two such expressions are commonly said to be 'Kleene equivalent' if the first is defined if and only if the second is, and in that case they are equal.

Clearly the conditions (sim 1) and (sim 2) follow immediately from the definition of $\leq^{kl}$. The conditions (sim 5) and (sim 6) are almost as straightforward, just needing the additional fact that $\leq^{kl}$ is reflexive (which is evident from the definition of $\leq^{kl}$).

To verify the condition (sim 4), suppose that $P \leq^{kl}_{\sigma_1 \times \sigma_2} P'$ holds. For any C, if fst$(P) \Downarrow C$ then this evaluation can only have been deduced by an application of rule ($\Downarrow$ fst) in Figure 3, so there are terms $M_i \in Exp_{\sigma_i}$ $(i = 1, 2)$ such that $P \Downarrow \langle M_1, M_2 \rangle$ and $M_1 \Downarrow C$. Then since $P \leq^{kl}_{\sigma_1 \times \sigma_2} P'$, it is the case that $P' \Downarrow \langle M_1, M_2 \rangle$ and hence that fst$(P') \Downarrow C$. Thus for any C, fst$(P) \Downarrow C$ implies fst$(P') \Downarrow C$, which is to say that fst$(P) \leq^{kl}_{\sigma_1}$ fst(P'). Similarly, one can deduce that snd$(P) \leq^{kl}_{\sigma_2}$ snd(P'). Thus condition (sim 4) does indeed hold.

The proof of the simulation condition at function types, (sim 3), is like that for product types, and is omitted. □

The following Kleene equivalences all follow immediately from the definition of evaluation in PCFL (where we have suppressed type information).

$$(\lambda x . M)A \cong^{kl} M[A/x]$$
$$\text{fst}(\langle M, M' \rangle) \cong^{kl} M$$
$$\text{snd}(\langle M, M' \rangle) \cong^{kl} M'$$
$$\text{case nil of } \{\text{nil} \to M \mid h :: t \to N\} \cong^{kl} M$$

$$\text{case } H :: T \text{ of } \{\text{nil} \to M \mid h :: t \to N\} \cong^{kl} N[H/h, T/t]$$
$$\text{if true then } M \text{ else } M' \cong^{kl} M$$
$$\text{if false then } M \text{ else } M' \cong^{kl} M'$$
$$\underline{n} \text{ op } \underline{n'} \cong^{kl} \underline{n \text{ op } n'}$$
$$\text{fix } x . M \cong^{kl} M[\text{fix } x . M/x].$$

By the proposition, these are also valid for PCFL similarity; and since $\preceq^\circ$ is defined from $\preceq$ by taking closed instantiations, it follows that $\preceq^\circ$ satisfies the β rules (2.13)–(2.18) and the unfolding rule (2.26). Thus by (one half of) Theorem 3.8, $\leq^{gnd}$ satisfies these rules as well.

Similarly, the fact that $\bot = \text{fix } x . x$ does not evaluate, immediately implies

$$\bot \leq^{kl}_\sigma M$$

holds for any $M \in Exp_\sigma$. Hence property (2.27) is also a consequence of the proposition combined with Theorem 3.8.

Proposition 3.10 (Co-induction at list types). *For any type τ, call a binary relation $\mathcal{R} \subseteq Exp_{[\tau]} \times Exp_{[\tau]}$ a $[\tau]$-bisimulation if whenever $L \mathcal{R} L'$*

$$L \Downarrow nil \Rightarrow L' \Downarrow nil \tag{3.8}$$

$$L' \Downarrow nil \Rightarrow L \Downarrow nil \tag{3.9}$$

$$L \Downarrow H :: T \Rightarrow \exists H', T' (H \cong_\tau^{gnd} H' \ \& \ T \mathcal{R} T') \tag{3.10}$$

$$L' \Downarrow H' :: T' \Rightarrow \exists H, T (H \cong_\tau^{gnd} H' \ \& \ T \mathcal{R} T'). \tag{3.11}$$

Then for any $L, L' \in Exp_{[\tau]}$, $L \cong_{[\tau]}^{gnd} L'$ if and only if there is some $[\tau]$-bisimulation $\mathcal{R}$ with $L \mathcal{R} L'$.

Proof. First note that by Theorem 3.8, $\cong^{gnd}$ is a PCFL bisimulation (since it coincides with $\sim$). In particular it satisfies conditions (bis 5a)–(bis 6b) of Figure 5, and therefore $\{(L, L') \mid L \cong_{[\tau]}^{gnd} L'\}$ is a $[\tau]$-bisimulation. This gives the 'only if' part of the proposition.

Conversely, if $\mathcal{R}$ is a $[\tau]$-bisimulation, then the fact that $\cong^{gnd}$ satisfies the conditions in Figure 5 and $\mathcal{R}$ satisfies (3.8)–(3.11) implies that

$$\mathcal{B}_\sigma \overset{def}{=} \begin{cases} \mathcal{R} \cup \{(L, L') \mid L \cong_{[\tau]}^{gnd} L'\} & \text{if } \sigma = [\tau] \\ \{(M, M') \mid M \cong_\sigma^{gnd} M'\} & \text{otherwise} \end{cases}$$

defines a PCFL bisimulation. Thus if $L \mathcal{R} L'$, then $L \mathcal{B}_{[\tau]} L'$, so $L \cong_{[\tau]}^{gnd} L'$ by Theorem 3.8. □

Examples

Here is a graded series of examples illustrating the use of the co-induction principle of Proposition 3.10.

Example 3.11. For any type τ, the following contextual equivalence is valid.

$$f : \tau \to \tau, x : \tau \vdash map\, f\, (iterate\, f\, x) \cong_{[\tau]}^{gnd} iterate\, f\, (f\, x) \tag{3.12}$$

where

$$map \overset{def}{=} fix\, m\,.\, \lambda f\,.\, \lambda \ell\,.$$
$$\text{case } \ell \text{ of } \{nil \to nil \mid h :: t \to (f\, h) :: (m\, f\, t)\}$$
$$iterate \overset{def}{=} fix\, i\,, \lambda f\,.\, \lambda x\,.\, x :: (i\, f\, (f\, x)).$$

(Note that $\emptyset \vdash map : (\tau \to \tau) \to ([\tau] \to [\tau])$ and $\emptyset \vdash iterate : (\tau \to \tau) \to \tau \to [\tau]$, for any type τ.)

Proof. Intuitively, *iterate f x* is a notation for the infinite list $[x, fx, f(fx), \ldots]$ and *map f* applies f to each component of a list. So one would expect that both *map f (iterate f x)* and *iterate f (f x)* denote the list $[fx, f(fx), f(f(fx)), \ldots]$. So the contextual equivalence (3.12) is intuitively reasonable. Let us see how to prove that it holds using the co-inductive characterisation of $\cong^{\mathrm{gnd}}$.

First note that in view of the extensionality property (2.19) of $\cong^{\mathrm{gnd}}$ (which as noted above, follows from Theorem 3.8), to prove (3.12) it suffices to show for all $\tau, F \in Exp_{\tau \to \tau}$, and $M \in Exp_\tau$ that

$$map\, F\, (iterate\, F\, M) \simeq_{[\tau]} iterate\, F\, (F\, M). \tag{3.13}$$

We deduce this from Proposition 3.10 by constructing a suitable $[\tau]$-bisimulation, $\mathcal{R}$. In fact we do not have to look very far for $\mathcal{R}$ in this case, since the pairs of terms we are interested in already constitute a $[\tau]$-bisimulation! Let us verify that for

$$\mathcal{R} \stackrel{\mathrm{def}}{=} \{(map\, F\, (iterate\, F\, M), iterate\, F\, (F\, M)) \mid F \in Exp_{\tau \to \tau}\, \&\, M \in Exp_\tau\}$$

if $L\, \mathcal{R}\, L'$, then conditions (3.8)–(3.11) are satisfied.

If $L\, \mathcal{R}\, L'$, then by definition of $\mathcal{R}$ we have that $L = map\, F\, (iterate\, F\, M)$ and $L' = iterate\, F\, (F\, M)$, for some terms M and F. Using the evaluation rules in Figure 3 together with the definitions of *iterate* and *map*, one obtains

$$iterate\, F\, M \Downarrow M :: (iterate\, F\, (F\, M))$$
$$L' = iterate\, F\, (F\, M) \Downarrow (F\, M) :: (iterate\, F\, (F\, (F\, M)))$$
$$L = map\, F\, (iterate\, F\, M) \Downarrow (F\, M) :: (map\, F\, (iterate\, F\, (F\, M))).$$

So by determinacy of evaluation (Proposition 2.4(i)), if $L \Downarrow C$, then $C = H :: T$ with $H = F\, M$ and $T = map\, F\, (iterate\, F\, (F\, M))$. But we know that $L' \Downarrow H' :: T'$ with $H' = F\, M = H$ and $T' = iterate\, F\, (F\, (F\, M))$, and hence with $H \cong^{\mathrm{gnd}}_\tau H'$ (since $\cong^{\mathrm{gnd}}$ is reflexive) and $T\, \mathcal{R}\, T'$ (by definition of $\mathcal{R}$). So conditions (3.8) and (3.10) are satisfied (the first one trivially, because by determinacy of $\Downarrow$, L does not evaluate to nil). A symmetrical argument starting with the assumption that $L' \Downarrow C'$ shows that conditions (3.9) and (3.11) are also satisfied by $\mathcal{R}$. So $\mathcal{R}$ is indeed a $[\tau]$-bisimulation, and since it relates the terms in which we are interested, the proof is complete. $\square$

The next example makes use of mathematical induction in order to verify that a particular relation has the properties required of a bisimulation.

Example 3.12. Define

$$zip \stackrel{\text{def}}{=} \text{fix } z \,.\, \lambda \ell \,.\, \lambda \ell' \,.\, \text{case } \ell \text{ of}$$
$$\{ \text{nil} \to \text{nil}$$
$$\mid h :: t \to \text{case } \ell' \text{ of } \quad \{ \text{nil} \to \text{nil}$$
$$\mid h' :: t' \to \langle h, h' \rangle :: z \, t \, t' \} \}$$

$$from \stackrel{\text{def}}{=} \text{fix } f \,.\, \lambda x \,.\, \lambda y \,.\, x :: (f \, (x + y) \, y)$$

$$suc \stackrel{\text{def}}{=} \lambda x \,.\, x + \underline{1}$$

$$plus \stackrel{\text{def}}{=} \lambda z \,.\, \text{fst}(z) + \text{snd}(z)$$

$$nats \stackrel{\text{def}}{=} \text{fix } \ell \,.\, \underline{0} :: (map \, suc \, \ell)$$

where *map* is as in the previous example. (Note that $\emptyset \vdash zip : [\sigma] \to ([\sigma'] \to [\sigma \times \sigma'])$ for any types σ and σ'; and $\emptyset \vdash from : int \to (int \to [int])$, $\emptyset \vdash suc : int \to int$, $\emptyset \vdash plus : (int \times int) \to int$, and $\emptyset \vdash nats : [int]$.) Then

$$map \, plus \, (zip \, nats \, nats) \cong^{\text{gnd}}_{[int]} from \, \underline{0} \, \underline{2} \tag{3.14}$$

Proof. Consider the following closed PCFL terms, defined by induction on $n \in \mathbf{N}$:

$$N_0 \stackrel{\text{def}}{=} \underline{0} \qquad\qquad E_0 \stackrel{\text{def}}{=} \underline{0} \qquad\qquad L_0 \stackrel{\text{def}}{=} nats$$
$$N_{n+1} \stackrel{\text{def}}{=} suc \, N_n \qquad E_{n+1} \stackrel{\text{def}}{=} E_n + \underline{2} \qquad L_{n+1} \stackrel{\text{def}}{=} map \, suc \, L_n.$$

From the definition of *from* and E_n it follows directly that

$$from \, E_n \, \underline{2} \Downarrow E_n :: (from \, E_{n+1} \, \underline{2}) \tag{3.15}$$

From the definition of *map*, *nats*, L_n, and N_n it follows by induction on n that

$$L_n \Downarrow N_n :: L_{n+1}$$

Therefore, using the definition of *zip*, we have that

$$zip \, L_n \, L_n \Downarrow \langle N_n, N_n \rangle :: (zip \, L_{n+1} \, L_{n+1})$$

and from the definition of *map* that

$$map \, plus \, (zip \, L_n \, L_n) \Downarrow plus \, \langle N_n, N_n \rangle :: (map \, plus \, (zip \, L_{n+1} \, L_{n+1})) \tag{3.16}$$

Finally, note that by induction on n, $plus \, \langle N_n, N_n \rangle$ is Kleene equivalent to E_n, and hence by Proposition 3.9

$$plus \, \langle N_n, N_n \rangle \cong^{\text{gnd}}_{int} E_n \tag{3.17}$$

So if we define $\mathcal{R} \subseteq Exp_{[int]} \times Exp_{[int]}$ by

$$\mathcal{R} \stackrel{\text{def}}{=} \{ (map \, plus \, (zip \, L_n \, L_n), from \, E_n \, \underline{2}) \mid n \in \mathbf{N} \}$$

then properties (3.15), (3.16), and (3.17) together with determinacy of evaluation (Proposition 2.4(i)) show that $\mathcal{R}$ is a $[int]$-bisimulation. Since by definition of L_0 and E_0, $\mathcal{R}$ relates the two terms of type $[int]$ in which we are interested, the proof of (3.14) via Proposition 3.10 is complete. $\qquad\square$

In the next example, in order to verify that a certain relation is a bisimulation we make use of the congruence property of $\cong^{\text{gnd}}$, namely that if two terms are contextually equivalent and they are substituted for a parameter in a context, the resulting terms are also contextually equivalent. (This is an easy consequence of the definition of contextual equivalence.)

Example 3.13 (The '*take*-lemma'). For any type τ and terms $L, L' \in Exp_{[\tau]}$, the following property holds.

$$\forall n \in \mathbf{N} \, (take \, \underline{n} \, L \cong^{\text{gnd}}_{[\tau]} take \, \underline{n} \, L') \Rightarrow L \cong^{\text{gnd}}_{[\tau]} L' \qquad (3.18)$$

where

$$take \overset{\text{def}}{=} \text{fix} \, f \, . \, \lambda x \, . \, \lambda \ell \, . \, \text{if} \, x = \underline{0} \, \text{then nil else}$$
$$\text{case} \, \ell \, \text{of} \, \{\text{nil} \to \text{nil} \mid h :: t \to h :: (f \, (x - \underline{1}) \, t)\}$$

(Note that $\emptyset \vdash take : int \to ([\tau] \to [\tau])$, for any type τ.)

This property allows one to establish instances of contextual equivalence between list expressions by appeal to mathematical induction: to prove $L \cong^{\text{gnd}}_{[\tau]} L'$, it suffices to prove

$$take \, \underline{0} \, L \cong^{\text{gnd}}_{[\tau]} take \, \underline{0} \, L' \qquad (3.19)$$

$$take \, \underline{n} \, L \cong^{\text{gnd}}_{[\tau]} take \, \underline{n} \, L' \Rightarrow take \, \underline{n+1} \, L \cong^{\text{gnd}}_{[\tau]} take \, \underline{n+1} \, L' \qquad (3.20)$$

For the informal theory of equality of functional programs discussed by Bird and Wadler (1988), this induction principle is called the '*take*-lemma' (see *loc. cit.*, section 7.5.1). It is used to justify equalities like the ones in the previous examples. But why is the *take*-lemma valid? As we now show, if "equal" means contextually equivalent, then one can prove the validity of this principle by appealing to the coinductive characterisation of $\cong^{\text{gnd}}$ at list types given by Proposition 3.10. (See also Gordon 1995b, Section 4.6.)

Proof. Fixing the type τ, define $\mathcal{R} \subseteq Exp_{[\tau]} \times Exp_{[\tau]}$ by:

$$\mathcal{R} \overset{\text{def}}{=} \{(L, L') \mid \forall n \in \mathbf{N} \, (take \, \underline{n} \, L \cong^{\text{gnd}}_{[\tau]} take \, \underline{n} \, L')\}$$

I claim that $\mathcal{R}$ satisfies the conditions (3.8)–(3.11) required of a $[\tau]$-bisimulation.

First note that the evaluation rules in Figure 3 imply the following properties of *take*. For all $n \in \mathbf{N}$, $H \in Exp_{\tau}$, and $L, T \in Exp_{[\tau]}$:

$$take \, \underline{n+1} \, L \Downarrow \text{nil} \Leftrightarrow L \Downarrow \text{nil} \qquad (3.21)$$

$$take \, \underline{n+1} \, L \Downarrow H :: T \Leftrightarrow \exists T' \, (L \Downarrow H :: T' \, \& \, T = take \, (\underline{n+1} - \underline{1}) \, T') \qquad (3.22)$$

Now suppose $L \, \mathcal{R} \, L'$, that is, for all $n \in \mathbf{N}$, $take \, \underline{n} \, L \cong^{\text{gnd}}_{[\tau]} take \, \underline{n} \, L'$.

To see that $\mathcal{R}$ satisfies (3.8), suppose $L \Downarrow \text{nil}$. Then by (3.21), $take \, \underline{1} \, L \Downarrow \text{nil}$. Since $L \, \mathcal{R} \, L'$, by definition of $\mathcal{R}$, $take \, \underline{1} \, L \cong^{\text{gnd}}_{[\tau]} take \, \underline{1} \, L'$. Since $\cong^{\text{gnd}}$ is a PCFL bisimulation (by Theorem 3.8), it follows that $take\,\underline{1}\,L'\Downarrow$ nil and hence by (3.21) again, that $L'\Downarrow$ nil. A symmetrical argument shows that $\mathcal{R}$ also satisfies (3.9).

To see that $\mathcal{R}$ satisfies (3.10), suppose $L\Downarrow H::T$. Then by (3.22), for any $n\in\mathbb{N}$ we have $take\,\underline{n+1}\,L\Downarrow H::(take\,(\underline{n+1}-\underline{1})\,T)$. Since $L\,\mathcal{R}\,L'$, by definition of $\mathcal{R}$, $take\,\underline{n+1}\,L\cong_{[\tau]}^{\mathrm{gnd}}take\,\underline{n+1}\,L'$. So since $\cong^{\mathrm{gnd}}$ is a PCFL bisimulation, it follows that there are terms H',T'' with

$$take\,\underline{n+1}\,L'\Downarrow H'::T''\ \&\ H\cong_{\tau}^{\mathrm{gnd}}H'\ \&\ take\,(\underline{n+1}-\underline{1})\,T\cong_{[\tau]}^{\mathrm{gnd}}T''.$$

By (3.22) again, $L'\Downarrow H'::T'$ for some term T' with $T''=take\,(\underline{n+1}-\underline{1})\,T'$. We have to check that $T\,\mathcal{R}\,T'$. Note that for all n we have $take\,(\underline{n+1}-\underline{1})\,T\cong_{[\tau]}^{\mathrm{gnd}}$ $T''=take\,(\underline{n+1}-\underline{1})\,T'$. To conclude from this that $\forall n\in\mathbb{N}(take\,\underline{n}\,T\cong_{[\tau]}^{\mathrm{gnd}}$ $take\,\underline{n}\,T')$, we use the congruence property (2.11) of $\cong^{\mathrm{gnd}}$ (which as we noted in section 2 is an easy consequence of the definition of $\cong^{\mathrm{gnd}}$). It allows us to infer $take\,(\underline{n+1}-\underline{1})\,T\cong_{[\tau]}^{\mathrm{gnd}}take\,\underline{n}\,T$ from the fact that $(\underline{n+1}-\underline{1})\cong_{int}^{\mathrm{gnd}}\underline{n}$. (The latter holds by Proposition 3.9, since evidently $\underline{n+1}-\underline{1}$ is Kleene equivalent to $\underline{n}$.) A symmetrical argument shows that $\mathcal{R}$ also satisfies (3.11).

We have now established that $\mathcal{R}$ is a $[\tau]$-bisimulation. So by Proposition 3.10, for all $L,L'\in Exp_{[\tau]}$, if $L\,\mathcal{R}\,L'$ then $L\cong_{[\tau]}^{\mathrm{gnd}}L'$, as required for (3.18).   □

The next example is somewhat more challenging than the previous ones, in as much as the verification of the bisimulation condition involves an induction on the **depths of proofs** of evaluation. We write

$$M\Downarrow^n C$$

to indicate that there is a proof tree for $M\Downarrow C$ (built out of the axioms and rules in Figure 3) whose depth is less than or equal to n. If the reader prefers, one can give a slightly more abstract definition of the relations $\Downarrow^n$ ($n\in\mathbb{N}$): they are simultaneously inductively defined by axioms and rules obtained from those in Figure 3 by replacing $\Downarrow$ by $\Downarrow^n$ in each axiom and each hypothesis of a rule, and by replacing $\Downarrow$ by $\Downarrow^{n+1}$ in the conclusion of each rule. Clearly it is the case that

$$M\Downarrow C\Leftrightarrow\exists n\in\mathbb{N}(M\Downarrow^n C)\qquad(3.23)$$

Example 3.14. For any type τ, the following contextual equivalence is valid.

$$u:\tau\to bool,v:\tau\to\tau,\ell:[\tau]\vdash$$

$$filter\,u\,(map\,v\,\ell)\cong_{[\tau]}^{\mathrm{gnd}}map\,v\,(filter\,(u\circ v)\,\ell)\quad(3.24)$$

where map is as in Example 3.11 and

$$filter\stackrel{\mathrm{def}}{=}\ \mathrm{fix}\,f\,.\,\lambda u\,.\,\lambda\ell\,.\,\mathrm{case}\,\ell\,\mathrm{of}$$
$$\{\mathrm{nil}\to\mathrm{nil}\mid h::t\to\mathrm{if}\,u\,h\,\mathrm{then}\,h::(f\,u\,t)\,\mathrm{else}\,f\,u\,t\}$$

$$u\circ v\stackrel{\mathrm{def}}{=}\lambda x\,.\,u\,(v\,x)$$

(Note that $\emptyset\vdash filter:(\tau\to bool)\to([\tau]\to[\tau])$ and that $u:\tau'\to\tau'',v:\tau\to\tau'\vdash u\circ v:\tau\to\tau''$, for any types τ,τ',τ''.)

Proof. Intuitively, the expression *filter u* is a notation for the function on lists which removes elements of the list which fail the boolean test u. It is an inherently partial function, because as one progressively evaluates an input lazy list, one may never find an element passing the boolean test with which to begin the output list. It is mainly for this reason that (3.24) is harder to prove than the previous examples.

Just as in Example 3.11, to prove (3.24) it suffices to prove for all types τ, and closed terms $U \in Exp_{\tau \to bool}$ and $V \in Exp_{\tau \to \tau}$, that

$$filter\ U\ (map\ V\ L) \simeq_{[\tau]} map\ V\ (filter\ (U \circ V)\ L) \qquad (3.25)$$

holds for all $L \in Exp_{[\tau]}$. Given τ, U, and V, define $\mathcal{R} \subseteq Exp_{[\tau]} \times Exp_{[\tau]}$ by:

$$\mathcal{R} \stackrel{\text{def}}{=} \{(filter\ U\ (map\ V\ L), map\ V\ (filter\ (U \circ V)\ L)) \mid L \in Exp_{[\tau]}\}.$$

To establish (3.25), by Proposition 3.10 it suffices to show that this $\mathcal{R}$ is a $[\tau]$-bisimulation. Instead of proving that the conditions (3.8)–(3.11) hold for $\mathcal{R}$ directly (which does not seem possible—try it and see), we can deduce them via (3.23), using the following properties of $\Downarrow^n$:

$$\forall L\ (filter\ U\ (map\ V\ L) \Downarrow^n nil \Rightarrow map\ V\ (filter\ (U \circ V)\ L) \Downarrow nil) \qquad (3.26)$$

$$\forall L\ (map\ V\ (filter\ (U \circ V)\ L) \Downarrow^n nil \Rightarrow filter\ U\ (map\ V\ L) \Downarrow nil) \qquad (3.27)$$

$$\forall L, H, T\ (filter\ U\ (map\ V\ L) \Downarrow^n H :: T \Rightarrow \qquad (3.28)$$
$$\exists T'\ (map\ V\ (filter\ (U \circ V)\ L) \Downarrow H :: T'\ \&\ T\ \mathcal{R}\ T'))$$

$$\forall L, H, T'\ (map\ V\ (filter\ (U \circ V)\ L) \Downarrow^n H :: T' \Rightarrow \qquad (3.29)$$
$$\exists T\ (filter\ U\ (map\ V\ L) \Downarrow H :: T\ \&\ T\ \mathcal{R}\ T'))$$

Each of (3.26)–(3.29) can be proved by induction on n. We give the argument for (3.28) and leave the other three as exercises.

So assume inductively that (3.28) holds for all $n < m$. If $filter\ U\ (map\ V\ L) \Downarrow^m H :: T$, then by definition of *filter*, $m \geq 2$ and there are terms H_1, T_1 so that

$$map\ V\ L \Downarrow^{m-2} H_1 :: T_1 \qquad (3.30)$$

$$\text{if } U\ H_1 \text{ then } H_1 :: (filter\ U\ T_1) \text{ else } filter\ U\ T_1 \Downarrow^{m-2} H :: T \qquad (3.31)$$

Then by definition of *map*, for (3.30) to hold, it must be the case that $m \geq 4$ and there are terms H_2, T_2 so that

$$L \Downarrow^{m-4} H_2 :: T_2 \qquad (3.32)$$

$$H_1 = V\ H_2 \quad \text{and} \quad T_1 = map\ V\ T_2. \qquad (3.33)$$

On the other hand, since (3.31) holds, it must be the case that either $U\ H_1 \Downarrow$ true or $U\ H_1 \Downarrow$ false. We treat each case separately.

Case $U\,H_1 \Downarrow$ true.   In this case (3.31) holds because

$$H = H_1 \quad \text{and} \quad T = \text{filter } U\,T_1. \tag{3.34}$$

Combining this with (3.33) we get $(U \circ V)\,H_2 \Downarrow$ true. Then together with (3.32), this yields

$$\text{filter } (U \circ V)\,L \Downarrow H_2 :: \text{filter } (U \circ V)\,T_2$$

and hence

$$\text{map } V\,(\text{filter } (U \circ V)\,L) \Downarrow V\,H_2 :: (\text{map } V\,(\text{filter } (U \circ V)\,T_2)).$$

Since by (3.33) and (3.34) we have $H = V\,H_2$ and $T = \text{filter } U\,(\text{map } V\,T_2)$, it follows that

$$\text{map } V\,(\text{filter } (U \circ V)\,L) \Downarrow H :: (\text{map } V\,(\text{filter } (U \circ V)\,T_2))$$
$$T\,\mathcal{R}\,\text{map } V\,(\text{filter } (U \circ V)\,T_2).$$

So the conclusion of the $n = m$ case of (3.28) holds with $T' = \text{map } V\,(\text{filter } (U \circ V)\,T_2)$.

Case $U\,H_1 \Downarrow$ false.   In this case (3.31) holds because $m \geq 3$ and $\text{filter } U\,T_1 \Downarrow^{m-3} H :: T$. Hence by (3.33), $\text{filter } U\,(\text{map } V\,T_2) \Downarrow^{m-3} H :: T$. So by induction hypothesis there is some T_3 with

$$\text{map } V\,(\text{filter } (U \circ V)\,T_2) \Downarrow H :: T_3 \tag{3.35}$$
$$T\,\mathcal{R}\,T_3. \tag{3.36}$$

By definition of map, for (3.35) to hold, it must be the case that there are terms H_4, T_4 with

$$\text{filter } (U \circ V)\,T_2 \Downarrow H_4 :: T_4 \tag{3.37}$$
$$H = V\,H_4 \quad \text{and} \quad T_3 = \text{map } V\,T_4. \tag{3.38}$$

Since we are assuming that $U\,H_1 \Downarrow$ false, by (3.33) we also have $(U \circ V)\,H_2 \Downarrow$ false. Then by (3.32) and (3.37), we have $\text{filter } (U \circ V)\,L \Downarrow H_4 :: T_4$ and hence

$$\text{map } V\,(\text{filter } (U \circ V)\,L) \Downarrow V\,H_4 :: (\text{map } V\,T_4).$$

So by (3.36) and (3.38)

$$\text{map } V\,(\text{filter } (U \circ V)\,L) \Downarrow H :: T_3 \ \& \ T\,\mathcal{R}\,T_3.$$

Thus the conclusion of the $n = m$ case of (3.28) holds with $T' = T_3$. $\square$

Exercises

Consider the following PCFL terms.

$$map \stackrel{\text{def}}{=} \text{fix}\, m \,.\, \lambda u \,.\, \lambda \ell \,.\, \text{case}\, \ell \,\text{of}\, \{\text{nil} \rightarrow \text{nil} \mid h :: t \rightarrow (u\, h) :: (m\, u\, t)\}$$

$$nats \stackrel{\text{def}}{=} \text{fix}\, \ell \,.\, \underline{0} :: map(\lambda x \,.\, x + \underline{1})\ell$$

$$from \stackrel{\text{def}}{=} \text{fix}\, f \,.\, \lambda x \,.\, \lambda y \,.\, x :: (f\, (x + y)\, y)$$

$$append \stackrel{\text{def}}{=} \text{fix}\, a \,.\, \lambda \ell \,.\, \lambda \ell' \,.\, \text{case}\, \ell \,\text{of}\, \{\text{nil} \rightarrow \ell' \mid h :: t \rightarrow h :: (a\, t\, \ell')\}$$

$$interleave \stackrel{\text{def}}{=} \text{fix}\, i \,.\, \lambda \ell \,.\, \lambda \ell' \,.\, \text{case}\, \ell \,\text{of}\, \{\text{nil} \rightarrow \ell' \mid h :: t \rightarrow h :: (i\, \ell'\, t)\}$$

$$val \stackrel{\text{def}}{=} \lambda x \,.\, x :: \text{nil}$$

$$lift \stackrel{\text{def}}{=} \text{fix}\, f \,.\, \lambda u \,.\, \lambda \ell \,.\, \text{case}\, \ell \,\text{of}\, \{\text{nil} \rightarrow \text{nil} \mid h :: t \rightarrow append(u\, h)(f\, u\, t)\}$$

$$u \circ v \stackrel{\text{def}}{=} \lambda x \,.\, u\, (v\, x).$$

Prove the following contextual equivalences.

$$\emptyset \vdash nats \cong^{\text{gnd}}_{[int]} from\, \underline{0}\, \underline{1} \tag{3.39}$$

$$x : int \vdash from\, x\, \underline{1} \cong^{\text{gnd}}_{[int]} interleave\, (from\, x\, \underline{2})\, (from\, (x + 1)\, \underline{2}) \tag{3.40}$$

$$x : \tau, u : \tau \rightarrow [\tau'] \vdash lift\, u\, (val\, x) \cong^{\text{gnd}}_{[\tau']} f\, x \tag{3.41}$$

$$\ell : [\tau] \vdash lift\, val\, \ell \cong^{\text{gnd}}_{[\tau]} \ell \tag{3.42}$$

$$u : \tau \rightarrow [\tau'], v : \tau' \rightarrow [\tau''], \ell : [\tau] \vdash$$

$$lift\, ((lift\, v) \circ u)\, \ell \cong^{\text{gnd}}_{[\tau'']} lift\, v\, (lift\, u\, \ell) \tag{3.43}$$

These last three equivalences are respectively the β, η and associativity identities
for the Kleisli triple corresponding to the (strong) monad structure of lazy lists (see
Moggi 1991 and Wadler 1992). Prove (3.41) by applying Proposition 3.9. Prove
(3.42) and (3.43) by constructing suitable bisimulations. (3.43) is quite challenging: you will need to employ techniques like those in Example 3.14, involving an
induction over depths of proofs of evaluation, in order to verify the bisimulation
conditions. (See also Gordon 1995b, Section 4.5.)

4 Rational Completeness and Syntactic Continuity

In this section we prove that the PCFL contextual preorder $\leq^{\text{gnd}}$ satisfies the properties (2.29) and (2.30) mentioned at the end of section 2—namely that each fixpoint
term fix $x \,.\, F$ is the least upper bound with respect to $\leq^{\text{gnd}}$ of a canonically associated chain of approximations, and these least upper bounds are preserved by the
PCFL language constructs.

Although it is beyond the scope of these notes to pursue the topic, these properties form the basis for transferring various domain-theoretic verification techniques (such as the induction principle of Scott 1993, section 3) from the denotational semantics of a functional language to the language itself equipped with an operational semantics. Which is not to say that the denotational semantics of a language is without its uses. Indeed one way to establish (2.29) and (2.30) is via a computationally adequate denotational semantics of PCFL: cf. (Pitts 1994). Here we give a proof directly from the operational semantics of PCFL, as specified by the evaluation relation of Figure 3. Mason, Smith, and Talcott (1996) achieve similar results for an untyped, call-by-value functional language, making use of a one-step transition relation rather than an evaluation relation. The differences between the language treated in *loc. cit.* and the one used in these notes are not particularly relevant to the proof of the properties in question: the method given below could easily be adapted to untyped languages and/or ones with call-by-value function application. It can also be used to prove completeness and continuity properties for some of the variations on contextual preordering and similarity mentioned in section 5.

As in *loc. cit.*, the proof of (2.29) and (2.30) given here hinges upon a certain 'compactness' property of $\Downarrow$ with respect to fixpoint terms (Corollary 4.6). However, we deduce this compactness property from an apparently stronger property of evaluation, Proposition 4.5, which seems to be new. Unfortunately, it is beyond the scope of these notes to present further applications of Proposition 4.5.

Notational conventions. Throughout this section we will consider a particular fixpoint term $\mathsf{fix}\, x\,.\, F$, of type τ say, and use the following abbreviations.

$$F_0 \stackrel{\text{def}}{=} \mathsf{fix}^{(0)} x\,.\, F \stackrel{\text{def}}{=} \bot \stackrel{\text{def}}{=} \mathsf{fix}\, x\,.\, x$$

$$F_{n+1} \stackrel{\text{def}}{=} \mathsf{fix}^{(n+1)} x\,.\, F \stackrel{\text{def}}{=} F[F_n/x]$$

$$F_\omega \stackrel{\text{def}}{=} \mathsf{fix}\, x\,.\, F\ .$$

We will only consider PCFL contexts involving parameters of type τ. As usual, we write $\mathcal{M}[\vec{p}]$ to indicate such a context whose parameters are contained in the list $\vec{p} = p_1, \ldots, p_k$ of pairwise distinct parameters. Given a k-tuple $\vec{n} = (n_1, \ldots, n_k)$ of natural numbers then we will make the following abbreviations.

$$C[F_{\vec{n}}] \stackrel{\text{def}}{=} C[F_{n_1}, \ldots, F_{n_k}]$$

$$C[F_\omega] \stackrel{\text{def}}{=} C[F_\omega, \ldots, F_\omega]\ .$$

Finally, the length of a list $\vec{p}$ of parameters will be denoted by $|\vec{p}|$.

Definition 4.1. For each k, we partially order the set $\mathbb{N}^k$ of k-tuples of natural numbers componentwise from the usual ordering on $\mathbb{N}$:

$$\vec{n} \le \vec{n}' \stackrel{\text{def}}{\Leftrightarrow} (n_1 \le n_1' \ \& \ \ldots \ \& \ n_k \le n_k')\ .$$

A subset $I \subseteq \mathbf{N}^k$ is said to be **cofinal** in $\mathbf{N}^k$ if and only if for all $\vec{n} \in \mathbf{N}^k$ there is some $\vec{n}' \in I$ with $\vec{n} \leq \vec{n}'$. We will write $\mathcal{P}_{\text{cof}}(\mathbf{N}^k)$ for the set of all such cofinal subsets of $\mathbf{N}^k$.

Note that by induction on n using (2.27) and (2.11), one can prove

$$F_n \leq^{\text{gnd}} F_{n+1} : \tau \quad \text{and} \quad F_n \leq^{\text{gnd}} F_\omega : \tau$$

and hence that for each unary context $C[\mathsf{p}]$, there is a $\leq^{\text{gnd}}$-ascending chain

$$C[F_0] \leq^{\text{gnd}} C[F_1] \leq^{\text{gnd}} C[F_2] \leq^{\text{gnd}} \cdots$$

bounded above by $C[F_\omega]$. We aim to show that $C[F_\omega]$ is in fact the least upper bound of this chain. If that is the case, then note that more generally if C involves several parameters $\vec{\mathsf{p}}$, then for any cofinal subset $I \subseteq \mathbf{N}^{|\vec{\mathsf{p}}|}$, $C[F_\omega]$ will be the least upper bound of the set $\{C[F_{\vec{n}}] \mid \vec{n} \in I\}$. In fact it turns out to be convenient to prove this stronger least upper bound property directly and then deduce (2.30) (and hence also (2.29)) as a special case.

The following notion of evaluation is somewhat technical: its introduction is justified below by Proposition 4.5.

Definition 4.2 (Evaluation of contexts, mod F). Given PCFL contexts $\mathcal{M}[\vec{\mathsf{p}}]$ and $C[\vec{\mathsf{p}}']$, we write $\mathcal{M}[\vec{\mathsf{p}}] \Downarrow^F C[\vec{\mathsf{p}}']$ to mean that for all $I \in \mathcal{P}_{\text{cof}}(\mathbf{N}^{|\vec{\mathsf{p}}|})$

$$\{\vec{n}\vec{n}' \mid \vec{n} \in I \ \& \ \mathcal{M}[F_{\vec{n}}] \Downarrow C[F_{\vec{n}'}]\} \in \mathcal{P}_{\text{cof}}(\mathbf{N}^{|\vec{\mathsf{p}}|+|\vec{\mathsf{p}}'|}) \ .$$

Note that the relation $\mathcal{M}[\vec{\mathsf{p}}] \Downarrow^F C[\vec{\mathsf{p}}']$ is preserved under renaming the parameters $\vec{\mathsf{p}}$ and, independently, the parameters $\vec{\mathsf{p}}'$. As the following lemma shows, the relation is also preserved under addition or subtraction of extra parameters.

Lemma 4.3.

$$\mathcal{M}[\vec{\mathsf{p}}] \Downarrow^F C[\vec{\mathsf{p}}'] \Leftrightarrow \mathcal{M}[\vec{\mathsf{p}}\vec{\mathsf{q}}] \Downarrow^F C[\vec{\mathsf{p}}'\vec{\mathsf{q}}'] \ .$$

Proof. This property follows from the definition of $\Downarrow^F$ together with simple properties of cofinal subsets of $\mathbf{N}^k$. $\qquad\qquad\square$

Lemma 4.4. *The relation $\Downarrow^F$ satisfies the following analogues of the axioms and rules for PCFL evaluation given in Figure 3.*

   (i) If C is in canonical form (that is, a constant, lambda abstraction, pair, or cons expression), then $C[\vec{\mathsf{p}}] \Downarrow^F C[\vec{\mathsf{p}}]$.

   (ii) If $\mathcal{B}[\vec{\mathsf{p}}] \Downarrow^F \text{true}[\,] $ and $\mathcal{M}_1[\vec{\mathsf{p}}] \Downarrow^F C[\vec{\mathsf{p}}']$, then $(\text{if } \mathcal{B} \text{ then } \mathcal{M}_1 \text{ else } \mathcal{M}_2)[\vec{\mathsf{p}}] \Downarrow^F C[\vec{\mathsf{p}}']$.

   (iii) If $\mathcal{B}[\vec{\mathsf{p}}] \Downarrow^F \text{false}[\,]$ and $\mathcal{M}_2[\vec{\mathsf{p}}] \Downarrow^F C[\vec{\mathsf{p}}']$, then $(\text{if } \mathcal{B} \text{ then } \mathcal{M}_1 \text{ else } \mathcal{M}_2)[\vec{\mathsf{p}}] \Downarrow^F C[\vec{\mathsf{p}}']$.

   (iv) If $\mathcal{M}_i[\vec{\mathsf{p}}] \Downarrow^F \underline{n_i}[\,]$ for $i = 1, 2$, then $(\mathcal{M}_1 \, \text{op} \, \mathcal{M}_2)[\vec{\mathsf{p}}] \Downarrow^F \underline{c}[\,]$, where $c = n_1 \, \text{op} \, n_2$.

(v) If $\mathcal{F}[\bar{p}] \Downarrow^F (\lambda x . \mathcal{M})[\bar{p}']$ and $\mathcal{M}[\mathcal{A}/x][\bar{p}\bar{p}'] \Downarrow^F C[\bar{p}'']$, then $(\mathcal{F}\,\mathcal{A})[\bar{p}] \Downarrow^F C[\bar{p}'']$.

(vi) If $\mathcal{M}[\text{fix}\,x . \mathcal{M}/x][\bar{p}] \Downarrow^F C[\bar{p}']$, then $(\text{fix}\,x . \mathcal{M})[\bar{p}] \Downarrow^F C[\bar{p}']$.

(vii) If $\mathcal{P}[\bar{p}] \Downarrow^F \langle \mathcal{M}_1, \mathcal{M}_2 \rangle[\bar{p}']$ and $\mathcal{M}_1[\bar{p}'] \Downarrow^F C[\bar{p}'']$, then $\mathsf{fst}(\mathcal{P})[\bar{p}] \Downarrow^F C[\bar{p}'']$.

(viii) If $\mathcal{P}[\bar{p}] \Downarrow^F \langle \mathcal{M}_1, \mathcal{M}_2 \rangle[\bar{p}']$ and $\mathcal{M}_2[\bar{p}'] \Downarrow^F C[\bar{p}'']$, then $\mathsf{snd}(\mathcal{P})[\bar{p}] \Downarrow^F C[\bar{p}'']$.

(ix) If $\mathcal{L}[\bar{p}] \Downarrow^F \mathsf{nil}[\,]$ and $\mathcal{M}_1[\bar{p}] \Downarrow^F C[\bar{p}']$, then

$$(\text{case } \mathcal{L} \text{ of } \{\mathsf{nil} \to \mathcal{M}_1 \mid h :: t \to \mathcal{M}_2\})[\bar{p}] \Downarrow^F C[\bar{p}'].$$

(x) If $\mathcal{L}[\bar{p}] \Downarrow^F (\mathcal{H} :: \mathcal{T})[\bar{p}']$ and $\mathcal{M}_2[\mathcal{H}/h, \mathcal{T}/t][\bar{p}\bar{p}'] \Downarrow^F C[\bar{p}'']$, then

$$(\text{case } \mathcal{L} \text{ of } \{\mathsf{nil} \to \mathcal{M}_1 \mid h :: t \to \mathcal{M}_2\})[\bar{p}] \Downarrow^F C[\bar{p}''].$$

Proof. Each property follows from combining the corresponding evaluation rule in Figure 3 with the definition of $\Downarrow^F$. We give the argument for the last case (x), and leave the others as exercises for the reader. So suppose

$$\mathcal{L}[\bar{p}] \Downarrow^F (\mathcal{H} :: \mathcal{T})[\bar{p}'] \tag{4.1}$$

$$\mathcal{M}_2[\mathcal{H}/h, \mathcal{T}/t][\bar{p}\bar{p}'] \Downarrow^F C[\bar{p}''] \tag{4.2}$$

In order to verify that $(\text{case } \mathcal{L} \text{ of } \{\mathsf{nil} \to \mathcal{M}_1 \mid h :: t \to \mathcal{M}_2\})[\bar{p}] \Downarrow^F C[\bar{p}'']$, we have to show for any $I \in \mathcal{P}_{\text{cof}}(\mathbb{N}^{|\bar{p}|})$ that

$$\{\vec{n}\vec{n}'' \mid \vec{n} \in I\ \&\ (\text{case } \mathcal{L} \text{ of } \{\mathsf{nil} \to \mathcal{M}_1 \mid h :: t \to \mathcal{M}_2\})[F_{\vec{n}}] \Downarrow C[F_{\vec{n}''}]\} \tag{4.3}$$

is a cofinal subset of $\mathbb{N}^{|\bar{p}|+|\bar{p}''|}$. But given such an I, by (4.1)

$$I' \stackrel{\text{def}}{=} \{\vec{n}\vec{n}' \mid \vec{n} \in I\ \&\ \mathcal{L}[F_{\vec{n}}] \Downarrow (\mathcal{H} :: \mathcal{T})[F_{\vec{n}'}]\}$$

is a cofinal subset of $\mathbb{N}^{|\bar{p}|+|\bar{p}'|}$. Then by (4.2) applied to I'

$$I'' \stackrel{\text{def}}{=} \{\vec{n}\vec{n}'\vec{n}'' \mid \vec{n}\vec{n}' \in I'\ \&\ \mathcal{M}_2[\mathcal{H}/h, \mathcal{T}/t][F_{\vec{n}\vec{n}'}] \Downarrow C[F_{\vec{n}''}]\}$$

is a cofinal subset of $\mathbb{N}^{|\bar{p}|+|\bar{p}'|+|\bar{p}''|}$ and hence

$$I''' \stackrel{\text{def}}{=} \{\vec{n}\vec{n}'' \mid \exists \vec{n}'\, (\vec{n}\vec{n}'\vec{n}'' \in I'')\}$$

is a cofinal subset of $\mathbb{N}^{|\bar{p}|+|\bar{p}''|}$.

Now if $\vec{n}\vec{n}'' \in I'''$, then $\vec{n} \in I$ and for some $\vec{n}'$ it is the case that

$$\mathcal{L}[F_{\vec{n}}] \Downarrow (\mathcal{H} :: \mathcal{T})[F_{\vec{n}'}] = \mathcal{H}[F_{\vec{n}'}] :: \mathcal{T}[F_{\vec{n}'}]$$

$$\mathcal{M}_2[F_{\vec{n}}][\mathcal{H}[F_{\vec{n}'}]/h, \mathcal{T}[F_{\vec{n}'}]/t] = \mathcal{M}_2[\mathcal{H}/h, \mathcal{T}/t][F_{\vec{n}\vec{n}'}] \Downarrow C[F_{\vec{n}''}]$$

and hence by ($\Downarrow$ case2)

$$(\text{case } \mathcal{L} \text{ of } \{\mathsf{nil} \to \mathcal{M}_1 \mid h :: t \to \mathcal{M}_2\})[F_{\vec{n}}] \Downarrow C[F_{\vec{n}''}].$$

Thus (4.3) contains I''' and hence is also a cofinal subset of $\mathbb{N}^{|\bar{p}|+|\bar{p}''|}$, as required. $\square$

Proposition 4.5. *For all PCFL contexts* $\mathcal{M}[\vec{p}]$, *if* $\mathcal{M}[F_\omega]\Downarrow C$ *then there is a context* $C[\vec{p}']$ *with* $C = C[F_\omega]$ *and* $\mathcal{M}[\vec{p}] \Downarrow^F C[\vec{p}']$.

Proof. The proof is by induction on the derivation of $\mathcal{M}[F_\omega] \Downarrow C$. More precisely, we show that

$$\mathcal{E} \stackrel{\text{def}}{=} \{(M, C) \mid \forall \mathcal{M}[\vec{p}]\, (M = \mathcal{M}[F_\omega] \Rightarrow \exists C[\vec{p}']\, (C = C[F_\omega]\ \&\ \mathcal{M}[\vec{p}] \Downarrow^F C[\vec{p}']))\}$$

is closed under the axioms and rules of Figure 3 inductively defining $\Downarrow$.

Case ($\Downarrow$ can). Since F_ω is not in canonical form, if C is a closed term in canonical form and $C = C[F_\omega]$, then the context C must itself be in canonical form, and hence $C[\vec{p}] \Downarrow^F C[\vec{p}]$ by Lemma 4.4(i). Hence $(C, C) \in \mathcal{E}$ for any closed canonical C.

Case ($\Downarrow$ fix). Suppose that $(M[\text{fix}\,x\,.\,M/x], C)$ is an element of $\mathcal{E}$; we wish to show that $(\text{fix}\,x\,.\,M, C)$ is too. So suppose

$$\text{fix}\,x\,.\,M = \mathcal{M}[F_\omega] \qquad (4.4)$$

for some context $\mathcal{M}[\vec{p}]$. We have to find $C[\vec{p}']$ such that $C = C[F_\omega]$ and $\mathcal{M}[\vec{p}] \Downarrow^F C[\vec{p}']$. For (4.4) to hold it must be the case that either

(A) $\mathcal{M} = \mathsf{p}_i$ is one of the parameters in $\vec{p}$ and $\text{fix}\,x\,.\,M = F_\omega(= \text{fix}\,x\,.\,F)$—without loss of generality we may assume that $M = F$;

or

(B) $\mathcal{M}$ is of the form $\text{fix}\,x\,.\,\mathcal{M}'[\vec{p}]$ and $M = \mathcal{M}'[F_\omega]$.

We consider each case in turn.

(A). Let $\mathcal{N}[\mathsf{p}]$ be the context $F[\mathsf{p}/x]$. Thus $\mathcal{N}[F_\omega] = F[F_\omega/x] = M[\text{fix}\,x\,.\,M/x]$. Then since by the induction hypothesis $(M[\text{fix}\,x\,.\,M/x], C) \in \mathcal{E}$, there is some context $C[\vec{p}']$ with

$$C = C[F_\omega] \qquad (4.5)$$
$$\mathcal{N}[\mathsf{p}] \Downarrow^F C[\vec{p}'] \qquad (4.6)$$

In view of (4.5), to complete this case it suffices to show that $\mathcal{M}[\vec{p}] \Downarrow^F C[\vec{p}']$. Since $\mathcal{M} = \mathsf{p}_i$, by Lemma 4.3 this is equivalent to showing that $\mathsf{p}[\mathsf{p}] \Downarrow^F C[\vec{p}']$. So for each $I \in \mathcal{P}_{\text{cof}}(\mathbf{N})$ we have to show that

$$\{n\vec{n}' \mid n \in I\ \&\ F_n \Downarrow C[F_{\vec{n}'}]\} \qquad (4.7)$$

is a cofinal subset of $\mathbf{N}^{1+|\vec{p}'|}$. But if I is cofinal in $\mathbf{N}$, so is

$$J \stackrel{\text{def}}{=} \{n \mid n+1 \in I\}$$

and hence from (4.6)

$$J' \stackrel{\text{def}}{=} \{n\vec{n}' \mid n \in J \,\&\, \mathcal{N}[F_n] \Downarrow C[F_{\vec{n}'}]\}$$

is a cofinal subset of $\mathbf{N}^{1+|\vec{p}'|}$. But if $n\vec{n}' \in J'$ then $n+1 \in I$ and

$$\mathcal{N}[F_n] = F[F_n/x] \qquad \text{by definition of } \mathcal{N}$$
$$= F_{n+1} \qquad \text{by definition of } F_{n+1}.$$

Thus if $n\vec{n}' \in J'$ then $(n+1)\vec{n}'$ is an element of (4.7). Since J' is cofinal, it follows that (4.7) is as well. This completes the induction step in case (A).

(B). By assumption, $M[\text{fix } x . M/x] = \mathcal{M}'[\text{fix } x . \mathcal{M}'/x][F_\omega]$. Then by the induction hypothesis $(M[\text{fix } x . M/x], C) \in \mathcal{E}$, there is some context $C[\vec{p}']$ with

$$C = C[F_\omega]$$
$$\mathcal{M}'[\text{fix } x . \mathcal{M}'/x][\vec{p}] \Downarrow C[\vec{p}']$$

and hence by Lemma 4.4(vi)

$$\mathcal{M}[\vec{p}] = \text{fix } x . \mathcal{M}'[\vec{p}] \Downarrow C[\vec{p}'].$$

This completes the induction step in case (B).

Thus in either case we have $(\text{fix } x . M, C) \in \mathcal{E}$, and so we have completed the induction step for case ($\Downarrow$ fix).

Case ($\Downarrow$ cond1). Suppose that (B, true) and (M_1, C) are both elements of $\mathcal{E}$. We have to show that $(\text{if } B \text{ then } M_1 \text{ else } M_2, C) \in \mathcal{E}$. So suppose

$$\text{if } B \text{ then } M_1 \text{ else } M_2 = \mathcal{M}[F_\omega] \tag{4.8}$$

for some context $\mathcal{M}[\vec{p}]$. We have to find $C[\vec{p}']$ such that $C = C[F_\omega]$ and $\mathcal{M}[\vec{p}] \Downarrow^F C[\vec{p}']$.

For (4.8) to hold it must be the case that $\mathcal{M} = \text{if } \mathcal{B} \text{ then } \mathcal{M}_1 \text{ else } \mathcal{M}_2$ for some contexts $\mathcal{B}$, and $\mathcal{M}_i$ $(i = 1, 2)$ satisfying

$$B = \mathcal{B}[F_\omega] \tag{4.9}$$
$$M_i = \mathcal{M}_i[F_\omega] \quad (i = 1, 2) \tag{4.10}$$

Since $(B, \text{true}) \in \mathcal{E}$, (4.9) implies that there is some context $C_1[\vec{p}_1]$ with

$$\text{true} = C_1[F_\omega] \tag{4.11}$$
$$\mathcal{B}[\vec{p}] \Downarrow^F C_1[\vec{p}_1] \tag{4.12}$$

Now (4.11) can only hold because C_1 = true, in which case from (4.12) and Lemma 4.3 we conclude that

$$\mathcal{B}[\vec{p}] \Downarrow^F \text{true}[\,] \tag{4.13}$$

Since $(M_1, C) \in \mathcal{E}$, (4.10) implies that there is some context $C[\vec{p}']$ with

$$C = C[F_\omega] \tag{4.14}$$

$$\mathcal{M}_1[\vec{p}] \Downarrow^F C[\vec{p}']. \tag{4.15}$$

Applying Lemma 4.4(ii) to (4.13) and (4.15) yields

$$\mathcal{M}[\vec{p}] = (\text{if } \mathcal{B} \text{ then } \mathcal{M}_1 \text{ else } \mathcal{M}_2)[\vec{p}] \Downarrow^F C[\vec{p}']$$

which together with (4.14) is the desired conclusion.

Remaining cases: they are all similar to the previous case, using the appropriate clause of Lemma 4.4 in each case. $\qquad\square$

Corollary 4.6 (A 'compactness' property of evaluation). *For any PCFL context* $\mathcal{M}[p]$ *of ground type, if* $\mathcal{M}[\text{fix}\, x\,.\, F] \Downarrow \underline{c}$, *then* $\mathcal{M}[\text{fix}^{(n)} x\,.\, F] \Downarrow \underline{c}$ *for some* $n \in \mathbb{N}$.

Proof. Suppose $\mathcal{M}[F_\omega] \Downarrow \underline{c}$. Then by the previous proposition there is a context $C[\vec{p}']$ such that $\mathcal{M}[p] \Downarrow^F C[\vec{p}']$ and $C[F_\omega] = \underline{c}$. The latter equation can only hold because $C = \underline{c}$, and hence (using Lemma 4.3) we have $\mathcal{M}[p] \Downarrow^F \underline{c}[\,]$. Taking $I = \mathbb{N}$ in the definition of $\Downarrow^F$, this means that $\{n \mid \mathcal{M}[F_n] \Downarrow \underline{c}\}$ is a cofinal subset of $\mathbb{N}$. So in particular it is a non-empty subset, that is, there is some $n \in \mathbb{N}$ with $\mathcal{M}[F_n] \Downarrow \underline{c}$, as required. $\qquad\square$

We can now complete the proof of the rational completeness (2.29) and syntactic continuity property (2.30) of the PCFL contextual preorder.

Theorem 4.7. *For any fixpoint term* fix $x\,.\, F \in Exp_\tau$, *define the terms* $\text{fix}^{(n)} x\,.\, F \in Exp_\tau$ $(n \in \mathbb{N})$ *by*

$$\text{fix}^{(0)} x\,.\, F \stackrel{\text{def}}{=} \bot \stackrel{\text{def}}{=} \text{fix}\, x\,.\, x$$

$$\text{fix}^{(n+1)} x\,.\, F \stackrel{\text{def}}{=} F[\text{fix}^{(n)} x\,.\, F/x].$$

Then for any type σ, *context* $C[-_\tau] \in Ctx_\sigma$, *and term* $M \in Exp_\sigma$

$$C[\text{fix}\, x\,.\, F] \leq^{\text{gnd}} M : \sigma \Leftrightarrow \forall n \in \mathbb{N}\, (C[\text{fix}^{(n)} x\,.\, F] \leq^{\text{gnd}} M : \sigma).$$

Proof. We mentioned at the beginning of this section that property (2.27) of $\perp$ combined with the precongruence property of $\leq^{\text{gnd}}$ imply that $\text{fix}^{(n)}x \, . \, F \leq^{\text{gnd}}$ $\text{fix} \, x \, . \, F \; : \; \tau$ and hence that $\mathcal{C}[\text{fix}^{(n)}x \, . \, F] \leq^{\text{gnd}} \mathcal{C}[\text{fix} \, x \, . \, F] \; : \; \sigma$. The $\Rightarrow$ direction of the theorem follows from this by transitivity of $\leq^{\text{gnd}}$.

Conversely, suppose $\mathcal{C}[\text{fix}^{(n)}x \, . \, F] \leq^{\text{gnd}} M : \sigma$ holds for all $n \in \mathbb{N}$. We wish to show that $\mathcal{C}[\text{fix} \, x \, . \, F] \leq^{\text{gnd}} M : \sigma$, that is, for any context $\mathcal{N}[-]$ of ground type and any constant $\underline{c}$, if $\mathcal{N}[\mathcal{C}[\text{fix} \, x \, . \, F]] \Downarrow \underline{c}$ then $\mathcal{N}[\mathcal{C}[M]] \Downarrow \underline{c}$. But if $\mathcal{N}[\mathcal{C}[\text{fix} \, x \, . \, F]] \Downarrow \underline{c}$, then by Corollary 4.6 applied to the context $\mathcal{N}[\mathcal{C}[-]]$, there is some $n \in \mathbb{N}$ with $\mathcal{N}[\mathcal{C}[\text{fix}^{(n)}x \, . \, F]] \Downarrow \underline{c}$. Since $\mathcal{C}[\text{fix}^{(n)}x \, . \, F] \leq^{\text{gnd}} M : \sigma$, it follows that $\mathcal{N}[M] \Downarrow \underline{c}$, as required. $\qquad\qquad\qquad\qquad\qquad\qquad\qquad\qquad\qquad\qquad\qquad\qquad\qquad\qquad\qquad\square$

Exercise 4.8. In view of the Operational Extensionality Theorem 3.8, we could have stated the above theorem using PCFL similarity, $\precsim$, rather than $\leq^{\text{gnd}}$. Give a direct proof that $\precsim$ satisfies the rational completeness and syntactic continuity properties by proving that $\mathcal{S} \in Rel$ is a PCFL simulation, where for each type σ we define

$$\mathcal{S}_\sigma \stackrel{\text{def}}{=} \{(M, M') \mid \exists \mathcal{M}[\vec{p}] \in Ctx_\sigma, I \in \mathcal{P}_{\text{cof}}(\mathbb{N}^{|\vec{p}|}) \, (M = \mathcal{M}[F_\omega] \, \& \\ \forall \vec{n} \in I \, (\mathcal{M}[F_{\vec{n}}] \precsim_\sigma M'))\}.$$

Exercise 4.9. Prove the following converse of Proposition 4.5, by induction on the derivation of $\mathcal{M}[F_{\vec{n}}] \Downarrow C$:

For all contexts $\mathcal{M}[\vec{p}]$ and all $\vec{n} \in \mathbb{N}^{|\vec{p}|}$, if $\mathcal{M}[F_{\vec{n}}] \Downarrow C$ then there is some canonical context $C[\vec{p}']$ and some $\vec{n}' \in \mathbb{N}^{|\vec{p}'|}$ with $C = \mathcal{C}[F_{\vec{n}'}]$ and $\mathcal{M}[F_\omega] \Downarrow \mathcal{C}[F_\omega]$.

5 Further Directions

In this section we discuss, very briefly and without going into details, the extent to which the co-inductive characterisation of PCFL contextual equivalence in terms of bisimilarity is stable with respect to change of program equivalence, or of programming language.

'Lazy' contextual equivalence

As the name suggests, the definition of PCFL ground contextual equivalence (Definition 2.9) involves observing convergence of evaluation only in contexts of *ground* type. A strictly finer notion of contextual equivalence is obtained if we relax this condition and observe convergence at any type.

$$\Gamma \vdash M \cong^{\text{lazy}} M' : \sigma \stackrel{\text{def}}{\Leftrightarrow} \forall \tau, \mathcal{C}[-_\sigma] \in Ctx_\tau \, (\mathcal{C}[M]\Downarrow \Leftrightarrow \mathcal{C}[M']\Downarrow)$$

where by $M\!\Downarrow$ we mean $\exists C\,(M \Downarrow C)$. Clearly

$$\Gamma \vdash M \cong^{\text{lazy}} M' : \sigma \Rightarrow \Gamma \vdash M \cong^{\text{gnd}} M' : \sigma.$$

However, the converse does not hold. For example we have

$$\lambda x\,.\,\bot \cong^{\text{gnd}} \bot : \sigma \to \sigma' \qquad (5.1)$$

by (2.21); but $\lambda x\,.\,\bot \not\cong^{\text{lazy}} \bot : \sigma \to \sigma'$, because the left-hand side does evaluate whereas the right-hand side does not. Similarly,

$$\langle \bot, \bot \rangle \cong^{\text{gnd}} \bot : \sigma \times \sigma' \qquad (5.2)$$

holds by (2.21), whereas $\langle \bot, \bot \rangle \not\cong^{\text{lazy}} \bot : \sigma \times \sigma'$.

It is possible to modify the notion of bisimulation to get a co-inductive characterisation of $\cong^{\text{lazy}}$.

Theorem 5.1. *Let $\simeq'$ be the greatest element of Rel satisfying conditions* (bis 1a), (bis 1b), (bis 2a), (bis 2b), (bis 5a), (bis 5b), (bis 6a), *and* (bis 6b) *from Figure 5 together with the following conditions at function and product types:*

$$(F\,\mathcal{B}_{\sigma \to \sigma'}\,F' \,\&\, F \Downarrow \lambda x\,.\,M) \Rightarrow \qquad \text{(bis 3a)}$$
$$\exists \lambda x\,.\,M'\,(F' \Downarrow \lambda x\,.\,M' \,\&\, \forall A \in Exp_\sigma\,(M[A/x]\,\mathcal{B}_{\sigma'}\,M'[A/x]))$$

$$(F\,\mathcal{B}_{\sigma \to \sigma'}\,F' \,\&\, F' \Downarrow \lambda x\,.\,M') \Rightarrow \qquad \text{(bis 3b)}$$
$$\exists \lambda x\,.\,M\,(F \Downarrow \lambda x\,.\,M \,\&\, \forall A \in Exp_\sigma\,(M[A/x]\,\mathcal{B}_{\sigma'}\,M'[A/x]))$$

$$(P\,\mathcal{B}_{\sigma \times \sigma'}\,P' \,\&\, P \Downarrow \langle M_1, M_2 \rangle) \Rightarrow \qquad \text{(bis 4a)}$$
$$\exists M_1', M_2'\,(P' \Downarrow \langle M_1', M_2' \rangle \,\&\, M_1\,\mathcal{B}_\sigma\,M_1' \,\&\, M_2\,\mathcal{B}_{\sigma'}\,M_2')$$

$$(P\,\mathcal{B}_{\sigma \times \sigma'}\,P' \,\&\, P' \Downarrow \langle M_1', M_2' \rangle) \Rightarrow \qquad \text{(bis 4b)}$$
$$\exists M_1, M_2\,(P \Downarrow \langle M_1, M_2 \rangle \,\&\, M_1\,\mathcal{B}_\sigma\,M_1' \,\&\, M_2\,\mathcal{B}_{\sigma'}\,M_2').$$

Defining $\simeq'^\circ$ from $\simeq$ as in Definition 3.7, then

$$\Gamma \vdash M \cong^{\text{lazy}} M' : \sigma \Leftrightarrow \Gamma \vdash M \simeq'^\circ M'.$$

The relation $\simeq'$ is a version for PCFL of Abramsky's notion of **applicative bisimulation** which he developed in his work with Ong on the untyped, 'lazy' lambda calculus (Abramsky 1990; Abramsky and Ong 1993). The above theorem can be proved using the operationally-based methods developed by Howe (1989, Howe (1996) and which we employ in the Appendix. to prove the coincidence of $\cong^{\text{gnd}}$ and $\simeq$.

Convergence testing

The η-rule (2.24) and the surjective pairing property (2.25) say that every closed PCFL term of function or product type is ground contextually equivalent to a term in canonical form. This is the essential difference between $\cong^{\text{gnd}}$ and $\cong^{\text{lazy}}$, and we can remove it by augmenting PCFL syntax with term-formers for testing convergence to canonical form at such types. Consider the extension of PCFL whose terms are given by the grammar of Figure 1 extended as follows:

$$M ::= \cdots \mid \text{ispr}(M) \mid \text{isfn}(M).$$

The type assignment and evaluation rules for ispr and isfn are:

$$\frac{\Gamma \vdash P : \sigma \times \sigma'}{\Gamma \vdash \text{ispr}(P) : bool} \qquad \frac{\Gamma \vdash F : \sigma \to \sigma'}{\Gamma \vdash \text{isfn}(P) : bool}$$

$$\frac{P \Downarrow \langle M_1, M_2 \rangle}{\text{ispr}(P) \Downarrow \text{true}} \qquad \frac{F \Downarrow \lambda x . M}{\text{isfn}(F) \Downarrow \text{true}}.$$

Then Theorem 5.1 continues to hold, but now it is the case that $\cong^{\text{lazy}}$ coincides with our original notion of ground contextual equivalence, $\cong^{\text{gnd}}$.

Note. Analogous convergence testers for ground and list types already exist in PCFL, namely

$$isbool[-_{bool}] \stackrel{\text{def}}{=} \text{if } -_{bool} \text{ then true else true}$$

$$isint[-_{int}] \stackrel{\text{def}}{=} \text{if } -_{int} = 0 \text{ then true else true}$$

$$islist[-_{[\sigma]}] \stackrel{\text{def}}{=} \text{case } -_{[\sigma]} \text{ of } \{\text{nil} \to \text{true} \mid h :: t \to \text{true}\}.$$

An alternative way to alter PCFL to make $\cong^{\text{lazy}}$ and $\cong^{\text{gnd}}$ coincide (while still retaining the validity of Theorem 5.1) is to use the elimination forms for product and function types which correspond systematically to their introduction forms of pairing and function abstraction respectively. (See Martin-Löf 1984, Preface; and the 'do-it-yourself' type theory of Backhouse, Chisholm, Malcolm, and Saaman 1989.)

For product types the eliminator takes the form

$$\text{split } P \text{ as } \langle x_1, x_2 \rangle \text{ in } E$$

with free occurrences of x_1 and x_2 in E bound in the elimination term. Its typing and evaluation rules are as follows.

$$\frac{\Gamma \vdash P : \sigma_1 \times \sigma_2 \qquad \Gamma, x_1 : \sigma_1, x_2 : \sigma_2 \vdash E : \sigma}{\Gamma \vdash \text{split } P \text{ as } \langle x_1, x_2 \rangle \text{ in } E : \sigma}$$

$$\frac{P \Downarrow \langle M_1, M_2 \rangle \qquad E[M_1/x_1, M_2/x_2] \Downarrow C}{\text{split } P \text{ as } \langle x_1, x_2 \rangle \text{ in } E \Downarrow C}$$

The projections fst and snd, and the convergence tester ispr are all definable from it:

$$p : \sigma_1 \times \sigma_2 \vdash \text{fst}(p) \cong^{\text{lazy}} \text{split } p \text{ as } \langle x_1, x_2 \rangle \text{ in } x_1 : \sigma_1$$

$$p : \sigma_1 \times \sigma_2 \vdash \text{snd}(p) \cong^{\text{lazy}} \text{split } p \text{ as } \langle x_1, x_2 \rangle \text{ in } x_2 : \sigma_2$$

$$p : \sigma_1 \times \sigma_2 \vdash \text{ispr}(p) \cong^{\text{lazy}} \text{split } p \text{ as } \langle x_1, x_2 \rangle \text{ in true} : bool$$

For function types, the systematic eliminator involves some extra syntactic complications. It is probably for this reason that it is less well-known in functional programming than in Type Theory. It takes the form

$$\text{funsplit } F \text{ as } \lambda x \,.\, \xi(x) \text{ in } E$$

where ξ belongs to a new syntactic category of **function variables**. Free occurrences of ξ in E are bound in the elimination term and x is a bound variable (really it is just a dummy variable to make the syntax more readable). The typing and evaluation rules for the function eliminator are as follows.

$$\frac{\Gamma \vdash F : \sigma_1 \to \sigma_2 \qquad \Gamma, \xi(\sigma_1) : \sigma_2 \vdash E : \sigma}{\Gamma \vdash \text{funsplit } F \text{ as } \lambda x \,.\, \xi(x) \text{ in } E : \sigma}$$

$$\frac{F \Downarrow \lambda x \,.\, M \qquad E[(x)M/\xi] \Downarrow C}{\text{funsplit } P \text{ as } \lambda x \,.\, \xi(x) \text{ in } E \Downarrow C}$$

The typing rule makes use of extended typing assumptions to the left of $\vdash$ that involve assigning 'arities' to function variables. For example, in the rule above $\xi(\sigma_1) : \sigma_2$ is an assumption that ξ is a unary function variable which applies to terms of type σ_1 to yield terms of type σ_2. The evaluation rule makes use of an extended notion of substitution, namely that of substituting a 'meta-abstraction' $(x)M$ for a function variable ξ in a term E: we leave its definition to the imagination of the reader. Function application and the convergence tester for function types are definable using the function eliminator:

$$f : \sigma_1 \to \sigma_2, a : \sigma_1 \vdash f\,a \cong^{\text{lazy}} \text{funsplit } f \text{ as } \lambda x \,.\, \xi(x) \text{ in } \xi(a) : \sigma_2$$

$$f : \sigma_1 \to \sigma_2 \vdash \text{isfn}(f) \cong^{\text{lazy}} \text{funsplit } f \text{ as } \lambda x \,.\, \xi(x) \text{ in true} : bool$$

Note. The systematically derived eliminator for list types is the case expression which we built into the original syntax of PCFL. We have been discussing how to augment the syntax of PCFL to make convergence at compound types more observable. Going in the opposite direction, it is possible to remove observability of convergence at list types, without reducing expressive power, by replacing the case expression by $\text{head}(L)$ and $\text{tail}(L)$ expressions, together with a semi-decision test for emptiness $\text{isnil}(L)$ (which is boolean-valued[2] and diverges unless $L \Downarrow \text{nil}$). The properties of $\cong^{\text{gnd}}$ are altered thereby—for example, an 'η-rule' for lists becomes valid:

$$L \cong^{\text{gnd}} \text{nil} : [\sigma] \quad \lor \quad \exists H, T \, (L \cong^{\text{gnd}} H :: T : [\sigma]).$$

In order to retain the validity of the Operational Extensionality Theorem 3.8, one has to change the notion of bisimilarity by replacing conditions (bis 5a), (bis 5b), (bis 6a), and (bis 6b) by one analogous to that for product types:

$$L \, \mathcal{B}_{[\sigma]} \, L' \Rightarrow$$
$$\text{isnil}(L) \, \mathcal{B}_{bool} \, \text{isnil}(L') \; \& \; \text{head}(L) \, \mathcal{B}_\sigma \, \text{head}(L') \; \& \; \text{tail}(L) \, \mathcal{B}_{[\sigma]} \, \text{tail}(L').$$

---

[2] Really $\text{isnil}(L)$ should be of unit type, but we did not include a unit type in PCFL.

Strict function application

The rule ($\Downarrow$ app) in Figure 3 describes **non-strict**, or **call-by-name** function application. The **strict**, or **call-by-value** rule is

$$\frac{F \Downarrow \lambda x . M \qquad A \Downarrow C \qquad M[C/x] \Downarrow D}{F A \Downarrow D}$$

If one alters the notion of evaluation by replacing ($\Downarrow$ app) by this rule, then of course the properties of $\cong^{gnd}$ change. The Operational Extensionality Theorem can be retained provided one alters the notion of bisimilarity at function types appropriately, by using conditions (bis 3a) and (bis 3b) given above with the universal quantification which occurs in them restricted to range over closed terms in *canonical form*. The proof of this and other operationally-based properties for strict functional languages can be developed along the lines indicated in these notes by systematically restricting the use of substitution of terms to substitution of terms in canonical form.[3] In other words, one carries along the idea that variables in strict languages implicitly range over values (that is, canonical forms). See also (Egidi, Honsell, and della Rocca 1992).

Recursive types, polymorphic types, no types

We built only one kind of recursive data—lazy lists—into our example language PCFL, because it is sufficient to illustrate some of the complications which such a feature introduces. An important complication is that in going from a simply typed language like PCF to ones with more complex type systems, one may loose the ability to define a notion of interest (such as some extensional notion of program equivalence, for example) by induction on the structure of the types. The co-inductive techniques used to prove the Operational Extensionality Theorem 3.8 for PCFL were originally developed for untyped languages. We have seen how they adapt to one simple form of recursive data, and in fact they extend very easily to give similar results for languages with general forms of recursively defined type. See Gordon (1995a, 1996), for example. As Rees (1994) shows, they can also be used to give operational extensionality results for languages with polymorphic types.

Languages with state

One can extend the methods described in this article to lambda-calculus based imperative programming languages—such as Idealised Algol (Reynolds 1981), Scheme (Abelson and Susman 1985), or Standard ML (Milner, Tofte, and Harper 1990). For work based directly on contextual equivalence for a Scheme-like language, see (Mason and Talcott 1991; Mason and Talcott 1992). For work employing various notions of bisimilarity and operationally-based logical relations applied

---

[3] so one should replace fixpoint terms by recursive *function* terms in a strict version of PCFL.

to ML- and Algol-like languages, see (Pitts and Stark 1993; Ritter and Pitts 1995; Stark 1995; Pitts 1996; Crole and Gordon 1996).

Concerning the status of Operational Extensionality theorems for functional languages with state, the situation is as follows. With some simplifying assumptions, an evaluation relation for such languages can take the general form

$$s, M \Downarrow s', C$$

where s is a state, M an expression to be evaluated, C the canonical form resulting from evaluation, and s' the state which results from the evaluation. A state might give the current values (which may well be complicated objects, such as closures, in the case of Scheme or Standard ML) of some storage locations, for example. If the language is such that it can be given an operational semantics in which the shape (the number of locations, say) of the final state s' is always the same as that of the initial state s, then it seems that a co-inductive characterisation of contextual equivalence can usually be given. This is the case if the language has global variables, but no constructs for locally declared state. Less trivially, it is also the case for 'block-structured' languages, such as Algol. On the other hand, languages like Standard ML, which involve dynamically created references, certainly do not have this nice property that the 'state shape' does not grow under evaluation. Accordingly, for Standard ML there are various notions of bisimilarity known which are congruences for the language and (hence) are contained in contextual equivalence, but so far none is known which actually coincides with contextual equivalence.

Refined notions of bisimulation

One very important topic has not been treated in these notes—namely the development of various refinements of the notion of bisimulation (such as 'bisimulation-up-to-bisimilarity') which can make the job of establishing specific instances of applicative bisimilarity much easier. This topic is addressed in (Gordon 1995b, section 4), to which the reader is referred.

A Proof of the Operational Extensionality Theorem

This appendix is devoted to the proof of Theorem 3.8, which says that the PCFL ground contextual preorder (Definition 2.9) coincides with the open extension of PCFL similarity (Definition 3.3). The proof will be split into two parts:

(a) Proof that the open extension $\preceq^{\circ}$ of similarity (Definition 3.7) is a PCFL precongruence.

(b) Proof that the ground contextual preorder $\leq^{\text{gnd}}$, when restricted to closed terms, is a PCFL simulation.

For part (a) we employ an adaptation of a method due to Howe (1989, Howe (1996). From part (a) we show that one can easily deduce that $\Gamma \vdash M \preceq^{\circ}_{\sigma} M'$ implies $\Gamma \vdash M \leq^{\mathrm{gnd}}_{\sigma} M'$, and part (b) gives the converse.

Congruence properties of similarity

Roughly speaking, a PCFL congruence is a binary relation between (open) terms which respects the usual laws of equational reasoning. Thus the relation should be an equivalence relation which is preserved by the operation of substituting a term for a parameter in a context. When dealing with typed terms (as we are) it is natural to restrict to relations which only relate terms of the same type. Since typing takes place in the presence of an assignment of types to free variables, we include some 'structural' properties (such as weakening and preservation under the operation of substituting terms for free variables) in the definition of congruence. Also, since we are interested in properties of the contextual preorder, we place the emphasis on the notion of 'precongruence'—which is a congruence minus the symmetry property. The following definition formulates the notion of PCFL precongruence solely with PCFL terms, rather than with PCFL contexts. The lemma which follows it gives the precise sense in which a precongruence respects the operation of substitution into contexts.

Suppose $\mathcal{R}$ is family of binary relations $\mathcal{R}_{\Gamma,\sigma} \subseteq Exp_{\sigma}(\Gamma) \times Exp_{\sigma}(\Gamma)$, indexed by variable typings Γ and types σ. As usual, we will write $\Gamma \vdash M\,\mathcal{R}_{\sigma}\,M'$ to indicate that a pair of terms (M, M') is in the relation $\mathcal{R}_{\Gamma,\sigma}$.

Definition A.1. $\mathcal{R}$ is a **PCFL precongruence relation** if it has the following properties.

$$(\Gamma \vdash M\,\mathcal{R}_{\sigma}\,M' \,\&\, \Gamma \subseteq \Gamma') \Rightarrow \Gamma' \vdash M\,\mathcal{R}_{\sigma}\,M' \tag{A.1}$$

$$(\Gamma \vdash M : \sigma \,\&\, \Gamma, x : \sigma \vdash N\,\mathcal{R}_{\sigma'}\,N') \Rightarrow \Gamma \vdash N[M/x]\,\mathcal{R}_{\sigma'}\,N'[M/x] \tag{A.2}$$

$$\Gamma \vdash M : \sigma \Rightarrow \Gamma \vdash M\,\mathcal{R}_{\sigma}\,M \tag{A.3}$$

$$(\Gamma \vdash M\,\mathcal{R}_{\sigma}\,M' \,\&\, \Gamma \vdash M'\,\mathcal{R}_{\sigma}\,M'') \Rightarrow \Gamma \vdash M\,\mathcal{R}_{\sigma}\,M'' \tag{A.4}$$

$$(\Gamma \vdash M\,\mathcal{R}_{\sigma}\,M' \,\&\, \Gamma, x : \sigma \vdash N : \sigma') \Rightarrow \Gamma \vdash N[M/x]\,\mathcal{R}_{\sigma'}\,N[M'/x] \tag{A.5}$$

$$\Gamma, x : \sigma \vdash M\,\mathcal{R}_{\sigma'}\,M' \Rightarrow \Gamma \vdash \lambda x . M\,\mathcal{R}_{\sigma \to \sigma'}\,\lambda x . M' \tag{A.6}$$

$$\Gamma, x : \sigma \vdash M\,\mathcal{R}_{\sigma}\,M' \Rightarrow \Gamma \vdash \mathsf{fix}\,x . M\,\mathcal{R}_{\sigma}\,\mathsf{fix}\,x . M' \tag{A.7}$$

$$\Gamma \vdash L\,\mathcal{R}_{\sigma}\,L' \,\&\, \Gamma \vdash M\,\mathcal{R}_{\sigma'}\,M' \,\&\, \Gamma, h : \sigma, t : [\sigma] \vdash N\,\mathcal{R}_{\sigma'}\,N'$$
$$\Rightarrow \Gamma \vdash (\mathsf{case}\,L\,\mathsf{of}\,\{\mathsf{nil} \to M \mid h :: t \to N\})\,\mathcal{R}_{\sigma'} \tag{A.8}$$
$$(\mathsf{case}\,L'\,\mathsf{of}\,\{\mathsf{nil} \to M' \mid h :: t \to N'\})$$

$\mathcal{R}$ is a **PCFL congruence relation** if in addition it is symmetric:

$$\Gamma \vdash M\,\mathcal{R}_{\sigma}\,M' \Rightarrow \Gamma \vdash M'\,\mathcal{R}_{\sigma}\,M.$$

Modulo (A.4), property (A.5) is equivalent to saying that the non variable-binding syntax constructors of PCFL preserve the precongruence relation. For example, for application one has:

$$(\Gamma \vdash F \, \mathcal{R}_{\sigma \to \sigma'} \, F' \, \& \, \Gamma \vdash A \, \mathcal{R}_\sigma \, A') \Rightarrow \Gamma \vdash (F \, A) \, \mathcal{R}_{\sigma'} \, (F' \, A').$$

Then (A.6)–(A.8) extend this preservation property to the variable-binding constructs of the language. As the following lemma shows, these properties are all special cases of preservation of the precongruence relation by the operation of substituting for a parameter in a context.

Lemma A.2. *Suppose that $\mathcal{R}$ is a PCFL precongruence relation. Suppose further that $\Gamma, \Gamma' \vdash M \, \mathcal{R}_\sigma \, M'$, that $\mathcal{C}[-_\sigma] \in Ctx_{\sigma'}(\Gamma)$, and that the variables in $dom(\Gamma')$ all occur as the bound variables of binders in $\mathcal{C}$ which contain the parameter $-_\sigma$ within their scope. (Cf. the statement of Lemma 2.8; in particular by that lemma, $\mathcal{C}[M]$ and $\mathcal{C}[M']$ are elements of $Exp_{\sigma'}(\Gamma)$.) Then $\Gamma \vdash \mathcal{C}[M] \, \mathcal{R}_{\sigma'} \, \mathcal{C}[M']$.*

Proof. The proof is by induction on the derivation of $\Gamma \vdash \mathcal{C}[-_\sigma] : \sigma'$, and is omitted. □

We aim to show:

Theorem A.3. *PCFL similarity, $\preceq^\circ$, is a precongruence, and hence (by Proposition 3.6(iii)) PCFL bisimilarity is a congruence.*

It is possible to prove Theorem A.3 by indirect means, making use of a domain-theoretic denotational semantics for PCFL. Abramsky (1990) takes such a route to prove the congruence property for his notion of applicative bisimulation for the untyped lambda calculus. The proof we give here is based directly upon the operational semantics of PCFL and is a minor adaptation of the method given by Howe (1989, Howe (1996). An adaptation is needed because Howe's proof concerns notions of bisimulation matching contextual equivalences in which convergence of function and product expressions to canonical form is observable. This is not the case for PCFL contextual equivalence as defined above. This is the reason why the η-rules (2.24) and (2.25) hold. It is pleasant that such properties hold, but the main reason for choosing to treat this variant of contextual equivalence here is to allow a direct comparison with Milner and Plotkin's classic work on PCF (Milner 1977; Plotkin 1977). Gordon (1995a) gets a result like Theorem 3.8 for PCFL contextual equivalence (indeed for a language with general forms of recursive type), but for a notion of bisimilarity (a very useful notion, as *loc. cit.* shows) based upon a certain labelled transition system.

Proofs of congruence for bisimilarities arising from labelled transition systems for reactive systems (such as for CCS (Milner 1989, 4.4), for example) suggest the following strategy for proving Theorem A.3. Let $\mathcal{S}$ denote the 'precongruence closure' of $\preceq^\circ$, that is, the smallest PCFL precongruence containing $\preceq^\circ$. To see that $\preceq^\circ$ is a precongruence, it would suffice to show that $\mathcal{S} = \preceq^\circ$; and by definition $\mathcal{S}$

$$\Gamma, x : \sigma \vdash x \preceq^* N : \sigma \quad \text{(if} \quad \Gamma, x : \sigma \vdash x \preceq^\circ_\sigma N) \qquad (\preceq^* \text{ var})$$

$$\Gamma, x : \sigma \vdash \underline{b} \preceq^*_{bool} N \quad \text{(if} \quad \Gamma \vdash \underline{b} \preceq^\circ_{bool} N) \qquad (\preceq^* \text{ bool})$$

$$\frac{\begin{array}{c} \Gamma \vdash B \preceq^*_{bool} B' \\ \Gamma \vdash M_1 \preceq^*_\sigma M_1' \\ \Gamma \vdash M_2 \preceq^*_\sigma M_2' \end{array}}{\Gamma \vdash \left(\begin{array}{c} \text{if } B \text{ then} \\ M_1 \text{ else } M_2 \end{array} \right) \preceq^*_\sigma N} \quad \text{(if} \quad \begin{array}{c} \Gamma \vdash \text{if } B' \text{ then} \\ M_1' \text{ else } M_2' \preceq^\circ_\sigma N) \end{array} \qquad (\preceq^* \text{ cond})$$

$$\Gamma \vdash \underline{n} \preceq^*_{int} N \quad \text{(if} \quad \Gamma \vdash \underline{n} \preceq^\circ_{int} N) \qquad (\preceq^* \text{ int})$$

$$\frac{\begin{array}{c} \Gamma \vdash M_1 \preceq^*_{int} M_1' \\ \Gamma \vdash M_2 \preceq^*_{int} M_2' \end{array}}{\Gamma \vdash M_1 \text{ op } M_2 \preceq^*_\gamma N} \quad \text{(if} \quad \Gamma \vdash M_1' \text{ op } M_2' \preceq^\circ_\gamma N) \qquad (\preceq^* \text{ op})$$

$$\frac{\Gamma, x : \sigma \vdash M \preceq^*_{\sigma'} M'}{\Gamma \vdash \lambda x . M \preceq^*_{\sigma \to \sigma'} N} \quad \text{(if} \quad \Gamma \vdash \lambda x . M' \preceq^\circ_{\sigma \to \sigma'} N) \qquad (\preceq^* \text{ abs})$$

$$\frac{\begin{array}{c} \Gamma \vdash F \preceq^*_{\sigma \to \sigma'} F' \\ \Gamma \vdash A \preceq^*_\sigma A' \end{array}}{\Gamma \vdash F A \preceq^*_{\sigma'} N} \quad \text{(if} \quad \Gamma \vdash F' A' \preceq^\circ_{\sigma'} N) \qquad (\preceq^* \text{ app})$$

$$\frac{\Gamma, x : \sigma \vdash M \preceq^*_\sigma M'}{\Gamma \vdash \text{fix} x . M \preceq^*_\sigma N} \quad \text{(if} \quad \Gamma \vdash \text{fix} x . M' \preceq^\circ_\sigma N) \qquad (\preceq^* \text{ fix})$$

Figure 6: Definition of $\preceq^*$, begun

contains $\preceq^\circ$, it would be enough to prove that $\mathcal{S} \subseteq \preceq^\circ$. Since $\mathcal{S}$ satisfies (A.2), to establish this inclusion, it is enough to prove that $\mathcal{S}$ restricted to closed terms is a PCFL simulation. Unfortunately, it is not clear how to prove this. Instead we follow Howe, and define an auxiliary relation, $\preceq^*$, which is not quite the precongruence closure (for one thing, it is not transitive), but which permits the proof-strategy we have outlined to go through.

Definition A.4. The relation

$$\Gamma \vdash M \preceq^*_\sigma N \qquad (M, N \in Exp_\sigma(\Gamma))$$

is inductively defined by the axioms and rules in Figures 6 and 7.

Lemma A.5. *(i) If* $\Gamma \vdash M \preceq^*_\sigma M'$ *and* $\Gamma \vdash M' \preceq^\circ_\sigma M''$, *then* $\Gamma \vdash M \preceq^*_\sigma M''$.

(ii) If $\Gamma \vdash M : \sigma$, *then* $\Gamma \vdash M \preceq^*_\sigma M$.

(iii) If $\Gamma \vdash M \preceq^\circ_\sigma M'$, *then* $\Gamma \vdash M \preceq^*_\sigma M'$.

$$\frac{\Gamma \vdash M_1 \preceq^*_\sigma M_1'}{\Gamma \vdash M_2 \preceq^*_{\sigma'} M_2'} \quad \text{(if} \quad \Gamma \vdash \langle M_1', M_2' \rangle \preceq^\circ_{\sigma \times \sigma'} N) \qquad (\preceq^* \text{ pair})$$

$$\frac{\Gamma \vdash P \preceq^*_{\sigma \times \sigma'} P'}{\Gamma \vdash \mathsf{fst}(P) \preceq^*_\sigma N} \quad \text{(if} \quad \Gamma \vdash \mathsf{fst}(P') \preceq^\circ_\sigma N) \qquad (\preceq^* \text{ fst})$$

$$\frac{\Gamma \vdash P \preceq^*_{\sigma \times \sigma'} P'}{\Gamma \vdash \mathsf{snd}(P) \preceq^*_{\sigma'} N} \quad \text{(if} \quad \Gamma \vdash \mathsf{snd}(P') \preceq^\circ_{\sigma'} N) \qquad (\preceq^* \text{ snd})$$

$$\Gamma \vdash \mathsf{nil} \preceq^*_\sigma N \quad \text{(if} \quad \Gamma \vdash \mathsf{nil} \preceq^\circ_\sigma N) \qquad (\preceq^* \text{ nil})$$

$$\frac{\Gamma \vdash H \preceq^*_\sigma H'}{\Gamma \vdash H :: T \preceq^*_{[\sigma]} N} \quad \text{(if} \quad \Gamma \vdash H' :: T' \preceq^\circ_{[\sigma]} N) \qquad (\preceq^* \text{ cons})$$

$$\frac{\begin{array}{c}\Gamma \vdash L \preceq^*_{[\sigma]} L' \\ \Gamma \vdash M_1 \preceq^*_{\sigma'} M_1' \\ \Gamma, h : \sigma, t : [\sigma] \vdash M_2 \preceq^*_{\sigma'} M_2' \end{array}}{\Gamma \vdash \left(\begin{array}{c} \mathsf{case}\ L\ \mathsf{of}\ \{\mathsf{nil} \to M_1 \\ \mid h :: t \to M_2 \} \end{array} \right) \preceq^*_{\sigma'} N} \quad \begin{array}{l}(\text{if } \Gamma \vdash \mathsf{case}\ L'\ \mathsf{of} \\ \{\mathsf{nil} \to M_1' \mid h :: t \to M_2' \} \\ \preceq^\circ_{\sigma'} N) \end{array} \qquad (\preceq^* \text{ case})$$

Figure 7: Definition of $\preceq^*$, completed

(iv) If $\Gamma \vdash M \preceq^*_\sigma M'$ and $\Gamma, x : \sigma \vdash N \preceq^*_{\sigma'} N'$, then $\Gamma \vdash N[M/x] \preceq^*_{\sigma'} N'[M'/x]$.

Proof. Part (i) is proved by induction on the derivation of $\Gamma \vdash M \preceq^*_\sigma M'$ from the axioms and rules in Figures 6 and 7. Part (ii) is proved by induction on the derivation of $\Gamma \vdash M : \sigma$ from the axioms and rules in Figure 2. Part (iii) follows from the first two parts. Part (iv) is proved by induction on the derivation of $\Gamma, x : \sigma \vdash N \preceq^*_{\sigma'} N'$, using part (iii) and the fact (evident from the definition of $\preceq^\circ$ from $\preceq$) that $\preceq^\circ$ satisfies property (A.2). $\square$

Lemma A.6.   *(i)* If $\emptyset \vdash \underline{b} \preceq^*_{bool} B$, then $B \Downarrow \underline{b}$.

(ii) If $\emptyset \vdash \underline{n} \preceq^*_{int} N$, then $N \Downarrow \underline{n}$.

(iii) If $\emptyset \vdash F \preceq^*_{\sigma \to \sigma'} F'$, then for all $A \in Exp_\sigma$, $\emptyset \vdash F A \preceq^*_{\sigma'} F' A$.

(iv) If $\emptyset \vdash P \preceq^*_{\sigma \times \sigma'} P'$, then $\emptyset \vdash \mathsf{fst}(P) \preceq^*_\sigma \mathsf{fst}(P')$ and $\emptyset \vdash \mathsf{snd}(P) \preceq^*_{\sigma'} \mathsf{snd}(P')$.

(v) If $\emptyset \vdash \mathsf{nil} \preceq^*_{[\sigma]} L$, then $L \Downarrow \mathsf{nil}$.

(vi) If $\emptyset \vdash H :: T \preceq^*_{[\sigma]} L$, then $L \Downarrow H' :: T'$ for some H', T' with $\emptyset \vdash H \preceq^*_\sigma H'$ and $\emptyset \vdash T \preceq^*_{[\sigma]} T'$.

Proof. For part (i), if $\emptyset \vdash \underline{b} \preceq^*_{bool} B$ holds, it must have been deduced using ($\preceq^*$ bool), so $\emptyset \vdash \underline{b} \preceq^\circ_{bool} B$ holds, that is, $\underline{b} \preceq_{bool} B$. Then since $\preceq$ is a simulation and $\underline{b} \Downarrow \underline{b}$, it follows from condition (sim 1) in Figure 4 that $B \Downarrow \underline{b}$, as required. The argument for parts (ii) and (v) is similar.

Part (iii) follows by applying rule ($\preceq^*$ app) from Figure 6 with $A' = A$ and $N = F\,A$, using the reflexivity of $\preceq^*$ (Lemma A.5(ii)) and $\preceq^\circ$ (via Proposition 3.6(i)). Similarly, part (iv) follows by applying the rules ($\preceq^*$ fst) and ($\preceq^*$ snd).

Finally for part (vi), if $\emptyset \vdash H :: T \preceq^*_{[\sigma]} L$ holds it can only have been deduced by an application of rule ($\preceq^*$ cons). So there are terms H'' and T'' with

$$\emptyset \vdash H \preceq^*_\sigma H'' \tag{A.9}$$

$$\emptyset \vdash T \preceq^*_{[\sigma]} T'' \tag{A.10}$$

$$\emptyset \vdash H'' :: T'' \preceq^\circ_{[\sigma]} L$$

and hence

$$H'' :: T'' \preceq_{[\sigma]} L. \tag{A.11}$$

The simulation property (sim 6a) of $\preceq$ applied to (A.11) and $H'' :: T'' \Downarrow H'' :: T''$ implies that there are further terms H' and T' with $L \Downarrow H' :: T'$, $H'' \preceq_\sigma H'$, and $T'' \preceq_{[\sigma]} T'$. The last two properties combined with (A.9), (A.10), and Lemma A.5(i) yield $\emptyset \vdash H \preceq^*_\sigma H'$ and $\emptyset \vdash T \preceq^*_{[\sigma]} T'$, as required. $\square$

The following lemma gives the key property of $\preceq^*$ permitting the proof of Theorem A.3 to go through. It is the analogue of (Howe 1989, Theorem 1). In the proof of the lemma we will make use of the Kleene preorder, $\leq^{kl}$, defined in Proposition 3.9 together with the fact, established in that proposition, that $\leq^{kl}$ is contained in PCFL similarity.

Lemma A.7. *If $M \Downarrow C$ and $\emptyset \vdash M \preceq^*_\sigma N$, then $\emptyset \vdash C \preceq^*_\sigma N$.*

Proof. The proof is by induction on the derivation of $M \Downarrow C$. For once we will give the details of the induction proof in some detail, since it is quite delicate. To be more precise, we will show that

$$\mathcal{E} \stackrel{\text{def}}{=} \{(M, C) \mid \forall \sigma, N\,(\emptyset \vdash M \preceq^*_\sigma N \Rightarrow \emptyset \vdash C \preceq^*_\sigma N)\}$$

is closed under the axioms and rules in Figure 3 and hence contains the evaluation relation, as required.

Case ($\Downarrow$ can). Trivial.

Case ($\Downarrow$ cond1). Suppose that (B, true) and (M_1, C) are in $\mathcal{E}$. We have to show that (if B then M_1 else $M_2, C) \in \mathcal{E}$. So suppose

$$\emptyset \vdash \text{if } B \text{ then } M_1 \text{ else } M_2 \preceq^*_\sigma N \tag{A.12}$$

This can only have been deduced by an application of rule ($\preceq^*$ cond), so there are terms B', M_1', and M_2' with

$$\emptyset \vdash B \preceq^*_{bool} B', \quad \emptyset \vdash M_i \preceq^*_\sigma M_i' \quad (\text{for } i = 1, 2) \tag{A.13}$$

and

$$\text{if } B' \text{ then } M_1' \text{ else } M_2' \preceq_\sigma N \tag{A.14}$$

Since $(B, \text{true}), (M_1, C) \in \mathcal{E}$, from (A.13) we get

$$\emptyset \vdash \text{true} \preceq^*_{bool} B' \tag{A.15}$$
$$\emptyset \vdash C \preceq^*_\sigma M_1' \tag{A.16}$$

By Lemma A.6(i), from (A.15) we have $B' \Downarrow \text{true}$. Hence by definition of $\leq^{kl}$,

$$M_1' \leq^{kl}_\sigma \text{if } B' \text{ then } M_1' \text{ else } M_2'$$

holds. Therefore by Proposition 3.9 we have

$$M_1' \preceq_\sigma \text{if } B' \text{ then } M_1' \text{ else } M_2'$$

which combined with (A.14) and transitivity of $\preceq_\sigma$ yields $M_1' \preceq_\sigma N$. Lemma A.5(i) plus (A.16) implies $\emptyset \vdash C \preceq^*_\sigma N$. So we have shown that (A.12) implies $\emptyset \vdash C \preceq^*_\sigma N$, for any N and σ. Thus (if B then M_1 else $M_2, C) \in \mathcal{E}$, as required.

Case ($\Downarrow$ cond2) is similar to the previous case.

Case ($\Downarrow$ op). Suppose $(M_i, \underline{n_i}) \in \mathcal{E}$ for $i = 1, 2$, and that

$$\emptyset \vdash M_1 \text{ op } M_2 \preceq^*_\gamma N \tag{A.17}$$

We must show that

$$\emptyset \vdash \underline{c} \preceq^*_\gamma N \tag{A.18}$$

where $c \stackrel{\text{def}}{=} n_1 \text{ op } n_2$. Now (A.17) must have been deduced by an application of rule ($\preceq^*$ op) to

$$\emptyset \vdash M_i \preceq^*_{int} M_i' \quad (i = 1, 2) \tag{A.19}$$
$$M_1' \text{ op } M_2' \preceq_\gamma N \tag{A.20}$$

for some terms M_1', M_2'. Since $(M_i, \underline{n_i}) \in \mathcal{E}$, from (A.19) it follows that $\emptyset \vdash \underline{n_i} \preceq^*_{int} M_i'$ and hence by Lemma A.6(ii) that $M_i' \Downarrow \underline{n_i}$. Thus by rule ($\Downarrow$ op), $M_1' \text{ op } M_2' \Downarrow \underline{c}$ and therefore $\underline{c} \leq^{kl}_\gamma M_1' \text{ op } M_2'$ (by definition of $\leq^{kl}$). Then from Proposition 3.9, (A.20), and transitivity of $\preceq$, we have that $\underline{c} \preceq_\gamma N$ and hence (by Lemma A.5(iii)) that (A.18) does indeed hold.

Case ($\Downarrow$ app).   Suppose $(F, \lambda x \,.\, M), (M[A/x], C) \in \mathcal{E}$ and that

$$\emptyset \vdash F A \preceq_{\sigma'}^* N \tag{A.21}$$

We must show that

$$\emptyset \vdash C \preceq_{\sigma'}^* N \tag{A.22}$$

Now (A.21) must have been deduced by an application of ($\preceq^*$ app) to

$$\emptyset \vdash F \preceq_{\sigma \to \sigma'}^* F' \tag{A.23}$$
$$\emptyset \vdash A \preceq_{\sigma}^* A' \tag{A.24}$$

and

$$F' A' \preceq_{\sigma'} N \tag{A.25}$$

for some terms F', A'. Since $(F, \lambda x \,.\, M) \in \mathcal{E}, \emptyset \vdash \lambda x \,.\, M \preceq_{\sigma'}^* F'$ holds by (A.23). This can only have been derived by an application of ($\preceq^*$ abs) to

$$x : \sigma \vdash M \preceq_{\sigma'}^* M' \tag{A.26}$$

and

$$\lambda x \,.\, M' \preceq_{\sigma \to \sigma'} F' \tag{A.27}$$

for some term M'. Applying Lemma A.5(iv) to (A.24) and (A.26), we have that $\emptyset \vdash M[A/x] \preceq_{\sigma'}^* M'[A'/x]$. Then since $(M[A/x], C) \in \mathcal{E}$, it follows from this that

$$\emptyset \vdash C \preceq_{\sigma'}^* M'[A'/x] \tag{A.28}$$

Since $\preceq$ is a PCFL simulation, from property (sim 3) in Figure 4 applied to (A.27), we get

$$(\lambda x \,.\, M')A' \preceq_{\sigma'} F' A' \tag{A.29}$$

Note that by definition of $\leq^{\mathrm{kl}}$, we always have $M'[A'/x] \leq_{\sigma'}^{\mathrm{kl}} (\lambda x \,.\, M')A'$ and hence by Proposition 3.9, $\emptyset \vdash M'[A'/x] \preceq_{\sigma'} (\lambda x \,.\, M')A'$. Combining this with (A.25), (A.29) and transitivity of $\preceq$, we get $M'[A, /x] \preceq_{\sigma'} N$. Lemma A.5(i) applied to this and (A.28) yields (A.22), as required.

Case ($\Downarrow$ fix). Suppose $(M[\text{fix } x \,.\, M/x], C) \in \mathcal{E}$ and that

$$\emptyset \vdash \text{fix } x \,.\, M \preceq^*_\sigma N \tag{A.30}$$

We must show that

$$\emptyset \vdash C \preceq^*_\sigma N \tag{A.31}$$

Now (A.30) must have been deduced by an application of ($\preceq^*$ fix) to

$$x : \sigma \vdash M \preceq^*_\sigma M' \tag{A.32}$$

and

$$\text{fix } x \,.\, M' \preceq_\sigma N \tag{A.33}$$

for some term M'. Applying ($\preceq^*$ fix) to (A.32) and $\text{fix } x \,.\, M' \preceq_\sigma \text{fix } x \,.\, M'$ (using the fact that $\preceq$ is reflexive), we get $\emptyset \vdash \text{fix } x \,.\, M \preceq^*_\sigma \text{fix } x \,.\, M'$. Applying Lemma A.5(iv) to this and (A.32) yields $\emptyset \vdash M[\text{fix } x \,.\, M/x] \preceq^*_\sigma M'[\text{fix } x \,.\, M'/x]$. Then since $(M[\text{fix } x \,.\, M/x], C) \in \mathcal{E}$, we deduce that

$$\emptyset \vdash C \preceq^*_\sigma M'[\text{fix } x \,.\, M'/x] \tag{A.34}$$

Note that by definition of $\leq^{kl}$, one always has $M'[\text{fix } x \,.\, M'/x] \leq^{kl}_\sigma \text{fix } x \,.\, M'$, and hence also $M'[\text{fix } x \,.\, M'/x] \preceq_\sigma \text{fix } x \,.\, M'$ (by Proposition 3.9). Combining this with (A.33), we get $M'[\text{fix } x \,.\, M'/x] \preceq_\sigma N$. Applying Lemma A.5(i) to this and (A.34) yields (A.31), as required.

Case ($\Downarrow$ fst). Suppose $(P, \langle M_1, M_2 \rangle), (M_1, C) \in \mathcal{E}$ and that

$$\emptyset \vdash \text{fst}(P) \preceq^*_{\sigma_1} N \tag{A.35}$$

We must show that

$$\emptyset \vdash C \preceq^*_{\sigma_1} N \tag{A.36}$$

Now (A.35) must have been deduced by an application of ($\preceq^*$ fst) to

$$\emptyset \vdash P \preceq^*_{\sigma_1 \times \sigma_2} P' \tag{A.37}$$

and

$$\text{fst}(P') \preceq_{\sigma_1} N \tag{A.38}$$

for some term P'. Since $(P, \langle M_1, M_2 \rangle) \in \mathcal{E}$, from (A.37) we get

$$\emptyset \vdash \langle M_1, M_2 \rangle \preceq^*_{\sigma_1 \times \sigma_2} P'.$$

This must have been deduced by an application of ($\preceq^*$ pair) to

$$\emptyset \vdash M_i \preceq^*_{\sigma_i} M'_i \quad (i = 1, 2) \tag{A.39}$$

$$\langle M'_1, M'_2 \rangle \preceq_{\sigma_1 \times \sigma_2} P' \tag{A.40}$$

for some terms M'_1, M'_2. Since $(M_1, C) \in \mathcal{E}$, from (A.39) we get

$$\emptyset \vdash C \preceq^*_{\sigma_1} M'_1 \tag{A.41}$$

Since $\preceq$ is a PCFL simulation, it satisfies property (sim 4) in Figure 4, and so (A.40) implies

$$\mathsf{fst}(\langle M'_1, M'_2 \rangle) \preceq_{\sigma_1} \mathsf{fst}(P') \tag{A.42}$$

Note that by definition of $\leq^{kl}$, one always has $M'_1 \leq^{kl}_{\sigma_1} \mathsf{fst}(\langle M'_1, M'_2 \rangle)$, and hence and hence also $M'_1 \preceq_{\sigma_1} \mathsf{fst}(\langle M'_1, M'_2 \rangle)$ (by Proposition 3.9). Combining this with (A.38) and (A.42) we get $M'_1 \preceq_{\sigma_1} N$. Applying Lemma A.5(i) to this and (A.41) yields (A.36), as required.

Case ($\Downarrow$ snd)   is similar to the previous case.

Case ($\Downarrow$ case1)   is similar to the case for ($\Downarrow$ cond1), but using the fact (evident from the definition of $\leq^{kl}$) that if $L' \Downarrow \mathsf{nil}$, then $M'_1 \leq^{kl}_{\sigma'} \mathsf{case}\ L'$ of $\{\mathsf{nil} \to M'_1 \mid h :: t \to M'_2\}$.

Case ($\Downarrow$ case2)   is similar to the case for ($\Downarrow$ app), but using the fact (evident from the definition of $\leq^{kl}$) that if $L' \Downarrow H' :: T'$, then

$$M'_2[H'/h, T'/t] \leq^{kl}_{\sigma'} \mathsf{case}\ L'\ \text{of}\ \{\mathsf{nil} \to M_1 \mid h :: t \to M_2\}.$$

This completes the proof of Lemma A.7.   □

Proposition A.8. *For all* Γ, σ, M, N

$$\Gamma \vdash M \preceq^\circ_\sigma N \Leftrightarrow \Gamma \vdash M \preceq^*_\sigma N.$$

Proof. We have already proved the left to right implication in part (iii) of Lemma A.5. For the converse, note that by part (iv) of that lemma, and by the construction of $\preceq^\circ$ from $\preceq$ (Definition 3.7), it suffices to prove the implication just for closed terms:

$$\emptyset \vdash M \preceq^*_\sigma N \Rightarrow M \preceq_\sigma N.$$

By the co-induction principle for $\preceq$ (Proposition 3.5), it suffices to show that $\mathcal{S}$ is a PCFL simulation, where

$$\mathcal{S}_\sigma \stackrel{\text{def}}{=} \{(M, N) \mid \emptyset \vdash M \preceq^*_\sigma N\}.$$

But the fact that $\mathcal{S} \leq \langle \mathcal{S} \rangle$ follows immediately by combining Lemmas A.6 and A.7.   □

We can now complete the proof of Theorem A.3.

Proof of Theorem A.3. We have seen that $\preceq$, and hence also $\preceq^\circ$, is reflexive and transitive. So it just remains to see that $\preceq^\circ$ has properties (A.1), (A.2), and (A.5)–(A.8) of Definition A.1. The weakening property (A.1) is an immediate consequence of the construction of $\preceq^\circ$ from $\preceq$. For the other properties, it suffices by Proposition A.8 to check that they hold for $\preceq^*$. The substitution properties (A.2) and (A.5) are both instances of Lemma A.5(iv) (using reflexivity of $\preceq^*$, established in part (ii) of that lemma). Finally, (A.6)–(A.8) hold for $\preceq^*$ by construction. For example, if $\Gamma, x : \sigma \vdash M \preceq^*_{\sigma'} M'$, then by ($\preceq^*$ abs) (taking $N = \lambda x \,.\, M'$ and using the fact that $\preceq^\circ$ is reflexive) one has $\Gamma \vdash \lambda x \,.\, M \preceq^*_{\sigma \to \sigma'} \lambda x \,.\, M'$. $\qquad\Box$

Corollary A.9. *For all* Γ, σ, M, N

$$\Gamma \vdash M \preceq^\circ_\sigma N \Rightarrow \Gamma \vdash M \leq^{\mathrm{gnd}}_\sigma N.$$

Proof. Suppose $\Gamma \vdash M \preceq^\circ_\sigma N$ and that $C[-_\sigma]$ is a context for which $C[M]$ and $C[N]$ are closed terms of ground type, γ say. Since by Theorem A.3 $\preceq^\circ$ is a precongruence relation, it follows from Lemma A.2 that $\emptyset \vdash C[M] \preceq^\circ_\gamma C[N]$, that is, $C[M] \preceq_\gamma C[N]$. So if $C[M] \Downarrow \underline{c}$, then by the simulation properties (sim 1) and (sim 2) of $\preceq$ it is also the case that $C[N] \Downarrow \underline{c}$. Since this holds for any $C[-_\sigma]$, we have that $\Gamma \vdash M \leq^{\mathrm{gnd}}_\sigma N$. $\qquad\Box$

The PCFL contextual preorder is a simulation

Referring back to the beginning of this section, we have now completed part (a) of the proof of Theorem 3.8, and it remains to prove part (b)—the fact that $\leq^{\mathrm{gnd}}$ is a PCFL simulation. The reader will be relieved to know that this part is quite straightforward in comparison with part (a).

Define $\mathcal{S} \in Rel$ by:

$$\mathcal{S}_\sigma \overset{\mathrm{def}}{=} \{(M, N) \mid \emptyset \vdash M \leq^{\mathrm{gnd}}_\sigma N\}.$$

We wish to show that $\mathcal{S} \leq \langle \mathcal{S} \rangle$. We check each of the simulation properties in Figure 4 in turn.

Property (sim 1). Suppose $M \, \mathcal{S}_{bool} \, N$ and that $M \Downarrow \underline{b}$. Applying the definition of $\leq^{\mathrm{gnd}}$ with the context $C[-_{bool}] \overset{\mathrm{def}}{=} -_{bool}$ shows that $N \Downarrow \underline{b}$.

Property (sim 2). is just like the previous case.

Property (sim 3).   Suppose $F \; \mathcal{S}_{\sigma \to \sigma'} \; F'$ and that $A \in Exp_\sigma$. Given any context $\mathcal{C}[-_{\sigma'}]$ for which $\mathcal{C}[F\,A]$ and $\mathcal{C}[F'\,A]$ are closed terms of ground type, let $\mathcal{C}'[-_{\sigma \to \sigma'}]$ be the context obtained by substituting $(-_{\sigma \to \sigma'})\,A$ for $-_{\sigma'}$ throughout $\mathcal{C}$. Thus $\mathcal{C}'[F] = \mathcal{C}[F\,A]$ and similarly with F' for F. Then

$$
\begin{aligned}
\mathcal{C}[F\,A] \Downarrow \underline{c} &\Rightarrow \mathcal{C}'[F] \Downarrow \underline{c} && \text{since } \mathcal{C}'[F] = \mathcal{C}[F\,A] \\
&\Rightarrow \mathcal{C}'[F'] \Downarrow \underline{c} && \text{since } \emptyset \vdash F \leq^{\mathrm{gnd}}_{\sigma \to \sigma'} F' \\
&\Rightarrow \mathcal{C}[F'\,A] \Downarrow \underline{c} && \text{since } \mathcal{C}'[F'] = \mathcal{C}[F'\,A].
\end{aligned}
$$

Thus $\emptyset \vdash F\,A \leq^{\mathrm{gnd}}_{\sigma'} F'\,A$, that is, $F\,A \; \mathcal{S}_{\sigma'} \; F'\,A$, as required.

Property (sim 4).   The proof is like the previous case, but using $\mathcal{C}'[-_{\sigma_1 \times \sigma_2}] \stackrel{\mathrm{def}}{=} \mathcal{C}[\mathsf{fst}(-_{\sigma_1 \times \sigma_2})]$, and then $\mathcal{C}'[-_{\sigma_1 \times \sigma_2}] \stackrel{\mathrm{def}}{=} \mathcal{C}[\mathsf{snd}(-_{\sigma_1 \times \sigma_2})]$.

Property (sim 5).   Suppose $L \; \mathcal{S}_{[\sigma]} \; L'$ and that $L \Downarrow \mathsf{nil}$. Consider the context

$$
\mathcal{C}[-_{[\sigma]}] \stackrel{\mathrm{def}}{=} \mathsf{case} \; -_{[\sigma]} \; \mathsf{of} \; \{ \mathsf{nil} \to \mathsf{true} \mid h :: t \to \mathsf{false} \}.
$$

Note that $\mathcal{C}[L] \Downarrow \mathsf{true}$ if and only if $L \Downarrow \mathsf{nil}$, and similarly for L'. So if $L \Downarrow \mathsf{nil}$, since $\emptyset \vdash L \leq^{\mathrm{gnd}}_{[\sigma]} L'$, it follows that $\mathcal{C}[L'] \Downarrow \mathsf{true}$ and hence $L' \Downarrow \mathsf{nil}$.

Property (sim 6).   Suppose $L \; \mathcal{S}_{[\sigma]} \; L'$ and that $L \Downarrow H :: T$. Arguing just as in the previous case, we have that $L \Downarrow H' :: T'$ for some terms H', T'. We have to show that $\emptyset \vdash H \leq^{\mathrm{gnd}}_{\sigma} H'$ and $\emptyset \vdash T \leq^{\mathrm{gnd}}_{[\sigma]} T'$.

We make use of PCFL expressions for the functions for taking the head and tail of a list:

$$
head \stackrel{\mathrm{def}}{=} \lambda \ell \, . \, \mathsf{case} \; \ell \; \mathsf{of} \; \{ \mathsf{nil} \to \bot \mid h :: t \to h \}
$$

$$
tail \stackrel{\mathrm{def}}{=} \lambda \ell \, . \, \mathsf{case} \; \ell \; \mathsf{of} \; \{ \mathsf{nil} \to \mathsf{nil} \mid h :: t \to t \}
$$

where

$$
\bot \stackrel{\mathrm{def}}{=} \mathsf{fix} \, x \, . \, x.
$$

Since $L \Downarrow H :: T$, it follows from the definition of $\cong^{\mathrm{kl}}$ (in Proposition 3.9) that

$$
\emptyset \vdash H \cong^{\mathrm{kl}}_{\sigma} head \, L \qquad \text{and} \qquad \emptyset \vdash T \cong^{\mathrm{kl}}_{[\sigma]} tail \, L
$$

and similarly for L', H', T'. We saw in Proposition 3.9 that $\leq^{\mathrm{kl}}$ is contained in $\preceq$. Hence by Corollary A.9 we have

$$
\emptyset \vdash H \cong^{\mathrm{gnd}}_{\sigma} head \, L \qquad \text{and} \qquad \emptyset \vdash T \cong^{\mathrm{gnd}}_{[\sigma]} tail \, L
$$

and similarly for L', H', T'. By an argument similar to that given above for property (sim 3) of $\leq^{\text{gnd}}$, the fact that $\emptyset \vdash L \leq^{\text{gnd}}_{[\sigma]} L'$ holds implies that

$$\emptyset \vdash head\ L \leq^{\text{gnd}}_{\sigma} head\ L' \quad \text{and} \quad \emptyset \vdash tail\ L \leq^{\text{gnd}}_{[\sigma]} tail\ L'.$$

Putting all these fact together we have:

$$H \cong^{\text{gnd}} head\ L \leq^{\text{gnd}} head\ L' \cong^{\text{gnd}} H'$$
$$T \cong^{\text{gnd}} tail\ L \leq^{\text{gnd}} tail\ L' \cong^{\text{gnd}} T'$$

so that $\emptyset \vdash H \leq^{\text{gnd}}_{\sigma} H'$ and $\emptyset \vdash T \leq^{\text{gnd}}_{[\sigma]} T'$, as required.

This completes the verification that $\leq^{\text{gnd}}$ restricted to closed terms is a PCFL simulation. Hence we have that it is contained in PCFL similarity:

$$\emptyset \vdash M \leq^{\text{gnd}}_{\sigma} N \Rightarrow \emptyset \vdash M \preceq^{\circ}_{\sigma} N \tag{A.43}$$

In order to complete the proof of the Operational Extensionality Theorem, we must extend this implication from closed to open terms. To do this we need to verify that the substitutivity property (2.12) holds for $\leq^{\text{gnd}}$. As mentioned on page 254, this property is essentially a consequence of the fact that β-conversion holds up to contextual equivalence for PCFL.

Lemma A.10. $\leq^{\text{gnd}}$ *satisfies property* (2.12), *that is, if* $\Gamma, x : \sigma \vdash N \leq^{\text{gnd}}_{\sigma'} N'$, *then it is the case that* $\Gamma \vdash N[M/x] \leq^{\text{gnd}}_{\sigma'} N'[M/x]$ *holds, for any* $M \in Exp_{\sigma}(\Gamma)$.

Proof. For any $C[-_{\sigma'}]$, since $C[(\lambda x . N)M]$ is of the form $C'[N]$ with $C'[-_{\sigma'}] \stackrel{\text{def}}{=} C[(\lambda x .)M]$, it follows that $\Gamma, x : \sigma \vdash N \leq^{\text{gnd}}_{\sigma'} N'$ implies

$$\Gamma \vdash (\lambda x . N)M \leq^{\text{gnd}}_{\sigma'} (\lambda x . N')M. \tag{A.44}$$

We noted on page 263 that as a consequence of Proposition 3.9 $\cong^{\circ}$ satisfies the β-rule for function application; hence by Corollary A.9 one has

$$\Gamma \vdash N[M/x] \leq^{\text{gnd}}_{\sigma'} (\lambda x . N)M \quad \text{and} \quad \Gamma \vdash (\lambda x . N')M \leq^{\text{gnd}}_{\sigma'} N'[M/x].$$

Combining these with (A.44) and transitivity of $\leq^{\text{gnd}}$ yields $\Gamma \vdash N[M/x] \leq^{\text{gnd}}_{\sigma'} N'[M/x]$. □

Suppose $x : \sigma_1, \ldots, x_n : \sigma_n \vdash M \leq^{\text{gnd}}_{\sigma} N$ holds. Then for any $M_i \in Exp_{\sigma_i}$ ($i = 1, \ldots, n$), by applying the lemma repeatedly we get $M[\vec{M}/\vec{x}] \leq^{\text{gnd}}_{\sigma} N[\vec{M}/\vec{x}]$, and hence by (A.43) that $M[\vec{M}/\vec{x}] \preceq_{\sigma} N[\vec{M}/\vec{x}]$. Thus by definition of $\preceq^{\circ}$, we have $\Gamma \vdash M \preceq^{\circ}_{\sigma} N$. Therefore the converse of Corollary A.9 does indeed hold and we have completed the proof of Theorem 3.8.

References

Abelson, H. and G. J. Susman (1985). *Structure and Interpretation of Computer Programs*. MIT Press.

Abramsky, S. (1990). The lazy λ-calculus. In D. A. Turner (Ed.), *Research Topics in Functional Programming*, Chapter 4, pp. 65–117. Addison Wesley.

Abramsky, S. and C.-H. L. Ong (1993). Full abstraction in the lazy lambda calculus. *Information and Computation 105*, 159–267.

Backhouse, R., P. Chisholm, G. Malcolm, and E. Saaman (1989). Do-it-yourself type theory. *Formal Aspects of Computing 1*, 19–84.

Barendregt, H. P. (1984). *The Lambda Calculus: Its Syntax and Semantics* (revised ed.). North-Holland.

Bird, R. and P. Wadler (1988). *Introduction to Functional Programming*. Prentice-Hall.

Crole, R. L. and A. D. Gordon (1996). Relating operational and denotational semantics for input/output effects. Technical Report 1996/5, University of Leicester Department of Mathematics and Computer Science.

de Roever, W. P. (1978). On backtracking and greatest fixed points. In E. J. Neuhold (Ed.), *Formal Description of Programming Concepts*, pp. 621–639. North-Holland, Amsterdam.

Dybjer, P. and H. P. Sander (1989). A functional programming approach to the specification and verification of concurrent systems. *Formal Aspects of Computing 1*, 303–319.

Egidi, L., F. Honsell, and S. R. della Rocca (1992). Operational, denotational and logical descriptions: a case study. *Fundamenta Informaticae 26*, 149–169.

Gordon, A. D. (1994). *Functional Programming and Input/Output*. Distinguished Dissertations in Computer Science. Cambridge University Press.

Gordon, A. D. (1995a). Bisimilarity as a theory of functional programming. In *Eleventh Conference on the Mathematical Foundations of Programming Semantics, New Orleans, 1995*, Volume 1 of *Electronic Notes in Theoretical Computer Science*. Elsevier.

Gordon, A. D. (1995b, June). Bisimilarity as a theory of functional programming. Minicourse. Notes Series BRICS-NS-95-3, BRICS, Department of Computer Science, University of Aarhus.

Gordon, A. D. and G. D. Rees (1996, January). Bisimilarity for a first-order calculus of objects with subtyping. In *Conference Record of the 23rd ACM Symposium on Principles of Programming Languages, St Petersburg Beach, Florida*, pp. 386–395. ACM Press.

Gunter, C. A. (1992). *Semantics of Programming Languages: Structures and Techniques*. Foundations of Computing. MIT Press.

Harper, R. (1995). A relational proof of correctness of CPS conversion. Draft Version of 9 June, 1995.

Howe, D. J. (1989). Equality in lazy computation systems. In *4th Annual Symposium on Logic in Computer Science*, pp. 198–203. IEEE Computer Society Press, Washington.

Howe, D. J. (1996, February). Proving congruence of bisimulation in functional programming languages. *Information and Computation 124*(2), 103–112.

Martin-Löf, P. (1984). *Intuitionistic Type Theory*. Bibliopolis, Napoli.

Mason, I. A., S. F. Smith, and C. L. Talcott (1996). From operational semantics to domain theory. *Information and Computation*. To appear. Revised and extended version of (Smith 1992).

Mason, I. A. and C. L. Talcott (1991). Equivalence in functional languages with effects. *Journal of Functional Programming 1*, 287–327.

Mason, I. A. and C. L. Talcott (1992). References, local variables and operational reasoning. In *Proceedings of the 7th Annual Symposium on Logic in Computer Science*, pp. 186–197. IEEE Computer Society Press.

Milner, R. (1977). Fully abstract models of typed lambda-calculi. *Theoretical Computer Science 4*, 1–22.

Milner, R. (1989). *Communication and Concurrency*. Prentice Hall.

Milner, R., M. Tofte, and R. Harper (1990). *The Definition of Standard ML*. MIT Press.

Moggi, E. (1991, July). Notions of computation and monads. *Information and Computation 93*(1), 55–92.

Park, D. (1981). Concurrency and automata on infinite sequences. In P. Deussen (Ed.), *Proceedings of the 5th GI-Conference on Theoretical Computer Science*, Volume 104 of *Lecture Notes in Computer Science*, pp. 167–183. Springer-Verlag, Berlin.

Paulson, L. C. (1991). *ML for the Working Programmer*. Cambridge University Press.

Pitts, A. M. (1994, December). Some notes on inductive and co-inductive techniques in the semantics of functional programs. Notes Series BRICS-NS-94-5, BRICS, Department of Computer Science, University of Aarhus. vi+135 pp, draft version.

Pitts, A. M. (1996). Reasoning about local variables with operationally-based logical relations. In *11th Annual Symposium on Logic in Computer Science*, pp. 152–163. IEEE Computer Society Press, Washington.

Pitts, A. M. and I. D. B. Stark (1993). Observable properties of higher order functions that dynamically create local names, or: What's new? In *Mathematical Foundations of Computer Science, Proc. 18th Int. Symp., Gdańsk, 1993*, Volume 711 of *Lecture Notes in Computer Science*, pp. 122–141. Springer-Verlag, Berlin.

Plotkin, G. D. (1977). LCF considered as a programming language. *Theoretical Computer Science 5*, 223–255.

Plotkin, G. D. (1981a). Post-graduate lecture notes in advanced domain theory (incorporating the "Pisa Notes"). Dept. of Computer Science, Univ. of Edinburgh.

Plotkin, G. D. (1981b). A structural approach to operational semantics. Technical Report DAIMI FN-19, Aarhus University.

298

Rees, G. (1994, April). Observational equivalence for a polymorphic lambda calculus. Unpublished note.

Reynolds, J. C. (1981). The essence of Algol. In J. W. de Bakker and J. C. van Vliet (Eds.), *Algorithmic Languages. Proceedings of the International Symposium on Algorithmic Languages*, pp. 345–372. North-Holland, Amsterdam.

Ritter, E. and A. M. Pitts (1995). A fully abstract translation between a λ-calculus with reference types and Standard ML. In *2nd Int. Conf. on Typed Lambda Calculus and Applications, Edinburgh, 1995*, Volume 902 of *Lecture Notes in Computer Science*, pp. 397–413. Springer-Verlag, Berlin.

Sands, D. (1995). Total correctness by local improvement in the transformation of functional programs. To appear (a short version appears in the proceedings of POPL'95).

Scott, D. S. (1982). Domains for denotational semantics. In M. Nielson and E. M. Schmidt (Eds.), *Automata, Languages and Programming, Proceedings 1982*, Volume 140 of *Lecture Notes in Computer Science*. Springer-Verlag, Berlin.

Scott, D. S. (1993). A type-theoretical alternative to ISWIM, CUCH, OWHY. *Theoretical Computer Science 121*, 411–440.

Smith, S. F. (1992). From operational to denotational semantics. In S. Brookes *et al* (Ed.), *7th International Conference on Mathematical Foundations of Programming Semantics, Pittsburgh PA*, Volume 598 of *Lecture notes in Computer Science*, pp. 54–76. Springer-Verlag, Berlin.

Stark, I. D. B. (1995). *Names and Higher-Order Functions*. Ph. D. thesis, University of Cambridge. Also published as Technical Report 363, University of Cambridge Computer Laboratory, April 1995.

Wadler, P. (1992). Comprehending monads. *Mathematical Structures in Computer Science 2*, 461–493.

Winskel, G. (1993). *The Formal Semantics of Programming Languages*. Foundations of Computing. Cambridge, Massachusetts: The MIT Press.

Categories in Concurrency

Glynn Winskel
Mogens Nielsen

Contents

1 Introduction

Computational behaviours are often distributed, in the sense that they may be seen as spatially separated activities accomplishing a joint task. Many such systems are not meant to terminate, and hence it makes little sense to talk about their behaviours in terms of traditional input-output functions. Rather, we are interested in the behaviour of such systems in terms of their often complex patterns of stimuli/response relationships varying over time. For this reason such systems are often referred to as *reactive systems*.

Many structures for modelling reactive systems have been studied over the past 20 years. Here we present a few key models. Common to all of them, is that they rest on an idea of atomic actions, over which the behaviour of a system is defined. The models differ mainly with respect to what behavioural features of systems are represented. Some models are more abstract than others, and this fact is often used in informal classifications of the models with respect to expressibility. One of our aims is to present principal representatives of models, covering the landscape from the most abstract to the most concrete, and to formalise the nature of their relationships by explicitly representing the steps of abstraction that are involved in moving between them. In following through this programme, category theory is a convenient language for formalising the relationships between models.

To give an idea of the role categories play, let us focus attention on transition systems as a model of parallel computation. A transition system consists of a set of states with labelled transitions between them. Assume the transition system has a distinguished initial state so that it can be presented by

$$(S, i, L, Tran)$$

where S is a set of states with initial state i, L is a set of labels and the transitions elements of $Tran \subseteq S \times L \times S$; a transition (s, a, s') is generally written as $s \xrightarrow{a} s'$. It then models a process whose transitions represent the process's atomic actions while the labels are action names; starting from the initial state, it traces out a computation path as transitions occur consecutively.

Processes often arise in relationship to other processes. For example, one process may refine another, or perhaps one process is a component of another. The corresponding relationships between behaviours are often expressed as morphisms between transition systems. For several models, there is some choice in how to define appropriate morphisms—it depends on the extent of the relationship between processes we wish to express. But here, we have an eye to languages like Milner's CCS, where communication is based on the synchronisation of atomic actions. From this viewpoint, we get a useful class of morphisms, sufficient to relate the behaviour of processes and their subcomponents, by taking a morphism from one transition system T to another T' to be a pair (σ, λ), in which

- σ is a function from the states of T to those of T' that sends the initial state of T to that of T',

- λ is a *partial* function from the labels of T to those of T' such that for any transition $s \xrightarrow{a} a'$ of T if $\lambda(a)$ is defined, then $\sigma(s) \xrightarrow{\lambda(a)} \sigma(s')$ is a transition of T'; otherwise, if $\lambda(a)$ is undefined, then $\sigma(s) = \sigma(s')$.

Morphisms respect a choice of granularity for actions in the sense that an action may only be sent to at most one action, and not to a computation consisting of several actions. By taking λ to be a *partial* function on labels, we in particular allow for the fact that projecting from a parallel composition of processes (*e.g.* in CCS) to a component may not only change action names, but also allow some actions to vanish if they do not correspond to those of the component, in which case their occurrence has no effect on the state of the component.

This definition of morphism is sufficient to express the relationship between a constructed process and its components as morphisms, at least within a language like CCS. But conversely the choice of morphisms also produces constructions. This is because transition systems and their morphisms form a category, and universal constructions (including limits and colimits) of a category are determined uniquely to within isomorphism, once they exist. In fact the universal constructions of the category of transition systems form the basis of a process description language. It is a little richer than that of CCS and CSP in the sense that their operations are straightforwardly definable within it.

When we consider other models as categories the same universal constructions yield sensible interpretations of the process-language constructs. Without categories this unity is lost; indeed, the denotations of parallel compositions, often nontrivial to define, have been invented in an *ad hoc* fashion for most of the models we present.

Categorical notions also come into play in relating different models. Another model, synchronisation trees, arises by ignoring repetitive behaviour. We can identify synchronisation trees with special transition systems (those with no loops, no distinct transitions *to* the same state, in which all states are reachable). Synchronisation trees inherit morphisms from transition systems, and themselves form a category. The inclusion of synchronisation trees in transition systems is a functor. But more, the inclusion functor is part of an adjunction; the inclusion functor (the left adjoint) is accompanied, in a uniquely-determined way, by a functor (the right adjoint) unfolding transition systems to synchronisation trees. A further step of abstraction, this time ignoring the branching of computation paths, takes us to languages as models of processes. A process is represented by the set of strings of actions it can perform. Languages can be identified with certain kinds of synchronisation trees and again this inclusion is part of an adjunction. As parts of adjunctions the functors enjoy preservation properties, which coupled with the understanding of process operations as universal constructions, are useful in relating different semantics.

We have discussed just the three simplest models, but the same general approach applies to other models. The main idea is that each model will be equipped with a notion of morphism, making it into a category in which the operations of process calculi are universal constructions. The morphisms will preserve behaviour, at the same time respecting a choice of granularity of actions in the description of processes. One role of the morphisms is to relate the behaviour of a construction on processes to that of its components. As we shall see, it turns out that certain kinds of adjunctions (reflections and coreflections[1]) provide a way to express that one model is embedded in (is more abstract than) another, even when the two models are expressed in very different mathematical terms. One adjoint will say how to embed the more abstract model in the other, the other will abstract away from some aspect of the representation. Importantly, we can use the preservation properties of adjoints to show how a semantics in one model translates to a semantics in another. The adjunctions not only provide an aid in the understanding of the different models and their relationships, but are also a vehicle for the transfer of techniques from one model to another, for example in extending the notion of bisimulation beyond

---

[1] A *reflection* is an adjunction in which the right adjoint is full and faithful, a *coreflection* one where the left adjoint is full and faithful.

transition systems to other models.[2]

2   Transition systems

Transition systems are a commonly used and understood model of computation. They provide the basic operational semantics for Milner's Calculus of Communicating Systems (CCS) and often underlie other approaches, such as that of Hoare's Communicating Sequential Processes (CSP). The constructions on transition systems used in such methods can frequently be seen as universal in a category of transition systems, where the morphisms can be understood as expressing the partial simulation (or refinement) of one process by another. By "abstract nonsense" the universal properties will characterise the constructions to within isomorphism. More strikingly, the same universal properties apply in the case of other models like Petri nets or event structures, which are seemingly very different in nature.

2.1   A category of transition systems

Transition systems consist of a set of states, with an initial state, together with transitions between states which are labelled to specify the kind of events they represent.

Definition: A *transition system* is a structure

$$(S, i, L, Tran)$$

where

- S is a set of *states* with *initial state* i,

- L is a set of *labels*, and

- $Tran \subseteq S \times L \times S$ is the
  transition relation.

Notation: Let $(S, i, L, Tran)$ be a transition system. We write

$$s \xrightarrow{\ a\ } s'$$

---

[2] A knowledge of basic category theory, up to an acquaintance with the notion of adjunction and monad, is sufficient for the notes. However a light acquaintance, and some goodwill, should suffice, at least for the earlier parts. Good introductory references are (van Oosten 1995; Pierce 1991; Barr and Wells 1990), while (MacLane 1971) remains the classic text.

to indicate that $(s, a, s') \in Tran$. This notation lends itself to the familiar graphical notation for transition systems. It is sometimes convenient to extend the arc-notation to strings of labels and write $s \xrightarrow{v} s'$, when $v = a_1 a_2 \cdots a_n$ is a, possibly empty, string of labels in L, to mean

$$s \xrightarrow{a_1} s_1 \xrightarrow{a_2} \cdots \xrightarrow{a_n} s_n,$$

for some states $s_1, \ldots, s_n$ with $s_n = s'$. A state s is said to be *reachable* when $i \xrightarrow{v} s$ for some string v.

Definition: Say a transition system $T = (S, i, L, Tran)$ is *reachable* iff every state in S is reachable from i and for every label a there is a transition $(s, a, s') \in Tran$. Say T is *acyclic* iff, for all strings of labels v, if $s \xrightarrow{v} s$ then v is empty.

It is convenient to introduce *idle* transitions, associated with any state. This has to do with our representation of the category of sets with partial functions. Assume that X and Y are sets not containing the reserved symbol $*$. Write $f : X \to_* Y$ for a function $f : X \cup \{*\} \to Y \cup \{*\}$ such that $f(*) = *$. When $f(x) = *$, for $x \in X$, we say $f(x)$ is *undefined* and otherwise *defined*. We say $f : X \to_* Y$ is *total* when $f(x)$ is defined for all $x \in X$. Of course, such total morphisms $X \to_* Y$ correspond to the usual total functions $X \to Y$, with which they shall be identified. For the category **Set**$_*$, we take as objects sets which do not contain $*$, and as morphisms functions $f : X \to_* Y$, with the composition of two such functions being the usual composition of total functions (but on sets extended by $*$). Of course, **Set**$_*$ is isomorphic to the category of sets with partial functions, as usually presented.

Definition: Let $T = (S, i, L, Tran)$ be a transition system. An *idle transition* of T typically consists of $(s, *, s)$, where $s \in S$. Define

$$Tran_* = Tran \cup \{(s, *, s) \mid s \in S\}.$$

Idle transitions help simplify the definition of morphisms between transition systems. Morphisms on transitions systems have already been discussed in the Introduction. There, a morphism $T \to T'$ between transition systems was presented as consisting of a pair, one component σ being a function on states, preserving initial states, and the other a partial function λ on labels with the property that together they send a transition of T to a transition of T', whenever this makes sense. More precisely, if (s, a, s') is a transition of T then $(\sigma(s), \lambda(a), \sigma(s'))$ is a transition of T' provided $\lambda(a)$ is defined; otherwise, in the case where $\lambda(a)$ is undefined, it is insisted that the two states $\sigma(s)$ and $\sigma(s')$ are equal. With the device of idle transitions and the particular representation of partial functions, the same effect is achieved with the following definition:

Definition: Let

$$T_0 = (S_0, i_0, L_0, Tran_0) \text{ and}$$
$$T_1 = (S_1, i_1, L_1, Tran_1)$$

be transition systems. A *morphism* $f : T_0 \to T_1$ is a pair $f = (\sigma, \lambda)$ where

- $\sigma : S_0 \to S_1$

- $\lambda : L_0 \to_* L_1$ are such that $\sigma(i_0) = i_1$ and

$$(s, a, s') \in Tran_0 \Rightarrow (\sigma(s), \lambda(a), \sigma(s')) \in Tran_{1*}.$$

The intention behind the definition of morphism is that the effect of a transition with label a in T_0 leads to inaction in T_1 precisely when $\lambda(a)$ is undefined. In our definition of morphism, idle transitions represent this inaction, so we avoid the fuss of considering whether or not $\lambda(a)$ is defined. With the introduction of idle transitions, morphisms on transition systems can be described as preserving transitions and the initial state. It is stressed that an idle transition $(s, *, s)$ represents inaction, and is to be distinguished from the action expressed by a transition (s, a, s') for a label a.

Morphisms preserve initial states and transitions and so clearly preserve reachable states:

Proposition 1 *Let $(\sigma, \lambda) : T_0 \to T_1$ be a morphism of transition systems. Then if s is a reachable state of T_0 then $\sigma(s)$ is a reachable state of T_1.*

Transition systems and their morphisms form a category which will be the first important category in our study:

Proposition 2 *Taking*

- *the class of objects to be transition systems,*

- *the class of morphisms to be those of transition systems,*

defines a category, where

- *the composition of two morphisms $f = (\sigma, \lambda) : T_0 \to T_1$ and $g = (\sigma', \lambda') : T_1 \to T_2$ is $g \circ f = (\sigma' \circ \sigma, \lambda' \circ \lambda) : T_0 \to T_2$—here composition on the left of a pair is that of total functions while that on the right is of partial functions, and*

- *the identity morphism for a transition system T has the form $(1_S, 1_L)$, where 1_S is the identity function on states S and 1_L is the identity function on the labelling set L of T.*

Definition: Denote by **T** the category of labelled transition systems given by the last proposition.

2.2 Constructions on transition systems

Transition systems are used in many areas. We focus on their use in modelling process calculi. The constructions used there can be understood as universal constructions in the category of transition systems. The point is not to explain the familiar in terms of the unfamiliar, but rather to find characterisations of sufficient generality that they apply to the other models as well. As we will see, the category of transition systems is rich in categorical constructions which furnish the basic combinators for a language of parallel processes.

2.2.1 Restriction

Restriction is an important operation on processes. For example, in Milner's CCS, labels are used to distinguish between input and output to channels, connected to processes at ports, and internal events. The effect of hiding all but a specified set of ports of a process, so that communication can no longer take place at the hidden ports, is to restrict the original behaviour of the process to transitions which do not occur at the hidden ports. Given a transition system and a subset of its labelling set, the operation of restriction removes all transitions whose labels are not in that set:

Definition: Let $T' = (S, i, L', Tran')$ be a transition system. Assume $L \subseteq L'$ and let $\lambda : L \hookrightarrow L'$ be the associated inclusion morphism, taking a in L to a in L'. Define the *restriction* $T' \upharpoonright \lambda$ to be the transition system $(S, i, L, Tran)$ with

$$Tran = \{(s, a, t) \in Tran' \mid a \in L\}.$$

Restriction is a construction which depends on labelling sets and functions between them. Seeing it as a categorical construction involves dealing explicitly with functions on labelling sets and borrowing a fundamental idea from fibred category theory. We observe that there is a functor $p : \mathbf{T} \to \mathbf{Set}_*$, to the category of sets with partial functions, which sends a morphism of transition systems $(\sigma, \lambda) : T \to T'$ between transition systems T over L and T' over L' to the partial function $\lambda : L \to_* L'$. Associated with a restriction $T' \upharpoonright L$ is a morphism $f : T' \upharpoonright L \to T'$, given by $f = (1_S, \lambda)$ where λ is the inclusion map $\lambda : L \hookrightarrow L'$. In fact the morphism f is essentially an "inclusion" of the restricted into the original transition system. The morphism f associated with the restriction has the universal property that:

> For any $g : T \to T'$ a morphism in $\mathbf{T}$ such that $p(g) = \lambda$ there is a unique morphism $h : T \to T' \upharpoonright L$ such that $p(h) = 1_L$ and $f \circ h = g$. In a diagram:

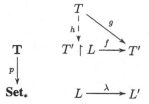

This says that the "inclusion" morphisms associated with restrictions are *cartesian*; the morphism f is said to be a *cartesian lifting* of λ with respect to T'.

Proposition 3 *Let* $\lambda : L \to_* L'$ *be an inclusion. Let* T' *be a labelled transition system, with states* S. *There is a morphism* $f : T' \upharpoonright L \to T'$, *given by* $f = (1_S, \lambda)$. *It is cartesian.*

Because an inclusion $\lambda : L \hookrightarrow L'$ has cartesian liftings for any T' with labelling set L', restriction automatically extends to a functor from transition systems with labelling set L' to those with labelling set L. To state this more fully, note first that a labelling set L is associated with a subcategory of transition systems $p^{-1}(L)$, called the *fibre* over L, consisting of objects those transition systems T for which $p(T) = L$ (*i.e.* whose labelling set is L) and morphisms h for which $p(h) = 1_L$ (*i.e.* which preserve labels). An explicit choice of cartesian lifting for each T' in $p^{-1}(L')$ (as is provided by the restriction operation) yields a functor between fibres $p^{-1}(L') \to p^{-1}(L)$—the functor's action on morphisms coming from the universal property of cartesian liftings.

2.2.2 Relabelling

In CCS, one can make copies of a process by renaming its port names. This is associated with the operation of relabelling the transitions in the transition system representing its behaviour. When $\lambda : L \to_* L'$ is total, the relabelling construction takes a transition system T with labelling set L to $T\{\lambda\}$, the same underlying transition system but relabelled according to λ.

Definition: Let $T = (S, i, L, Tran)$ be a transition system. Let $\lambda : L \to L'$ be a total function. Define the *relabelling* $T\{\lambda\}$ to be the transition system $(S, i, L', Tran')$ where

$$Tran' = \{(s, \lambda(a), s') \mid (s, a, s') \in Tran\}.$$

The operation of relabelling is associated with a construction dual to that of cartesian lifting, that of forming a *cocartesian lifting*. Letting the transition system T have states S, there is a morphism $f = (1_S, \lambda) : T \to T\{\lambda\}$. Such a morphism is a cocartesian lifting of λ in the sense that:

> For any $g : T \to T'$ a morphism in **T** such that $p(g) = \lambda$ there is a unique morphism $h : T\{\lambda\} \to T'$ such that $p(h) = 1_{L'}$ and $h \circ f = g$.
> In a diagram:

$$
\begin{array}{ccc}
 & & T' \\
 & \nearrow^{g} & \uparrow{\scriptstyle h} \\
\mathbf{T} & T \xrightarrow{f} & T\{\lambda\} \\
\Big\downarrow{\scriptstyle p} & & \\
\mathbf{Set}_* & L \xrightarrow{\ \lambda\ } & L'
\end{array}
$$

Proposition 4 *Let* $\lambda : L \to L'$ *be a total function. Let* T *be a labelled transition system, with states* S. *There is a morphism* $f : T \to T\{\lambda\}$, *given by* $f = (1_S, \lambda)$ *which is cocartesian.*

Relabelling extends to a functor $p^{-1}(L) \to p^{-1}(L')$, where $\lambda : L \to L'$ is a total function.

2.2.3 Product

Parallel compositions are central operations in process calculi; they set processes in communication with each other. Communication is via actions of mutual synchronisation, possibly with the exchange of values. Precisely how actions synchronise with each other varies enormously from one language to another, but for example in CCS and Occam processes are imagined to communicate over channels linking their ports. In these languages, an input action to a channel from one process can combine with an output action to the same channel from the other to form an action of synchronisation. The languages also allow for processes in a parallel composition to reserve the possibility of communicating with a, yet undetermined, process in the environment of both.

Parallel compositions in general can be derived, with restriction and relabelling, from a product operation on transition systems. In itself the product operation is a special kind of parallel composition in which all conceivable synchronisations are allowed. Because morphisms of transition systems have a component which is a partial function on labelling sets, it is not surprising that the labelling set of the product of two transition systems, which individually have labelling sets L_0 and L_1, is the product $L_0 \times_* L_1$ in **Set**$_*$.

Definition: Assume given transition systems $T_0 = (S_0, i_0, L_0, Tran_0)$ and $T_1 = (S_1, i_1, L_1, Tran_1)$. Their *product* $T_0 \times T_1$ is $(S, i, L, Tran)$ where

- $S = S_0 \times S_1$, with $i = (i_0, i_1)$, and projections $\rho_0 : S_0 \times S_1 \to S_0$, $\rho_1 : S_0 \times S_1 \to S_1$

- $L = L_0 \times_* L_1 =$
  $\{(a, *) \mid a \in L_0\} \cup \{(*, b) \mid b \in L_1\} \cup \{(a, b) \mid a \in L_0, b \in L_1\}$,
  with projections π_0, π_1, and

- $(s, a, s') \in Tran_* \Leftrightarrow$
  $(\rho_0(s), \pi_0(a), \rho_0(s')) \in Tran_{0*}$ & $(\rho_1(s), \pi_1(a), \rho_1(s')) \in Tran_{1*}$.

Define $\Pi_0 = (\rho_0, \pi_0)$ and $\Pi_1 = (\rho_1, \pi_1)$.

Example: Let T_0 and T_1 be the following transition systems

where T_0 has $\{a\}$ and T_1 has $\{b\}$ as labelling set. The product of these labelling sets is

$$\{a\} \times_* \{b\} = \{(a, *), (a, b), (*, b)\}$$

with projections λ_0 onto the first coordinate and λ_1 onto the second. Thus $\lambda_0(a, *) = \lambda_0(a, b) = a$ and $\lambda_0(*, b) = *$. Their product takes the form:

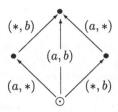

Intuitively, transitions with labels of the form (a, b) represent synchronisations between two processes set in parallel, while those labelled $(a, *)$ or $(*, b)$ involve only one process, performing the transition unsynchronised with the other. Clearly, this is far too "generous" a parallel composition to be useful as it stands, allowing as it does all possible synchronisations and absences of synchronisations between two processes. However, a wide range of familiar and useful parallel compositions can be obtained from the product operation by further applications of restriction (to remove unwanted synchronisations) and relabelling (to rename the results of synchronisations).

The product of transition systems T_0, T_1 has projection morphisms $\Pi_0 = (\rho_0, \pi_0) : T_0 \times T_1 \to T_0$ and $\Pi_1 = (\rho_1, \pi_1) : T_0 \times T_1 \to T_1$. They together satisfy the universal property required of a *product in a category*; *viz.* given any morphisms $f_0 : T \to T_0$ and $f_1 : T \to T_1$ from a transition system T there is a unique morphism $h : T \to T_0 \times T_1$ such that $\Pi_0 \circ h = f_0$ and $\Pi_1 \circ h = f_1$:

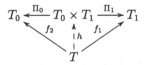

Proposition 5 *Let T_0 and T_1 be transition systems. The construction $T_0 \times T_1$ above, with projections $\Pi_0 = (\rho_0, \pi_0)$, $\Pi_1 = (\rho_1, \pi_1)$, is a product in the category* **T**. *A state s is reachable in $T_0 \times T_1$ iff $\rho_0(s)$ is reachable in T_0 and $\rho_1(s)$ is reachable in T_1.*

Although we have only considered binary products, all products exist in the category of transition systems. In particular, the empty product is the *nil* transition system

$$nil = (\{i\}, i, \emptyset, \emptyset),$$

consisting of a single initial state i. In this special case the universal property for products amounts to:

For any transition system T, there is a unique morphism $h : T \to nil$,

that is, *nil* is a *terminal* object in the category of transition systems. The transition system *nil* is also an *initial* object in the category of transition systems:

For any transition system T, there is a unique morphism $h : nil \to T$.

We remark that the product-machine construction from automata theory arises as a *fibre product*, *viz.* a product in a fibre. Recall a fibre $p^{-1}(L)$ is a category which consists of the subcategory of transition systems with a common labelling set L, in which the morphisms preserve labels.

2.2.4 Parallel compositions

In the present framework, we do not obtain arbitrary parallel compositions as single universal constructions. Generally, they can be obtained from the product by restriction and relabelling; a parallel composition of T_0 and T_1, with labelling sets L_0, L_1 respectively, is got by first taking their product, to give a transition system $T_0 \times T_1$ with labelling set $L_0 \times_* L_1$, then restricting by taking $(T_0 \times T_1) \restriction S$ for an inclusion $S \subseteq L_0 \times_* L_1$, followed by a relabelling $((T_0 \times T_1) \restriction S)\{r\}$ with respect to a total function $r : S \to L$. In this way, using a combination of product, restriction and relabelling we can represent all conceivable parallel compositions which occur by synchronisation.

In general parallel compositions are derived using a combination of product, restriction and relabelling. We can present the range of associative, commutative parallel compositions based on synchronisation in a uniform way by using *synchronisation algebras*. A synchronisation algebra on a set L of labels (not containing the distinct elements $*, 0$) consists of a binary, commutative, associative operation $\bullet$ on $L \cup \{*, 0\}$ such that

$$a \bullet 0 = 0 \text{ and } (a_0 \bullet a_1 = * \Leftrightarrow a_0 = a_1 = *)$$

for all $a, a_0, a_1 \in L \cup \{*, 0\}$. The role of 0 is to specify those synchronisations which are not allowed whereas the composition $\bullet$ specifies a relabelling. (It may be helpful to look at the example ahead of the synchronisation algebra of CCS.) For a synchronisation algebra on labels L, let $\lambda_0, \lambda_1 : L \times_* L \to_* L$ be the projections on its product in **Set**$_*$. The parallel composition of two transition systems T_0, T_1, labelled over L, can be obtained as $((T_0 \times T_1) \restriction D)\{r\}$ where $D \subseteq L \times_* L$ is the inclusion of

$$D = \{a \in L \times_* L \mid \lambda_0(a) \bullet \lambda_1(a) \neq 0\}$$

determined by the 0-element, and $r : D \to L$ is the relabelling, given by

$$r(a) = \lambda_0(a) \bullet \lambda_1(a)$$

for $a \in D$.

We present one synchronisation algebra as an example, in the form of tables—more, including those for value-passing, can be found in (Winskel 1982; Winskel 1985).

Example: *The synchronisation algebra for pure CCS:* In CCS (Milner 1989) events are labelled by $a, b, \cdots$ or by their complementary labels $\bar{a}, \bar{b}, \cdots$ or by the label τ. The idea is that only two events bearing complementary labels may synchronise to form a synchronisation event labelled by τ. Events labelled by τ cannot synchronise further; in this sense they are invisible to processes in the environment, though their occurrence may lead to internal changes of state. All labelled events may occur asynchronously. Hence the synchronisation algebra for CCS takes the following form. The resultant parallel composition, of processes p and q say, is represented as $p|q$ in CCS.

$\bullet$	$*$	a	$\bar{a}$	b	$\bar{b}$	$\cdots$	τ	0
$*$	$*$	a	$\bar{a}$	b	$\bar{b}$	$\cdots$	τ	0
a	a	0	τ	0	0	$\cdots$	0	0
$\bar{a}$	$\bar{a}$	τ	0	0	0	$\cdots$	0	0
b	b	0	0	0	τ	$\cdots$	0	0
$\cdot$		$\cdot$	$\cdot$	$\cdot$	$\cdot$	$\cdots$	$\cdot$	$\cdot$

2.2.5 Sum

Nondeterministic sums in process calculi allow a process to be defined with the capabilities of two or more processes, so that the process can behave like one of several alternative processes. Which alternative can depend on what communications the environment offers, and in many cases, nondeterministic sum plays an important role like that of the conditional of traditional sequential languages.

With the aim of understanding nondeterministic sums as universal constructions we examine coproducts in the category of transition systems.

Definition: Let $T_0 = (S_0, i_0, L_0, Tran_0)$ and $T_1 = (S_1, i_1, L_1, Tran_1)$ be transition systems. Define $T_0 + T_1$ to be $(S, i, L, Tran)$ where

- $S = (S_0 \times \{i_1\}) \cup (\{i_0\} \times S_1)$ with $i = (i_0, i_1)$, and injections in_0, in_1,

- $L = L_0 \uplus L_1$, their disjoint union, with injections j_0, j_1 (this a coproduct in the category **Set**$_*$ of sets with partial functions),

- transitions

$$t \in Tran \Leftrightarrow \exists (s, a, s') \in Tran_0.\, t = (in_0(s), j_0(a), in_0(s')) \text{ or}$$
$$\exists (s, a, s') \in Tran_1.\, t = (in_1(s), j_1(a), in_1(s')).$$

The construction $T_0 + T_1$ on transition systems T_0, T_1 has injection morphisms $I_0 = (in_0, j_0) : T_0 \to T_0 + T_1$ and $I_1 = (in_1, j_1) : T_1 \to T_0 + T_1$. They together satisfy the universal property required of a *coproduct in a category*; *viz.*. . given any morphisms $f_0 : T_0 \to T$ and $f_1 : T_1 \to T$ to a transition system T there is a unique morphism $h : T_0 + T_1 \to T$ such that $h \circ I_0 = f_0$ and $h \circ I_1 = f_1$:

$$
\begin{array}{ccc}
& T & \\
{\scriptstyle f_0} \nearrow & {\scriptstyle\uparrow h} & \nwarrow {\scriptstyle f_1} \\
T_0 \xrightarrow{\ I_0\ } & T_0 + T_1 & \xleftarrow{\ I_1\ } T_1
\end{array}
$$

Proposition 6 *Let T_0 and T_1 be transition systems. Then $T_0 + T_1$, with injections $(in_0, j_0), (in_1, j_1)$, is a coproduct in the category of transition systems. A state s is reachable in a coproduct iff there is s_0 reachable in T_0 with $s = in_0(s_0)$ or there is s_1 reachable in T_1 with $s = in_1(s_1)$.*

The coproduct is not quite of the kind used in modelling the sum of CCS for example, because in the coproduct labels are made disjoint. We look to coproducts in a fibre.

For a labelling set L, each fibre $p^{-1}(L)$ has coproducts. Recall $p^{-1}(L)$ is that subcategory of **T** consisting of transition systems over a common labelling set L with morphisms those which project to the identity on L. In form fibre coproducts are very similar to coproducts of transition systems in general—they differ only in the labelling part.

Definition: Let $T_0 = (S_0, i_0, L, Tran_0)$ and $T_1 = (S_1, i_1, L, Tran_1)$ be transition systems over the same labelling set L. Define $T_0 +_L T_1 = (S, i, L, Tran)$ (note it is over the same labelling set) where:

$S = (S_0 \times \{i_1\}) \cup (\{i_0\} \times S_1)$ with $i = (i_0, i_1)$, and injections in_0, in_1, and

$$
t \in Tran \Leftrightarrow \exists (s, a, s') \in Tran_0. \ t = (in_0(s), a, in_0(s')) \ \text{or}
$$
$$
\exists (s, a, s') \in Tran_1. \ t = (in_1(s), a, in_1(s')).
$$

Proposition 7 *Let T_0 and T_1 be transition systems over L. The transition system $T_0 +_L T_1$ with injections $(in_0, 1_L)$ and $(in_1, 1_L)$, as defined above, is a coproduct in the subcategory of transition systems consisting of the fibre $p^{-1}(L)$.*

Neither the coproduct or fibre coproduct of transition systems quite match the kind of sums used in modelling processes, for example, in CCS. The coproduct changes the labels, tagging them so they are disjoint, while the fibre coproduct, seemingly more appropriate because it leaves the labels unchanged, assumes that the transition systems have the same labelling set. A more traditional sum is the following:

Definition: Let T_0 and T_1 be transition systems over L_0 and L_1 respectively. Define their *sum* $T_0 \oplus T_1$ to be $(S, i, L_0 \cup L_1, Tran)$ where

$S = (S_0 \times \{i_1\}) \cup (\{i_0\} \times S_1)$ with $i = (i_0, i_1)$, and injections in_0, in_1, and

$$t \in Tran \Leftrightarrow \exists(s, a, s') \in Tran_0. \ t = (in_0(s), a, in_0(s')) \text{ or}$$
$$\exists(s, a, s') \in Tran_1. \ t = (in_1(s), a, in_1(s')).$$

This sum can be understood as a fibre coproduct, but where first we form cocartesian liftings of the inclusion maps into the union of the labelling sets; this simply has the effect of enlarging the labelling sets to a common labelling set, their union, where we can form the fibre coproduct:

Proposition 8 *Let T_0 and T_1 be transition systems over L_0 and L_1 respectively. Let $j_k : L_k \hookrightarrow L_0 \cup L_1$ be the inclusion maps, for $k = 0, 1$. Then*

$$T_0 \oplus T_1 \cong T_0\{j_0\} +_{(L_0 \cup L_1)} T_1\{j_1\}.$$

Only coproducts of two transition systems have been considered. All coproducts exist in fibres and in the category of all transition systems. Thus there are indexed sums of transition systems of the kind used in CCS. The sum construction on transition systems is of the form required for CCS when the transition systems are "nonrestarting", *i.e.* have no transitions back to the initial state. In giving and relating semantics we shall be mindful of this fact.

Example: The fibred coproduct $T_0 +_L T_1$ of

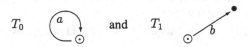

both assumed to have the labelling set $L = \{a, b\}$, takes the form:

The sum can behave like T_0 but then on returning to the initial state behave like T_1.

2.2.6 Prefixing

The categorical constructions form a basis for languages of parallel processes with constructs like parallel compositions and nondeterministic sums. The cartesian and cocartesian liftings give rise to restriction and relabelling operations as special cases, but the more general constructions, arising for morphisms in the base category which are truly partial, might also be useful constructions to introduce into a programming language. This raises an omission from our collection of constructions; we have not yet mentioned an operation which introduces new transitions from scratch. Traditionally, in languages like CCS, CSP and Occam this is done with some form of prefixing operation, the effect of which is to produce a new process which behaves like a given process once a specified, initial action has taken place. Given a transition system, the operation of prefixing $a(-)$ introduces a transition, with label a, from a new initial state to the former initial state in a copy of the transition system. One way to define prefixing on transition systems concretely is by:

Definition: Let a be a label (not $*$). Define the *prefix* $aT = (S', i', L', Tran')$ where

$$S' = \{\{s\} \mid s \in S\} \cup \{\emptyset\},$$
$$i' = \emptyset,$$
$$L' = L \cup \{a\},$$
$$Tran' = \{(\{s\}, b, \{s'\}) \mid (s, b, s') \in Tran\} \cup \{(\emptyset, a, \{i\})\}.$$

Because we do not ensure that the prefixing label is distinct from the former labels, prefixing does not extend to a functor on all morphisms of transition systems. However, it extends to a functor on the subcategory of label-preserving morphisms, *i.e.* those morphisms $(\sigma, \lambda) : T \to T'$ between transition systems for which $\lambda : L \hookrightarrow L'$ is an inclusion function. As a special case, prefixing $a(-)$ extends to a functor between fibres $p^{-1}(L) \to p^{-1}(L \cup \{a\})$.

3 A process language

A process language **Proc** and its semantics can be built around the constructions on the category of transition systems. Indeed the process language can be interpreted in all the models we consider. Its syntax is given by

$$t ::= nil \mid at \mid t_0 \oplus t_1 \mid t_0 \times t_1 \mid t \upharpoonright \Lambda \mid t\{\Xi\} \mid x \mid rec\, x.t$$

where a is a label, Λ is a subset of labels and Ξ is a total function from labels to labels. We have seen how to interpret most of these constructions in transition systems, which in particular will yield a labelling set for each term. It is convenient to broaden the understanding of a restriction $t \upharpoonright \Lambda$ so it means the same as $t \upharpoonright \Lambda \cap L$

in the situation where the labelling set L does not include Λ. The denotation of $t\{\Xi\}$ is obtained from the cocartesian lifting with respect to t of the function $\Xi : L \to \Xi L$, so that t with labelling set L is relabelled by Ξ cut down to domain L. The new construction is the recursive construction of the form $rec\ x.t$, involving x a variable over processes.

The presence of process variables means that the denotation of a term as a transition system is given with respect to an environment ρ mapping process variables to transition systems. We can proceed routinely, by induction on the structure of terms, to give an interpretation of syntactic operations by those operations on transition systems we have introduced, for example we set

$\mathbf{T}[\![nil]\!]\rho = nil$, for a choice of initial transition systems

$\mathbf{T}[\![t_0 \oplus t_1]\!]\rho = \mathbf{T}[\![t_0]\!]\rho \oplus \mathbf{T}[\![t_1]\!]\rho$, the nondeterministic sum of section 2.2.5

ω-colimits are used to interpret $\mathbf{T}[\![rec\ x.t]\!]\rho$, but here we won't go into the details, and refer to (Winskel and Nielsen 1995).

Proc can also be given an operational semantics in agreement with the denotational semantics above—see (Winskel and Nielsen 1995), where the proof that the two semantics correspond assumes that in recursive process terms of the form $rec\ x.t$ the variable x is guarded.

4   Synchronisation trees

We turn to consider another model. It gives rise to our first example illustrating how different models can be related through the help of adjunctions between their associated categories.

In his foundational work on CCS (Milner 1980), Milner introduced synchronisation trees as a model of parallel processes and explained the meaning of the language of CCS in terms of operations on them. In this section we briefly examine the category of synchronisation trees and its relation to that of labelled transition systems. This illustrates the method by which many other models are related, and the role category theoretic ideas play in formulating and proving facts which relate semantics in one model to semantics in another.

A synchronisation tree is a tree together with labels on its arcs. Formally, we define synchronisation trees to be special kinds of labelled transition systems, those for which the transition relation is acyclic and can only branch away from the root.

Definition: A *synchronisation tree* is a transition system $(S, i, L, Tran)$ where

- every state is reachable,

- if $s \xrightarrow{v} s$, for a string v, then v is empty (*i.e.* the transition system is acyclic), and

- $s' \xrightarrow{a} s$ & $s'' \xrightarrow{b} s \Rightarrow a = b$ & $s' = s''$.

Regarded in this way, we obtain synchronisation trees as a full subcategory of labelled transition systems, with a projection functor to the category of labelling sets with partial functions.

Definition: Write **S** for the full subcategory of synchronisation trees in **T**.

In fact, the inclusion functor **S** $\hookrightarrow$ **T** has a right adjoint ts : **T** $\to$ **S** which has the effect of unfolding a labelled transition system to a synchronisation tree.[3]

Definition: Let T be a labelled transition system $(S, i, L, Tran)$. Define $ts(T)$ to be $(S', i', L, Tran')$ where:

- The set S' consists of all finite, possibly empty, sequences of transitions

$$(t_1, \cdots, t_j, t_{j+1}, \cdots, t_{n-1})$$

such that $t_j = (s_{j-1}, a_j, s_j)$ and $t_{j+1} = (s_j, a_{j+1}, s_{j+1})$ whenever $1 < j < n$. The element $i' = ()$, the empty sequence.

- The set $Tran'$ consists of all triples (u, a, v) where $u, v \in S'$ and $u = (u_1, \ldots, u_k)$, $v = (u_1, \ldots, u_k, (s, a, s'))$, obtained by appending an a transition to u.

Define ϕ : $S' \to S$ by taking $\phi(()) = i$ and $\phi((t_1, \cdots, t_n)) = s_n$, where $t_n = (s_{n-1}, a_n, s_n)$.

Theorem 9 *Let T be a labelled transition system, with labelling set L. Then $ts(T)$ is a synchronisation tree, also with labelling set L, and, with the definition above, $(\phi, 1_L) : ts(T) \to T$ is a morphism. Moreover $ts(T), (\phi, 1_L)$ is cofree over T with respect to the inclusion functor **S** $\hookrightarrow$ **T**, i.e. for any morphism $f : V \to T$, with V a synchronisation tree, there is a unique morphism $g : V \to ts(T)$ such that $f = (\phi, 1_L) \circ g$:*

$$T \xleftarrow{(\phi, 1_L)} ts(T)$$
$$\nwarrow_{f} \qquad \uparrow_{g}$$
$$V$$

It follows that the operation ts extends to a functor which is right adjoint to the inclusion functor from **S** to **T** and that the morphisms $(\phi, 1_L) : ts(T) \to T$ are the counits of this adjunction (see MacLane 1971, Theorem 2, p. 81). This makes **S** a (full) coreflective subcategory of **T**, which implies the intuitively obvious fact that

---

[3] Because we shall be concerned with several categories and functors between them we name the functors in a way that indicates their domain and range.

a synchronisation tree T is isomorphic to its unfolding $ts(T)$ (see MacLane 1971, p.88).

Like transition systems, synchronisation trees have been used to give semantics to languages like CCS and CSP (see *e.g.* (Milner 1980), (Brookes 1983)). Nondeterministic sums of processes are modelled by the operation of joining synchronisation trees at their roots, a special case of the nondeterministic sum of transition systems. We use $\sum_{i \in I} S_i$ for the sum of synchronisation trees indexed by $i \in I$. For the semantics of parallel composition, use is generally made of Milner's "expansion theorem" (see (Milner 1980)). In our context, the expansion of a parallel composition as a nondeterministic sum appears as a characterisation of the product of synchronisation trees.

Proposition 10 *The product of two synchronisation trees S and T of the form*

$$S \cong \sum_{i \in I} a_i S_i \quad and \quad T \cong \sum_{j \in J} b_j T_j.$$

is given by

$$S \times T \cong \sum_{i \in I} (a_i, *) S_i \times T \oplus \sum_{i \in I, j \in J} (a_i, b_j) S_i \times T_j \oplus \sum_{j \in J} (*, b_j) S \times T_j.$$

The coreflection between transition systems and synchronisation trees is fibrewise in that it restricts to adjunctions between fibres over a common labelling set. For example, for this reason its right adjoint of unfolding automatically preserves restriction because it is associated with a cartesian lifting (see Appendix B of Winskel and Nielsen 1995). Right adjoints, such as the operation of unfolding a transition system to a tree, do not necessarily preserve colimits like nondeterministic sums.

5 Languages

Synchronisation trees abstract away from the looping structure of processes. Now we examine a yet more abstract model, that of languages, which further ignores the nondeterministic branching structure of processes.

Definition: A *language* over a labelling set L consists of (H, L) where H is a nonempty subset of strings L^* which is closed under prefixes, *i.e.* if $a_0 \cdots a_{i-1} a_i \in H$ then $a_0 \cdots a_{i-1} \in H$.

Thus for a language (H, L) the empty string ε is always contained in H. Such languages were called *traces* in (Hoare 1981) and for this reason, in the context of modelling concurrency, they are sometimes called *Hoare traces*. They consist however simply of strings and are not to be confused with the traces of Mazurkiewicz, to be seen later.

Morphisms of languages are partial functions on their alphabets which send strings in one language to strings in another:

Definition: A partial function $\lambda : L \rightarrow_* L'$ extends to strings by defining

$$\widehat{\lambda}(sa) = \begin{cases} \widehat{\lambda}(s)\lambda(a) & \text{if } \lambda(a) \text{ defined}, \\ \widehat{\lambda}(s) & \text{if } \lambda(a) \text{ undefined}. \end{cases}$$

A *morphism* of languages $(H, L) \rightarrow (H', L')$ consists of a partial function $\lambda : L \rightarrow_* L'$ such that $\forall s \in H.\ \widehat{\lambda}(s) \in H'$.
We write **L** for the category of languages with the above understanding of morphisms, where composition is our usual composition of partial functions.

Ordering strings in a language by extension enables us to regard the language as a synchronisation tree. The ensuing notion of morphism coincides with that of languages. This observation yields a functor from **L** to **S**. On the other hand any transition system, and in particular any synchronisation tree, gives rise to a language consisting of strings of labels obtained from the sequences of transitions it can perform. This operation extends to a functor. The two functors form an adjunction from **S** to **L** (but not from **T** to **L**).

Definition: Let (H, L) be a language. Define $ls(H, L)$ to be the synchronisation tree $(H, \varepsilon, L, tran)$ where

$$(h, a, h') \in Tran \Leftrightarrow h' = ha.$$

Let $T = (S, i, L, Tran)$ be a synchronisation tree. Define $sl(T) = (H, L)$ where a string $h \in L^*$ is in the language H iff there is a sequence, possibly empty, of transitions

$$i \xrightarrow{a_1} s_1 \xrightarrow{a_2} \cdots \xrightarrow{a_n} s_n$$

in T such that $h = a_1 a_2 \cdots a_n$. Extend sl to a functor by defining $sl(\sigma, \lambda) = \lambda$ for $(\sigma, \lambda) : T \rightarrow T'$ a morphism between synchronisation trees.

Theorem 11 *Let (H, L) be a language. Then $ls(H, L)$ is a synchronisation tree, with labelling set L, and, $1_L : sl \circ ls(H, L) \rightarrow (H, L)$ is an isomorphism. Moreover $sl \circ ls(H, L), 1_L$ is cofree over (H, L) with respect to the functor $sl : \mathbf{S} \rightarrow \mathbf{L}$, i.e. for any morphism $\lambda : sl(T) \rightarrow (H, L)$, with T a synchronisation tree, there is a unique morphism $g : T \rightarrow ls(H, L)$ such that $\lambda = 1_L \circ sl(g)$:*

$$(H, L) \xleftarrow{\ 1_L\ } sl \circ ls(H, L)$$
$$\overset{\lambda}{\nwarrow} \qquad \uparrow{sl(g)}$$
$$sl(T)$$

This demonstrates the adjunction $\mathbf{S} \rightarrow \mathbf{L}$ with left adjoint sl and right adjoint ls; the fact that the counit is an isomorphism makes the adjunction a (full) reflection. Let $r : \mathbf{L} \rightarrow \mathbf{Set}_*$ be the functor sending a morphism $\lambda : (H, L) \rightarrow (H', L')$ of languages to $\lambda : L \rightarrow_* L'$. Let $q : \mathbf{S} \rightarrow \mathbf{Set}_*$ be the functor sending synchronisation trees to their labelling sets (a restriction of the functor p from transition systems). With respect to these projections the adjunction is fibred.

We can immediately observe some categorical constructions. The product of two languages $(H_0, L_0), (H_1, L_1)$ takes the form

$$(\widehat{\pi_0}^{-1} H_0 \cap \widehat{\pi_1}^{-1} H_1, L_0 \times_* L_1),$$

with projections $\pi_0 : L_0 \times_* L_1 \to_* L_0$ and $\pi_1 : L_0 \times_* L_1 \to_* L_1$ obtained from the product in **Set$_*$**. The coproduct of languages $(H_0, L_0), (H_1, L_1)$ is

$$(\widehat{j_0} H_0 \cup \widehat{j_1} H_1, L_0 \uplus L_1)$$

with injections $j_0 : L_0 \to L_0 \uplus L_1, j_1 : L_1 \to L_0 \uplus L_1$ into the left and right component of the disjoint union. The fibre product and coproduct of languages over the same alphabet are given simply by intersection and union respectively.

The expected constructions of restriction and relabelling arise as (strong) cartesian and cocartesian liftings.

6   Relating semantics

We can summarise the relationship between the different models by recalling the coreflection and reflection (and introducing a little notation to depict such adjunctions):

$$\mathbf{L} \longleftarrow\!\!\lhd \mathbf{S} \longleftrightarrow\!\!\rhd \mathbf{T}$$

The coreflection and reflection are associated with "inclusions", embedding one model in another—the direction of the embedding being indicated by the hooks on the arrows, whose tips point in the direction of the left adjoint. Each inclusion has an adjoint; the inclusion of the coreflection has a right and that of the reflection a left adjoint. These functors from right to left correspond respectively to losing information about the looping, and then in addition the nondeterministic branching structure of processes.[4]

Such categorical facts are useful in several ways. The coreflection $\mathbf{S} \hookrightarrow \mathbf{T}$ tells us how to construct limits in $\mathbf{S}$ from those it $\mathbf{T}$. In particular, we have seen how the form of products in $\mathbf{S}$ is determined by their simpler form in $\mathbf{T}$. We regard synchronisation trees as transition systems via the inclusion functor, form the limit there and then transport it to $\mathbf{S}$, using the fact that right adjoints preserve limits. Because the adjunctions are fibrewise, the right adjoints also preserve cartesian liftings and left adjoints preserve cocartesian liftings (see *e.g.* Appendix B in (Winskel and Nielsen

---

[4]**Warning:** We use the term ' 'coreflection" to mean an adjunction in which the unit is a natural isomorphism, or equivalently (by theorem 1, p.89 of (MacLane 1971)) when the left adjoint is full and faithful. Similarly, "reflection" is used here to mean an adjunction for which the counit is a natural isomorphism, or equivalently when the right adjoint is full and faithful. While the same usage can be found in the literature, it is not entirely standard.

1995)). The fact that the embedding functors are full and faithful ensures that they reflect limits and colimits, as well as cartesian and cocartesian morphisms because the adjunctions are fibrewise.

Imagine giving semantics to the process language **Proc** of section 3 in any of the three models. Any particular construct is interpreted as being built up in the same way from universal constructions. For example, product in the process language is interpreted as categorical product, and nondeterministic sum in the language as the same combination of cocartesian liftings and coproduct we use in transition systems. Constructions are interpreted in a uniform manner in any of the different models. Prefixing for languages requires a (straightforward) definition. Recursion requires a separate treatment, omitted here. With respect to an environment ρ_S from process variables to synchronisation trees we obtain a denotational semantics yielding a synchronisation tree

$$\mathbf{S}[\![t]\!]\rho_S$$

for any process term t. And with respect to an environment ρ_L from process variables to languages the denotational semantics yields a language

$$\mathbf{L}[\![t]\!]\rho_L$$

for a process term t. What is the relationship between the three semantics

$$\mathbf{T}[\![-]\!], \quad \mathbf{S}[\![-]\!], \quad \text{and} \quad \mathbf{L}[\![-]\!]?$$

Consider the relationship between the semantics in transition systems and synchronisation trees. Letting ρ be an environment from process variables, to transition systems, the two semantics are related by

$$ts(\mathbf{T}[\![t]\!]\rho) = \mathbf{S}[\![t]\!]ts \circ \rho$$

for any process term t. This is proved by structural induction on t. The cases where t is a product or restriction follow directly from preservation properties of right adjoints. The other cases require special, if easy, argument. For example, the fact that

$$ts(\mathbf{T}[\![t_0 \oplus t_1]\!]\rho) = \mathbf{S}[\![t_0 \oplus t_1]\!]ts \circ \rho$$

depends on $\mathbf{T}[\![t_0]\!]\rho$, $\mathbf{T}[\![t_1]\!]\rho$ being nonrestarting. A similar relationship,

$$sl(\mathbf{S}[\![t]\!]\rho) = \mathbf{L}[\![t]\!]sl \circ \rho$$

for a process term t, and environment ρ to synchronisation trees, holds between the two semantics in synchronisation trees and languages. This time the structural induction is most straightforward in the cases of nil, nondeterministic sum and relabelling (because of the preservation properties of the left adjoint sl). However, simple arguments suffice for the other cases.

In summary, the operations on processes are interpreted in a uniform manner (with the same universal constructions) in the three different semantics. The preservation properties of adjoints are useful in relating the semantics. Less directly, a knowledge of what we can and cannot expect to be preserved automatically provides useful guidelines in itself. The failure of a general preservation property can warn that the semantics of a construct can only be preserved in special circumstances. For instance, we cannot expect a right adjoint like ts to always preserve a colimit, like a nondeterministic sum. Accordingly, the semantics of sums is only preserved by ts by virtue of a special circumstance, that the transition systems denoted are nonrestarting. The advantages of a categorical approach become more striking when we turn to the more intricate models of the non-interleaving approach to concurrency, but where again the same universal constructions will be used.

7 Trace languages

All the models we have considered so far have identified concurrency, or parallelism, with nondeterministic interleaving of atomic actions. We turn now to consider models where concurrency is modelled explicitly in the form of independence between actions. In some models, like Mazurkiewicz traces, the relation of independence is a basic notion while in others, like Petri nets, it is derived from something more primitive. The idea is that if two actions are enabled and also independent then they can occur concurrently, or in parallel. Models of this kind are sometimes said to capture "true concurrency", an irritatingly biased expression. They are also often called "noninterleaving models" though this again is inappropriate; Petri nets and event structures can be described as forms of transition systems. A much better term is "independence models" for concurrent computation, though this is not established. Because in such models the independence of actions is not generally derivable from an underlying property of their labels, depending rather on which occurrences are considered, we will see an important distinction basic to these richer models. They each have a concept of *events* distinguished from that of *labels*. Events are to be thought of as atomic actions which can support a relation of independence. Events can then bear the further structure of having a label, for instance signifying which channel or which process they belong to.

A greater part of the development of these models is indifferent to the extra labelling structure we might like to impose, though of course restriction and relabelling will depend on labels. Our treatment of the models and their relationship will be done primarily for the unlabelled structures. Later we will adjoin labelling and provide semantics in terms of the various models and discuss their relationship.

7.1 A category of trace languages

The simplest model of computation with an in-built notion of independence is that of Mazurkiewicz trace languages. They are languages in which the alphabet also possesses a relation of independence. As we shall see, this small addition has a striking effect in terms of the richness of the associated structures. It is noteworthy that, in applications of trace languages, there have been different understandings of the alphabet; in Mazurkiewicz's original work the alphabet is thought of as consisting of events (especially events of a Petri net), while some authors have instead interpreted its elements as labels, for example standing for port names. This remark will be elaborated later on in section 7.2.

Definition: A *Mazurkiewicz trace language* consists of (M, L, I) where L is a set, $I \subseteq L \times L$ is a symmetric, irreflexive relation called the *independence* relation, and M is a nonempty subset of strings L^* such that

- *prefix closed*: $sa \in M \Rightarrow s \in M$, for all $s \in L^*, a \in L$,

- *I-closed*: $sabt \in M$ & $aIb \Rightarrow sbat \in M$, for all $s, t \in L^*, a, b \in L$.

We say that a trace language is *coherent* when, in addition, it satisfies:

- *coherent*: $sa \in M$ & $sb \in M$ & $aIb \Rightarrow sab \in M$, for all $s \in L^*, a, b \in L$.

The alphabet L of a trace language (M, L, I) can be thought of as the set of actions of a process and the set of strings as the sequences of actions the process can perform. Some actions are independent of others. The axiom of I-closedness expresses a consequence of independence: if two actions are independent and can occur one after the other then they can occur in the opposite order.

Given that some actions are independent of others, it is to be expected that some strings represent essentially the same computation as others. For example, if a and b are independent then both strings ab and ba represent the computation of a and b occurring concurrently. More generally, two strings $sabt$ and $sbat$ represent the same computation when a and b are independent. This extends to an equivalence relation between strings, the equivalence classes of which are called *Mazurkiewicz traces*. There is an associated preorder between strings of a trace language which induces a partial order on traces.

Definition: Let (M, L, I) be a trace language. For $s, t \in M$ define $\approx$ to be the smallest equivalence relation such that

$$sabt \approx sbat \text{ if } aIb$$

for $sabt, sbat \in M$. Call an equivalence class $\{s\}_\approx$, for $s \in M$, a *trace*. For $s, t \in M$ define

$$s \lesssim t \Leftrightarrow \exists u.\ su \approx t.$$

Proposition 12 *Let (M, L, I) be a trace language with trace equivalence $\approx$. If $su \in M$ and $s \approx s'$ then $s'u \in M$ and $su \approx s'u$. The relation $\lesssim$ of the trace language is a preorder. Its quotient $\lesssim / \approx$ by the equivalence relation $\approx$ is a partial order on traces.*

The partial order $\lesssim$ / $\approx$ of a trace language can be associated with a partial order of causal dependencies between event occurrences. This structure will be investigated in the next section.

Morphisms between trace languages are morphisms between the underlying languages which preserve independence:

Definition: A *morphism* of trace languages $(M, L, I) \rightarrow (M', L', I')$ consists of a partial function $\lambda : L \rightarrow_* L'$ which

- *preserves independence*: aIb & $\lambda(a)$ defined & $\lambda(b)$ defined $\Rightarrow \lambda(a)I'\lambda(b)$ for all $a, b \in L$,

- *preserves strings*: $s \in M \Rightarrow \widehat{\lambda}(s) \in M'$ for all strings s.

It is easy to see that morphisms of trace languages preserve traces and the ordering between them:

Proposition 13 *Let* $\lambda : (M, L, I) \rightarrow (M', L', I')$ *be a morphism of trace languages. If* $s \lesssim t$ *in the trace language* (M, L, I) *then* $\widehat{\lambda}(s) \lesssim \widehat{\lambda}(t)$ *in the trace language* (M', L', I').

Definition: Write **TL** for the category of trace languages with composition that of partial functions.

7.2 Constructions on trace languages

We examine some categorical constructions on trace languages. The constructions generalise from those on languages but with the added consideration of defining independence.

Let (M_0, L_0, I_0) and (M_1, L_1, I_1) be trace languages. Their *product* is (M, L, I) where $L = L_0 \times_* L_1$, the product in **Set$_*$**, with projections $\pi_0 : L \rightarrow_* L_0$ and $\pi_1 : L \rightarrow_* L_1$, with

$$aIb \Leftrightarrow (\pi_0(a), \pi_0(b) \text{ defined } \Rightarrow \pi_0(a)I_0\pi_0(b)) \ \& $$
$$(\pi_1(a), \pi_1(b) \text{ defined } \Rightarrow \pi_1(a)I_1\pi_1(b)),$$

and

$$M = \widehat{\pi}_0^{-1}M_0 \cap \widehat{\pi}_1^{-1}M_1.$$

Their *coproduct* is (M, L, I) where $L = L_0 \uplus L_1$, the disjoint union, with injections $j_0 : L_0 \rightarrow L, j_1 : L_0 \rightarrow L$, the relation I satisfies

$$aIb \Leftrightarrow \exists a_0, b_0.\ a_0 I_0 b_0 \ \& \ a = j_0(a_0) \ \& \ b = j_0(b_0) \text{ or}$$
$$\exists a_1, b_1.\ a_1 I_1 b_1 \ \& \ a = j_1(a_1) \ \& \ b = j_1(b_1)$$

and

$$M = \widehat{\jmath_0} M_0 \cup \widehat{\jmath_1} M_1.$$

What about restriction and relabelling? Restriction appears again as a cartesian lifting of an inclusion between labelling sets. Its effect is simply to cut down the language and independence to the restricting set. However, the relabelling of a trace language cannot always be associated with a cocartesian lifting. To see this consider a function $\lambda : \{a, b\} \to \{c\}$ sending both a, b to c. If a trace language T has $\{a, b\}$ as an alphabet and has a, b independent then, λ cannot be a morphism of trace languages, and hence there is no cocartesian lifting of λ with respect to the trace language T; because independence is irreflexive, independence cannot be preserved by λ. The difficulty stems from our implicitly regarding the alphabet of a Mazurkiewicz trace language as a set of labels of the kind used in the operations of restriction and relabelling. Although the alphabet can be taken to have this nature, it was not the original intention of Mazurkiewicz. Here it is appropriate to discuss the two ways in which trace languages are used to the model parallel processes.

One way is to use trace languages in the same manner as languages. This was implicitly assumed in our attempts to define the relabelling of a trace language, and in the example above. Then a process, for example in CCS, denotes a trace language, with alphabet the labels of the process. This regards symbols of the alphabet of a trace language as labels in a process algebra. As we have seen in the treatment of interleaving models labels can be understood rather generally; they are simply tags to distinguish some actions from others. However this general understanding of the alphabet conflicts with this first approach. As the independence relation is then one between labels, once it is decided that say a and b are independent in the denotation of a process then they are so throughout its execution. However, it is easy to imagine a process where at some stage a and b occur independently and yet not at some other stage. To remedy this some have suggested that the independence relation be made to depend on the trace of labels which has occurred previously. But even with this modification, the irreflexivity of the independence relation means there cannot be independent occurrences with the same label; in modelling a CCS process all its internal τ events would be dependent!

The other approach is to regard the alphabet as consisting, not of labels of the general kind we have met in process algebras, but instead as consisting of *events*. It is the events which possess an independence relation and any distinctions that one wishes to make between them are then caught through an extra labelling function from events to labels. True, this extra level of labelling complicates the model, but the distinction between events and the labels they can carry appears to be fundamental. It is present in the other models which capture concurrency directly as independence. This second view fits with that of Mazurkiewicz's trace-language semantics of Petri nets. When we come to adjoin the extra structure of labels, restriction will again be associated with a cartesian lifting and relabelling will reappear as a cocartesian lifting.

There remains the question of understanding the order $\lesssim / \approx$ of trace languages.

We shall do this through a representation theorem which will show that $\lesssim / \approx$ can be understood as the subset ordering between configurations of an event structure.

8 Event structures

There is most often no point in analysing the precise places and times of events in a distributed computation. What is generally important are the significant events and how the occurrence of an event causally depends on the previous occurrence of others. For example, the event of a process transmitting a message would presumably depend on it first performing some events, so it was in the right state to transmit, including the receipt of the message which in turn would depend on its previous transmission by another process. Such ideas suggest that we view distributed computations as event occurrences together with a relation expressing causal dependency, and this we may reasonably take to be a partial order. One thing missing from such descriptions is the phenomenon of nondeterminism. To model nondeterminism we adjoin further structure in the form of a consistency relation specifying those finite subsets of events can occur together in a computation.

Definition: Define an *event structure* to be a structure $(E, \leq, Con)$ consisting of a set E, of *events* which are partially ordered by $\leq$, the *causal dependency relation*, and a *consistency relation* Con consisting of finite subsets of events, which satisfy

$$\{e' \mid e' \leq e\} \text{ is finite,}$$
$$\{e\} \in Con,$$
$$Y \subseteq X \in Con \Rightarrow Y \in Con,$$
$$X \in Con \& e \leq e' \in X \Rightarrow X \cup \{e\} \in Con,$$

for all events e, e' and their subsets X, Y.

We say two events $e, e' \in E$ are *concurrent*, and write $e \ co \ e'$, iff

$$(e \not\leq e' \ \& \ e' \not\leq e \ \& \ \{e, e'\} \in Con).$$

The finiteness assumption restricts attention to discrete processes where an event occurrence depends only on finitely many previous occurrences. The axioms on the consistency relation express that all singletons of events are consistent, and that the relation is closed under subsets and downwards with respect to the causal dependency relation.

Say an event structure $E = (E, \leq, Con)$ is *coherent* if the consistency relation Con is determined by consistency on pairs of events, or alternatively if there is a, necessarily unique, binary conflict relation $\#$ on events such that

$$X \in Con \Leftrightarrow \forall e_1, e_2 \in X. \ \neg e_1 \# e_2.$$

We can describe coherent event structures by a triple $(E, \leq, \#)$ where, as before, E is a set of *events* partially ordered by a causal dependency relation $\leq$, and $\#$, the *conflict relation*, is a binary, symmetric, irreflexive relation on events, which satisfy

$$\{e' \mid e' \leq e\} \text{ is finite,}$$
$$e \# e' \leq e'' \Rightarrow e \# e''$$

for all $e, e', e'' \in E$. The property of $\#$, that two events causally dependent on conflicting events are themselves in conflict, follows from those of Con. We shall take the liberty of identifying $(E, \leq, \#)$, presenting a coherent event structure, with the associated event structure $(E, \leq, Con)$; in other words, $(E, \leq, \#)$ should be understood as referring to the event structure $(E, \leq, Con)$ it determines.

Guided by our interpretation we can formulate a notion of computation state of an event structure $(E, \leq, Con)$. Taking a computation state of a process to be represented by the set x of events which have occurred in the computation, we expect that if an event has occurred then all events on which it causally depends have occurred too, and also all finite subsets of events in the same computation are consistent.

Definition: Let $(E, \leq, Con)$ be an event structure. Define its *configurations*, $\mathcal{D}(E, \leq, Con)$, to consist of those subsets $x \subseteq E$ which are

- *downwards-closed:* $\forall e, e'. \, e' \leq e \in x \Rightarrow e' \in x$, and

- *consistent:* $\forall X. \, X \text{ finite } \& \, X \subseteq x \Rightarrow X \in Con$.

In particular, define $\lceil e \rceil = \{e' \in E \mid e' \leq e\}$. (Note that $\lceil e \rceil$ is a configuration as it is consistent.)

Write $\mathcal{D}^0(E, \leq, Con)$ for the set of finite configurations.

Events manifest themselves as atomic jumps from one configuration to another, and later it will follow that we can regard such jumps as transitions in an asynchronous transition system.

Definition: Let $(E, \leq, Con)$ be an event structure. Let x, x' be configurations. Write

$$x \xrightarrow{e} x' \Leftrightarrow e \notin x \, \& \, x' = x \cup \{e\}.$$

Proposition 14 *Two events e_0, e_1 of an event structure are in the concurrency relation co iff there exist configurations x, x_0, x_1, x' such that:*

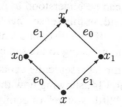

8.1 A category of event structures

From the previous we have seen how an event structure $ES = (E, \leq, Con)$ determines a transition system $(\mathcal{D}^0(ES), \emptyset, E, Tran)$, where

$$(x, e, x') \in Tran \Leftrightarrow x \xrightarrow{e} x',$$

for finite configurations x, x' and events e. It would thus seem reasonable to define a morphism of event structures from ES to ES' as a morphism between their associated transition systems, in more detail, as a pair (σ, η), where

- σ is a function from finite configurations of ES to those of ES', sending the empty configuration of ES to the empty configuration of ES', and

- η is a partial function from events of ES to events of ES', such that

$x \xrightarrow{e} x'$ in ES implies $\sigma(x) \xrightarrow{\eta} (e)\sigma(x')$ when $\eta(e)$ is defined, and $\sigma(x) = \sigma(x')$ otherwise.

By considering chains of transition in ES

$$\emptyset \xrightarrow{e_1} x_1 \xrightarrow{e_2} \cdots \xrightarrow{e_n} x_n = x$$

up to an arbitrary configuration x, it is easy to see that this definition constrains the function σ to act like the direct-image function associated with η and, moreover, that no two distinct events in a configuration of ES can have a common, defined image under η. So, in fact, we can equivalently define morphisms on event structures as follows (see (Nielsen, Rozenberg, and Thiagarajan 1992)):

Definition: Let $ES = (E, \leq, Con)$ and $ES' = (E', \leq', Con)$ be event structures. A *morphism* from ES to ES' consists of a partial function $\eta : E \to_* E'$ on events which satisfies that for all $x \in \mathcal{D}(ES)$

$\eta x \in \mathcal{D}(ES')$ &
$\forall e_0, e_1 \in x.\ \eta(e_0), \eta(e_1)$ both defined & $\eta(e_0) = \eta(e_1) \Rightarrow e_0 = e_1$.

A morphism $\eta : ES \to ES'$ between event structures expresses how behaviour in ES determines behaviour in ES'. The partial function η expresses how the occurrence of an event in ES implies the simultaneous occurrence of an event in ES'; the fact that $\eta(e) = e'$ can be understood as expressing that the event e' is a "component" of the event e and, in this sense, that the occurrence of e implies the simultaneous occurrence of e'. If two distinct events in ES have the same image in ES' under η then they cannot belong to the same configuration.

Morphisms of event structures preserve the concurrency relation. This is a simple consequence of proposition 14, showing how the concurrency relation holding between events appears as a "little square" of configurations.

Proposition 15 *Let ES be an event structure with concurrency relation co and ES' an event structure with concurrency relation co'. Let $\eta : ES \to ES'$ be a morphism of event structures. Then, for any events e_0, e_1 of ES,*

$$e_0 \ co \ e_1 \ \& \ \eta(e_0), \eta(e_1) \ both \ defined \Rightarrow \eta(e_0) \ co' \ \eta(e_1).$$

Morphisms between event structures can be described more directly in terms of the causality and conflict relations of the event structure:

Proposition 16 *A morphism of event structures from $(E, \leq, Con)$ to $(E', \leq'$, $Con')$ is a partial function $\eta : E \to_* E'$ such that*

(i) $\eta(e)$ defined $\Rightarrow \lceil \eta(e) \rceil \subseteq \eta \lceil e \rceil$ and

(ii) $X \in Con \Rightarrow \eta X \in Con'$ and for all $e_0, e_1 \in x$
   $\eta(e_0), \eta(e_1)$ both defined $\& \eta(e_0) = \eta(e_1) \Rightarrow e_0 = e_1$.

The category of event structures possesses products and coproducts useful in modelling parallel compositions and nondeterministic sums.

Proposition 17 *Let $(E_0, \leq_0, Con_0)$ and $(E_1, \leq_1, Con_1)$ be event structures. Their coproduct in the category $\mathbf{E}$ is the event structure $(E_0 \uplus E_1, \leq, Con)$ where*

$$e \leq e' \Leftrightarrow (\exists e_0, e_0'. \ e_0 \leq_0 e_0' \ \& \ j_0(e_0) = e \ \& \ j_0(e_0') = e') \ or$$
$$(\exists e_1, e_1'. \ e_1 \leq_1 e_1' \ \& \ j_1(e_1) = e \ \& \ j_1(e_1') = e')$$

and

$$Con = \{j_0 X \mid X \in Con_0\} \cup \{j_1 X \mid X \in Con_1\},$$

with injections $j_0 : E_0 \to E_0 \uplus E_1, j_1 : E_1 \to E_0 \uplus E_1$ the injections of E_0 and E_1 into their disjoint union.

It is tricky to give a direct construction of product on event structures. However, a construction of the product of event structures will follow from the product of trace languages and the coreflection from event structures to trace languages (see corollary 30), and we postpone the construction till then.

Ordered by inclusion the configurations of an event structure form a dI-domain in the sense of Berry (1979) and, in fact, all dI-domains can be represented in this way (see Winskel and Nielsen 1995; Winskel 1988 for further details).

8.2 Event structures and trace languages

8.2.1 A representation theorem

Throughout this section assume (M, L, I) is a trace language. In this section we study the preorder

$$s \lesssim t \Leftrightarrow \exists u. \ su \approx t$$

of a trace language and show that its quotient $\lesssim / \approx$ can be represented by the finite configurations of an event structure.[5]

We use $a, b, c, \ldots$ for symbols in L and $s, t, u, \ldots$ for strings in L^*. Write $N(b, s)$ for the number of occurrences of b in the string s. We write $a \in s$ to mean a occurs in s, *i.e.* $N(a, s) > 0$. As an abbreviation, we write sIt if aIb for every symbol a in s and b in t.

Events of (M, L, I), to be thought of as event occurrences, are taken to be equivalence classes of nonempty strings with respect to the equivalence relation $\sim$ now defined.

Definition: The relation $\sim$ is the smallest equivalence relation on nonempty strings such that

$$sa \sim sba \quad \text{if} \quad bIa, \text{ and}$$
$$sa \sim ta \quad \text{if} \quad s \approx t$$

for $sa, sba, ta \in M$.

The next lemma yields an important technique for reasoning about trace languages.

Lemma 18 *Suppose* $sa, ta \in M$.

$$\neg(aIb) \ \& \ sa \sim ta \Rightarrow N(b, s) = N(b, t).$$

As $\neg(aIa)$ the lemma in particular yields

$$sa \sim ta \Rightarrow N(a, s) = N(a, t)$$

for $sa, ta \in M$. Thus different occurrences of the same symbol in a string of M are associated with different events:

Proposition 19 *Suppose* $s_0 a, s_1 a$ *are prefixes of* $t \in M$ *such that* $s_0 a \sim s_1 a$. *Then* $s_0 a = s_1 a$.

We can now show how the preorder of trace languages coincides with the order of inclusion on the associated sets of events:

Definition: Let $s \in M$. Define the events of s, to be

$$ev(s) = \{\{u\}_\sim \mid u \text{ is a nonempty prefix of } s\}.$$

---

[5]The proof here generalises that of (Winskel and Nielsen 1995) in that it applies to trace languages which are not necessarily coherent. We only include proofs when we differ from (Winskel and Nielsen 1995).

Lemma 20 *Let* $s, t \in M$. *Then*

$$s \lesssim t \Leftrightarrow ev(s) \subseteq ev(t).$$

The next lemma shows that traces with upper bounds have least upper bounds.

Lemma 21 *Letting* $s, t, u \in M$,

$$s \lesssim u \ \& \ t \lesssim u \Rightarrow \exists v, w.u \approx vw \ \& \ ev(v) = ev(s) \cup ev(t).$$

Proof: Assume $s, t \lesssim u$. Without loss of generality suppose $u = su'$. We show by induction of the size of t that

$$\exists v', w. \ u \approx sv'w \ \& \ ev(sv') = ev(s) \cup ev(t). \tag{†}$$

For the basis, when $t = \epsilon$, take $v' = \epsilon$ and $w = u'$.

Now consider the induction step, when $t = t'c$. Inductively, there are v', w for which

$$u \approx sv'w \ \& \ ev(sv') = ev(s) \cup ev(t').$$

There are now two cases to consider:

(i) $t'c \in ev(s)$

(ii) $t'c \notin ev(s)$.

In case (i), taking v', w as above for t', we fulfil (†) for t. Suppose otherwise, that case (ii), when $t'c \notin ev(s)$. As $t \lesssim u \approx sv'w$, by lemma 20, we know

$$\{t'c\}_\sim \in ev(t) \subseteq ev(sv'w)$$

Because in this case $\{t'c\}_\sim \notin ev(sv')$, there must exist w_0, w_1 for which

$$w = w_0 c w_1 \ \& \ sv'w_0 c \sim t'c$$

Now $u \approx sv'w_0 c w_1$. We argue that $w_0 I c$:
Suppose otherwise that $b \in w_0$ and $\neg(b_0 I c)$. Then

$$N(b, sv'w_0) > N(b, sv') \geq N(b, t'),$$

the latter inequality following because $ev(sv') \supseteq ev(t')$. However, $sv'w_0 c \sim t'c$ so $N(b, sv'w_0) = N(b, t')$ by lemma 18, a contradiction. Hence, $w_0 I c$.

Finally, we observe that

$$u \approx s(v'c)(w_0 w_1) \ \& \ ev(s(v'c)) = ev(s) \cup ev(t'c),$$

which concludes the induction step. $\qquad\qquad\square$

Here we make a slight detour to remark that in the case where the trace language is coherent we can refine the previous lemma; when the trace language is coherent incompatibility between traces stems from a lack of independence between events (as shown in Winskel and Nielsen 1995).

Lemma 22 *Assume that the trace language* (M, L, I) *is coherent. Then, letting* $s, t \in M$,

$$\exists u \in M.\ ev(u) = ev(s) \cup ev(t)$$

iff

$$\forall v \in M, a, b \in L.\ \{va\}_\sim \in ev(s)\ \&\ \{vb\}_\sim \in ev(t) \Rightarrow a(I \cup 1_L)b.$$

We return to the main line of the proof. The following lemma says that each event has a $\lesssim$-minimum representative.

Lemma 23 *For all events* e *there is* $sa \in e$ *such that*

$$\forall ta \in e.\ sa \lesssim ta.$$

The minimum representatives are used in defining the event structure associated with a trace language.

Definition: Let $T = (M, L, I)$ be a trace language.
Define

$$tle(M, L, I) = (E, \leq, Con)$$

where

- E is the set of events of (M, L, I),

- $\leq$ is a relation between events e, e' given by $e \leq e'$ iff $e \in ev(sa)$ where sa is a minimum representative of e', and

- $X \in Con$ iff $\exists s \in M.\ X \subseteq ev(s)$.

Furthermore, define $\lambda_T : E \to L$ by taking $\lambda_T(\{sa\}_\sim) = a$. (From the definition of $\sim$, it follows that λ_T is well-defined as a function.)

Lemma 24 *Let* $T = (M, L, I)$ *be a trace language. Then the structure* $tle(T) = (E, \leq, Con)$ *given by the definition above is an event structure for which*

$$e \leq e' \text{ iff } \forall s \in M.\ e' \in ev(s) \Rightarrow e \in ev(s). \tag{1}$$

Furthermore, if e_1 *co* e_2 *in* $tle(T)$, *then* $\lambda_T(e_1) I \lambda_T(e_2)$ *in* T.

If T *is a coherent trace language, then* $tle(T)$ *is a coherent event structure with conflict relation* $\#$ *satisfying:*

$$e\#e' \text{ iff } \forall s \in M.\ e \in ev(s) \Rightarrow e' \notin ev(s). \tag{2}$$

Proof: First, (1) follows by considering the minimal representatives of events provided by lemma 23:

"$\Rightarrow$": Suppose $e \leq e'$ and $e' \in ev(s)$. Letting va be a minimal representative of e' we see $va \lesssim s$, so $ev(va) \subseteq ev(s)$. From the definition $e \leq e'$ we have that $e \in ev(va)$, so $e \in ev(s)$.

"$\Leftarrow$": This direction follows directly by taking s to be a minimal representative of e'.

From (1) and the definition of Con it is now easy to check that $tle(T)$ is an event structure.

That λ_T sends concurrent events to independent symbols will follow provided that, for $a, b \in L$ and strings u, v over L,

$$\neg(aIb) \ \& \ uavb \in M \Rightarrow \{ua\}_\sim \leq \{uavb\}_\sim.$$

Assume $\neg(aIb)$ and $uavb \in M$. Let $e_1 = \{ua\}_\sim$ and $e_2 = \{uavb\}_\sim$. Let wb be a $\lesssim$-minimal representative of e_2. As both are representatives of e_2,

$$wb \sim uavb. \tag{i}$$

We argue by contradiction to show $e_1 \leq e_2$. Assume otherwise, that $e_1 = \{ua\}_\sim \notin ev(wb)$. Because wb is a minimal representative, $wb \lesssim uavb$, so there must be strings s, s' such that

$$wbsas' \approx uavb$$

where

$$wbsa \sim ua. \tag{ii}$$

Recall $\neg(aIb)$. By lemma 18, from (i),

$$N(b, w) = N(b, uav) \geq N(b, u)$$

while from (ii),

$$N(b, w) < N(b, wbs) = N(b, u)$$

—a contradiction. Thus $e_1 \leq e_2$.

It remains to show that assuming T is a coherent trace language, the event structure $tle(T)$ is coherent, with conflict given by (2). Guided by lemma 22, we define a conflict relation, $e \# e'$ to hold between events e, e' iff

$$\exists e_0, e_0'. \ e_0 \#_0 e_0' \ \& \ e_0 \leq e \ \& \ e_0' \leq e'$$

where, by definition,

$$e_0 \#_0 e_0' \ \text{iff} \ \exists v, a, b. \ va \in e_0 \ \& \ vb \in e_0' \ \& \ \neg(a(I \cup 1_L)b).$$

Lemma 22 ensures that the conflict relation induces the consistency relation of $tle(T)$, *i.e.*

$$X \in Con \Leftrightarrow \forall e, e' \in X. \ \neg(e \# e') :$$

"⇐": Assuming $\forall e, e' \in X.\ \neg(e\#e')$, repeated use of lemma 22 on minimal representatives of events of X yields $u \in M$ for which $X \subseteq ev(u)$, witnessing $X \in Con$.

"⇒": If $X \in Con$ then $X \subseteq ev(u)$ for some $u \in M$. Let $e, e' \in X$. For $e_0 \leq e$ and $e'_0 \leq e'$, let s, t be minimal representatives of e_0, e'_0. The set $ev(u)$ is downwards-closed by (1). Hence $ev(s), ev(t) \subseteq ev(u)$, so $s, t \lesssim u$. By lemma 21, there is v such that $ev(v) = ev(s) \cup ev(t)$. This entails $\neg(e_0\#_0e'_0)$ by lemma 22. Thus $\neg(e\#e')$.

In particular, $\{e, e'\} \in Con \Leftrightarrow \neg(e\#e')$, *i.e.*

$$\exists s \in M.\ \{e, e'\} \subseteq ev(s) \text{ iff } \neg(e\#e'),$$

the contraposition of which yields (2).   □

We now present the representation theorem for trace languages. We write $(M/\approx, \lesssim / \approx)$ for the partial order obtained by quotienting the preorder $\lesssim$ by its equivalence $\approx$.

Theorem 25 *Let* $T = (M, L, I)$ *be a trace language. Let* $tle(T) = (E, \leq, Con)$. *There is an order isomorphism*

$$Ev : (M/\approx, \lesssim / \approx) \to \mathcal{D}^0(E, \leq, Con)$$

where $Ev(\{s\}_\approx) = ev(s)$.
  Moreover, for $s \in M$, $x \in \mathcal{D}^0(E, \leq, Con)$ *and* $a \in L$,

$$(\exists e.\ ev(s) \xrightarrow{e} x \text{ in } \mathcal{D}^0(E, \leq, Con) \ \& \ \lambda_T(e) = a) \Leftrightarrow (sa \in M \ \& \ ev(sa) = x). \tag{†}$$

Proof: Let $s \in M$. Clearly $ev(s)$ is a consistent subset of events. By lemma 24(1), $ev(s)$ is downwards-closed with respect to $\leq$. The fact that Ev is well-defined, 1-1, order preserving and reflecting follows from lemma 20. To establish that Ev is an isomorphism it suffices to check Ev is onto. To this end we first prove (†).

The "⇐" direction of the equivalence (†) follows directly, as follows. Assume $sa \in M$, and $ev(sa) = x$. Then taking $e = \{sa\}_\approx$ yields an event for which $ev(s) \xrightarrow{e} x$ and $\lambda_T(e) = a$. To show "⇒", assume $ev(s) \xrightarrow{e} x$ and $\lambda_T(e) = a$. Let ta be a minimum representative of the event e. As x is downwards-closed

$$ev(t) \subseteq ev(s).$$

Because x is consistent and finite, there is $u \in M$ with $x \subseteq ev(u)$. Now, $ev(ta) \subseteq ev(u)$ and $ev(s) \subseteq ev(u)$. Hence $ta \lesssim u$ and $s \lesssim u$. By lemma 21, there is $v \in M$ such that $v \lesssim u$ and

$$ev(u) = ev(s) \cup ev(ta) = x.$$

Hence $s \lesssim v$, *i.e.* $sw \approx v$ for some string w. But $ev(s) \xrightarrow{e} ev(sw)$, so w must be a with $sa \in e$.

Now a simple induction on the size of $x \in \mathcal{D}^0(E, \leq, Con)$ shows that there exists $s \in M$ for which $ev(s) = x$. From this it follows that Ev is onto, and consequently that Ev is an order isomorphism. $\qquad\square$

The representation theorem for trace languages establishes a connection between trace languages and the *pomset* languages of Pratt (1986). Via the representation theorem, each trace of a trace language $T = (M, L, I)$ corresponds to a labelled partial order of events (a *partially ordered multiset* or *pomset*)—the partial order on events in the trace is induced by that of the event structure and the labelling function is λ_T. The trace language itself then corresponds to a special kind of pomset language; it is special chiefly because the concurrency relations in the pomsets arise from a single independence relation on the alphabet of labels, so consequently pomsets of traces have no *autoconcurrency*—no two concurrent events have the same label. (See (Bloom and Kwiatkowska 1992), (Rozoy and Thiagarajan 1991) and (Grabowski 1981) for more details.)

8.2.2 A coreflection

The representation theorem extends to a coreflection between the categories of event structures and trace languages.[6]

Definition: Let ES be an event structure with events E. Define $etl(ES)$ to be (M, E, co), where $s = e_1 \ldots e_n \in M$ iff there is a chain

$$\emptyset \xrightarrow{e_1} x_1 \xrightarrow{e_2} x_2 \ldots \xrightarrow{e_n} x_n$$

of configurations of ES.

Let η be a morphism of event structures $\eta : ES \to ES'$. Define $etl(\eta) = \eta$.

Proposition 26 *etl is a functor* $\mathbf{E} \to \mathbf{TL}$.

The function λ_T, for T a trace language, will be the counit of the adjunction.

Proposition 27 *Let* $T = (M, L, I)$ *be a trace language. Then,*

$$\lambda_T : etl \circ tle(T) \to T$$

is a morphism of trace languages.

---

[6]Where the proofs are simple modifications of those in (Winskel and Nielsen 1995) (which restricts attention to coherent models) they are omitted.

Lemma 28 *Let $ES = (E, \leq, Con)$ be an event structure, such that $etl(ES) = (M, E, co)$. Let $\lambda : etl(ES) \to T'$ be a morphism in **TL**. If $\lambda(e)$ is defined then for all $se, s'e \in M$*

$$\hat{\lambda}(se) \sim \hat{\lambda}(s'e)$$

in $T' = (M', L', I')$.

Theorem 29 *Let $T' = (M', L', I')$ be a trace language. Then the pair $etl \circ tle(T')$, $\lambda_{T'}$, is cofree over T' with respect to the functor etl. That is, for any event structure ES and morphism $\lambda : etl(ES) \to T'$ there is a unique morphism $\eta : ES \to tle(T')$ such that $\lambda = \lambda_{T'} \circ etl(\eta)$.*

Proof: Let $ES = (E, \leq, Con)$, $tle(T') = (E', \leq', Con')$ and $etl(ES) = (M, E, co)$. Define $\eta : E \to_* E'$ by

$$\eta(e) = \begin{cases} * & \text{if } \lambda(e) = * \\ \{\hat{\lambda}(se)\}_\sim, & \text{where } se \in M, \text{ if } \lambda(e) \neq * \end{cases}$$

It follows from lemma 28 that η is a well-defined partial function from E to E'. We need to prove that

    (a) η is a morphism $ES \to tle(T')$

    (b) $\lambda = \lambda_{T'} \circ \eta$

    (c) η is unique satisfying (a) and (b).

(a): To prove (a), that η is a morphism, it suffices by proposition 16 to prove (i) and (ii) below.

(i) For every $e \in E$, if $\eta(e)$ is defined then $\lceil \eta(e) \rceil \subseteq \eta(\lceil e \rceil)$
Choose $se \in M$ such that the occurrences in s equal $\lceil e \rceil$ (in ES). Assume $x'a' \in M'$ such that

$$\{x'a'\}_\sim \leq \{\hat{\lambda}(se)\}_\sim \text{ in } tle(T'). \tag{$*$}$$

We have to prove the existence of $e_0 \in \lceil e \rceil$ in E such that $\{x'a'\}_\sim = \eta(e_0)$. But from $(*)$ we may choose a minimal prefix s_0e_0 of se such that $x'a' \sim \hat{\lambda}(s_0e_0)$, with $e_0 \in \lceil e \rceil$ from which we conclude the desired property.

(ii) For all $X \in Con$ we require that $\eta X \in Con'$ and that for all $e_1, e_2 \in X$ if $\eta(e_1) = \eta(e_2)$ (both being defined) then $e_1 = e_2$.
Assume $X \in Con$, i.e. there is $s \in M$ such that $X \subseteq ev(s)$. We see that $\hat{\lambda}(s) \in M'$ and $\eta X \subseteq ev(\hat{\lambda}(s))$, which ensures $\eta X \in Con'$. Now assume (to obtain a contradiction) that e_1, e_2 are distinct events in X for which both $\eta(e_1), \eta(e_2)$ are defined and $\eta(e_1) = \eta(e_2)$. There is either a prefix of s of the form ue_1ve_2 or ue_2ve_1. Without loss of generality, assume ue_1ve_2 a prefix of s. From the definedness and equality $\eta(e_1) = \eta(e_2)$ we obtain $\lambda(e_1) = \lambda(e_2)$ and $\hat{\lambda}(ue_1) \sim \hat{\lambda}(ue_1ve_2)$—a contradiction by lemma 18. This completes the proof of (a).

(b): If $\lambda(e) = *$ then $\eta(e) = *$, so $(\lambda_{T'} \circ \eta)(e) = *$. If $\lambda(e)$ defined then $\eta(e) = \{\lambda(se)\}_\sim$ for some $se \in M$. This implies $\lambda_{T'}(\eta(e)) = \lambda(e)$ by the definition of $\lambda_{T'}$. Hence $\lambda = \lambda_{T'} \circ \eta$.

(c): We now show the uniqueness of η. Assume η' is any morphism from E to $tle(T)$, such that $\lambda_{T'} \circ \eta' = \lambda$. We want to show $\eta(e) = \eta'(e)$ for all $e \in E$. Let $x \xrightarrow{e} x \cup \{e\}$ in ES, and assume inductively that η and η' agree on all elements of x. Firstly, from the assumption $\lambda_{T'}\circ\eta' = \lambda$ we get $\eta'(e)$ defined iff $\lambda(e)$ defined (since $\lambda_{T'}$ is total) and hence iff $\eta(e)$ defined. So, assume $\eta'(e)$ is defined and equal to e'. Then $\eta'(x) \xrightarrow{e'} \eta'(x \cup \{e\})$ in $tle(T')$ (since η' morphism) and $\lambda_{T'}(e') = \lambda(e)$. However, from the representation theorem for trace languages, it follows that there is exactly one event in $tle(T')$ satisfying these requirements—the one picked by η, and hence $\eta(e) = \eta'(e)$. □

Corollary 30 *The operation tle on trace languages extends to a functor, right adjoint to etl, forming a coreflection* $\mathbf{E} \hookrightarrow \mathbf{TL}$*; the functor tle sends the morphism* $\lambda : T \to T'$ *to* $\eta : tle(T) \to tle(T')$ *acting on events* $\{sa\}_\sim$ *of tle(T) so that*

$$\eta(\{sa\}_\sim) = \begin{cases} * & \text{if } \lambda(a) \text{ undefined}, \\ \{\widehat{\lambda}(sa)\}_\sim & \text{if } \lambda(a) \text{ defined}. \end{cases}$$

The coreflection cuts down to one between subcategories of coherent trace languages and coherent event structures.

The coreflection expresses the sense in which the model of event structures "embeds" in the model of trace languages. Because of the coreflection we can restrict trace languages to those which are isomorphic to images of event structures under *etl* and obtain a full subcategory of trace languages equivalent to that of event structures.

The existence of a coreflection from event structures to trace languages has the important consequence of yielding an explicit product construction on event structures, which is not so easy to define directly. The product of event structures E_0 and E_1 can be obtained as

$$tle(etl(E_0) \times etl(E_1)),$$

that is by first regarding the event structures as trace languages, forming their product as trace languages, and then finally regarding the result as an event structure again. That this result is indeed a product of E_0 and E_1 follows because the right adjoint *tle* preserves limits and the unit of the adjunction is a natural isomorphism (*i.e.* from the coreflection). In a similar way we will be able to obtain the product of event structures from that of nets, asynchronous transition systems, or indeed more general event structures, from the coreflections between categories of event structures and these models.

The existence of a *coreflection* from the category of event structures to the category of trace languages might seem surprising, at least when seen alongside the analogous interleaving models, where we might think of trace languages as the analogue of languages. There is a *reflection* from the category of languages to the category of synchronisation trees.

This mismatch can be reconciled by recalling the two ways of regarding trace languages (*cf.* the discussion of section 7.2). One is where the alphabet of a trace language is thought of a consisting of events; this view is adopted in establishing the coreflection. Alternatively, the alphabet can be thought of as a set of labels. With the latter view a more correct analogy is:

• Labelled event structures generalise synchronisation trees.

• Trace languages generalise languages.

This analogy can be formalised in a diagram of adjunctions—see (Winskel and Nielsen 1995).

What model is to generalise both transition systems and labelled event structures? A suitable model would consist of labels attached to certain structures; a fitting structure should allow loops in the behaviour and have events on which it is possible to interpret a relation of independence. There are several candidates for the appropriate structures, and we turn now to consider one closely related to Petri nets.

9   Asynchronous transition systems

Asynchronous transition systems[7] were introduced independently by Bednarczyk (1988) and Shields (1985). Their transitions are to be thought of as occurrences of events which bear a relation of independence. This interpretation is supported by axioms which essentially generalise those from Mazurkiewicz trace languages.

Definition: An *asynchronous transition system* consists of $(S, i, E, I, Tran)$ where $(S, i, E, Tran)$ is a transition system and $I \subseteq E^2$, the *independence relation*, is an irreflexive, symmetric relation on the set E of *events* such that

(1) $e \in E \Rightarrow \exists s, s' \in S. \ (s, e, s') \in Tran$

(2) $(s, e, s') \in Tran \ \& \ (s, e, s'') \in Tran \Rightarrow s' = s''$

(3) $e_1 I e_2 \ \& \ (s, e_1, s_1) \in Tran \ \& \ (s_1, e_2, u) \in Tran$
      $\Rightarrow \exists s_2. \ (s, e_2, s_2) \in Tran \ \& \ (s_2, e_1, u) \in Tran.$

Say an asynchronous transition system is *coherent* if it also satisfies

---

[7] Our treatment of asynchronous transition systems follows that of (Winskel and Nielsen 1995) closely and the proofs omitted here are a simple amendment of those given there. In contrast to *loc. cit.*, the asynchronous transition systems here need not be coherent.

(4) $e_1 I e_2$ & $(s, e_1, s_1) \in Tran$ & $(s, e_2, s_2) \in Tran$
$\Rightarrow \exists u. (s_1, e_2, u) \in Tran$ & $(s_2, e_1, u) \in Tran.$

Axiom (1) says every event appears as a transition, and axiom (2) that the occurrence of an event at a state leads to a unique state. Axioms (3) and (4) express properties of independence: if two independent events can occur one immediately after the other then they should be able to occur with their order interchanged (3); if two events can occur independently from a common state then they can occur together and in so doing reach a common state (4). Both situations lead to an "independence square" associated with the independence $e_1 I e_2$:

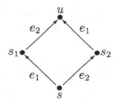

Morphisms between asynchronous transition systems are morphisms between their underlying transition systems which preserve the additional relations of independence.

Definition: Let $T = (S, i, E, I, Tran)$ and $T' = (S', i', E', I', Tran')$ be asynchronous transition systems. A *morphism* $T \to T'$ is a morphism of transition systems

$$(\sigma, \eta) : (S, i, E, Tran) \to (S', i', E', Tran')$$

such that

$$e_1 I e_2 \text{ & } \eta(e_1), \eta(e_2) \text{ both defined } \Rightarrow \eta(e_1) I' \eta(e_2).$$

Morphisms of asynchronous transition systems compose as morphisms between their underlying transition systems, and are readily seen to form a category.

Definition: Write **A** for the category of asynchronous transition systems.

The category **A** has categorical constructions which essentially generalise those of transition systems and Mazurkiewicz traces. Here are the product and coproduct constructions for the category **A**:

Definition: Assume asynchronous transition systems $T_0 = (S_0, i_0, E_0, I_0, Tran_0)$ and $T_1 = (S_1, i_1, E_1, I_1, Tran_1)$. Their *product* $T_0 \times T_1$ is $(S, i, E, I, Tran)$ where $(S, i, E, Tran)$ is the product of transition systems $(S_0, i_0, E_0, Tran_0)$ and $(S_1, i_1, E_1, Tran_1)$ with projections (ρ_0, π_0) and (ρ_1, π_1), and the independence relation I is given by

$$a I b \Leftrightarrow (\pi_0(a), \pi_0(b) \text{ defined } \Rightarrow \pi_0(a) I_0 \pi_0(b)) \text{ &}$$
$$(\pi_1(a), \pi_1(b) \text{ defined } \Rightarrow \pi_1(a) I_1 \pi_1(b)).$$

Definition: Assume asynchronous transition systems $T_0 = (S_0, i_0, E_0, I_0, Tran_0)$
and $T_1 = (S_1, i_1, E_1, I_1, Tran_1)$. Their *coproduct* $T_0 + T_1$ is $(S, i, E, I, Tran)$
where $(S, i, E, Tran)$ is the coproduct of transition systems $(S_0, i_0, E_0, Tran_0)$ and
$(S_1, i_1, E_1, Tran_1)$ with injections (in_0, j_0) and (in_1, j_1), and the independence relation I is given by

$$a I b \Leftrightarrow (\exists a_0, b_0.\ a = j_0(a_0)\ \&\ b = j_0(b_0)\ \&\ a_0 I_0 b_0)\ \text{or}$$
$$(\exists a_1, b_1.\ a = j_1(a_1)\ \&\ b = j_1(b_1)\ \&\ a_1 I_1 b_1).$$

9.1 Asynchronous transition systems and trace languages

That asynchronous transition systems generalise trace languages is backed up by
a straightforward coreflection between categories of trace languages and asynchronous transition systems. To obtain the adjunction we need to restrict trace
languages to those where every element of the alphabet occurs in some trace
(this matches property (1) required by the definition of asynchronous transition
systems).

Definition: Define $\mathbf{TL}_0$ to be the full subcategory of trace languages (M, E, I)
satisfying

$$\forall e \in E \exists s.\ se \in M.$$

A trace language forms an asynchronous transition system in which the states
are traces.

Definition: Let (M, E, I) be a trace language in $\mathbf{TL}_0$, with trace equivalence $\approx$.
Define $tla(M, E, I) = (S, i, E, I, Tran)$ where

$$S = M/\approx \text{ with } i = \{\epsilon\}_\approx$$
$$(t, e, t') \in Tran \Leftrightarrow \exists s, se \in M.\ t = \{s\}_\approx\ \&\ t' = \{se\}_\approx$$

Let $\eta : (M, E, I) \to (M', E', I')$ be a morphism of trace languages. Define
$tla(\eta) = (\sigma, \eta)$ where

$$\sigma(\{s\}_\approx) = \{\hat\eta(s)\}_\approx.$$

(Note this is well-defined because morphisms between trace languages respect $\approx$—
this follows directly from proposition 13.)

Proposition 31 *The operation tla is a functor* $\mathbf{TL}_0 \to \mathbf{A}$.

An asynchronous transition system determines a trace language:

Definition: Let $T = (S, i, E, I, Tran)$ be an asynchronous transition system. Define $atl(T) = (Seq, E, I)$ where Seq consists of all strings of events, possibly
empty, $e_1 e_2 \ldots e_n$ for which there are transitions

$$(i, e_1, s_1), (s_1, e_2, s_2), \ldots, (s_{n-1}, e_n, s_n) \in Tran$$

Let $(\sigma, \eta) : T \to T'$ be a morphism of asynchronous transition systems. Define
$atl(\sigma, \eta) = \eta$.

Proposition 32 *The operation atl is a functor* $A \to TL_0$.

In fact, the functors *tla, atl* form a coreflection:

Theorem 33 *The functor tla* : $TL_0 \to A$ *is left adjoint to atl* : $A \to TL_0$.

Let $L = (M, E, I)$ *be a trace language. Then atl* $\circ$ *tla* $(M, E, I) = (M, E, I)$ *and the unit of the adjunction at* (M, E, I) *is the identity* 1_E : $(M, E, I) \to$ *atl* $\circ$ *tla*(M, E, I).

Let T *be an asynchronous transition system, with events* E. *Then* $(\sigma, 1_E)$: *tla* $\circ$ *atl*$(T) \to T$ *is the counit of the adjunction at* T, *where* $\sigma(t)$, *for a trace* $t = \{e_1 e_2 \dots e_n\}_{\approx}$, *equals the unique state* s *for which* $i \xrightarrow{e_1 e_2 \dots e_n} s$.

The coreflection does not extend to an adjunction from **TL** to **A**—TL_0 is a reflective and not a coreflective subcategory of **TL**.

We note that a coreflection between event structures and asynchronous transition systems follows by composing the coreflections between event structures and trace languages and that between trace languages and asynchronous transition systems. It is easy to see that the coreflection $E \hookrightarrow TL$ restricts to a coreflection $E \hookrightarrow TL_0$. The left adjoint of the resulting coreflection, is the composition

$$E \xrightarrow{etl} TL_0 \xrightarrow{tla} A.$$

A left adjoint of the coreflection can however be constructed more directly. The composition *tla* $\circ$ *etl* is naturally isomorphic to the functor yielding an asynchronous transition system directly out of the configurations of the event structure, as is described in the next proposition.

Proposition 34 *For* $ES = (E, \leq, Con)$ *an event structure, define*

$$\Gamma(ES) = (\mathcal{D}^0(ES), \emptyset, E, co, Tran)$$

where the transitions between configurations, Tran, consist of (x, e, x') *where* $e \notin x$ & $x' = x \cup \{e\}$. *For* η : $ES \to ES'$ *a morphism of event structures, define* $\Gamma(\eta) = (\sigma, \eta)$ *where* $\sigma(x) = \eta x$, *for* x *a configuration of ES. This defines a functor* Γ : $E \to A$. *Moreover,* Γ *is naturally isomorphic to tla* $\circ$ *etl.*

9.2 Asynchronous transition systems and Petri nets

Asynchronous transition systems are closely related to Petri nets. In fact, an asynchronous transition system possesses enough structure from which to construct a Petri net (its conditions are taken to be certain subsets of transitions and states). Provided the asynchronous transition system satisfies some restrictions (entailing coherence) the constructed net will behave like the original asynchronous transition system. This equivalence between certain asynchronous transition systems and Petri nets works at the level of categories of the models; adjunctions and coreflections between asynchronous transition systems and categories of Petri nets are exhibited in (Winskel and Nielsen 1995; Nielsen and Winskel 1996).

10   Labelled models and bisimulation

The presentation of models for concurrency as categories allows us to apply a general notion of bisimulation, obtained from a span of open maps, proposed in (Joyal, Nielsen, and Winskel 1994).

10.1   Labelled models and their relationship

The semantics of processes in languages like CCS are given by labelled structures. There is a general way of introducing labels to models in such a way that one may carry over adjunctions between unlabelled models to their labelled counterparts. We sketch the idea, applicable to the categories of Mazurkiewicz trace languages, asynchronous transition systems and event structures. We assume a category $\mathbf{X}$ of structures each of which possesses a distinguished set of events and where morphisms have as a component a partial function between sets of events.

  (i) Add to structures X an extra component of a (total) labelling function l : $E \to L$ from the structure's set of events E to a set of labels L; we obtain labelled structure as pairs (X, l).

 (ii) We assume morphisms $f : X \to X'$ of unlabelled structures include a component η between sets of events. A morphism of labelled structures $(X, l) \to (X', l')$ is a pair (f, λ) where $f : X \to X'$ is a morphism on the underlying unlabelled structures and $\lambda : L \to_* L'$ is a partial function on the label sets such that $\lambda \circ l = l' \circ \eta$. Composition of morphisms is done coordinatewise.

Morphisms between labelled structures are of this generality in order to obtain operations of process calculi as universal constructions. However, for our purpose of studying bisimulation, it suffices to work with subcategories of structures having a common set of labels L, and restrict to morphisms as above, but with the extra condition that the component λ is the identity on L—this implies that the event component η is total. We call the resulting category $\mathbf{X}_L$; this subcategory is the fibre over L with respect to the obvious functor projecting labelled structures to their label sets. For emphasis:

  • The objects of $\mathbf{X}_L$ consist of structures (X, l) where X is an object of $\mathbf{X}$, and $l : E \to L$ is a (total) labelling function from E the events of X to the labelling set L

  • The morphisms of $\mathbf{X}_L$ from (X, l) to (X', l') correspond to morphisms f : $X \to X'$ of $\mathbf{X}$ of which the event component η preserves labels, i.e. $l' \circ \eta = l$.

Correspondingly, for a set of labels L, we denote the fibres over L in the labelled versions of the categories of asynchronous transition systems and event structures by $\mathbf{A}_L$, and $\mathbf{E}_L$ respectively. Similarly the category of transition systems over label set L, with morphisms having the identity as label component, will be denoted $\mathbf{T}_L$, and its full subcategory of synchronisation trees $\mathbf{S}_L$. We remark that *synchronisation trees* can be identified with those event structures having empty *co*-relation.

It follows for general reasons (Winskel and Nielsen 1995) (and is easy to see) that the adjunctions between models given earlier lift to a adjunctions between the labelled versions. The modified adjoints are essentially the adjoints presented in the previous sections, simply carrying the label parts across from one model to the other.

$$\mathbf{S}_L \overset{st}{\to} \mathbf{T}_L$$
$$se\downarrow$$
$$\mathbf{E}_L \underset{ea}{\overset{\to}{\to}} \mathbf{A}_L$$

When specifying a functor of one of the coreflections above, we adopt a convention; for example the left adjoint from $\mathbf{S}_L$ to $\mathbf{T}_L$ is denoted st while its right adjoint is ts. The left adjoints, drawn above, embed one model in another. The functor se identifies a synchronisation tree with its corresponding labelled event structure; its right adjoint es takes a labelled event structures to its synchronisation-tree serialisation whose branches correspond to sequences of event occurrences of the event structure. Irritatingly, there is not a coreflection from transition systems $\mathbf{T}_L$ to labelled asynchronous transition systems $\mathbf{A}_L$. This is simply because, unlike transition systems, labelled asynchronous transition systems allow more than one transition with the same label between two states. This stops the natural bijection required for the "inclusion" of transition systems to be a left adjoint.

10.2   Path-lifting morphisms

In this section we briefly present some of the main ideas, definitions and results from (Joyal, Nielsen, and Winskel 1994), providing a general notion of bisimulation applicable to a wide range of models.[8]

Informally, a computation path should represent a particular run or history of a process. For transition systems, a computation path is reasonably taken to be a sequence of transitions. Let's suppose the sequence is finite. For a labelling set L, define the category of branches $\mathbf{Bran}_L$ to be the full subcategory of transition systems, with labelling set L, with objects those finite synchronisation trees with one maximal branch; so the objects of $\mathbf{Bran}_L$ are essentially strings over alphabet L. A computation path in a transition system T, with labelling set L, can then be represented by a morphism

$$p : P \to T$$

in $\mathbf{T}_L$ from an object P of $\mathbf{Bran}_L$. How should we represent a computation path of a labelled asynchronous transition system or event structure? To take into account the explicit concurrency exhibited by an event structure, it is reasonable to represent a

---

[8]For the missing proofs we refer to (Joyal, Nielsen, and Winskel 1994).

computation path as a morphism from a partial order of labelled events, that is from a *pomset*. Note that Pratt's *pomsets*, with labels in L, can be identified with special kinds of labelled event structures in $\mathbf{E}_L$, those with consistency relation consisting of all finite subsets of events. Define the category of pomsets $\mathbf{Pom}_L$, with respect to a labelling set L, to be the full subcategory of $\mathbf{E}_L$ whose objects consist exclusively of finite pomsets. A computation path in an event structure E, with labelling set L, is a morphism

$$p : P \to E$$

in $\mathbf{E}_L$ from an object P of $\mathbf{Pom}_L$. What about computation paths in asynchronous transition systems? The left adjoint ea of the coreflection $\mathbf{E}_L \to \mathbf{A}_L$ embeds labelled event structures, and so pomsets, in labelled asynchronous transition systems. This enables us to identify pomsets P in $\mathbf{Pom}_L$ with their images $ea(P)$ in $\mathbf{A}_L$. Now, we can take a computation path in an A, with labelling set L, to be a morphism

$$p : P \to A$$

in $\mathbf{A}_L$ from a pomset P, with labelling set L—where the pomset P is understood as the corresponding labelled asynchronous transition system in $\mathbf{A}_L$. In future, when discussing labelled asynchronous transition systems, we will deliberately confuse pomsets with their image in $\mathbf{A}_L$ under the embedding.

Generally, assume a category of models $\mathbf{M}$ (this can be any of the categories of labelled structures we are considering) and a choice of path category, a subcategory $\mathbf{P} \hookrightarrow \mathbf{M}$ consisting of path objects (these could be branches, or pomsets) together with morphisms expressing how they can be extended. Define a *computation path* in an object X of $\mathbf{M}$ to be a morphism

$$p : P \to X,$$

in $\mathbf{M}$, where P is an object in $\mathbf{P}$. A morphism $f : X \to Y$ in $\mathbf{M}$ takes such a path p in X to the path $f \circ p : P \to Y$ in Y. The morphism f expresses the sense in which Y simulates X; any computation path in X is matched by the computation path $f \circ p$ in Y.

We might demand a stronger condition of a morphism $f : X \to Y$ expressed succinctly in the following *path-lifting condition*:

Whenever, for $m : P \to Q$ a morphism in $\mathbf{P}$, a "square"

$$\begin{array}{ccc} P & \xrightarrow{p} & X \\ m\downarrow & & \downarrow f \\ Q & \xrightarrow{q} & Y \end{array}$$

in $\mathbf{M}$ commutes, *i.e.* $q \circ m = f \circ p$, meaning the path $f \circ p$ in Y can be extended via m to a path q in Y, then there is a morphism p' such that in the diagram

$$\begin{array}{ccc} P & \xrightarrow{p} & X \\ m\downarrow & \nearrow^{p'} & \downarrow f \\ Q & \xrightarrow{q} & Y \end{array}$$

the two "triangles" commute, *i.e.* $p' \circ m = p$ and $f \circ p' = q$, meaning the path p can be extended via m to a path p' in X which matches q. When the morphism f satisfies this condition we shall say it is **P**-*open*.

It is easily checked that **P**-open morphisms include all the identity morphisms (in fact, all isomorphisms) of **M** and are closed under composition there; in other words they form a subcategory of **M**.

For the well-known model of transition systems open morphisms are already familiar:

Proposition 35 *With respect to a labelling set L, the* **Bran**$_L$-*open morphisms of* $\mathbf{T}_L$ *are the "zig-zag morphisms" of (Bentham 1984), the "p-morphism" of (Segerberg 1968), the "abstraction homomorphisms" of (Castellani 1985), and the "pure morphisms" of (Benson and Ben-Shachar 1988), i.e. those label-preserving morphisms* $(\sigma, 1_L) : T \to T'$ *on transition systems over labelling set L with the property that for all reachable states s of T*

if $\sigma(s) \xrightarrow{a} s'$ in T' then $s \xrightarrow{a} u$ in T and $\sigma(u) = s'$, for some state u of T.

Let us return to the general set-up, assuming a path category **P** in a category of models **M**. Say two objects X_1, X_2 of **M** are **P**-*bisimilar* iff they are connected by **P**-open morphisms, *i.e.* there are **P**-open morphisms $f_1, \cdots, f_n$

$$X_1 \xleftarrow{f_1} Y_1 \xrightarrow{f_2} Y_2 \cdots \xleftarrow{f_{n-1}} Y_{n-1} \xrightarrow{f_n} X_2.$$

The relation of **P**-bisimilarity is clearly an equivalence relation between objects of **M**—it is reflexive because identities are **P**-open.

In the case where **M** has pullbacks the **P**-open morphisms connecting **P**-bisimilar objects can be standardised to a simple *span* of **P**-open morphisms. In other words, two objects X_1, X_2 of **M** are **P**-bisimilar iff there is a *span* of **P**-open morphisms f_1, f_2:

$$\begin{array}{ccc} & X & \\ f_1 \swarrow & & \searrow f_2 \\ X_1 & & X_2 \end{array}$$

This is because:

Proposition 36 *Pullbacks of* **P**-*open morphisms are* **P**-*open.*

So, by repeatedly applying the proposition above, a connecting chain of **P**-open morphisms can be converted to a span of **P**-open morphisms, when **M** has pullbacks as is so for all the models we consider:

Proposition 37 *The categories* $\mathbf{T}_L, \mathbf{S}_L, \mathbf{N}_L, \mathbf{A}_L,$ *and* $\mathbf{E}_L$ *have pullbacks.*

Proof: See (Nielsen and Winskel 1996). □

For the interleaving models of transition systems and synchronisation trees with path category **P** taken to be branches, **P**-bisimulation coincides with Milner's strong bisimulation:

Theorem 38 *Two transition systems (and so synchronisation trees), over the same labelling set L, are* Bran$_L$-*bisimilar iff they are strongly bisimilar in the sense of (Milner 1989).*

We present a few general facts from (Joyal, Nielsen, and Winskel 1994; Nielsen and Winskel 1996) about how open morphisms and bisimilarity are preserved and reflected by functors, especially when part of a coreflection. For notational simplicity we shall assume the left adjoints of the coreflections are inclusions. It follows that for the coreflections of section 10.1 in which the two categories of models share the same choice of path category, open morphisms and bisimilarity are preserved in both directions of the adjunction.

Proposition 39 *Let* M *be a full subcategory of* N*, and* P *a subcategory of* M*. A morphism f of* M *is* P*-open in* M *iff f is* P*-open in* N*.*

Lemma 40 *Let* M *be a coreflective subcategory of* N *with R right adjoint to the inclusion function* M $\hookrightarrow$ N *and* P *a subcategory of* M*. Then:*

(i) *A morphism f of* M *is* P*-open in* M *iff f is* P*-open in* N*.*

(ii) *The components of the counit of the adjunction* $\varepsilon_X : R(X) \to X$ *are* P*-open in* M*.*

(iii) *A morphism f is* P*-open in* N *iff* $R(f)$ *is* P*-open in* M*.*

Corollary 41 *Let* M *be a coreflective subcategory of* N *with R right adjoint to the inclusion function* M $\hookrightarrow$ N *and* P *a subcategory of* M*. Then:*

(i) M_1, M_2 *are* P*-bisimilar in* M *iff* M_1, M_2 *are* P*-bisimilar in* N*.*

(ii) N_1, N_2 *are* P*-bisimilar in* N *iff* $R(N_1), R(N_2)$ *are* P*-bisimilar in* M*.*

10.3   Pomset bisimulation

We have already seen (lemma 35, theorem 38) that for the well-known model of transition systems, the general definition of **P**-open morphism and **P**-bisimilarity coincide with familiar notions; in particular, we recover the equivalence of strong bisimilarity central to Milner's work. Here we explore how the general definitions specialise to the models of event structures and labelled asynchronous transition systems, with nonsequential paths in the form of pomsets.

We start by characterising Pom$_L$-open morphisms on labelled asynchronous transition systems. Following our convention, we identify pomsets with their image under the embedding $\mathbf{E}_L \to \mathbf{A}_L$.

Lemma 42 *The* Pom_L*-open morphisms of* $\mathbf{A}_L$ *are precisely those which satisfy the "zig-zag" condition of proposition 35 and which, in addition, reflect consecutive independence, i.e. morphisms satisfying:*

η *is total and label preserving*

whenever $(\sigma(s), e', u') \in tran_2$ *then there exists* $(s, e, u) \in tran_1$ *such that* $\eta(e) = e'$ *and* $\sigma(u) = u'$

whenever $(s, e, u), (u, e', v) \in Tran_1$, *with* s *reachable, and* $\eta(e) I_2 \eta(e')$ *in* T_2, *then* $e I_1 e'$ *in* T_1.

Proof: The proof of this lemma is a straightforward modification of the proof of the corresponding result for transition systems with independence from (Joyal, Nielsen, and Winskel 1994). □

Now to the question of bisimulations. In (Joyal, Nielsen, and Winskel 1994) it was shown that in the case of event structures taking the path category **P** to be pomsets one gets a reasonable strengthening of a previously studied equivalence, that of *history-preserving bisimulation*. Its definition depends on the simple but important remark, that a configuration of an event structure can be regarded as a pomset, with causal dependency relation and labelling got by restricting that of the event structure.

Definition: (Rabinovich and Trakhtenbrot 1988, Glabeek and Goltz 1989)

A *history-preserving bisimulation* between two event structures E_1, E_2 consists of a set H of triples (x_1, f, x_2) where x_1 is a configuration of E_1, x_2 a configuration of E_2 and f is a isomorphism between them (regarded as pomsets), such that $(\emptyset, \emptyset, \emptyset) \in H$ and, whenever $(x_1, f, x_2) \in H$

(i) if $x_1 \xrightarrow{a} x_1'$ in E_1 then $x_2 \xrightarrow{a} x_2'$ in E_2 and $(x_1', f', x_2') \in H$ with $f \subseteq f'$, for some x_2' and f'.

(ii) if $x_2 \xrightarrow{a} x_2'$ in E_2 then $x_1 \xrightarrow{a} x_1'$ in E_1 and $(x_1', f', x_2') \in H$ with $f \subseteq f'$, for some x_1' and f'

We say a history-preserving bisimulation H is *strong* when it further satisfies

(I) $(x, f, y) \in H$ & $x' \subseteq x$, for a configuration x' of E_1 implies $(x', f', y') \in H$, for some $f' \subseteq f$ and $y' \subseteq y$.

(II) $(x, f, y) \in H$ & $y' \subseteq y$, for a configuration y' of E_2, implies $(x', f', y') \in H$, for some $f' \subseteq f$ and $x' \subseteq x$.

In (Joyal, Nielsen, and Winskel 1994) it is shown that $\mathbf{Pom}_L$-bisimilarity of event structures in $\mathbf{E}_L$ coincides with their being strong history-preserving bisimilar. However, this in itself does not show that $\mathbf{Pom}_L$-bisimilarity of event structures in the smaller category $\mathbf{E}_L^0$ of coherent event structures also coincides with strong history-preserving bisimilarity. There might conceivably be a span of open morphisms, $f_1 : E \to E_1, f_2 : E \to E_2$, from a noncoherent event structure E relating two coherent event structures E_1, E_2 which could never be replaced by a span of open morphisms from a coherent event structure. In fact, such is not the case, because for any event structure E in $\mathbf{E}_L$ there is an open morphism $f : E' \to E$ from a *coherent* event structure E' (lemma 43). Hence a span of open morphisms $f_1 : E \to E_1, f_2 : E \to E_2$ in $\mathbf{E}_L$, with E_1, E_2 coherent, can always be converted to a span of open morphisms $f_1 \circ f : E' \to E_1, f_2 \circ f : E' \to E_2$ in $\mathbf{E}_L^0$. Consequently, $\mathbf{Pom}_L$-bisimilarity in the subcategory of coherent event structures $\mathbf{E}_L^0$ coincides with strong history-preserving bisimilarity. This result has implications for $\mathbf{Pom}_L$-bisimilarity between Petri nets because of the coreflection from coherent event structures to nets—see (Nielsen and Winskel 1996).

Although we have not insisted on it, a reasonable requirement on event structures (and the other objects we consider here) is that they be countable. One might view with suspicion any result which depended crucially on allowing event structures to be uncountable. For this reason, some care is taken to give countable constructions.

Lemma 43 *Let* $A = (A, \leq, Con, l)$ *be a labelled event structure. Then, there is a labelled coherent event structure* $E = (E, \leq', \#', l')$ *and an open morphism* $g : E \to A$.

Moreover, if A *is countable/finite then so can* E *be taken to be countable/finite respectively.*

Proof: See (Nielsen and Winskel 1996). $\square$

Now we can show that restricting the category of event structures to those which are coherent does not effect the relation of bisimilarity.

Corollary 44 *Let* E_1, E_2 *be coherent event structures with labelling sets* L. *The following are equivalent:*

(i) E_1, E_2 *are* $\mathbf{Pom}_L$*-bisimilar in* $\mathbf{E}_L^0$.

(ii) E_1, E_2 *are* $\mathbf{Pom}_L$*-bisimilar in* $\mathbf{E}_L$.

(iii) E_1, E_2 *are strong history-preserving bisimilar.*

Via the coreflection between event structures and Petri nets, we can draw characterisations of $\mathbf{Pom}_L$-bisimilarity on nets—see (Nielsen and Winskel 1996).

10.4 Presheaf models

Given a path category $\mathbf{P}$ we can build the category $\widehat{\mathbf{P}}$ of presheaves over $\mathbf{P}$.[9] The objects of $\widehat{\mathbf{P}}$ consist of functors $\mathbf{P}^{op} \to \mathbf{Set}$, to the category of sets. The morphisms of $\widehat{\mathbf{P}}$ are natural transformations between functors. Intuitively a presheaf F : $\mathbf{P}^{op} \to \mathbf{Set}$ can be thought of as specifying for a typical path object P the set $F(P)$ of paths from P. It acts on a morphism $m : P \to Q$ in $\mathbf{P}$ to give a function $F(m) : F(Q) \to F(P)$ saying how Q-paths restrict to P-paths.

Let us see how a model, like a transition system or a labelled event structure, gives rise to a presheaf. Consider a category of models $\mathbf{M}$ and a choice of path category forming a subcategory $\mathbf{P} \hookrightarrow \mathbf{M}$. There is a *canonical functor* from the category of models $\mathbf{M}$ to the category of presheaves $\widehat{\mathbf{P}}$. The functor

$$\mathbf{M} \to \widehat{\mathbf{P}}$$

takes an object X of $\mathbf{M}$ to the presheaf $\mathbf{M}(-, X)$—more intuitively, it takes the model X to the to the presheaf which for each path object P yields the set of paths $\mathbf{M}(P, X)$ from P into X. The canonical functor takes a morphism $f : X \to Y$ in $\mathbf{M}$ to the natural transformation

$$\mathbf{M}(-, f) : \mathbf{M}(-, X) \to \mathbf{M}(-, Y)$$

whose component at an object P of $\mathbf{P}$ is the function $\mathbf{M}(P, X) \to \mathbf{M}(P, Y)$ taking p to $f \circ p$—intuitively, a path $p : P \to X$ in X is taken to a path $f \circ p : P \to Y$ in Y.

Theorem 45

  (i) The canonical functor from $\mathbf{S}_L$ to $\widehat{\mathbf{Bran}_L}$ is full, faithful and dense.

  (ii) The canonical functor from $\mathbf{E}_L$ to $\widehat{\mathbf{Pom}_L}$ is full faithful and dense.

There are more objects in the presheaf categories than in the original models. In the case where path objects are branches, objects of the presheaf category $\widehat{\mathbf{Bran}_L}$ consist of "synchronisation forests", *viz.* collections of synchronisation trees. Such a collection may be empty. The embedding has as image all those collections which are singletons. The collections carry a computational intuition similar to that of synchronisation trees—there is no longer simply one initial state. The embeddings, being full, faithful and dense, preserve limits, so products in the larger category of presheaves coincide with the fibre product on synchronisation trees, though coproducts will differ, amounting to disjoint union of forests in $\widehat{\mathbf{Bran}_L}$. The extra objects in $\widehat{\mathbf{Pom}_L}$, over those presheaves corresponding to event structures, are more

---

[9]Proofs for presheaf models can be found in (Joyal, Nielsen, and Winskel 1994). A good introduction to presheaves can be found in Chapter 1 of (MacLane and Moerdijk 1992).

difficult to explain, though some are representable via models such as general Petri nets.

The embeddings of theorem 45 extend the Yoneda embedding of $\mathbf{P} \rightarrow \widehat{\mathbf{P}}$, regarding a path object P as the presheaf $\mathbf{P}(-, P) = \mathbf{M}(-, P)$ because, in these cases, the subcategory $\mathbf{P} \hookrightarrow \mathbf{M}$ is full. Now, if we regard presheaves as the model $\mathbf{M}'$ and the image of $\mathbf{P}$ under the Yoneda embedding as its path category $\mathbf{P}'$, we can apply the general definition of section 10.2, to obtain the class of $\mathbf{P}'$-open morphisms of the presheaf category. They form a category of *open maps* of the topos $\widehat{\mathbf{P}}$, in the sense of Joyal and Moerdijk.[10] The two notions of $\mathbf{P}$-open and open map agree for the models of synchronisation trees and event structures, because generally:

Proposition 46. *Let* $\mathbf{P}$ *be a dense, full subcategory of* $\mathbf{M}$. *A morphism* $f : X \rightarrow Y$ *of* $\mathbf{M}$ *is* $\mathbf{P}$-*open iff the morphism* $\mathbf{M}(-, f) : \mathbf{M}(-, X) \rightarrow \mathbf{M}(-, Y)$ *is an open map (in the sense of (Joyal and Moerdijk 1994)).*

So, in particular, a morphism f of event structures is $\mathbf{Pom}_L$-open iff the corresponding morphism $\mathbf{E}(-, f)$ in the presheaf category $\widehat{\mathbf{Pom}_L}$ is an open map.

When it comes to relating notions of bisimilarity, care must taken. It is not the case that two event structures are $\mathbf{Pom}_L$-bisimilar iff their associated presheaves are related by a span of open maps in $\widehat{\mathbf{Pom}_L}$. This is because there are many more objects in the presheaf category, and, in particular, there is always a span of open maps between any two presheaves subtended from the initial (always empty) presheaf. One way to get a correspondence is to define bisimilarity in the entire presheaf category via spans of *epimorphic* open maps.

Another way to get a correspondence is to restrict the objects in the presheaf category. In the situation where the path category $\mathbf{P}$ of a model $\mathbf{M}$ has an initial object I, a *rooted presheaf* is a presheaf F in which $\widehat{F(I)}$ is a singleton. As remarked, the full subcategory of rooted presheaves of $\widehat{\mathbf{Bran}_L}$ is equivalent to the category $\mathbf{S}$. Note incidentally, that in the full subcategories of rooted presheaves of $\widehat{\mathbf{Bran}_L}$ and $\widehat{\mathbf{Pom}_L}$, the coproduct glues presheaves together at a common initial state; thus there the construction coincides with that required to represent Milner's sum of processes.

Proposition 47

(i) *Two synchronisation trees, over labelling set* L, *are* $\mathbf{Bran}_L$-*bisimilar (i.e. strong bisimilar) iff their corresponding presheaves, under the canonical embedding, are related by a span of open maps in the full subcategory of rooted presheaves of* $\widehat{\mathbf{Bran}_L}$.

---

[10]See (Joyal and Moerdijk 1994) P.3, Example 1.1, though there the definition is expressed in terms of the existence of certain quasi-pullbacks; its equivalence with $\mathbf{P}'$-openness, expressed as a path-lifting property, follows by the Yoneda Lemma.

(ii) Two event structures, over labelling set L, are $\mathbf{Pom}_L$-bisimilar (i.e. strong history-preserving bisimilar) iff their corresponding presheaves, under the canonical embedding, are related by a span of open maps in the full subcategory of rooted presheaves of $\widehat{\mathbf{Pom}_L}$.

As indicated in (Joyal, Nielsen, and Winskel 1994), and further justified by work of Gian-Luca Cattani, for general reasons presheaf models support operations of refinement familiar from process algebras, as in (Glabbeek 1990). Presheaves are also helpful in generalising Hennessy-Milner logic to the new notions of bisimulation. Roughly the idea is to have modalities indexed by morphisms in the path category; in the case of a simple path category like $\mathbf{Bran}_L$ this amounts to modalities associated with strings of labels, easily reduced to the modalities of Hennessy and Milner. Like Hennessy-Milner logic the general logic, parameterised by the path category $\mathbf{P}$, is characteristic for the equivalence of $\mathbf{P}$-bisimulation (see Joyal, Nielsen, and Winskel 1994).

10.5 Weak bisimulation

Recall that in Milner's work (see *e.g.* (Milner 1989)) the label τ has a special status. It is used to label internal actions. Weak bisimulation is an equivalence relation taking account of the invisibility of τ actions. We follow Milner and reduce weak bisimulation to strong bisimulation via a construction on transition systems. Recall Milner defines two transition systems X and Y to be *weakly bisimilar* iff $\mathcal{T}(X)$ and $\mathcal{T}(Y)$ are strongly bisimilar, where the construction $\mathcal{T}$ is defined as follows: for a transition system $U = (S, i, L, Tran)$

$$\mathcal{T}(U) = (S, i, L, Tran')$$

with

$$s \xrightarrow{a} s' \text{ in } \mathcal{T}(U) \Leftrightarrow s(\xrightarrow{\tau})^*(\xrightarrow{a})(\xrightarrow{\tau})^* s' \text{ in } U, \text{ when } a \neq \tau,$$
$$s \xrightarrow{\tau} s' \text{ in } \mathcal{T}(U) \Leftrightarrow s(\xrightarrow{\tau})^* s' \text{ in } U.$$

Let L be a set of labels containing τ. It is a simple matter to extend $\mathcal{T}$ to a functor on $\mathbf{T}_L$. For a morphism $(\sigma, 1_L) : U \to V$ between transition systems U, V take $\mathcal{T}(\sigma, 1_L) = (\sigma, 1_L)$. In fact it is an equally simple matter to check that $\mathcal{T}$ forms a monad with unit $\eta_U = (1_S, 1_L) : U \to \mathcal{T}(U)$ and multiplication $\mu_U = (1_S, 1_L) : \mathcal{T}^2(U) \to \mathcal{T}(U)$ at a transition system U in $\mathbf{T}_L$ with states S.

Because $\mathcal{T}$ forms a monad it opens the door to another way to define weak bisimulation. We can form the Kleisli category $(\mathbf{T}_L)_{\mathcal{T}}$. Its objects are transition systems and its morphisms $U \to V$ are morphisms $U \to \mathcal{T}(V)$ in $\mathbf{T}_L$ which compose as follows: If $f : U \to V$ and $g : V \to W$ are morphisms in the Kleisli category we define their composition to be $\mu_W \circ \mathcal{T}(g) \circ f : U \to W$. For general reasons, there is an adjunction from $\mathbf{T}_L$ to the Kleisli category $(\mathbf{T}_L)_{\mathcal{T}}$, in which the left adjoint $F : \mathbf{T}_L \to (\mathbf{T}_L)_{\mathcal{T}}$ takes a morphism $f : U \to V$ of $\mathbf{T}_L$ to the morphism $\eta_V \circ f : U \to V$ of the Kleisli category $(\mathbf{T}_L)_{\mathcal{T}}$. Because the unit of the monad consists of monics, the functor F is essentially an inclusion allowing us to identify $\mathbf{T}_L$ with a subcategory of $(\mathbf{T}_L)_{\mathcal{T}}$. With this identification we can view the path category $\mathbf{Bran}_L$ as a subcategory of the Kleisli category $(\mathbf{T}_L)_{\mathcal{T}}$, and hence ask for the meaning of $\mathbf{Bran}_L$-bisimulation in the Kleisli category. In fact, $\mathbf{Bran}_L$-bisimulation in $(\mathbf{T}_L)_{\mathcal{T}}$ coincides with weak bisimulation (a fact observed implicitly in (Cheng and Nielsen 1996)). This coincidence arises for abstract reasons. The particular case of transition systems falls within the following abstract picture.

Assume a category of models $\mathbf{M}$ and a choice of path category forming a subcategory $\mathbf{P} \hookrightarrow \mathbf{M}$. Assume a monad $\mathcal{T}$ on $\mathbf{M}$ with unit η and multiplication μ. We can define two objects X and Y of $\mathbf{M}$ to be $\mathcal{T}$-weak $\mathbf{P}$-bisimilar iff $\mathcal{T}(X)$ and $\mathcal{T}(Y)$ are $\mathbf{P}$-bisimilar.

Generally, there is an adjunction from $\mathbf{M}$ to the Kleisli category $\mathbf{M}_{\mathcal{T}}$. If the components of the unit η are monics then via the left adjoint we can identify $\mathbf{P}$ with a path category in $\mathbf{M}_{\mathcal{T}}$.[11] The relation of $\mathbf{P}$-bisimulation in the Kleisli category $\mathbf{M}_{\mathcal{T}}$ coincides with $\mathcal{T}$-weak $\mathbf{P}$-bisimulation provided:

- the functor $\mathcal{T}$ of the monad preserves $\mathbf{P}$-open morphisms, *i.e.* if f is a $\mathbf{P}$-open morphism of $\mathbf{M}$, then so is $\mathcal{T}(f)$,

- the components of the multiplication of the monad are $\mathbf{P}$-open, *i.e.* for each object X of $\mathbf{M}$, the component μ_X is $\mathbf{P}$-open.

In fact, $\mathbf{P}$-bisimilarity in the Kleisli category implies $\mathcal{T}$-weak $\mathbf{P}$-bisimilarity without these extra conditions—roughly because right adjoints preserve openness.

We can try to follow the same abstract pattern in formulating notions of weak bisimulation for independence models, and, in particular, for event structures. But here there are difficulties due to independence. Roughly, just as there are not enough event structures so that the projection $\mathbf{E} \to \mathbf{Set}_*$ forms a fibration, so it appears that we need to broaden the category of event structures to be able to define a suitable monad for weak bisimulation. Presheaf models over pomsets are an appropriate generalisation.

11   The future

To conclude we present some remarks on research directions in the semantics of concurrent computation. These views are admittedly biased, and quite possibly limited—to some extent they represent natural continuations of our recent work.

The paper (Cattani and Winskel 1996) parallels the work here, but for presheaf models, obtaining abstract results for a whole class of presheaf models, which can

---

[11] Although for simplicity we have assumed that path categories are subcategories of the categories of models, this assumption can easily be relaxed and with it the need for components of the unit of the monad to be monics.

then be transferred to concrete models like event structures. In particular, it presents abstract grounds for the operations of process-calculi preserving open maps. A games account of strong history-preserving bisimulation is given in (Nielsen and Clausen 1994); a good deal of the preliminary work and definitions of that paper could have been done in greater generality at the level of presheaf models.

But probably the most important motivation for presheaf models is the hope they give of making concurrency less separate a study in the semantics of programming languages. Through presheaf models we are trying to bring concurrency theory within domain theory, which is so successful in handling higher-order and recursive features. Here the term "domain theory" should be understood liberally enough to include generalisations of domain theory like those envisaged in "axiomatic domain theory", being developed by Fiore and Plotkin (Fiore 1994; Plotkin 1995). The paper (Winskel 1996) is a step in this programme; it shows how presheaf models can be extended to higher-order process languages, where processes are transmitted along channels, and along similar lines, incorporating ideas of (Stark 1996; Fiore, Moggi, and Sangiori 1996), a presheaf semantics can be obtained for Milner's Pi-calculus (Milner, Parrow, and Walker 1992). At present, it is not known how to combine systematically higher-order features with independence models.

The question of logics for concurrent processes looms large. The categorical account of bisimulation does accompany a scheme for generalising of Hennessy-Milner logic with respect to a path-category (Joyal, Nielsen, and Winskel 1994). But its generality is a mixed blessing, pushing a lot of choices for the logic over to presentations of the path-category. It's to be expected that recursively-defined path categories, as introduced in (Winskel 1996), provide more informative logics, based on a few constructions on logics for basic operations on path-categories. What, if any, the relations are with *ad hoc* logics of event structures such as those in (Thiagarajan 1994; Ramanujam 1996) is unknown.

Several fundamental algorithmic questions remain, such as the computability and complexity of deciding bisimulation equivalences on finite state independence models. It is encouraging that independence models in many different settings have be found useful in obtaining feasible model-checking algorithms (*e.g.* McMillan 1993; Godefroid and Wolper 1994; Valmari 1990; Peled 1993; Alur, Peled, and Penzek 1995).

References

Alur, R., D. Peled, and W. Penzek (1995). *Model-Checking of Causality Properties.* Proceedings of LICS'95.

Barr, M. and C. Wells (1990). *Category theory for Computer Science.* Prentice Hall.

Bednarczyk, M. A. (1988). *Categories of asynchronous systems.* PhD thesis in Computer Science, University of Sussex, report no. 1/88.

Benson, D. B. and O. Ben-Shachar (1988). *Bisimulation of automata.* Information and

Computation, 79.

Bentham, J. V. (1984). *Correspondence theory.* the Handbook of Philosophical Logic, Vol.II, ed. Gabbay and Guenther, Reidel.

Berry, G. (1979). *Modèles completement adéquats et stables des λ-calculs typées.* Thèse de Doctorat d'Etat, Université Paris VII.

Bloom, B. and M. Kwiatkowska (1992). *Trade-offs in true concurrency: Pomsets and Mazurkiewicz traces,* Brookes, S., Main, M., Melton, A., Mislove, M., and Schmidt, D., (eds), *Mathematical Foundations of Programming Semantics.* Springer LNCS 598.

Brookes, S. D. (1983). *On the relationship of CCS and CSP.* Diaz, J. (ed.), Icalp '83, Springer LNCS 154.

Castellani, I. (1985). *Bisimulation and abstraction homomorphisms.* Proc. of CAAP 85, Springer Lecture Notes in CS.

Cattani, G. L. and G. Winskel (1996). *Presheaf models for concurrency.* To appear as a BRICS report.

Cheng, A. and M. Nielsen (1996). *Open Maps (at) Work.* BRICS report RS-95-23, 1995. In Proc. of 15th Conference, FST&TCS '95, Springer Lecture Notes in CS.

Fiore, M., E. Moggi, and D. Sangiori (1996). *A fully abstract model for the Pi-calculus.* To appear in the Proc. of LICS'96.

Fiore, M. P. (1994). *Axiomatic Domain Theory in Categories of Partial Map.* Ph.D. Thesis, Department of Computer Science, University of Edinburgh.

Glabbeek, R. J. V. (1990). *Comparative concurrency semantics and refinement of actions.* PhD thesis, CWI Amsterdam.

Glabeek, R. J. V. and U. Goltz (1989). *Equivalence notions for concurrent systems and refinement of actions.* Proc of MFCS, Springer Lecture Notes in CS vol.379.

Godefroid, P. and P. Wolper (1994). *A partial Approach to Model Checking.* Information and Computation 110 (2), pp. 305 – 326.

Grabowski, J. (1981). *On partial languages.* Fundamenta Informaticae, IV, 2.

Hoare, C. A. R. (1981). *A model for communicating sequential processes.* Technical Report PRG-22, Programming Research Group, University of Oxford Computing Lab.

Joyal, A. and I. Moerdijk (1994). *A completeness theorem for open maps.* In Annals of Pure and Applied Logic 70.

Joyal, A., M. Nielsen, and G. Winskel (1994). *Bisimulation from open maps.* Journal version of LICS93 article. BRICS report RS-94-7, Aarhus University.

MacLane, S. (1971). *Categories for the Working Mathematician, Graduate Texts in Mathematics.* Springer.

MacLane, S. and I. Moerdijk (1992). *Sheaves in geometry and logic: a first introduction to topos theory.* Springer.

McMillan, K. L. (1993). *Symbolic Model Checking.* Kluwer Academic Publishers.

Milner, A. R. G. (1980). *Calculus of communicating systems.* Springer LNCS 92.

Milner, A. R. G. (1989). *Communication and concurrency.* Prentice Hall.

Milner, A. R. G., J. Parrow, and D. Walker (1992). A calculus of mobile processes, parts I and II. *Information and Computation 100,* 1–77.

Nielsen, M. and C. Clausen (1994). *Bisimulations, Games and Logic.* Springer LNCS 812.

Nielsen, M., G. Rozenberg, and P. S. Thiagarajan (1992). *Elementary transition systems.* Theoretical Computer Science 96.

Nielsen, M. and G. Winskel (1996). *Petri Nets and Bisimulation.* TCS 153.

Pierce, B. C. (1991). *Category theory for computer scientists.* the Foundations of Computing Series, The MIT Press.

Peled, D. (1993). *All from One, One for All: On Model Checking Using Representatives.* 5th Conference on Computer Aided Verification, Springer LNCS 697.

Plotkin, G. (1995). Algebraic Completeness and Compactness in an Enriched Setting. *Handwritten Notes.*

Pratt, V. R. (1986). *Modelling concurrency with partial orders.* International Journal of Parallel Programming, 15,1.

Rabinovich, A. and B. A. Trakhtenbrot (1988). *Behaviour Structure and Nets.* Fundamenta Informaticae, XI, 4.

Ramanujam, R. (1996). *Locally linear time temporal logic.* To appear in proc. LICS'96.

Rozoy, B. and P. S. Thiagarajan (1991). *Event structures and trace monoids.* Theoretical Computer Science, 91, 2.

Segerberg, K. (1968). *Decidability of S4.1.* Theoria 34.

Shields, M. W. (1985). *Concurrent machines.* Computer Journal, vol. 28.

Stark, I. (1996). *A fully abstract domain model for the Pi-calculus.* To appear in the Proc. of LICS'96.

Thiagarajan, P. S. (1994). *A trace based extension of propositional linear time temporal logic.* Proc LICS'94.

Valmari, A. (1990). *A Stubborn Attack on State Explosion.* Proc. 2nd Conference on Computer Aided Verification, Springer LNCS 531, pp. 156 – 165.

van Oosten, J. (1995). *Basic Category Theory.* BRICS Lecture notes LS-95-1.

Winskel, G. (1982). *Event structure semantics of CCS and related languages.* Nielsen, M. and Schmidt, E.M. (eds), Icalp '82, Springer LNCS 140. A full version with proofs appears as DAIMI PB-159, Computer Science Department, University of Aarhus, 1983.

Winskel, G. (1985). *Synchronisation trees.* Theoretical Computer Science, 34.

Winskel, G. (1988). *An introduction to event structures.* de Bakker, de Roever and Rozenberg (eds.), Linear Time, Branching Time and Partial Orders in Logics and Models for Concurrency, Springer LNCS 354.

Winskel, G. (1996). *A Presheaf semantics for Value Passing.* To appear as a BRICS report.

Winskel, G. and M. Nielsen (1995). *Models for concurrency.* vol.4 of the Handbook of Logic in Computer Science, Oxford University Press. A draft appears as BRICS Report RS-94-12, 1994.

Index